Chu Hsi
and
Neo-Confucianism

Chu Hsi (Zhuxi)
1130–1200

Chu Hsi
and
Neo-Confucianism

EDITED BY

Wing-tsit Chan

UNIVERSITY OF HAWAII PRESS

HONOLULU

Library of Congress Cataloging in Publication Data

Main entry under title:

Chu Hsi and Neo-Confucianism.

  "Papers presented at the International Conference
on Chu Hsi, held July 6–15, 1982, in Honolulu"—Introd.
  Sponsored by the University of Hawaii and the
American Council of Learned Societies.
  Bibliography: p.
  Includes index.
  1. Chu, Hsi, 1130–1200—Congresses. 2. Neo-
Confucianism—Congresses. I. Chan, Wing-tsit, 1901–
II. International Conference on Chu Hsi (1982 :
Honolulu, Hawaii) III. University of Hawaii (Honolulu)
IV. American Council of Learned Societies.

B128.C54C48   1986   181'.11   85–24532
ISBN 0–8248–0961–0

FRONTISPIECE: A copy of Chu Hsi's self-portrait carved on stone and preserved in the Chu family, made by Chu Hsi's sixteenth-generation descendant Chu Yü 朱玉 (*fl.* 1722) and published in his *Chu Tzu wen-chi ta-ch'üan lei-pien* 朱子文集大全類編 (A classified compilation of the complete collection of literary works of Master Chu). It is maintained that Chu Hsi painted the portrait while facing the mirror at sixty. A number of portraits, not all identical, have been claimed to be copies of the stone portrait.

This volume is dedicated

to

Dr. Hung Wo Ching

whose unusual insight, generous support,

and outstanding leadership have made possible several

East-West Philosophers' Conferences

including the

International Conference on Chu Hsi

Contents

Preface

THE INTERNATIONAL CONFERENCE on Chu Hsi was made possible by many people from many countries. Dr. Hung Wo Ching raised all the funds for the conference. The response from various directions was overwhelming. The University of Hawaii and the American Council of Learned Societies became sponsors. The support of President Fujio Matsuda of the University of Hawaii was extremely generous. Thirty-six senior scholars, all specialists on Neo-Confucianism, came from several continents, including the 86-year-old Fung Yu-lan. Thirty-three younger scholars selected through an international competition also attended, as well as fourteen interested scholars who came as observers. The conference committee, with Dr. Wm. Theodore de Bary as chairman and Professors Irene Bloom, Wing-tsit Chan, Chung-ying Cheng, and Wei-ming Tu as members, planned the roster of participants and the program. Dr. Stephen Uhalley, Jr., Acting Director of the Center for Asian and Pacific Studies at the University of Hawaii, served as administrative director of the conference. He took care of all the business administration and readily mobilized all the resources of the Center. His assistant, Ms. Peggy Blumenthal, in her capacity as the assistant administrative director of the conference, conducted the daily operation with an efficiency and smoothness seldom seen in an international gathering. All members sang her praise, and we now add our encore. University of Hawaii faculty members chaired the various sessions and served as members of the Local Committee. Others performed duties on the Committee of Conference Historians, as interpreters, and as translators of papers from Chinese and Japanese into English. The East-West Center opened its facilities to us. To all these people and institutions, we reverently bow our heads three times.

Regarding the editing of this anthology, we have not insisted on uniformity or consistency, for scholars from diverse backgrounds must be free to express themselves in their own way. We have respected their styles as we have honored their opinions. At the same time, we want to accommodate our future readers, who may not be specialists in Neo-Confucianism. We have therefore reduced transliteration to a minimum. When transliteration is used, a translation is provided in parentheses or in a footnote. Officially we have followed the Wade-Giles system of transliteration, but any scholar who wanted to use the *p'in-yin* system was free to do so.

Translation of Chinese terms is always a controversial matter, since no Chinese word corresponds exactly to an English word. Inevitably, in any translation some Chinese meanings and implications are left out and some extraneous English meanings and implications creep in. The best one can do is to choose the English word that comes closest to the Chinese. When a scholar prefers his own translation, his choice is final. Thus *li* may be variously rendered as "principle," "reason," "pattern"; *ch'i* as "material force," "vital force," "ether," "breath"; and *wu-hsing* as "five agents," "five elements," "five phases." In such cases, however, either the original Chinese term or an alternate translation is given for ready identification, and cross references in the index will remove any possible confusion. Fortunately, a particular translation has been used in most cases. Thus there is a high degree of uniformity and consistency after all.

Dates are provided for dynasties and historical persons at the first occurrence in each chapter, on the assumption that the reader may consult different chapters at different times. In a few cases scholars do not agree on these dates, and dates for such people as Confucius may seem unnecessary to the specialist, but we do not want to ignore the general reader, who may need some kind of time framework. At any rate, it is difficult to draw the line regarding what the reader does and does not know. The Oriental year is simply equated with the Western year, except in such cases as Lu Hsiang-shan and Wang Yang-ming, who died at the end of the Oriental year that happened to be the beginning of the following Western year. Asian ages are counted according to the Asian tradition, that is, by calendar year instead of twelve months. Names of historical persons follow the Oriental order with the family name first. For modern and contemporary writers, however, we have followed the author's own preference as to whether the family name or private name comes first. We refer to people in history by their private names except in the cases of Lu Chiu-yüan and Wang Shou-jen because practically all Asian writers have called them by their honorific names, that is, Lu-Hsiang-shan and Wang Yang-ming, respectively. Diacritical marks over personal names follow the usage of the persons themselves.

We have tried to identify all people and places mentioned, translate all titles, explain all terms, trace all sources of quotations, and give the specific editions and page references. Abbreviated titles have been avoided except the following two:

SPPY   *Ssu-pu pei-yao* 四部備要 (Essentials of the Four Libraries)
SPTK   *Ssu-pu ts'ung-k'an* 四部叢刊 (Four Libraries series)

Chinese characters for Asian names, titles, and terms are found in the glossary at the end of each chapter except for dynasties, provinces, and well-known cities.

WING-TSIT CHAN
陳榮捷

1

Introduction

WING-TSIT CHAN

THE PRESENT ANTHOLOGY consists of papers presented at the International Conference on Chu Hsi held July 6–15, 1982, in Honolulu. The symposium, convened as one of the continuing East-West Philosophers' Conferences and in conjunction with the seventy-fifth anniversary of the University of Hawaii, was the first on this Neo-Confucian thinker. A word may be appropriate to explain the reason for the event.

The main reason is Chu Hsi himself. He was the most influential Chinese philosopher since the time of Confucius (551–479 B.C.) and Mencius (372–289 B.C.?). He was not only the crystalization of the Neo-Confucian movement that dominated China for 800 years but also the only thinker in the Christian era to influence many phases of Asian life throughout East Asia. Asian scholars have called him the "chi ta-ch'eng"[a] of Neo-Confucianism, using Mencius' description of Confucius as "a complete concert,"[1] an orchestra in which all perfect notes blend together in a harmonious whole. However, because *chi* means "to gather" and *ta-ch'eng* means "great accomplishment," the Chinese phrase is usually rendered in English as "great synthesis." This translation gave rise to the general understanding in the West that Chu Hsi merely put together the philosophies of the early Sung (960–1279) Neo-Confucianists, notably Chou Tun-i[b] (1017–1073), Chang Tsai[c] (1020–1077), Ch'eng Hao[d] (1032–1085), and his brother Ch'eng I[e] (1033–1107), especially the last. But I preferred to translate the word *ch'eng* literally, namely, "to complete." When I wrote "Chu Hsi's Completion of Neo-Confucianism" for the Sung Project in Paris,[2] I did not mean to suggest that the philosophical system of Chu Hsi was perfect. Scholars have pointed out many difficulties. But it is unfair to say that Chu Hsi did not offer anything new. As I pointed out in my essay, he reconstructed Neo-Confucianism in an original way in three areas. First was his completion of the concept of the Tradition of the Way (*tao-t'ung*[f]). He did this by leaving out the Confucianists of the Han (206 B.C.–A.D. 220) and T'ang (618–907) dynasties and a number of Sung Neo-Confucianists, notably Shao Yung[g] (1011–1077), Chang Tsai, Ssu-ma Kuang[h] (1019–1086), and even his own teacher, Li T'ung[i] (1093–1163), affirming a direct line from

the ancient sages to Chou Tun-i and the Ch'eng brothers, chiefly on the
ground that Chou developed the doctrine of the Great Ultimate (*T'ai-chi*[j]) and
the Ch'engs developed the doctrine of *li*[k] (principle).[3] He reestablished the
tao-t'ung primarily on philosophical grounds, that is, on the basis of *li*. As
Ch'eng I before him, he built his entire system on this concept. The idea of *li*
became so central in the whole Neo-Confucian movement that in Chinese it
has been called *Li-hsüeh*[l] (the Learning or School of Principle). Second, in
1190 he grouped the *Great Learning,* the *Analects,* the *Book of Mencius,* and
the *Doctrine of the Mean* as the Four Books. The grouping provided a methodology in the study of the Classics for the first time in Chinese history, beginning with the blueprint in the *Great Learning,* through the applications in the
Analects and the elaboration in the *Mencius,* to the wonder and mystery of the
Mean. Even more important, he took the student back to the direct sources of
Confucian teachings, because the Four Books contain the words of Confucius
and Mencius whereas the Five Classics,[4] which had dominated Confucianism
in previous centuries, were but indirect sources.[5] At once this created a new
approach and a new spirit in Confucian studies. The Four Books and Chu
Hsi's commentaries on them were made basic and official texts in civil service
examinations in 1313 and thus controlled Chinese thought as well as the
selection of government officials for 600 years until 1905.

His third innovation was the most important of all, namely, his completion
of Neo-Confucian philosophy.[6] This he did in four different ways. First, he
determined the direction of Neo-Confucianism by choosing the philosophy of
li of the Ch'eng brothers as the foundation of Neo-Confucian thought. Had he
preferred Buddhism or Taoism, the course of Chinese history would have
been different. Even if he had sided with the philosophy of material force
(*ch'i*[m]) of Chang Tsai or the philosophy of form and number (*hsiang-shu*[n]) of
Shao Yung, the complexion of Chinese thought would not have been the
same. But he guided Chinese thought in the direction of principle, and Chinese thought has by and large remained that way since.

Second, he clarified the relation between principle and material force.
Ch'eng I provided the doctrine that *li* is one but its manifestations are many
(*li-i fen-shu*[o]),[7] but he never explained why things differ. By borrowing the
concept of material force from Chang Tsai, Chu Hsi was able to explain the
variation of man and things by saying that the interaction of the two material
forces, yin[p] or negative cosmic force, and yang[q] or positive cosmic force, differs in every case and therefore everyone's endowment in material force is different.

Third, he developed the concept of the Great Ultimate. Chou Tun-i had
modified a diagram of the Great Ultimate that he received from a Taoist priest
and had written a short explanation of it (*T'ai-chi-t'u shuo*[r]). The treatise had
remained obscure until Chu Hsi placed it at the head of the *Chin-ssu lu*[s]
(Reflections on things at hand[8]) which he and Lü Tsu-ch'ien[t] (1137–1181)
compiled in 1175. As the first anthology of its kind, it became the best state-

ment of Neo-Confucianism. Under his influence it also became the opening passage in the *Hsing-li ta-ch'üan*ᵘ (The great collection of Neo-Confucianism) and the *Hsing-li ching-i*ᵛ (The essentials of Neo-Confucianism), both of which are basic sources on Neo-Confucianism.[9] Chu Hsi had to use the diagram of the Great Ultimate in spite of its Taoist origin because the concept of the Great Ultimate is necessary to account for the operation of principle and material force. According to Chou Tun-i, the Great Ultimate produces the two material forces, yin and yang, the interaction of which in turn engenders all things. According to Chu Hsi's interpretation, the Great Ultimate is the sum total of principles. Principle does not produce anything, but as there are the principles of tranquility and activity, or yin and yang, there must be their actuality. Yin and yang naturally have to interact to produce things. This is the process of perpetual production and reproduction, resulting in an endless variety of things and affairs.

Fourth, Chu Hsi developed the concept of *jen*ʷ (humanity) to its highest point in Chinese history. Confucius had taught *jen* not only as a particular virtue but as the general virtue out of which all virtues emerge. To Mencius *jen* meant compassion. And to Han Yü*ˣ (768–824), it meant universal love.[10] Being more rational, Ch'eng I maintained that *jen* is the basic and universal virtue because it is creative, giving rise to all other virtues, just as *jen* as a seed grows into leaves and flowers.[11] Chu Hsi went still further to describe *jen* as "the mind of Heaven and Earth to create things."[12] In so doing, he combined philosophy, religion, and ethics as one. In all these ways, he "completed" Neo-Confucianism as no one else had done before or has done since.

If Chu Hsi's accomplishment were limited to completing Neo-Confucian philosophy, he would have been but a Chinese Spinoza or St. Thomas Aquinas with whom he has been compared.[13] But he achieved much more. His influence on the examination system has been noted. He wrote, commented on, compiled, and edited almost one hundred works. Aside from his commentaries on the Confucian Classics, his works on social and religious rites shaped Chinese, Korean, and Japanese behavior for hundreds of years. His work on history has become a standard. And the *Hsiao-hsüeh*ʸ (Elementary education), which was compiled by his students under his direction, served as the basic primer in education. He established public granaries to relieve famine and thus inaugurated a social institution that still exists in many communities today. He rebuilt the White Deer Hollow Academy and the Yüeh-luᶻ Academy, two famous educational centers that had come to ruin, and founded many new ones himself, besides lecturing at many others. These academies, together with those which his pupils founded or headed or where they lectured, became a concerted movement that was to change the nature and extent of private education. In rejecting the "Prefaces" of the *Book of Odes* as inauthentic,[14] in insisting that 24 of the 305 odes are but love songs instead of didactic verses,[15] in overthrowing the authenticity of the ancient version of the *Book of History*,[16] in asserting that the *Book of Rites* is but the Han Confucianists' explanations of the *I-li*[aa] (Book of ceremonial),[17] and in regarding the three commentaries on the *Spring and Autumn Annals* as twice or thrice removed from the author, Confucius,[18] Chu Hsi brought the skepticism toward ancient Classics to new heights and thus pioneered the movement of *k'ao-chu*[ab] (evidential research) that flourished in the Ch'ing dynasty (1644–1912). In addition he was a renowned poet and calligrapher.

Chu Hsi's works reached Korea and Japan soon after his death. The West, however, had to wait for several hundred years. Western studies of Neo-Confucianism in general, and Chu Hsi in particular, did not start until the seventeenth century, when Christian missionaries, especially the Jesuits, were looking for something in Chinese thought to support their Christian doctrines. Chu Hsi's works were translated into English, French, and German between 1836 and 1889.[19] The study stopped when Emperor K'ang-hsi[ac] (r. 1662–1722) expelled the missionaries from China as a result of the Rites Controversy in which the Pope prohibited Chinese Christians from performing religious rites before their ancestors and the Chinese emperor exercised his prerogatives as the sovereign of the land. Neo-Confucianism was then at its height, for the *Chu Tzu ch'üan-shu*[ad] (The complete works of Master Chu) was compiled by imperial order in 1714 and the *Hsing-li ching-i* was compiled by imperial order in 1715. Since the Four Books had been made official in 1313, the Neo-Confucianism of Chu Hsi began to enjoy the position of orthodoxy, especially in government; and the compilation of the *Hsing-li ta-ch'üan* in 1415, also by imperial order, further affirmed this orthodoxy. Under Emperor K'ang-hsi and later Ch'ien-lung[ae] (r. 1736–1795), imperial patronage of Chu Hsi reached its height. By this time, Chu Hsi's influence had extended to Korea and Japan for centuries.

Unfortunately, Neo-Confucianism was too closely associated with the monarchical system. When the Chinese overthrew the system in 1911, Chinese tradition came under attack. In the ensuing intellectual revolution from 1917 on, Neo-Confucianism was denounced as a "metaphysical devil." The strongest attacks were directed at Ch'eng I and Chu Hsi. Two quotations were cited to attack them. When asked whether a lonely and poor widow should remarry, Ch'eng had answered, "To starve to death is a minor matter but to lose one's integrity is a very serious matter."[20] Intellectual rebels were unanimous in declaring that this was a clear proof of Neo-Confucian suppression of women. The rebellious mood was too strong for them to realize that Ch'eng I was talking about the choice between righteousness and profit as a way of life, an issue raised by Mencius long before.[21] Of course in the Confucian tradition women had been subordinated, but Ch'eng I was by no means insensitive to their misfortune. In his biography of his father, he praised him for arranging the marriage of his father's widowed niece.[22] When Chu Hsi was asked about the conflict between Ch'eng I's praise of his father and his own prohibition of a widow's remarrying, Chu Hsi answered, "The general principle is like that, but human beings sometimes cannot fulfill it."[23] In other words, one should live by moral principles, but there are always circumstances that prevent the ideal from being fulfilled. In the Confucian tradition, integrity demanded that a woman should remain devoted to her husband, living or dead, although no such requirement was made of men. Modern reform has changed that tradition, but critics of Ch'eng I still apply a modern standard to the eleventh century. Philosophically, the choice is always between righteousness and profit. In practical life, one often faces a situation about which Chu Hsi was asked.

A favorite attack on Chu Hsi is that of Yen Yüan[af] (1635–1704), who asserted that Chu Hsi "taught people to sit quiet half of the day and to read books the other half of the day."[24] Yen Yüan meant that the doctrines of Chu Hsi served no practical purposes. Modern critics of Chu Hsi love to repeat Yen Yüan, just as the Chinese saying that goes, "a hundred dogs bark at the noise when one dog barks at the shadow." What Yen Yüan saw was a shadow indeed. As Ch'ien Mu[ag] has pointed out, Chu Hsi gave this advice to his pupil Kuo Yu-jen (Kuo Te-yüan[ah]) only once, and he never taught any other pupil to act so.[25] Chu Hsi gave this unusual advice to this pupil because Kuo was too rash and neglected his studies.[26] As usual in teaching his pupils, Chu Hsi was like a physician prescribing a specific medicine for a particular ailment.[27]

When the political situation became more settled in China in the 1930s, scholars began to have second thoughts about Neo-Confucianism. The tide seemed to turn in its favor. In 1939, for example, Fung Yu-lan[ai] published his *Hsin-li-hsüeh*[aj] (New learning of principle), in which he poured Western wine into the old Chinese bottle of Chu Hsi's Neo-Confucianism.[28] After the Communists got control of mainland China in 1949, the reaction to Neo-Confucianism took opposite directions. Chinese scholars who went to Hong Kong and later to Taiwan, such as Ch'ien Mu, Hsü Fu-kuan,[ak] Tang Chun-i,[al] and Mou Tsung-san,[am] published a large number of articles and books of high quality on the subject and trained a number of brilliant young scholars who now teach Neo-Confucianism in Hong Kong, Taiwan, and the United States. On the mainland, Neo-Confucianism was at first ignored. Of the 213 books published between 1949 and 1963, only one was on Chu Hsi and it dealt with the Chu Hsi school in Japan; and of the 756 articles published during the same period, the six on the Ch'eng brothers and Chu Hsi were generally accusatory, while Chang Tsai's philosophy of *ch'i* was hailed as materialism.[29] In 1980 the quotation from Ch'eng I regarding the widow still dominated the description of him in the Historical Museum in Peking. In October 1981, however, 262 scholars attended a symposium on Neo-Confucianism in Hangchow. I was invited to attend with Professor Wm. Theodore de Bary from the United States in a total of seven from outside China. In the section on Chu Hsi in which I participated, discussions were strictly on scholarly grounds and appraisal was reasonably objective. Naturally, Chu Hsi was still regarded as serving feudal society, and consideration was given to how he could be made to contribute to Marxism.

Two books on Chu Hsi's life and thought appeared shortly before and after the Hangchow conference. They were written from the scholarly point of view and approached him from both favorable and unfavorable standpoints. They acknowledged certain contributions Chu Hsi had made. Although the authors have accepted the fabricated stories of Shen Chi-tsu,[an] who, at the height of the Court's attack on the Chu Hsi School as *wei-hsüeh*[ao] (false learning), accused Chu Hsi of taking two nuns to be his concubines and of marrying Liu Kung's[ap] daughter for her dowry[30] when in fact Chu Hsi married the daughter of Liu Mien-chih[aq] (1091–1149), and although they have misinterpreted Chu Hsi's thanks to the emperor[31] as a confession of his evil deeds, they have also pointed out some of Shen's falsehood.[32] They have tried to be fair. Generally speaking, the attitude toward Chu Hsi is remarkably different from a decade ago when he was totally denounced. Neo-Confucianism as a whole is still considered to be a tool of feudalism, but the appraisal has taken a new turn. Chu Hsi relics destroyed during the Cultural Revolution are being restored. The restorations at Fukien, in the White Deer Hollow Academy, and in the Yüeh-lu Academy impressed me tremendously. All in all, Chu Hsi's fortune in Asia has turned for the better.

In the meantime, interest in Neo-Confucianism, particularly in Chu Hsi, was revived in the West. Father Graf translated the *Chin-ssu lu* into German and wrote a definitive book, *Tao*[ar] *und Jen* (The Way and humanity), on the two concepts central to Neo-Confucian philosophy.[33] The Sung Project in Paris, with the collaboration of scholars around the world, produced indispensable works on Sung bibliography and biography.[34] For a time Europe was the center for studies of the Sung period. Eventually, the center shifted to the United States. Following World War II, Asian studies programs developed rapidly in American universities. Outstanding institutions like Harvard and Columbia produced a number of young specialists on Neo-Confucian thought. Professor de Bary organized several conferences on Neo-Confucianism, and the Columbia University Press published a series of books on the subject.[35]

Since American studies on Neo-Confucianism had reached the point where an entire conference could concentrate on an individual philosopher, scholars felt a need for a conference on Chu Hsi. As early as 1962 a national conference in Changsha was devoted to Wang Fu-chih[as] (1619–1692) in commemoration of the 270th anniversary of his death;[36] in 1972 an international conference on Wang Yang-ming (Wang Shou-jen,[at] 1472–1529) was held in Honolulu in celebration of the 500th anniversary of his birth.[37] But Chu Hsi was too important a historical figure for us to wait for any such anniversary of his. I therefore took the initiative to organize a meeting on him. The response from all quarters was overwhelming. Dr. Hung Wo Ching[au] of Honolulu single-handedly raised funds in ample amount, the University of Hawaii and the American Council of Learned Societies readily agreed to sponsor the conference, and scholars from several continents offered unreserved support.

The conference was not intended to cover all areas in which Chu Hsi was concerned. From the start, the conference committee rejected the textbook or encyclopedia approach. We simply wanted to gather together internationally known authorities on Chu Hsi and renowned scholars on Neo-Confucianism to discuss questions of their own choice and to share their scholarship with others. By no means can we claim that all authorities on Chu Hsi were at the conference. Professors Liang Shuming[av] and Ch'ien Mu, both in their late eighties, for example, were expected to come but finally did not attend. Fortunately, they did prepare papers. We dare say that there has never been so much accumulated expertise at a conference devoted to a Chinese thinker.

As the scholars were free to choose their own subjects, there were bound to be some overlapping and some omissions. The topic of the Great Ultimate, for instance, was discussed again and again, probably out of balance in relation to other topics. As matters turned out, however, the topic was approached from different angles, and monotonous repetition was reduced to a minimum. On the other hand, a number of topics were not covered: Chu Hsi's government service, Chu Hsi's religious practice, Chu Hsi as a poet, Chu Hsi and science, to name but a few. On the latter, we had fully expected Dr. Joseph Needham, surely the world authority on the subject, to lead a workshop on science, but he was unable to come. The result was that the conference committee decided to cancel the workshop. This is regrettable, for Neo-Confucianism has often been regarded as an obstacle to science, and yet Chu Hsi discovered the nature of fossils, three hundred years ahead of the discovery in Europe.[38] Thus there are many gaps. A comprehensive conference on Chu Hsi covering all aspects will have to wait for decades when there are enough specialists to embrace all phases of this great thinker. It is hoped that even the gaps will play a constructive role by highlighting the need for and stimulating research.

The conference was an open forum, with no doctrine to propagate and no issue to resolve. All scholars came as individuals, not as representatives of any organization. There were as many scholars from the mainland as from Taiwan, and the numbers of Westerners and Chinese, and senior and younger scholars, were equal. It was feared that because of the political situation, scholars from the mainland and from Taiwan would find their encounter unpleasant. The fear was real, because this was to be the first meeting of these scholars on Chinese thought. In such a meeting, political ideology could easily emerge. But as soon as they met at the customs area at the airport, they seemed like old friends. In fact, some of them had been acquainted, and many had been aware of each other's publications on Chu Hsi. Throughout the conference no political issue ever arose.

Unlike an international congress on science where a new theory is announced or a medical meeting where a new discovery is reported, few earth-shaking ideas have emerged from meetings in the humanities, for philosophical ideas are not subject to quantitative analysis, develop very slowly, and are well known among colleagues. We cannot claim anything new from the Chu

Hsi conference. However, since the study of Chu Hsi is still in its infancy in the West, the conference did open up territories that have been scarcely traversed. I have in mind Professor Okada Takehiko's[aw] discussion of Chu Hsi's idea of wisdom as hidden and stored (chapter 13), Professor Sato Hitoshi's[ax] deliberation on Chu Hsi's "Treatise on *Jen*" (chapter 14), Professor Wei Cheng-t'ung's[ay] paper on Chu Hsi's theory of the standard and the expedient (chapter 16), Professor Chang Liwen's[az] analysis of Chu Hsi's system of thought of *I* (changes) (chapter 18), Professor Kao Ming's[ba] essay on Chu Hsi's discipline of propriety or system of rites (chapter 19), and Professor Richard Lynn's presentation on Chu Hsi as a literary critic (chapter 20). Chu Hsi's interpretation of wisdom as hidden and stored has not been studied even in China or Japan, let alone the West.

It is not surprising that three-fourths of the conference papers deal with the Great Ultimate in one way or another, and six papers elaborate on it at length. Several of the six may be said to be entirely devoted to it, but they approach the subject from different angles—Professor Stanislaus Lokuang[bb] from what is prior to physical form and what is posterior to it (chapter 6), Professor Yu Yamanoi[bc] from principle and material force (chapter 7), Professor Teng Aimin[bd] from substance and function and other pairs of opposites (chapter 8), Professor Chiu Hansheng[be] from the Principle of Heaven and nature (chapter 9), Professor Tomoeda Ryūtarō[bf] from the ground-providing principle of nature and man (chapter 11), and Professor Chang Liwen from the operation of Changes (chapter 18). Nowhere else is there such a concentrated study of the Great Ultimate.

It is expected that anyone who discusses Chu Hsi's philosophy will refer to the Great Ultimate, for it is the foundation of his thought. Neo-Confucianism is called *Li-hsüeh* in Chinese, suggesting that *li* is the keynote. In a general sense, it is. Ch'eng I inaugurated it as the basis of his whole philosophy, and Chu Hsi inherited it from him, expanded it, and refined it. But Ch'eng I only emphasized the unity of principle. Although he taught that principle is one but its manifestations are many, he never explained how the differentiation came about. Chu Hsi had to fill this gap. For an explanation he borrowed the concept of material force from Chang Tsai. According to Chu Hsi, material force, in its operation as yin and yang, endows man and things differently so that some endowments are substantial and balanced and others are meager and unbalanced. Thus no two things are exactly alike. To account for the relationship between principle and material force, Chu Hsi resorted to Chou Tun-i's "Explanation of the Diagram of the Great Ultimate." In Chou's philosophical scheme, the Ultimate of Nonbeing *(wu-chi)*,[bg] which is soundless and odorless, produces the Great Ultimate, which in turn produces yin and yang out of whose interaction all things emerge. Since Ch'eng I never mentioned the Great Ultimate,[39] Chu Hsi believed that although he learned it from his teacher, Chou Tun-i, he did not transmit it because no pupil was ready to receive the knowledge.[40] Although Lu Hsiang-shan (Lu Chiu-yüan,[bh] 1139–

1193) strongly objected to the diagram because it came from a Taoist priest and because the term *wu-chi* is of Taoist origin,[41] Chu Hsi's metaphysical structure built on the Great Ultimate prevailed. Students of Neo-Confucianism have long accepted it.

It came as a surprise, therefore, when Professor Yamanoi pronounced that the Great Ultimate "remained an alien element in Chu Hsi's theoretical system" and that it "has never been woven into the fabric of his philosophy" (chapter 7). Professor Yamanoi's arguments are that "the word *t'ai-chi* was used nowhere in the *Ssu-shu chi-chu*"[bi] (Collected commentaries on the Four Books), that "nowhere did Chu Hsi use the word *t'ai-chi* to annotate or elucidate the Four Books," and that he discussed *t'ai-chi* only in connection with Chou's diagram of the Great Ultimate and the *Book of Changes*. Professor Yamanoi had expressed this opinion to his Japanese colleagues, but it surprised the international audience. Since the *Ssu-shu chi-chu* is Chu Hsi's most important work, Professor Yamanoi has a point. Chu Hsi spent decades on the work and was still revising his commentary on the *Great Learning* three days before he died.[42] A number of his key concepts came from the *Ssu-shu chi-chu*, such as *jen* as "the character of the mind and the principle of love"[43] and propriety (or rites) as "the restraint and beautiful ornament according to the Principle of Heaven and the form and law of human affairs."[44] Still, Chu Hsi spoke a great deal in his conversations and letters about the Great Ultimate without reference to Chou's diagram or the *Book of Changes*,[45] and it is very difficult to conceive that they are not part of his thought system. However, Professor Yamanoi has given us an interesting idea to consider, and that is what a conference is all about.

As the Great Ultimate is the totality of principle, any discussion on the Great Ultimate necessarily involves principle. Of special interest are Professor A. C. Graham's discussion of it in connection with human nature (chapter 10) and Professor Chung-ying Cheng's[bj] analysis of *li* into six different types (chapter 12).

One troublesome problem is whether principle produces material force. Chu Hsi is often quoted as having said that "principle produces material force."[46] But as Professor Yamanoi has correctly pointed out, the quotation cannot be found in Chu Hsi's works. This raises the question whether the quotation is authentic. A year after the conference, in August 1983, I acquired some significant information. While attending a meeting at the Institute of Philosophy of the Chinese Academy of Social Science in Peking, I was given a journal in which an article states that the quotation is found in Lü Nan's[bk] (1479–1542) *Chu Tzu ch'ao-shih*[bl] (Selections from Master Chu explained). In the preface Lü wrote that he took the sayings from the *Chu Tzu yü-lüeh*[bm] (A simple selection of sayings from Master Chu), compiled by Chu Hsi's pupil Yang Yü-li.[bn] The writer of the article surmises that the editor of the *Chu Tzu yü-lei*, Li Ching-te[bo] (*fl.* 1263), must have seen the compilation but probably attached no importance to it.[47] But I rather think that Li Ching-te deliberately

excluded the saying from the *Chu Tzu yü-lei* because it is inconsistent with
Chu Hsi's theory. Chu Hsi said, "*Li* has no feeling or intention, does no calculation, and does not create."[48] In his philosophical system the process of
creation is natural. The Great Ultimate is the sum total of principles. As there
are principles of yin and yang, there must be their actuality. In other words,
there must be the interaction of activity and tranquility, which means creation. But principle itself does not create. Since Chu Hsi's conversations took
place over several decades, there is bound to be some inconsistency. And yet it
is surprising how little inconsistency there is in Chu Hsi's words or thinking.
I prefer to think that Yang Yü-li misunderstood his teacher, and Professor
Yamanoi's skepticism is fully justified.

In Chu Hsi's philosophy, principle must be thoroughly investigated in
order to understand it. This is his central doctrine of the investigation of
things. He deliberately "amended" the commentary of the fifth chapter of the
Great Learning to make the Neo-Confucian system complete. The topic of the
investigation of things has been taken up in a number of papers. In two of
them, however, it has received special attention. To Professor Liang Shuming,
Chu Hsi's doctrine has the drawback of applying the mind to external things
(chapter 3). One is reminded of Wang Yang-ming's criticism of Chu Hsi on
this ground.[49] He set forth his criticism in a letter to Lo Ch'in-shun[bp] (1465–
1547). But as Lo replied, the value of the investigation of things is to see that
principle is one but its manifestations are many *(li-i fen-shu).* That is to say,
from the point of view of principle, things and the self are a unity, and there is
no distinction between the internal and the external.[50] The controversy over
whether Chu Hsi externalized the mind to investigate things outside has been
an issue for several hundred years and is yet unsettled. The phrase *li-i fen-shu*
is cited in many of the papers (chapters 7, 8, 9, 12, 15, 16, 30) and the concept
is discussed in even more.

A great deal of confusion and misunderstanding has arisen in the translation
of this expression. The expression comes from Ch'eng I.[51] The word *fen* is
pronounced in the fourth tone, meaning one's lot, one's share, one's endowment, and the like, and not in the first tone, meaning to divide. In Morohashi
Tetsuji's[bq] *Daikanwa jiten*[br] (Great Chinese-Japanese dictionary), 7:929, *fen* is
explained as *fu-yü*[bs] (endowment) and not "to divide." In the 1702 edition of
the *Ssu-shu ta-ch'üan*[bt] (Great collection on the Four Books), page 110b, there
is a sign over the character on the upper right hand corner to indicate that it is
pronounced in the fourth tone and there is also a note, "fu-wen chieh,"[bu] to
show the pronunciation. In the *Chu Tzu yü-lei*, chapter 98, section 100, page
4014; the *Chung-yung huo-wen*[bv] (Questions and answers on the *Doctrine of the
Mean*), comment on chapter 22; and the *Meng Tzu huo-wen*[bw] (Questions and
answers on the *Book of Mencius*), comment on 1A:8, *li* and *fen* are used as
nouns in parallel construction; *fen* is not used as a verb. However, in the process of elaborating on the term, *fen* is also pronounced in the first tone meaning to divide. A case in point is the *Chu Tzu yü-lei,* chapter 98, section 88,

page 4004. My translation, "Principle is one but its manifestations are many," is meant to indicate as many meanings of *fen* (lot, endowment, and the like) as possible. "Diverse particularization" will do, except it may lead the reader to pronounce *fen* in the first tone.

Regarding human nature, another cardinal concept in Neo-Confucian thought, Professor A. C. Graham (chapter 10) approaches the subject from the point of view of the Great Ultimate, principle, and material force, while Professor Julia Ching[bx] couples nature with the emotions and goes into a discussion of reverence, self-conquest, meditation, and good and evil (chapter 17). The discussion of human nature leads to the discussion of *jen* (humanity), since it is the chief quality of human nature.

In the last decade or so, *jen* has become a favorite subject in discussions of Chu Hsi, since it is a cardinal concept in his philosophy. His ideas on *jen* are fully developed, though succinctly expressed, in his "Treatise on *Jen*."[52] This essay, which took him more than ten years of thought and correspondence with friends to complete, had never been discussed in English until this conference, although a year before I had published a long article in Chinese on it.[53] Professor Sato Hitoshi's treatise deserves special attention, especially as he has related Chu Hsi to other Neo-Confucianists in China and Japan (chapter 14).

Chu Hsi begins his "Treatise on *Jen*" with the sentence "the mind of Heaven and Earth is to produce things, and in the birth of man and things, each receives this mind of Heaven and Earth to be his mind." In other words, humanity, or to love and to be humane, is derived from the spirit of life-giving in Heaven and Earth. Similarly, rites are derived from Heaven. As stated before, Chu Hsi defined rites in terms of the Principle of Heaven. He took religious and social rites very seriously. When he became keeper of records or magistrate at the age of twenty-four, he regulated religious and marriage ceremonies. The day before he died, he wrote on his deathbed requesting that his son-in-law and a pupil complete his work of compiling books on rites. In a most learned and most comprehensive discussion on the subject in English, Professor Kao Ming deals with Chu Hsi's works on rites and makes it clear that one of these at least, the *Family Etiquette,* exerted tremendous influence. We may add that this influence extended far into Korea and Japan (chapter 19).

If rites are norms for proper human behavior, *ching*[by] and *ch'üan*[bz] are guidelines for right human behavior. The topic of the standard *(ching)* and the expedient *(ch'üan)* is of more than academic interest, for Chu Hsi regarded it as a matter of great concern in his life. He religiously directed his life with the standard, which is based on righteousness, and avoided the expedient, which is based on profit. He repeatedly declined government service when he considered it wrong to serve, and he strongly attacked Ch'en Liang[ca] (1143–1194) for his utilitarianism, which Chu Hsi considered to have been motivated by profit at the sacrifice of righteousness. When Lu Hsiang-shan visited him in

1181 and lectured at the White Deer Hollow Academy on the Confucian saying that the superior man understands righteousness and the inferior man
understands profit,[54] it must have pleased him greatly. *Chin-ssu lu* contains a
chapter on serving or not serving in the government. As taught by Ch'eng I
and other Northern Sung (960–1126) Neo-Confucianists, the issue must be
decided in favor of righteousness over profit. Only when we perfectly understand this doctrine of Chu Hsi's can we evaluate his political behavior correctly. To this end, Professor Wei Cheng-t'ung's chapter on the standard and the
expedient (chapter 16) is a great help.

We regret not having a paper on Chu Hsi's political life. In fact, the conference was long on his ideas but short on his personal life. Even Professor Ren
Jiyu's[cb] essay on Chu Hsi and religion (chapter 21) deals mostly with Chu
Hsi's theoretical system. On the practical side, it explains how Confucian religion served feudalism but not how Chu Hsi practiced religion himself. Fortunately, we do have Dr. Brian McKnight's account of the world Chu Hsi
lived in (chapter 23). In describing the economic and political situation, the
kinship and the land systems, and the position of the elite, Professor Mc-
Knight has given us a vivid picture of the world in which Chu Hsi lived, thus
enabling us to understand him more adequately as a teacher, a patriot, an
advisor to the emperor, and a local reformer. If more details about his life are
needed, Appendix A contains the biography that I wrote for *Sung Biographies.*

As to his relations with other Neo-Confucianists, we have a paper on
Ch'eng I and one on Hu Hung[cc] (1106–1161). In spite of the fact that Chu Hsi
derived many ideas from Ch'eng I, so much so that his school is often called
the Ch'eng-Chu School, Professor Hsü Fu-kuan makes it very clear (chapter
5) that there are many differences between Chu Hsi and his mentor.

On the other hand, Chu Hsi not only differed with Hu Hung but was
directly opposed to him. According to Hu, nature is beyond the distinction of
good and evil, and Heavenly Principle and human selfish desires are similar
in substance though different in function. To Chu Hsi, original human nature
is good, and human selfish desires cannot be good in substance because good
substance cannot perform an evil function.[55] This is but one issue on which
the two philosophers are diametrically opposed. A thorough examination on
their differences may throw a significant light on why Chu Hsi's doctrine
became dominant while Hu's school soon disappeared. Unfortunately, Western scholars have shown no interest in Hu, and there is practically nothing in
English on him. We therefore welcome Professor Conrad Schirokauer's presentation on this philosopher (chapter 26).

Hu Hung is also dealt with in Professor Ts'ai Jen-hou's[cd] paper (chapter
25), along with other Northern and Southern Sung Neo-Confucianists. By
and large Professor Ts'ai reflects the viewpoint of his teacher, Professor Mou
Tsung-san. In recent years Professor Mou has vigorously argued that Neo-
Confucianism in the Southern Sung should be divided into three schools, the
Hunan School of Hu Hung in addition to the Chu Hsi and Lu Hsiang-shan

schools.[56] In terms of ideas about the mind and the nature, Professor Mou is correct, because the three schools do represent three different viewpoints. In terms of ideas in general, however, his theory is unsound because it leaves out the Utilitarian School of Ch'en Liang and the Historical School of Lü Tsu-ch'ien. Scholars are not in error in dividing the Southern Sung Neo-Confucian Schools into two, namely that of Chu Hsi, which holds that the nature is principle and that of Lu Hsiang-shan, which holds that the mind is principle. Hu Hung's school was a passing phenomenon so far as history is concerned, because he had very few followers and their influence did not reach beyond their local area.

Professor Mou has advanced another theory, which is absolutely new and original. He agrees that Chu Hsi's ideas came from Ch'eng I but argues that Lu Hsiang-shan's ideas came directly from Mencius and that Lu is therefore more representative of Confucian orthodoxy. In his paper "The Problem of Orthodoxy in Chu Hsi's Philosophy," Professor Shu-hsien Liu[ce] examines Mou's thesis critically but generally agrees with his conclusion (chapter 14). In their view, in other words, Chu Hsi was "the side branch that takes over the position of the orthodoxy" (*pieh-tzu wei-tsung*[cf]).

Whether this theory will win acceptance by the majority of Neo-Confucian scholars remains to be seen. It has already rendered valuable service in the study of Neo-Confucianism. For one thing, it helps to overthrow the domination of the Neo-Confucian movement by the Ch'eng-Chu School. For another, Professor Liu strikes down the opposition between the Ch'eng-Chu School and the Lu-Wang School. As he has indicated, "honoring the moral nature" and "following the path of inquiry and study"[57] are not mutually exclusive, but in the case of Chu Hsi, the latter merely serves as the means to the former. Most important of all, although Professor Mou labels Chu Hsi as *pieh-tzu wei-tsung* (literally "a second son in the direct line of descent"), he implies that Chu Hsi and Lu Hsiang-shan are in the same family after all.

By not contrasting "honoring the moral nature" and "following the path of inquiry and study," Professor Liu shows the new spirit of harmony between the Chu Hsi and Lu Hsiang-shan schools. For centuries there has been a partisan spirit among Neo-Confucianists. Followers of Ch'eng I and Chu Hsi, on the one hand, and followers of Lu Hsiang-shan and Wang Yang-ming, on the other, have attacked each other in bitter terms. According to the traditional account, the feud began at the Goose Lake Temple in 1175 when Lü Tsu-ch'ien arranged for Chu Hsi and Lu Hsiang-shan to meet. They had heard of each other and wanted very much to get acquainted. Chu Hsi had by this time become the leading figure in the intellectual world. Lu, ten years younger, brilliant, and self-confident, attracted many followers and was becoming a strong rival to Chu Hsi. According to the traditional account, Chu Hsi advocated "following the path of inquiry and study" while Lu advocated "honoring the moral nature," and the meeting was to "resolve their philosophical differences." Their seven or eight letters in subsequent years have usually been cited to show their differences on this issue and also on their opposite attitudes toward Chou Tun-i's "Explanation of the Diagram of the Great Ultimate," which Chu Hsi took as the foundation of Neo-Confucian metaphysics and Lu regarded as having no place in the Neo-Confucian system. That they held opposite views on the Great Ultimate cannot be denied. But in my studies I have found that besides the seven or eight correspondences usually cited, they wrote to each other almost once a year, totaling twenty-one times in each direction. In these letters they talked about private affairs, such as building a study or the loss of an infant daughter. The letters show mutual respect and genuine friendship. My conclusion was that while the two firmly held on to their philosophical views and were frank and strong in their criticism of each other's ideas, they were courteous and warm in personal dealings.[58] The meeting at the Goose Lake Temple was by no means one to resolve philosophical differences. To be sure, in the gathering there were arguments over Chu Hsi's emphasis on book learning, but the issue was not one of knowledge versus morality. I have found that while Lu went with his brother and several pupils, Chu Hsi went alone. Besides, in the informal gathering of a week or so, they talked about the order of hexagrams, Lü Tsu-ch'ien's commentary on the *Book of History*, Lu's brother's new treatise, and interpretations of the word *i* in the title of the *I ching* (Book of changes). I was forced to conclude that the meeting was not at all confined to the issue of "honoring the moral nature" and "following the path of inquiry and study" but ranged over many subjects. The meeting, therefore, was not designed to resolve any philosophical difference but simply to get acquainted. If it was to be a debate between the two schools, pupils in equal number should have been mobilized.[59] Nevertheless, most likely the meeting sowed the seed of discord. The need of the time for a new philosophy provided a fertile ground, and Lu's pupils who shuttled between Lu and Chu added the necessary water and fertilizer with their distorted reports of the two teachers. The upshot was bias of one school toward the other, especially after the death of the two Masters. This antagonism continued throughout Chinese history until recent decades, with the Chu Hsi School triumphant because it represented orthodoxy. When orthodoxy was overthrown early this century, however, the partisan spirit began to die.

It is in the light of this development that three papers presented at the conference take on special significance. In his opening remarks (chapter 2) Professor Fung Yu-lan strikes the note of the Neo-Confucian unity of "this side" and "the other side," which he considers "a contribution to the development of the human intellect and the advancement of human happiness." Professor Ch'ien Mu's "A Historical Perspective on Chu Hsi's Learning" (chapter 4) not only stresses Chu Hsi's emphasis on the similarities among early Sung Neo-Confucianists rather than their differences but also calls attention to the fact that throughout Chinese history, philosophers have sought convergence rather than divergence. He suggests that there are more similarities than differences between Chu Hsi and Lu Hsiang-shan. Many papers deal with Chu Hsi's amended commentary on the *Great Learning* (chapters 10, 15, 17, 21, 24). Professor Liang Shuming alone (chapter 6) saw in it "a major flaw."

Professor Ying-shih Yü[ch] did not address himself to the problem of Chu Hsi's "following the path of inquiry and study" and Lu Hsiang-shan's "honoring the moral nature," but rather the close relationship between these two approaches in Chu Hsi's own philosophy (chapter 15). We do not need to go into his careful analysis of Chu Hsi's methodology of book learning and Chu Hsi's interpretation of Confucian Classics. It is enough to cite Professor Yu's repeated statement that for Chu Hsi, knowledge is the foundation of morality. Once this is understood, it will be absurd to say that Chu Hsi stands for one approach while Lu Hsiang-shan stands for the other.

Chu Hsi often characterized Lu Hsiang-shan as a Meditation (*Ch'an*[ci]) Buddhist. He was even more critical of Buddhism. In fact, he was very much afraid of it. In this respect he was uncompromising, oftentimes going too far. Professor Charles Wei-hsun Fu[cj] has subjected his criticism to a careful analysis strictly on philosophical grounds (chapter 22). Chu Hsi's critique of Buddhist metaphysics, the Buddhist theory of mind and nature, and the Buddhist method of personal cultivation leading to sudden enlightenment is carefully examined, pointing out both its strengths and its weaknesses.

Turning to the historical development of Chu Hsi's philosophy, we welcome Professor Mao Huaixin's[ck] account of the Chu Hsi Schools in his native province, Fukien (chapter 27). Although brief, the account shows the development of Chu Hsi's teachings in different directions. This prepares the way for further Western studies on the development of the Chu Hsi School, for so far the subject has not been touched upon in English. For later development, we are fortunate to have Professor Liu Ts'un-yan's[cl] paper on the Yüan period (1279–1368). It is a comprehensive treatment with full documentary support (chapter 28). The author discusses the role played by the Four Books, the *Hsiao-hsüeh*, and the civil service examinations, as well as the promulgation of Chu Hsi's teaching, its revision, and the reconciliation of conflicting interpretations of Chu Hsi's doctrines. We wish we had a similar paper to cover the Ming (1368–1644) and Ch'ing (1644–1912) dynasties. However, Professor Li Zehou's[cm] presentation (chapter 29) does deal briefly with some Ming and Ch'ing Neo-Confucianists and brings us to some thinkers of the People's Republic after a general survey of Neo-Confucian metaphysics.

We wish we had done more on Chu Hsi's role in Korea and Japan, but that would require a separate conference. In the meantime, several conferences have been held in which Chu Hsi's influence in Korea and Japan has been discussed at least to a limited extent. As far as this conference is concerned, by focusing on the debate between Han Won-jin[cn] (1682–1751) and Yi Gan[co] (1677–1727), Professor Youn Sa-soon[cp] (chapter 30) brings out one of the two basic issues in Korean study of Chu Hsi's thought: the controversy over the nature of man and things, a natural and logical outgrowth of the earlier debate on the relationship between nature based on principle and feeling based on material force. Professor Yamazaki Michio's[cq] concentration on Inaba Mokusai[cr] (1732–1799) (chapter 31) may be taken as a case study on Chu Hsi's doctrine of the learning of the Way in Japan.

All in all, we believe the conference covered a good deal of ground and did much to promote the further study of Chu Hsi. Indeed, one of its purposes was to look to the future. This was the reason for the innovative program of awarding fellowships to young scholars through an international competition. Most of the young scholars chosen had received their Ph.D.'s in Neo-Confucian studies; several had published books. Three workshops were set up for them, and there is no question but that the intimate association with senior scholars has given them tremendous inspiration and strong stimulation. It is not fantastic to expect that a new generation of Chu Hsi scholars will emerge from this conference.

Four books were published just before the conference, three exclusively on Chu Hsi[60] and one on Neo-Confucianism in general.[61] They were presented to members of the conference. In the two years since the conference, a participant has published a book on Chu Hsi's thoughts on the *Book of Changes*.[62] In addition, a number of articles on Chu Hsi have appeared in mainland China, Taiwan, the United States, and elsewhere. At least one professor in Peking has begun to lecture on Neo-Confucianism at two universities. Courses on Neo-Confucianism or Chu Hsi have been added at several universities in the United States and Taiwan. A conference on Neo-Confucianism and education, under the direction of Professor de Bary, was held in the fall of 1984. It was a delayed reaction, one might say, from the workshop that Professor de Bary led at the conference. We cannot claim credit for all this, but studies on Chu Hsi are certainly growing rapidly.

Notes

1. *Book of Mencius*, 5B:1.

2. In Francoise Aubin, ed., *Étude Song-Sung Studies im memoriam Étienne Balazs*, Ser. II, no. 1, 1973, pp. 59–90.

3. See "Chu Hsi's Completion of Neo-Confucianism," sec. 2.

4. The *Book of Odes*, the *Book of History*, the *Book of Changes*, the *Book of Rites*, and the *Spring and Autumn Annals*.

5. See "Chu Hsi's Completion of Neo-Confucianism," sec. 3.

6. *Ibid.*, sec. 1.

7. *I-ch'uan wen-chi*[cs] [Collection of literary works of Ch'eng I], 5:12b, and *I chuan*[ct] [Commentary on the *Book of Changes*], 1:48a and 3:3b, both in the *Erh-Ch'eng ch'üan-shu*[cu] [Complete works of the two Ch'engs], (SPPY ed.).

8. The *Chin-ssu lu* contains the sayings of Chou Tun-i, Ch'eng Hao, Ch'eng I, and Chang Tsai. I have translated the work into English under the title *Reflections on*

Things at Hand. It was published by the Columbia University Press, New York, in 1967.

9. For the latter, see my "The *Hsing-li ching-i* and the Ch'eng-Chu School in the Seventeenth Century," in Wm. Theodore de Bary, ed., *The Unfolding of Neo-Confucianism* (New York: Columbia University Press, 1975), pp. 543–579.

10. For details, see my "The Evolution of the Confucian Concept *Jen*," *Philosophy East and West*, 4 (1955), pp. 295–319.

11. *I-shu*[cv] [Surviving works], 2A:12b and 18:2a, in the *Erh-Ch'eng ch'üan-shu*.

12. *Chu Tzu wen-chi*[cw] [Collection of literary works of Master Chu], (SPPY ed.), 67:20a, "Treatise on *Jen*."

13. J. P. Bruce, *Chu Hsi and His Masters* (London: Probsthain, 1923), pp. 148 and 241; Olaf Graf, *Tao und Jen: Sein und Sollen im sungchinesischen Monismus* (Wiesbaden: Otto Harrassowitz, 1970), pp. 243, 277, 317–341, 350–352.

14. *Chu Tzu yü-lei*[cx] [Classified conversations of Master Chu], (Taipei: Cheng-chung[cy] Book Co. ed., 1970), ch. 80, sec. 36–43, pp. 3294–3303.

15. In the *Shih chi-chuan*[cz] (Collected commentaries on the *Book of Odes*), odes nos. 42, 48, 64, 72, 74, 76, 81, 83–95, 137, 139, 140, 143.

16. *Chu Tzu yü-lei*, ch. 78, sec. 25 and 26, p. 3153.

17. *Ibid.*, ch. 84, sec. 28, p. 3469.

18. *Ibid.*, ch. 83, sec. 39, p. 3413.

19. See my "The Study of Chu Hsi in the West," *Journal of Asian Studies*, vol. 30, no. 4 (Aug. 1976), pp. 555–577.

20. *I-shu*, 22B:3b.

21. *Book of Mencius*, 6A:10. Mencius said, "I like life, and I also like righteousness. If I cannot have both, I will let life go and choose righteousness."

22. *I-shu* 8:4b.

23. *Chu Tzu yü-lei*, ch. 96, sec. 60, p. 3928.

24. *Chu Tzu yü-lei p'ing*[da] [Criticism of Master Chu's classified sayings], in the *Yen-Li ts'ung-shu*[db] [Yen Yüan and Li Kung series], p. 24a.

25. *Chu Tzu hsin hsüeh-an*[dc] [New anthology and critical accounts of Master Chu], (Taipei: San-min[dd] Book Co., 1971), Vol. II, p. 293.

26. *Chu Tzu yü-lei*, ch. 116, sec. 55, p. 4474. For the disciple, see the *Sung-Yüan hsüeh-an pu-i*[de] [Supplement to the *Anthology and Critical Accounts of the Neo-Confucianists of the Sung and Yüan Dynasties*], (Taipei: The World Book Co. ed.), 69:190b.

27. See his instructions to pupils, *Chu Tzu yü-lei*, chs. 113–121.

28. For a discussion and translation of selections from this work, see my *Source Book in Chinese Philosophy* (Princeton, N.J.: Princeton University Press, 1963), ch. 42.

29. See my *Chinese Philosophy, 1949–1963* (Honolulu: East-West Center Press, 1967), pp. 38 and 190–194.

30. Yeh Shao-weng,[df] *Ssu-ch'ao wen-chien lu*[dg] [What was heard and seen during the four reigns], 4th collection, 4:3b.

31. *Chu Tzu wen-chi*, 85:19a.

32. Yang T'ien-shih,[dh] *Chu Hsi chi-ch'i che-hsüeh*[di] [Chu Hsi and his philosophy], (Peking: Chung-hua[dj] Book Co., 1982), pp. 69–70; Chang Liwen, *Chu Hsi ssu-hsiang yen-chiu*[dk] [Study of Chu Hsi's thought] (Beijing: Chinese Social Sciences Press, 1981), pp. 78–79.

33. Olaf Graf, trans., *Dschu Hsi*,[dl] *Djin si lu*,[dm] *die Sungkonfuzianische Summa mit*

dem Kommetar des Yä Tsai[dn] (Tokyo: Sophia University, 1953); *Tao und Jen: Sein und Sollen im sungchinesischen Monismus* (Wiesbaden: Otto Harrassowitz, 1970).

34. Yves Hervouet, ed., *A Sung Bibliography* (Hong Kong: The Chinese University Press, 1978); Herbert Franke, ed., *Sung Biographies* (Wiesbaden: Franz Steiner Verlag, 1976), 4 vols.

35. The conference volumes are: Wm. Theodore de Bary, ed., *Self and Society in Ming Thought,* 1970; de Bary, ed., *The Unfolding of Neo-Confucianism,* 1975; de Bary and Irene Bloom, eds., *Principle and Practicality, Essays in Neo-Confucianism and Practical Learning,* 1979; and Hok-lam Chan[do] and de Bary, eds., *Yüan Thought: Chinese Thought and Religion under the Mongols,* 1982; all published by the Columbia University Press.

36. Conference papers were published as *Wang Ch'uan-shan hsüeh-shu t'ao-lun chi*[dp] [Anthology of the symposium on the learning of Wang Fu-chih], (Peking: Chung-hua Book Co., 1963).

37. Papers presented at the conference were published in a special issue of *Philosophy East and West,* vol. 23, nos. 1–2 (Jan. & Apr. 1973).

38. *Chu Tzu yü-lei,* ch. 94, sec. 16, p. 3759.

39. The only place in Ch'eng I's works where *t'ai-chi* is mentioned is in the "Preface to Changes," which is generally considered unreliable. For a discussion of this question, see A. C. Graham, *Two Chinese Philosophers: Ch'eng Ming-tao and Ch'eng Yi-ch'uan* (London: Lund Humphrey, 1958), Appendix I; and my "Patterns for Neo-Confucianism: Why Chu Hsi Differed from Ch'eng I," *Journal of Chinese Philosophy,* 5 (1978), pp. 108–109.

40. *Chu Tzu yü-lei,* ch. 94, sec. 109, p. 3790.

41. *Hsiang-shan ch'üan-chi*[dq] [Complete works of Lu Chiu-yüan], (SPPY ed.), 2:6a–b, "Letter to Chu Yüan-hui[dr] [Chu Hsi]."

42. Wang Mao-hung,[ds] *Chu Tzu nien-p'u*[dt] [Chronological biography of Master Chu], (World Books Co. ed.), p. 216 (under the third month of 1200), and pp. 341–342.

43. Commentary on the *Analects,* 1:2.

44. Commentary on the *Analects,* 1:12.

45. *Chu Tzu yü-lei,* ch. 1, sec. 1, 4, pp. 1–2; ch. 6, sec. 13, p. 161; ch. 100, sec. 31, p. 4050; and *Chu Tzu wen-chi,* 36:8b–9a–12a; 67:16a–b.

46. For example, in ch. 1 of the *Chou Tzu ch'üan-shu*[du] [Complete works of Master Chou Tun-i].

47. Ch'en Lai,[dv] "Kuanyü Ch'eng-Chu li-ch'i hsüeh-shuo liang-t'iao tzu-liao ti k'ao-cheng"[dw] [Investigation on two pieces of material in connection with the theories on principle and material force of Ch'eng I and Chu Hsi], *Chung-kuo che-hsüeh shih yen-chiu*[dx] [Studies in the history of Chinese philosophy], 1983, no. 2, pp. 85–86.

48. *Chu Tzu yü-lei,* ch. 1, sec. 13, p. 5.

49. *Instructions for Practical Living,* trans. Wing-tsit Chan (New York: Columbia University Press, 1963), sec. 172.

50. *K'un-chih chi*[dy] [Knowledge painfully acquired], (1528 ed.), supplement, 5:3a.

51. *I-ch'uan wen-chi,* 7:12b; *I chuan,* 1:48a and 3:3b.

52. *Chu Tzu wen-chi,* 67:20a–21b.

53. In my *Chu-hsüeh lun-chi*[dz] [Collected essays on Chu Hsi studies], (Taipei: Student Book Co., 1982), pp. 37–68.

54. *Analects,* 4:16.

55. *Chu Tzu wen-chi,* 73:40b–47b, "Doubts on Hu Hung's *Knowing Words.*"

56. Mou Tsung-san, *Hsin-t'i yü hsing-t'i*[ea] [The substance of the mind and the substance of the nature], (Taipei: Cheng-chung Book Co., 1969), Vol. 1, p. 49.

57. *Doctrine of the Mean,* ch. 27.

58. For these correspondences, see my "A Detailed Account of the Correspondences between Chu and Lu," *Chu-hsüeh lun-chi,* pp. 251–269.

59. For the meeting, see my "Supplementary Information on the Goose Lake Temple Meeting," *ibid.,* pp. 233–249.

60. My *Chu-hsüeh lun-chi* and *Chu Tzu men-jen*[eb] [Chu Hsi's pupils], and Shu-hsien Liu's *Chu Tzu che-hsüeh ssu-hsiang ti fa-chen yü wan-ch'eng*[ec] [The development and maturity of Master Chu's philosophical thought], all published by the Student Book Co. of Taipei in 1982.

61. Ts'ai Jen-hou, "Hsin Ju-chia ti ching-shan fang-hsiang"[ed] [The spiritual direction of Neo-Confucianism], (Taipei: Student Book Co., 1982).

62. Tsang Chun-hai,[ee] *Hui-an I-hsüeh t'an-wei*[ef] [An investigation into the subtleties of Chu Hsi's philosophy of *Changes*], (Taipei: Fu Jen[eg] Catholic University Press, 1983).

Glossary

a	集大成	ac	康熙	be	邱漢生
b	周敦頤	ad	朱子全書	bf	友枝龍太郎
c	張載	ae	乾隆	bg	無極
d	程顥	af	顏元	bh	陸象山九淵
e	程頤	ag	錢穆	bi	四書集註
f	道統	ah	郭友仁德元	bj	成中英
g	邵雍	ai	馮友蘭	bk	呂柟
h	司馬光	aj	新理學	bl	朱子抄釋
i	李侗	ak	徐復觀	bm	朱子語略
j	太極	al	唐君毅	bn	楊與立
k	理	am	牟宗三	bo	黎靖德
l	理學	an	沈繼祖	bp	羅欽順
m	氣	ao	僞學	bq	諸橋轍次
n	象數	ap	劉珙	br	大漢和辭典
o	理一分殊	aq	劉勉之	bs	賦與
p	陰	ar	道	bt	四書大全
q	陽	as	王夫之	bu	扶問切
r	太極圖說	at	王陽明守仁	bv	中庸或問
s	近思錄	au	程慶和	bw	孟子或問
t	呂祖謙	av	梁漱溟	bx	秦家懿
u	性理大全	aw	岡田武彥	by	經
v	性理精義	ax	佐藤仁	bz	權
w	仁	ay	韋政通	ca	陳亮
x	韓愈	az	張立文	cb	任繼愈
y	小學	ba	高明	cc	胡宏
z	嶽麓	bb	羅光	cd	蔡仁厚
aa	儀禮	bc	山井湧	ce	劉述先
ab	考據	bd	鄧艾民	cf	別子爲宗

cg	易	cz	詩集傳	ds	王懋竑
ch	余英時	da	朱子語類評	dt	朱子年譜
ci	禪	db	顏李叢書	du	周子全書
cj	傅偉勳	dc	朱子新學案	dv	陳來
ck	冒懷辛	dd	三民	dw	關於程朱理氣學說兩
cl	柳存仁	de	宋元學案補遺		條資料的考証
cm	李澤厚	df	葉紹翁	dx	中國哲學史研究
cn	韓元震	dg	四朝聞見錄	dy	困知記
co	李東	dh	楊天石	dz	朱學論集
cp	尹絲淳	di	朱熹及其哲學	ea	心體與性體
cq	山崎道夫	dj	中華	eb	朱子門人
cr	稻葉默齋	dk	朱熹思想研究	ec	朱子哲學思想的發展
cs	伊川文集	dl	朱熹		與完成
ct	易傳	dm	近思錄	ed	新儒家的精神方向
cu	二程全書	dn	葉采	ee	曾春海
cv	遺書	do	陳學霖	ef	晦庵易學探微
cw	朱子文集	dp	王船山學術討論集	eg	輔仁
cx	朱子語類	dq	象山全集		
cy	正中	dr	朱元晦		

2

A General Statement on Neo-Confucianism

Fung Yu-lan

I AM VERY HAPPY to be here to participate in the International Conference on Zhu Xi. Beside what I shall learn from other scholars coming from many countries, I will also have a chance to renew my memory of thirty-five years ago, when I had the privilege of being a visiting professor at this university. During the Christmas vacation, a friend with his family and I engaged a yacht to travel to the other islands. Everywhere I was impressed by the beauty of the land and the hospitality of the people. The conference now gives me a chance to see these old places and to meet old friends.

I take this opportunity to express my congratulations on the seventy-fifth anniversary of the University of Hawaii. The islands of Hawaii are midway between the West and the Far East. Taking advantage of this geographical location, this university considers itself a suitable meeting place for cultural exchange and interflow between East and West. The university has done much work in that respect. This conference is an example of such work. Under the sponsorship of the University of Hawaii and the American Council of Learned Societies, the conference will promote cultural exchange between East and West in general and the study of Zhu Xi in particular.

Zhu Xi was a leader of what is known in the West as Neo-Confucianism. I shall here try to make a general statement of what I take to be the essence of Neo-Confucianism.

Neo-Confucianism may be called "the learning of man." It deals with such topics as man's place and role in the universe, the relation between man and nature, and the relations between man and man and between human nature and human happiness. Its aim is to achieve unity of opposites in the life of man, and to show how to accomplish this.

Generally speaking, there are two sets of fundamental opposites, hence, two fundamental contradictions. They are fundamental because they are common to everything in the universe.

In the universe, every thing, big or small, is an individual, human beings included. Being an individual, it must be an individual of some kind. It must have some qualities. Nothing is without qualities. The individual is a particular; its quality is the universal inherent in it. The contradiction between universality and particularity thus exists in everything. This is one kind of contradiction.

Being an individual, the individual must consider itself as the subject and others as objects. This is another kind of contradiction, the contradiction between subjectivity and objectivity.

These two kinds of contradiction are the consequence of the same fact that an individual is an individual. This fact is common to everything. What is peculiar in man is that he is conscious of it. In this respect, the outstanding representative is the philosopher; the learning of man is the philosophy of the philosophers.

In philosophy, there are three ways to approach the above fact: the ontological, the epistemological, and the ethical.

In the West, Plato was the representative of the ontological approach. Inspired by the suggestion of mathematics, he introduced his theory of Ideas. Geometry defines the circularity of circles, only to find that among concrete circles, no one circle is exactly in accordance with the definition. That is to say, among concrete circles, no one is perfectly circular. The definition is not merely words of geometry, nor merely the thought of the mathematician. The definition of circularity expresses the objective standard of criticism and action. With this standard people could say this or that circle is more or less circular, pointing out its defects and imperfections. With this standard people could strive to correct its defects and imperfections. Plato pointed out that the standard is the Idea, the original of circularity, while concrete circles are mere imitations, mere copies of circularity. An imitation can never be exactly the same as the original.

Plato made clear the contradiction between universality and particularity, only to show that the contradiction is much sharper and more acute than what is generally understood. In consequence, he considered those aspects of human life that are due to particularity—such as sensuous desires, for example —to be by nature base and evil. Reason is by nature superior to and higher than the sensuous, just as slavemasters were by nature superior to and higher than the slaves. The order of nature is that the higher should control the lower.

Kant started with the opposites of subjectivity and objectivity. According to him, the subject could know the object only through its own subjective forms and categories. What is known through subjective forms and categories is only the phenomena, not the noumena. Even with regard to man's own spiritual world, what is known to him is also only a phenomenon, because that also is known through his subjective forms and categories. Kant made clear the contradiction between subjectivity and objectivity only to show that the contradiction is much sharper and more acute than what is understood by the common people.

According to Kant there is something like a flashlight through which man could have a glance at the noumena. The flashlight is the moral conduct of man. According to Kant, moral conduct is moral because it represents a universal law. Through this universal law, which man legislates for himself, he could have a glance at the noumena, God, immortality and freedom. By logical inference through the accumulation of moral conduct man could have a complete knowledge of noumena or a whole experience of it. Kant, however, did not make this inference but regarded the noumena as the "other side." What men could know and experience is "this side." To Kant, the "other side" was beyond the reach of man.

The Neo-Confucianists approached the problem from the ethical angle. They did not altogether neglect the ontological approach, however, for without the ontological approach the contradiction between universality and particularity could not be made clear. In fact, Zhu Xi himself was one of the great ontologists in the history of Chinese philosophy. But the Neo-Confucianists did not stop with the ontological approach. They did not stop with the analysis of the opposites of universality and particularity but tried to achieve a unity of the two. For them the way to achieve such a unity was through the accumulation of moral conduct.

According to the Neo-Confucianists the universal is inherent in the particular. The particular is not merely the imperfect imitation of the universal, but rather the realization of the universal. The realization may be imperfect, but without the particular the universal could not exist at all. On this point the different schools of Neo-Confucianism were not in agreement. Even Zhu Xi himself was inconsistent in his sayings. But I think this point correctly represents the conclusions of Neo-Confucianism.

For the Neo-Confucianists the nature of man is that which distinguishes man from other animals. It is the universal of man inherent in man as a particular. The nature of man is not equivalent to the instinct of man. The nature of man is a logical concept, not a biological concept. It includes the biological instincts but is not these instincts. It is in this sense that Neo-Confucianism insisted that human nature is good. It could not be otherwise.

Even sensuous desires as such are not by nature base and evil as Plato thought, for they derive from the body, the material foundation of human existence. According to Neo-Confucianism what is bad and evil is not these desires themselves but the selfishness associated with them. The standard for judging a conduct moral or immoral is whether the conduct is "for private," or "for public." If it is "for private," it is immoral or nonmoral; if it is "for public," it is moral. Moral conduct means that the selfishness of man is reduced. The accumulation of moral conduct means the accumulation of this diminution of selfishness. When the accumulation of the diminutions reaches a certain point, selfishness is completely overcome, and a unity of particularity and universality comes as a result. This point is what Zhu Xi called the "thorough understanding" (*huo-jan kuan-t'ung*[a]) and what Ch'an[b] Buddhism called "sudden enlightenment" (*tun-wu*[c]). "With the thorough understand-

ing . . . the complete nature and the great function of the mind are illuminated," as Zhu Xi said.[1] When selfishness is overcome, the sensuous desire is
not abolished altogether; what is abolished is the selfishness associated with it.
With this unity there comes also the unity of subjectivity and objectivity.

The Neo-Confucianists considered benevolence (humanity, 'jen'[d]) as the
first of Four Fundamental Virtues, or even including all four.[2] Benevolence
means love for others. The man who loves others is called the "benevolent
man." According to Neo-Confucianism the spiritual world of the benevolent
man merges into a whole with the universe. He considers all men as his
brothers and everything as his companion. The Chinese words for "benevolence" and for "man" (*jen*[e]) have the same sound. In the Classics, the two
words mutually defined each other. The learning of man may thus be defined
as the learning of benevolence.

According to Neo-Confucianism, when this kind of unity is achieved, there
comes supreme happiness. It is a kind of happiness different in quality from
sensuous pleasures. It is an enjoyment of emancipation and freedom from the
boundaries and limitations of particularity and subjectivity. It is an emancipation—not in the political sense, but an emancipation from the finite to the
infinite, from time to eternity. What Kant said about the three important matters in the world of noumena—God, immortality, and freedom—is similar.

Plato offered a parable telling of a man who, imprisoned in a cave for life,
escaped from the cave. He immediately began to see the brilliance of the sun
and the beauty of the world. His view broadened, he experienced a joy that he
had never experienced before. Plato used this parable to illustrate the mind of
the man who has gained the insight of the world of Ideas. What the Neo-Confucianists called "supreme happiness" is something like this.

Such supreme happiness may be called intellectual happiness, because it is
the result of the activity of the intellect. It differs in quality from sensuous
pleasures resulting from the satisfaction of the sense organs. In order to
achieve this state, one does not have to do anything special, to leave society or
abandon one's family. Nor is there need for worship and prayer. One just
accumulates moral conduct in daily life, always keeps in mind the need to
fight against selfishness. That is all. In this way, the "this side" becomes the
same as the "other side," the "other side" resides in "this side." This synthesis is the contribution of Neo-Confucianism toward the development of the
human intellect and the advancement of human happiness.

Any moral conduct, as a particular, is unavoidably associated with the existing social institutions and involved in the social regulations of the time. The
Neo-Confucianists lived in the feudal society of China. What they considered
as moral was naturally associated with and involved in feudal institutions and
regulations. This association also shows the contradiction between universality and particularity. Concrete moral conduct is the particular; the character
of being "for public" is the universal. The universal is inherent in the particular. Thus in the feudal society of China, the ruling class honored Neo-Con-

fucianism as the ruling philosophy; in the time of antifeudalism, Neo-Confucianism is denounced as reactionary. Neither position is without reason; both are the consequences of the dialectical development of history. The points I have made are confined to the philosophical aspect of Neo-Confucianism.

In this limited space I did not quote much from the sayings of the Neo-Confucianists to illustrate my points. Instead I talked about Plato and Kant, Western philosophers who considered the same problems as did the Neo-Confucianists. This shows that East and West, although separated by oceans, face the same problems in life, which are reflected in philosophy.

Notes

1. Introduction to his *Chung-yung chang-chü*[f] [Commentary on the *Doctrine of the Mean*].

2. *Book of Mencius*, 2A:2, 6A:6. The Four Fundamental Virtues are benevolence, righteousness, propriety, and wisdom.

Glossary

[a] 豁然貫通

[b] 禪

[c] 頓悟

[d] 仁

[e] 人

[f] 中庸章句

3

Chu Hsi's Contribution to Confucian Learning and the Flaws in His Theoretical Thinking

Liang Shuming

To BEGIN WITH, we must clarify what kind of learning Confucianism is. Having done so, we can then evaluate Chu Hsi's contribution to this tradition. I shall proceed with my discussion in this sequence.

Describing his own process of learning and intellectual maturity, Confucius (551–479 B.C.) once remarked, "At fifteen I set my mind on learning. At thirty I had established myself. At forty I no longer had perplexities. At fifty I understood the Decree of Heaven. At sixty I became at ease with whatever I heard. At seventy I could follow my heart's desires without transgressing moral principles."[1] It is thus evident that what Confucius called learning is both a conscious reflection upon one's life and one's manner of living and a search for gradual improvement of both. Scholars in the past have offered various conjectures to interpret the different stages of development outlined by Confucius. To explain the sentence, "At sixty I became at ease with whatever I heard," for example, some scholars have suggested something like "When the sound enters, the mind is penetrated." This is a highly inappropriate explanation. When we reflect upon the matter seriously, even Confucius himself did not know what stage of development he would reach before he actually reached it. How can we venture any reckless guess? We should strictly observe the dictum that "when we do not know, we acknowledge our ignorance."[2] What we do know, however, is that Confucian learning is nothing other than the conscious reflection upon one's life and one's manner of living.

The way Confucius' disciple Yen Hui[a3] (c. 521–490 B.C.) undertook his study is the best illustration of Confucian learning:

> When Duke Ai[b] of Lu[c] asked him which of his disciples was fond of learning, Confucius replied, "There was one Yen Hui who was fond of learning. He did not vent his anger upon an innocent party, nor did he make the same mistake twice. Unfortunately his allotted span of life was a short one and he died. Now there is no one. I have not come across another as fond of learning as he was."[4]

What is meant by "not venting anger upon an innocent party"? What is meant by "not making the same mistake twice"? From Confucius' tone of approval in the above quote, we can surmise that Yen Hui's accomplishment in learning must have been most impressive. We must not follow the example of later scholars, however, Chu Hsi included, to conjecture purely from the superficial meaning of the words used what these phrases really say. To do so will be to claim knowledge when actually we are ignorant. What we are sure about, however, is that Yen Hui was unmatched precisely because of his understanding and appreciation of life and the manner of living, and nothing else.

As representative of the Sung (960–1279) scholars, Chu Hsi has certainly made major contributions to the propagation and perpetuation of Confucian learning. In particular, I have in mind his shrewd and insightful selection from among the fifty chapters of the *Book of Rites* the two chapters that best illustrate the true essence of Confucian teaching, namely, the *Great Learning* and the *Doctrine of the Mean,* and his combination of them with the *Analects* and the *Book of Mencius* to form the Four Books, which constitute the most basic reading for all students in later generations. This accomplishment of Chu will be further discussed below.

Confucianism was, in the beginning, only one of the contending schools of thought. During the Warring States period (403–222 B.C.), the miscellaneous practices of the hegemon were widely adopted. In Western Han (206 B.C.–A.D. 8), the tradition of Huang-Lao[d] (Taoist statecraft) was popular. A cursory reading of the chapter "Liu-chia yao-chih"[e] (Essential doctrines of the six schools) in the *Shih-chi*[f] (Historical records) will reveal that Confucianism was very much in eclipse during this time. We can generally state that from Han (206 B.C.–A.D. 220) to T'ang (618–907) there were only classical, canonical studies, but no authentic, practicing Confucianists. It was only after the challenge of Taoism and Buddhism in the T'ang dynasty that Confucianists began to reemerge in Sung and Ming (1368–1644) to revive their long obscured tradition.

When this Confucian tradition was revived in the Sung period, it was at one time known as *Tao-hsüeh*[g] (The learning of immutable Way). It had another name of *Li-hsüeh*[h] (The learning of principles). Beginning with Chou Tun-i[i] (1017–1073), it was transmitted through Chang Tsai[j] (1020–1077), the two brothers Ch'eng Hao[k] (1032–1085) and Ch'eng I[l] (1033–1107), and the two brothers Lu Chiu-ling[m] (1132–1180) and Lu Chiu-yüan (Lu Hsiang-shan,[n] 1139–1193). When Chu Hsi appeared on the scene, he enjoyed great esteem for having synthesized the ideas of these Sung masters into an integrated whole.

Chu Hsi's creation of an integrated synthesis must be seen in the light of the decision made by the ruling authorities in Ming and Ch'ing (1644–1912). Both dynasties recruited officials through the civil service examination. It was Chu Hsi's *Ssu-shu chang-chü chi-chu*[o] (Commentaries on the Four Books) that was designated to be the basis for all compositions in these examinations.

Since the consolidation of Chu Hsi's authoritative position relied on the political support of the ruling dynasty, the teachings of Confucius and Mencius (372–289 B.C.?), which originally represented only one school of thought and not a religion, were turned into a "Religion of Confucianism" (*K'ung-chiao*[p]) through the manipulation of the authorities. Chu Hsi himself was exalted as the representative of this religion. The "religion of rituals" (*li-chiao*[q]), or the "religion of titles and statuses" (*ming-chiao*[r]), which espouse the Three Bonds and the Five Constancies (*san-kang wu-ch'ang*[s]),[5] was thus established. The true spirit of Confucian teaching became suffocated and lost. The abuses of this new religion had been given an impassioned denunciation by Tai Chen[t] (1723–1777) in the Ch'ing period. In fairness to Chu Hsi, however, he was not entirely to blame for these later developments.

The *Doctrine of the Mean* and the *Great Learning* best exemplify the quintessence of Confucian teaching because they both clearly reveal that this teaching centers on the notions of *hsiu-shen*[u] (cultivation of the self) and *shen-tu*[v] (vigilance in solitude). This focus on inner cultivation is also called *hsiu-chi*[w] (self-cultivation). *Hsiu-chi, hsiu-shen,* and *shen-tu* are evidently identical in meaning. Have we not pointed out earlier that the essence of Confucian learning is this conscious reflection on one's life and one's manner of living? All of this is made clear in Confucius' reply to a question put to him by his disciple Tzu-lu[x] (c. 542–480 B.C.).

> Tzu-lu asked about the gentleman. The Master said, "He cultivates himself with reverential seriousness." Tzu-lu further inquired, "Is that all?" The Master answered, "He cultivates himself and thereby brings peace and security to his fellow men." Tzu-lu asked again, "Is that all?" The Master replied, "He cultivates himself so as to bring peace and security to the common people. Even Yao[y] and Shun[z] would have found this task of bringing peace and security to the common people difficult to perform!"[6]

The solemn exaltation of the *Doctrine of the Mean* and the *Great Learning* by grouping them with the *Analects* and the *Book of Mencius* to form the Four Books that provide the basis for education for all later generations—this is the contribution of the Sung scholars. At the same time, it is the contribution of Chu Hsi. It is regrettable, however, that Chu Hsi's annotations on the Four Books contain numerous errors and misinterpretations. Early Ch'ing scholars such as Yen Yüan[aa] (1635–1704) and Li Kung[ab] (1659–1733) were highly critical of the Sung Confucianists, Chu Hsi included. Later in the Ch'ing period, Ch'en Li's[ac] (1810–1882) *Tung-shu tu-shu chi*[ad] (Reading notes from the Eastern Studio) and Li Tzu-ch'i's[ae] *Ssu-shu chih-i*[af] (Queries on the Four Books) both pointed out some of the errors and provided corrections. Mao Ch'i-ling's[ag] (1623–1716) *Ssu-shu kai-ts'uo*[ah] (Rectifying mistakes on the Four Books) offered even more scathing criticisms of Chu Hsi's mistakes. To be sure, Chu Hsi was earnest and industrious in his studies and was well versed in many schools of thought. However, he had also over-extended himself and become negligent in some areas. In addition, he had excessively strong subjective views. It is thus conceivable that some of his commentaries show signs of carelessness and crude understanding.

Finally, I would like to touch upon what I perceive to be a major flaw in Chu Hsi's theoretical reasoning. This flaw is revealed most glaringly in a passage in his "supplemental commentary" on the *Great Learning* (*pu-chuan*[ai]):

> The human mind is sentient, so none lacks the capacity to know. At the same time, not a single thing in the world is devoid of principle. It is only because the principles of things are not fully and exhaustively investigated that human knowledge itself is incomplete. For this reason, the *Great Learning* begins its instruction for each learner by admonishing him that, with regard to all things in the world, he should proceed from what he already knows about their principles, and should investigate further until he reaches the limit. After exerting himself in this manner for an extended period of time, he will one day abruptly arrive at a penetrating comprehension of all things. Then every aspect of these things, whether external or internal, refined or coarse, will be apprehended; and the mind, in its entire substance and great function, will be perfectly enlightened. This is called the investigation of things. This is called the perfection of knowledge.[7]

We have to keep in mind that in this world there is *wu-li*[aj] (principle of things), and then there is *ch'ing-li*[ak] (principle of feelings). The two are entirely different. Unfortunately, Chu Hsi has failed to make any distinction between them. When we observe the phenomena of evolution and natural selection in the animal and plant worlds, we notice that they are characterized by the strong dominating the weak and the many overpowering the few. Even in the human world the situation is similar. This objective reality in nature is indicative of the principle of things. Yet emotionally we find this reality repulsive. We always sympathize with the weak and demand fairness and justice for them. Occasionally we are moved by righteous outrage and stand up for the downtrodden and the unfairly treated. In such cases the principle of feelings is at work. This principle of feelings is identical with what we commonly call the Principle of Heaven (*T'ien-li*[al]) or conscience (*liang-hsin*[am]), which inheres in our subjective preference. Moreover, what our common sayings often refer to as the sense of moral justice (*cheng-i kan*[an]) is clearly a feeling, which is exactly the opposite of the principle of things. The latter is external, objective, and is derived entirely from detached observation and experimentation. It will tolerate no intermixing with any subjective feeling or preference.

From the perspective of our analysis outlined above, let us reexamine Chu Hsi's writing on the investigation of things in the *Great Learning*. Since he mentions such terms as "thing in the world," "the external and internal," and "the refined and coarse of all things," he is evidently talking about the principle of things. The application of the mind to investigate external things will surely enable one to observe their operating principles and to produce natural sciences as well as social sciences. But does not this orientation represent a departure from the focus on conscious reflection on the meaning of life and the manner of living, which we have determined to be the central concern of Confucian learning? How then can one attain the goal of what Chu Hsi has referred to as "the perfect enlightenment of the entire substance and great function of the mind"? We should know that in order to attain this goal, the way to follow is what has already been mentioned in the original text of the *Great Learning*—the way of manifesting the clear character (*ming ming-te*[ao]).[8] Manifesting the clear character lies precisely in *hsiu-shen* and *shen-tu;* and to observe and handle all affairs in real life is fundamentally the undertakings of *hsiu-shen* and *shen-tu*. Both will reveal and develop the entire substance and great function of our mind. If we begin our learning by applying the mind to external things, will it not run counter to the central teaching of the Confucian tradition we have described above? Chu Hsi has therefore failed to avoid committing a serious mistake in his theoretical thinking. I await the judgment and comment of my readers whether I, too, have committed any serious mistakes in this evaluation.

Translated by Richard Shek[ap]

Notes

1. *Analects*, 2:4.
2. *Ibid.*, 2:17.
3. Confucius' most virtuous pupil, c. 521–490 B.C.
4. *Analects*, 6:2.
5. The Three Bonds were the ruler as the standard for the minister, the father as the standard for the son, and the husband as the standard for the wife. The Five Constancies were the five relations between father and son, ruler and minister, brothers, husband and wife, and friends, with the traditional emphasis on loyalty to the ruler and filial piety toward the father.
6. *Analects*, 14:15. Yao and Shun were legendary sage-emperors.
7. Commentary in the fifth chapter of his *Ta-hsüeh chang-chü*[aq] [Commentary on the *Great Learning*].
8. The beginning sentence of the *Great Learning*.

Glossary

a	顏回	i	周敦頤	q	禮教
b	哀	j	張載	r	名教
c	魯	k	程顥	s	三綱五常
d	黃老	l	程頤	t	戴震
e	六家旨要	m	陸九齡	u	修身
f	史記	n	陸九淵象山	v	慎獨
g	道學	o	四書章句集註	w	修己
h	理學	p	孔教	x	子路

y 堯

z 舜

aa 顏元

ab 李珠

ac 陳澧

ad 東塾讀書記

ae 栗子奇

af 四書質疑

ag 毛奇齡

ah 四書改錯

ai 補傳

aj 物理

ak 情理

al 天理

am 良心

an 正義感

ao 明明德

ap 石漢椿

aq 大學章句

4

A Historical Perspective on Chu Hsi's Learning

CH'IEN MU

THERE EXISTS a characteristic in Chinese learning that can also be considered as the characteristic of Chinese civilization as a whole. It is to place value on similarity and convergence rather than on difference and divergence. Let me begin by examining Confucius (551–479 B.C.). Confucius described his own learning as an effort "to transmit and not to innovate, to trust and to delight in antiquity."[1] It is evident that for Master K'ung,[a] learning involves trusting and taking delight in what is being learned. He regarded as learning that which one has derived from the ancients, not that which one has arrived at independently to distinguish oneself from the ancients. Hence he lamented, "How far I have degenerated! It has been a long time since I last dreamt of the Duke of Chou [d. 1056 B.C.]!"[b2] It can be seen that what Confucius had sought to learn, and what he had pursued ceaselessly day and night, was the Way of the Duke of Chou. Likewise, Mencius (372–289 B.C.?) also proclaimed that "what I wish to do is to learn to be like Confucius!"[3] There is a common thread that runs through the Duke of Chou, Confucius, and Mencius, and it creates the Confucian tradition in China.

Mencius also remarked that "Shun[c] the sage practiced virtue with others. He regarded virtue as the common property of himself and others . . . and delighted to learn from others to practice what was virtuous."[4] It is therefore obvious that the Chinese consider similarity with others (t'ung[d]) as good. Thus the Great Similarity (ta-t'ung,[e] also translated as Great Unity) is at the same time the Supreme Good (chih-shan[f]). To engage in learning is to learn to be human. The great way of humanity resides in the commonality, and not the diversity, among man.

Indeed, this line of thinking was not confined to the Confucianists. It was shared by the Mohists. The Mohist philosophers advocated universal love, viewing the father of others as their own father and arguing for the "Will of Heaven" and "Agreement with the Superiors." They also insisted that if one did not subscribe to the Way of the sage Yü,[g5] one would be unworthy to be a Mohist. Mo Tzu's[h] (468–376 B.C.?) exaltation of Yü is analogous to Confucius' elevation of the Duke of Chou. Mo Tzu, like Confucius, was a transmitter and not an innovator. He too trusted and took delight in antiquity.

Following the Confucianists and the Mohists, the Taoists appeared on the scene. Their teaching focused even more on the search for unity and not variance. Lao Tzu[i] commented in the *Tao-te ching*[j] (Classic of the Way and Virtue) that "similarity is called mystery; mystery upon mystery—the gateway of manifold secrets."[6] For this reason the Taoists chose among the ancients the Yellow Emperor as the exemplar. The thinking was that the more distant past to which the individual belongs, the more similarity he shares with other men. Thus the Taoists were equally concerned with transmission and not innovation and harkened back to as well as delighted in antiquity. Eventually Confucianism and Taoism formed the two principal traditions of learning in China. This is my reason for identifying the characteristic of Chinese learning with the characteristic of China's civilization itself.

The Han (206 B.C.–A.D. 220) Confucianists assigned special distinction to the Five Classics,[7] suppressed contending schools of thought, and accorded sole veneration to the Duke of Chou and Confucius. By the Wei-Chin period (220–420), however, the Taoists enjoyed a revival. The notion that Confucius and Lao Tzu were "just about the same" (*chiang wu-t'ung*[k]) was a celebrated observation. After Buddhism was introduced to China, its adherents turned out to be transmitters and not innovators. It therefore formed a triumvirate with Confucianism and Taoism. At the same time, Confucius, Lao Tzu, and Sakyamuni[l] enjoyed equal respect from the Chinese people.

When the Neo-Confucianists appeared in the Sung dynasty (960–1279), they dispelled heterodox ideas and doctrines and singled out the Confucian tradition for veneration. Yet they also subscribed, as the scholars before them did, to the ideal of transmission of ancient ideas and not the innovation of new ones. For this reason, they did not attach any great value to creative theories and individualized doctrines. Even the writing of books was not emphasized. To be sure, Confucius himself authored the *Spring and Autumn Annals,* but it was meant to be a historical record, not an exposition of his personal views. The *Analects,* a collection of his daily conversations and actions recorded and circulated by his disciples, was committed to writing only after a few generations. It was not completed until more than a century after Confucius' death. The case of Mo Tzu was almost identical. Mo Tzu himself never wrote any book. The book bearing his name was compiled by his disciples and later followers.

The *Book of Mencius,* with its seven books, was the product of the joint effort between Mencius and some of his disciples such as Wan Chang[m] and Kung-sun Ch'ou.[n] On the whole, its format resembles that of the *Analects,* in that it records the daily conversations and deeds of the Master. This is a far cry from the systematic and organized exposition of inventive and unique views.

Only Chuang Tzu[o] (c. 369–c. 286 B.C.) and Lao Tzu, because of their retreat from social involvement and their refusal to gather a following like the Confucianists and the Mohists, compiled books as individuals. The seven inner chapters of the *Chuang Tzu* and the two parts of the *Tao-te ching* thus started the tradition for book writing by individual Chinese thinkers. But the *Chuang Tzu* is replete with metaphors, and it teaches withdrawal from the world. The book *Lao Tzu* was inspired by its namesake mentioned in the *Chuang Tzu*. It too is a form of metaphor, and the author's name or identity remains obscure. Later on special treatises appeared that reflected the synthesis of Confucian and Taoist teachings. Works such as the *Doctrine of the Mean* (*Chung-yung*[p]) and the commentary and appendices to the *Book of Changes* are examples of works whose date of completion and authorship were never known. Likewise, the "Great Learning," the "Record of Music," and the "Evolution of Rites" chapters of the *Book of Rites* have no known authorship or definite time of completion. We can only surmise that they were composed after the *Lao Tzu* and the *Chuang Tzu*. Hence it can once again be proven that Chinese scholars concentrated mostly on transmitting ancient ideas rather than innovating new ones. The urge to strive for inventiveness, individual expressiveness, and self-fame was absent. Even the later Taoists, unlike Lao Tzu and Chuang Tzu, placed no emphasis on the individual composition of books.

Scholars in China rarely wrote books as individuals to express their personal ideas. Examples of individual authorship, however, do exist. In addition to historical works, literary compositions such as Ch'ü Yüan's[q] (343–277 B.C.) "Encountering Sorrow" (*Li-sao*[r]) immediately come to mind. This poetic piece actually set the pattern for later literary works. Others were written in response to certain needs. Chia I's[s] (201–169 B.C.) "Memorial on Government Affairs" (*Ch'en cheng-shih shu*[t]) in early Han and Tung Chung-shu's[u] (176–104 B.C.) "Answers to Questions on Heaven and Man" (*T'ien-jen tui-ts'e*[v]) are such specific pieces. They differ in nature from works intended to be expressions of personal ideas meant for posterity. As Tung Chung-shu failed to make further headway in politics, he authored the *Luxuriant Gems of the Spring and Autumn Annals* (*Ch'un-ch'iu fan-lu*[w]). Yang Hsiung[x] (53 B.C.–A.D. 18) led an undistinguished political life when Wang Mang[y] (45 B.C.–A.D. 23) founded the Hsin dynasty (9–23). He therefore composed the two works of *Model Sayings* (*Fa-yen*[z]) and the *Classic of Supreme Mystery* (*T'ai-hsüan*[aa]). The *Ch'un-ch'iu fan-lu* was aimed at the elucidation of the deeper meaning of the *Spring and Autumn Annals*, while the *Fa-yen* and the *T'ai-hsüan* were conscious imitations of the *Book of Changes* and the *Analects*. They clearly and unequivocally identified their source of inspiration and intellectual lineage. Thus these works are still different from those written by individuals with the purpose of expounding their unique, personal views. By the Sui period (581–618), Wang T'ung (Wen-chung Tzu,[ab] 584–617) was believed to have compiled the *Wen-chung Tzu*. Yet this work was given final organization by Wang's followers, who even decided upon the title itself. As this text is principally concerned with the consolidation of one particular intellectual tradition, it is still a transmission and not an innovation. It is apparent that, more so than the works of

Tung Chung-shu and Yang Hsiung, Wang T'ung's book is not an original, inventive piece of writing. Tung, Yang, and Wang were three of the most outstanding Confucianists of all times. If their writings all shared this common feature of seeking to blend in with an established tradition rather than creating a totally new one, then those of their lesser fellow scholars should go without saying.

In addition to historical and literary writing, the compilation of commentaries on classical texts was a major undertaking of the Han Confucianists. Cheng Hsüan[ac] (127–200) was known for his achievement in synthesizing the various schools of commentary in the Han period. Furthermore, Wang Pi[ad] (226–249) annotated the *Book of Changes* and the *Lao Tzu*, while Ho Yen[ae] (190–249) provided exegesis on the *Analects* and Kuo Hsiang[af] (d. 312) did the same for the *Chuang Tzu*. Even such a political wizard as Ts'ao Ts'ao[ag] (155–220) wrote a commentary on the *Military Strategem by Master Sun* (*Sun Tzu ping-fa*[ah]). After Buddhism was introduced to China, eminent Chinese monks were actively involved in writing commentaries on the Buddhist texts in addition to translating them. In T'ang (618–907) China, commentaries on the commentaries of the Five Classics appeared. This was apparently a practice inspired by the Buddhists. Mahayana sects such as T'ien-t'ai[ai] and Hua-yen[aj] undoubtedly represented new movements, yet they insisted on evolving their doctrines from one basic scripture instead of composing brand new texts. In Ch'an[ak] there were only recorded sayings (*yü-lu*[al]). When one comes to think of it, is not the *Analects* the *yü-lu* of Confucius?

In the Sung dynasty, the Neo-Confucianists enjoyed tremendous growth. But only Chou Tun-i[am] (1017–1073) and Chang Tsai[an] (1020–1077) authored books. Yet Chou's *Penetrating the Book of Changes* (*T'ung-shu*[ao]) was a commentary on the *Book of Changes*. Chang Tsai's *Correcting Youthful Ignorance* (*Cheng-meng*[ap]) was also based on the *Book of Changes*. Its aim, as the title suggests, is to enlighten the ignorant young. It is by no means a piece of writing composed *ex nihilo* and unrelated to previous ideas. The two Ch'eng brothers (Ch'eng Hao,[aq] 1032–1085 and Ch'eng I,[ar] 1033–1107) did not even write books. Ch'eng I's most celebrated treatise is his *Commentary on the Book of Changes* (*I-chuan*[as]), which again is not an entirely original work.

Chu Hsi inherited the tradition of Chou, Chang, and the two Ch'engs and became a great synthesizer of Sung Neo-Confucianism. His most memorable work is the *Collected Commentaries on the Four Books* (*Ssu-shu chang-chü chi-chu*[at]). Next in importance is the *Reflections on Things at Hand* (*Chin-ssu lu*[au]), which is merely an annotated and categorized anthology of the teachings of the four Northern Sung (960–1126) masters mentioned above. Chu Hsi also wrote commentaries on Chou Tun-i's *An Explanation of the Diagram of the Great Ultimate* (*T'ai-chi-t'u shuo*[av]) as well as Chang Tsai's "Western Inscription" (*Hsi-ming*[aw]). He provided annotations on the *Book of Odes* and the *Book of Changes*. His historical writings include an outline (*kang-mu*[ax]) for Ssu-ma Kuang's[ay] (1019–1086) *General Mirror for Aid in Government* (*Tzu-chih t'ung-*

chien[az]). In literature he commented on Ch'ü Yüan's *"Li-sao,"* analyzed Han Yü's[ba] (768–824) works, and studied the Taoist text *Ts'an-t'ung ch'i*[bb] (The three ways unified and harmonized). In terms of breadth and quantity, as we have seen, Chu Hsi was unsurpassed in the entire history of Chinese scholarship. But none of his writings dealt with subjects unique or original to himself. When his followers compiled his recorded sayings, they managed to fill 140 chapters. His poems and literary compositions also amounted to more than 100 chapters. These were all spontaneous outpourings of sentiments in different times, under different circumstances, and in the company of different people. They were definitely not an organized and systematic exposition of totally original ideas. Thus in the single example of Chu Hsi, one characteristic of Chinese learning is made manifest. This characteristic values unity and identity but belittles particularity and diversity.

But to say that one identifies with the ancients implies that there is an individual self that does the identifying. It does not mean that the existence of this self is contingent upon the existence of the ancients. From the outset Confucius advocated learning for the self and showed great contempt for the complacent and convention-minded scholars (*hsiang-yüan*[bc]) [who presumably engaged in learning for the sake of others]. Both in terms of space and time, each individual born into this world has a unique self. Furthermore, each self is different from other selves. Confucius could never be wholly identified with the Duke of Chou; this much he had to concede. The *Analects* is in fact a highly personalized and self-revealing portrayal of Confucius. Yet Confucius insisted that he received his inspiration from the Duke of Chou and that everything he meant to say had been handed down to him from the Duke of Chou.

Mencius' modelling after Confucius did not mean the complete obliteration of his own individuality either. Tzu-kung[bd] (c. 520–456 B.C.), a disciple of Confucius, once remarked that the master never dealt with the two topics of nature (*hsing*[be]) and the Way of Heaven (*T'ien-tao*[bf]).[8] Yet Mencius made a strong case for the goodness of nature, a doctrine evidently not advocated by Confucius himself. Still, Mencius never boasted that this was his own creation and never made it a distinguishing point between himself and Confucius. Such self-effacement made Mencius who he was. Mencius further observed that the sages were people who had attained an identity with our minds. This being the case, it follows that what we seek to learn from the ancient sages is precisely this identical mind. When we think and act in complete accord with this mind, we will then become identical with the ancient sages. It can thus be seen that Mencius never sought dissimilarity or difference.

Both the "Commentary" on the *Book of Changes* and the *Doctrine of the Mean* discourse on nature and the Way of Heaven. This betrays the intrusion of Taoist ideas. Yet the two works belong obviously to the Confucian tradition. Their authors never claimed that they stood for a new departure, nor did they boast that they represented a new synthesis of Confucian and Taoist doctrines. They actually opted for deliberate obscurity by not revealing their identity. Furthermore, they insisted that the ideas found in their works were those of the ancients, and not their own. Nevertheless, the two works reveal genuine individual insights and a new synthesizing outlook.

The teachings of the four Northern Sung masters also display individual variations. Chu Hsi combined and synthesized them to form a great Neo-Confucian movement in the three dynasties of Sung, Yüan (1277–1368), and Ming (1368–1644). This, combined with the teachings of Confucius and Mencius in the pre-Ch'in period (221–206 B.C.), actually created a new Confucian tradition. One of the trickiest problems in the study of Chu Hsi's thought is the difficulty in identifying those elements that are uniquely his or representative of his individual thinking. What we generally find is Chu Hsi's bringing together of various teachings and his heaping praises on earlier scholars to the point of completely obscuring his own ideas or the original views he held. If, however, there is indeed such a thing as a unique Chu Hsi style of scholarship, then this scholarship is, from the Chinese point of view, the property of one individual and is therefore insignificant.

Ssu-ma Ch'ien's[bg] (145–86 B.C.?) writing of the *Historical Records* (*Shih-chi*[bh]) was undertaken in the tradition of Confucius' *Spring and Autumn Annals*. Yet he declared boldly that the purpose of his project was to "illuminate the encounter between Heaven and man, understand the changes from antiquity to contemporary times, and formulate the establishment of a school of thought."[9] Is it not true that the entity that does the "illuminating" and the "understanding" is the individual self? In China, one's disciples are known as one's *ti-tzu*[bi] (junior members in the family), and they are as close to oneself as one's own kin. In blood relations, the transmission from generation to generation forms a lineage family. In scholarship and learning, this also holds true. Thus the transmission of one's ideas through generations of disciples forms a "school of thought" (*i-chia*[bj]). All the twenty-five official histories in China were compiled in the tradition of Ssu-ma Ch'ien's *Shih-chi*, which was perceived and venerated as the ancestral model. In this respect Ssu-ma Ch'ien had indeed formed a school of thought. If his ideas were unique to him, without precedent and successor, then they represented the scholarship of one man. How could they have become a "school of thought?" Moreover, Ch'ien's father T'an[bk] (d. 110 B.C.) was the author of the *Essentials of the Six Schools of Thought* (*Liu-chia yao-chih*[bl]), in which he gave an impartial treatment of each of the ancient schools, including Confucianism. But Ch'ien venerated Confucius above all others and included his biography among those of the "hereditary princely families" (*shih-chia*[bm]). On this matter it is evident that Ch'ien differed from his father. Yet he made no attempt to conceal the fact and made no issue of it. Later historians also felt no necessity to comment on this difference, but instead focused their attention on following the pattern set by Ch'ien.

Contemporary scholars studying Chu Hsi are fond of pointing out the differences between his ideas and those of the early masters. In fact, however, Chu Hsi himself was also fully cognizant of the variations in the teaching of his intellectual predecessors. A case in point is the teaching of the two Ch'eng brothers. The two brothers had four outstanding disciples, Yang Kuei-shan (Yang Shih,[bn] 1053–1135) being one of them. Yang's teachings were inherited by Li Yen-p'ing (Li T'ung,[bo] 1093–1163), who was the master of Chu Hsi. To be sure, Chu paid his teacher the highest respect, but it would be erroneous to conclude that his appreciation and further development of the teaching of the two Ch'engs was limited to the Yang-Li branch.

Later scholars often mention Chu Hsi and the two Ch'engs together, especially the younger brother Ch'eng I. It is true that Chu Hsi's veneration for Ch'eng I was deep and immense. The latter's *Commentary on the Book of Changes* was quoted repeatedly in Chu's *Reflections on Things at Hand*. Yet Chu also wrote his own *Original Meaning of the Book of Changes of Chou (Chou-i pen-i[bp])* in which he argued that this ancient classic was originally nothing more than a book of divination. This line of thinking differed greatly from that of Ch'eng I. But Chu Hsi did not stress this difference at all. Even in his *Collected Commentaries (chi-chu[bq])* on the *Analects* and the *Book of Mencius* Chu showed numerous disagreements with the views held by the two Ch'eng brothers. We should, however, note that the spirit of Chu Hsi's scholarship lies in harmonious synthesis and interconnectedness, and that it seeks to identify points of convergence with the ancients. It deliberately downplays the expression of personal opinions and individual differences. If we insist on looking for dissimilarities and individual unique views, we are likely to miss the mark in our apprehension of the spirit of Chu Hsi's learning.

Some people might question that if indeed the spirit of their scholarship is to seek similarity, why then were the Neo-Confucians so emphatic in their criticism of heterodox ideas? This is because of their realization that to seek similarity one must first identify that which is dissimilar. Between the two actions, however, the task to seek similarity was ultimately considered to be primary, while to identify dissimilarities was only secondary. Since some pre-Ch'in schools such as that of Mo Tzu and Hsün Tzu[br] (313–328 B.C.?) focused more on the latter, they were eventually abandoned by later scholars. Since the *Lü-shih ch'un-ch'iu*[bs] (Spring and Autumn Annals of Mr. Lü) and *Huai-nan Tzu*[bt]10 were compiled by groups of advisors and assistants to feudal lords, their emphasis was on harmonious synthesis, and they have been more valued by scholars than the writings of Mo Tzu and Hsün Tzu. As already mentioned, the commentary and appendices to the *Book of Changes* and the *Doctrine of the Mean* represent the synthesized view of Confucianism and Taoism. They provided much inspiration for Chou Tun-i and Chang Tsai. Even both of the two Ch'engs were well versed in Confucian and Taoist concepts. The Neo-Confucians had adopted much from the Buddhist school of Ch'an, and Chu Hsi specifically showed Hua-yen's influence. From these admissions modern scholars speculate that the Neo-Confucians have all made forays into the Taoist and Buddhist camps and been tainted by them. This is precisely the strong point of the Neo-Confucians, and not their weakness. To harmonize and synthesize in order to seek a broad, unified consensus—this is precisely where the Neo-Confucians exerted their greatest effort.

Lu Hsiang-shan (Lu Chiu-yüan,[bu] 1139–1193) was adamantly opposed to Chu Hsi. Yet Chu merely characterized the difference between them as one between his insistence on *"tao wen hsüeh"*[bv] (following the path of study and inquiry) and Lu's emphasis on *"tsun te hsing"*[bw] (honoring moral nature). Chu further exhorted his followers to adopt Lu's strong points to supplement his own teaching and to avoid doctrinal squabbles. When Lu died, Chu lamented the loss of his Kao Tzu[bx] (c. 420–c. 350 B.C.), an obvious comparison of his debate with Lu to that between Mencius and Kao Tzu.[11] It can thus be seen that though Chu Hsi disagreed with Lu Hsiang-shan, he was never blind to the latter's contribution. His attitude toward Taoism and Buddhism was similar. When Wang Yang-ming (Wang Shou-jen,[by] 1472–1529) appeared in the Ming dynasty, he subscribed to Lu Hsiang-shan's argument and opposed Chu Hsi. In his "Master Chu's Final Conclusions Arrived at Late in Life" (*Chu Tzu wan-nien ting-lun*[bz]),[12] however, Wang ultimately sought to prove the similarity between Chu and Lu. This is another proof that scholars in China value convergence of views rather than divergence.

Among Chu Hsi's works, the one most susceptible to objection and debate is his "Supplementary Commentary" on the *ko-wu*[ca] (investigation of things) chapter of the *Great Learning*.[13] In using his own ideas to fill the gap that existed in the interpretation of this Classic, Chu Hsi has obviously violated the dictum of "transmitting but not innovating" in China's tradition of learning. Even though Chu defended his action by claiming that his supplement was based on Master Ch'eng's ideas, he could not justify how he deemed it proper to use Master Ch'eng's interpretation to speculate on the intended meaning of the ancient sages. The Master Ch'eng mentioned here is Ch'eng I, not Ch'eng Hao. Thus when later scholars rejected Chu Hsi, by extension they also rejected Ch'eng I. The commentary and appendices to the *Book of Changes* and the *Doctrine of the Mean*, on the other hand, rallied behind the authority of Confucius, even though they embodied substantial Taoist ideas. They were thus far less open to criticism. It is for this reason that Ch'ing (1644–1912) Confucianists supported Han Learning and disparaged Sung Scholarship. They put equal emphasis on textual analysis (*k'ao-chü*[cb]) and philosophic inquiry (*i-li*[cc]).Chu Hsi's aforementioned "Supplementary Commentary" on the *ko-wu* chapter of the *Great Learning* could claim only philosophic validity, not textual support. Hence it was not readily accepted by later scholars. These conflicts are all due to the nature of China's scholastic tradition. We can state that what a scholar in China studies is the history of Chinese learning itself, and not any independently created academic discipline. We can also state that this history of learning was initiated by Confucius, and that the most accomplished organizer and synthesizer of this history was Chu Hsi. This is what I mean by treasuring similarity and disparaging dissimilarity. It is analogous to the total absence of any proponent of new religious doctrines after Jesus in the Christian tradition.

Ku Yen-wu[cd] (1613–1682), Huang Tsung-hsi[ce] (1610–1695), and Wang Fu-chih[cf] (1619–1692) in early Ch'ing all based their scholarship on Sung-Ming Neo-Confucianism. Ku levelled scathing criticisms against Wang Yang-ming without mercy; but Huang Tsung-hsi was partial to Yang-ming. In his later life Wang Fu-chih singled out Chang Tsai for veneration, but was critical of Ch'eng-Chu. All three scholars sought to identify sameness, not contrariness. They valued identity with the ancients, not individual uniqueness. In this practice they were no different from others.

I personally feel that the role played by Confucius in China is similar to that played by Jesus in the West, while Chu Hsi was comparable to Martin Luther. Chu's greatest contribution to the Confucian tradition was his compilation of the Four Books[14] with commentaries, and his designating to them an importance far beyond the Five Classics of the Han-T'ang period. At the same time, the *Proper Meaning of the Five Classics* (*Wu-ching cheng-i*[cg]) of the T'ang era became, by the Sung dynasty, the *Commentaries and Sub-commentaries of the Thirteen Classics* (*Shih-san-ching chu-shu*[ch]). This illustrates that the more attempt is made at synthesis, the more harmonious consensus can be attained, and the more the underlying unity can be revealed. This is the characteristic of Chinese learning; it is also the characteristic of Chinese civilization.

The Ch'ing scholars in the eighteenth century were very much like the Catholic Counter-Reformation leaders who adamantly rejected Luther's Protestantism. In China, however, the Protestantism (of Chu Hsi) finally won out. In the T'ung-chih[ci] (1862–1874) and Kuang-hsü[cj] (1875–1908) periods of the nineteenth century, Tseng Kuo-fan[ck] (1811–1872) wrote the essay *Accounts of Sketches of Sages and Wise Men* (*Sheng-che hua-hsiang chi*[cl]), and Ch'en Li[cm] (1810–1882) authored the book *Reading Notes of the Eastern Studio* (*Tung-shu tu-shu chi*[cn]). Both focused on unity instead of disagreement in their views on learning, and both emphasized transmission rather than innovation. They never regarded themselves to be superior to the ancients. In this practice they followed the ancient tradition.

But Confucius was not a religious founder in China. What he had his faith and took delight in, as well as what he had transmitted, was antiquity itself. His focus was on mankind, not on God, who is suprahuman. Hence he never thought of himself as superior to the ancients. This is the spirit of Chinese learning and Chinese civilization. In fact, the position of Confucius in China surpassed that of Jesus in the West. If we can grasp this point in our study of Chu Hsi's scholarship, then we are apt to find the true spirit of his learning.

Translated by Richard Shek[co]

Notes

1. *Analects*, 7:1.
2. *Ibid.*, 7:5. The duke established social and governmental institutions of the Chou dynasty (1111–249 B.C.).
3. *Book of Mencius*, 2A:2.
4. *Ibid.*, 2A:8. Shun was a legendary sage-emperor.
5. Legendary sage-emperor, founder of the Hsia dynasty (c. 2183–1752 B.C.).
6. *Tao-te ching*, ch. 1.
7. The *Book of Odes*, the *Book of History*, the *Book of Changes*, the *Book of Rites*, and the *Spring and Autumn Annals*.
8. *Analects*, 5:12.
9. His autobiographic preface.
10. The former attributed to Lü Pu-wei[cp] (d. 235 B.C.) and the latter to Liu An[cq] (d. 122 B.C.).
11. For details, see the *Book of Mencius*, 2A:2, 6A:1–4, 6.
12. For an English translation, see Wing-tsit Chan,[cr] trans., *Instructions for Practical Living and Other Neo-Confucian Writings by Wang Yang-ming* (New York: Columbia University Press, 1963), pp. 263–267.
13. In his *Ta-hsüeh chang-chü*[cs] [Commentary on the *Great Learning*].
14. The *Great Learning*, the *Analects*, the *Book of Mencius*, and the *Doctrine of the Mean*.

Glossary

a 孔	x 楊雄	au 近思錄
b 周	y 王莽	av 太極圖説
c 舜	z 法言	aw 西銘
d 同	aa 太玄	ax 綱目
e 大同	ab 王通文中子	ay 司馬光
f 至善	ac 鄭玄	az 資治通鑑
g 禹	ad 王弼	ba 韓愈
h 墨子	ae 何晏	bb 參同契
i 老子	af 郭象	bc 鄉愿
j 道德經	ag 曹操	bd 子貢
k 將毋同	ah 孫子兵法	be 性
l 釋迦牟尼	ai 天台	bf 天道
m 萬章	aj 華嚴	bg 司馬遷
n 公孫丑	ak 禪	bh 史記
o 莊子	al 語錄	bi 弟子
p 中庸	am 周敦頤	bj 一家
q 屈原	an 張載	bk 談
r 離騷	ao 通書	bl 六家要旨
s 賈誼	ap 正蒙	bm 世家
t 陳政事疏	aq 程顥	bn 楊龜山時
u 董仲舒	ar 程頤	bo 李延平侗
v 天人對策	as 易傳	bp 周易本義
w 春秋繁露	at 四書章句集註	bq 集註

br 荀子
bs 呂氏春秋
bt 淮南子
bu 陸象山九淵
bv 道問學
bw 尊德性
bx 告子
by 王陽明守仁
bz 朱子晚年定論
ca 格物

cb 考據
cc 義理
cd 顧炎武
ce 黃宗羲
cf 王夫之
cg 五經正義
ch 十三經注疏
ci 同治
cj 光緒

ck 曾國潘
cl 聖哲畫像記
cm 陳澧
cn 東塾讀書記
co 石漢椿
cp 呂不韋
cq 劉安
cr 陳榮捷
cs 大學章句

5

A Comparative Study of Chu Hsi and the Ch'eng Brothers

Hsü Fu-kuan

Special Characteristics of Sung-Ming Neo-Confucianism

CHU HSI'S IDEAS originated with the Ch'eng brothers, Ch'eng Hao[a] (1032–1085) and Ch'eng I[b] (1033–1107), especially the latter. That is why ever since the beginning of the Yüan dynasty (1217–1368) their names were linked together. In this paper I would like to show first the similarities between Chu Hsi and Ch'eng I and then the significant differences. The Ch'eng brothers seem to have developed a "human world which stretches on the same plane," while Chu Hsi seems to have developed a "human world which unites the world beyond and this world." Before we may enter into a discussion of such problems in any depth, however, we must first try to define the special characteristics of Sung-Ming Neo-Confucianism.

Both Ch'eng I and Chu Hsi claimed that they had inherited the orthodoxy from Confucius (551–479 B.C.) and Mencius (372–289 B.C.?). Is there a basis for them to make such claims, or are these claims merely emotional exaggerations on their part without any real foundation? We must give an answer to this question before we can expect to have any understanding of the common characteristics of Sung-Ming Neo-Confucianism. A review of the development of Confucian thought is in order.

"Knowledge for the sake of action" was the fundamental principle of Chinese philosophy since the early Chou dynasty (1111–479 B.C.). Confucius also followed the same principle by putting special emphasis on the pursuit of knowledge. His contribution lies in his being interested not only in the accumulation of knowledge in general but in "knowledge for the self," something distinctly different from what he called "knowledge for others," which emphasized intellectual achievements to be useful for and ardently sought after by others.[1] Confucius believed that the primary goal of knowledge is to discover, develop, and elevate the self in order to bring about self-realization. In learning he urges us "to begin from a humble start in order to reach a lofty goal."[2] Such an approach shows that Confucius is not merely concerned with knowledge of external objects; the essence of learning for him is to transform the self from a biological organism into a rational, moral being under whose guidance the other selves and things are united with the self. His ideal that "the whole world turns to humanity" (jen^c)[3] implies the Neo-Confucian ideal that "a man of humanity regards Heaven, Earth and myriad things as one body." Realizing that most people do things for the sake of self-interest, Confucius nevertheless urges us to "overcome the self"[4] and "transcend the ego."[5] Also he advocates that "A man of humanity, wishing to establish his own character, also establishes the character of others, and wishing to be prominent himself, also helps others to be prominent."[6] Obviously then, knowledge for Confucius cannot mean just knowledge acquired through our perceptions and conceptions, even though he does value highly the information collected by such means.[7] Instead, he leads us in a new direction. He says, "When you see a worthy person, you would love to become like him. But when you see someone who is no good, then you would turn inward to reflect [on your own shortcomings]."[8] Here objective knowledge is transformed into a kind of knowledge that is deeply concerned with the self. This is indeed a radical breakthrough, as moral knowledge now finds its root in the self. What Confucius develops is a "human world seen through the eyes of an organic moral self." And it is the realization of humanity that characterizes the realization of the self, even though Confucius himself has not elaborated on the point enough to develop a comprehensive theory of human nature.

Subsequent development of Confucian thought shows that the author of the *Doctrine of the Mean* declares that "what Heaven (T'ien^d) imparts to man is called human nature. To follow our nature is called the Way (Tao^e). Cultivating the Way is called education."[9] Although the idea of Heaven may appear to be a traditional one, yet Heaven's decree is now internalized in human nature and it is clear that the emphasis has been shifted to the idea of human nature. The *Doctrine of the Mean* says,

> Only those who are absolutely sincere can fully develop their nature. If they can fully develop their nature, they can fully develop the nature of others. If they can fully develop the nature of others, they can then fully develop the nature of things. If they can fully develop the nature of things, they can then assist in the transforming and nourishing process of Heaven and Earth. If they can assist in the transforming and nourishing process of Heaven and Earth, they can thus form a trinity with Heaven and Earth.[10]

Furthermore, the *Doctrine of the Mean* shows us the steps to self-realization. It says, "Study it [the way to be sincere] extensively, inquire into it accurately, think it over carefully, sift it clearly, and practice it earnestly."[11] The first four steps must lead to the last step so that knowledge external and abstract would be truly embodied in the self.

Mencius went even further by stating explicitly that human nature is good and that it is manifested in the four beginnings of humanity, righteousness, propriety, and wisdom.[12] For Mencius there is no need to depart from human ways in order to reach Heaven. He says, "He who exerts his mind to the utmost knows his nature. He who knows his nature knows Heaven. To preserve one's mind and to nourish one's nature is the way to serve Heaven."[13] The focus is laid on knowledge of the self; as Mencius says, "All things are already complete in oneself. There is no greater joy than to examine oneself and be sincere."[14]

But beginning with the middle of the Warring States period (403–222 B.C.), the emphasis was shifted to cosmological speculation. Theories of yin-yang[f] (passive and active cosmic forces) and the Five Agents (Metal, Wood, Water, Fire, and Earth) were developed and completed in the early Han period (206 B.C.–A.D.220), and scholars' attention also turned to problems concerning social institutions. Even though it is still true that the discipline of the self was considered important by all Confucian scholars since Hsün Tzu[g] (313–238 B.C.?), yet the focusing point was no longer the realization of the self.

It was not until the Ch'eng brothers, during the Sung dynasty (960–1279), revived the line of thought transmitted through Confucius and Mencius that knowledge of the self regained its position of primary importance. Scholarly learning was now considered of only secondary importance. It became the aim of the investigation of things and the extension of knowledge to achieve a unification between what is internal and what is external. It is here that we can find the essential characteristics of Sung-Ming Neo-Confucian philosophies. Without any doubt, realization of the self is the primary goal for truly committed Neo-Confucian scholars.

What Chu Hsi Inherited from Ch'eng I

Chu Hsi was indebted to both Ch'eng brothers, whose ultimate concerns do not seem to differ. There are, however, certain significant differences other than merely temperamental differences between the two. For example, Ch'eng Hao emphasizes the discipline of the self through tranquillity, while Ch'eng I stresses discipline through seriousness; in the understanding of *jen*, Ch'eng Hao realizes it in the self as a spiritual state, while Ch'eng I takes it to be the concrete embodiment of impartiality; on investigation of things, Ch'eng Hao proceeds with the attitude of artistic contemplation, while Ch'eng I approaches the problem with the attitude of empirical observation and reflection. Chu Hsi put some distance between himself and Ch'eng Hao, but he was indeed greatly indebted to Ch'eng I.

Chu Hsi studied under Li T'ung[h] (1093–1163), who was a disciple of Lo Ts'ung-yen[i] (1072–1135), who in turn studied under Yang Shih[j] (1053–1135), one of the most famous disciples of Ch'eng I. But we should not understand the relationship between Chu Hsi and Ch'eng I through this line of transmission. In his later years Chu Hsi criticized his teacher's approach to look for enlightenment through sitting and meditating as onesided and unsatisfactory.[15] He went back to Ch'eng I's own teachings for guidance. Ch'eng I put much greater emphasis on seriousness than on tranquillity. It was only after a long search that Chu Hsi finally claimed that he had discovered the true meanings of Ch'eng I's teachings on discipline of the self through the realization of equilibrium and harmony.[16] These served as the guidelines of his thought throughout his life.

In their earlier views the Ch'eng brothers attached importance to the idea of seriousness, as they advocated "seriousness to straighten the internal life and righteousness to square the external life."[17] But the view is not without its difficulties, as it presupposes a duality between seriousness and righteousness. Furthermore, there seems to be a hidden emphasis on tranquillity that was taught by the Ch'eng brothers' one-time teacher Chou Tun-i[k] (1017–1073),[18] who might have exerted great influences on their thoughts. But when Ch'eng I developed his mature views later in his career, he shifted the emphasis from tranquillity to seriousness, and he coined a new dictum, which says that "self-cultivation requires seriousness; the pursuit of learning depends on the extension of knowledge."[19] Now one may hold on to seriousness in activity or in tranquillity; in other words, seriousness is now regarded as that which applies to both the world of activity and that of tranquillity. He says, "Seriousness without fail is the state of equilibrium before the feelings of pleasure, anger, sorrow, and joy are aroused. Seriousness is not equilibrium itself. But seriousness without fail is the way to attain equilibrium."[20] Activity is now regarded as the essence of life. One should discipline himself by engaging in things and becoming involved in events. Seriousness means none other than concentrating without being led away by distractions. Such thoughts exerted the most profound influence on Chu Hsi, who said,

> It is necessary to talk much about the doctrine of holding fast to seriousness. One has only to brood over these sayings [of Ch'eng I] thoroughly: "Be orderly and dignified," "Be grave and austere," "Be correct in movement and appearance and be orderly in thoughts and deliberations," and "Be correct in your dress and dignified in your gaze," and make real effort. Then what [Ch'eng] called straightening the internal life and concentrating on one thing will naturally need no manipulation, one's body and mind will be serious, and the internal and external will be unified.[21]

Secondly, Ch'eng I had always stressed that to learn one must follow proper steps. Chu Hsi also adopted such an attitude. Ch'eng I says, "When you study a work, the first step is to understand the meaning of the text; then you may be able to recover its intention. It is simply impossible to get at the intention without even understanding the meaning."[22] Ch'eng I thought that scholars should begin with the study of the *Great Learning*.[23] Chu Hsi followed this instruction almost religiously. He not only wrote the commentary for the document, but placed it as the first of the Four Books ahead of the *Analects* and the *Book of Mencius* and the *Doctrine of the Mean*. But when one understands Cheng I's thought as a whole, it seems that the *Analects* could serve as a better starting point; or at least one need not begin with the *Great Learning* as rigidly as Chu Hsi claimed. Both the Ch'eng brothers were most indebted to the *Analects;* in fact the principles of their philosophies were derived from the *Analects*. But after Ch'eng Hao died, Ch'eng I tended to put more emphasis on the effort to investigate things and to extend knowledge. Consequently, he said that the *Great Learning* is the gate through which the beginning student enters into virtue. Chu Hsi simply took this for granted. For him, the way of learning started with investigating principles, while the essentials of investigating principles lay in studying the Classics. It was he who established a definite program of study. But surely his ideas must be traced back to Ch'eng I.

Finally, on the problem of the relation between knowledge and action, Ch'eng I believed that knowledge is prior to action[24] but also that knowledge in its last or highest stage must imply action. Chu Hsi also followed the lead of Ch'eng I but developed his theory in greater detail and in more precise terms.

How can knowledge be translated into action? To answer the question Ch'eng I draws certain distinctions in our understanding of knowledge. For example, he says, "Hear it, know it, get it, have it."[25] In the first two stages, hearing and knowing, the knowing subject makes an effort to understand the object. But when the information collected by hearing and knowing is thoroughly digested by the self through the thinking process, one has got it. And when what is external is completely transformed into something internal, one has it. It is only at this stage that "true knowledge" is acquired. Such knowledge must imply action, and it is to be kept distinct from "ordinary knowledge."

> True knowledge and ordinary knowledge are different. I once saw a farmer who had been wounded by a tiger. When someone said that a tiger was hurting people, everyone was startled. But in his facial expression the farmer reacted differently from the rest. Even a young boy knows that tigers can hurt people, but his is not true knowledge. It is true knowledge only if it is like the farmer's. Therefore when men know evil and still do it, this also is not true knowledge. If it were, they would surely not do it.[26]

True knowledge must be completely appropriated by the self and find its root in one's life.

Chu Hsi also believed that knowledge is prior to action. If one does not even know what is the right thing to do, how can he ever cultivate his self? One who doesn't know right is in danger of "taking a thief as one's father." But true knowledge is not static; it always implies action. Only when one's knowledge is still shallow would he fail to act according to his knowledge. Chu Hsi says, "Knowledge and action always require each other. It is like a person who cannot walk without legs although he has eyes, and who cannot see without eyes although he has legs. With respect to order, knowledge comes first, and with respect to importance, action is more important."[27] Chu Hsi starts with investigation of things, especially things near at hand. But in the end knowledge must be realized in one's life. His ultimate goal is not different from Ch'eng I's. For that reason he quoted more than once Ch'eng I's story about the farmer's reaction to talk about the tiger.

The Ch'eng brothers, especially Ch'eng I, were devoted to investigation of things and extension of knowledge. They revived the traditional emphasis on knowledge that existed since the time of Confucius and opened up new dimensions not even covered by Mencius. Neither Ch'eng I nor Chu Hsi excluded the investigation of natural things. But ultimately, they pointed out, knowledge must be realized in the self. For Ch'eng I, investigation of things and extension of knowledge are intellectual activities, while rectification of the mind and making one's will sincere are moral activities. Ch'eng I insisted that investigation of things and extension of knowledge must be prior to rectification of the mind and making the will sincere. Chu Hsi wholeheartedly endorsed this view. Even though methodologically speaking one must start with investigation of things and events, knowledge cannot be just piecemeal study of external things, but must be rooted in one's life.

The Ch'eng Brothers' Human World That Stretches on the Same Plane

Having seen the similarities between Ch'eng and Chu, we turn now to the differences. It seems to me that the Ch'eng brothers have tried to develop a human world that stretches on the same plane, while Chu Hsi has tried to develop a human world that unites the world beyond and this world. In order to make my meanings clear, we must again have a historical review of the development of Confucian thought.

In the early Chou, T'ien (Heaven) and Ti[i] (Lord) still retained their religious character. But the Duke of Chou[m] (d. 1094 B.C.) made the crucial change, shifting the emphasis on Heaven or Lord to emphasis on man, as he believed that human behaviors determine the good and evil fortunes of man. This development marked the beginning of a new humanistic spirit. In the Spring and Autumn period (722–481 B.C.), Heaven was preferred to Lord; henceforth it became the symbol of the highest moral existence or the origin of morality in man. Heaven was understood not from a religious point of view but rather from a moral point of view. This may be said to be the result of the process of "the humanization of Heaven." As Heaven still pertains to the world beyond and above this world, we may say that the human world shows the character of having two levels.

Confucius felt awe before the Mandate of Heaven, and he claimed that at fifty he knew the Mandate of Heaven.[28] He seemed to believe that by opening up an organic human world of moral life man can relate himself to the world beyond. His emphasis was on moral cultivation rather than on religious worship. The *Doctrine of the Mean* explicitly states that "what Heaven imparts to man is called human nature,"[29] showing that the world beyond penetrates into this world of ours. Mencius believed that Heaven imparts to man a mind that has the seeds of humanity, righteousness, propriety, and wisdom in it.[30] From this philosophy, moral reason has its root in man. When Mencius said that it is necessary "to know one's nature in order to know Heaven,"[31] on the surface it may appear that Mencius still believed in the two levels of the human world; but Mencius' Heaven must be understood through man; consequently, it became merely a shadow without substance. Thus it is by no means strange for Hsün Tzu to say that "the sage does not even care to know Heaven."[32] To see Heaven from a naturalistic viewpoint is a natural development of Confucian thought from Confucius to Hsün Tzu, even though Hsün Tzu's theory of human nature contradicts that developed by Mencius.

Since the middle of the Warring States period, however, the Yin-Yang School employed the ideas of yin and yang to explain the way of Heaven. This explanation had great attraction for a culture based on agriculture.[33] Again the way of Heaven became closely related to man, only in a different fashion. Han scholars went even further, combining the ideas of yin-yang and the Five Agents and trying to formulate a new theory to understand the relation of human nature to the way of Heaven. While Confucius wanted to find the origin of values within man himself, the Han scholars turned around and tried to look for it in Heaven. They believed that there are patterns in nature that should serve as models for man to follow. They demanded that human rulers follow these patterns, lest disasters strike. Not only did they believe in the two levels of the human world; Heaven now became a much more prominent factor than man. It was not until the Ch'eng brothers that the trend was reversed and attention turned again to man.

The Ch'eng brothers returned to Mencius, who taught that humanity, righteousness, propriety, and wisdom have their roots in the mind. But they went even further than Mencius. They said, "The mind alone is Heaven. When you exhaust your mind, you would know your nature. When you know your nature, you would know Heaven. Realize it here and now. There is no need to look for it elsewhere."[34] Heaven is now completely embodied in man. But we must be careful to understand Heaven in this context as Heaven realized from a moral perspective, not Heaven investigated from a scientific point of view. The Ch'eng brothers made a sharp distinction between man's moral nature and physical nature. Man as a biological organism is related to Heaven in a naturalistic sense. Ch'eng I never associated physical nature with Heaven as moral reason. As moral reason is rooted in the mind, there is no need for an upper level. The human world the Ch'eng brothers developed stretches on the same plane and includes the individual, the social and political, and even the scientific.

The Ch'eng brothers said, "Innate knowledge and innate ability have no other sources than Heaven. They are not manufactured by man."[35] When the Ch'eng brothers said that Heaven and man are one, what they really meant was that man, as moral reason, is Heaven.[36] Ch'eng I said, "What Heaven imparts to man is nature. This refers to the principles inherent in nature. . . . To say that they come from Heaven means that they are natural principles."[37] This shows that when Ch'eng I used the word *T'ien-li*[n] (Heavenly Principles), he used the word *T'ien* merely as an adjective meaning "natural."

Furthermore, the Ch'eng brothers did not even want to maintain the distinction between what is metaphysical and what is mundane taught by the "Appended Remarks" of the *Book of Changes*. They said, "What exists before physical form [and is therefore without it] constitutes the Way. What exists after physical form [and is therefore with it] constitutes concrete things. Nevertheless, though we speak in this way, concrete things are the Way and the Way is concrete things."[38] Ch'eng I elaborated on the point in various ways. He said, "Substance and function come from the same source, and there is no gap between the manifest and the hidden."[39] Principles are hidden while things are manifest, but we must learn about principles through things; there is simply no gap between the two. Yin and yang are material forces, but Ch'eng I believed that there is no Way apart from yin and yang. In his later years he especially emphasized that we must "investigate principles to the utmost by studying things at hand." Naturally, one must use inference to reach what is hidden and abstract. But we must use it with great caution. Otherwise we may even succumb to hearsay and superstitions. Ch'eng I's thought, then, is rooted in this world; he has shown no interest for what is metaphysical. What he cares about is the human world, which for him stretches on the same plane. The actions of inference and reasoning he values are also relevant for this world alone.

Chu Hsi's Human World That Unites the World Beyond and This World

Although Chu Hsi followed Ch'eng I's general principles closely, there were significant differences between the two. As the Ch'eng brothers developed a human world that stretches on the same plane, Chu Hsi believed that there is an upper level of the world the message of which must penetrate into this world. He therefore devoted himself to developing a human world that unites the world beyond and this world. One indication of this belief lies in Chu Hsi's endorsing Chou Tun-i's "An Explanation of the Diagram of the Great Ultimate."[40] The Ch'eng brothers never mentioned the essay, though Chou had taught the Ch'eng brothers for some time when they were young. The essay presupposes a distinction between the metaphysical and the mundane world. Maybe it was for this reason that the Ch'eng brothers could not accept the essay. Their rejection had nothing to do with the diagram's Taoist origin.

The essay was clearly a Confucian document that synthesized the theories of yin-yang and the Five Agents in the Han period. In the essay Chou finds a metaphysical foundation for this world and argues that the metaphysical penetrates into the world here and now. Such a picture of the world clearly contradicts the Ch'eng brothers' picture of the world that stretches on the same plane. Chu Hsi, on the other hand, further developed Chou's world view. But before we can discuss the problem in any depth, we must examine the differences between their understanding of human nature. It is false to assume that Chu Hsi's view of human nature was the same as Ch'eng I's.

Let us first look at the views of the Ch'eng brothers. They went straight back to Mencius, who declared that human nature is good. Although the Ch'eng brothers also believed that essential human nature is good, they introduced more complications into their theories. For example, Ch'eng Hao said, "What is inborn is called nature. Nature is the same as material force and material force is the same as nature. They are both inborn. According to principle, there are both good and evil in the material force with which man is endowed at birth. . . . Man's nature is of course good, but it cannot be said that evil is not his nature."[41] Ch'eng Hao refused to draw a sharp line of demarcation between material force and nature. When a person is born, his endowment must have something to do with material force. When Mencius talked about human nature, he merely emphasized in what ways man is distinct from other animals. But the aspect of material force should not be neglected. Therefore Ch'eng I said, "It would be incomplete to talk about the nature of man without including material force and unintelligible to talk about material force without including nature."[42] The two aspects should be kept distinct but not separated. Only by referring to material force can the evils of man be accounted for. But the Ch'eng brothers were by no means fatalists. For them the very aim of education is to transform one's temperament through discipline of the self.

Chu Hsi followed this general outline. He also identified nature as principle but he went a step further. He identified mind as material force, and hence he taught something quite different from what the Ch'eng brothers had taught. For the Ch'engs, nature as principle and nature as material force could not be separated. And if principle and material force are inseparable, the one cannot be said to be prior to the other. But for Chu Hsi, even though principle and material force are inseparable, from an ontological point of view principle is said to be prior to material force. Principle is metaphysical while material force is physical. Mind is constituted by subtle material force. It has the ability to understand principles, but it still belongs to the physical level while principles belong to the metaphysical level. From Chu Hsi's point of view, for Ch'eng Hao to say that mind is nature, nature is Heaven, Heaven is nature, and nature is mind without qualifications was wrong, as these statements fail to make certain necessary distinctions.[43]

Now we understand why Chu Hsi praised Chou Tun-i's essay "An Explanation of the Diagram of the Great Ultimate." Myriad things in the world may be traced back to the Five Agents and the two material forces, yin and yang, while these in turn can be traced back to the Great Ultimate, which has no physical shape but has principles inherent in it. True, the metaphysical principles must be embodied in things, and what is transcendent must penetrate into this world. But still there is the implicit assertion of a hierarchy in the world. Such a view is implied by Chou's essay but contradictory to what the Ch'eng brothers taught. Here it is clear that Chu Hsi deviated from the teachings of the Ch'eng brothers and followed Chou Tun-i instead to develop a human world that unites the world beyond and this world.

The Implications of Ch'eng I's World of One Level and Chu Hsi's World of Two Levels

Ch'eng Hao died before his brother. Apart from recorded sayings he left us only some short essays and letters. Ch'eng I was more productive, but even he wrote only one book in his whole career, The *I-chuan*[o] (Commentary on the *Book of Changes* by Ch'eng I). As he spent his whole life preparing this work, it is an extremely important document for anyone who wants to understand his thought. Chu Hsi wrote two books on the *Book of Changes:* the *Chou-i pen-i*[p] (The original meanings of the *Book of Changes*) was completed when he was forty-eight years old, and the *I-hsüeh ch'i-meng*[q] (Study of the *Book of Changes* for beginning students) was completed when he was fifty-seven years old. A comparison of Ch'eng's and Chu's different interpretations of the *Book of Changes* will show the implications of their different world views.

The special characteristic of Ch'eng I's approach to the *Book of Changes* lies in that he refused to have anything to do with divination. He was interested only in the philosophical principles implied in the so-called ten wings (ten commentaries) of the *Book of Changes.* In the preface to his book he made it clear that all the principles are included in the commentaries; the only way to understand the intended meanings was to study these commentaries. Although the *Book of Changes* does have a system of symbols that were developed in ancient time by the priest class to tell the good or evil fortunes of man, since Confucius the rational elements were abstracted from the Classic, and Confucius and his followers wrote the commentaries to formulate a philosophy of creativity based on rational philosophical principles. During the Han dynasty scholars concentrated on the deduction and interpretations of the symbolic system, which became a source of superstitions and ambiguous messages. It was not until the Wei dynasty (220–265) that Wang Pi[r] (226–249) started a radically new approach, giving a philosophical interpretation to the Classic based on Taoist insight. Ch'eng I followed Wang Pi's example, but gave it a thoroughly new Confucian interpretation instead.

As Ch'eng I never believed that there is another world beyond and above this world, it was impossible for him to believe in divination. To him moral discipline and its cultivation were important, not the reading of symbols; hence, he paid only lip service to the traditional practice of divination. For Ch'eng I, substance and function come from the same source, and there is no gap between the manifest and the hidden. He showed no interest whatsoever in the world of spirits and deities or messages from beyond through a proper reading of symbols. For him, there is just a human world that stretches on the same plane.

Chu Hsi's approach was different. On the surface it seems that he had endorsed Ch'eng I's view of substance and function, the hidden and the manifest. He gave his interpretation of Ch'eng's dictum as follows:

> That substance and function come from the same source means that from the perspective of principles, principles are the substance and forms are the function; as principles have forms, so they come from the same source. That there is no gap between the manifest and the hidden means that from the perspective of forms, forms are manifest and principles are hidden; as forms have principles, so there is no gap between the two.[44]

If Chu Hsi's interpretation were correct, then principles and forms would be inseparable, and it would be impossible for Ch'eng I to talk about principles only. But in fact Ch'eng I hardly ever discussed forms. Chu Hsi actually was reading his own thought into Ch'eng I's dictum. No wonder he went on to say that "after all, the distinction between substance and function and the manifest and the hidden must be maintained." This shows that he held a different view. When he was sixty-two years old he wrote a letter to a friend saying,

> When modern scholars discussed the *Book of Changes,* they had nothing to say about divination, but talked about philosophical principles alone. In so doing the meanings of the texts were twisted and could not be substantiated anymore. Such malpractices lasted for a long time. We must start with divination, recover the original meanings of the text, . . . so that we would not fall into empty talks and false reasonings.[45]

Chu Hsi's criticisms had to apply to Ch'eng I's interpretation of the *Book of Changes,* too. The key difference between the two lies in that Chu Hsi believed that there is a world beyond, and the only way to reach it is through divination and the correct reading of symbols and forms. It was reported that he practiced divination in his own life on two occasions when he had important decisions to make.[46]

Because of their difference in world views they also held different attitudes toward spirits and deities. The Ch'eng brothers did not believe in the existence of spirits and deities; they warned people not to trust rumors. Their attitude toward life and death was very close to Confucius' attitude: "If we do not yet know about life, how can we know about death?"[47] Although Chu Hsi followed Chang Tsai[s] (1020–1077) in understanding the phenomena of spirits and deities in terms of natural causes and thought that they resulted from the interaction of the two material forces, at least he conceded the existence of spirits and deities. For him it is natural for a man to turn into a ghost or spirit after he dies. Chu Hsi might have had some religious purpose for believing in the two levels of the world. But his main emphasis was on metaphysics. He might have gone a bit too far in his inferences and in effect contradicted somewhat his own rigorous demand to investigate things and extend knowledge on an objective basis.

Some Clues to Move Away from Metaphysical Speculation in Chu Hsi's Thought

To review Chu Hsi's philosophy as a whole, his disciple as well as son-in-law Huang Kanᵗ (1152–1221) said, "Be serious in order to establish the foundation, investigate principles in order to extend knowledge, and practice in order to realize in the self. Seriousness is that which runs through these three items; it is the beginning as well as the ending point."[48] These words are well said. For Chu Hsi, furthermore, to investigate principles means none other than to investigate things. Thus investigation of principles has as its object things in the empirical world; the more one is involved with investigation of principles, the less he would have anything to do with the transcendent metaphysical world and the world of spirits and deities. No matter whether it was the study of classics or the practice of moral behaviors, Chu Hsi always wanted to keep his feet on the solid ground, which is none other than the human world that stretches on the same plane. Therefore, the core of his thought was not that much different from that of the Ch'eng brothers. In fact, it seems that he changed his attitude toward the Diagram of the Great Ultimate in his later years. When he was sixty-two, he reinterpreted Chou Tun-i's ideas as follows:

> Master Chou's understanding of the Ultimate of Nonbeing and the Great Ultimate are inseparable from the daily practice, and his theories of yin, yang and the Five Agents are inseparable from humanity, righteousness, propriety, wisdom, strength, weakness, good and evil. He realizes that substance and function come from the same source and that there is no gap between the manifest and the hidden; nobody had a better understanding of the principle than him since Ch'in (221–206 B.C.) and Han dynasties. But what he transmits are nothing but what have been taught by the Six Classics, the *Analects*, the *Doctrine of the Mean*, the *Great Learning* and the *Book of Mencius*. And the so-called Great Ultimate is but the common name of the principles of Heaven, Earth, and myriad things in the world.[49]

What is remarkable about this essay is that Chu Hsi no longer treated the Great Ultimate as the origin of things, but rather as the common name of the principles of Heaven, Earth, and myriad things in the world. Under such an interpretation the metaphysical implication of the Diagram of the Great Ultimate is greatly reduced and the hierarchy of worlds disappears.

Only a month or two before his death at seventy-one he scolded Liao Tzu-hui (Liao Te-ming,[u] 1169 *cs*), a disciple, who appeared to take the Ultimate of Nonbeing or Great Ultimate to be a metaphysical entity, something shining and rolling like a mercury ball. Chu Hsi believed that it never paid to reflect on the mind in itself; what is important is to realize the principles grasped by the mind in one's life.[50] This must be considered his definitive idea on the subject. Therefore, it is by no means an accident that he criticized strongly the Buddhist position and showed a strong distaste for metaphysical language in general.

To conclude, his main concern was the human world, the here and now, and he put equal emphasis on theory and practice. And yet some contemporary writers still condemn him as giving only empty, mysterious talks, accuse him of covering his Buddhist views with a Confucian cloak, and attack him as representing the interests of the landlord class to suppress the common people. These are unfounded criticisms; they fail to appreciate the true spirit of Chu Hsi's philosophy.

Notes

I am indebted to Professor Liu Shu-hsien[v] who agreed to edit and translate my article in English. Owing to limited space the English version of my paper must omit the details and almost three-fourths of the notes. For a better understanding of my views readers are requested to consult the Chinese version of my paper. See Hsü Fu-kuan, "Ch'eng Chu i-t'ung" in *Chung-kuo ssu-hsiang-shih lun-chi hsü-p'ien*[w] [Supplement to a collection of essays on history of Chinese thought], (Taipei: China Times Publishing Co., 1982), pp. 569–611.

1. *Analects*, 14:15.
2. *Ibid.*, 14:37.
3. *Ibid.*, 12:1.
4. *Ibid.*
5. *Ibid.*, 9:4.
6. *Ibid.*, 6:28. Quoted from Wing-tsit Chan,[x] *A Source Book in Chinese Philosophy* (Princeton, N.J.: Princeton University Press, 1963), p. 3. Hereafter, Chan, *Source Book*.
7. *Ibid.*, 2:18. For example, Confucius urged his disciple Tzu-chang[y] (503–c. 450 B.C.?) to hear a great deal and see a great deal so that he would make few mistakes and have few regrets. *Analects*, 2:18.
8. *Ibid.*, 4:17.
9. *Doctrine of the Mean*, ch. 1; Chan, *Source Book*, p. 98.
10. *Ibid.*, ch. 22; Chan, *Source Book*, pp. 107–108.
11. *Ibid.*, ch. 20; Chan, *Source Book*, p. 107.
12. *Book of Mencius*, 2A:6, 6a:6, Chan, *Source Book*, pp. 54, 65–66.
13. *Ibid.*, 7A:1; Chan, *Source Book*, p. 78.
14. *Ibid.*, 7a:4; Chan, *Source Book*, p. 79.

15. *Chu Tzu yü-lei*[z] [Classified conversations of Master Chu], (Taipei: Cheng-chung[aa] Book Co., 1970), 120:1, pp. 4127–4128.

16. Cf. Wang Mou-hung,[ab] *Chu Tzu nien-p'u*[ac] [Chronological biography of Master Chu], under Chu Hsi's forty-first year.

17. *Book of Changes*, commentary on the second hexagram, *k'un*[ad] (earth, female).

18. I am referring to Chou Tun-i's famous essay "An Explanation of the Diagram of the Great Ultimate." The essay is found in the *Chou Tzu ch'üan-shu*[ae] [Complete works of Master Chou], ch. 1. For an English translation, see Chan, *Source Book*, pp. 463–465.

19. *I-shu*[af] [Surviving works], 18:5b, in the *Erh-Ch'eng ch'üan-shu*[ag] [Complete works of the two Ch'engs], (SPPY ed.); Chan, *Source Book*, p. 562.

20. *Ibid.*, 2A:23b; Chan, *Source Book*, p. 552.

21. *Chu Tzu yü-lei*, 12:11a, p. 337; Chan, *Source Book*, p. 607.

22. *I-shu*, 22A:14a.

23. *Ibid.*, 22A:1a.

24. *Ibid.*, 3:6a.

25. *Ibid.*, 15:2b.

26. *Ibid.*, 2A:2b–3a; Chan, *Source Book*, p. 551.

27. *Chu Tzu yü-lei*, 9:1a, p. 235; Chan, *Source Book*, p. 609.

28. *Analects*, 2:4; Chan, *Source Book*, p. 22.

29. *Doctrine of the Mean*, ch. 1; Chan, *Source Book*, p. 98.

30. *Book of Mencius*, 2A:6; Chan, *Source Book*, p. 65.

31. *Ibid.*, 7A:1; Chan, *Source Book*, p. 78.

32. *Hsün Tzu*, ch. 17; Chan, *Source Book*, p. 118.

33. The ideas of yin and yang were used to explain seasonal changes as concrete manifestations of the Way of Heaven the understanding of which had a great deal to do with farmers whose crops depended on good weather conditions.

34. *I-shu*, 2A:2b.

35. *Ibid.*, 2A:6a.

36. *Ibid.*, 2A:5b.

37. *Ibid.*, 2A:2a.

38. *Ibid.*, 1:3b; Chan, *Source Book*, p. 527. The quotation is from the *Book of Changes*, "Appended Remarks," pt. 1, ch. 12.

39. Preface to his *I-chuan*, in the *Erh-Ch'eng ch'üan-shu;* Chan, *Source Book*, p. 570.

40. Chan, *Source Book*, pp. 463–465.

41. *I-shu*, 1:7b; Chan, *Source Book*, pp. 527–528. The quotation is a saying by Kao Tzu[ah] (c. 420–c. 350 B.C.) in the *Book of Mencius*, 6A:3.

42. *I-shu*, 6:2a; Chan, *Source Book*, p. 552.

43. "Essentials of *The Mencius*," in the *Chu Tzu wen-chi*[ai] [Collection of literary writings of Master Chu], ch. 74. Translator's note: This reference was given in original note 135. But I cannot find Chu Hsi's criticism of Ch'eng Hao's view that mind, nature, and Heaven are one in the essay. I suspect that this could be a mistake. Unfortunately there was no way to consult Professor Hsü as he had passed away. But it is quite true that Chu Hsi's view was different from Ch'eng Hao's as Chu Hsi believed that mind is constituted of material force (*Chu Tzu yü-lei*, 5:3b, p. 138) while nature is regarded as principle (*Chu Tzu yü-lei*, 5:1b, p. 134), their ontological status are different. But generally Chu Hsi seemed to deliberately avoid any direct, harsh criticisms of Ch'eng Hao.

44. *Chu Tzu wen-chi* (SPPY ed.), 40:38b, twenty-ninth letter to Ho Shu-ching.[aj]

45. *Ibid.*, separate collection, 3:9b, third letter to Sun Chi-ho.[ak]

46. Original note 148 pointed out that these divinations were practiced when Chu Hsi was sixty-six years old and eixty-eight years old. See Wang Mou-hung, *Chu Tzu nien-p'u.*

47. *Analects,* 11:11; Chan, *Source Book,* p. 36.

48. Huang Kan, "Chu Tzu hsing-chuang"[al] [Biography of Chu Hsi] in the *Mien-chai chi*[am] [Collected works of Huang Kan], (Precious works of the Four Libraries ed.), 36:30b.

49. *Chu Tzu wen-chi,* 78:18b–19a, "An Essay in Commemoration of Master Chou Tun-i." The Six Classics were the *Book of Odes, History, Rites, Changes, Chou-li* [Rites of Chou], and the *Spring and Autumn Annals.* The ancient Six Classics had the *Book of Music,* now lost, instead of the *Chou-li.*

50. *Ibid.,* 45:42b, eighteenth letter to Liao Tzu-hui.

Glossary

6

Chu Hsi's Theory of Metaphysical Structure

STANISLAUS LOKUANG

Introduction

IN THE HISTORY of Chinese philosophy, there is no term for metaphysics. There is only the term *hsing-shang*, of which scholars throughout the centuries have had different interpretations. The terms *hsing-erh-shang*[a] (prior to physical form) and *hsing-erh-hsia*[b] (posterior to physical form) originally are derived from the *I-ching*[c] (Book of changes). According to its "Appended Remarks," "That which is *hsing-erh-shang* is called the Way (*Tao*[d]); that which is *hsing-erh-shia* is called a concrete thing (*ch'i*[e])."[1] The *Book of Changes* did not give explanation or interpretation to these two terms; neither did scholars devoted to the study of the Classics in the Han dynasty (206 B.C.–A.D. 220) pay much attention to these two sentences.

Han K'ang-po[f] (332–380) commented on the sentence from the "Appended Remarks," part 1, chapter 2, "That which is visible we then call *hsiang* (form). That which has form we then call *ch'i*."[2] Han's commentary reads: "That which becomes form is called a concrete thing."[3] He takes *hsing-erh-shang* as that which does not yet have form and *hsing-erh-hsia* as that which has form.

Hsün Shuang's[g] (128–190) commentary explained the sentence in question as follows: "It is said that the sun, moon, and stars that manifest themselves in the heavens become *hsiang*. The myriad things produced and grown on the earth have form and can be taken as concrete things."[4] Han K'ang-po's comment is based on this explanation, but neither Han nor Hsün commented on the terms *hsing-erh-shang* and *hsing-erh-hsia*.

Finally, in the Sung dynasty (960–1279) scholars of the School of Principle (*Li-hsüeh*[h]) who studied principle (*li*[i]) and material force (*ch'i*[j]) began to pay attention to the problem of *hsing-erh-shang* and *hsing-erh-hsia*.

Chang Tsai's[k] (1020–1077) *I-shuo*[l] (Commentary on the *Book of Changes*) took *hsing-erh-shang* as a formless body and *hsing-erh-hsia* as a body with form. He said,

Hsing-erh-shang is that which is formless. Therefore *hsing-erh-shang* is called the Way. *Hsing-erh-hsia* is that which has form. Therefore *hsing-erh-hsia* is called a concrete thing. That which has no form or leaves no trace is the Way, like great virtue which strengthens moral ties between humans. That which has form and leaves traces is a concrete thing, visible from fact and reality, like ceremony and etiquette. All that which is *hsing-erh-shang* is called the Way. Only because of this is it difficult to understand the connection between the point which divides being (*yu*[m]) and nonbeing (*wu*[n]) and physical form (*hsing*[o]) and formlessness (*wu-hsing*[p]). It is at this crucial point that material force begins. Therefore that which is material force can unite being and nonbeing. Out of nonbeing material force naturally arises. This is the Way and the Change.[5]

The opinions of Ch'eng I (Ch'eng I-ch'uan,[q] 1033–1107) and Ch'eng Hao (Ch'eng Ming-tao,[r] (1032–1085) differ from Chang Tsai's opinion: "Tzu-hou[s] [Chang Tsai] takes *ch'ing-hsü-i-ta*[t] (the one great pure vacuity) to mean the Way of Heaven (*T'ien-tao*[u]). Therefore he considers it not from the viewpoint of *hsing-erh-shang*, but from concrete things."[6] In Chang Tsai's thinking, formlessness is *hsing-erh-shang*. And because he advocated that the material force of the Great Vacuity is formless material force it follows that the material force of the Great Vacuity (*T'ai-hsü*[v]) is *hsing-erh-shang*. As Chang noted: "Material force originated from vacuity, and therefore it should originally be formless. Having been affected, it was produced. Thus congregating, it became form (*hsiang*[w])."[7] Ch'eng I and Ch'eng Hao did not agree with Chang's taking material force as *hsing-erh-shang;* moreover, the Way which is formless and the concrete thing which has form cannot exist in the same physical body. Therefore, that which has form and that which does not have form cannot explain *hsing-erh-shang* and *hsing-erh-hsia*. Even if material force is the material force of the Great Vacuity, it is still *hsing-erh-hsia*.

Chu Hsi follows what Ch'eng I and Ch'eng Hao advocated. He takes *hsing-erh-shang* as "prior to physical form" and *hsing-erh-hsia* as "posterior to physical form." These two can coexist in the same object.

> That which is prior to physical form refers to principle. That which is posterior to physical form refers to facts and things.[8]

> Someone asked, "Why do you explain *hsing-erh-shang* and *hsing-erh-hsia* in terms of *shang* and *hsia?*"
> Chu Hsi replied, "Because it is most appropriate. Suppose you use 'form' and 'formlessness.' Then you sever the relationship of things and principle. Therefore when you use *shang* and *hsia* to describe the difference clearly, you are only drawing a clear distinction, not separating them from each other. A concrete thing is also the Way. The Way is also a concrete thing. They are distinct but not separate."[9]

The difference between Chu Hsi and Chang Tsai consists in Chang Tsai's taking the constituting material force of the Great Vacuity as formless, while Chu Hsi takes anything that has material force as *hsing-erh-hsia*.

In heaven and earth there are principle and material force. Principle is the Way which is prior to physical form, the root of the creation of things. As for material force, it is the constitutive elements of what is posterior to physical form. It is the implement of the creation of things. For this reason the creation of man and things has to possess this principle and then there is the nature *(hsing)*. It has to possess this material force, and then there is physical form *(hsing)*.[10]

> *Hsing-shang* and *hsing-hsia* merely refer to the separation, fusion, and distinction of form. This is precisely the point of demarcation. If you merely say "existing prior to" or "existing posterior to," then that separates them into two separate entities.[11]

In the beginning of the Ch'ing dynasty (1644–1912), Wang Fu-chih[x] had his own opinion on *hsing-shang* and *hsing-hsia*. He used "hidden" (*yin*[y]) and "manifest" (*hsien*[z]) to interpret these two terms.

> The Way which is hidden is not nonexistence. Then how can it be found in the vast emptiness? That which is *hsing-erh-shang* is hidden; that which is *hsing-erh-hsia* is manifest. As soon as you speak the term *hsing-erh-shang*, you presuppose there is the word *hsing* (physical form) which leaves a trace that can be followed and can be referred to.[12]

> That which is formless is the darkness which cannot be seen by man. Formlessness is not really formless. Man's eyesight is circumscribed by the obscurity, so it is seen as obscure. The capacity of the mind is circumscribed by the vastness of what it contemplates. The power of eyesight and hearing are circumscribed by minuteness.[13]

Wang Fu-chih takes the Great Ultimate (*T'ai-chi*[aa]) as the material force of the Great Harmony (*T'ai-ho*[ab]). The material force of the Great Harmony already possesses yin[ac] (passive cosmic force) and yang[ad] (active cosmic force), but it is not yet manifest because there is no material force prior to yin and yang. If there is material force, yin and yang exist. The material force of the Great Harmony is then the material of which yin and yang are not yet made manifest. Human eyesight cannot perceive yin and yang; therefore they are labeled as formless. When the two material forces of yin and yang are made manifest, then they are said to have form.

Tai Chen[ae] (1723–1777) of the Ch'ing dynasty had another opinion. He thought that formlessness and having form should refer to "prior to form" and "posterior to form." "Form refers to the entity which has already become concrete. *Hsing-erh-shang* is like saying 'prior to form' and *hsing-erh-hsia* is like saying 'posterior to form.' The yin yang that has not become an entity with form is said to be *hsing-erh-shang*. It is clear that it is not *hsing-erh-hsia*."[14]

The School of Principle explains *hsing-shang* and *hsing-hsia* by using the terms "having form" and "becoming form" and "manifesting form." These are all based on material force. If material force is the only element comprising the universe and the myriad things in it, and if the distinction between *hsing-shang* and *hsing-hsia* is based on material force, then material force is either concrete or not yet concrete. That which is concrete is yin yang, is "posterior to form." That which is not yet concrete is *hsing-erh-shang*. Wang Fu-chih divided the substance of material force into yin and yang. There is no material force that is not divided into yin and yang. He distinguished between *hsing-erh-shang* and *hsing-erh-hsia* in terms of the "hidden" and the "manifest." Chu Hsi advocated the dualism of principle and material force. He took principle to be that which is *hsing-erh-shang* and material force as that which is *hsing-erh-hsia*. It seems to me that Chu Hsi's interpretation is closer to that which the "Appended Remarks" of the *Book of Changes* referred to as *hsing-erh-shang* and *hsing-erh-hsia*. The "Appended Remarks" takes the Way as *hsing-erh-shang* and concrete things as *hsing-erh-hsia*. The Way, we can say, is equal to principle, but we cannot say it is equal to the material force of the Great Vacuity. When we say principle is *hsing-erh-shang*, we mean that *hsing-erh-shang* is called the Way.

In Chinese philosophy we translate Aristotle's First Philosophy as *hsing-shang-hsüeh*,[af] but we cannot take *hsing-shang* as the object of the study of First Philosophy metaphysics. The metaphysics of Aristotle researches the highest principle or the ultimate principle of everything. The highest principle of everything is the First Principle of everything. Therefore, Western metaphysics studies "Being." "Being" is the substance of everything. Metaphysics studies the substance.

On Substance

Western ontology studies "Being" in the aspect of "Being" as an idea. "Being" is the simplest idea. It has the least intensional or connotative meaning. It can be neither analyzed nor explained. We can explain "Being" in terms of its character and its relationships. Truth, beauty, and goodness are the characteristics of Being; the law of identity, the law of contradiction, and the law of causality are its ontological relationships.

Ontology in the *Book of Changes* studies the metamorphosis of "being," that is, it studies the concrete "existence" of being, becoming (*ch'eng*[ag]) or actus (*hsing*[ah]). Becoming or actus is the metamorphosis (*hua*[ai]). Metamorphosis was called change in the *Book of Changes*. *I* means change and change means metamorphosis (*hua-sheng*[aj]) or production by the perpetual renewal of life (*sheng-sheng*[ak]).

Things that are produced by metamorphosis are becoming or actus; they are also existence. On the perpetual renewal of life, the *Book of Changes* states that from the Great Ultimate, yin and yang are produced. From yin and yang, the Four Phenomena (*ssu-hsiang*[al]) or the Five Agents (*wu-hsing*[am])[15] are produced. From the Four Phenomena or the Five Agents are produced things, which are "existence." Ontology in the *Book of Changes* is an ontology of actus. It studies actus. It is a philosophy of actus.

Although Chu Hsi's ontology studies production by metamorphosis and the perpetual renewal of life, he pays more attention to the structure of things as things. He analyzes things and advocates that things contain two elements, principle and material force. In Western philosophy, things fall within the boundary of cosmology. Both Aristotle and St. Thomas Aquinas advocated that things contained forma and materia. "Being" in ontology of course is *hsing-shang*, because it has no physical form; things belong to *hsing-hsia* because they have matter. The subject of ontology in Western philosophy is "Being"; therefore it is certainly the science of *hsing-shang*. The subject of Western cosmology is "things"; therefore it is certainly the science of *hsing-hsia*. But since the ontology of both the *Book of Changes* and Chu Hsi studies material force as its subject, therefore it cannot but be the science of *hsing-hsia*. But the substance of things belongs to the field of the science of *hsing-shang*. Therefore the ontology of the *Book of Changes* and Chu Hsi should be viewed as the science of *hsing-shang-hsüeh* (metaphysics).

Although the terms of *t'i*[an] (substance) and *yung*[ao] (function) appeared in philosophical thought before the Sung dynasty, they were not in widespread use. These two terms were in common use in Buddhist scriptures and commentaries on the scriptures. The scholars of the School of Principle in the Sung, Ming (1368–1644), and Ch'ing dynasties were much influenced by Buddhist thought and widely used these two terms.

Chu Hsi discussed substance and function on many occasions, but his discussions on the substance of things are few. In discussing substance and function he focused for the most part on facts and events:

> What one should do is called substance. What one does is called function. For example, a fan consists of the spine, handle, and paper. This is substance. Fanning it then is function. Another example is a ruler and a scale which has lines and dots. These are substance. We use them to measure and weight things. That is function.[16]

The substance in question is the subject, the function in question is the usage. There are many elements in the subject. Some of them belong to substance; some of them belong to accident:

> The spines of the fan themselves are substance. The flow or stagnancy of water or the waves of the water are function. The water itself can flow or be stagnant, can be stirred up into waves. This is substance.

> Take for example, our body. It is substance. Seeing wih the eyes and hearing with the ears and moving with the limbs are function. Or take the hand. It is substance, and pointing and carrying and other movements of the fingers are function.[17]

This substance means subjectum. The accident of the subjectum is function. But when Chu Hsi discussed the substance of things, he used Way or principle to refer to substance. He said:

Substance is the principle and function is the usage, like the seeing of the eyes and the hearing of the ears. It is naturally so. This is principle. We use our eyes to see things. We use ears to hear sounds. That is function.[18]

> *Someone asked,* "Are substance and function always different?"
> *Chu Hsi replied,* "Take this signpost. It is one principle. It points out a direction down the road this way or that way. Or take this house. It is one principle. It has sitting rooms and halls. There are Chang San[ap] and Li Ssu.[aq] Li Ssu can't be Chang San. Chang San can't be Li Ssu. Take yin and yang. The 'Western Inscription' (*Hsi-ming*[ar]) says that 'the principle is one but its manifestations are many.' The meaning is the same here." *Chu Hsi also said,* "The more things are differentiated, the greater the principle appears."[19]

Chu Hsi takes principle as substance because first there is substance and then there is function. Function is consistent with (in accordance with) principle. But with respect to original substance, what is important is not the relationship of substance and function but the relationship of principle and existence. What does the existence of this thing take as its original substance? The original substance of something's existence. The reason of something's existence must be within the nature of that thing. This thing is this thing because of its nature. The existence of something should have its own original substance, because existence is the existence of the original substance. Original substance is the subject of existence. Besides the original substance, the existing subject also contains many accidentals. Chu Hsi said in relation to original substance,

> Therefore when we Confucianists speak of the original substance of the nature, it means only the reality of humanity, righteousness, propriety, and wisdom (*jen i li chih*[as]) . . .[20] If it is not that the original substance contains these, how can they develop from function? There is no point we can grasp the original substance; we can only look for the original substance from its function.[21]

In this quotation Chu Hsi takes humanity, righteousness, propriety, and wisdom as the endowment of nature. The meaning of original substance and the meaning of the original substance of the mind that has not yet begun to work are the same. Here the substance means entity.

> *Someone asked,* "What is the difference between the mind not yet working and its nature?"
> *Chu Hsi replied,* "Mind contains substance and function. Before the mind begins to work it is substance. When it is working, it is function."[22]

Chu Hsi advocated that the mind consists of its feeling and its nature. The original substance of its nature is the substance of the mind and the principle of humanity, righteousness, propriety, and wisdom. In the same way the original substance of the mind is also the principle of humanity, righteousness, propriety, and wisdom. "When we talk solely about the virtue of the mind,

then the mind not yet functioning is substance and the mind already functioning is function. When we talk only of the principle of love, then humanity is
the substance and compassion is the function."[23]

When we take principle or the Way as substance, we contrast it to function
and not to existence. According to Chu Hsi, that by which a thing exists has
to have principle and material force. The original substance of a thing is
therefore formed by the fusion of principle and material force. This original
substance then is the root of the thing; all other substance and functions are
dependent upon this original substance.

Chu Hsi took principle and material force as the original substance of
things, equivalent to things in Western cosmology, not being in Western ontology. But from the point of view of Chinese philosophy, Chu Hsi's thing
which consists of principle and material force is what the *Book of Changes*
spoke of as becoming and actus. The two terms in the *Book of Changes* refer to
the myriad things in the universe, which were formed by change. The becoming and actus of the myriad things are not absolute actus. The absolute actus
exhibits no change. It has no element of the perpetual renewal of life. The
actus of the myriad things in the universe is formed by fusion and the perpetual renewal of the elements. The *Book of Changes* took the myriad things to be
formed by the material force of yin and yang. Within the material force there
is naturally the principle of union. Chu Hsi advocated that principle did not
contain material force, but was in opposition to it. The metamorphosis of the
myriad things has its own principle of becoming and its own material force of
becoming. If there is a certain principle, there is a certain material force. Principle and material force unite and form the myriad things. The *Book of
Changes* takes material force to be the original substance of things. Within
material force there is principle. Chu Hsi took principle and material force as
the substance of things. Principle and material force are two, but they are not
separate.

Chu Hsi's theory of metaphysics, therefore, does not use the categories
of *hsing-erh-shang* and *hsing-erh-hsia* but begins with original substance.
Although material force is *hsing-erh-hsia,* it is still one element in the original
substance of things. Therefore it still belongs to the metaphysics. Things in
Western epistemology have two elements: forma and materia. Materia belongs
to material; therefore it belongs to the universe. Material force in Chinese
philosophy does not mean material. Therefore it belongs to the science of
hsing-erh-shang.

Principle and Material Force

In studying the substance of the myriad things, Chu Hsi was following
Ch'eng I's thought, which advocated that the myriad things are composed of
principle and material force. Principle forms the nature of the thing and material force forms the form of the thing. "*Someone asked, 'Is the nature the mate-*

rial of life?' *Chu Hsi replied,* 'No, the nature is the principle of life. Material force is the material of life, and already has form and figure.' "[24]

The things of the universe are called the myriad things, yet things are not necessarily all material. Things represent that which actually exists. Everything has principle by which it is formed and also has "existence" which formed each thing. "Existence" is the concrete thing, that is, the reality of the thing. And principles are abstract. Abstract principle which forms reality has to have "material." Material is concrete, and therefore it must have form. Material comes from material force. Therefore everything has both principle and material force.

The word *hsing* (physical form) was originally written as *hsing,*[a] which means a model. In ancient China people made bricks by first mixing clay, then spreading it evenly, then taking a wooden model and pressing it on the clay to separate it into squares. After baking in the sun, the square clay turned into square bricks. If we use this word *hsing* (model) to explain the substance of things, then this *hsing* (physical form) is equivalent to the forma in Western scholastic philosophy. This forma then is equivalent to Chu Hsi's principle but not to material force. Therefore the *hsing* in "material force forms the *hsing* of things" does not mean model but physical form. As the form depends on the material, it is said, "Material force forms the physical form of things." Physical form is the characteristic of material force, but principle has no form and moreover can't have form. Therefore, Chu Hsi advocated that principle is *hsing-erh-shang* and *hsing-erh-hsia.*

Material force is the material, equivalent to materia in Western scholastic philosophy. This is speaking of it in terms of function and not from the point of view of its original nature. Material force has the function of materia in the substance of things. Materia in original nature is always of a material nature but material force is not. Material force may be material or may be immaterial.

Things have their own principle to form things. Principle is the nature of the thing. Things have their own material which is material force. "As there is such principle, then there is such material force."[25]

A thing becomes a certain thing because the principle for it exists; if the principle exists, then so does the material force. For example, a particular person became that particular person because there exists principle of the person and then the material force of the person. The "this" of the person is the characteristic of the person and also the principle of the person. Because the particular principle exists, so does the material force. Chu Hsi often said that principle and material force should not be seen as sequential; but in theory, principle must come first. "*Someone asked,* 'Does principle come first and material force follow it?' *Chu Hsi replied,* 'Principle and material force as such are not sequential; but when we are reasoning, principle comes first and material force follows it.' "[26]

This means that principle conditions material force. Principle determines material force. There is a little similarity to the forma determining materia in scholastic philosophy. Materia is an undetermined material; having forma added to it, it becomes materia of the things. But in Chu Hsi's philosophy, the relationship of principle and material force is not like this. Chu Hsi advocated that principle is one but its manifestations are many. Originally principle is one, but because of material force it is manifested as many. In this way of speaking, material force determines principle. First there is a unified principle, but then according to the differences of material force, the things formed are different. The differences of things do not come from principle but from material force.

The thought that principle is one but its manifestations are many comes from Ch'eng I, but Chang Tsai already had this kind of thought. Chu Hsi strongly supported it.

Someone asked, "What are principle and material force?" Chu Hsi replied, "I-ch'uan (Ch'eng I) said it well: 'Principle is one but manifestations are many.'[27] If you take all of heaven and earth and myriad things together, there is only one principle. But each person has his own principle."[28]

" 'The Western Inscription' from beginning to end is explaining this concept that principle is one but manifestations are many."[29]

Chu Hsi takes the Great Ultimate as the supreme principle; but it is not the highest principle of the universe, and it is not the origin of the universe. The Great Ultimate is the most relevant principle of everything. Chu Hsi taught that there is only one Great Ultimate in the universe but that everything has its own Great Ultimate. This is the meaning that principle is one but its manifestations are many.

Chu Hsi said, "The Great Ultimate is only the principle of heaven, earth, and the myriad things. Within heaven and earth, there is the Great Ultimate. Within the myriad phenomena, each phenomenon has its own Great Ultimate."[30]

"The Great Ultimate is only the best and most perfect principle; everyone has a Great Ultimate and everything has a Great Ultimate."[31]

How do we explain this seeming contradiction? Fung Yu-lan[au] said,

According to this, in everything besides principle which forms the thing itself, there is the Great Ultimate. That is, the whole principle of everything.[32] As I have written, "This explanation is not correct. Chu Hsi does not separate principle and the Great Ultimate as two different kinds of principle. There is only one principle. The Great Ultimate represents the supreme principle, that is, the whole principle. One thing cannot contain two principles, or else it can't be one thing but two. The principle of a thing is the whole principle of the Principle of Heaven. It is only manifested to a different degree. Chu Hsi made an analogy: 'There is only one moon but the moons reflected in the rivers, lakes, and streams are different.' "[33]

But the problem is here. Principle forms the nature of a thing; it is the principle by which a thing gets its physical form. When the principle is the same, then the nature should be the same. When the nature is the same, the thing is the same. Suppose there is only one principle for all myriad things in the universe. Then there is only one nature. If there is only one nature, then there is only one thing. Then the result of Chu Hsi's thought would be similar to the result of Chuang Tzu's[av] (c. 369–c. 286 B.C.) "Ch'i-wu lun" (On the equality of things), that is, the myriad things are the same. Only the surface appearance differs. All of the substance is the same. For example, the nature of human beings is the same. All persons are human. Only their quantity and quality differ.

But this is not the conclusion Chu Hsi wanted. He still brought forth the theory that principle is one but its manifestations are many. But if the principle is one, how can it be manifested differently? If we want to explain this, we must analyze and clarify the content of principle.

The traditional thought of Confucianists took the universe as the flux of life and everything possessing life. Life to them was simply the existence of things. From the point of view of existence, everything is existent, just as everything is being. The existence of the myriad things was formed by the fusion of yin and yang in their operations. The operations of yin and yang never cease. They are continuous and unceasingly combine to produce the myriad things. We call their operations the perpetual renewal of life. The *Book of Changes* says, "The perpetual renewal of life is called Change."[34]

Because every existence is formed from the operation of yin and yang, each existence is a life. The *Book of Changes* says, "One yin and one yang is called the Way. That which continues it is goodness. That which is formed is the nature." Yin and yang not only revolve unceasingly in the universe; they also revolve unceasingly in the physical body of each thing. The existence of each physical body never ceases motion. It is a kind of existence of on-going movement. Therefore we call it life.

The whole universe is composed of the operations of yin and yang. Yin and yang have their own principle of operations. This principle is the principle of perpetual renewal of life. It is also the Great Ultimate that comprises the universe. Chu Hsi thought that the universe has a Great Ultimate. In addition, every physical body also has the principle of the operations of yin and yang. This principle also is the principle of perpetual renewal of life. This is also the Great Ultimate in every physical body. The principle of perpetual renewal of life in everything and in the universe is the same. But the principle of perpetual renewal of life of each thing is different. Therefore Chu Hsi said, "Principle is one but its manifestations are many."

Originally the principle of perpetual renewal of life in each thing is the same principle. Then why is it different? It is different because the material force that each physical body possesses is different. Material force is differentiated into purity and turbidity. The degree of purity or turbidity also has countless varieties and diversifications. The effect of purity and turbidity consists in concealing or making manifest the principle of perpetual renewal of life. Turbid material force conceals the principle of perpetual renewal of life. Pure material force makes manifest the principle of perpetual renewal of life. The difference in the degree of purity or turbidness determines the degree to which the principle of perpetual renewal of life will be concealed or made manifest. The most turbid material force completely conceals the principle of perpetual renewal of life, causing the physical body not to manifest the slightest amount of life. The lower the degree of turbidness, the lower the degree of concealment of the principle of perpetual renewal of life. Therefore life is more able to be made manifest. Take, for example, plants. On them the degree of turbidness being low, the degree of concealment of the principle of perpetual renewal of life will be low, and this principle will be manifest. The material force of man, on the other hand, is pure, and therefore man's principle of perpetual renewal of life can be manifested. This is what Chu Hsi meant when he said that things, that is, animals, obtained only part of principle, but man obtained the whole of principle.

> *Someone asked,* "If someone asked if material force which is upright and unobstructed constitutes man and material force which is oblique and obstructed constitutes things, what would you say?"
> *Chu Hsi replied,* "The coming into existence of things must necessarily depend on the coagulation of material force and then have form. That which possesses pure material force is man; that which possesses turbid material force is a thing. . . ."
> *Someone else asked,* "What do you think of this: Material force has purity and turbidness but their principle is the same?"
> *Chu Hsi replied,* "It is certainly like that. The principle is like a precious jewel. When possessed by a saint or wise man, it is like being placed in clear water. Its brilliance naturally can be seen. When it is possessed by stupid or unworthy persons, it is like being placed in turbid water. The water must be made clear and the mud and sand removed before its brilliance can be seen."[35]

Even though man's material force may be pure, there are still differences in the degree of purity. Therefore Chu Hsi advocated the nature of the quality of material force. The purity or turbidness of material force makes human nature good or evil. Compared to that of man, the material force of things is turbid, and the principle that things possess is oblique and obstructed. The material force of man, on the other hand, is pure; thus the principle that man possesses is upright and unobstructed.

Principle and material force fuse to form the substance of things. Substance possesses the nature of the thing and its form. In his ontology, St. Thomas Aquinas takes forma and materia to form the nature of things. Nature and existentia fuse to form "reality," which is a concrete thing. The structure of substance for Chu Hsi and St. Thomas Aquinas are similar but there are differences. Figure 1 shows those differences.

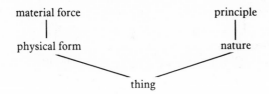

FIGURE I
Chu Hsi's Theory of Substance

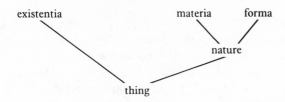

St. Thomas Aquinas' Theory of Substance

Existentia in St. Thomas Aquinas' theory of substance brings with it the individuality of quantity and quality; besides characteristics in common, the concrete thing has its individuality. Material force in Chu Hsi's theory of substance brings individuality with it, too. Individuality consists of the Five Agents. Chu Hsi calls these Five Agents quality. Quality is formed by material force: "Yang changes and yin fuses with it and then Water, Fire, Wood, Metal and Earth are produced. Yin and yang are the material force which produces the quality of these Five Agents. When Heaven and Earth produced things, the Five Agents came into existence first."[36]

Chou Tun-i[aw] (1017–1073) in his "Explanation of the Diagram of the Great Ultimate" (*T'ai-chi-t'u shuo*[ax]) advocated that the Ultimate of Nonbeing (*wu-chi*[ay]) begat the Great Ultimate. The Great Ultimate produced yin and yang, which produced the Five Agents. The Five Agents produced male and female. Male and female produced the myriad phenomena. Even though Chu Hsi defended Chou Tun-i's "Explanation of the Diagram of the Great Ultimate," he did not make use of it. He did not advocate that the Great Ultimate produced yin and yang but said that the Great Ultimate was the principle and yin and yang were the material force. The fusion of principle and material force produced things. The fusing of principle and material force produced the Five Agents which are the quality of things. When asked about the theory of the "Explanation of the Diagram of the Great Ultimate" Chu Hsi replied, "In speaking of man's physical body, the breath in breathing is the yin and yang. The body, the blood, and the flesh are the Five Agents. Their nature is the principle."[37]

Chu Hsi's theory of substance is as shown in Figure 2. Material force is

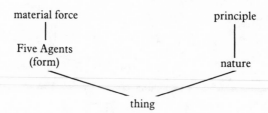

FIGURE 2
Chu Hsi's Theory of Substance

hsing-hsia and the Five Agents are *hsing-hsia*. Principle then is *hsing-shang*. Therefore the substance of things contains *hsing-shang* and *hsing-hsia*. As Chu Hsi advocated, there is a distinction between *hsing-shang* and *hsing-hsia*, but they cannot be separated.[38] In Chu Hsi's metaphysical structure of the substance, *hsing-shang* and *hsing-hsia* are mutually connected.

The Principle of Perpetual Renewal of Life

There is only one principle in Heaven and Earth, yet each thing has a principle. Principle is one but its manifestations are many. This principle is the principle of perpetual renewal of life. What does it involve? Although the principle of perpetual renewal of life which Chu Hsi spoke of is the principle of life, it is different from the principle of life in Western philosophy in general. Although life as spoken of in Western philosophy has various different explanations, the most common explanation is that life is autonomous. Life grows by itself. Chu Hsi spoke of life in the unswerving Confucian tradition as life of the mind. Mencius (372–289 B.C.?) said that man has smaller parts and greater parts. The smaller parts are the organs like ears and eyes. The greater part is the organ of the mind and thought.[39] The difference between man and animals is in this greater part. Mencius said, "The difference between the superior man and the common people is that he preserves and fosters his mind."[40]

The human mind is unobstructed and flexible; it can know and think and make determinations. It commands nature and feeling. Therefore the mind contains the whole principle of perpetual renewal of life. As Chu Hsi noted, "The whole of the mind is clear and open; it contains myriad principles."[41] "The mind is the myriad principles; only the one who can preserve the mind can probe to the root of the principle."[42] "Nature is the principle which the mind possesses, and the mind is the place where the principles converge."[43]

Chu Hsi takes the mind as commanding the nature of the thing and its feeling. The nature is the substance of the mind; feeling is the usage of the mind. The principle of the nature comprises humanity, righteousness, propriety, and wisdom. The usage of the mind comprises the feeling of commiseration, shame, right and wrong, and humility.

> *Someone asked* about mind, nature and feeling. *Chu Hsi replied,* "Mencius said the feeling of commiseration of the mind is the beginning of humanity. From this one section all becomes clear. The feeling of commiseration, shame, right and wrong, and humility are all feelings. Humanity, righteousness, propriety, and wisdom are the substance of the nature. Within the nature there are only humanity, righteousness, propriety, and wisdom. It is expressed as the feeling of commiseration, shame, humility, right and wrong. Therefore it is the feeling of the nature."[44]

This section makes it clear that the principle contained in the human mind is the nature. The nature is then humanity, righteousness, propriety, and wisdom. The principle of perpetual renewal of life for Chu Hsi is humanity, righteousness, propriety, and wisdom. These four qualities generalized are humanity. Mencius said, "Humanity is the human mind."[45] He also said, "As for humanity, it is man; combining the two forms the Way."[46] Chu Hsi explains the mind of man being humanity as man possessing the mind of Heaven and Earth as his mind. Heaven and Earth take the creation of things as their mind. The mind of man therefore is humanity. Humanity is creation *(sheng)*. To clarify the meaning of the word "mind," Chu Hsi said,

> One word can cover it all. That is simply creation. The great virtue of Heaven and Earth is creation. Man receives the element of Heaven and Earth and is created. Therefore this mind must be humane. Humanity is then creation.[47]

> Heaven and Earth take creation of things as their mind. And the creation of man and things likewise take the mind of Heaven and Earth as their mind. Therefore we say that although the virtue of the mind encompasses all and there is nothing which it does not contain, one word can cover it all. Thus I say simple humanity.[48]

The principle possessed by Heaven and Earth (the Great Ultimate of Heaven and Earth) is the principle that produces and reproduces the myriad things. It is called the mind of Heaven and Earth, that is, the principle of perpetual renewal of life of Heaven and Earth.

Man possesses the material force of yin and yang, of Heaven and Earth, and thus possesses the principle of perpetual renewal of life. Man's principle of perpetual renewal of life is called humanity. The myriad things all possess the principle of perpetual renewal of life of Heaven and Earth: "The mind of Heaven which produces things never ceases. . . . The Way of *ch'ien*[32] (Heaven)[49] changes and perpetually renews life. Each thing obtains its proper nature and life. Therefore it makes each grass and tree obtain its principle."[50]

But the myriad things don't have the faculty of mind and thought. They cannot recognize the principle of perpetual renewal of life and cannot experience it, much less manifest and develop it. Man has the faculty of mind and thought. Man has feeling; he knows to love his own life and the life of other men and things. Chu Hsi takes humanity as the principle of love: "Love is not humanity; the principle of love is humanity. The mind is not humanity; its virtue is humanity."[51]

Humanity is the principle of love. This kind of love is not lust for things but for virtue. The mind of man puts into practice the virtue of humanity and love. Therefore man has the feeling of commiseration, shame and dislike, right and wrong, and humility. Chu Hsi takes feeling as emanating from the nature; that is, emanating from the principle of the mind. Commiseration, shame and dislike, right and wrong, and humility are feelings. Thus the mind's action is the beginning of virtue. Mencius said, "The feeling of commiseration of the mind is the beginning of humanity. The feeling of shame and dislike of the mind is the beginning of righteousness. The feeling of humility of the mind is the beginning of propriety. The feeling of right and wrong of the mind is the beginning of wisdom. Man has these four beginnings just as he has four limbs."[52]

The nature possessed by man's substance is the principle of humanity, righteousness, propriety, and wisdom. The material force possessed by man's substance is the feeling of commiseration, shame and dislike, right and wrong, and humility. The substance of man is the goodness of ethical morality. Man, according to his substance, is moral. The principle of perpetual renewal of life is the principle of humanity, righteousness, propriety, and wisdom. What is called perpetual renewal of life is spiritual life, is the activity of the mind and spirit.

Heaven and earth and all the myriad things of the universe possess this kind of principle. The degree of manifestation of the principle of spiritual life is different depending on whether the material force that forms it is either pure or turbid. The material force of man is pure, and thus his spiritual life can be manifested. Therefore it is said that the principle man possesses is complete, upright, and unobstructed. However, within the material force of man there are differences of degree of purity. A lower degree of purity in the material force produces turbid material force. Men who possess this kind of material force are evil. The material force possessed by sages is the purest. The spiritual life of sages is thus completely manifested. The "Appended Remarks" of the *Book of Changes* says, "The great virtue of Heaven and Earth is creation. The great preciousness of saints is called rank. How to preserve this rank is called humanity."[53]

The virtue of the humanity of sages matches the virtue of creation of Heaven and Earth. Thus the *Book of Changes* says, "As for the great man, his virtue matches that of Heaven and Earth, his brightness matches that of the sun and moon, his orderliness matches that of the four seasons, and his auspiciousness and inauspiciousness matches that of ghosts and spirits."[54] Chu Hsi said,

The universe is only the flowing of one material force. The myriad things are naturally produced and naturally grow and form and have their own color. Are they one by one decorated thus? A sage is only a flowing out from the great origin. His vision is naturally clear. His hearing is naturally sharp. His disposition is naturally gentle. His appearance is naturally respectful. The relation of father and son is therefore humane. The relationship of ruler and minister is therefore righteousness. The many principles flowing out of the great origin are only this one from beginning to end.[55]

The sage represents the whole meaning of the principle of perpetual renewal of life. He is also the whole expression of that principle. Sages and Heaven and Earth match each other. Heaven and Earth are characterized by creation, and sages are characterized by humanity. Creation and humanity match each other.

The Metaphysical Basis of Morality

Morality is the expression of spiritual life. When Chu Hsi spoke of morality, he often talked about the Five Constant Virtues of humanity, righteousness, propriety, wisdom, and faithfulness. The Five Constant Virtues are man's spiritual life. In his theory of substance, Chu Hsi took principle and material force to be the metaphysical structure. Principle becomes the nature; material force becomes concrete form. The form of material force first has yin and yang, then the Five Agents. Afterwards comes the individuality of things. In the universe yin and yang become the Five Agents, which operate as Origination, Flourish, Advantage, and Firmness (*yüan heng li chen*[ba]).[56] Within humans, yin and yang become the Five Agents, which correspond to humanity, righteousness, propriety, wisdom, and faithfulness.

Origination, Flourish, Advantage, and Firmness are the nature; birth, growth, harvest, and storage are feelings. As for the mind, it takes Origination to create; it takes Flourish to grow; it takes Advantage to harvest; and it takes Firmness to store. As for the nature, it is humanity, righteousness, propriety, wisdom, and faithfulness. As for feeling, it is commiseration, shame and dislike, humility, and right and wrong. As for the mind, it takes humanity to love, it takes righteousness to dislike, it takes propriety to be humble, and it takes wisdom to be wise. As for the nature, it is the principle of the mind. As for feeling, it is the function of the mind.[57]

Humanity, righteousness, propriety, wisdom, and faithfulness match Wood, Fire, Metal, Water, and Earth. Earth is the basis of Wood, Fire, Metal, and Water. When the Five Agents match the five directions, the earth matches the center; when the Five Agents match the four seasons, earth is the central point of the year. When the Five Agents match the Five Constant Virtues, Earth matches faithfulness. Faithfulness is the common condition of humanity, righteousness, propriety, and wisdom, that is, sincerity in nature. Thus, the usage of the Five Constant Virtues only has the Four Virtues of humanity, righteousness, propriety, and wisdom. The Four Virtues then match Origination, Flourish, Advantage, and Firmness.

The great virtue of Heaven and Earth is called creation. Heaven and Earth produce the myriad things through a process of birth, growth, harvest, and storage. Origination is the birth, Flourish is the growth, Advantage is the harvest, and Firmness is the storage. The external form of Origination, Flourish, Advantage, and Firmness is the four seasons of spring, summer, autumn, and winter. Therefore it is said that in the spring there is birth, in the summer there is growth, in the autumn there is harvest, and in the winter there is storage. Man's spiritual life also has its own process, which is humanity, righteousness, propriety, and wisdom.

Ethical morality is not only ethical behavior and the habit of humanity. Western ethics takes goodness as the habit of being good fostered by charitable action. It has no relationship to the theory of substance. Good or evil in man does not influence his basic nature. Men who do evil actions do not decrease their substance. Good men are men; evil men are also men. In Chinese philosophy, such as in Chu Hsi's philosophy, morality is not only humane action, but it is also the expression of a man's substance. In the *Doctrine of the Mean* it is called full development of one's nature, that is, developing one's own human nature. The *Doctrine of the Mean* says, "Only people of the utmost sincerity under Heaven can develop fully their nature; developing fully this nature can thus develop fully the nature of others; developing fully the nature of others thus can develop fully the nature of things."[58] Chu Hsi said,

> By utmost sincerity in the universe is meant the reality of the virtue of the sage. The universe cannot add to it. As one who fully develops his nature, his virtue is solid. Because he possesses no selfish human desires and because the Mandate of Heaven is within him, he can be aware of it, follow it whether it be great or small, coarse or refined. There is not even the slightest bit that will not be developed. The nature of man and things is also my nature; but since they are endowed with different material force and physical forms, so there are differences. He who can fully develop is said to know with clarity and to handle without impropriety.[59]

The nature of man is humanity. Fully developing one's nature then is to develop humanity and love, to love one's own life, to love the life of others, and to love the life of the myriad things. The *Doctrine of the Mean* says, "He who can develop the nature of things can then assist Heaven and Earth in renewing and fostering. He who can assist Heaven and Earth in renewing and fostering can then be in the same rank of Heaven and Earth."[60] Developing humanity and love is to assist Heaven and Earth in the perpetual renewal of the myriad things. Man thus can be in the same rank as Heaven and Earth. In the "Appended Remarks" we read, "As for the great man, his virtue matches with Heaven and Earth."[61]

Ethical morality is connected to the metaphysical substance. Ethical morality takes substance as its basis. Western ethics takes morality as rooted in human nature, for in human nature there are rules of morality. The ethics of Chu Hsi and the Confucianists take morality to originate in the substance of man; morality is the development of human life, because the principle of humanity, righteousness, propriety, and wisdom is the principle of perpetual renewal of life. The principle of perpetual renewal of life is the principle of the substance of man.

The principle of man and things is the same. The nature of man and things is also my nature, but since they are endowed with different material force and physical forms, so there are differences. The myriad phenomena in the universe all have the principle of humanity. It is only because of the turbidness of their material force that it cannot be made manifest. The material force of man is pure. Thus it can manifest the principle of humanity.

Conclusion

Chu Hsi's theory of metaphysical structure concerns the substance of things. The substance of things was formed by principle and material force. Principle became the nature of the thing and material force became the form of the thing. The nature of the thing is the principle of why a particular thing is itself. The form is the material of why it became itself. Material comes from material force. Material force first forms the Five Agents, and then from the Five Agents it forms the material.

The principle of things is one principle. Chu Hsi advocated that principle is one but its manifestations are many. The principle of things is the principle of actual "existence."

The existence of things is formed by the union of yin and yang. The union of yin and yang then is the continuous operations of "becoming." The operations of yin and yang, which never cease, produce the myriad things. The principle of the union of yin and yang is the principle of perpetual renewal of life.

The principle of perpetual renewal of life in the myriad things of the universe, in each of the phenomena, is the same principle. Yet because the material force endowed by each is different, the principle manifested in the myriad things appears to be different. Material force can be pure or turbid. Turbid material force conceals the principle of perpetual renewal of life. Pure material force manifests the principle of perpetual renewal of life. The material force of things is turbid. The material force of man is pure.

The principle of perpetual renewal of life manifested in man is humanity, righteousness, propriety, and wisdom in spiritual life; generalized, these become humanity. Man's principle of perpetual renewal of life then is humanity.

The principle of Heaven and Earth is perpetual renewal of life. The principle of man is humanity. From creation there is humanity. In the myriad things of the universe there is creation, and in man there is humanity. Perpetual renewal of life in Heaven and Earth passes through four processes which are Origination, Flourish, Advantage, and Firmness. The spiritual life of man also passes through four processes, which are humanity, righteousness, propriety, and wisdom. These belong to the substance of man and the characteristics of the substance. Thus ethical morality and the characteristics of the substance connect with each other. Chu Hsi's theory of metaphysical structure combined substance and morality, and connected ethics and ontology. Thus, although the philosophy of Chinese Confucianism seems to have only ethics, actually its ethics are the continuation of ontology. Its ethics and ontology are mutually connected.

Notes

1. *Book of Changes*, "Appended Remarks," pt. 1, ch. 12.
2. *Ibid.*, ch. 11.
3. Han's commentary is found in the Thirteen Classics edition.
4. Comment on *ibid.*
5. *I-shuo,*[bb] 11:15b–16a, in the *Chang Tzu ch'üan-shu*[bc] [Complete works of Chang Tsai], (SPPY ed.).
6. *I-shu*[bd] [Surviving works], 11:1b, in the *Erh-Ch'eng ch'üan-shu*[be] [Complete works of the two Ch'engs], (SPPY ed.). The text does not mention Chang Tsai specifically, but the reference is clearly implied, for no one else but Chang Tsai had said that.
7. *Cheng-meng*[bf] [Correcting youthful ignorance], ch. 1.
8. *Chu Tzu yü-lei,*[bg] [Classified conversations of Master Chu], (Taipei: Cheng-chung[bh] Book Co., 1970), 75:20a, p. 3077.
9. *Ibid.*, 75:19b, p. 3067.
10. *Chu Tzu wen-chi*[bi] [Collection of literary works of Master Chu], (SPPY ed. entitled *Chu Tzu ta-ch'üan*[bj] [Complete collection of Master Chu], 58:4b, first reply to Huang Tao-fu.[bk]
11. *Chu Tzu yü-lei*, 94:4a, p. 3761.
12. *Tu Ssu-shu ta-ch'üan shuo*[bl] [On reading the *Great Completion of the Four Books*], ch. 2, commenting on the *Doctrine of the Mean*, ch. 11.
13. *Cheng-meng chu*[bm] [Commentary on the *Cheng-meng*], p. 12, in the *Ch'uan-shan i-shu*[bn] [Surviving works of Wang Fu-chih], (Taipei: Tzu-yu[bo] Press, 1972).
14. *Meng Tzu tzu-i shu-cheng*[bp] [Commentary on the meaning of terms in the *Book of Mencius*], in Hu Shih,[bq] *Tai Tung-yüan ti che-hsüeh*[br] [The philosophy of Tai Chen], (Shanghai: Commercial Press, 1927), sec. 17, p. 73.
15. Metal, Wood, Water, Fire, and Earth. *Wu-hsing* has also been translated as "Five Elements."
16. *Chu Tzu yü-lei*, 6:3a, p. 163.
17. *Ibid.*, 6:2b, p. 162.
18. *Ibid.*, 6:2b–3a, pp. 162–163.
19. *Ibid.*, 6:3b, p. 164.

20. The Four Virtues are taught in the *Book of Mencius,* 2A:6 and 6A:6.

21. *Chu Tzu wen-chi,* 61:2a–b, third reply in Lin Te-chiu.[bs]

22. *Chu Tzu yü-lei,* 5:7b, p. 146.

23. *Ibid.,* 20:17b, p. 752.

24. *Ibid.,* 137:10a, p. 1239.

25. *Ibid.,* 1:1b, p. 2.

26. *Ibid.,* 1:2b, p. 4.

27. *I-ch'uan wen-chi*[bt] [Collection of literary works by Ch'eng I], 5:12b, in the *Erh-Ch'eng ch'üan-shu.*

28. *Chu Tzu yü-lei,* 1:1b, p. 2.

29. *Ibid.,* 98:15a, p. 4009.

30. *Ibid.,* 1:1a, p. 1.

31. *Ibid.,* 94:62, p. 3765.

32. *Chung-kuo che-hsüeh shih*[bu] [History of Chinese philosophy], (Shanghai: Commercial Press, 1934), p. 902.

33. *Chu Tzu yü-lei,* 94:35b, p. 3824; Lokuang, *Chung-kuo che-hsüeh ssu-hsiang shih: Sung-tai p'ien*[bv] [History of Chinese philosophical thought: the Sung period], (Taipei: Student Book Co., 1978), p. 499.

34. *Book of Changes,* "Appended Remarks," pt. 1, ch. 5.

35. *Chu Tzu yü-lei,* 17:4a–5b, pp. 600–601.

36. *Ibid.,* 94:3a, p. 3759.

37. *Ibid.,* 94:11b–12a, pp. 3776–3777.

38. See above, n. 9.

39. *Book of Mencius,* 6A:14–15.

40. *Ibid.,* 4A:28.

41. *Chu Tzu yü-lei,* 5:11a, p. 153.

42. *Ibid.,* 9:6a, p. 245.

43. *Ibid.,* 5:6a, p. 143.

44. *Ibid.,* 5:8b, p. 148.

45. *Book of Mencius,* 6A:11.

46. *Ibid.,* 7B:16.

47. *Chu Tzu yü-lei,* 5:3b, p. 138.

48. *Chu Tzu wen-chi,* 67:20a, "A Treatise on Humanity."

49. The first hexagram in the *Book of Changes.*

50. *Chu Tzu yü-lei,* 27:18b, p. 1108.

51. *Ibid.,* 20:24a, p. 765.

52. *Book of Mencius,* 2A:6.

53. *Book of Changes,* "Appended Remarks," pt. 2, ch. 10.

54. *Book of Changes,* the main commentary on the first hexagram, *ch'ien.*

55. *Chu Tzu yü-lei,* 45:2a–b, pp. 1825–1826.

56. The Four Qualities of the first hexagram, *ch'ien,* in the *Book of Changes.*

57. *Chu Tzu wen-chi,* 67:1a, "A Treatise on Origination, Flourish, Advantage, and Firmness."

58. *Doctrine of the Mean,* ch. 22.

59. *Chung-yung chang-chü*[bw] [Commentary on the *Doctrine of the Mean*], comment on ch. 22.

60. *Doctrine of the Mean,* ch. 22.

61. *Book of Changes,* the main commentary on the first hexagram, *ch'ien.*

Glossary

a	形而上	aa	太極	az	乾
b	形而下	ab	太和	ba	元亨利貞
c	易經	ac	陰	bb	易説
d	道	ad	陽	bc	張子全書
e	器	ae	戴震	bd	遺書
f	韓康伯	af	形上學	be	二程全書
g	孫爽	ag	成	bf	正蒙
h	理學	ah	行	bg	朱子語類
i	理	ai	化	bh	正中
j	氣	aj	化生	bi	朱子文集
k	張戴	ak	生生	bj	朱子大全
l	易説	al	四象	bk	黃道夫
m	有	am	五行	bl	讀四書大全説
n	無形	an	體	bm	正蒙註
o	形	ao	用	bn	船山遺書
p	無形	ap	張三	bo	自由
q	程頤伊川	aq	李四	bp	孟子字義疏證
r	程顥明道	ar	西銘	bq	胡適
s	子厚	as	仁義禮智	br	戴東原的哲學
t	清虛一大	at	型	bs	林德久
u	天道	au	馮友蘭	bt	伊川文集
v	太虛	av	莊子	bu	中國哲學史
w	象	aw	周敦頤	bv	中國哲學思想史宋代篇
x	王夫之	ax	太極圖説	bw	中庸章句
y	隱	ay	無極		
z	顯				

7

The Great Ultimate and Heaven in Chu Hsi's Philosophy

YU YAMANOI

Introduction

IT HAS BEEN SAID that Chu Hsi's philosophy is a *li-ch'i*[a] dualism. The *li* (principle) and *ch'i* (material force) are not merely juxtaposed in Chu's philosophy. *Li* is more fundamental and essential; it is superior to *ch'i* and is seen as the ultimate principle of existence in the universe. In other words, *li* is one of the most important concepts in the theoretical system of Chu Hsi's philosophy.

But holding the view that *li* is the supreme notion in Chu Hsi's philosophical theory poses some problems. One cannot accept it without reservations, for other concepts in his philosophy have played an important role, especially *T'ai-chi*[b] (Great Ultimate) and *T'ien*[c] (Heaven).

First, *T'ai-chi* is generally acknowledged as a concept equally as important as, or even more important than, *li*. Many scholars have accepted this interpretation, but I cannot regard *T'ai-chi* in the same way, because the word "*t'ai-chi*" never appeared in Chu Hsi's serious discussions on philosophical issues.

Second, it seems to me that *T'ien* has been neglected when considering Chu Hsi's philosophy. There are not a few examples in Chu's philosophical writings in which *T'ien* is obviously superior to *li*, if we interpret the original texts without regard to traditional interpretations. Hence, I think that we ought to reconsider the relationship between *li* and *T'ien* in a new light.

The Great Ultimate (*T'ai-chi*)

T'ai-chi and *li* have been understood to stand on the same level because *T'ai-chi* can be thought of as the Great Ultimate from which everything is generated and in which everything exists. But a higher place, a place superior to *li*, can be given to *T'ai-chi* because it is "the ultimate of *li*" or "the totality of *li*." This is a fairly prevalent way of understanding of Chu Hsi's philosophical system.

In Japan, Uno Tetsuto,[d] for example, wrote in his *Lectures on the History of Chinese Philosophy*, "Chu Hsi, combining Chou Tun-i's[e] [1017–1073] 'T'ai-chi-t'u shuo'ᶠ [Explanation of the diagram of the Great Ultimate] with Ch'eng I's^g (1033–1107) *li-ch'i* dualism, made *T'ai-chi* what he called the substance of the universe, and with a full use of the notion of *T'ai-chi*, he tried to bring the *li-ch'i* dualism into an integrated whole."[1] In his *A History of Chinese Philosophy: Early modern Confucianism,* Uno also commented that "while proclaiming *T'ai-chi* as the substance, Chu Hsi did not displace the *li-ch'i* dualism" because "by the notion of *T'ai-chi,* Chu Hsi made an attempt to bring this *li-ch'i* dualism into an integrated whole."[2] In this citation Chu Hsi is spoken of as a philosopher calling *T'ai-chi* the substance of the universe. Hence it follows that Chu Hsi's *T'ai-chi* is the Ultimate One synthesizing the *li-ch'i* dichotomy.

In China the following comment can be found in *A General History of Chinese Thought,* edited by Hou Wai-lu^h: "A key to investigating Chu Hsi's complex theoretical system is the notion of *li* which he originated as the absolute subject, or the notion of *T'ai-chi* as totality of *li.*" In Chu Hsi's philosophy "the ultimate of the myriad *li*s" is equal to "*T'ai-chi* as the totality of *li* in the universe." Moreover, it shows an illustration accounting for the interrelationship between *T'ai-chi* and other notions: *li, ch'i, chih*^i (physical nature), yin-yang^j (passive and active cosmic forces), *wu-hsing*^k (the Five Agents or elements of Metal, Wood, Water, Fire, and Earth), and so forth.[3] According to this explanation, *li* is to *ch'i* what *T'ai-chi* is to yin-yang, and it is worth noting that Chu Hsi's *T'ai-chi* is taken as "the totality of *li.*"

In the Western world, H. G. Creel writes in his *Chinese Thought from Confucius to Mao Tse-tung*^l as follows: "Principles or *li,* Chu Hsi says, are 'without birth and indestructible.' They never change in any way. They are all really part of the one great *li,* the Supreme Ultimate [Great Ultimate] which Chu Hsi sometimes equates with the Tao."^m" According to this interpretation man's nature, which, according to Chu Hsi, is his *li,* is a part of the Supreme Ultimate.[4]

These three authors, Japanese, Chinese, and Western, offer to us the common mode of understanding what Chu Hsi called *T'ai-chi.* This understanding seems fairly prevalent, indeed, even dominant in the academic world; a similar assumption of *T'ai-chi* can be found in many academic research publications besides those I have mentioned. To understand that Chu Hsi thought of *T'ai-chi* as *li* or that *T'ai-chi* is the ultimate of all creation is quite justifiable; it is not the object of my criticism. But to say that *T'ai-chi* does not simply mean *li* but is "the ultimate *li*" or "the totality of *li*" is more than misleading; it is wrong. Hence, even to say that the concept of *T'ai-chi* is superior to that of *li* in Chu Hsi's philosophical theory will give rise to misunderstanding; it is wrong also. Furthermore, to understand that Chu Hsi gave the name *T'ai-chi* to the ultimate of all creation will lead to obvious misunderstanding.

The reason that what Chu Hsi called *T'ai-chi* has been understood to mean "the ultimate *li*" or "the totality of *li*" is probably due to several remarks that Chu Hsi himself made as an explanation of the notion of *T'ai-chi.* He said:

1. "*T'ai-chi* . . . is nothing but *li*, and it can be called *T'ai-chi* because it is ultimate (*chi*[n]) *li*."[5]
2. "What *T'ai-chi* means is just that *li* is the ultimate *(chi)* of everything."[6]
3. "Since *li* is the ultimate *(chi)*, we call it ultimate *(chi)*."[7]
4. "It is *T'ai-chi* that synthesizes the *li* of heaven and earth and all things."[8]
5. "*T'ai-chi* has all the *li* of yin-yang and *wu-hsing*."[9]

But "the ultimate" mentioned in the first three passages does not mean *li* is *T'ai-chi*. This can be made clear by distinguishing what is the ultimate *li* and what is the rudimentary *li*. *Li* is originally the ultimate form of existence; what these passages try to do is to offer some explanation concerning the nature of *li*, explanations based solely on the meaning of the word *chi* by saying that "*li* can be called *T'ai-chi* because it is the ultimate." Hence *T'ai-chi* is equal to *li* but never transcends *li*.

In the fourth and fifth passages Chu Hsi spoke of *T'ai-chi* as that which contains every *li*. Certainly *T'ai-chi* seen thus means that it is the whole of every individual *li*, but at the same time it means that *T'ai-chi* is also an individual *li*. In other words, *T'ai-chi* is the *li* of *li-i* (Principle is one) when spoken of as *li-i fen-shu*[o] (Principle is one but its manifestations are many) and at the same time the *li* of *fen-shu*. Chu Hsi himself said, "Generally speaking, all creations as a whole share one *T'ai-chi*. Analytically speaking, every creature has its own proper *T'ai-chi*."[10] So, *T'ai-chi* is none other than *li*. Suffice it to say that *T'ai-chi* is *li*. It is unnecessary to add to this definition any other provision; it hardly matters. What is worse, to do that will do great harm to the understanding of Chu Hsi's philosophy.

Furthermore, Chu Hsi's conception of *T'ai-chi* does not exhaust his conception of *li*, which has all-inclusive as well as complex implications. *T'ai-chi* is included in this notion of *li*, but it fails to acquire a stable and proper position there, which I will consider in some detail below.

Although, as I have already mentioned, it is undoubtedly a fact that Chu Hsi thought of *T'ai-chi* as *li*, Chu Hsi himself never said that *T'ai-chi* meant such and such; he never said something to the effect that "the origin of all creation is *T'ai-chi*," or that "*li* as *raison d'etre* can be called *T'ai-chi*." The word *t'ai-chi* is used by Chou Tun-i in his "T'ai-chi-t'u shuo," which comes from the "Appended Remarks" of the *Book of Changes*[11] and is not Chu Hsi's original term. What Chu Hsi did was to interpret the term *t'ai-chi* (which had been defined and used by other philosophers) in terms of his own understanding of *li*. Although *li* was a philosophical term that had been handed down to him, Chu Hsi endowed it with his own meaning and used the word as his own key word. He built his philosophical system around the term *li* as its central core. Even though almost all of his philosophical terms—such as *ch'i*, *hsin*[p] (mind), *hsing*[q] (nature), *ch'ing*[r] (feeling), *yü*[s] (desire)—were inherited from his precursors with their existing definitions, Chu Hsi wove these terms into his own theoretical system, assigning every one of them to its own position within the system. And he interpreted the various sayings in classical works as well as various phenomena in both the natural and mundane worlds by applying his own theoretical system as the standard, and accounted for them with a liberal use of many key words, including those mentioned above.

Unlike such terms as *li, ch'i, hsin,* and *hsing,* the case of the term *t'ai-chi* is quite different. The word *t'ai-chi* was neither woven closely into Chu Hsi's philosophical system nor given its proper place within it. For Chu Hsi's theoretical system, the word *t'ai-chi* is not an indispensable one.

Chu Hsi used Chou Tun-i's "T'ai-chi-t'u shuo" when he built his own philosophical system. It is because he attached great importance to the "T'ai-chi-t'u shuo" that he published his "T'ai-chi-t'u shuo chieh" (Commentary on the "Explanation of the Diagram of the Great Ultimate"). In this sense the word *t'ai-chi* played an important role in his philosophy, having a great deal of bearing on him. Were it not so, he would never have become so enthusiastic as to discuss and explain it incessantly. But we should keep in mind that when he spoke of the word *t'ai-chi* he merely treated it as a prevailing and accepted term. He did not weave the concept into his theoretical system in order to account for something in terms of the word *t'ai-chi.*

If we examine the *Chu Tzu wen-chi*[t] (Collection of literary works of Master Chu) and *Chu Tzu yü-lei*[u] (Classified conversations of Master Chu) for the use of the word *t'ai-chi* we find that it appears about 260 times in the former and about 350 times in the latter. Perhaps one cannot say that the word is used "a great many" times, but one can say "not a few." And notice that almost all of the cases in which this term is used belong to the contexts where Chu Hsi interpreted the word *t'ai-chi* described in the "T'ai-chi-t'u shuo" or in the "Appended Remarks" of the *Book of Changes,* or to the contexts where he discussed some philosophical issues relevant to these works. There are very few instances where Chu Hsi used this term when he developed his own theory or expressed his own opinions without any regard to the "T'ai-chi-t'u shuo" or the *Book of Changes.* But one must admit that there are a few cases that have nothing to do with these two works. The following passages are remarks that seem to bear comparatively little relationship to the "T'ai-chi-t'u shuo" or the *Book of Changes:*

1. "It is necessary to see *T'ai-chi* within the ever-moving *ch'i* and to see the original nature (*pen-hsing*[v]) within the ever-working mind. To depart from the ever-moving *ch'i* in order to seek for *T'ai-chi* or to depart from the ever-working mind in order to seek for the original nature will probably lead to the absurdity of the Buddhists and Taoists."[12]

2. "If it were not for *T'ai-chi,* heaven and the earth would not move."[13]

3. "What the 'Hsi-ming'[w] (Western inscription) sets forth is the principle of physical transformation and the nature which is the source of all things.[14] Since *T'ai-chi* pushes its way from the outside into this culminating point, there is no further point to go and one can therefore call it the Great Ultimate."[15]

4. "From major matters like heaven and earth and the ten thousand things to minor matters of everyday life at home all are the *li* of *T'ai-chi* and yin-yang."[16]

One cannot be certain that these four quotations express Chu Hsi's philosophical views without only direct relationship to the *Book of Changes* and the "T'ai-chi-t'u shuo." However the possibility exists that they stand by themselves without any special references to these two works. The very fact that there are only four examples among hundreds bespeaks my point that the word *t'ai-chi* did not become one of the words that could sustain Chu Hsi's philosophical system.

More decisive on this issue is that the word *t'ai-chi* was used nowhere in the *Ssu-shu chi-chu*[x] (Collected commentaries on the Four Books).[17] Even in the *Ssu-shu huo-wen*[y] (Questions and answers on the Four Books), the word *t'ai-chi* is not used except in the brief remark that "When Master Chou [Chou Tun-i] appeared, he advocated the doctrines of *T'ai-chi*, yin-yang, and the Five Agents."[18] Moreover, even this one example belongs to the context where Chu Hsi pointed out the greatness of what Chou Tun-i's "T'ai-chi-t'u shuo" had achieved. Never did he aim at elucidating Mencius' doctrine of nature by the notion of *T'ai-chi* there. Nowhere did Chu Hsi use the word *t'ai-chi* to annotate or elucidate the Four Books. If Chu Hsi had regarded *T'ai-chi* in the way many scholars have thought he did, he would have used the word *t'ai-chi* frequently in the *Collected Commentaries on the Four Books* and the *Questions and Answers on the Four Books;* the frequency in the use of this word must have been at least as great as the frequency in the use of the words yin-yang and *wu-hsing*, it seems to me. For a testimony to this point, now check the examples of yin-yang and *wu-hsing:*

1. "Heaven and earth accumulate essence. That which acquires the excellent elements of *wu-hsing* becomes man."[19]

2. "Blood and vital power are what give physical form to things. Blood is yin and vital power is yang."[20]

3. "Heaven gives rise to everything through the functioning of yin-yang and *wu-hsing*."[21]

4. "Speaking of two *ch'i*s, *kuei*[z] (negative cosmic force) is the spirit of yin and *shen*[aa] (positive cosmic force) is the spirit of yang."[22]

5. "All the beginning and end of things are caused by the colletion and distribution of yin-yang."[23]

6. "All the collection and distribution of yin-yang is none other than truth."[24]

However small the number of these examples may be, Chu Hsi showed his masterful use of these terms to interpret the text of the Four Books as if they were his own original philosophical terms. While the words *yin-yang, wu-hsing* were used thus, the word *t'ai-chi* was never used in the same way.

Also in the *Questions and Answers on the Four Books,* the contexts in which the words yin-yang and *wu-hsing* are used are almost the same as in the examples cited above. Especially helpful is the following:

> When the revolution of the Way of Heaven gives rise to and brings up everything, what functions as a creative force is yin-yang and *wu-hsing.* But it is not until *li* exists that these *ch'i*s can come into being; it is not until *ch'i* collects that nature can come into being. If, in this process, man and things come into existence, they cannot constitute the [two qualities] nature of strength and obedience[25] and the Four Virtues of humanity, righteousness, propriety, and wisdom[26] until they acquire *li;* they cannot constitute bodies connsisting of the heavenly and earthly parts of the soul, the five internal organs and the skeleton until they acquire *ch'i.* When Master Chou remarked that "When the reality of the Ultimate of Nonbeing and the essence of yin-yang and *wu-hsing* come into mysterious union, integration ensues,"[27] he meant exactly this. However, from the viewpoint of *li,* the origin of everything is all the same; there is no difference between man and things, the noble and the vulgar. But from the view-point of *ch'i* . . . [28]

The former part of this passage describes the way everything comes into being through the functioning of yin-yang and *wu-hsing.* If the notion of *T'ai-chi* had acquired in his philosophical theory such a position as is generally supposed, that very word, *t'ai-chi,* must have been used here. Instead of it, the word *T'ien-tao*[ab] (Way of Heaven) or *li* is used here. Whether or not Chu Hsi avoided using the word *t'ai-chi* with that intention when he quoted from the "T'ai-chi-t'u shuo," one cannot be sure. But the fact remains that by taking up "the reality of the Ultimate of Nonbeing," which is substantially an equivalent for *T'ai-chi,* Chu Hsi treated it as a quotation from Chou Tun-i, a mere quotation which would serve to support his own theory, instead of weaving it into the framework of his theory for further discussions.

To repeat my point: Although *T'ai-chi* serves as an important clue to Chu Hsi's formation of his own philosophical theory, the examples above show us that it is not closely woven into Chu Hsi's philosophical theory.

Why did this happen? There seem to be two reasons. First, in Chu Hsi's philosophy the two notions *li* and *ch'i* can serve sufficiently to account for the generation and existence of all creation (in addition to them, the physical nature of *wu-hsing* is advanced as a supplement completing the function of *ch'i*). Hence, there is no room in his philosophy for *T'ai-chi. T'ai-chi* need not have been added to his established theoretical system.

Second, we will need to consider the history of the word *t'ai-chi.* This word, as is generally known, has its origin in the "Appended Remarks" of the *Book of Changes.* "In the system of Change, there exists *T'ai-chi,* which gives rise to the Two Modes, which gives rise to the Four Forms, which gives rise to the Eight Trigrams."[29] This part of the "Appended Remarks" has been regarded as an account for the generative process of all the components in the universe, as well as an account for the patterns of the Eight Trigrams. From the time of the *Book of Changes,* from the period of Han (206 B.C.–A.D. 220) through the period of T'ang (618–907) the word *t'ai-chi* has been open to various kinds of interpretation in various philosophical schools. In the generative theories offered by these philosophical schools, *T'ai-chi* was commonly regarded as *yüan-ch'i*[ac] (the ultimate or original material force). Although *T'ai-chi* has sometimes been regarded as a metaphysical existence transcending the *yüan-ch'i,* no great numbers of such examples can be found. According to the generative theory of the so-called Five Evolution (*wu-yün*[ad]) theory from "Great Change" to "Great Beginning" to "Great Origin" to "Great Simplicity" to "Great Ultimate" (*T'ai-i, T'ai-ch'u, T'ai-shih, T'ai-su, T'ai-chi*[ae]) set forth in *Hsiao-ching kou-ming-chüeh*[af] (Prophetic commentary on the *Classic of Filial Piety*), for instance, *T'ai-chi* is described as the origin of everything that existed before heaven and earth were separated from each other. But note that *T'ai-chi* is not ascribed the place of ultimate existence but the fifth place, which is regarded as the place closest to individual things in the real word, the place, according to this theory, where "physical nature and physical form are already provided."[30]

This is the history that the term *t'ai-chi* has gone through; it has been understood to possess the character of *ch'i.* Chou Tun-i's use of *t'ai-chi* in his "T'ai-chi-t'u shuo," must have been inherited from traditional interpretations; the term must have referred to "the ultimate *ch'i.*" It was Chu Hsi who interpreted it to be *li.*

As has been often pointed out, Chu Hsi's ontology is a *li-ch'i* dualism. But even though it is dualism, Chu Hsi took *li* as the supreme principle of existence, placing *li* over *ch'i.* It is no wonder that he took *T'ai-chi* as *li,* because *T'ai-chi* had been defined as the ultimate origin of all creation in the universe as in the saying, "Wu-chi er t'ai-chi"[ag] (the Ultimate of Nonbeing and the Great Ultimate).[31] That he interpreted the *t'ai-chi* of the "Appended Remarks" of the *Book of Changes* as *li,* therefore, needs no explanation. According to Chu Hsi's interpretation, this part of the "Appended Remarks" states the process in which *T'ai-chi* (that is, the *li* of the transformation of yin-yang) makes it possible for the Two Modes (—— and — —), and the Four Forms (⚌ ⚍ ⚎ ⚏) and the Eight Trigrams, both of which can be produced from the combination of the two modes, to evolve in succession. Briefly speaking, Chu Hsi understood this part of the "Appended Remarks" to refer to the purely diagrammatic problem caused by the Eight Trigrams in the *Book of Changes.*

Since *T'ai-chi* in the "T'ai-chi-t'u shuo" was clearly defined as the ultimate origin of the generative process of all things in the universe, Chu Hsi, who proclaimed himself to be an inheritor of the philosophy of the "T'ai-chi-t'u shuo," could not but apprehend the notion of *T'ai-chi* in terms of his notion of *li.* But there remains a slight difference between the *T'ai-chi* of Chuo Tun-i and the *li* of Chu Hsi after all. In Chou Tun-i *T'ai-chi* was defined as the ultimate origin of existence, the origin which "gives rise to yang in its motion and gives rise to yin in its stationary state."[32] Chu Hsi's *li*, on the other hand, is different because while it is the ultimate origin of existence, it is by no means the ultimate origin from which everything generates. Worthy of special mention is the notion of *li*. Chu Hsi said, "*Li* has neither emotion nor will; neither planning ability nor creative ability. . . . *Li* is a thoroughly clean world of emptiness; it has no form and no ability to create anything."[33] Thus seen, *li*, which cannot move, stop, or create anything, is a purely metaphysical entity. In this respect, Chou Tun-i's *T'ai-chi* and Chu Hsi's *li* differ markedly. Although on a certain occasion, Chu Hsi, in answer to a disciple's question concerning the motion and repose of *T'ai-chi*, said that what moves and stops is none other than *li*,[34] his answer is an awkward one. Rather than this answer, Chu Hsi's view on the movement seems to have been more definitely shown when he said, "*T'ai-chi* is *li*, and what moves and halts is *ch'i*. If *ch'i* moves, then *li* accompanies it."[35] The agent of this movement is *ch'i* rather than *li*. As for the *li* which, Chu Hsi said, can give rise to yin-yang, there are some examples where he said that "*li* creates *ch'i*": "*Ch'i* is created by *li*. But once *ch'i* comes into being, *li* can no longer control it,"[36] and that "*T'ai-chi* creates yin-yang means that *li* creates *ch'i*."[37] To my knowledge, however, these are the only remarks Chu Hsi made on the subject; they can therefore be regarded as exceptional. It is absolutely impossible to take these remarks as true expressions of Chu Hsi's philosophy, for even if one can admit that *li* sustains the existence of *ch'i* or that *li* determines the mode of the existence of *ch'i*, one cannot admit that *ch'i* can be created directly out of *li*. That is hardly possible.

Let me summarize what I have found. Chou Tun-i's *T'ai-chi* was originally "the ultimate *ch'i*." It can be the ultimate origin of all things because, being the ultimate *ch'i*, it can "give rise to yang in its motion and give rise to yin in its stationary state." Chu Hsi interpreted this *t'ai-chi* to be *li*. As a result, Chu Hsi's notion of *T'ai-chi* can no longer fit itself to what he thought of *li*. Moreover, Chu Hsi never accorded the concept of *T'ai-chi* a stable position in his theoretical system.

Furthermore, when Chu Hsi spoke of *T'ai-chi* as *li*, the latter has such a wide-spread conceptual range that *T'ai-chi* is really part of *li*, for *li* is conceived as the ultimate origin of yin-yang, *wu-hsing*, and all creations in the universe. Thus *li* includes *T'ai-chi*. Hence, when Chu Hsi spoke of *li* in discussing and accounting for something, his *li* could cover all the implications *T'ai-chi* could have. In fact, it can be said that Chu Hsi's concept of *li* makes it unnecessary for him to use the word *t'ai-chi* in the discursive contexts.

But this view of mine cannot settle all the issues entirely. The statement that *T'ai-chi* is part of the totality of *li* and is contained within the conceptual range of *li*, provides only a rough outline of the complicated relationship between *li* and *T'ai-chi*. In some respects, *T'ai-chi* cannot even be included and covered by *li*. To be more exact, *T'ai-chi* is doomed to remain an alien element in Chu Hsi's theoretical system. The concept seems to have made him uneasy, and for that reason he may have tried to avoid using the term.

But in the contexts where Chu Hsi attempted to discuss and interpret the

"Appended Remarks" of the *Book of Changes* and the "T'ai-chi-t'u shuo," he discussed and elucidated every possible meaning of the word *t'ai-chi*. It is no wonder that in doing so Chu Hsi considered the issues in terms of his own philosophical principles, discussing them by applying his own notions to them. Moreover, he put a great emphasis upon the "ultimate" quality that the term *t'ai-chi* was supposed to have, over and over again. This fact, combined with his philosophical activities as an admirer of the greatness that the "T'ai-chi-t'u shuo" had achieved and as a commentator on the work, seems to have caused misunderstanding that *T'ai-chi* is the supreme notion in Chu Hsi's philosophical system.

However important the word *t'ai-chi* may be in Chu Hsi's philosophical writing, it has never been woven into his philosophy. It was not his own term; he used it exclusively in the contexts in which he interpreted the word *t'ai-chi* as defined and used by other philosophers.

Heaven *(T'ien)*

There is another ill-fitted word in Chu Hsi's theoretical system, the word *t'ien* (sometimes, *t'ien-ti*[ah] or Heaven and Earth).

According to Chu Hsi's description, at the genesis of the universe, through the process of the revolution of *ch'i* (*yüan-ch'i* or the original *ch'i*), while light and transparent *ch'i* expanded and became Heaven, the dregs coagulated into a solid core and became Earth. Heaven and Earth were thus created by the *li*, as is shown in the following passage: "There is only one great *li* in the universe. Heaven acquires it and becomes Heaven; the Earth acquires it and becomes Earth."[38] Heaven and Earth can exist in so far as they follow their own proper *li*—the *li* of Heaven and the *li* of Earth.

This sort of Heaven (or Heaven and Earth) fits adequately into Chu Hsi's theory of the universe, which depends on the *li-ch'i* theory. But we can find not a few examples in which the concept of Heaven and Earth will not fit into the theoretical frame of the *li-ch'i* philosophy.

The term *T'ien-li*[ai] (Principle of Heaven) in the phrase *T'ien-li jen-yü*[aj] (Principle of Heaven and selfish human desires) is, contrary to the above definition, not the *li* that is supposed to give Heaven its own basis of existence and to govern its operation. The *li* in the phrase *T'ien-li* means the *li* based on *T'ien* or the *li* following *T'ien*. Thus the priority between *T'ien* and *li* is reversed. Hence *li* in this case refers to that which would be justifiable from the moral point of view. Judging from the definition of the term *T'ien-li*, *T'ien* has an authority over *li* and guarantees its existence. *T'ien*, regarded thus, seems to be superior to *li*. "As for the '*t'ien-ch'i ti-chih*' in this passage: Nature is equal to *li*. But where there is no *t'ien-ch'i ti-chih*[ak] (the material force of Heaven and the physical nature of Earth), there is no place for *li* to stay in."[39] Here *t'ien-ch'i ti-chih* means neither the *ch'i* nor the *chih* that is supposed to constitute Heaven and Earth and sustain their existence but the *ch'i-chih* (endowed physical nature) that is distributed to man and things by Heaven and Earth. "Or notice the following remark, for instance: Heaven and Earth have no other thing to do but to produce things. The *ch'i* of one source creates every kind of thing in its incessant movement."[40] Here the notion that Heaven and Earth give rise to everything through the movement of *ch'i* is clearly shown.

The Heaven or Earth spoken of in the above examples is regarded as superior to both *li* and *ch'i*. Therefore, it is evident that *T'ien* is neither the *t'ien* nor the *ti* that is supposed to have been formed by *li* and *ch'i*.

This relationship between *T'ien* and *li-ch'i* is more definitively given in the following examples:

1. "Nature is the *li* that man receives from *T'ien*. Life is *ch'i* that man receives from *T'ien*."[41]
2. "In order that man and things can be born, both of them must receive the *li* of *T'ien-ti* to form their nature, and must receive the *ch'i* of *T'ien-ti* to constitute their physical form."[42]
3. "Nature is equal to *li* that the mind possesses, and *T'ien* is the origin of *li*."[43]

Although these passages deal with nature, their theories refer to *T'ien* as the ultimate existence superior to both *li* and *ch'i*. Man and things are supposed to be born by the power of *li* and *ch'i*. Be that as it may, there is *T'ien*, which is spoken of as superior to *li* and *ch'i*. It follows that man and things cannot come into being until they are given *li* and *ch'i* by *T'ien*.

One can readily notice a paradox here. Although *T'ien* (*T'ien-ti*) and its mode of existence are decided by *li* because *t'ien* is one with all creation in the universe and is made to come into being by *ch'i*, *T'ien* is at the same time spoken of as having ultimate existence superior to both *li* and *ch'i* because it can give both *li* and *ch'i* to all creation in the universe. This is hardly possible; this is a paradox. One must admit that Chu Hsi's theory, *qua* theory, contradicts itself. How do we resolve the contradiction?

It seems that the *t'ien* as spoken of by Chu Hsi has a double meaning, one as a natural object in the universe and one as the creator or organizer of the universe. While *t'ien*, so far as it can be defined as one of all creation in the universe, can remain in the frame of the *li-ch'i* philosophy, *T'ien* as the creator or organizer of the universe exists beyond the realm of *li-ch'i*, jutting out of the frame of the *li-ch'i* philosophy.

Where did this transcendental nature of *T'ien* jutting out of Chu Hsi's philosophical frame come from? Obviously, it came from the Chinese Classics of Confucianism. Remarks such as *T'ien* "gave rise to," "created," or "commanded" man and things can frequently be found in the Four Books, which bear a specially close relationship to Chu Hsi's philosophy, as well as in the *Book of History* and the *Book of Odes*.[44] The idea that *T'ien* is the creator or organizer of the natural and human world was so powerful in the Confucian tradition that Chu Hsi could not escape from its influence. Even his wide-scale *li-ch'i* philosophy could not encompass this notion successfully, it would seem.

Thus, *T'ien* could not fit itself into Chu Hsi's *li-ch'i* philosophy. But the long tradition I have mentioned permitted this notion of *T'ien* to occupy a highly respectable place within that philosophy. Moreover, the infusion of *T'ien* into his philosophical theories made it possible for the notion of *T'ien* to acquire sufficient force and great power of applicability. While the word *t'ai-chi* failed to enter Chu Hsi's philosophy and has seldom been used in his discussions on *li-ch'i*, mind and nature, the word *t'ien* has been used many times in the *Collected Commentaries on the Four Books* and the *Questions and Answers on the Four Books*. It may be that the word *t'ien* was used because it was used in the original texts of the Four Books. But more important is that Chu Hsi treated this word exhaustively when he argued over philosophical issues; it was alive in Chu Hsi's philosophy.

Regarding the usage of the word *T'ien-li*, both *T'ien-li* and *T'ai-chi* have a similar history. The term *t'ien-li* comes from the "Records of Music" chapter of the *Book of Rites*. This is the only source, and it came to be used frequently by the Ch'eng brothers (Ch'eng Hao,[al] 1032–1085, and Ch'eng I). The terms hardly differ. In Chu Hsi's philosophy they both refer to *li* and both are included in *li* because the range of reference of both words is narrower than that of *li*. But the word *t'ien-li*, as compared with the word *t'ai-chi*, is a more fully digested philosophical term, it having been used more freely and exhaustively. In the *Chu Tzu wen-chi*, for instance, the word *t'ai-chi* appears about 260 times, while *t'ien-li* occurs about 340 times. If we compare the numbers only, there seems to be no marked difference. But while the word *t'ai-chi* is used in contexts that almost always bear some relationship to the "Appended Remarks" of the *Book of Changes* or the "T'ai-chi-t'u shuo," the word *t'ien-li* is used less frequently in contexts that bear some relationship to the "Records of Music" of the *Book of Rites* or to the *t'ien-li* used and defined by the Ch'eng brothers than in contexts free from such relationships. Such usage implies that Chu Hsi used the word *t'ien-li* as his own original philosophical term.

Finally, I would like to submit one definitive example for further consideration. In the *Collected Commentaries on the Book of Mencius*, Chu Hsi wrote, "*Nature* is the *li* which man received from the *T'ien*."[45] In another context he explained, "*Nature* is the *T'ien-li* which man received at birth."[46] There is a slight difference between the first and the second passages, but both must be understood to mean the same thing. Thus we see that Chu Hsi used the term *t'ien-li* in various ways, used it freely, and was not influenced by its classical and traditional usages. What a rich and powerful applicability the words *t'ien-li*, *t'ien*, and *li* have in Chu Hsi's philosophy!

Conclusion

As has been shown above, Chu Hsi failed to enclose the concepts of *T'ai-chi* and of *T'ien* in his theoretical system of *li-ch'i* philosophy. In addition, the two concepts have broken through the theoretical, referential frame of his philosophy in strikingly different ways. Chu Hsi seldom used the word *t'ai-chi* in his original philosophical remarks because the wide discrepancy between his *T'ai-chi* and his *li* deprived the word *t'ai-chi* of its rich applicability. The word *t'ien*, on the other hand, could maintain its strong power because it is in harmony with the key notions of *li-ch'i* even though in some respects it cannot be encompassed entirely by the notion of *li* or *ch'i*. Thus we see much difference in usage between the word *t'ai-chi* and the word *t'ien*.

It is the concept of *li* that occupies the supreme position in Chu Hsi's philosophy. Hence the concept of *T'ai-chi* is not superior to that of *li*. Neither does Chu Hsi use the term *T'ai-chi* in its transcendental sense as "the ultimate *li*" very often in his commentaries. What should be placed in the position superior to *li*, whether or not Chu Hsi ever thought of it, would be the notion of *T'ien* and not the notion of *T'ai-chi*. *T'ien (t'ien-ti)*, however, was an exceptional notion in Chu Hsi's philosophy. Chu Hsi, after all, built and rebuilt his system of philosophical theories within the frame of reference that had *li* and *ch'i* as its central core.

Translated by Ohasi Yoichi[am]

Notes

1. Uno Tetsuto, *Shina tetsugakushi kōwa*[an] (Tokyo: Daidōkan,[ao] 1914), p. 290.

2. Uno Tetsuto, *Shina tetsugakushi: kinsei jugaku*[ap] (Tokyo: Hōbunkan,[aq] 1954), p. 175.

3. Hou Wai-lu, *Chung-kuo ssu-hsiang t'ung-shih*[ar] (Peking: Jen-min[as] Press, 1960), vol. 4, pt. 2, pp. 600–605.

4. H. G. Creel, *Chinese Thought from Confucius to Mao Tse-tung* (London: Eyre & Spottiswoode, 1954), p. 218.

5. *Chu Tzu yü-lei* [Classified conversations of Master Chu], (Taipei: Cheng-chung[at] Book Co., 1962), 94:6a.

6. *Chu Tzu wen-chi* [Collection of literary works of Master Chu], (SPTK ed.) 37:34a, third reply to Ch'eng K'o-chiu.[au]

7. *Ibid.*, 36:9b, fifth reply to Lu Tzu-ching.[av]

8. *Chu Tzu yü-lei*, 94:9b.

9. *Ibid.*, 94:2b.

10. "T'ai-chi-t'u shuo chieh"[aw] [Commentary on the "Explanation of the Diagram of the Great Ultimate"], in the *Chou Tzu ch'üan-shu*[ax] [Complete works of Master Chou], (Wan-yu wen-k'u[ay] [Universal Library] ed.), 1:1a.

11. "Appended Remarks," pt. 1, ch. 11.

12. *Chu Tzu wen-chi*, 32:14a, reply to Chang Ching-fu.[az]

13. *Chu Tzu yü-lei*, 1:1b.

14. The "Western Inscription" was written by Chang Tsai[ba] (1020–1077) and became a key document in Neo-Confucian thought. It occupies the first chapter of the *Chang Tzu ch'üan-shu*[bb] [Complete works of Master Chang]. Chu Hsi's passage quoted here is obscure.

15. *Ibid.*, 98:17b.

16. *Ibid.*, 6:5a.

17. The *Great Learning*, the *Analects*, the *Book of Mencius*, and the *Doctrine of the Mean*.

18. *Meng Tzu huo-wen*[bc] [Questions and answers on the *Book of Mencius*], (*Chu Tzu i-shu*[bd] [Surviving works of Master Chu] ed.), comment on the *Book of Mencius*, 6A:6.

19. *Lun-yü chi-chu*[be] [Collected commentaries on the *Analects*], comment on *Analects*, 6:3. Chu Hsi was quoting Ch'eng I. *I-ch'uan wen-chi*[bf] [Collection of literary writings of Ch'eng I] (SPPY ed.), 4:1a, "What Yen Tzu[bg] loved to learn."

20. *Ibid.*, comment on *Analects*, 16:7.

21. *Chung-yung chang-chü*[bh] [Commentary on the *Doctrine of the Mean*], comment on ch. 1.

22. *Ibid.*, comment on ch. 16.

23. *Ibid.*

24. *Ibid.*

25. The two qualities are those of the first two hexagrams in the *Book of Changes*.

26. The Four Virtues are taught in the *Book of Mencius*, 2A:6 and 6A: 6.

27. "Explanation of the Diagram of the Great Ultimate." See above, n. 10.

28. *Ta-hsüeh huo-wen*[bi] in the *Ssu-shu ta-ch'üan*[bj] [Complete commentaries on the Four Books], (1698 ed.), p. 7b.

29. *Book of Changes*, "Appended Remarks," pt. I, ch. 11. The two modes are yin-yang, the Four Forms are lesser and greater yin-yang, and the Eight Trigrams consists of yin, or broken, and yang, or continuous lines.

30. *Hsiao-ching kou-ming-chüeh*, in *Isho shusei*[bk] [Collection of books of prophecy], (Tokyo: Meitoka[bl] Press, 1973), 5:76.

31. "T'ai-chi-t'u shuo." See above, n. 10.

32. *Ibid.*

33. *Chu Tzu yü-lei*, 1:3a.

34. *Ibid.*, 94:9a.

35. *Ibid.*, 94:10a.

36. *Ibid.*, 4:13b.

37. Collected commentaries added to Chu Hsi's "Commentary on the 'Explanation of the Diagram of the Great Ultimate' " in the *Chou Tzu ch'üan-shu*, ch. 1. The *Chou Lien-hsi chi*[bm] [Collected works of Chou Tun-i], edited by Chang Po-hsing[bn] (1651–1725) (Kuo-hsüeh chi-pen ts'ung-shu[bo] ed.), 1:6; the *Chou Tzu ch'üan-shu*, edited by Tung Yung[bp] (1711–1760), p. 7; as well as the *Hsing-li ching-i*[bq] [Essential ideas of nature and principle], compiled by Li Kuang-ti[br] (1642–1718), (SPPY ed.) 1:4a., quoted it as Chu Hsi's remark, but I have not yet been able to identify its original source. I shall be profoundly grateful if I am informed of it.

38. *Chu Tzu wen-chi*, 70:5a.

39. *Chu Tzu yü-lei*, 4:9b.

40. *Ibid.*, 1:3b.

41. *Meng Tzu chi-chu*[bs] [Collected commentaries on the *Book of Mencius*], comment on the *Book of Mencius*, 6A:3.

42. *Ibid.*, comment on the *Book of Mencius*, 4B:19.

43. *Ibid.*, comment on the *Book of Mencius*, 7A:2.

44. For example, *Book of Odes*, ode n. 260; *Book of History*, ch. 27, "The Great Oath," sec. 7; the *Analects*, 7:23; the *Book of Mencius*, 5A:7, the *Doctrine of the Mean*, chs. 1 and 17.

45. *Meng Tzu chi-chu,* comment on the *Book of Mencius,* 6A:3.
46. *Ibid.,* comment on the *Book of Mencius,* 6A:1.

Glossary

a 理氣
b 太極
c 天
d 宇野哲人
e 周敦頤
f 太極圖説
g 程頤
h 侯外廬
i 質
j 陰陽
k 五行
l 毛澤東
m 道
n 極
o 理一分殊
p 心
q 性
r 情
s 欲
t 朱子文集
u 朱子語類
v 本性
w 西銘
x 四書集註

y 四書或問
z 鬼
aa 神
ab 天道
ac 元氣
ad 五運
ae 太易太初太始太素太極
af 孝經鈎命訣
ag 無極而太極
ah 天地
ai 天理
aj 天理人欲
ak 天氣地質
al 程顥
am 大橋洋一
an 支那哲學史講話
ao 大同館
ap 支那哲學史近世儒學
aq 寶文館
ar 中國思想通史
as 人民
at 正中
au 程可久

av 陸子靜
aw 太極圖説解
ax 周子全書
ay 萬有文庫
az 張敬夫
ba 張載
bb 張子全書
bc 孟子或問
bd 朱子遺書
be 論語集註
bf 伊川文集
bg 顏子
bh 中庸章句
bi 大學或問
bj 四書大全
bk 緯書集成
bl 明德
bm 周濂溪集
bn 張伯行
bo 國學基本叢書
bp 董榕
bq 性理精義
br 李光地
bs 孟子集註

8

On Chu Hsi's Theory of
the Great Ultimate

TENG AIMIN

THE PHILOSOPHY OF CHU HSI should be considered the summation of idealism in old China. His doctrine was accepted as the official philosophy,
possessing unquestionable authority and serving the interests of feudalistic
dynasties for more than seven hundred years, from the late Southern Sung
(1127–1279) to the end of the Ch'ing dynasty (1644–1912). Chu Hsi's philosophy also had a tremendous influence in Korea and Japan.

Compared with the West, Chinese feudal society developed more fully and
lasted much longer. In its late period, the development of science and technology was slow, and the emergence of capitalist production lagged much behind
Western society. Chu Hsi's doctrine, being the dominant official philosophy,
evidently had negative effects in this respect.

Since the beginning of the modern period (1840–1949), China has passed
from a semifeudal and semicolonial society to socialism through revolutionary
transformation. The influence of Chu Hsi's philosophy, however, has persisted. Even now, feudal ideology remains an obstacle to the modernization of
China.

Since Chu Hsi was so influential, we should make an unbiased evaluation
of his achievements and draw useful lessons from them, instead of merely
emphasizing the negative aspect of his philosophy. This paper is a preliminary study of Chu Hsi's theory of the Great Ultimate from this approach.

Some researchers of Chu Hsi's philosophy have used the *Chu Tzu yü-lei*[a]
(Classified conversations of Master Chu) as the main text. It is true that the
Chu Tzu yü-lei, as the record of his dialogues, treats some problems more concretely than do his other writings, as well as reflecting his thoughts in his late
years. However, since there are discrepancies among the records of different
disciples, these records are not as reliable as his own writings. Therefore,
although I shall also use the *Chu Tzu yü-lei* as an important reference, I prefer
the "T'ai-chi-t'u shuo chieh"[b] (Commentary on the "Explanation of the Diagram of the Great Ultimate") as the main text for this discussion, because in
this writing Chu Hsi himself systematically elucidated his theory of the Great

Ultimate. This work was written around 1173 but was not expounded to his disciples until 1188. He taught it once again in 1200—the year of his death[1]— showing that this text also contains examples of his later thought.

Chu Hsi's Description of the Great Ultimate

According to Chu Hsi, the Great Ultimate is the highest being or substance (*pen-t'i*[c]) of the universe. The whole world together with the myriad things are generated by it. He said, "The operations of Heaven (*T'ien*[d]) have neither sound nor smell, and yet this is really the axis of creation and the origin of things of all kind."[2] The substance of the universe, so far as it has neither sound nor smell and is incapable of being grasped by perceptual cognition, is called the Ultimate of Nonbeing (*wu-chi*[e]). The same substance, so far as it is capable of generating the world together with the myriad things, is called the Great Ultimate. For this kind of substance, "If this substance is said not to be the Ultimate of Nonbeing, then the Great Ultimate would be considered a finite thing and unable to be the origin of the myriad things. If it is said not to be the Great Ultimate, the Ultimate of Nonbeing would perish in emptiness (*k'ung*[f]) and absolute quiet (*chi*[g]) and unable to be the origin of the myriad things."[3] This is why the expression "the Ultimate of Nonbeing and also the Great Ultimate" was used to describe it. In short, this expression means that it lacks shape but contains principle (*li*[h]). It does not mean that outside of the Great Ultimate there is an Ultimate of Nonbeing.

After asserting this, Chu Hsi considered that the Great Ultimate is the mystery of naturalness (*pen-jan chih miao*[i]). He elaborated the characteristics of it as follows: First, the Great Ultimate is naturally as it is and not the result of the action and effect of other beings. Thus it is supreme. In other words, it is what is in itself and conceived through itself. It possesses mystical energy and effect, and is capable of generating all beings. It is, as he said, "the highest, the subtlest, the finest and the most mystical."[4]

Following the Neo-Taoists of the Wei and Chin dynasties (220–420), Chu also used the terms being (*yu*[j]) and nonbeing (*wu*[k]) to characterize it. On the one hand, he maintained that the Great Ultimate is both being and nonbeing or the synthesis of being and nonbeing. He said, "The operations of Heaven have neither sound nor smell, that is to say, nonbeing exists in being. The Ultimate of Nonbeing is also the Great Ultimate, that is to say, being exists in nonbeing."[5] On the other hand, the Great Ultimate could be considered as neither being nor nonbeing, that is, something transcending both being and nonbeing. In his opinion, " 'The Ultimate of Nonbeing and also the Great Ultimate' means that in the Ultimate of Nonbeing, all things are luxuriantly present. Therefore, it cannot be called nonbeing. The Great Ultimate is fundamentally the Ultimate of Nonbeing, that is, the Great Ultimate as substance is empty and tranquil and without any sign. Therefore, it cannot be called being." Then he added that the Great Ultimate "has no relation to being and nonbeing."[6] In other words, the Great Ultimate is both a synthesis of being versus nonbeing and transcends being versus nonbeing.

Second, the Great Ultimate is infinite and eternal. Consider this statement: "The Great Ultimate is a large thing. The four directions together with above and below are called space (*yü*[l]). The past, the present, and the future together are called time (*chou*[m]). Nothing is as large as space, extending infinitely into four directions, above and below. How large it is! Nothing is as lasting as time, enduring from the ancient past to the coming future. It is eternal."[7] Chu Hsi attempted here to characterize the Great Ultimate as infinite and eternal, like the universe, because the universe itself is generated from it. Thus it is also absolute. As he declared, "The Great Ultimate is one with nothing equal to it."[8] Originally the Great Ultimate has no such appellation; it is merely an expression of its character.[9]

Third, the Great Ultimate is the highest good and perfect. Chu Hsi said, "The Great Ultimate is simply an utterly excellent and supremely good normative principle. . . . The Great Ultimate is an appellation for all that is good in Heaven and Earth, and among men and things."[10] The principle of a thing is the supremely good archetype of that thing. This is the meaning of the word "Ultimate" as used in the statement "For every thing or object, there is an Ultimate which is the normative principle [of that thing or object] in its highest ultimate form."[11] The principles of all things within the universe, brought into one whole, constitute the Great Ultimate. The Great Ultimate thus stands as the highest archetype and becomes the final purpose of all things in the universe. The universe is orderly because it has the Great Ultimate to serve as its archetype and purpose. Without the Great Ultimate the universe would be something other than itself. Therefore, "If there exists no Great Ultimate, the universe, so to speak, would be turned upside down."[12] The Great Ultimate may thus be regarded as the final cause of all things.

The Great Ultimate as the highest archetype and final purpose of all things is similar to the top of a house or the zenith of the sky, beyond which point there is no more. It is the ultimate of principle.[13] It comes into being and acts by itself and for itself, not by others and for others. Therefore, the Great Ultimate has been forever spontaneous; it lacks volition, plan, and creative means.[14]

Finally, the Great Ultimate possesses activity (*tung*[n]) and tranquillity (*ching*[o]). Chu Hsi said, "The activity and tranquillity of the Great Ultimate are the Mandate of Heaven (*T'ien-ming*[p]) in its universal operation."[15] He also said that the Ultimate through movement generates yang[q] (active cosmic force), through tranquillity generates yin[r] (passive cosmic force), so it "gives rise to the distinction of yin and yang, and the two modes are thus established."[16] Here Chu Hsi explained that activity is the activity of the Great Ultimate and tranquillity is also its tranquillity.

Chu Hsi also elucidated more explicitly the point that the Great Ultimate is active. That is, the Great Ultimate as substance already contained within itself activity and tranquillity from the standpoint of universal operation. However, the Great Ultimate cannot be reduced to activity and tranquillity nor be identified with them. If we identify the Great Ultimate with activity and tranquillity, then the assertion that the Great Ultimate serves as the basis of change would be superfluous.[17] Chu Hsi further pointed out that the assertion "taking the Great Ultimate as the substance, activity and tranquillity are the function" is defective, because "tranquillity is the substance of the Great Ultimate while activity is the function of the Great Ultimate."[18]

Chu Hsi also made the distinction between activity and tranquillity pertaining to things existing after physical form (*hsing-erh-hsia*[s]) and that pertaining to principle existing before physical form (*hsing-erh-shang*[t]). He said, "Things cannot be tranquil while active or active while tranquil." This refers to material objects existing after physical form. That which exists after physical form cannot mutually penetrate. Therefore, while acting, it is not tranquil; while tranquil, it is not active. Furthermore, 'being active without activity and tranquil without tranquillity' does not mean that it is neither active nor tranquil. It refers to principle which existed before physical form. Principle is unfathomable, like spirit. While acting, it cannot be said that it is not tranquil; therefore it is called nonactivity. While tranquil it cannot be said that it is not active; therefore it is called nontranquillity. There is tranquillity in activity and activity in tranquillity. It is tranquil but able to act and active but also tranquil."[19] Chu Hsi here accepted and expounded the view of Chou Tun-i[u] (1017–1073) that principle or the Great Ultimate, like spirit, can be active and tranquil, but it is a kind of activity and tranquillity exactly opposite that of things. The activity and tranquillity of the Great Ultimate consists in the unity of their opposition. Because of this point, the Great Ultimate is "mysterious and profound" and also "infinitely complicated." It possesses the ability for production and reproduction (*sheng-sheng*[v]), and so the whole universe is generated from it.

Whether the Great Ultimate conceived by Chu Hsi should be interpreted as being capable of movement is a controversial question among specialists. For instance, Fung Yu-lan[w] once asserted that Chu Hsi thought that neither movement nor tranquillity may be postulated for the Great Ultimate. The principle of motion exists in the Great Ultimate while the material force (*ch'i*[x]) that moves according to this principle constitutes the material force of yang. The principle of motion itself, however, does not move.[20]

Fung cited two supporting quotations from Chu Hsi. One is the following passage recorded by his student:

Once there is the principle governing movement, there can then exist the movement to produce yang. Once there is the principle of tranquillity, there can then exist the tranquillity to produce yin. When there is movement, there is principle within this movement. When there is tranquillity, there is principle within the tranquillity.

Question: Movement and tranquillity pertain to material force. Is it then correct to say that it is because there is this principle which governs material force, that material force can therefore operate in this manner?

Answer: It is.[21]

From the above passage Fung concluded that movement and tranquillity pertain to material force.[22] He also cited a passage from a letter:

Question: In the "T'ai-chi-t'u shuo" it is stated: "The Great Ultimate through movement generates yang. When its activity reaches its limit, it becomes tranquil. Through tranquillity the Great Ultimate generates yin." But the Great Ultimate is principle, and how can principle be in a state of activity and tranquillity? What has shape may have such activity and tranquillity. But the Great Ultimate has no shape, and therefore it seems as if one should not speak of it in terms of activity and tranquillity. Yet Nan-hsien [Chang Shih,[y] 1133-1180] says that the Great Ultimate cannot but have such activity and tranquillity. I do not understand him.

Answer: It is only because principle is in possession of activity and tranquillity that material force thus has activity and tranquillity. For if principle is not in possession of activity or tranquillity, how could material force in itself have such activity and tranquillity?[23]

From the above passage Fung concluded that "yang and yin both pertain to what exists after physical form, whereas the principle of activity or tranquillity is what exists before physical form. Hence it has neither activity nor tranquillity. Therefore one should not speak of it in terms of activity and tranquillity."[24]

We have already indicated the point that Chu Hsi followed Chou Tun-i's view that the Great Ultimate is capable of activity or motion. On this point the idea of principle has different implications for Chu Hsi and Ch'eng I[z] (1033-1107). Ch'eng I held that "all principles are plainly lying down there."[25] He also maintained that "the constant principle remains changeless. It is never in activity. Being inactive, it is said to remain in the state of absolute quiet."[26]

Fung held that Chu Hsi advocated that the Great Ultimate has either activity or tranquillity. The first quotation cited, however, only confirms the interpretation that Chu Hsi advocated that material force has activity and tranquillity. It does not prove that Chu Hsi advocated the view that principle is incapable of either activity or tranquillity. Chu maintained that principle has activity and tranquillity and material force or things also have activity and tranquillity; the nature of two kinds of activity and tranquillity, however, are different.

Furthermore, Chu Hsi sometimes asserted explicitly that activity and tranquillity can be spoken of only in relation to principle or the Great Ultimate and not in reference to yin and yang or material force. As he said when asked if activity and tranquillity are predicated about the Great Ultimate or yin and yang, "It refers to principle which is capable of undergoing activity or tranquillity."[27]

Neither does the second citation above prove Fung's point. The statement that "the Great Ultimate has no shape, and therefore it seems as if one should not speak of it in terms of activity and tranquillity" is a part of the question put forth by a disciple of Chu Hsi and not Chu's answer. It seems logically deficient to rely upon the question to interpret the doctrine of the master.

Furthermore, Chu's answer was that "it is only because principle is in possession of activity and tranquillity that material force thus has activity and tranquillity. For if principle is not in possession of activity or tranquillity, how could material force in itself have such activity and tranquillity?" This answer is interpreted by Fung to mean that "material force undergoes actual phases of activity and tranquillity, but only because there are implanted in it principles governing this activity and tranquillity, which themselves pertain to the Great Ultimate."[28] Here the idea of "activity and tranquillity" has been replaced by that of "principles governing this activity and tranquillity." More simply, Fung here uses "principles of activity and tranquillity" instead of "activity and tranquillity" in his interpretation and thus some unfounded conjecture has slipped in.

One should interpret the above quotation, I think, as the Great Ultimate being in possession of activity and tranquillity, having activity and tranquillity, and consequently generating material force. As principle and material force, there result activity and tranquillity. If principle is not in possession of activity and tranquillity and incapable of being active and tranquil, then material force could not be generated, and thus there would be no material force to be active or tranquil.

Fung has deleted the last two sentences of the original passage which run as follows: "And in the present context, humanity (jen[aa]) is activity and righteousness, (i[ab]) is tranquillity. It has nothing to do with material force."[29] It is quite clear that Chu maintained here that activity and tranquillity only pertain to principle (such as humanity or righteousness) or the Great Ultimate itself, and not to material force. Fung attempts to assert the opposite. But this attempt cannot be based on the letter he quoted without distorting the original connotation of the letter.

To be sure, according to the *Chu Tzu yü-lei* some of Chu's conversations seem to show that activity and tranquillity only pertain to material force and not to the Great Ultimate. Once he said, "Yang is active and yin is tranquil, but the Great Ultimate is neither active nor tranquil, . . . It is simply that there are the principles of activity and tranquillity. Principle is not visible, it becomes visible through yin and yang. Principle holds itself upon yin and yang just as a man sits astride a horse."[30] Or as he said, "*T'ai-chi* is only *li*, and *li* cannot be spoken of in terms of activity and tranquillity."[31] It means the same thing. When material force is in action, then the Great Ultimate also is in action. But this idea appears only in the records or interpretations of his disciples. It cannot be found in his own writings, such as the "T'ai-chi-t'u shuo chieh." Besides, as Ts'ao Tuan[ac] (1376–1434) pointed out long ago, this idea is not rational, for if so, the horse is a living horse, but the man is a dead man. How can something dead be the origin of the myriad things in the universe?[32]

In recent years, Ch'ien Mu's[ad] *Chu Tzu hsin hsüeh-an*[ae] (New anthology and critical accounts of Master Chu) has aroused great interest. Ch'ien's viewpoint is diametrically opposed to that of traditional formulation and Fung Yu-lan.

Ch'ien Mu said, "Many of the scholars concerned are usually of the opinion that since the Ch'eng-Chu School advocated the view that nature is identical with principle while the Lu-Wang [Lu Chiu-yüan, Lu Hsiang-shan,[af] 1139–1193 and Wang Shou-jen, Wang Yang-ming,[ag] 1472–1529] School maintained that mind is identical with principle, it would be appropriate to designate the former as the School of Principle and the latter as the School of Mind. This distinction is somewhat imprecise, because Chu Hsi seems to be best at elucidation of the concept of mind."[33] Therefore according to Ch'ien, "Chu's philosophy is a detailed system of the school of mind."[34] He also maintained that the philosophy of Chang Tsai[ah] (1020–1077), who himself considered it the continuation of some ancient learning that had been interrupted, was also nothing but a sort of school of mind.

It seems that Ch'ien's classification of all schools that lay special emphasis on the elucidation of the concept of mind to the category of the School of Mind has the advantage of clarifying better the common feature of different schools of Neo-Confucianism in the Sung and Ming (1368–1644) dynasties, that is, their special emphasis on philosophy of life. Important distinctions in their theories of cosmology, however, would be blurred, if this criterion were consistently used. Such a criterion would not only force us to classify the Ch'eng-Chu School into the School of Mind but also compel us to do the same with Chang Tsai and even Wang Fu-chih[ai] (1619–1692). This kind of classification would lead to difficulties. Therefore I recommend examining their cosmological views for distinctions.

The cosmology systematically developed by Chu Hsi in his "Commentary on the 'Explanation of the Diagram of the Great Ultimate'" is a kind of objective idealism that is coherent with the view he consistently held that "nature is identical with principle." This makes Chu Hsi's philosophy different from the subjective idealism of the Lu-Wang School, which advocated the view that "mind is identical with principle." From the perspective of the history of philosophy, this distinction between the two schools is more important than are their similarities.

Substance and Function in Chu Hsi's Philosophy

In Chu Hsi's philosophy substance (*t'i*[aj]) and function (*yung*[ak]) come from the same source and there is no gap between the manifest and the hidden (*t'i-yung i-yüan,*[al] *hsien-wei wu-chien*[am]). According to Chu, the Great Ultimate is the substance that generates the universe. He described this process of generation as follows: "With the existence of the Great Ultimate, the two modes resulted from activity and tranquillity; and with the existence of yin and yang, the Five Agents (*wu-hsing,*[an] Metal, Wood, Fire, Water, Earth) resulted from transformation and unification. For the Five Agents, however, the corporal matter is embodied in earth, while material force operates in heaven . . . Things resulting from the transformation of the Five Agents are infinite and inexhaustible, but they all belong to the scope of yin and yang. It is the natural property of the Great Ultimate that makes it so and there is no deficiency and no gap."[35]

According to Chu Hsi, the Great Ultimate is *causa sui.* Given the existence of the Great Ultimate, its activity and tranquillity are manifested as a kind of force of generation. This necessarily results in the appearance of yin and yang, that is, the two modes. The two modes actually are only the condensation and universal operation of the single material force, which interact upon each other, being in incessant change. Thus Chu Hsi said, "Yin and yang consist of a single material force. Yang results from the universal operation of yin and yin results from the condensation of yang. It is not the case that there are two things in reality opposing each other."[36] The Five Agents together with the myriad things result from the various actions of yin and yang, which, in turn, result from the Great Ultimate.

In the process during which the myriad things are generated from yin-yang and the Five Agents, which, in their turn, are produced from the Great Ultimate, the Great Ultimate and yin-yang are fused and there is no gap between them. This is what is said to be one splitting into two and two combining into one. For the process, there is neither beginning nor end. In Chu's terms "activity and tranquillity have no beginning and yin and yang have no starting point."[37] In this process, the Great Ultimate and yin-yang are always fused. From the perspective of the universal operation of the substance, Chu noted that "Substance and function come from the same source, and there is no gap between the manifest and the hidden."[38] Chu said,

> The Great Ultimate is the Way that stands before physical form. Yin and yang are the concrete things that exist after physical form. Hence, if it [the Great Ultimate] is considered in its prominent (*hsien*[ao]) aspects, we find that activity and tranquillity do not coexist in time, nor do yin and yang coexist in space; whereas the Great Ultimate itself, on the contrary, is to be found everywhere. But if it is considered in its obscure (*wei*[ap]) aspects, we find that the Great Ultimate is something empty, tranquil, and without any sign; yet it contains fully within itself the principles governing the visible manifestations of activity and tranquillity, yin and yang.[39]

That is to say, from the perspective of its obscure aspect of possessing the power of generating the universe, although the Great Ultimate is empty, tranquil, and without any sign, the principles of activity, tranquillity, and yin-yang are implied as well as the principle of the universe. From the prominent aspect of the process by which the Great Ultimate creates the universe, activity and tranquillity or yin and yang are interacting upon each other. Sometimes there is activity but no tranquillity and at other times there is tranquillity but no activity. Sometimes there is yin but no yang and at other times there is yang but no yin. The Great Ultimate, however, persists through all time and all spaces of this transformation process. Therefore, Chu Hsi said, "From the perspective of existing things, yin and yang embrace the Great Ultimate. In tracing their origin, yin and yang are generated from the Great Ultimate."[40]

The doctrine of substance-function was originally put forth by Ch'eng I, who used it to explain the relation between principle and symbol (*hsiang*[aq]). Chu Hsi associated substance-function with Chou Tun-i's theory of the Great Ultimate and applied it to illustrate the relation between the Great Ultimate and yin-yang, in other words, between principle and material force. Thus Chu Hsi established a systematic cosmogony developing the philosophy of Ch'eng I. Through his cosmogony Chu Hsi assimilated Chang Tsai's materialistic theory of material force, making the concept of material force an important component of his theory of the Great Ultimate. In other words, Chang Tsai's concept of a material *ch'i*, when it was used by Chu Hsi as an interpretation of the generation and change of the universe, was encompassed by a system that was a kind of objective idealism. This is the first feature of the doctrine that Chu summarized in the substance-function proposition.

Chu Hsi's second interpretation of the doctrine of substance-function proceeds from Ch'eng I's view of the relation between principle and symbol or things.

> Master Ch'eng had already illustrated in detail the proposition that "Substance and function come from the same source." By the proposition that "Substance and function come from the same source" we mean that, so far as the principle of the most hidden is concerned, it is empty and tranquil and without any sign and yet all things are luxuriantly present. The assertion that "There is no gap between the manifest and the hidden" means that, so far as the forms of the most manifest are concerned, the principle is omnipresent in all facts and things. In principle, substance is prior to function because the principle of the function comes together with that of substance. Therefore, they are said to be from the same source. As for facts, the manifest is prior to the hidden, because substance of the principle is seen in the facts. Therefore, it could be said that there is no gap. Thus, by "same source" we do not mean that there is no distinction in fineness and no order in sequence. It is said, after all, that function prevails only after substance is set up and it is allowable to have one thing being followed by another.[41]

In this passage, Chu Hsi maintained that myriad concrete things were implied when one talked about the highest principle. That is to say, function is implied in substance and they are unified into one. When we are talking about concrete things, principle is embodied in each of them. That is to say, the hidden is implied in the manifest and there is no gap between the manifest and the hidden. It seems that Chu Hsi gave an ontological interpretation of the substance-function proposition.

Chu Hsi discussed two different theoretical questions in his interpretation of the proposition that "Substance and function come from the same source." The first question concerns the relationship between the absolute and the relative. The proposition "substance and function come from the same source" means that the absolute is embodied in the relative and the relative contains the absolute. They are unified and inseparable. Substance is the highest absolute. The pursuit of the absolute could be realized only through the existing things, concrete and relative. It is impossible to attain the absolute without knowledge of the relative.

The second question concerns the relationship between noumenon and phenomenon or reality and process. So far as relations between things in the universe as a whole are concerned, this relationship is the same as that between the absolute and the relative discussed above. So far as concrete things are concerned, we are here actually dealing with the relationship between essence and appearance or that between substance and accidents or attributes.

By the proposition that substance and function come from the same source, we mean that the essence of a thing is manifested in all appearances and each appearance also contains its essence. The two are unified and inseparable. We could perhaps put it in another way, saying that substance and accidents of a thing are unified and inseparable. In this connection, Chu Hsi appeared to be aware that substance and function form a unity of opposition, but he failed to recognize the dialectical relationship between the two. His words "Function prevails only after substance is set up and it is allowable to have one thing following another," show that he actually left the two separated.

Finally, Chu Hsi interpreted the substance-function proposition from the perspective of ethics. He said, "From now on, I know that in the process of the extensive transformation of the universe, everybody can find a resting place for himself, that is a place to settle down in spiritual life and to make the way for himself and a place to control his consciousness. This is the pivotal point upon which the great foundation is laid and from which the universal path leads out. This explains the proposition 'Substance and function come from the same source and there is no gap between the manifest and the hidden.' "[42] That is to say, if one is endeavouring to "lay the great foundation and go along the universal path" with the aim of attaining the highest truth, then one must work hard at controlling his own consciousness. This is what Chu Hsi meant when he said that "when you perceive the principle, you should consider mind (hsin[ar]) as the master."[43] If one places special emphasis upon seriousness (ching[as]), both before and after the feelings have been aroused (wei-

fa,[at] *i-fa*[au]); and if one is on one's good behavior, quiet *(chi)* yet constantly acted upon *(kan*[av]) and being acted upon yet constantly quiet, then the state wherein "substance and function come from the same source and there is no gap between the manifest and the hidden" is realized. Chu added, "This explains why the mind is constantly both quiet and acted upon and substance and function have always remained inseparable."[44] According to Chu, mind, including both the state before and after feelings are aroused, is nothing but the manifestation of the Great Ultimate. He said that "before feelings are aroused, [mind is the manifestation of] the Great Ultimate in its state of tranquillity, that is, being yin; and after feelings have been aroused, [mind is the manifestation of] the Great Ultimate in the state of activity, that is, being yang."[45] If one keeps himself constantly in the state of seriousness either when active or tranquil, then he attains sagehood. The sage's mind is identical with principle, and as an individual he is identical with the universe. This is what Chu Hsi said: "The sage, the Great Ultimate in its entirety, could not help but naturally attain the highest state of the Mean *(chung*[aw]), correctness *(cheng*[ax]), humanity and righteousness, without depending on self-cultivation, either when he is active or when he is tranquil."[46]

The doctrine originating with Ch'eng I that "substance and function come from the same source and there is no gap between the manifest and the hidden" took on new meanings after being extended by Chu Hsi into cosmology, ontology, and ethics. In connection with this doctrine, Chu Hsi discussed the relationship between the absolute and the relative and that between essence and appearance. There are some rational elements in his theory.

If, however, we examine Chu Hsi's theory as a philosophical system, we notice that he considered the Great Ultimate as the supreme substance of the Way (Tao[ay]). This spiritual substance of the Way existed prior to the beginning of the universe, being the origin of its generation. In his doctrine concerning substance and function, and the manifest and the hidden, both the schism between substance and function and the gap between the manifest and the hidden remain. Students of Chinese philosophy are given a lesson here. Questions such as the relationship between the absolute and the relative and between essence and appearance, that is, questions relating to unity of opposition, could not be properly dealt with in an idealistic philosophical system.

Some Chinese scholars thought that the speciality of Chinese philosophy could be summarized as reaching brilliant heights but following the path of the Mean, leading to sageliness within and kingliness without. This is the ideal of the sage, proposed by Chu Hsi, in whom the Great Ultimate is realized in totality, leading to identification with the absolute. This is based on the doctrine of substance-function. But it is nothing but a fiction of an idealistic system. Although the purpose of this theory might be the pursuit of the ideal of the sage, its shortcoming is that it places the sage at an undue height and unduly deifies a particular person. It could easily be turned into a tool to serve the interest of the feudal autocracy.

Chu Hsi's Theory of Principle

Important also to Chu Hsi's theory of the Great Ultimate is the proposition that principle is one but its manifestations are many (*li-i fen-shu*[az]). We mentioned above that according to Chu Hsi the two material forces and the Five Agents are generated from the Great Ultimate and the myriad things are produced in the interaction of the two material forces and the Five Agents while everything has in itself the Great Ultimate. Chu said, "Things generated from the Five Agents are distinct in mind owing to differences in physical nature (*ch'i-chih*[ba]). This is what we mean by saying that things are distinct in nature. Since things are distinct in nature, the Great Ultimate in its entirety exists in each individual thing. This also indicates that nature is ubiquitous."[47] This is the interpretation of his saying "Everybody has in him the Great Ultimate and everything has in it the Great Ultimate."[48]

According to Chu Hsi, each thing has its own principle, and the principle of the universe is a synthesis of principles inherent in myriad things. This synthesis, however, is not a mechanical one; principles inherent in myriad things are not separate and disconnected but interrelated to form an organic whole. "When all principles of heaven and earth and the myriad things are put together, then you have the Great Ultimate."[49]

Chu Hsi's saying "every person has in him the Great Ultimate; everything has in it the Great Ultimate" is the same saying that principle is one but its manifestations are many. Chu further explained: "From the angle of the male and the female, they have their own natures; yet the male and the female each has its own Great Ultimate. From the angle of the myriad things, each has its own nature and each its own Great Ultimate. The myriad things, taken together, consist of one Great Ultimate separately. It is adequately shown here that there is nothing in the universe that lies beyond the scope of nature and nature is ubiquitous."[50] Chu has said here that the myriad things as a whole have one Great Ultimate, and therefore we can say that principle is one; and each individual thing has in it its own Great Ultimate which is nothing but its nature, and thus we can say that the manifestations are many. Principles of the individual things are obtained from the one principle.

How do they partake of this one principle? According to Chu, principles of individual things do not result from sectioning the one principle, because after the generation of principles of individual things, the one principle remains the Great Ultimate in its entirety while these principles of individual things are also the Great Ultimate. Chu Hsi once explained this point to his students.

Question: [You said,] "Principle is a single, concrete entity, and the myriad things partake of it as their substance. Hence each of the myriad things also possesses in it a Great Ultimate." According to this theory, does the Great Ultimate not split up into parts?

> *Answer:* Fundamentally there is only one Great Ultimate, and yet each of the myriad things has been endowed with it and each in itself possesses the Great Ultimate in its entirety. This is similar to the fact that there is only one moon in the sky but when its light is scattered upon rivers and lakes, it can be seen everywhere. It cannot be said that the moon has been split.[51]

In characterizing this relation in terms of the metaphor of the moon's reflection in streams, Chu was showing that the relation between one and many is neither that between the whole and the part, nor that between genus and species, nor that between the universal and the particular.

But the myriad things are distinct in nature. If each individual thing "has in it its own Great Ultimate which is complete," how can we distinguish the nature of distinct things? To solve this problem, Chu Hsi introduced the concept of material force and explained the distinction of the natures of things in terms of distinctions in modes of combination of principle and material force. He said, "When considering that all things come from one source, we see that their principle is the same but their material force is different. Looking at their various substances, we see that their material force is similar but their principle utterly different. The difference in material force is due to its purity or impurity, whereas the difference in principle is due to its completeness or partiality."[52] That is to say that the myriad things come from the combination of principle and material force. Considering that the principle of the myriad things comes from the same source, principles of all things at the beginning are the same. Material force differs in its degree of purity. Considering that the myriad things, inheriting the principle from the same source, are distinct from one another, the difference in material force is minor, and yet the difference in principle is great because of its completeness or partiality. Thus individual things are different in nature.

Chu gave some examples to illustrate this point. He remarked that, for instance, so far as material force is concerned, the difference between man and animal is minor; therefore they both have the sense of cold and hunger. But so far as principle is concerned, the difference is great. Man has the nature of humanity, righteousness, rites (*li*[bb]), and wisdom while "in the case of love, for example, in tigers and wolves, or in the sacrificial rites in the wolf and otter, or in the righteousness in bees and ants, only the obstruction to a particular part of their nature is penetrated, just as light penetrates only a crack."[53] This example shows that, according to him, animals also partake some of the nature of humanity, righteousness, rites, and wisdom and also possess the Great Ultimate in entirety. But owing to difference in material force, ants and bees have only a little bit of the nature of righteousness, and tigers and wolves only a little humanity.

Chu Hsi also distinguished his doctrine of one-many (or principle-one/manifestations-many) from the doctrine of one-and-all of the Hua-yen[bc] School. In Chu Hsi's system, material force is more emphasized. By the operation of material force, he explained, principle becomes many manifestations. That is to say, his doctrine of one-many means that the many copies of the one principle existing as manifestations are distinct from one another. According to the one-and-all doctrine of the Hua-yen School, one is all and all is one, one is in all and all is in one. That is to say, all the copies of the one principle existing as manifestations are the same. Furthermore, in Chu Hsi's opinion, principle is obtained from Heaven and then becomes embodied in the mind. According to the Hua-yen School, all phenomenal things depend upon the mind to be manifested.

Chu Hsi criticized the doctrine of one-and-all of the Hua-yen School. He held that if all copies of the one principle existing as manifestations were the same, the differences of all things could not be sufficiently explained. He said, "The Sage did not speak of the doctrine of one-and-all but only of one-many. It is only by concentrating upon the particularity of the principles of facts and things that one can reach their inevitability and then know the principle running through them. If one does not understand that there are as many principles as the ten thousand manifestations, but only asserts that there is one principle, how can one know how this one principle manifests?"[54] With the doctrine of one-and-all which lays the foundation for the theory of life, the Hua-yen School also affirmed that all living beings are equal. This meant casting off the ethics of social distinctions. Chu Hsi attacked this doctrine as violating Confucian tradition and agreed with his teacher Li T'ung[bd] (1093–1163) that the difference between Confucianism and Buddhism was the doctrine of one-many versus the doctrine of one-and-all. Since the doctrine of one-and-all denied that the many copies of the one principle existing as manifestations do have distinctions, it was a heterodox (*i-tuan*[be]) one.[55]

From the difference between Chu Hsi's doctrine and the Hua-yen School, we can see that to explain the relation of one principle with many manifestations in terms of the metaphor of the moon reflecting itself in ten thousand streams was not suitable. Thus Chu Hsi often illustrated his theory in terms of the metaphor of the growing plant. Once he said,

> There is one principle which the myriad things divide to form their substance. Then each thing embodies principle separately; it is called the way of *ch'ien*[bf] (male) which is "changing and transforming so that everything will reach its correct nature and destiny (*ming*[bg])." Everything taken together, there is only one principle. The one principle manifests everywhere as an integral whole, just as one grain of millet comes up as a seedling, which produces flowers that run to fruit and form seeds again. There are a hundred grains on an ear of millet. Every grain is perfect in nature. As a hundred grains are sown, each grain grows into a hundred grains again. It produces and reproduces unceasingly. But at the beginning, there is only one grain to grow. Each thing has its principle. To summarize, there is only one principle.[56]

This metaphor is a more suitable characterization of Chu Hsi's one-many doctrine. At the same time, it also explains well feudal ethics for different stations of persons. As Chu said, "The myriad things have this principle; all principles come from the same origin, but they are in different positions. Therefore the functions of principles are different. For example, as a ruler, one must be humane; as a minister, one must be reverent; as a son, one must be filial (*hsiao*[bh]); as a father, one must love deeply (*tz'u*[bi]). Each thing has its respective principle and each affair a different function. Yet among all these things and affairs, there is none that is not the universal operation of one principle."[57]

Chu Hsi advocated the doctrine of one-many not only to draw a clear distinction from the doctrine of one-and-all of the Hua-yen School, but also to lay a theoretical foundation for criticizing Yang Chu[bj] (440–360 B.C.?) and Mo Ti[bk] (*fl.* 479–438 B.C.). Mencius (372–289 B.C.?) criticized Yang and Mo only from the standpoint of ethics, showing that their denial of the special relationships with the ruler and the father respectively would degrade man to an animal. Chu criticized them in terms of the doctrine of one-many. Mo Ti advocated universal love (*chien-ai*[bl]), which means an affirmation of one principle but a denial of the various manifestations. Yang Chu advocated egoism, which means an affirmation of individual manifestations but a denial of one principle. They both took an erroneous, one-sided approach. Chu said,

> It is the meaning of the "Western Inscription" (*Hsi-ming*[bm]). Master Ch'eng I regarded it as illuminating the doctrine of one-many. He actually capsulized it in a single sentence. When *ch'ien* is regarded as the father, *k'un*[bn] (female) as the mother, and this applies to all classes of living beings without exception, such is the statement that principle is one. Yet among men and all other living beings with blood in their veins, each loves his own parents as parents and treats his own son as a son, how can its manifestations not then be many? Once there is this unity which yet leads to myriad manifestations, then even though the whole world is a single family and China is a single person, we do not drift into the error of universal love. And once there are these myriad manifestations which may yet be reduced to a single unity, then even though the feelings expressed toward those close to us and those remote from us may differ and even though class distinctions may exist between those of honorable and those of humble station, nevertheless we are not shackled by the selfishness of each one for himself.[58]

By means of this criticism, Chu made it clear that the doctrines of Yang and Mo not only would not lead to good, but also were untrue in themselves. Chu developed the thought of Mencius at the same metaphysical level upon which he criticized Yang and Mo. He turned Mencius' doctrine into a total truth and regarded it as the Confucian orthodox tradition. In this way he hoped to avoid drifting into the error of Mo's universal love advocating that the whole world is a single family. At the same time he would not be shackled by Yang's egoism advocating the doctrine of class distinction.

By the doctrine of one-many, Chu Hsi indicated not only the relation between one principle and many principles, that is, "the ten thousand principles end in one,"[59] but also the relation between principle and things, that is, principle is one but its manifestations are the ten thousand things. This relation, too, is the relation between substance and function. He said, "That which is absolutely sincere and ceaseless is the substance of the Way. This is why the ten thousand differentiations can be one substance. The ten thousand things are well adjusted in their places and this is the function of the Way. This is why one substance becomes the ten thousand differentiations (*i-pen wan-shu*[bo])."[60] In other words, the substance of the Way is sincere and real, not emptiness and absolute quiet alleged by Buddhism. The function of the Way is the multiplicity of the myriad things, not the illusion held by Buddhism. The substance of the Way is unceasing production and reproduction. The function of the Way is its varied manifestations.

Chu Hsi also pointed out that the central idea of the *Doctrine of the Mean* is that of the "Western Inscription"—one principle but many manifestations. "It speaks of one principle at the beginning, which disperses and becomes the myriad things. They at last reunite to become one principle. When released, it expands to fill the entire universe; but when rolled up, it is contained within one's innermost being. It is all practical learning (*shih-hsüeh*[bp])."[61] Here Chu showed that the relation between substance and function is that of one principle with many manifestations. The identity of substance and function is the same as the identity of one principle with many manifestations. Therefore he said, "When we speak of one principle, it is as it runs through many manifestations."[62]

The doctrine of one-many originated with Ch'eng I but was developed systematically by Chu Hsi. It was he who identified one principle with its various manifestations, and through it substance with function and principle with things. But while following Ch'eng I's theory of principle, he also used Chang Tsai's doctrine of material force to solve some problems imperfectly answered by Ch'eng. His theory exerted great influence, escaping criticism until Tai Chen[bq] (1723–1777) made a direct attack. Tai said it impeded investigation of the laws of the objective world. He pointed out:

> The Sung Neo-Confucianists knew also how to seek principle in things, but because they were attracted to Buddhism, they have applied what the Buddhists used to designate spiritual consciousness (*shen-shih*[br]) to designate principle. Therefore they look upon principle as if it were a thing. They not only talk about the principle of things, but also say that principle lies scattered through events and things. Since principle is that of things, it can be discovered only after things have been analyzed to the minutest detail. And since principle lies scattered through events and things, they therefore seek it through deep and quiet concentration of the mind. They said the substance is one but it has ten thousand manifestations, and when released, it expands to fill the entire universe; but when rolled up, it is contained within one's innermost being."[63]

Tai Chen was not accurate in alleging that Chu's principle is the same as the spiritual consciousness of Buddhism. But he showed the unacceptable mysticism of the assertions that "the substance is one but it has ten thousand manifestations" and that "principle can be sought through deep and quiet concentration of the mind." For these were contrary to Tai's method of investigating principle by analyzing things themselves to the minutest detail. They were not helpful in obtaining scientific knowledge. Tai's exposure was correct.

According to Chu Hsi, principle and material force are two different entities, but they are merged into one and are inseparable. Because of this concept, some scholars compare his philosophy to that of Aristotle. For instance, Fung Yu-lan has asserted that principle and material force in Chu's system correspond to form and matter in Aristotle's.[64] Though this comparison is worthy of serious consideration, yet Aristotle did not suggest a mysticism of the doctrine of one-many. This difference between them is an important one.

Several scholars also have compared the philosophy of Chu Hsi with that of Leibniz. Knowing that Leibniz had read Confucian philosophy and debated with his correspondent on Chu Hsi's view of Shang-ti[bs] (God on High), Needham believes that Leibniz was influenced by Chu Hsi. Furthermore, Leibniz's idea of the monad and preestablished harmony of the universe are strikingly close to the ideas of Chu Hsi that everything has its own Great Ultimate and that principle is an organic order.[65] Considering the doctrine of one-many, this comparison is sufficiently warranted. Indeed, Chu Hsi repeatedly asserted that his Great Ultimate is an organic order, which grows and develops like a plant. For example, he said, "The Great Ultimate is like a plant which grows out of the root into stem and branches. The leaves and flowers are generated from the stem and branches. It is in the condition of production and reproduction until the fruits come into being. In the fruits there are infinite principles of production and reproduction, by means of which also grow out infinite Great Ultimates. This process never ceases."[66] That is to say, the Great Ultimate is a spiritual substance. It is as active as the monad of Leibniz. The Great Ultimate is an organic whole like a tree, in each node of which exists also a Great Ultimate. Just as every monad reflects the universe, all the monads together constitute the whole organic universe as a result of preestablished harmony. Here the similarities end and important differences begin.

In my opinion, Chu Hsi is a philosopher of feudalism. His system was established as the basis of feudal social hierarchy. He preferred practical or moral reason to intellectual or pure reason. And the main components of his moral reason are the morals of feudal society. He neglected the importance of scientific knowledge, especially of the universal and necessary knowledge of the physical world. All these ideas are reflected in his theory of the Great Ultimate.

On the other hand, Leibniz was a philosopher of the bourgeoisie. Though his idealism is unacceptable to us, yet he stressed the freedom of man and thought highly of pure reason and the importance of natural science. As helpful to the progress of society, these thoughts are also reflected in his system of monadology. But the significance and function of the two philosophers within their own contexts are very different. Essentially, every philosopher exists as part of a certain class and within the cultural tradition of his nation. When we compare theories of Chinese philosophers with those of philosophers in the West, we should not forget their social and historical contexts. It is as Wing-tsit Chan[bt] states, "These comparisons show that in any comparative study, similarities are usually accompanied by dissimilarities. The important point to note is that Chu Hsi is neither Platonic nor Aristotelian. The usual Western polarities do not apply in Chinese philosophy."[67] It is the case with Plato and Aristotle, and it is also the case with Leibniz.

Conclusion

To sum up briefly, Chu Hsi's theory of the Great Ultimate gathered all the main idealistic doctrines of substance in ancient China into a harmonious whole and achieved great completion. Classical Confucianism in general is an ethical system, but it provided no explicit philosophical foundation for its morals. As Tzu-kung[bu] (520–450 B.C.) said, "We cannot hear our Master's views on human nature and the Way of Heaven (*T'ien-tao*[bv])."[68] Chu Hsi combined the Great Ultimate of Chou Tun-i and the principle of Ch'eng I, added some ideas of Taoism and Buddhism, and then established a systematic ontology and cosmology as the metaphysical foundation for Confucian ethics. Thus he developed classical Confucianism to a new stage.

Chu Hsi held that the Great Ultimate is supreme, infinite, and the highest good, and that it possesses activity and tranquillity. All things in the universe are generated from it. It also stands as their archetype and purpose. He asserted that the Great Ultimate is prior to yin and yang and that principle is prior to material force. All these viewpoints are idealistic. He also advocated the doctrine of one-many. This idea brought a mystic flavor to his idealism.

It is evident that Chu Hsi's theory of the Great Ultimate applied to politics at that time was reactionary. In laying the metaphysical foundation for feudal ethics such as the Three Standards (*san-kang*[bw]) and the Five Constant Virtues (*wu-ch'ang*[bx]),[69] this theory set up their absolute authority. Hence it strengthened feudalism in China. It was criticized by some later progressive philosophers. Tai Chen pointed out that Sung Neo-Confucianists killed a person with principle. He said, "If someone is killed for violating the law, perhaps he will be pitied. If he is killed with principle, who will take pity on him!"[70] T'an Ssu-t'ung[by] (1865–1898) complained that "the Three Standards advocated by Sung Neo-Confucianists could strike into somebody so much terror as to put his soul to death!"[71] These criticisms are no exaggeration.

Chu Hsi's theory of the Great Ultimate also had more negative influence than positive influence on the development of science in China. He maintained that each individual thing must have its individual principle and that one should come into contact with things to gain an exhaustive knowledge of their principle. From this point of view, the so-called principles seem somewhat scientific. But when he declared that the Great Ultimate is the sum total of all principles and that each thing possesses the Great Ultimate in its entirety, principle cannot be laws of nature. Furthermore, he asserted that some of the main components of the Great Ultimate are feudal morals such as the Three Standards, taking the meaning of principle even further from the laws of nature in modern science. Hu Shih[bz] (1891–1962) asserted that the purpose of natural science is, as advocated by Chu Hsi, the investigating of principles of all things.[72] This assertion does not quite correspond to Chu Hsi's theory of principle.

Needham points out that according to Chu Hsi, principle is the dynamic pattern embodied in all living things, in human relationships, and in the highest human values. It lacks the sense of universality of a formulated law. Indeed, a law in the Newtonian sense was far from Chu Hsi's mind. Under the influence of Chu Hsi's organic philosophy, Chinese science never awoke from its empirical slumbers. From the meanings of principle, Needham concludes that Chu Hsi's theory of the Great Ultimate impeded the development of science in China.[73] This analysis is a direct hit.

But in Chu Hsi's theory of the Great Ultimate there are many positive factors that had no strict connection with feudal politics. He said that considering the present world, yin and yang imply the Great Ultimate and principle and material force are merged one with the other; in tracing their origin, the Great Ultimate generated yin and yang. That is to say, the Great Ultimate is both transcendent and immanent in the universe. It is a kind of pantheism directly opposed to the Taoist nonbeing and Buddhist emptiness. To go a step further, it was to be transformed into naturalism or materialism, the latter an achievement of Wang Fu-chih. Wang's philosophy of materialism helped to shift the central concern from an early emphasis on the practical learning *(shih-hsüeh)* of moral substantiality to that of functional practicality. It was conducive to the development of modern science in China.

The Great Ultimate is also said to possess activity and tranquillity. It is the first necessary cause of the universe. The Great Ultimate generates yang through movement and generates yin through tranquillity, and then generates all things in the universe. Within the Great Ultimate lie the contradictions of activity and tranquillity, yang and yin. Thus the Great Ultimate embodies a dynamic force or the power of production and reproduction. This power was said to be the essence of humanity. Thus the traditional concept of humanity acquired a metaphysical character, leading to the concept of fraternity and humanism in the bourgeois revolution.

In addition, according to Chu Hsi, the universe is a macrocosm, while each man is a microcosm. This theory provides the metaphysical foundation for sagehood. A sage is a man who realizes the real principles in the Great Ultimate and then becomes identical with the Great Ultimate, his microcosm forming one body with the macrocosm. It requires the unity of investigating principle to the utmost and fully developing one's nature. Though there were some elements in this theory favorable to feudalism in China, as stated above, yet it consistently developed a philosophy of man and tried to establish an ultimate standard for man.

Chu Hsi also analyzed the interdependent relations of such pairs of opposites as the Ultimate of Nonbeing and the Great Ultimate, being and nonbeing, activity and tranquillity, yin and yang, substance and function, principle and material force, the Way and concrete thing (ch'i^{ca}), and what exists before physical form and after physical form. Although in general he did not acknowledge that two opposites can transfer themselves into one another, yet his clear and penetrating analysis of these categories promoted the process of cognition of objective reality.

In the history of Chinese philosophy, Chu Hsi's theory of the Great Ultimate remains an indispensible link. The naturalism, secularism, and humanism in his theory were developed by later philosophers. These significant contributions may also be used for reference today.

Translated by Wu Yun-zeng[cb]

Notes

1. Wang Mao-hung[cc] (1669–1741), *Chu Tzu nien-p'u*[cd] [Chronological biography of Master Chu], under Chu Hsi's age of 71.

2. Chu Hsi, "T'ai-chi-t'u shuo chieh," in *Chou Tzu ch'üan-shu*[ce] [Complete works of Master Chou], (*Wan-yu wen-k'u*[cf] [Universal library] ed.), p. 5. Hereafter cited as *Shuo chieh*.

3. *Chu Tzu wen-chi*[cg] [Collection of literary works of Master Chu], (SPPY ed. entitled *Chu Tzu ta-ch'üan*[ch] [Complete literary works of Master Chu]), 36:3b. Hereafter cited as *Wen-chi*.

4. *Chu Tzu yü-lei* (1880 ed.), 94:4b–5a. Hereafter cited as *Yü-lei*.

5. *Wen-chi*, 36:14a.

6. "Collected Conversations of Master Chu," in *Chou Tzu ch'üan-shu*, p. 13.

7. *Yü-lei*, 94:6a.

8. *Ibid.*, 100:7b.

9. *Ibid.*, 94:11a.

10. *Ibid.*, 94:7a.

11. *Ibid.*, 94:11a.

12. *Ibid.*, 1:1b.

13. *Ibid.*, 94:10a.

14. *Ibid.*, 1:3a.

15. *Shuo chieh*, p. 6.

16. *Ibid.*, p. 7.

17. *Wen-chi*, 45:12a.

18. *Yü-lei*, 94:7b–8a.

19. *Ibid.*, 94:35b–36a.

20. Fung Yu-lan, *Chung-kuo che-hsüeh shih*[ci] [A history of Chinese philosophy], (Shanghai: Commercial Press, 1934), p. 907.

21. *Yü-lei*, 94:9a–b.

22. *Chung-kuo che-hsüeh shih*, pp. 901–902.

23. *Wen-chi*, 56:33b–34a.

24. *Chung-kuo che-hsüeh shih*, pp. 901–902.

25. Ch'eng Hao[cj] (1032–1085) and Ch'eng I, *I-shu*[ck] [Surviving works], 2a:16a, in the *Erh-Ch'eng ch'üan-shu*[cl] [Complete works of the two Ch'engs], (SPPY ed.).

26. *Ibid.*, 2A:22b.

27. *Yü-lei*, 94:10b.

28. *Chung-kuo che-hsüeh shih*, p. 901.

29. *Wen-chi*, 56:34a.

30. *Yü-lei*, 94:10a.

31. *Ibid.*, 94:5a.

32. Ts'ao Tuan, *Pien-li*[cm] [Refuting the unreasonable], in *Ts'ao Yüeh-ch'uan Hsiensheng i-shu*[cn] [Surviving works of Master Ts'ao Tuan], 1:17b–18a.

33. Ch'ien Mu, *Chu Tzu hsin-hsüeh-an* (Taipei: San-min[co] Book Co., 1971), Bk. III, p. 48.

34. *Ibid.*, Bk. II, p. 1.

35. *Shuo chieh*, p. 11.

36. *Wen-chi*, 50:1b.

37. Chu Hsi often quotes from Ch'eng I's *Ching-shuo*[cp] [Explanations of the Classics], 1:2a, in the *Erh-Ch'eng ch'üan-shu*.

38. Chu also often quotes from Ch'eng I's preface to his *I-chuan*[cq] [Commentary on the *Book of Changes*] in the *Erh-Ch'eng ch'üan-shu*.

39. *Shuo chieh*, p. 7.

40. *Yü-lei*, 75:17b–18a.

41. *Shuo chieh*, p. 34.

42. *Wen-chi*, 32:4b. For the great foundation and the universal path, see the *Doctrine of the Mean*, ch. 1.

43. *Ibid.*, 32:24b.

44. *Ibid.*, 32:25a.

45. *Ibid.*, 40:36a.

46. *Shou chieh*, p. 26.

47. *Ibid.*, p. 13.

48. *Yü-lei*, 94:7a.

49. *Ibid.*, 94:11a.

50. *Wen-chi*, 37:31b.

51. *Yü-lei*, 94:41b–42a.

52. *Wen-chi*, 46:11b.

53. *Yü-lei*, 4:3a.

54. *Ibid.*, 27:9a.

55. *Yen-p'ing ta-wen*[cr] [Li Tung's answers to questions], (*Chu Tzu i-shu*[cs] [Surviving Works of Master Chu] ed.), Postscript, p. 9b.

56. *Yü-lei*, 94:9b. The quotation on *ch'ien* (male), the first hexagram in the *Book of Changes*, is from its commentary on the hexagram.

57. *Ibid.*, 18:9a.

58. Chu Hsi, "Hsi-ming chieh"[ct] [Commentary on the "Western Inscription"], in the *Chang Tzu ch'üan-shu*[cu] [Complete Works of Master Chang], (*Kuo-hsüeh chi-pen ts'ung-shu*[cv] [Basic Sinological series] ed.), p. 8. *K'un* is the second hexagram in the *Book of Changes*.

59. *I-shu*, 18:10b.

60. *Lun-yü chi-chu*[cw] [Collected commentaries on the *Analects*], comment on *Analects* 4:15.

61. *Chung-yung chang-chü*[cx] [Commentary on the *Doctrine of the Mean*], introductory remark. The passage is a summary of Ch'eng I's remarks in the *I-shu*, 7:3b, 14:1a, and 18:30a, *Wai-shu*[cy] [Additional work], 11:1b, in the *Erh-Ch'eng ch'üan-shu*.

62. *Wen-chi*, 37:29b.

63. Tai Chen, *Meng Tzu tzu-i shu-cheng*[cz] [Commentary on the meanings of terms in the *Book of Mencius*], in Hu Shih's *Tai Tung-yüan ti che-hsüeh*[da] [Philosophy of Tai Chen], (Shanghai: Commercial Press, 1927), p. 128.

64. *Chung-kuo che-hsüeh shih*, p. 903.

65. Joseph Needham, *Science and Civilisation in China*, Vol. II, *History of Scientific Thought* (Cambridge: Cambridge University Press, 1956), pp. 496–505.

66. *Yü-lei*, 75:19a–b.

67. Wing-tsit Chan, *A Source Book in Chinese Philosophy* (Princeton, N. J.: Princeton University Press, 1963), p. 641.

68. *Analects*, 5:12. Tsu-kung was a Confucian pupil.

69. The Three Standards were the Three Bonds with the ruler as the standard of minister, the father as the standard for the son, and the husband as the standard for the wife. The Five Constant Virtues are affection between father and son, righteousness between ruler and minister, order between seniors and juniors, separate functions between husband and wife, and good faith among friends.

70. *Meng Tzu tzu-i shu-cheng*, in Hu Shih's *Tai Tung-yüan ti che-hsüeh*, p. 56.

71. T'an Ssu-t'ung, *Jen-hsüeh*[db] [Philosophy of humanity] in *T'an Ssu-t'ung ch'üan-chi*[dc] [Complete works of T'an Ssu-t'ung], (Peking: San-lien[dd] Book Co., 1954), p. 65.

72. Hu Shih, *Hu Shih wen-ts'un*[de] [Collected works of Hu Shih], (Shanghai: The Oriental Book Co., 1931), Vol. II, p. 208.

73. *Science and Civilisation in China*, Vol. II, p. 579.

Glossary

a 朱子語類	r 陰	ai 王夫之
b 太極圖説解	s 形而下	aj 體
c 本體	t 形而上	ak 用
d 天	u 周敦頤	al 體用一源
e 無極	v 生生	am 顯微無間
f 空	w 馮友蘭	an 五行
g 寂	x 氣	ao 顯
h 理	y 南軒張栻	ap 微
i 本然之妙	z 程頤	aq 象
j 有	aa 仁	ar 心
k 無	ab 義	as 敬
l 宇	ac 曹端	at 未發
m 宙	ad 錢穆	au 已發
n 動	ae 朱子新學案	av 感
o 靜	af 陸九淵象山	aw 中
p 天命	ag 王守仁陽明	ax 正
q 陽	ah 張載	ay 道

az 理一分殊
ba 氣質
bb 禮嚴
bc 華嚴
bd 李侗
be 異端
bf 乾
bg 命孝
bh 孝
bi 慈
bj 楊朱
bk 墨翟
bl 兼愛
bm 西銘
bn 坤
bo 一本萬殊
bp 實學震
bq 戴震
br 神識
bs 上帝

bt 陳榮捷
bu 子貢
bv 天道
bw 三綱
bx 五常
by 譚嗣同
bz 胡適
ca 器
cb 吳允曾
cc 王懋竑
cd 朱子年譜
ce 周子全書
cf 萬有文庫
cg 朱子文集
ch 朱子大全
ci 中國哲學史
cj 程顥
ck 遺書
cl 二程全書

cm 辯庋
cn 曹月川先生遺書
co 三民
cp 經說
cq 易傳
cr 延平答問
cs 朱子遺書
ct 西銘解
cu 張子全書
cv 國學基本叢書
cw 論語集註
cx 中庸章句
cy 外書
cz 孟子字義疏證
da 戴東原的哲學
db 仁學
dc 譚嗣同全集
dd 三聯
de 胡適文存

9

Zhu Xi's Doctrine of Principle

CHIU HANSHENG

IN THIS SHORT ESSAY, I do not attempt to expound comprehensively Zhu Xi's Doctrine of Principle (*lixue*[a]); I have limited myself to a discussion of his theory of the Principle of Heaven (*tianli*[b]) and his theory of nature (*xing*[c]).

Zhu Xi's Theory of the Principle of Heaven

The Principle of Heaven

The core and highest philosophical category of Zhu Xi's doctrine of principle is his theory of the Principle of Heaven. He inherited this theory from Cheng Yi[d] (1033–1107) and developed it into a more concise, precise, and profound concept.

Zhu Xi believed that principle or the Principle of Heaven is the origin or foundation of the universe. "The sum of all creation and the universe when taken together is but the one principle."[1] "Before heaven and earth existed, there was certainly only principle. As there is this principle, therefore there are heaven and earth. If there were no principle, there would also be no heaven and earth, no man, no things, and in fact, no containing or sustaining [of things by heaven and earth] to speak of. As there is principle, there is therefore material force (*qi*[e]), which operates everywhere and nourishes and develops all things."[2] Clearly, according to Zhu Xi, the principle is the origin of the universe. The universe exists because of principle, as do men and objects. The universe and all creation in the universe, taken as a whole, comes to this one principle.

In his introduction to the *Zhongyong zhangju*[f] (Commentaries on the *Doctrine of the Mean*), Zhu Xi cited passages from Cheng Yi which said that the *Doctrine of the Mean* "first speaks of one principle, then proceeds to cover all creation and finally returns and gathers them all under one principle. This principle saturates the universe when diffused; collected, it recedes and lies hidden in minuteness."[3] This principle reigns over all creation and all creation unites in one principle. Regarded in its macroscopical aspect, the principle saturates the whole universe, embraces and covers the whole universe, its immensity allowing nothing above or beyond it. Regarded in its microscopical aspect, it recedes into seclusion, its minuteness allowing no interior. The passages cited by Zhu Xi provide a programmatic discourse on the world view of the Cheng-Zhu School of Principle: the theory of the Principle of Heaven. It puts forward principle as the highest philosophical category of his system of thought, and in elucidating the relationship between principle and all creation maintains that principle is all-comprehensive and omnipresent. Many of Zhu Xi's discourses on principle are connected with these passages.

Zhu Xi said, "After all, there is the principle before there is the universe."[4] Then again, "After all, the principle will remain even if the mountains and rivers and the earth itself all cave in."[5] The principle has no beginning or ending. There is a beginning for the universe, but not for the principle; there is an ending for the universe, but not for the principle. The principle exists before the universe. After the universe caves in, the principle will remain. The principle exists independently and eternally, not relying on the universe or the creation in it.

Zhu Xi described the relationship between principle and material force. He maintained that "there is material force since there is principle, but principle is the basis."[6] He added, "In the universe there has never been any material force without principle or principle without material force. When a form is created by material force, principle is found in that form at that very moment."[7] "It is asked: Must principle then precede material force? The answer is: Fundamentally, principle and material force cannot be spoken of as prior or posterior. But if we must trace their origin, we are obliged to say that principle is prior. However, principle is not a separate entity. It exists in material force. Without material force, principle would have nothing to adhere to."[8]

In letters answering Huang Daofu[g] and Liu Shuwen,[h] Zhu Xi explained the relationship between principle and material force.

Throughout the universe there are both principle and material force. Principle refers to the Way, which is above the realm of corporeality and is the source from which all things are produced. Material force refers to material objects, which are within the realm of corporeality; it is the concrete object by which things are produced. Therefore in the production of man and things, they must be endowed with principle before they have their material force, and they must be endowed with material force before they have corporeal form. While this nature and this form are integrated within one and the same body, the distinction between the Way and concrete objects is very marked and must not be confused.[9]

What are called principle and material force are certainly two different things. But considered from the standpoint of things, the two things are merged one with the other and cannot be separated with each in a different place. But we do not say that the two things are each a single thing. When considered from the standpoint of principle, before things existed their principles of being had already existed. Only their principles existed, however, but not yet really the things themselves. Generally speaking, we must make distinctions when examining such matters, and take in the whole process lest we err.[10]

"When the reality of the Ultimate of Nonbeing (wuji[i])," said Master Zhou (Zhou Dunyi,[j] 1017–1073), "and the essence of yin[k] (passive cosmic force) and yang[l] (active cosmic force), and the Five Agents (Water, Fire, Wood, Metal and Earth) come into mysterious union, integration ensues." What he calls "reality" is principle, and what he calls "essence" is material force.[11]

Commenting on this statement found in Zhou Dunyi's "An Explanation of the 'Diagram of the Great Ultimate'" (Taijitu yishuo[m]), Zhu Xi wrote "'Reality' is principle and 'essence' is material force. Because principle and material force merge, a form is created."[12] From this and the several citations from his *Classified Conversations* we can summarize Zhu Xi's theory of principle and material force into five main points:

1. Principle and material force exist in the universe, principle being the basis of the two.

2. Principle is the Way, which existed before physical form and is the root from which all things are originated. Material force is material objects, which existed after physical form; it is the instrument by which things are produced. The distinction between principle and material force is very marked and must not be confused.

3. The principle of an object exists before the object itself does; what exists is only the principle, not yet the object itself. This is to say that principle precedes object and it also precedes material force.

4. Principle and material force are intermingled and cannot be separated. We cannot say which of the two precedes the other. But if one were to insist upon sequence, we must say that principle precedes.

5. Take the coming into being of man and things as an example. When the reality of the Ultimate of Nonbeing (principle) and the essence of yin and yang and the Five Agents (material force) come into mysterious union, integration ensues. "Principle and material force combine, and thus a form is created." "Yin and yang are material force and the Five Agents are physical substances, and the existence of these physical substances makes it possible for things to come into being."[13]

Zhu Xi's discourse on principle and material force is the main content of this theory of the Principle of Heaven. A clear exposition of the essence and form of expression of this discourse is therefore of great importance in elucidating the Principle of Heaven.

Zhu Xi believed that the Great Ultimate (taiji[n]) is the ultimate principle of the myriad things of heaven and earth. "With respect to heaven and earth, there is the Great Ultimate in them. With respect to the myriad things, there is the Great Ultimate in each and every one of them."[14] "Should there be no Great Ultimate, would not the heaven and earth turn upside down?"[15] In Zhu Xi's system of philosophy the Great Ultimate is synonymous with principle or the Principle of Heaven. Without the Great Ultimate, there would be no Principle of Heaven, and the universe, heaven and earth, would turn upside down. By "the Great Ultimate is the principle of the universe, and all creation,"[16] Zhu Xi meant that it is the order of the universe and of all creation.

"Cheng Yichuan° [Cheng Yi] expressed it very well when he said that principle is one but its manifestations are many (*liyi fenshu*ᵖ).[17] When heaven, earth and the myriad things are spoken of together, there is only one principle. As applied to man, however, there is in each individual a particular principle."[18] That is to say, there is one principle for the universe; yet there is still one principle for every individual being, which, joined together, incarnate the one Principle of Heaven. This one principle is the general name for the principles of the myriad things in heaven and earth, which is the Great Ultimate, that is, the ultimate principle.

According to the above, Zhu Xi's principle or Principle of Heaven is endowed with the following characteristics:

1. Principle exists independently of any thing or matter. It has no beginning or ending and exists eternally. The coming into being and destruction of the universe and all creation does not apply to principle.

2. Principle is the origin and foundation of the universe, the origin and foundation of all creation of the universe, and the general principle of all creation of the universe.

3. Principle and material force are related. "Where there is principle there is material force, which operates and brings into being all creation."[19] Principle is the origin, while material force is the material substance forming heaven and earth and all creation, which must operate depending on principle. Yet if there is no material force, principle will have nothing to adhere to. Principle is only a "clean, empty, and boundless space,"[20] having no shape or trace, and doing nothing. It embraces everything and is omnipresent.

4. Principle is synonymous with the Great Ultimate as presented by Zhou Dunyi in "An Explanation of the Diagram of the Great Ultimate" based on the "Appended Remarks" (Commentary on the *Book of Changes*).[21]

There is, apart from the material world, a principle, or a Principle of Heaven, which does not depend on the material world and which exists independently and eternally. It is the origin and foundation of the material world. It is a "clean, empty, and boundless space"; yet it contains and covers all creation of the universe and is incarnated in each and every one of the myriad things in the universe. Such a principle or Principle of Heaven is not a law abstracted from the objective world and has no material basis. It should be noted, however, that concepts in fact mirror the material world. Concepts that exist independently and do not rely on the material world can only be fabrications of the imagination.

If principle, or the Principle of Heaven, is interpreted as an objective law, such a law should be derived from the development of all physical and spiritual life. If we believe that such a law embodies life, then it is undoubtedly true. But that is not Zhu Xi's view. He thought just the opposite, holding that the development of physical and spiritual life embodies the Principle of Heaven. Thus the Principle of Heaven "becomes the creator of Nature." In this way Zhu Xi's theory of the Principle of Heaven is endowed with the character of objective idealism.

Principle Is One but Its Manifestations Are Many

According to Zhu Xi, the idea that principle is one but its manifestations are many means that there is one general principle governing all the specific principles. He likened it to the one single moon sending down its beams to the myriad rivers, lakes, streams, and seas, producing myriad reflections;[22] this is one side of the picture. On the other side, all the principles come together to make up the one general principle, just as the myriad reflections all find in the one single moon their common origin. Thus a single Great Ultimate ramifies to become the Great Ultimate of each and every specific being, which, in their totality, go back to make up the original Great Ultimate. Zhu Xi said, "The Great Ultimate is simply the principle of the highest good. Each and every person has in him the Great Ultimate and each and every thing has in it the Great Ultimate."[23] This Great Ultimate, which is found in everybody and everything, is connected with the general Great Ultimate, that is, the one principle. It clearly interprets the relationship between one general principle and the specific principles of things.

Zhu Xi's idea that principle is one but its manifestations are many was written in reference to Zhou Dunyi's *Yitong*[q] (*Tongshu*[r]) (Penetrating the *Book of Changes*). Zhu Xi said,

According to Master Zhou, "The Five Agents constitutes the differentiation [of things], while the cosmic dual forces yin and yang constitute the activity; the two forces are fundamentally one. The substance is expressed in the myriad, and the one substance and the myriad things all become correct, while the largeness or smallness of each has its own definiteness."[24] Tracing from bottom to top, the Five Agents are nothing but the two material forces [yin and yang], which in their turn are nothing but the principle. Tracing from top to bottom, there is only this one principle which the myriad objects share to serve as their substance. The myriad objects embody in themselves, each and every one, their own principle. This is what is meant by the "changes in Heavenly Way resulting in each possessing its correct nature, life, and destiny."[25] But at all events there is only one principle that permeates every being. It is like a grain of millet, which grows to be a seedling which produces a flower. When the flower bears seeds which become millet again, the original figure is restored. One ear will bear 100 grains and each grain is integral to itself. Have the 100 grains sown and each in time will produce again 100 grains. They will go on producing like this eternally. At the beginning there is only one grain, which keeps propagating. Every object has its principle, but all of these principles are one and the same principle.[26]

"The one substance is expressed in the myriad" means "one principle with many manifestations." "The one and the myriad are all integral to themselves" means "every object possesses one Great Ultimate." When one grain of millet becomes 100 grains, the one grain is integral and each of the 100 grains is also integral to itself. "Tracing from top to bottom" signifies one principle ramifying to form the substance of the myriad objects. "Tracing from bottom to top" signifies the restoring of the principle from the bodies of the myriad objects to become this one principle.

Zhu Xi related his theory of one principle with many manifestations to Cheng Yi's explanation of Zhang Zai's[s] (1020–1077) "Western Inscription," (*Ximing*[t]).[27] Cheng Yi held that the thesis of cosmic brotherhood described in the "Western Inscription" had elucidated the logic of one principle with many manifestations.[28] Zhu Xi said that in the "Western Inscription" "every sentence signifies one principle with many manifestations."[29] "Reading the text as a whole, we find one principle; perusing the text sentence by sentence, we find the many manifestations."[30] In relating the theory of one principle with many manifestations of Zhou Dunyi's *Penetrating the Book of Changes* to Zhang Zai's "Western Inscription" and Cheng Yi's interpretation, Zhu Xi held that all these famous Neo-Confucianists of the Northern Song dynasty (960–1126) were early advocates of this theory.

Zhu Xi also used this theory to annotate the Four Books.[31] His comment on the *Doctrine of the Mean* reads,

The sky covers, the ground bears, and all creation are bred in between to coexist and not to harm one another. The four seasons, the sun and the moon, alternately replace one another in rotation and are not mutually exclusive. That they are not mutually harmful or mutually exclusive is because the small virtues run incessantly like streams. That they coexist and function side by side is because of the working of the grand virtue. The small virtues are the many manifestations of the totality, and the grand virtue is the origin of the myriad manifestations.[32]

Zhu Xi's discussion here of "the Way of Heaven" cited from the *Doctrine of the Mean* is an exposition of his own philosophy of nature by the theory of "one principle with many manifestations." The grand virtue, that is, the origin of the myriad manifestations, signifies the one principle. The small virtues are the specific manifestations derived from the totality of the universe, signifying the ramifications of the totality. These concepts—the grand virtue and the small virtues, the origin of the myriad manifestations and the ramifications of the totality—are nothing but the theory of one principle with many manifestations. Commenting on the chapter in the *Analects* that begins with the sentence "My doctrines have one thread which runs through them all" (4:15) in his *Lunyu jizhu*ᵘ (Collected commentaries on the *Analects*) Zhu Xi said, "Absolute and constant sincerity is the entity of the Way, which explains why there is only one origin for the myriad manifestations. That the myriad objects all find their proper places is the function of the Way, which explains why the one origin should have myriad manifestations." The origin of the different manifestations of the myriad objects is thus traced and recognized to be the one principle; this is to prove that these manifestations are derived from this one principle. The different manifestations of the myriad objects are understood from the original one principle. This is to prove that this one principle stipulates the manifestations of the myriad objects.

In this sense, mankind, grass, trees, birds, and animals with all their different manifestations are derived from one origin; in this is found their identification with one another: they share the same origin, the same one principle. Yet at the same time they differ from one another in their manifestations, the difference lying in that each has its particular share of the principle, and each has its specific quality. Therefore, Zhu Xi added, "When mankind, grass, trees, birds, and animals come into being, each does so with its own seed."[33] "If Heaven and Earth had no intention, then a cow would give birth to a horse and peach flowers would blossom on plum trees. However, they each have their own stipulations."[34] It is this "seed," this "stipulation," which has caused the many manifestations.

Zhu Xi's theory of "the principle is one, but the manifestations are many" is an important component of his philosophy of nature. It elucidates the relationship between the entity and its various ramifications, between the universe and all creation, and between the one principle and the principle found in each and every being. The theory is originated from the theory of principle and manifestation preached by the Huayanᵛ School of Buddhism. It is of important theoretical significance in the history of the Neo-Confucianism of the Song and Ming dynasties (1368–1644).

Movement of Transformation and Nourishment

"Movement of transformation and nourishment" (*huayu liuxing*ʷ), otherwise termed movement of the Principle of Heaven (*tianli liuxing*ˣ), signifies the operating of the Principle of Heaven to bring all things into existence. In the *Daxue huowen*ʸ (Questions and answers on the *Great Learning*) Zhu Xi said, "As I am told, all are objects that possess sound, color and shape, and are produced and brought into being through the operation of the Heavenly Way" (2:10a). The Heavenly Way is the Principle of Heaven, or the Way which is above the realm of corporeality. By "objects" is meant all creation, all the beings that possess sound, color, and shape and that inhabit the universe. The Way, which is above the realm of corporeality, operates, producing and bringing into being all objects in the world.

Why is it that the operation of the Principle of Heaven can produce and bring into being all creation? The *Questions and Answers on the Great Learning* provides the following answer:

> The Heavenly Way is able to create the myriad things in its operations of producing and nourishing because there are yin and yang and the Five Agents. With regard to yin and yang and the Five Agents, there must be principle before there is material force. When things are produced, the material force must first integrate before a form is created. Therefore, when man is born, he must first be bestowed with the principle so that he will possess the nature of strength and obedience and those of humanity, righteousness, propriety, and wisdom.[35] He must also be bestowed with material force before he will possess in his person a spirit (or soul), the viscera, and the skeleton. This is just what Zhou Zi called "when the reality of the Ultimate of Nonbeing and the essence of yin and yang, and the Five Agents come into mysterious union, integration ensues."[36]

Here is discussed the law by which mankind and animals and plants come into being. According to Zhu Xi, when the material forces of yin and yang and the Five Agents gather together and coagulate, the figures and bodies of mankind and animals and plants, and the mind, the viscera, and the skeleton of animals are formed. As material force accompanies principle, as material force gathers and coagulates in the creation of man and things, it must have been endowed at the same time with principle, and possess strength and obedience as well as humanity, righteousness, propriety, and wisdom. And so, movement of transformation and nourishment or movement of the Principle of Heaven means simply that the material forces of yin and yang and the Five Agents accompany principle in producing and bringing into being all creation in the universe.

For the same concept, Zhu Xi sometimes used another expression, "movement of material force in transformation" (*qihua liuxing*^{z}). Commenting on the *Book of Mencius*, 6A:8, on the beautiful trees on Ox Mountain in his *Mengzi jizhu*[aa] (Collected commentaries on the *Book of Mencius*) Zhu Xi notes, "The material force operates to transform and nourish without even stopping, and so objects keep growing day and night." This is to say that the uninterrupted operation of the material forces of yin and yang and the Five Agents is the basis for all creation (trees on Ox Mountain) to keep growing day and night.

"Movement of transformation and nourishment" signifies the uninterrupted movement of the universe. Zhu Xi's comment in the *Collected Commentaries on the Analects*, 9:16, reads, "The operation of the universe goes on without a moment's interruption; no sooner is the past gone than the coming has arrived to continue the movement. Such is the fundamental nature of the essence of the Way. The best example that can both be designated and easily seen is the flow of a stream. Therefore, Confucius made use of it to give his instruction, calling on scholars always to scrutinize and reflect in their hearts without a moment's interruption." Following this, Zhu Xi cited Cheng Yi:

"This is the essence of the Way. Heaven operates ceaselessly. When the sun goes down, the moon rises. Winter passes by and summer follows. The stream flows continuously. Objects come into being with no end. All these take the Way for their essence, and are in motion day and night without stop. And so, the superior man takes this for his model and makes ceaseless efforts to aspire after the sublime."

Zhu Xi took the constant movement of the universe and all creation for the innate function of the essence of the Way of Nature, that is, for the innate function of the Principle of Heaven. Zhu Xi's thinking would be very close to materialism if this comment could be stripped of the idealist system of his theory of the Principle of Heaven. However, these words were said within the context of his system of his theory of the Principle of Heaven. The "Way" in the fundamental nature of the essence of the "Way" is a kind of Heavenly Principle suspended in the air, not a law abstracted from the objective world. These discourses of Zhu Xi and Cheng Yi are actually forcing conjectures of the Principle of Heaven on the movement of the true essence of the universe and all creation. Such a system is inverted materialism.

The purpose of these theories of Cheng Yi and Zhu Xi is to borrow the so-called unceasing movement in the realm of Nature to give the instruction that superior men should model themselves on Nature and make constant efforts to aspire after the sublime. "Scholars should always scrutinize and reflect in their hearts without a moment's interruption." They should ceaselessly perceive in their inner hearts the Principle of Heaven.

The ultimate purpose of recognizing the transformation of the universe is to require the individual to have the Principle of Heaven operating within his inner heart so that he will "be at peace with the world and flow in the same current with all creation and the universe." A comment in his *Comment on the Analects*, 11:25, about Confucian pupils Zilu,[ab] Zeng Xi,[ac] Ran You,[ad] and Gongxi Hua[ae][37] sitting by the Master reads, "Zeng Dian[af][37] holds that Heaven's principle operates at the point when [selfish] human desires are completely eradicated. It saturates everywhere, leaving no empty space. . . . Such a person has peace in his inner bosom and is able to flow in the same current with all creation and the universe." Upward, all creation and the universe flow in the Principle of Heaven. Downward, the inner hearts of men flow also in the Principle of Heaven. That is what is meant by "flowing upward and downward in the same current." When human desires are completely eradicated, their subjective world will be saturated fully with the Principle of Heaven and flow in the same current with all creation and the universe of the objective world. This is a mysterious realm, elusive and difficult to appreciate.

How can this be achieved? Zhu Xi maintained that it depends on "tacit understanding." His *Commentary on the Doctrine of the Mean*, chapter 32, reads, "The virtue of the sage is extreme honesty and freedom from falsehood. He is in tacit understanding with the transformation and nourishment of the universe because of his extreme honesty and freedom from falsehood, which is not restricted to what he has gained from hearing and seeing in person." According to Zhu Xi, the sage is able to reach a tacit understanding with the work and function of the universe by virtue of his extreme honesty and freedom from falsehood, which realizes entirely his nature unmixed with the least bit of the hypocrisy of human desires. And where human desires are completely eradicated, the Principle of Heaven will prevail. Likewise, the "transformation and nourishing of the universe" in the objective world is also "extremely honest and uncontaminated by falsehood." And since both the subjective and the objective are "extremely honest and free from falsehood," it is but natural that a tacit understanding occurs. Such an understanding, existing above and beyond the world of the senses and independent of what can be seen or heard, is something mysterious, visionary and nonexistent. The origin of this theory can be traced to the creed of Huayen that the principle and the phenomenon identify tacitly and do not differ from each other.[38]

Further, Zhu Xi's theory of the operation of the Principle of Heaven stresses that human ethics and practice cannot depart from this operation of the Principle of Heaven. He said in his *Questions and Answers on the Doctrine of the Mean,* chapter 2,

> The operation of the Way is found between heaven and earth; it is omnipresent. Above, it is found in the kite's approaching the sky in its flight; below, it is found in the fish's leaping out of the deep. In the world of man, it is found in his daily practice and his relationships with his fellow beings, in what can be learned and practiced between husband and wife yet not necessarily known or done by the sage. One can say that all these, which are found between heaven and earth, are quite conspicuous.

In sum, the theory of the operation of the Principle of Heaven maintains that man must practice introspection and self-scrutiny in his daily practice and relationships with his fellow men to eradicate completely human desires so that the same Principle of Heaven will operate within him.

Zhu Xi's theory of the transformation and nourishment of the Principle of Heaven is related to his theory on the formation of the universe in his theory of the Principle of Heaven, and constitutes an important part of his philosophy of Nature. It complements the theory of one principle with many manifestations. The theory of the transformation and nourishment of the Principle of Heaven elucidates the coming into being of the universe, while the theory of one principle with many manifestations elucidates the relationship between the totality and the ramifications. A clear description of the two provides us with a lucid sketch of the basic contents of Zhu Xi's philosophy of Nature.

No Starting Point for Activity and Tranquillity and No Beginning for Yin and Yang

Cheng Yi said in his *Jingshuo* (Explanation of the Classics), "There is no starting point for activity and tranquillity and no beginning for yin and yang.[39] Only he who knows the Way can recognize it." Zhu Xi systematized and developed Cheng Yi's theory. *Classified Conversations* reads as follows:

> *Question:* There are activity and tranquillity in the Great Ultimate. Which of the two precedes the other?
> *Answer:* There are endless cycles for movement and quietude. There would be no tranquillity without movement, and no movement without tranquillity. This is just like the breath of man which goes on in and out at all times. Breathing-in starts when breathing-out ends. Breathing-out starts when breathing-in ends. This is just as it should be.[40]

Zhu Xi further said,

> The Great Ultimate through movement generates yang, and through quietude generates yin. It is not the case that yang is produced after movement and yin after tranquillity. It only means that the movement of the Great Ultimate itself is yang and the tranquillity of the Great Ultimate itself is yin. When it moves, tranquillity is not seen, and when it is quiet, activity is not seen. However, to say that movement generates yang is just by way of describing the circle since there is another link before movement and yang. From this it can readily be seen what Cheng Yi meant when he said "no starting point for activity and tranquillity and no beginning for yin and yang."[41]

Again he said,

> When it is not moving, it is tranquil; when it is not tranquil, it is moving again; when it is not moving, it is tranquil again. Yichuan said, "No starting point for activity and tranquillity and no beginning for yin and yang. Only he who knows the Way can recognize it." When activity reaches its limit, then tranquillity comes into being. When tranquillity reaches its limit, then activity resumes in its course. . . . As a matter of fact, before activity there exists tranquillity; before tranquillity, activity goes on. This is just like the situation when daytime has passed away, night ensues. After night has passed away, the daytime of tomorrow will come. That is to say, there is night before daytime today, and there is daytime before last night.[42]

The idea of no starting point for activity and tranquillity and no beginning for yin or yang expounded in Yichuan's remarks the so-called initial thrust and the so-called beginning of the universe. In the Middle Ages of China, this was very valuable thinking. This thinking is certainly not unrelated to the concepts of yin and yang and of activity and tranquillity as presented by Zhou Dunyi in his "Explanation of the Diagram of the Great Ultimate," but the former was clearer than the latter. In his analysis Zhu Xi obviously integrated Cheng Yi's thinking with Zhou Dunyi's, believing that Cheng Yi's thinking conformed with the latter; it inherited and generalized the theories of yin and yang and activity and tranquillity expressed in the "Explanation of the Diagram of the Great Ultimate." This is a contribution of Zhu Xi in the history of the development of Neo-Confucianism. It also reveals his painstaking efforts to link the thinking of Zhou Dunyi and Cheng Yi.

The following points can be deduced from Zhu Xi's discourse:

1. Movement has no so-called initial beginning. "Before movement there exists tranquillity; and before tranquillity, activity goes on." From activity to tranquillity endless cycles repeat themselves. Therefore we say that "there is no starting point for activity or tranquillity." Activity and tranquillity are the movement.

2. Activity and tranquillity are not isolated from each other. "There would be no tranquillity without movement and no movement without tranquillity." This is just like material force. Breathing-in starts when breathing-out expires. Breathing-out starts when breathing-in expires. They cannot be arbitrarily divided into two.

3. Yin and yang are material forces and have no beginning. The Great Ultimate possesses the principle of activity, which produces yang, and the principle of tranquillity, which produces yin. That the Great Ultimate through movement produces yang and through tranquillity produces yin does not mean that it produces yang after it has moved and produces yin after it has become tranquil. Activity is yang, and tranquillity yin. Thus, yin and yang, activity and tranquillity, are not separated. Since there is no starting point for activity and tranquillity, so there is no beginning for yin and yang.

4. The Great Ultimate is the original fundamental principle (Principle of Heaven), and activity and tranquillity are the mechanism undertaken by it. The existence of activity and tranquillity in the material forces of yin and yang originates from activity and inactivity of the Great Ultimate.

5. There is movement before tranquillity and tranquillity before movement. Tracing backward, there is no beginning. Tracing forward to the fathomless future, there will be no ending.

If we take Zhu Xi's material forces of yin and yang as substance, and activity and tranquillity as movement, then his theory of activity and tranquillity having no starting point and yin and yang having no beginning has touched upon the problem of the relationship between movement and substance. Movement is the form of the existence of substance. It is an extremely important and indispensable characteristic of substance. The world is an eternally moving substance. The source of movement lies in the substance itself. But Zhu Xi believed that both the transformation and the rise and fall of yin and yang have no ending. This is an eternal and unfailing truth. The source of movement of yin and yang lies in that there are activity and tranquillity in the principle of the Great Ultimate. Zhu Xi said,

The Great Ultimate is nothing other than principle, and yin and yang are material forces. Principle does not take form, but material force leaves traces. Since there are activity and tranquillity now, how can the principle of the Great Ultimate not be invested with activity and tranquillity? I formerly perceived the Great Ultimate as substance, and activity and tranquillity as function. There are flaws in this expression and I have lately changed to say: The Great Ultimate is the wonder as it is originally, and activity and tranquillity are the mechanism through which it operates. Such a description may be approximately to the point.[43]

The first half of the above passage is comparatively well written and clear, and shines with the beams of truth of materialism. But the second half is difficult to understand, and the expression "activity and tranquillity are the mechanism through which it operates" is rather obscure. Zhu Xi wanted to attribute to the movement of yin and yang the inevitability of the Principle of Heaven, but this principle transcends substance, time, and space, and is only a "clean, empty and spacious world." So he again turned toward idealism. This is the tragedy in which Zhu Xi's theory sank into the mire of objective idealism.

In the field of philosophy of nature, Zhu Xi elaborated his theory of the Principle of Heaven, which embraces the concepts discussed above such as the relationship between principle and material force, principle being one but its manifestations many, movement of transformation and nourishment, no starting point for activity and tranquillity, no beginning for yin and yang, and so on. In so doing he aimed at rendering Nature into the Principle of Heaven.

Zhu Xi claimed that feudal moral codes, rites, music, and justice all came from the Principle of Heaven. For instance, in the field of ethical relations Zhu Xi maintained that moral codes, such as filial piety and love for brothers, come from "the principle of what should be" in one's nature. And feudal rites, music, and justice result from embellishing, tailoring, and fabricating the "principle of what should be," and thus also arise from the Principle of Heaven. Zhu Xi thus subsumed the yoke of feudalism within his Principle of Heaven. In the sociopolitical field Zhu Xi also applied the Principle of Heaven to explain historical development and contemporary human society. This is the entire content of Zhu Xi's Principle of Heaven.

Zhu Xi said,

There is only this one principle in the universe. Being endowed with it, heaven becomes the heaven; being endowed with it, earth becomes the earth. When those which exist between heaven and earth are endowed with it, they take it for their nature. With mankind, it is extended to become the Three Bonds (*sangang*[ag])—the proper relations between ruler and ministers, between father and son, and between husband and wife—and regulated to become the Five Constant Virtues (*wuchang*[ah]) [humanity, righteousness, propriety, wisdom, and faithfulness]. All these constitute the movement of this principle which is found everywhere. Coming and going, ebbing and surging, it keeps on moving in endless cycles from the time when nothing existed, up to the time when mankind vanishes and objects are exhausted; all the while an end is always followed by a beginning and a beginning by an end without any interruption. Since scholars have already been endowed with this principle in their original hearts, then a moment's negligence will not be tolerated between interior and exterior and between fineness and coarseness. They should cultivate their own moral character and guide others, serve as models for the world and institute doctrine to teach others without allowing the least bit of selfishness or hypocrisy. Therefore by dint of this natural principle, they will naturally accomplish the last. Thus, they are in a position to stand in line with Heaven and Earth and participate in transformation and nourishment. Accordingly not a single object, obscure or conspicuous, large or small, is left uncared for.[44]

The principle is the basis of the universe and all creation. It is also the basis of human society and the Three Bonds and Five Constant Virtues. Self-cultivation, guiding others, serving as models and establishing schools to teach moral codes, and politics—all are based on this "Principle of Nature (*Tian*[ai])" (Principle of Heaven), whereby the work of Nature is accomplished. Principle is the sole basis of the universe and all creation. Human society is also embraced in the universe and all creation and is subject to the control of this principle. If scholars will abide by this "Principle of Nature" to fulfill the "work of Nature," they will be able to realize "the grandeur of the entire principle in the universe" through "standing in line with Heaven and Earth and participating in transformation and nourishment."

Zhu Xi's Theory of Nature

The Nature of Man and the Nature of Things

Zhu Xi holds that nature (*xing*[ai]) is the Principle of Heaven embodied in all living things, such as grass and trees, birds and animals, insects and mankind. The Principle of Heaven bestowed by Heaven to all living things is the principle they depend on for living. In his *Collected Commentaries on the Book of Mencius*, 4b:26, he said, "Nature is the principle on which mankind and things depend for living." Mankind and things are of two different categories. Things refer to birds, animals, and insects, with grass and trees sometimes included, sometimes not.

Zhu Xi held that nature is the principle by which mankind and things can live; in this respect mankind is no different from things. For instance, mankind and objects are similar in physical functions like consciousness and movement. Yet in terms of social morality, the nature of mankind and that of things are not similar in all respects. In commenting on 6A:3, Zhu Xi said,

Nature is the principle mankind has acquired from Heaven. Life is the breath (*qi*[ak]) mankind has acquired from Heaven. Nature refers to what existed before physical form, and material force refers to what exists after physical form. In coming into being, man and things are all imbued with such nature and such material force. In terms of material force, man and things are not different in consciousness and movement. In terms of principle, could things be fully endowed with all the humanity, righteousness, propriety, and wisdom? That is why the nature of man is always perfect and why man is the most intelligent of all creatures. Now Gaozi[al45] did not know that nature is principle and tried to replace it with material force. He merely knew that in innate consciousness and movement man and things are similar but did not know that in the purity of humanity, righteousness, propriety, and wisdom man and things are different.

In this comment Zhu Xi demonstrates, by opposing principle to material force, the similarity and difference between the nature of mankind and of things. As innate endowment, nature consists of two factors: principle and material force. Man receives a complete endowment of principle whereas birds, animals, and insects do not. Therefore man has comprehensively acquired the essence of virtue, namely, humanity, righteousness, propriety, and wisdom, while birds, animals, and insects have not acquired them completely. This marks the difference between the nature of mankind and that of things. There is no difference between the endowment of material force in mankind and in birds, animals, and insects. Thus, in innate consciousness and movement, the understanding of mankind is similar to that of birds, animals, and insects. Mankind has consciousness and movement, which birds, animals, and insects also share. This is the core of Zhu Xi's theory of nature.

Similar statements can be found in his comment on 4B:19:

Man and things, in coming into being similarly acquire the principle of Heaven and Earth to constitute their nature, and similarly acquire the material force of Heaven and Earth to constitute their physical forms. The difference lies in that man alone has acquired the correct material force and physical form and is capable of rendering perfect his nature. This is where man is somewhat different. Although the difference is somewhat small, yet the distinction between man and things really lies here.

Zhu Xi maintains that mankind and material objects are similar in "acquiring the principle of Heaven and taking it for their own nature" and "acquiring the material force of Heaven and taking it for their physical form." The difference between them lies in that while man has acquired the positive of material force for physical form, and is therefore capable of rendering perfect his nature, birds and animals have not, and therefore are not capable of rendering perfect their nature. This is where mankind and objects are different. The *Classified Conversations* contains passages that corroborate this view. For instance, bees and ants "observe justice between rulers and subjects." "This is only because there is one point of light in their 'righteousness.'" Tigers and wolves "observe the parental love between fathers and sons." "This is only because there is one point of light in their 'humanity.'" In them other points of virtues are entirely absent. "This is likened to a mirror. With the exception of only one or two points of light, all other places on its surface are dark."[46] This is to say that the humanity, righteousness, propriety, and wisdom of birds, animals, and insects are all partial and incomplete. Only mankind can have all these virtues and attain perfection in nature.

In a class society human nature is of a class nature. Humanity, righteousness, propriety, and wisdom are class virtues. In his discourse on nature, Zhu Xi took the difference between man's acquisition of class virtues such as humanity, righteousness, propriety, and wisdom, and the acquisition of these virtues by birds, animals, and insects, as differences in completeness of endowment. Obviously his explanation is wrong.

Worthy of note is that Zhu Xi described here the influence of principle and material force upon human nature. He developed Zhang Zai's theory of the nature of Heaven and the physical nature. We should not underestimate the tremendous influence on human ethics and education which Zhu Xi's thoughts on these matters had upon subsequent generations.

Expansion of Zhang Zai's Nature of Heaven and Physical Nature

Zhang Zai discussed the nature of Heaven and the physical nature in *Zhengmeng*[am] (Correcting youthful ignorance). In the chapter "Enlightenment Resulting from Sincerity" (Chengming pian[an]) he wrote, "Only with physical form is there physical nature. If one can skillfully return to his nature, the nature of Heaven and Earth will be preserved. So, men of virtue will deny that the physical nature is the original nature."

Cheng Yi and Zhu Xi especially approved Zhang Zai's statement about the nature of Heaven and the physical nature. Cheng Yi said, "To discuss nature but not material force will not be complete. To discuss material force but not nature will not be clear. It is not correct to separate the two."[47] Zhu Xi further explained this concept in accordance with Cheng Yi's comment.

> If we only say that humanity, righteousness, propriety, and wisdom are nature, how can we explain that there are many who are born deprived? This is merely due to the endowment of material force. So, if we do not take into consideration material force, the argument will not be comprehensive. Hence, it is not complete if we only talk about the endowment of material force, that so and so is good and so and so is evil, but do not talk about the one origin which is the same principle, or the argument will not be clear.[48]

Zhu Xi maintained that since Zhang Zai and Cheng Yi "discovered the nature of material force," they "made a tremendous contribution to the Confucian School and were of great help to later scholars."[49]

Zhu Xi apparently developed his thinking on the Principle of Heaven and the material force of Heaven from Zhang Zai's nature of Heaven and the nature of material force. In his *Collected Commentaries on the Four Books*, Zhu Xi stated, "Nature is the principle of Heaven." A comment in his *Collected Commentaries on the Book of Mencius*, 6A:2, reads, "Nature is the principle of

Heaven; it has never been evil." Again he said in 6A:1, "Nature is the Principle of Heaven with which mankind has been endowed in life." A comment in 7A:4 says, "Large things like the relationship between rulers and subjects, and father and son, small things like fine and tiny things, are all furnished with the principle of what they should be within their nature." A comment in 6B:2 reads, "Within the nature, the myriad principles are embodied." Zhu Xi reiterated his argument: "Human nature is none other than the Principle of Heaven." He inherited Mencius' theory of the goodness of human nature. This is again a development of the theory of the two Chengs that "nature is none other than the Principle of Heaven" and of Zhang Zai's belief that it is "the nature of Heaven and Earth" and that "nature is good in everyone." Starting from this theory, the conclusion can be drawn that "letting nature work on its own is following the principle of Heaven." Again in his *Daxue zhangju*³⁰ (Commentary on the *Great Learning*) Zhu Xi called the "nature of Heaven" the "nature from Heaven's mandate," which is a "command from Heaven," thus attributing a sacred character to the nature of man.

Zhang Zai maintained that one would do well to fight against physical nature. This is to say, one should apply self-cultivation to restore the nature of Heaven from physical nature—consequently the saying "As to physical nature, there are cases when gentlemen do not take it as nature."

Zhu Xi, however, recognized the nature of material force as nature and offered many arguments to sustain his view. Men were classified into four categories in *Analects* 16:9: those who are born with knowledge, those who learn to get knowledge, those who learn when they are hard pressed, and those who do not learn even when they are hard pressed. Commenting on this, Zhu Xi said, "These four categories of men derive from the difference in their physical nature." He attributed this classification to the differences in physical nature. Physical nature signifies the physical nature of Heaven and Earth. It was also said that yin and yang are the material force and the Five Agents are physical stuff. Man's spiritual character and behavior are determined by yin and yang and the Five Agents they are endowed with. Those who are completely equipped with the Five Agents and with harmonized yin and yang will become sages. If a man lacks some of these things, his spiritual character and behavior will not be proper. There are detailed explanations of this point in his *Classified Conversations*.

> Nature is principle only. However, without the material force and physical stuff of the universe, principle would have nothing in which to inhere. When material force is received in its state of cleanness and clearness, there will be no obscurity or obstruction, and principle will express itself freely. The Principle of Heaven will dominate if the obstruction is small, and selfish desire will dominate if the obstruction is great. From this we know that original nature is perfectly good ... It is only sometimes blurred by the turbid substance of the physical nature.⁵⁰

Zhu Xi added,

The nature of all men is good, and yet there are those who are good from their birth and those who are evil from their birth. This is because of the difference in material force with which they are endowed. When the sun and moon are clear and bright and the climate temperate and reasonable, the man born at such a time and endowed with the material force that is clear, bright, well-blended, and strong, would be a good man. But if the sun and moon are darkened and gloomy, and the temperature abnormal, all this is evidence of violent material force. There is no doubt that if a man is endowed with such material force, he will be a bad man. Since my nature seems to be good, why is it that I have not been able to become a sage and a man of virtue? It is because that I have been impaired by this material force I have been endowed with. If the endowed material force inclines toward being sturdy, then I will tend to be tough. If it inclines toward being soft, then I will tend to be irresolute. . . . We must know the harm done by endowed material force and try our best to overcome it. It is advisable to suppress the aggressiveness and stop at the mean.[51]

He said moreover,

Those endowed with refined and brilliant material force will become sages and men of virtue, and will be enabled to acquire a comprehensive and correct principle. Those endowed with clear and bright material force will become talented and forthright. Those endowed with simple and rich material force will become mild. Those endowed with pure and lofty material force will become noble. Those endowed with full and thick material force will become rich. Those endowed with long lasting material force will live long. Those endowed with thin and turbid material force will become foolish, unworthy, poor, humble, and short-lived.[52]

He said further,

Although nature is the same in all men, it is inevitable that in most cases the various elements in their material endowment are unbalanced. In some men the material force of Wood predominates. In such cases, the feeling of commiseration is generally uppermost, but the feeling of shame and dislike, of deference and compliance, and of right and wrong are impeded by the predominating force and do not emanate into action. In others, the material force of Metal predominates. In such cases, the feeling of shame and dislike is generally uppermost, but the other feelings are impeded and do not emanate into action. So with the material forces of Water and Fire. It is only when yin and yang are harmonized and the Five Moral Natures [of Humanity, Righteousness, Propriety, Wisdom, and Good Faith] are all complete that men have the qualities of the Mean and correctness and become sages and men of virtue.[53]

According to Zhu Xi's theory, the nature of Heaven (nature from Heavenly mandate) determines that the nature of mankind should be perfectly good. Yet because of the endowment of material force, there will be good and evil. Moreover, the firmness and softness of men is also influenced by material force. Likewise is wisdom and stupidity, high and low station, longevity and short life. Material force influences temperament, intelligence, social status, and the life span of men. Weather conditions and the state of the sun and moon at the time of birth and the disposition of yin and yang and the Five Agents constitute the conditions under which men receive the endowment of Heaven. These affect certain aspects of men as well as their whole lives. This assertion is in no way different from the humbug of a fortune teller. One comment in his *Classified Conversations* is more plain and direct in this respect.

Question: How do you explain the fact that a father like Yao[ap] begot a son like Danzhu,[aq] and a father like Gun[ar] begot a son like Yü[bs]?[54]

Answer: This is again due to the operation of yin and yang and the Five Agents. Their transformation and movement often vary; sometimes they are bright and sometimes turbid. These conditions cause human qualities to vary from man to man. Just like a fortune teller conjecturing on the five stars and the material forces of yin and yang, if a propitious sign is hit upon, the character of the man or the object will be good; otherwise it will be evil. This is certainly beyond the control of the material force of men [meaning heredity].[55]

Zhu Xi held that the qualities of the physical nature are connected with man's material desires. He said, "Yang is good and yin is evil. Therefore yang imparts clearness and brightness and yin darkness and turbidity." "If the brightness of yang prevails, then the nature of morality will find its application. If the turbidity of yin prevails, material desires will have their way." "If man's mind is sober and quiet, it will naturally become clear and bright. If it is blurred by material desires it will become dark and turbid." Since material desires are the source of darkness and turbidity, their suppression will be an effort to transform the physical nature.

Zhu Xi's statements on physical nature are a development of the theory of human nature under feudal hierarchy. He tried to attribute men's sagacity, stupidity, goodness, and evil to the differences in endowment of inborn material force, with a view of explaining that there are innate grounds for standards of good and evil, and for the judgment of right and wrong in feudal society. I would like to point out that Zhu Xi's thesis on good and evil, firmness and softness, and other qualities in human nature was inherited from Zhou Dunyi's *Yitong* in which human nature was classified into five types: firm, soft, good, evil, and mean.[56]

Another problem raised by Zhu Xi is that concerning the pure or stained state of human nature. He maintained that nature is innately pure, but after it has mingled with miscellaneous desires and habits, it cannot help being stained. Therefore, it is necessary to cleanse it to recover its original nature. Zhu Xi held at the same time that the nature of material force is the source of material desires. If the Principle of Heaven is to be maintained, it is necessary to restrain lust. All of this constitutes the evolution of a theoretical basis for Zhu Xi's advocacy of self-examination and self-mastery. Zhu Xi's theory of nature also includes such aspects of mind as feeling, desire, will, aspiration, and talents. His statements crystallize his predecessors' theory of human nature, and develop the theory to a higher plane in terms of depth and precision.

Zhu Xi built a comprehensive system of Neo-Confucianism centering on the theory of Heaven. His system embraces the theories of the Principle of Heaven, nature, extension of knowledge and investigation of things, philosophy of history, politics, education, and the tradition of orthodox transmission of the Way (*Daotong*[at]). Theories of the Principle of Heaven and nature belong or are relevant to cosmology. Extension of knowledge, investigation of things, and reverence belong to the theory of knowledge or method of self-cultivation. Philosophy of history and education are applications of his philosophical thought to sociopolitics, history, and education. The tradition of orthodox transmission seeks to defend the dominant position of his philosophical thought in the ideological field. Zhu Xi's Principle of Heaven is the core of the ideological system of his philosophy. The theories of nature, extension of knowledge, investigation of things and reverence are also very important. Together with the Principle of Heaven, these form the mainstay of the ideological system of Zhu Xi's philosophy. These are the categories and topics that most concerned the Neo-Confucianists and were constantly elaborated and discussed by them. They permeate the whole history of Neo-Confucianism.

Notes

1. *Zhuzi yulei*[au] [Classified conversations of Master Zhu], (1603 ed.), 1:2a.

2. *Ibid.*, 1:1b.

3. *Yishu*[av] [Surviving works], 7:3b, 14:1a, 18:30a, in the *Erh-Cheng chuanshu*[aw] [Complete works of the two Chengs], (SPPY ed.).

4. *Zhuzi yulei*, 1:1b.

5. *Ibid.*, 1:4a.

6. *Ibid.*, 1:2a.

7. *Ibid.*

8. *Ibid.*, 1:3a.

9. *Zhuzi wenji*[ax] [Collection of literary works of Master Zhu], (SPTK ed.), 58:5a, "In answer to Huang Daofu."

10. *Ibid.*, 46:26a, "In answer to Lin Shuwen."

11. *Ibid.*, 58:5a, "In answer to Huang Daofu."

12. *Ibid.*, 46:27a, "In answer to Lin Shuwen."

13. *Zhuzi yulei*, 1:9a.

14. *Ibid.*, 1:1a.

15. *Ibid.*, 1:1b.

16. *Ibid.*, 1:1a.

17. *Yichuan wenji*[ay] [Collection of literary works of Cheng Yi], 5:12a, in the *Erh-Cheng chuanshu*.

18. *Zhuzi yulei*, 1:2a.

19. *Ibid.*, 1:1b.

20. *Ibid.*, 1:3b.

21. *Book of Changes*, "Appended Remarks," pt. 1, ch. 11.

22. *Zhuzi yulei*, 94:49a.

23. *Ibid.*, 94:8a.

24. *Yitong*, ch. 22.

25. *Book of Changes*, the first hexagram.

26. *Zhuzi yulei*, 94:11a–b.

27. *Zhangzi chuanshu*[az] [Complete works of Master Zhang], ch. 1.

28. *Yichuan wenji*, 5:12a, "In answer to Yang Shi[ba] on the 'Western Inscription.' "

29. *Zhuzi yulei*, 98:19b.

30. *Ibid.*, 98:20a.

31. The *Great Learning*, the *Analects*, the *Book of Mencius*, and the *Doctrine of the Mean*.

32. *Zhongyong zhangju*, comment on the *Doctrine of the Mean*, ch. 30.

33. *Zhuzi yulei*, 1:3b.

34. *Ibid.*, 1:4b.

35. Strength and obedience referring to the first hexagram, *qian*[bb] (Heaven, male, strength), and the second hexagram, *gun*[bc] (Earth, female, weakness), of the *Book of Changes*, and the Four Virtues of humanity, etc., are taught in the *Book of Mencius*, 2A:6.

36. *Taijitu yishuo*, in the *Zhou Zi chuanshu*[bd] [Complete works of Master Zhou], ch. 1.

37. Zilu's (c. 542–480 B.C.) family name was Zhong[be] and private You.[bf] Noted for courage, he was only nine years younger than Confucius. Zengxi (c. 505–436 B.C.) was Zeng Zi's[bg] father. Ron You's (c. 522–462) private name was Ziu[bh] and courtesy name Ronji.[bi] Gongxi Hua (b. c. 509 B.C.) was known by his courtesy name Jihua[bj] and private name Chi.[bk]

38. *Dazengjing*,[bl] ch. 45, pt. 2, *Huayan yicheng fajie tu*[bm] [Diagram of the Law of the Great Vehicle of the Huayan School].

39. *Jingshuo*[bn] [Commentary on the Classics], 1:2a, in the *Erh-Zheng chuanshu*.

40. *Zhuzi yulei*, 94:6b.

41. *Ibid.*, 94:10a.

42. *Ibid.*, 94:10a.

43. *Zhuzi wenji*, 45:11a–12a, 1st letter in answer to Yang Zishi.[bo]

44. *Ibid.*, 70:5a–b, "Reading the Great Historical Records."

45. Gaozi (c. 420–350 B.C.) was Mencius' opponent in the theory of human nature. To him, what is inborn is nature, which is neither good nor evil, and righteousness comes from the outside. See the *Book of Mencius*, 6A:1–4.

46. *Zhuzi yulei*, 4:2b.

47. *Yishu*, 6:2a.

48. *Zhuzi yulei*, 4:18a.

49. *Ibid.*

50. *Ibid.*, 4:13a.

51. *Ibid.*, 4:16a–b.

52. *Ibid.*, 4:26a.

53. *Ibid.*, 4:23a.

54. According to ancient Chinese legend, Yao was an ideal emperor. He begot Danzhu, who was a very bad man. For that reason he did not pass his throne to his son but asked an able and virtuous minister Shun[bp] to succeed him. Yu, a sage-king, was the son of Gun, a very bad father. Hence the question.

55. *Zhuzi yulei*, 4:23b.

56. *Yitong*, ch. 22.

Glossary

a 理學
b 天理
c 性
d 程頤
e 氣
f 中庸章句
g 黄道夫
h 劉叔文
i 無極
j 周敦頤
k 陰
l 陽
m 太極圖易説
n 太極
o 程伊川
p 理一分殊
q 易通
r 通書
s 張載
t 西銘
u 論語集註
v 華嚴
w 化育流行

x 天理流行
y 大學或問
z 氣化流行
aa 孟子集註
ab 子路
ac 曾晳
ad 冉有
ae 公西華
af 曾點
ag 三綱
ah 五常
ai 天
aj 性
ak 氣
al 告子
am 正蒙
an 誠明篇
ao 大學章句
ap 堯
aq 丹朱
ar 鯀
as 禹
at 道統

au 朱子語類
av 遺書
aw 二程全書
ax 朱子文集
ay 伊川文集
az 張子全書
ba 楊時
bb 乾
bc 坤
bd 周子全書
be 仲
bf 由
bg 曾子
bh 求
bi 冉子
bj 子華
bk 赤
bl 大藏經
bm 華嚴一乘法界圖
bn 經説
bo 楊子直
bp 舜

10

What Was New in the Ch'eng-Chu Theory of Human Nature?

A. C. GRAHAM

AT THE TIME of the rise of Neo-Confucianism there was one philosophical problem that had long obsessed Confucians and upon which they seemed destined never to reach agreement, the goodness or badness of human nature. Man's nature being what he is born with and can do nothing about, it must, like everything else independent of his will, be the work of Heaven; in the words of the opening sentence of the *Chung-yung*ᵃ *(Doctrine of the Mean)*, "It is the destined by Heaven that is meant by the 'nature.' " Should it not follow then that it is by following his own nature that man obeys Heaven, his highest authority? If so, either human nature is good, or morality is baseless. How then do we reconcile the demand for morality with the evidence of common experience that the evil in man is at least as natural to him as the good? When Mencius (372–289 B.C.) defended the goodness of human nature in the late fourth century B.C, three other doctrines were already current: that it is neutral, can become good or bad, is good or bad in different individuals.[1] In the next century Hsün-tzuᵇ (313–238 B.C.) pronounced it bad. Later, Yang Hsiungᶜ (53 B.C.–A.D. 18) thought it a mixture of good and bad. This profoundly troubling issue, a threat to the foundations of Confucian moralism, continued to be discussed, urgently and fruitlessly, even at the times when Confucians showed least interest in philosophical abstractions. Thus during the T'ang dynasty (618–907) Han Yüᵈ (768–824) argued that there are three grades of human nature: good, intermediate, and bad; his disciple Li Aoᵉ (fl. 792) sided with Mencius, Tu Muᶠ (b. 803) with Hsün-tzu.[2]

The controversy continued right up to the Sung, even among the earlier of those later classed as Neo-Confucians. Chou Tun-yiᵍ (1017–1073) treated human nature as mixed.[3] Chang Tsaiʰ (1020–1077) and Ch'eng Haoⁱ (1032–1085) approximated the Mencian doctrine, but both seem to have shared a position commonly held in the early Sung, for example by Su Shihʲ (1036–1101) and early in the twelfth century by Hu Hungᵏ (1106–1161) that although it is good to act according to the nature, the term "good" cannot properly be applied to the nature itself.[4] But with Ch'eng Yiˡ (1033–1107) something fundamentally new entered the discussion. In defending the goodness of human nature, he elevated *li,*[m5] the pattern which runs through all things and joins man to the universe, to the central place among Confucian concepts, the reinterpreted Heaven and Nature as aspects of *li.* Chu Hsi inherited this new conceptualization of the Mencian theory of human nature, and with the victory of his school it became Confucian orthodoxy. Henceforth, whatever new issues arose to divide Confucians, the problem of human nature was generally assumed to be solved.

How are we to explain this sudden decisive resolution of a controversy that had continued without result for a millenium and a half? It would seem that the restatement of the problem in terms of *li* was an event comparable with those paradigm shifts that Thomas S. Kuhn has demonstrated in the history of Western science.[6] Scientists go on arguing inconclusively over a problem insoluble within the current conceptual frame until, quite suddenly, there is a conceptual revolution, and the problem is seen from a new direction and definitively solved. Not, of course, that it is solved for eternity, there being no reason to suppose that we can ever reach a perfect system of concepts that fits everything; according to Kuhn a scientific revolution may even reopen questions already satisfactorily answered yet triumph over the old system because the questions it does enable one to answer are those that at the time have come to the forefront. A Westerner interested in original sin or natural goodness can see that Confucians are not dealing with exactly the same problem as Augustine or Rousseau, and that a Chinese solution might be wholly successful and yet not able to be transplanted to our own culture. It is none the less possible for us to ask whether and why the Ch'eng-Chu[n] solution was definitive in its own terms. If nothing else, such questions are of great help in penetrating the conceptual structures of Chinese philosophy.

The problem of human nature, and more generally of the relation between Heaven and Man, is one of the places where one is most conscious of elusive differences between Western and Chinese preconceptions that frustrate understanding from deep down in the foundations of thought. As a Westerner, or at any rate as a Western post-Kantian, I explore my own nature by trying to detach myself from spontaneous desires and aversions and to examine them objectively, as I would any other natural phenomenon. I try to shrink myself to a point of observing Ego, which is perhaps only a fiction, but if so seems to be a fiction necessary to objective thinking. However, necessary or not, Mencius and Chu Hsi do not seem to share it, or to be doing this kind of thinking about man. Nor, if I look back into my origins as an infant as spontaneous as an animal, is it easy to understand how I came to be doing so myself.

Suppose we imagine, as the first dawning of objective thought, a child wanting another helping at dinner, remembering having been sick, and telling himself what he has often been told by his mother, "Don't or you'll be ill." Previously he would have immediately acted out spontaneous impulse; now he is beginning to choose in the light of objective facts combined with imperatives. But we have the problem, familiar to Westerners since Hume, of how the imperative seems somehow to draw its authority from the facts of the case. When I apply the example to myself, in detachment from my infant greed and nausea, it is as though I could validly argue like this.

> Shall I eat it or not?
> You don't like being sick.
> Another helping will make you sick.
> Therefore don't eat it.

Then, as the situation recurred, I could generalize the imperative to "Never eat too much," which applied to everyone is equivalent to "One ought not to eat too much," and my prudential value judgments would be safely launched. The trouble is, of course, that it is a fallacy to draw an imperative conclusion from purely factual premises, and the nausea that could have moved me spontaneously to refrain is now detached from me in the factual statement that I don't like being sick. To escape the fallacy one seems to be driven to R. M. Hare's solution that "You don't like being sick" is itself a logical imperative ("Don't get sick") disguised by the grammatically indicative mood, a claim which implies that in advancing from spontaneity to rational choice the child mysteriously finds himself confronted by imperatives to pursue every goal to which he already spontaneously inclines.[7]

Do Mencius and Chu Hsi look as we do at the situation that gives rise to this puzzle? Now the retrospection that has trapped me in the dichotomy of "is" and "ought" is crucially different from my viewing of the situation as an infant. In first waking to the pressures of unwelcome fact, I was still being spontaneously pulled between nausea when I remembered being sick and desire when I forgot. To take the step from spontaneity to deliberate choice, I would have required only one objective fact, that overeating makes me ill, and only one imperative, "Face facts," which would begin to exert its authority from the first recognition of the obstinate resistance of external circumstance to my desires. The form of my thought would have been something like this:

> Overlooking the fact I am moved to eat; facing the fact I am moved to refrain.
> In which direction shall I let myself be moved?
> Face facts.
> Therefore let yourself be moved to refrain.

"Face facts" is an imperative that moral philosophers would acknowledge but dismiss as trivial, since no prescriptive conclusions can follow merely from the facts to be faced. But to suppose it trivial is to assume the highly artificial model of an ideally rational agent who in thinking is not already responding to the situation in which he finds himself. In the case of the child, appetite is hindering awareness of the fact that would move him to refrain; to force himself to obey "Face facts" is to let himself be moved to refrain. So there were none of the consequences that seemed to emerge in retrospect, no jump from "is" to "ought" and no fallacy; he required no imperative but "Face facts" to choose between his spontaneous tendencies. It is by no means the case then that from an imperative to face facts, prefer reality to illusion, be wise not foolish, no further prescriptive consequences can follow. Provided that I am content to appeal to reason alone when conflict arises between spontaneous inclinations already in motion, a simple "Know!" will tell me what to do. If the child succumbs after all to temptation and does get sick, a sufficient scolding would be "You ought to have known better" or "You should have had more sense." As for generalizing to a standard of conduct, very likely it would be in the form of "Sensible people don't eat too much"; it would be a factual generalization which assumes imperative force because we cannot deny the value of acting sensibly rather than foolishly.

It seems then that in advancing from spontaneous animal to reasoning man I was at first choosing only between spontaneous inclinations, in the light of an imperative to deal with things as they really are, and that in due course I derived further imperatives after the model of "One ought not to eat too much" ("Sensible people don't eat too much"). The sphere of reason was at first a tiny island in the ocean of the spontaneous. It was only later that I got to the point of shrinking myself to that ideal Ego detached from desire and aversion, from which reason can radiate to explain and predict even the spontaneous in myself. Or did I in fact ever get to that point? That would be an interesting question if we were discussing the foundations of ethics in general. Since in practice we are always being pulled in reconcilable or conflicting directions by spontaneous tendencies that vary from moment to moment with fluctuating awareness, why not build an ethic on one's spontaneous reactions in awareness of oneself and external conditions, and sidestep the whole problem of getting from "is" to "ought"? In discussing Chu Hsi, however, all that matters is that Western philosophy has assumed that we should get to that point of perfect objectivity and start again from zero to develop imperatives independent of spontaneity, while in the case of the Chinese tradition nothing obliges us to take it for granted, except in the most rationalizing schools, the Sophists and Later Mohists before the Han dynasty (206 B.C.–A.D. 220), that the ideal would even be conceivable. It is a commonplace that in all other schools reason is practical, confined within the same limits as it is with ourselves in the conduct of ordinary life; rationality does not, as in Western philosophy since the Greeks, expand until in theory it permeates universally, throughout all that is spontaneous even in the reasoner himself.

Might we think of Chinese philosophy as a tradition in which reason still functions inside spontaneous process (which is from our "Nature" and beyond it from "Heaven"), choosing between one tendency and another, but never except perhaps in a brief episode about 300 B.C., expanding to pull everything spontaneous within its range? Let us explore this possibility, putting aside the question whether it was the Chinese or ourselves who got off on the wrong foot. In the first place, it does seem to be a reasonable generalization about moral philosophizing in China that it starts from the spontaneous reaction. The terms *kan*[o] and *ying*,[p] so oddly similar to Pavlov's "stimulate" and "respond," are as prominent in Confucianism as in Taoism, from not later than the third century B.C. Confucians, unlike Taoists, discipline the response by rules, but the rules are to ensure that we are not moved inappropriately or too much or little. To quote what is for Neo-Confucians a crucial passage from the *Chung-yung*, "Before pleasure or anger, grief or joy, emerge, one speaks of the 'Mean'; when, emerging, all accord with measure, one speaks of 'Harmony.' The 'Mean' is the ultimate root of the world, 'Harmony' is the universal way of the world."[8] As for the rules that bring spontaneity into accord with measure, although there are words such as pre-verbal *tang*[q] that correspond to "ought," the tendency is to say not "One ought to do X" but "The gentleman/wise man/sage does X." If one wants to know whether the child's first rule of conduct would be expressed in the form "One ought not to overeat" or "Sensible people don't overeat," the answer is in the very first chapter of the *Analects:* "The gentleman in eating does not seek repletion."[9] The authority of the rule derives from the wisdom of the sage or the gentleman, who regularly behaves in this manner; what the man who knows in fact does, all who recognize knowledge as better than ignorance must recognize is better to do. It will be objected, perhaps, that the wise man knows not only what is but what ought to be, so that the appeal to wisdom smuggles in other imperatives surreptitiously. But that does not necessarily follow; on the argument we are pursuing, even knowing what he ought to do would be reducible to self-awareness as to how he is in fact spontaneously moved when most aware of his circumstances.

On this approach, the grounds for preferring one's unselfish to one's selfish reactions would have to be the claim that the wisest men, with the widest information, most balanced judgment, deepest understanding of mankind, *do* respond unselfishly. The issue for moral philosophy would be posed as the question why the man who knows responds to the misfortunes of others as he does to his own, and be answered by trying to show that each individual is in some sense one with others. Now it does appear that the Chinese tradition follows this line. The earliest formulation is perhaps the Sophist Hui Shih's[r] (380–305 B.C.) tenth thesis: "Love the myriad creatures indiscriminately; heaven and earth are one body."[10] The paradoxes in the preceding theses, which show that dividing leads to self-contradiction, are apparently intended as proofs that everything is one, so that the man who knows will respond to all with the same love that he feels for himself. The theme of oneness is continued in Taoism and in Neo-Confucianism, where Ch'eng Hao compares insensitivity to others to numbness in a member, individuals being like limbs of a single body.[11] By this analogy, to be selfish is to respond in ignorance of one's unity with others, as though ignoring injury to a numbed limb because one does not feel it. But in full awareness of the unity, one has only to trust to spontaneity. "Nothing in a gentleman's learning is as important as to be completely impartial towards everything, and respond in accordance with things as they come."[12]

Obviously I am in no position to demonstrate my grand generalization about a difference between China and the West within the space of this paper; in any case, the whole point of such generalizations is to open up stimulating prospects before finally sinking under the weight of criticisms and qualifications. However, at the risk of seeming to go a long way round before reaching Chu Hsi, I shall briefly try out the proposal on the period about 300 B.C., when the Later Mohists on the one hand and Chuang-tzu[s] (c. 369–c. 256 B.C.) on the other were carrying rationalism and antirationalism to their farthest points within the Chinese tradition. The Mohist ethic, which resembles Utilitarianism in testing all moral principles by their practical effects, is systematized in the *Canons* of the Later Mohists by deriving definitions of the moral terms directly or indirectly from *li*[t] 'benefit' and *hai*[u] 'harm,' themselves dependent on the undefined *yü*[v] 'desire' and *wu*[w] 'dislike.'[13] The procedure is similar to that by which the definition of the circle is derived by stages from the undefined *jo*[x] 'like' (distances from the center being alike), the likeness of objects called by the same name being the basis of the nominalist theory of naming in the *Canons*. From a couple of stray references to the circle as "known *beforehand*" (*hsien-chin*[y]) and to the good and the bad as "what the sage desires and dislikes *beforehand* on behalf of men" (*sheng-jen so hsien wei-jen yü wu*[z]), it appears that the Mohists were quite consciously treating such concepts as derivable a priori from those chosen as basic and unimpugnable.[14] In grounding their highly rationalized ethic in the actual desires and dislikes of men, the Mohists seem at first sight to provide an actual example of the confusion of "is" and "ought" for which Western Utilitarianism is criticized. Certainly it is the Mohists, if anyone, who came near enough to ourselves to make the same mistakes. But the *Canons* do not in fact use any normative verb comparable to "ought," and they prescribe the virtues not as what everyone desires but as what the *sage* desires on behalf of men. It seems then that even for the Mohists action begins from the spontaneity of desire, and the good is what the wisest do in fact desire, the value of choosing wisely between desires being taken as self-evident.

Turning now to Chuang-tzu, the great Taoist rejects all the grounds upon which Confucians and Mohists judge between good and bad, and recommends us to act without premeditation in accord with the Tao.[aa] It seems at first sight that in discarding all traditional imperatives he substitutes a new one, "Be spontaneous." However, can there be any such thing as a recommendation of spontaneity as such, simply to let things slide, rather than of one kind of spontaneity against another? Western romanticism extols intensity of spontaneous emotion, without regard for its distortions of reality by subjectivity; Taoism on the other hand insists on the clear-headed response when reflecting the situation objectively as though in a mirror. One might say that the Taoist agrees with the Confucian in assuming that action starts from spontaneity; but instead of laying down rules by which the wise man adjusts his spontaneity to due measure, he reduces wisdom itself to its essence, the dispassionate mirroring of things as they objectively are. The metaphor of the mirror, introduced in the "Inner Chapters" attributable to Chuang-tzu himself,[15] is most fully developed in one of the "Outer Chapters," "The Way of Heaven:"

> When the sage is still, it is not that he is still because he says to himself "It is good to be still"; he is still because none among the myriad things is sufficient to disturb his heart. If water is still, its clarity lights up the hairs of beard and eyebrows, its evenness is plumb with the carpenter's level: the greatest of craftsmen take their standard from it. If mere water clarifies when it is still, how much more the stillness of the quintessential-and-daemonic, the heart of the sage! It is the reflector of heaven and earth, the mirror of the myriad things.
>
> Emptiness and stillness, calm and indifference, quiescence, Doing Nothing, are the even level of heaven and earth, the utmost reach of the Way and the Power; therefore emperor, king, or sage finds rest in them. At rest he empties, emptying he is filled, and what fills him sorts itself out. Emptying he is still, in stillness he is moved, and when he moves he succeeds.[16]

Reflecting with perfect clarity, the sage allows himself to be moved; "and when he moves he succeeds." One might ask how success is judged unless in relation to an end approved by some standard. But that would be to miss the point. The Taoist sage has only the fluid goal to which he spontaneously inclines in his perfect awareness of the situation of the moment; and the only imperative needed for preferring it at that moment is "Mirror with perfect clarity."

In writings of the school of Chuang-tzu we find some of the earliest significant uses of the term *li* 'pattern' which long afterwards became central in Neo-Confucianism. The "Autumn floods" dialogue, of the third if not the second century B.C., which is perhaps the fullest and clearest of all expositions of Chuang-tzu's form of Taoism, at one point actually formulates the question that a reader sinking in its morass of scepticism and relativism will have been longing to ask, "If so, then what is there to value in the Tao?" The answer is at first sight disappointing: "The man who knows the Tao is sure to fathom the *li*, the man who fathoms the *li* is sure to be clear-sighted in weighing, the man who is clear-sighted in weighing will not use other things to his own harm."[17] One is tempted to ask by what standard the sage judges advantage and harm to himself, and to feel frustrated when the discourse almost at once meanders off into aphorisms about Heaven and man: "Heaven is within, man is without, and the Power (*te*[ab]) goes on residing in what is from Heaven." But this would be to lose track of a line of thought that has been fairly easy to follow up to this point. It has been assumed right from the start of this beautifully organized dialogue that one is already being moved by Heaven on a course of spontaneous change. In the preceding exchange, when the Lord of the River asked " 'on what final consideration am I to refuse or accept, prefer or discard?' " the seagod had answered by showing how to "sort out the *li* of the myriad things," and concluded by saying, " 'What shall we do? What shall we not do? It is inherent in everything that it will transform of itself.' "[18] The point is that, having sorted out the *li*, the patterns in which things are organized (which is the thinking that belongs to the realm of man), I have only to respond to them in their interrelations as I am prompted by Heaven from within. The "weighing" is like that of the child hesitating whether or not to eat another helping. Having grasped a *li*, the recurring pattern in affairs that excess regularly leads to nausea, he is moved by Heaven to stop eating. On the other hand, "One ought not to overeat" would presumably not be a *li* for the Taoist, as it would be for a Neo-Confucian. The patterns mentioned in the "Autumn Floods" that may be presumed to come under the heading of *li* include, for example, the relative positions of heaven and earth and the alternations of yin[ac] and yang[ad] (passive and active cosmic forces), rise and fall, birth and death; they do not include standards of conduct, which a Taoist denies in principle.

Coming at last to the Sung philosophy as perfected by Chu Hsi, it reinterprets traditional formulae by regrouping them around two concepts, which are both complex and coherent: on the one hand *li*, the universal pattern branching by division from the Supreme Ultimate (*T'ai-chi*[ae]), setting the lines along which things move; on the other *ch'i*,[af] the universal fluid out of which things condense and into which they dissolve, freely moving when fine or inert when coarse, active as the yang or passive as the yin. Inanimate things are immobilized by the density of their solidified *ch'i*, the animate vitalized by the light and pure circulating inside them; in man the activating *ch'i* at his center, from which all his behavior starts, attains a degree of tenuity as mind (*hsin*[ag]), which at its utmost ceases to be distinguishable from the patterned void that is pure *li*.

How far does Neo-Confucianism fit our proposal to treat Chinese ethical thinking as pursuit of the wisdom that imposes measure on spontaneity? We may note in the first place the fundamental importance for all Neo-Confucian schools of the famous sentence-sequence in the *Ta-hsüeh*[ah] *(Great Learning)* deriving good order in state, family, and person from "extending knowledge to the utmost" (*chih-chih*[ai]), itself dependent on that eternal crux *ke-wu*,[aj] understood by Chu Hsi as *chih-wu*[ak] 'arriving at the thing.' If we look for the imperative at the basis of the value system, it must still be "Know!" Knowing is identified with comprehension of the patterns that regularize things and events, their *li*:

> What is meant by "Extending knowledge to the utmost depends on arriving at the thing" is that the enterprise of extending to the utmost my own knowledge

depends on exhausting the *li* in the thing itself. The point is that man's mind never lacks the efficacy for knowing, and the things in the world are never without *li;* it is only because the *li* have not yet been exhausted that there are gaps in his knowledge. That is why the *Ta-hsüeh* starts its teaching by insisting that the learner, in all the things of the world themselves whatever they may be, proceed progressively from the *li* he already knows toward exhausting them all, seeking to reach the ultimate in them. When effort has been sustained for a long time, and quite suddenly I burst through to the interrelations (*kuan-t'ung*[al] 'threading together and permeating'), there will be nothing outside or inside the multitudinous things however coarse or fine that I shall not reach, and nothing in the total substance and universal function of my mind that will not be plain. This is what is meant by "arriving at the thing," this is what is meant by the utmost of knowledge.[19]

It is still assumed, however, as in earlier philosophy, that the knower is already in spontaneous interaction with other things. The familiar passage we quoted from the *Chung-yung* about the harmonious emission of the passions remains the classic account of the springs of human behavior and its adjustment to norms, and man's reactions to his circumstances are seen as belonging with physical interactions within the universal process of *kan-ying* 'stimulation and response.'

Ch'eng Hao said that "between heaven and earth there is nothing but a single stimulation and response"[20]—the point being that the alterations and transformations of yin and yang, the engendering and coming to completion of the myriad things, the interchanges of the true and the false, the end and start of enterprises, if from one side they are stimulation from the other they are response; turning in circles they alternate, which is why they go on forever.[21]

Although Chu Hsi insists on the importance of endeavor in extending knowledge, for him one does not truly know until one does spontaneously what one ought to do. "Spontaneity" (*tzu-jan*[am] 'being so of itself'), which for Taoists discredits learning, is for Chu Hsi the proof of success in learning.

In everything the sage's learning depends on the mind to exhaust the *li*, and accords with the *li* to respond to things, like the body employing the fingers. Its Way is smooth and everywhere accessible, its dwelling is broad and safe, its *li* are real and its exercise spontaneous.[22]

Why is it that I have to struggle before this lucid spontaneity is attainable? To the extent that I remain ignorant, the dense *ch'i* of my organism runs blindly in the broad channels of the *li* where it happens to be; but by moral training I refine my substance to greater transparency and penetrate into the finer veins of the universal pattern, so that my spontaneous reactions change as the rarified *ch'i* out of which the denser goes on being generated adjusts to newly perceived *li*. The assumption is that if I still fail to respond in the full light of my

knowledge, it is because a *li* has permeated just far enough to awaken a spontaneous inclination along its path but not yet to articulate the motions of the
organism as a whole. The varying permeability of the *ch'i* is the whole explanation of the ignorance of animals and the varying degrees of knowledge in man.

> Therefore in the generating of men and other things there is a difference of
> coarse and fine. Speaking in terms of the *ch'i* as one, both men and other things
> are generated by receiving this *ch'i*. Speaking in terms of the coarse and the fine,
> men get *ch'i* that is well adjusted and permeable, other things *ch'i* that is ill
> adjusted and impeding. Because man alone gets the well adjusted, the *li* in per-
> meating him are nowhere impeded; because other things get the ill adjusted, the
> *li* being impeded they know nothing. . . . But speaking in terms of man's own
> endowment, here too there is a difference of dull and bright, clear and murky.
> Therefore the highest in knowledge, who know from birth, are so constituted
> that the *ch'i* is clear, bright, pure, choice, and without a trace of the dull and
> murky. As for the next in degree, being secondary to the knowers from birth,
> they have to learn before they know, have to practice before they attain.[23]

To return to that implicit imperative "Know!" it is only when a *li* shows up
through the obstructing denseness of my *ch'i* that I truly know it. I do not genuinely know, however glibly I repeat the words, until I do spontaneously
react. Ch'eng Yi had a vivid illustration of this point.

> Genuine knowledge (*chen-chih*[an]) is different from everyday knowledge (*ch'ang-
> chih*[ao]). I once saw a farmer who had been mauled by a tiger. Someone said a tiger
> was mauling people; everyone was startled, but only the farmer had an expres-
> sion on his face different from the rest. That a tiger can maul people everyone
> knows, even a little boy, but they have never genuinely known; it is only genuine
> knowledge if it is like the farmer's. So when men go on doing what they know to
> be bad, they too have never genuinely known; if they did genuinely know,
> decidedly they would not do it.[24]

The importance to Chu Hsi of Chou Tun-yi's "Diagram of the Supreme Ultimate" (which the Ch'eng brothers had ignored) is as a plan for interrelating
the multiple *li*, showing how they ramify by binary division from one (the
Supreme Ultimate) to two (yin and yang), and then to four constellated
around a fifth in the middle (*wu-hsing*[ap] 'Five Phases'),[25] and so on to the ten
thousand things. To the extent that Neo-Confucians go into the detail of the
cosmic scheme, they retain the symmetries and correspondences of the traditional cosmology. The aspiration, as in the older systems, is to elucidate an
order in which the individual's spontaneous joy and sorrow, pleasure and
anger, the behavior of father and son, ruler and minister, the cycles of day and
night and the four seasons, are so organized as to avoid conflict and to
strengthen mutual support. In modern terms, this resembles not unification
by the explanatory-predictive laws of physics but rather by that man-oriented
coordination of ecology, biology, and psychology with which many people

nowadays seek the lines along which to harmonize themselves with community and with nature. The analysis of complex interrelations in these modern sciences and quasi sciences is of course a very recent achievement; in earlier thought, Western and Eastern, the interdependence of things is approachable only by laying out simple schemes that separate and put in sequence the conflicting (spring, summer, autumn, winter; Wood, Fire, Earth, Metal, Water) and juxtapose the mutually supportive (spring, wood, green, Benevolence [*jen*ᵃᑫ]; autumn, Metal, white, Duty [*yi*ᵃʳ]). The effect is to establish for each person both symmetries within which he fits and rhythms with which he is in step, implanting that assurance of belonging within a cosmos which modern science denies us. The assurance comes, as it does for ourselves in the case of belonging to a community (where however carefully one obeys the rules an involuntary gesture can mark one as an outsider), not simply from knowing what one ought to do, but from the harmony of one's own spontaneity with community and cosmos. Thus the prescription that the emperor wears green and pardons in spring, wears white and punishes in autumn, does not, as a Western moral philosopher might suppose, depend on a false logic combining feeble arguments from analogy with a gigantic leap from "is" to "ought." The emperor will spontaneously be most inclined to pardon in the mildness of spring, to punish in the chill of autumn, and the color of his robes is one of the signals alerting himself and the empire to this and other seasonal changes; if he breaks the rhythm it will be less easy for him to respond fully to both the conflicting pulls, to be both perfectly benevolent and perfectly dutiful.

Systems current since the Han had tried to build a cosmos upwards from rigid sets of countable units, twos, fours, fives, or more. The Ch'eng-Chu system, on the other hand, by working downwards from *li* as a whole, escapes dependence on these artificial simplifications and allows a more fluid approach to placing man inside a complex and dynamic order of changing interrelationships. It is, as Needham says, the culmination of what he calls the Chinese "philosophy of organism" (a description which, as Donald Munro has recently shown, had better not be used without the caveat that the Chinese metaphors for cosmic relations derive from the family much more than from the body and its organs).[26] Although Chu Hsi finds places in the ramifications of *li* for older classifications such as the Five Phases which the Ch'engs seldom find occasion to mention, even for him the only one crucial to his thinking is the basic binary division of yin and yang. Chu Hsi often reminds us that in the universal pattern it is largely a matter of convenience how one divides up and counts subpatterns.[27] Moreover, since *li* runs through a three-dimensional world of things condensing out of *ch'i*, it is itself conceived as a vast three-dimensional structure which looks different from different angles. In laying down the lines along which everything moves, it appears as the Way *(Tao)*; in that the lines are independent of my personal desires, it imposes itself on me as Heaven (*T'ien*ᵃˢ); as a pattern which from my own viewpoint spreads out from the subpattern of my own profoundest reactions, it appears as my own basic Nature (*hsing*ᵃᵗ). Looking down from the Supreme

Ultimate, the apex at which its branches join, it first divides as the Way of the first two diagrams of the *Book of Changes*, *ch'ien*[au] (heaven, male) and *k'un*[av] (earth, female), patterning the *ch'i* in its yang and yin phases; but from my own viewpoint, the major lines that connect me with the whole are the principles of conduct: Benevolence, Duty, Manners, Wisdom. Each person, peering into the vast web from his own little corner of it, may, if his *ch'i* is perfectly transparent, see all the way to the Supreme Ultimate at its farthest limits. In the words of our very first quotation from Chu Hsi,[28] he proceeds "from the *li* he already knows towards exhausting them all, seeking to reach the *ultimate* in them" (*chi* of *T'ai-chi* 'Supreme Ultimate'). To the question whether the Supreme Ultimate could belong to the Nature of everyone without being divided, Chu Hsi answers,

> It's just that at bottom it is only the single Supreme Ultimate, but each of the myriad things has an endowment; moreover, each in itself fully comprises the single Supreme Ultimate, just as there is only one moon in the sky, but when it is scattered in the rivers and lakes it is visible eveywhere. It can't be said that the moon has been divided.[29]

The conception of the universal structure of *li* as both pervading everything and potentially visible in its entirety from every viewpoint, everywhere discoverable by using its regularities to infer (*t'ui*[aw]) from the known to the unknown, enables Chu Hsi to give a coherent account of that unity of self and others that, we have suggested, has to be postulated in some form in any philosophical justification of morality that starts from spontaneity guided by an imperative to know.

> Ch'eng Hao's passage to the effect that from the "Hands and feet being unfeeling (*pu-jen*[ax])" of medical books one can get to the substance of Benevolence—drawing out its implications, the point he is making is that if Benevolence is the mind with which heaven and earth generate things, and which men and other things get (*te*[ay]) as their own mind, it follows that heaven and earth, men and other things, all without exception share this mind, and the mind's powers (*te*, 'capacity-to-get') never fail to interrelate (*kuan-t'ung*). Although, as heaven or as earth, as man or as another thing, each has its dissimilarities from the rest, in reality there is a single vein (*mo-lo*[az]) threading them together (*kuan*[ba]). Therefore if you can acknowledge this mind as embodied in yourself, and have the means to preserve and nurture it, the *li* in the mind will reach everywhere, and spontaneously (*tzu-jan*) you will love everyone. As soon as you have the least selfish desire obscuring it, you are broken off from the rest, and love fails to reach all. Therefore the callousness and ungenerosity in the world results simply from being blinkered and clogged up by selfish desires, so that one never recognizes the *li* by which one's own mind interrelates with the minds of heaven and earth and the myriad things.[30]

As an individual, I find from the beginning of consciousness regularities in my spontaneous reactions that belong to *li;* and with every advance in penetrating my turbid *ch'i* farther into the network of interrelations, the reactions themselves change. My subjective pursuit of the *li* to "extend knowledge to the utmost" can reach as far as the Supreme Ultimate, so that everything falls into place as interconnected, and down again into other branches to the *li* in other persons, so that I empathize their woes and respond from their viewpoints with compassion, shame, or reverence. This self-education, beginning in my own subjectivity, relates me to other subjective viewpoints, to the minds of other persons and things, and to that mysterious "mind of Heaven and Earth" (*t'ien-ti chih hsin*[bb]) mentioned in the *Book of Changes*,[31] which would be the final subject which sees everything as inside itself. If on the contrary I use a *li* simply as an objectivized abstraction, to explain and predict another person's behavior for purposes of my own, I arbitrarily exclude it from the subjectively experienced interrelations which guide my reactions; I cannot be said even genuinely to know it, since there can be no genuine knowledge without reacting like Ch'eng Yi's peasant mauled by the tiger or, to take another illustration that he borrows from the *Analects*,[32] "seeing evil as though you were dipping in hot water." In relation to the objectivity of Western science, we may see Chu Hsi as just as much a subjectivist as Lu Hsiang-shan (Liu Chiu-yüan,[bc] 1139–1193) and Wang Yang-ming (Wang Shou-jen,[bd] 1472–1529). He demands investigation of the *li* in external affairs rather than awakening to them by self-searching, but he denies that one has fully grasped them until they begin to show through one's progressively clarifying *ch'i* and make one react differently. That for Chu Hsi knowledge of the *li* in another person implies, to use English idioms, "putting oneself in his place," "seeing his point of view," may be illustrated from the comments in his *Lun-yü chi-chu*[be] (Collected commentaries on the *Analects*) on the last episode of *Analects* ch. 6.

Confucius: The Benevolent, wishing himself to stand helps others to stand, wishing himself to succeed helps others to succeed.

Chu Hsi: To use one's own case to arrive at the other man's belongs to the mind of the Benevolent. By observing it here in his own case, he can see the universal flow of Heaven's *li* and no longer be separated from it. There could be no more pointed description of the substance of Benevolence.

Confucius: Being able to pick an analogy close at hand may be called the secret of Benevolence.

Chu Hsi: Picking it close at hand in your own person, you find in what you desire yourself an analogy for what is in the other man, and know that what he desires will be the same. As for proceeding to extend what he desires to mankind, that is the practice of Consideration (*shu*[bf]) and the secret of Benevolence. If you make the effort here in yourself, you have the means to conquer the partiality of your human desires and keep intact the impartiality of your *li* from Heaven. [Chu Hsi continues by again quoting Ch'eng Hao.] "The Benevolent regards heaven and earth and the myriad things as one substance, so that nothing is not himself. If you can recognize them as yourself, which of them will be beyond your range? If you do not have them in yourself, of course they do not concern yourself, as when hands and feet are unfeeling *(pu-jen)*, and the *ch'i* has failed to circulate, so that they all cease to belong to oneself.[33]

In introducing a new conceptualization of knowledge as permeation of *ch'i* by *li*, it may seem that Neo-Confucians fail to distinguish within *li* the physical principles by which one explains and predicts and the moral principles on which one acts. I myself always supposed them confused on this point until I embarked on the present study. But if the Chinese assumption has been that "One ought to do X" is equivalent to "The wise man is spontaneously inclined to do X," we must change our angle of vision. Let us go back to our original example, of the child at the dinner table. He is moved to eat another helping, but then the regularity in the patterning of things by which overeating is followed by nausea bursts through his obscuring *ch'i*, and he is impelled in the opposite direction by the impulse to refrain. In so reacting in fuller knowledge, he is being spontaneously moved along another *li*, that the wise do not overeat. But it might be that even in foreseeing the consequences he still, because of unevenness in the quality of his *ch'i*, finds it hard to resist his greed. Then the new *li* imposes itself as the path he *ought* to follow, because not to do so is unwise. Formerly, when he was still ignorant of these two lines in the pattern of things, his dense *ch'i* blindly flowed in the channel of the first of them, so that he simply ate and vomited; but now that both permeate the finer *ch'i* out of which his coarser substance is being generated and vitalized, he reacts ahead, aware of the pattern of interrelations. On this analysis, there is no confusion in Neo-Confucian thought between physical and moral principles, which its terminology in any case clearly distinguishes as *so-yi jan chih li*[bg] (pattern by which something is so) and *tang-jan chih li*[bh] (pattern by which something should be so). "The wise man does not overeat" verbalizes the pattern as *so-yi jan chih li*, which at a banquet attended by Confucius might be used to explain or to predict his moderation; but for anyone who acknowledges the authority of "Be wise!" or "Know!" the pattern is also a *tang-jan chih li*, verbalizable as "Don't overeat."

So far our example has illustrated not morality but prudence. The next step will be for the wise child to discover that the same *li* runs through others and himself; all tend to vomit when they overeat and to eat more moderately when they know that. He now has two alternative courses, which in terms of the grand simplification we are trying out in this paper, are the Western and the Chinese.

Objectivizing, Western. He thinks of the knowing of a *li* as detachable from the reactions it patterns. Then he can know that everyone tends to avoid overeating when aware of the consequences, but as an objective fact, irrelevant to his actions unless combined with an imperative, in dealing with himself prudential ("Don't hurt yourself"), in dealing with others moral ("Don't stand by and let others hurt themselves").

Subjectivizing, Chinese. He thinks of the knowing of a *li* as inseparable from the reactions it patterns. Then in knowing that someone is eating too much he feels nausea and is moved to abstain or warn, the nausea being immediate if the eater is himself and empathetic if it is someone else. He can choose to abstain or to warn without applying any imperative to himself except "Know the *li*."

Either approach is self-consistent. What is not consistent is to apply the latter to oneself, or to oneself and those nearest to one, but the former to everyone else. That would be failure to "interrelate," self-separation from "the universal flow of Heaven's *li*." It may be seen from this analysis that Chu Hsi's parallel to St. Paul's "we are members one of another" is by no means a rhetorical appeal to sympathize with each other that is finally unsupported by the philosophy, as might perhaps be urged against Ch'eng Hao's striking analogy of callousness to paralysis of a limb. Chu Hsi's conception of the oneness of self and other as the foundation of morality is firmly rooted in the logical structure of his entire system.

We now arrive at last at Chu Hsi's theory of human nature. He recognizes that the term *hsing* 'Nature' is often applied to the individual's innate endowment of *ch'i*, both as pure, freely circulating and vitalizing, and in the dense, inert state in which it is specified as *chih*[bi] 'matter.' He distinguishes this endowment, which varies from person to person and may be good, mixed, or bad, by a term borrowed from Chang Tsai, *ch'i-chih chih hsing*[bj] (nature which is *ch'i* and matter). The basic nature (*pen-hsing*[bk]), on the other hand, is the *li* as it is progressively discovered inside oneself, starting from the pattern of one's own spontaneous reactions. One of the fullest expositions of the basic nature is in a letter to a pupil.

The nature is the substance of the Supreme Ultimate as a whole; it is fundamentally unsayable in terms of names. But it contains within it all the myriad *li*, of which the greatest of the arterial *li (kang-li*[bl] 'large-rope-of-net *li')* amount to four, which therefore have been given names, Benevolence, Duty, Manners, Wisdom (*jen yi li chih*[bm]).[34] The disciples of Confucius never said all there was to say about it; that no one did so before Mencius was because in the time of Confucius the principle *(li)* of the goodness of the nature was taken for granted, and even if they did not detail its ramifications (*t'iao*[bn]) there was nothing which needed explanation. By the time of Mencius heresies were teeming, and it was common to deem the nature bad. Mencius was alarmed that the principle remained unclear, and pondered how to clarify it. If he were merely to say that it is "the complete substance as a whole," he was afraid that it would seem like a steelyard without grading marks, a foot-measure without the inches, and would never be adequate to enlighten the world. So he made distinctions in speaking about it, splitting it up into four divisions, and the doctrine of the Four Beginnings (*ssu-tuan*[bo])[35] was established as a result. For before the emergence of the Four Outcomes, although in its quiescence it does not stir, of itself it has inside it ramifying *li*, of itself it has inside it a structure (*chien-chia*[bp] 'rooms and house-frame'), it is not that it is homogeneous with nothing in it at all. Therefore as soon as it is stimulated from outside it responds from within. If the occurrence of a child falling into a well stimulates, the *li* of Benevolence responds, and then [from among the Four Beginnings] a compassionate mind is manifested; if the occurrence of passing through shrine or court stimulates, the *li* of Manners responds, and a reverent mind is manifested. The point is that the multitudinous *li* are wholly at our disposal from inside it, every one of them clearly distinct. Hence they respond as they are stimulated by whatever they happen on outside, with the consequence that when the Four Beginnings emerge each is differently expressed on the surface. This is why Mencius breaks up into four, in order to show scholars that, if they know that inside the complete substance as a whole there is such a variety of ramifications, the goodness of the nature becomes evident.

But before the Four Beginnings emerge, what we called "the complete substance as a whole" has no describable sound or smell, no visible shape or image; how do we know that it has such a variety of ramifications? Because, when it comes to the verifiability of a certain *li*, it can be verified in the same way through the emergence itself. Things must all have roots to them, and although the *li* in the nature are without shape, the actual emergence is fully verifiable. Hence through someone's compassion one knows for sure that there is Benevolence in him, through his shame that there is Duty in him, through his reverence that there are Manners in him, through his approval and disapproval that there is Wisdom in him. Supposing that at the root of it there were not this *li* within, how could there be this Beginning outside? Through his having the Beginning on the outside one knows for sure that he has the *li* within, without possibility of deception. Hence Mencius said, "As far as the passions are concerned, they have the possibility of becoming good; that is what is meant by its being good,"[36] which shows that when Mencius speaks of the goodness of the nature it is simply that he knows it by tracing it to the source by going back through the passions.[37]

This passage more than once mentions the goodness of human nature as itself a *li*, in which cases we translate by "principle." But "principle" as a regular equivalent[38] throughout would get us into difficulties when Chu Hsi refers to *li* as stimulated and responding. Even "pattern" would be inadequate, since what is stimulated and responding must be, not abstracted pattern, but patterned *ch'i* in its ultimate purity. Among Chu Hsi's regular assumptions are that *li* is not detachable from *ch'i*, that there is no void other than the perfectly rarified *ch'i* out of which the solid condenses and into which it dissolves, and that the finer the *ch'i* the more delicately it stimulates and responds. These assumptions explain why he everywhere treats the passions as disturbances of the nature (how would a principle be disturbed?), how he can accept without demur the statement in Chou Tun-yi's "Explanation of the Diagram of the Supreme Ultimate"[39] that the Supreme Ultimate (which for himself is *li*) generates the yin and yang (which are *ch'i*), and why Neo-Confucians in general tend to be vague or inconsistent as to whether the mind and the passions, which are of a high degree of tenuity, should be classed as *li* or as *ch'i*.[40] Here similarly the nature, which is *li*, responds as the Four Beginnings, passions (*ch'ing*[bq]), which in showing outwardly enable us to infer the presence of the corresponding *li* inside the man. We must think of them as generated in response to the stimulating occurrence by the finest *ch'i* inside the man, so that in condensing out of it they are structured by its distinctive pattern, which in the case of compassion will be Benevolence, of shame Duty, of reverence Manners, of approval and disapproval Wisdom. It is this structured tenuity, in which Benevolence and the rest are the main lines leading outward from self to the rest of the universal pattern, which is man's nature.

Let us now try to identify that "paradigm-shift" by which the Ch'eng-Chu doctrine established itself as the definitive Chinese solution of the problem of human nature. Historically, the creative moment was in the thought of Ch'eng Yi, who reinterpreted the problem in terms of *li* while his brother Ch'eng Hao stayed stuck in confusions and contradictions inherited from the older scheme of thought.[41] Earlier thinkers had understood nature as the spontaneous tendency of human reactions, and had wandered round in circles without reaching a formula that would reconcile its derivation from Heaven with the demand for morality. As far as spontaneous tendency is concerned, Ch'eng Yi and Chu Hsi abandon the search for such a formula, and admit the simple fact that individuals have natures that are mixtures of all degrees of good and bad. "Nature" in that sense, however, is the constitution of an individual's *ch'i*, Chang Tsai's "nature which is *ch'i* and matter." Behind it is the basic nature, the structural pattern of human reactions in general, their *li*. But man is a being whose reactions change with knowledge; the pattern of each person's own reactions is just a corner of the universal pattern, which enters his knowledge and modifies his reactions from selfish to impartial to the extent that he succeeds in penetrating the obscuring cloud of his *ch'i* to win a comprehensive view of the whole. The decisive novelty in the new conceptual scheme is the equation of knowledge with permeation of the *ch'i* by *li*. "Know!" we have argued, is the starting point of Chinese ethical thinking, the ultimately unchallengeable imperative, imposing only that obligation to recognize things as they are without which we cannot live. Then from the permeability of *ch'i* by *li* as the first good it follows that reacting along the pattern that from my own viewpoint is my nature will also be good, and that the unselfishness that characterizes it when you "extend knowledge to the utmost" will be good as well. At the same time the varying permeability of people's *ch'i* explains why the spontaneous tendency of their reactions is so often bad. It would still have been possible to decide, with Su Shih and Hu Hung, that "good" is not properly applicable to *li* or nature, only to action in accordance with them. But that is a sophisticated variation on the Mencian theory. With the reorganization of the traditional concepts around the poles of *li* and *ch'i*, is any other than a basically Mencian solution possible?

Notes

1. *Book of Mencius*, 6A:6.

2. *Han Ch'ang-li chi*[br] [Collected writings of Han Yü], (Kuo-hsueh chi-pen ts'ung-shu[bs] [Basic Sinological series] ed.), 3:64–65; *Li Wen-kung chi*[bt] [Collected writings of

Li Ao], (SPTK ed.), ch. 2; *Fan-ch'uan wen-chi*[bu] [Collected literary writings of Tu Mu], (SPTK ed.), 6:11b–12b.

3. *T'ung-shu*, ch.7. Chu Hsi's comment that Chou Tun-yi means by "Nature" the endowment of *ch'i* assumes his own distinction between the basic nature and the "nature which is *ch'i* and matter," already made by Chang Tsai and Ch'eng Yi, but not yet attested in the writings of Chou Tun-yi.

4. Cf. A. C. Graham, *Two Chinese Philosophers: Ch'eng Ming-tao*[bv] and *Ch'eng Yi-ch'uan*[bw] (London: Lund Humphries, 1958), pp. 45–47, 131–140, for the evidence that the early Neo-Confucians were not committed to the Mencian position. For Su Shih and Hu Hung, see *Su-shih yi-chuan*[bx] [Su's commentary on the *Book of Changes*], (*Ts'ung-shu chi-ch'eng*[by] ed.), pp. 159, l. 13 and 160, l. 6; *Hu-tzu chih-yen*[bz] [Hu Hung being knowledgeable with words], (Yüeh-ya-t'ang ts'ung-shu[ca] ed.), *Yi-yi*[cb] [Questions raised] p. 7b, ll. 4–8.

5. The use of "principle" for *li* in *Two Chinese Philosophers* has considerable disadvantages. "Principle" suggests a truth formulated in words in order to make deductions, while *li* suggests rather a pattern running through things, even sharing their three dimensions, and variously describable in words. In more recent translations, when having to choose an equivalent for *li* I have preferred "pattern."

6. *The Structure of Scientific Revolutions* (Chicago: University of Chicago Press, 1962).

7. *The Language of Morals* (Oxford: Oxford University Press, 1952), Vol. I, ch. 3, p. 2.

8. James Legge, *The Chinese Classics* (Oxford: Oxford University Press, 1893), The *Doctrine of the Mean*, ch. 1, pp. 384–385.

9. *Analects*, 1:14.

10. *Chuang-tzu* [Harvard-Yenching sinological index series], p. 93, l. 73–74.

11. *Ho-nan Ch'eng-shih yi-shu*[cc] [Book of remains of the Ch'engs], (Kuo-hsüeh chi-pen ts'ung-shu ed.), pp. 15, ll. 5–7; 34, l. 2; 81, ll. 1–4; 132, ll. 11–14.

12. Ch'eng Hao, "Ting-hsing shu"[cd] [Letter on stabilizing the nature], in *Ming-tao wen-chu*[ce] [Collected literary writings of Ch'eng Hao], ch. 3.

13. I have argued this claim in *Later Mohist Logic, Ethics and Science* (Hong Kong and London: Chinese University of Hong Kong Press, 1978), pp. 47–50. It may be noticed that I then assumed that the Mohist ethic is open to the objection that it "confused value with the psychological fact of desire" (p. 52), wrongly as it now appears.

14. *Later Mohist Logic*, pp. 57–58, 188–189.

15. *Chuang-tzu*, ch. 21, p. 7, ll. 32–33. I have tried out the present approach to Chuang-tzu in "Taoist Spontaneity and the Dichotomy of 'Is' and 'Ought' " in Victor H. Mair, ed., *Experimental Essays on Chuang-tzu* (Honolulu: University of Hawaii Press, 1983).

16. *Ibid.*, ch. 13, p. 33, ll. 2–6.

17. *Ibid.*, ch. 17, p. 44, l. 48.

18. *Ibid.*, ch. 17, p. 44, l. 47.

19. *Ta-hsüeh chang-chü*[cf] [Commentary on the *Great Learning*], on *ke-wu*.

20. *Ho-nan Ch'eng-shih yi-shu*, ch. 15, p. 168, l. 1, from a chapter attributable rather to Ch'eng Yi (*Two Chinese Philosophers*, 142).

21. *Chu-tzu yü-lei*[cg] [Classified conversations of Master Chu] (1872 ed.), 95:23a.

22. "Kuan-hsin shuo"[ch] [Explanation of observing the mind], in *Chu-tzu wen-chi*[ci] [Collection of literary works of Master Chu], (SPPY ed. entitled *Chu-tzu ta-ch'üan*[cj] [Complete collection of Chu Hsi]), 67:19b.

23. *Chu-tzu yü-lei*, 4:10b.

24. *Ho-nan Ch'eng-shih yi-shu*, 16:2-4.

25. The *wu-hsing*, traditionally translated "Five Elements" (Wood, Fire, Earth, Metal, Water), serve for explaining cyclic changes rather than physical constitution; I therefore follow Nathan Sivin in preferring as English equivalent "Five Phases."

26. Joseph Needham, *Science and Civilisation in China*, Vol. II (Cambridge: Cambridge University Press, 1956), p. 465*ff.*; Donald J. Munro, "The Family Network and the Stream of Water: Picturing Persons in Sung Confucianism," paper delivered at the Individualism and Wholism Conference, Breckinridge Center, York, Maine, June 24-29, 1981.

27. Cf. our last quotation from Chu Hsi below, and *Two Chinese Philosophers*, pp. 57-58.

28. See above, n. 19.

29. *Chu-tzu yü-lei*, 94:41b.

30. *Ibid.*, 95:10a.

31. *Book of Changes*, commentary on the twenty-fourth hexagram *fu*[ck] (to return).

32. *Ho-nan Ch'eng-shih yi-shu*, p. 163, l. 1. Cf. *Analects*, 16:11.

33. *Ssu-shu chang-chü chi-chu*[cl] [Collected commentaries on the Four Books], commenting on the *Analects*, 6:28.

34. *Book of Mencius*, 2A:6.

35. The "Four Beginnings" (*Mencius* 2A:6) are the four emotions (compassion, shame, deference, approval/disapproval) corresponding to the virtues Benevolence, Duty, Manners, and Wisdom. Chu Hsi understands them as the "beginnings" in perceptible behavior from which one traces the virtues that lie behind them.

36. *Book of Mencius*, 6A:6.

37. *Chu-tzu wen-chi*, 58:21a-22b, second letter to Ch'en Ch'i-chih (Ch'en Chih[cm]).

38. See above, n. 5.

39. *Chou-tzu ch'üan-shu*[cn] [Complete works of Chou-Tun-yi], ch. 1.

40. I failed to appreciate this point in *Two Chinese Philosophers*, where I supposed that the Sung philosophers were confused by difficulties in imposing the dualism of *li* and *ch'i* on to older concepts (*Two Chinese Philosophers*, pp. 50-53, 64-66, 162-164). This may be true to some extent of Ch'eng Yi (who did not identify *li* with the Supreme Ultimate), but Chu Hsi's application of the dichotomy now seems to be consistent even in these marginal cases.

41. Cf. the accounts of the theories of human nature of the two Ch'eng brothers in *Two Chinese Philosophers*, pp. 44-60, 131-140.

Glossary

[a] 中庸	[i] 程顥	[q] 當
[b] 荀子	[j] 蘇軾	[r] 惠施
[c] 揚雄	[k] 胡宏	[s] 莊子
[d] 韓愈	[l] 程頤	[t] 利
[e] 李翱	[m] 理	[u] 害
[f] 杜牧	[n] 程朱	[v] 欲
[g] 周敦頤	[o] 感應	[w] 惡
[h] 張載	[p] 應	[x] 若

y 先知

z 聖人所先為人欲惡

aa 道

ab 德

ac 陰陽

ad 太極

ae 氣

af 心

ag 大學

ah 致知

ai 格物

aj 至物

ak 貫通

al 自然

am 真知

an 常知

ao 五行

ap 仁

aq 義

ar 天

as 性

at 乾

av 坤

aw 推

ax 不仁

ay 得

az 脈絡

ba 貫

bb 天地之心

bc 陸象山九淵

bd 王陽明守仁

be 論語集註

bf 恕

bg 所以然之理

bh 當然之理

bi 質

bj 氣質之性

bk 本性

bl 綱理

bm 仁義禮智

bn 條

bo 四端

bp 間架

bq 情

br 韓昌黎集

bs 國學基本叢書

bt 李文公集

bu 樊川文集

bv 程明道

bw 程伊川

bx 蘇氏易傳

by 叢書集成

bz 胡子知言

ca 粵雅堂叢書

cb 疑義

cc 河南程氏遺書

cd 定性書

ce 明道文集

cf 大學章句

cg 朱子語類

ch 觀心說

ci 朱子文集

cj 朱子大全

ck 復

cl 四書章句集註

cm 陳器之埴

cn 周子全書

11

The System of
Chu Hsi's Philosophy

Tomoeda Ryūtarō

WHAT IS THE SYSTEM of Chu Hsi's philosophy? In this essay I shall try to elucidate its outline by reexamining my past studies.

The Ground-providing Principle

At forty years of age, Chu Hsi established his theory of "diffusion and convergence (*i-fa wei-fa*[a]) of mind," and then started writing a commentary on the "Explanation of the Diagram of the Great Ultimate," which he completed at the age of forty-four.[1] Tracing the process of his theoretical development, we see that he first asserted the identity of man and nature, and later came to recognize that they are both controlled by the same principle of *wu-chi erh t'ai-chi*[b] (the Ultimate of Nonbeing and also the Great Ultimate). In a letter to Wu I (Wu Hui-shu,[c] 1129–1177) he states, "Change (*i*[d]) means transformation, denoting movement-quiescence and diffusion-convergence. *T'ai-chi* (Great Ultimate) is the principle of movement-quiescence and diffusion-convergence."[2]

The *T'ai-chi* controls the tranquillity of the passive principle (*yin-ching*[e]) and the activity of the active principle (*yang-tung*[f]) of nature and the *i-fa wei-fa* of the human mind. It is the ground-providing principle of man and nature which is maintained orderly and harmoniously. Elucidating Chou Tun-i's (Chou Lien-ch'i,[g] 1017–1073) concept of *wu-chi erh t'ai-chi*, Chu Hsi states, "The operation of Heaven is devoid of sound or smell. It is indeed the pivot (*shu-niu*[h]) of creation and the ground (*ken-ti*[i]) of everything."[3]

Shu-niu means a central point on which something turns; *ken-ti* means a ground, basis, or foundation. In the *Chu Tzu yü-lei*[j] (Classified conversations of Master Chu), Chu Hsi said that the heavenly body was rounding the line of the South and North poles, and so he called that line "a pivot of heaven"[4] and in the *Lun-yü chi-chu*[k] (Collected commentaries on the *Analects*), he called the North pole (*pei-ch'en*[l]) "a pivot of heaven."[5]

I think that the heavenly body cannot be born from the pivot of heaven. So ether (*ch'i*[m] 'material force'), yin yang[n] (passive and active cosmic forces), and everything cannot be formed from the principle of the Great Ultimate. The phrase "the pivot of creation and the ground of everything" shows that the Great Ultimate is neither nil nor nonbeing, but rather the pivot of heaven and earth and the ground of different species in the world of man and other creatures.

The intention of Chu Hsi is not to distinguish the principle that controls man as *sollen* (becoming) and the principle that controls nature as *sein* (being). For Chu Hsi, the Great Ultimate or principle is devoid of volition, plan, or creative power, being a pure, empty, and vast world, but *ch'i* 'ether' has a function of condensation and production.[6] The principle of *wu-chi erh t'ai-chi* itself is not a fixed entity but is rather indefinite. In his "Commentary on the 'Explanation of the Diagram of the Great Ultimate' " (*T'ai chi-t'u chieh*[o]) Chu Hsi states, "*Wu-chi erh t'ai-chi* is the substance with which yin[p] remains quiet and yang[q] moves, but it cannot exist separately from yin yang. The Great Ultimate points to the entity of yin yang and is expressed in conformity with yin yang but is not mixed with yin yang."[7] I think Chu Hsi used the phrase *wu-chi erh t'ai-chi* to point out the ground and pivot of the actual world of yin yang, and so it is undoubtedly a misunderstanding for Lo Ch'in-shun[8] (Lo Cheng-an,[r] 1465–1547) and Tai Chen[9] (Tai Tung-yüan,[s] 1723–1777) to regard it as one thing which exists before yin yang.

Chu Hsi said in a poem,

> Yin and yang never cease to function,
> Chill and heat replace each other,
> One principle (*li*[t]) harmoniously controls,
> A principle not obscure but clear.[10]

> I look on the changing movement of yin and yang,
> Up and down in heaven and earth.
> Looking behind, there is no beginning.
> Looking ahead, there is no ending.
> The finest principle exists here,
> The present is eternal.[11]

The Great Ultimate is one principle, is the finest principle in yin yang and chill-heat, and is a pivot of the actual world. The present world has the finest pivot and so it is eternal. In the poem, Chu Hsi does not say that principle produces yin yang and the chill or heat.

In the postscript of his "Commentary on the 'Explanation of the Diagram of the Great Ultimate' " Chu Hsi states,

We surely cannot say there are two principles between yin yang and the Great Ultimate, but the Great Ultimate has no shape and yin yang has ether. Therefore there is a difference between the metaphysical and the physical.[12] When we talk about principle, we express substance first and function second, because when substance is mentioned, the principle of function is inherent in it. That is why substance and function have the same origin. When we talk about affairs, we express phenomenon first and noumenon second, because when phenomenon is mentioned, we can find the substance of principle inherent there. That is why there is no gap between phenomenon and noumenon.[13]

There is a dialectic relationship between the Great Ultimate and yin yang, and principle and ether are neither separate nor mixed, neither one nor two. It is sure that there is no one thing that precedes yin yang, ether, and affairs. This postscript was written when he was forty-four years old; perhaps the poem was written at about the same time.

Chu Hsi's theory of the Great Ultimate became clear in his letters to the Lu[u] brothers. When he was fifty-seven years old, he sent a letter to Lu Chiu-shao (Lu So-shan,[v] *fl.* 1150) stating, "Unless the term 'the Ultimate of Non-being' *(wu-chi)* is used, the Great Ultimate will lose its qualification as the basic principle of myriad beings and become merely one of them. If the expression *t'ai-chi* is not used, *wu-chi* will be reduced to naught and will not be able to serve as the basic principle of all being."[14]

The characteristics of the ground-providing principle cannot be described without using the five characters *wu-chi erh t'ai-chi. Wu-chi* represents the all-embracing and transcendent aspect of the ground-providing principle, while *t'ai-chi* shows its ground-providing aspect. Since principle is indefinite and yet definite, it is able to embrace all beings and to provide a firm ground for them. Thus Chu Hsi understood the meaning of *wu-chi erh t'ai-chi*. It was necessary for Chu Hsi in defining the character of the ground-providing principle to use the expression *wu-chi erh t'ai-chi.*

At fifty-nine years of age Chu Hsi sent a letter to Lu Chiu-yüan (Lu Hsiang-shan,[w] 1139–1193), younger brother of Chiu-shao, stating, "Why did Master Chou use the term 'the Ultimate of Nonbeing'? It is because the Great Ultimate has no place or shape, exists where there is nothing and where there is something, is both inside and outside of yin yang, is in the whole existence, and has neither sound, nor smell, nor shadow originally."[15] In contrast to yin yang, the Great Ultimate is transcendent and immanent. This means there is a dialectic relationship between the Great Ultimate (principle) and yin yang. It is impossible that the Great Ultimate produces yin yang and all things. It is not a theory that yin yang and every thing emanate from the Great Ultimate, but a structural theory of the Great Ultimate and yin yang.

The principle of the Great Ultimate, according to the Lu brothers, is contained in the actual world which is described as being "within shapes" *(hsing-erh-hsia)*, and it is devoid of the power to transcend the actual world. Chu Hsi, on the other hand, postulated the ground-providing principle as an entity pertaining to the metaphysical world which is described as being "above shape" *(hsing-erh-shang)*, which provides ground for the world "within shapes."

When compared with the concept of the Great Ultimate of the Lu brothers, the character of Chu Hsi's *wu-chi erh t'ai-chi* becomes clear.

Nature

How have heaven, earth, and nature been formed? How is the nonexistent ground-providing principle manifested in them? Chu Hsi regarded the original state of heaven, earth, and nature as a flux of ether, which is an endless action of ether characterized by the cycle of active and passive yin and yang and cold and heat. To him, the generation of heaven, earth, and nature was entirely due to the movement and the condensation of such ether. Whereas ether has a function of condensation and production, principle is devoid of such a material function.

Principle manifests itself on the operation of ether as the latter flows up and down and conglomerates. When expressed in terms of the cycle of the four seasons of the year, there are the ether of Wood of spring, the ether of Fire of summer, the ether of Metal of autumn, and the ether of Water of winter; their principles are the principle of Origination (*yüan*[x]), the principle of Flourish (*heng*[y]), the principle of Advantage (*li*[z]), and the principle of Firmness (*chen*[aa]). The indefinite ground-providing principle displays itself in the natural world of four seasons corresponding to Origination, Flourish, Advantage, and Firmness.[16]

Let us see Chu Hsi's own views according to the description in the *Classified Conversations of Master Chu:*

> In the beginning of heaven and earth, there existed only the yin ether and the yang ether. This ether underwent rotary movement. As its speed increased, a great deal of sediment was sealed inside, and having no place to go, the sediment came to form the earth at the center. The clearer part of ether, on the other hand, came to form the sky, sun, moon, and stars. Staying outside of the earth, they perpetually go round it. The earth, lying at the center, does not move. Nevertheless, it does not lie under heaven.[17]

Although this view of Chu Hsi was greatly influenced by Chang Tsai (Chang Heng-ch'ü,[ab] 1020–1077), it is characteristic in that he propounds a kind of nebular hypothesis by maintaining the rotation of the earth and centripetal force. He further states,

> In the beginning of heaven and earth, when they were still undifferentiated and in state of chaos, there were only water and fire. Presumably the part where the sediments from water piled up came to form the earth. If one climbs to a high spot and views the mountains, they invariably represent the form of waves, which undoubtedly suggest that the water had drifted in this way. However, we do not know when solidification of earth took place. At first it was exceedingly soft whereas later it came to be solidified.[18]

This image of the beginning of heaven and earth conceived by Chu Hsi was exceedingly vivid. He thought that the earth drifted in the center while water surrounded it and its outskirts conjoined with heaven. According to him, the only reason why the earth stays in the center without falling is that the whole sky surrounding it is constantly rotating. Chu Hsi further compared the celestial sphere to two bowls joining together, calling the joint the red path (*ch'ih-tao*[ac] 'equator') and the path of the sun the yellow path (*huang-tao*[ad]). Moreover, heaven was thought to rotate with both the South and North poles as axes.[19]

Furthermore, Chu Hsi calculated in detail the movements of the sun, moon, and fixed stars, and supported the theory of seven intercalary months in nineteen years. The formulas of calculation are shown in Figure 1.

Chu Hsi also made detailed observations on the waxing and waning of the moon by adopting Shen Kuo's[ae] (1029–1093) theory, touching also on the problem of solar and lunar eclipses.[21]

In a letter to Ts'ai Yüan (Ts'ai Po-ching,[af] 1156–1236), Chu Hsi virtually devised a planetarium.

Open holes on a large globe so as to make them look like stars, and cut the part of the globe that hides those stars (the portion inside a circle drawn with a radius at

FIGURE I

$$365 \frac{1}{4} = 365 \frac{235}{940}$$ 1 rotation of the sun (1 solar year)

$$365 \frac{1}{4} \div 12 \frac{7}{19} = 29 \frac{499}{940}$$ 1 rotation of the moon (1 lunar year)

$$29 \frac{499}{940} \times 12 = 354 \frac{348}{940}$$ 1 rotation of the moon × 12 (1 lunar year)

$$365 \frac{235}{940} - 354 \frac{348}{940} = 10 \frac{827}{940}$$ intercalary days

$$10 \frac{827}{940} \times 19 = 206 \frac{673}{940}$$ intercalary days in 19 years

$$206 \frac{673}{940} \div 29 \frac{499}{940} = 7$$ 7 intercalary months in 19 years[20]

36° from the South Pole) like the mouth of an earthen pot. Then attach a short axis to the North Pole to make the globe rotate and a short rod on the north side of the South Pole to sustain the mouth of the pot. Finally, place a four-legged ladder at the mouth, and entering inside the globe, lay a board at the end of the ladder horizontally to the north and look up at the holes on the wall of the globe and they are opened in such a way as to resemble the actual stars.[22]

As it is evident from the above, Chu Hsi clearly perceived that movements of the celestial body maintained order and harmony according to perpetual principles and laws, which are nothing but the manifestation of the ground-providing principle of the Great Ultimate. Precisely because of its indefinite character, it manifests itself as the principle that gives order to the natural world. Chu Hsi defined the ground-providing principle of the Great Ultimate as *so-i-jan chih ku*[ag] (the basic principle of all things and their laws) and perpetual principles and laws as *so-tang-jan chih tse*[ah] (the principle that makes things what they should be). The latter, according to Chu Hsi, is manifested in the human as well as the natural world.

Man

How did man come to exist, and what form of existence does he assume? Chu Hsi maintained that man was first formed by evolutions of the ether, but once formed, he propagates generation after generation in the same image by means of germs.[23]

Man is endowed with the ground-providing principle of the Great Ultimate at the time he is born into the world. This principle becomes his nature, determining his strength (*chien*[ai]), obedience (*shun*[aj]), humanity (*jen*[ak]), righteousness (*i*[al]), propriety (*li*[am]), and wisdom (*chih*[an]). The ether of man conglomerates into his body equipped with organs, with the distinction of male and female, and possessing various feelings such as commiseration, shame and dislike, deference and compliance, right and wrong, pleasure, anger, sorrow, joy. Man becomes a sage or a mediocrity depending on whether the ether he receives at the time of his birth is pure or impure.[24]

Metaphorically speaking, just as a gemstone in clear water glitters, whereas that in contaminated water is invisible, man's nature, although the same when endowed, differs according to the disposition of those who receive it. The qualities of humanity, righteousness, propriety, and wisdom, for instance, are properly manifested in some people and not directly in others. This is what causes man either to be a sage or a mediocrity.[25]

As we have seen before, the movements of celestial bodies are exceedingly regular, conforming to perpetual principles and laws. Even natural phenomena of heaven and earth, however, are not always reliable, occasionally violating "the principle that makes things what they should be" in minute points as exemplified by the casualties and damages wrought by natural disasters such as an unusual change of weather.[26] This being the case, although saints and sages may fully master and practice "the principle that makes man what he should be," mediocrities are always exposed to the danger of violating that principle. That is, however, by no means the proper state in which man should be.

Chu Hsi therefore seeks "the principle that makes man what he should be," and concludes that "the principle that makes things what they should be" manifested in the natural world is also applicable to the human world. For instance, just as the principles of Origination, Flourish, Advantage, and Firmness correspond to the ethers of Wood, Fire, Metal, and Water in nature, so do the nature of humanity, righteousness, propriety, and wisdom correspond to the feelings of commiseration, shame and dislike, deference and compliance, and right and wrong in man.[27] Here, too, we discover that nature and man can be understood according to the same pattern. Thus, humanity, righteousness, propriety, and wisdom are the fundamentals of the principle that makes man what he should be. Besides these, however, there are certain subsidiary principles such as clearness in seeing, distinctiveness in listening, respectfulness in appearance, agreeableness in speech, as well as righteousness between ruler and the ruled, affection between parent and child, attention to separate functions between husband and wife, order among seniors and juniors, and truthfulness among friends. These are all regarded as the principle that makes man what he should be. There are, of course, subsidiary principles governing daily conduct such as dressing, eating, acting, and resting.[28]

The principles that make man what he should be, which include humanity, righteousness, propriety, wisdom, and so on, are the key to maintaining order and harmony in the human world. If so, "the principle that makes man what he should be" must have a basis that transcends human temper, feeling, and desires. That is the nature of man, which unifies all the principles that makes man what he should be, and this nature, understood metaphysically, is the Great Ultimate. The indefinite ground-providing principle of the Great Ultimate is manifested in the human world as the principle that makes man what he should be such as humanity, righteousness, propriety, wisdom, and so on.

If man's nature and emotions were always in harmony, cultivation of mind would be unnecessary. In reality, however, they frequently contradict each other. Thus, the method of cultivating the human mind is to restore harmony between human nature and emotion by overcoming all the contradictions between them.

What is to be noted here, however, is that the consciousness of original sin as seen in Christianity is missing in Chu Hsi's theory or Chinese thought in general. Furthermore, there is no gap between man and the ground-providing principle of the Great Ultimate as there is in the case between man and God in Christianity. It is not that a divine being called the Great Ultimate creates man and the myriad beings.

Since the ground-providing principle of the Great Ultimate, when the emotions of pleasure, anger, sorrow, and joy are not activated, is inherent in the human mind as nature, it is sufficient, in cultivating one's mind, just to grasp and hold this nature without exercising the senses. Furthermore, when the emotions are about to be activated, it is necessary to consider consciously and discern whether such emotional movement complies with the principle that makes man what he should be. Although man's nature and emotions may conflict with each other at this stage, man can ultimately achieve harmony through the cultivation of his mind.[29]

Are grasping, holding, and discerning sufficient? In order to make the emotions conform with one's nature, it is necessary to know the criteria for discerning the good from evil. Hence, Chu Hsi, interpreting the investigation of things (*ko-wu*[ao]) in the *Great Learning* as the investigation of principles (*ch'iung-li*[ap]), proposed the learning of *ch'iung-li* as a science to study the principles; this was to be done objectively by reviewing the knowledge thereof.[30] Such pursuit of the principles of all things and matters through reflection and discernment, which has a scientific character, was a powerful weapon against the Meditation School of Buddhism since such a principle was unknown to them.

It was probably impossible for Chu Hsi, as a government official, to carry out his official duties without this method of investigation of principle through reflection and discernment. His accomplishments in establishing granaries for famine relief, setting a pattern for cultivating paddy rice, organizing measures against famine, formulating a plan for land reform, and recommending various measures in domestic and foreign affairs were closely related to the science of the investigation of principle.[31] As a scholar, his spirit of the investigation of principle was an essential element in his study of the Classics.

We must investigate the principles that make things what they should be in the daily world of man and nature; such investigation belongs to the reflective cognizance of our mind. Then we can grasp the basic principle of all things and their laws; such understanding belongs to the enlightenment of our mind. At this point, we attain a pure, empty and vast world which is filled with the Great Ultimate or ground-providing principle. In his epistemology, Chu Hsi propagated the ground-providing principle as the basic principle of all things and their laws, while in his ontology, he propagated it as the Great Ultimate. The Great Ultimate or the basic principle of all things and their laws manifests itself in all things and matters as the principles that make things what they should be. This is the dual character of principle *(li)* in Chu Hsi's philosophy. Many scholars, including Lo Ch'in-shun, Wang Yang-ming[aq] (Wang Shou-jen, 1472–1529), and Tai Chen, could not understand this dual character of principle.

Matteo Ricci (1552–1610), the author of the *T'ien-chu shih-i*[ar] (True idea of God), asserted that God was the origin and the foundation of all things,[32] and that the real bodies such as heaven, earth, spirits (*kuei-shen*[as]), and man were independent, while the forms or principles such as the five cardinal virtues, the five colors, and the five musical scales were dependent. If we thus interpret the Great Ultimate as principle or form, the Great Ultimate was not the origin and the foundation of all things.[33] Furthermore, Ricci accepted the Heavenly God (*Shang-t'ien*,[at] *Shang-ti*[au]) in the Classics of ancient China and equated the Christian God with this Heavenly God.[34] For this reason Ricci upheld his Catholic theology. The Christian God has personality and created everything, he thought, while Chu Hsi's ground-providing principle of the Great Ultimate had no personality and did not create everything. In studying comparative philosophy, we recognize the differential characters of the thought between East and West, but my religious experience tells me that the Christian God and the Great Ultimate, whether they have personality or not, are all the same, since the principles of our daily conduct in the actual world are controlled by them.

Conclusion

Let me conclude by briefly restating my main points.

The principle of *wu-chi erh t'ai-chi* is postulated as the foundation of nature and man. This ground-providing principle, although indefinite by itself, is manifested in man and nature as *so-tang-jan chih tse* or "principles that make man (nature) what he (it) should be" precisely because of its nonexistent character. In short, *li* or principle possesses a dual character of *so-i-jan* (foundation) and *so-tang-jan* (principle and law).

While Chu Hsi's theory resembles Meditation Buddhism, on the one hand, in that it teaches cultivation of the mind before the emotions are aroused and enlightenment through sudden penetration, it has, on the other hand, a progressive and intellectual character in that it proposes a scientific method, encouraging the investigation of the principles that make things what they should be.

Although Chu Hsi employs elaborate logic because of his long secluded life, his philosophy is practical in nature because of his position as a government official of the Sung dynasty.

Comparing Eastern and Western philosophy we see differences in character between God and the Great Ultimate, but my religious experience teaches me that they are the same.

Notes

1. Postscript to "T'ai-chi-t'u shuo chieh"[av] [Commentary on the "Explanation of the Diagram of the Great Ultimate"] in *Chou Lien-ch'i chi*[aw] [Collected works of Chou Tun-i], (Kuo-hsüeh chi-pen ts'ung-shu[ax] [Basic Sinological Studies] ed. 1937,) p. 29.

2. *Chu Tzu wen-chi*[ay] [Collection of literary works of Master Chu], (SPTK ed.), 42:14a.

3. *Chou Lien-ch'i chi*, p. 4.

4. *Chu Tzu yü-lei* (Taipei: Cheng-chung[az] Book Co., 1970), 2:6b, p. 30.

5. *Lun-yü chi-chu*[ba] [Collected commentaries on the *Analects*], (Taipei: I-wen[bb] Press, 1978), 1:8a, commentary on the *Analects*, 1:2.

6. *Chu Tzu yü-lei*, 1:3a, p. 5.

7. *Chou Lien-ch'i chi*, p. 2.

8. *Kun-chih chi*[bc] [Knowledge painfully acquired], (Kyoto: Chubun[bd] Press, 1975), ch. 8, pt. 1, 6a.

9. *Meng-tzu tzu-i su-cheng*[be] [Commentary on the meanings of terms in the *Book of Mencius*] in *Tai Tung-yüan Hsien-sheng ch'üan-chi*[bf] [Complete works of Tai Chen], (Taipei: Ta-hua[bg] Book Co., 1978), p. 289.

10. *Chu Tzu wen-chi*, 4:10a.

11. *Ibid.*, 4:10b.

12. *Chou Lien-ch'i chi*, p. 27.

13. *Ibid.* The sentences about the same origin and no gap are quotations from Ch'eng I's[bh] (1033–1107) preface to his *I-chuan*[bi] [Commentary on the *Book of Changes*].

14. *Chu Tzu wen-chi*, 36:3b.

15. *Ibid.*, 36:10ab.

16. The Four Virtues of the first hexagram in the *Book of Changes*. *Lun-yü huo-wen*[bj] [Questions and answers on the *Analects*] (Kyoto: Chubun Press, 1977), 1:7b; *Chu Tzu wen-chi*, 67:22b.

17. *Chu Tzu yü-lei*, 1:4b, p. 8.

18. *Ibid.*, 1:5b, p. 10.

19. See Tomoeda Ryūtarō, *Shushi no siso keisei*[bk] [The formation of Master Chu's thoughts], (Tokyo: Shunjusha,[bl] 1969), pp. 303–304.

20. *Ibid.*, pp. 309–310; *Chu Tzu yü-lei*, 2:4ab, pp. 25–26.

21. *Shushi no siso keisei*, pp. 311–313.

22. *Chu Tzu wen-chi*, supplementary collection, 3:7b.

23. *Chou Lien-ch'i chi*, pp. 3–12.

24. *Ta-hsüeh huo-wen*[bm] [Questions and answers on the *Great Learning*], (Kyoto: Chubun Press, 1977), 3a; the preface to the *Ta-hsüeh chang-chü*[bn] (Taipei: I-wen Press, 1978), 1a.

25. *Chu Tzu yü-lei*, 4:15a–b, pp. 117–118.

26. *Chung-yung chang-chü*[bo] [Commentary on the *Doctrine of the Mean*], (Taipei: I-wen Press, 1978), 12:8a.

27. *Chu Tzu wen-chi*, 67:22b–23a, "Jen-shuo"[bp] [Treatise on humanity], 74:20ab–21a and "Yü-shan chiang-i"[bq] [Lecture at Yü-shan]; *Lun-yü huo-wen*, 1:7b.

28. *Ta-hsüeh huo-wen*, 19a–b, commentary on ch. 5 on investigation of things and extension of knowledge; *Shih chi-chüan*[br] [Collected commentaries on the *Book of Odes*], (SPTK ed.), 18:24b, comment on ode no. 260, *Chung-yung huo-wen*, 9a.

29. *Chu Tzu wen-chi*, 67:12a–b, "I-fa wei-fa shuo"[bs] [Treatise on the emotions before and after they are aroused].

30. *Ta-hsüeh chang-chü*, 2a–b, 6a–b.

31. See Tomoeda, *Shushi no siso keisei*, ch. 3, sec. 2, "Theory of *ko-wu* and Political Practices."

32. *T'ien-chu shih-i* (Taipei: Kuo-fang yen-chiuyüan ch'u-pan-pu,[bt] 1967), pt. 1, 7a.
33. *Ibid.*, pt. 1, 15b–16a.
34. *Ibid.*, pt. 1, 20a–b.

Glossary

a	已發未發	y	亨	aw	周濂溪集
b	無極而太極	z	利	ax	國學基本叢書
c	吳翌晦叔	aa	貞	ay	朱子文集
d	易	ab	張載橫渠	az	正中
e	陰靜	ac	赤道	ba	論語集註
f	陽動	ad	黃道	bb	藝文
g	周敦頤濂溪	ae	沈括	bc	困知記
h	樞紐	af	蔡淵伯靜	bd	中文
i	根柢	ag	所以然之故	be	孟子字義疏證
j	朱子語類	ah	所當然之則	bf	戴東原先生全集
k	論語集注	ai	健	bg	大化
l	北辰	aj	順	bh	程頤
m	氣	ak	仁	bi	易傳
n	陰陽	al	義	bj	論語或問
o	太極圖解	am	禮	bk	朱子の思想形成
p	陰	an	智	bl	春秋社
q	陽	ao	格物	bm	大學或問
r	羅欽順整菴	ap	窮理	bn	大學章句
s	戴震東原	aq	王陽明守仁	bo	中庸章句
t	理	ar	天主實義	bp	仁說
u	陸	as	鬼神	bq	玉山講義
v	陸九韶梭山	at	上天	br	詩集傳
w	陸九淵象山	au	上帝	bs	已發未發說
x	元	av	太極圖說解	bt	國防研究院出版部

12

Chu Hsi's Methodology and Theory of Understanding

Chung-ying Cheng

Significance and Methodology of "Investigating Things"

ALTHOUGH CHU HSI'S PHILOSOPHY is traditionally called the philosophy or learning of principle (*li-hsüeh*[a]), the goal of his philosophy is to realize the potential nature of mind and eventually to realize the true nature of heaven and earth or the Way (Tao[b]). In this sense his philosophy should be more properly titled philosophy or learning of original substance (*pen-t'i-chih-hsüeh*[c]). But there is nevertheless great significance in calling his philosophy that of *li*[d] (principle). This significance lies in marking out both a methodological involvement and an ontological commitment as designated by the term "principle." As we have seen, *li* is no doubt ontologically denotative: it is the ordering and the resulting ordered structure of a thing. But we also point out that there is a subject-oriented meaning for *li*: *li* is the ordering activity of mind, and consequently in this sense we can say that mind exhibits *li* as a function and as a capacity. We may naturally conceive *li* in this sense as rationality or intelligence. It is the investigating power of mind. It is composed of perceptive, discernmental, judgmental, and thinking activities of mind, and yet it remains a unity of all these. This irreducible unity of mind is what provides mind the inexhaustible resources to continue its many mental activities. We may simply regard mind as having both the analytical and the synthetic capacities: in the employment of these capacities order and structure are revealed and their significances and relevances recognized. *Li* can be therefore said to be the logical-scientific or analytical-synthetic activity and capacity of mind.

A third significance of *li* is this: *Li* is the resulting concept or system of concepts of intellectual activities of mind, which not only reveal the order and ordered structures of things, but provide clarity for whatever corresponding ideas there are in one's mind. As we have seen, mind in its ontological dimension has *li* as its nature, or more precisely, has principle and vitality (*li-ch'i*[e]) as its nature (*hsing*[f]). Thus *li* inherent in mind can be said to be clarified in light of the resulting conceptual systems from the mind-activities. This latent *li*, however, as we shall see, is more complicated. It must be dialectically conceived as it is related to the ultimate *li* or the Great Ultimate (*T'ai-chi*ᵍ) in Chu Hsi's philosophy. It is the internal *li,* capable of being developed, realized, made explicit, and fully integrated on both conceptual and ontological levels.

Fourth, we may introduce another meaning of *li: li* as the pattern of design or "pattern of organization." In this sense *li* is the proto-idea for man to construct an artifact such as a fan or a bed. In this sense *li* is the technological design that underlies all scientific and technological or technical inventions.[1] *Li* in this sense is an intentional plan and a procedure for creating an order or a structure.

Finally, there is *li* in the sense of ordering and organizing our conduct and society. *Li* in this sense is the value and norm that we recognize as essential to fulfilling the ontological goal of human life and the life of society. It consists of those nomological-axiological principles that we use to shape and transform our life and society. *Li* in this sense has both an ontological and a pragmatic dimension: it is ontological as it presupposes recognition of an ultimate order and structure in the ontological sense. It is pragmatic as it can apply through the agency of mind to practice for guidance of life. There is no doubt that Chu Hsi and in fact all Neo-Confucianists have conception of *li* in this sense. For them *li* is considered the *li* of life and therefore moral and ethical principle *par excellence.* They also conceive moral norms and principles of conduct as all rooted in the ontology of the great ultimate or the Tao.

If, following Chu Hsi, we add the notion of *li* as indicating the total and ultimate reality and the source of all things, we may say that there is the ultimate ontological notion of *li.* Then we may summarize the meanings and types of *li* as follows:

1. ontological *li* of the Great Ultimate
2. objective *li* of things—order, structure, and laws of things
3. rational *li* of mind—the ordering and analytical-synthetic activities of mind
4. latent *li* of mind—the ideas and concepts in mind
5. the technological *li* of mind and things—design of artifacts
6. nomological *li* of mind-conduct-pattern of moral conduct and correct social behavior

These six meanings and types of *li* are related in a fundamental network that can be said to be architechtonic. In the first place, all *li* are ultimately rooted in the ontological *li,* which provides the rationale for the distinctions of *li.* In this mode of ontological understanding, *li* is the objective principles inherent in things, and yet is conceived by Chu Hsi as ultimately one. This is the doctrine of *li-i fen-shu*ʰ (*li* is one and is distributed in different things). Chu Hsi articulated this doctrine in the following statements: "*li-i fen-shu.* If we speak of heaven, earth and ten thousand things together, there is only one *li.* When we come to individual persons, there is one *li* for each person."[2] Asked about whether each of ten thousand things has a *li* and if ten thousand *li* come from the same source, Chu Hsi said, "One general *tao-li*ⁱ is one *tao-li*. It is like rain. The big hole contains water in the big hole, the small hole contains water in the small hole. The wood has water-on-the-wood; the grass has water-on-the-grass. Though in different places, it is the same water."[3] These two statements seem to identify the oneness of *li* in two different senses: *li* as universal concrete and *li* as universal abstract. In the first sense, *li* is the principle according to which the totality of things comes into being, and each thing in the totality partakes of this principle. In this sense the *li* is individuated in each thing and yet it is the same *li* that individuates each thing; in the second sense, *li* is the universal property each thing exemplifies: thus one can speak of the "same water" for all waters. What individuates individual waters is not the water itself: It is something else, namely the *ch'i*,ʲ as we shall see. It seems that Chu Hsi has conceived *li* sometimes as concrete universal and sometimes as abstract universal, and this creates unexpected difficulties for his metaphysics of *li*. Insofar as he conceived *li* as basically one, yet not divisible and in rest, he conceived *li* as basically a universal abstract; but insofar as he wanted to treat *li* as logically primary and prior to *ch'i* as the principle of change and transformation, he seemed to conceive *li* as a concrete universal, namely as something ontologically self-subsistent and self-contained. In either case it is clear that *li* is conceived as the principle of unity and identity by which everything can be said to share the same *li*. Even different things may have different *li*, but the ontologies of these different *li* are the same; they have the *li*-ness of *li* and therefore are abstractly the same; but they are also concretely the same, for each *li* is the same ultimate *li* that gives rise to each individual *li*. Chu Hsi appealed to the Ch'anᵏ Buddhist image "one moon casts the same print in ten thousand waters" (*Yüeh-yin wan-ch'uan*ˡ). This image occurs in the Ch'an poem *Yung-chia cheng-tao ko*ᵐ (Yung-chia song of vindication of Tao): "One moon universally appears in all waters, all water moons are absorbed in one moon (in the sky)" to illustrate the doctrine of *'li-i fen-shu*.*[4] The gist of this image is that one principle divides into many principles yet retains the same identity of the one principle, and thus many principles are unified in one principle. It leads to the Hua-yenⁿ conclusion that one penetrates many and many unifies into one, so that there is interpenetration of one and many. But the image leaves no doubt that the many retaining the qualitative sameness as the one are not qualitatively many but only numerically many. Thus all differences in things are merely numerical differences in terms of *li*, and there is homogeneity of *li* among all things.

It is in this sense of principle of ultimate identity for all things, as well as in the sense of principle of oneness of totality of all things, that *li* is the *T'ai-chi* (the Great Ultimate). He says, "The *T'ai-chi* is not a thing, it is in yin-yangº (passive and active cosmic forces) where yin-yang is; it is in *wu-hsing*ᵖ (the Five Powers, Metal, Wood, Water, Fire, and Earth) where *wu-hsing* is; it is in *all things* where all things are. It is only a *li*. But in so far as it reaches the ultimate, it is the *T'ai-chi*."[5] Therefore, the ultimate *li* is the *T'ai-chi*. It is the ultimate identity of things and the ultimate unity which things share. It is in this sense that "every person has a *T'ai-chi* and everything has a *T'ai-chi*,"[6] because every person and everything has a *li* that makes it what it is and that represents the same ultimate *li*.

From the dialectical point of view, mind and things may be regarded as the yang and yin of the *T'ai-chi* which contains the ontological *li*. Therefore, the objective *li* of things and the latent *li* of mind can be said to be mutually opposite and yet mutually complementary to each other and in this sense mutually dependent. To say that they are opposite is to say that one belongs to the objective order of things external to mind and the other belongs to the subjective structure of mind apart from external things. Yet they are complementary, for each requires the other for making possible the actuality of knowledge of things in mind which corresponds to reality. Thus they are organically interrelated as if belonging to a structured totality. Ontologically speaking, it might be said that they share one structure in common, and this should explain why mind may develop knowledge of things and things can be understood by mind. Although there is something that mind and things may be said to share, it takes the activity of mind to manifest this something and thus to extend and elaborate it. This activity of mind can be said to be the rational *li* of the mind, which is subjectively the rational logical-methodological or methodologizing functioning, and which results in the creation of the logic and methodology of thinking and sciences. When this intellectual activity of mind applies to things, it gives rise to knowledge of things and therefore realizes the objective *li* of things. When it applies to mind in reference to the objective *li* of things, mind comes to understanding in terms of acquiring ideas, concepts, and views. But must mind apply to things in order to have understanding of mind? Or must mind apply to mind itself in order to have understanding of things? If we remember the dialectical statement that "motion and rest has no inception and yin and yang has no beginning,"[7] then we can see that it is futile to pursue this question, for there cannot be any definite answers. The fact is that since mind and things have shared an underlying ontological unity and an implicit ontological structure, they have mutual influences on each other.

Following a common view of contemporary philosophical hermeneutics,[8] we may say that mind has a preunderstanding of things so that it may have deeper understanding of itself; and because of this deeper understanding of mind itself, it can further apply to things and acquire a deeper understanding of things and this can continue *ad infinitum*. Similarly, the mind can have a preunderstanding of itself that needs to be developed through the preunderstanding of things by mind. This interactive and mutually reinforcing process between the objective *li* of things and the latent *li* of mind indeed forms a hermeneutical circle.[9] As a result knowledge and truth as realized by mind is indeed an interplay between mind and things. This hermeneutical interplay is made possible by the ontological unity underlying both, and the interplay becomes necessary in light of the ontological *li* of the Great Ultimate. Hence the hermeneutical circle between the *li* of mind and the *li* of things is basically onto-hermeneutical, that is, hermeneutical or meaning-determining and meaning-interpretive on the basis of ontological understanding. For onto-hermeneutics is nothing but the possibility of ontological interaction and the possibility of meaning, truth, and understanding based on ontology and ontological interaction. It is clear that the onto-hermeneutical understanding of mind by way of things and the onto-hermeneutical understanding of things by way of mind become one if mind comes to realize the ontological source of these two, and thus comes to understanding the ultimate truth of the ultimate reality through the dialectics of the unity and division of the Great Ultimate. The rational *li* of mind begins with the onto-hermeneutical interaction between mind and things, and by this process transforms itself into ontological understanding of the ultimate reality. The technological *li* of mind consists in the application of knowledge of things to things themselves, whereas the nomological *li* of conduct consists in applying knowledge of mind to life and conduct. Both are pragmatic and practical aspects of the onto-hermeneutical activity of mind as well as the ontological interaction between mind and things.

In light of the above analysis of Chu Hsi's understanding of the ontological *li* as the *T'ai-chi*, it is clear that *li* (in the ontological sense of the *T'ai-chi*) can be diversified into different types and orders of things, which consequently manifest different types and orders of *li*: the objective *li*, the rational *li*, the latent *li* of mind, the technological *li*, and the nomological *li*. If one queries how and why these five types of *li* result from the *T'ai-chi*, the answer can only be that they form the very basis for understanding natural objects, mind (mind-activities), knowledge, invention of things (material civilization and technology), and creation of moral society (spiritual civilization and values), or in other words, these five types of *li* provide respective definitions of the natural sciences, the psychological sciences, human science and philosophy, technological studies, and morals. These five types of *li* are unified in the ontological *li* of the *T'ai-chi* and yet exhibit an architectonic interrelationship which is presupposed in the human understanding of man and his world. It is clear that the objective *li* of things are disclosed in the findings of natural sciences and that the rational *li* of mind can be obtained only through a process of personal introspection and the self-reflection of an individual mind. While philosophy and science as systems of concepts and ideas are results of thinking and speculation of mind, which are distinguishable from the process and activities of thinking, they are not to be identified with engineering designs in architectural planning, which are intended for a special practical end. Finally the nomological-axiological *li* simply refers to *li* of norms and values, which are the vital concerns of moral philosophy and social ethics.

In light of the above abstract discussion on the relation between the six types of *li*, we can now correctly and fully appreciate the renowned doctrine of *ko-wu*q (investigating things) of Chu Hsi. This doctrine, which appears in the supplements to the commentary on *ko-wu* in the *Great Learning*, says,

> The proposition that extension of knowledge consists in investigation of things means that if we want to extend our knowledge, we must exhaust (fully understand) the *li* of things right at things (*chi-wu erh ch'iung ch'i li*r). For the intelligence of mind, it can have all knowledge, and for all things under heaven, there is none without *li*. It is because *li* has not been exhausted (fully understood) that knowledge is not completed. Thus the beginning teaching of the *Great Learning* must urge scholars to do the following: With regard to all things under heaven, to always exhaust the *li* of them on the basis of the *li* mind already knows, so that it may reach understanding of *li* to the utmost. Once one has exercised efforts in this way for long, one will all of a sudden integrate (*huo-jan kuan-t'ung*s) all *li*. Then one's knowledge will cover the outside and the inside, the fine and the rough, of the things, and the great function of my total mind (*ch'üan-t'i ta-yung*t) will not be unilluminated. This is called *wu-ko*u and this is the utmost of knowledge.

Several observations are in order. First, it is to be noticed that Chu Hsi followed Ch'eng I-ch'uan (Ch'eng I,v 1033–1107) in interpreting the investigation of things as fully understanding (exhausting) the *li (ch'iung-li)*.[10] But Chu Hsi is highly innovative in suggesting that one has to fully understand the *li* of things right at things (*chi-wu*w). This means that one should not think of *li* as apart from things nor one can fully understand the *li* of things without closely investigating things. To confront things is the beginning of understanding the *li* of things. This again implies that one should not look for things far away for investigation. Things at hand that are given in life are a good starting point of investigation. Thus Chu Hsi's proposal contains an effective and concrete procedure which Ch'eng I-ch'uan's original interpretation lacks. Second, Chu Hsi stresses explicitly the innate capacity for understanding and knowing in human mind, and suggests that it is only when the *li* has not been fully understood that the knowledge of mind is not complete. This suggestion means that *ch'iung-li* is not simply full understanding of *li*, but understanding of the full *li* or complete *li* of all things.[11] The question can be raised as to whether full understanding of *li* is the same as understanding of full *li*. The answer seems to me to be that for Chu Hsi to fully understand *li* is to have understanding of full *li* and vice versa. In fact, Chu Hsi emphasizes the importance of the empirical scope of investigation, for he suggests that one should investigate all things under heaven, and therefore believes that the larger the scope of one's investigation, the better understanding of things one will have and the more complete the knowledge of mind will be. This means that *ch'iung-li* is to widen and deepen one's understanding of *li*.[12] Chu Hsi further stresses the importance of continuity of investigation and knowledge. He urges seeking understanding of the *li* of things based on the *li* that one comes to know.

Knowledge is therefore conceived as an evergrowing circle of knowing the *li*, and all *li* are linked together to form a holistic unity. This means that knowledge of *li* is basically integrational and should be developed as an interaction and interplay between what one knows and what one comes to know in the process of investigation. The hermeneutical circle is implicitly suggested, but unfortunately it has not been elaborated on other occasions.

Finally, the notion of "sudden integration" *(huo-jan kuan-t'ung)* is highly significant.[13] It suggests that the ever-enlarging circle of investigating and knowing is not a matter of mechanical and arithmetical growth but a matter of organic and geometrical development: The *li* one has discovered in the process of investigation will sooner or later dawn upon the potential structure of mind so that mind may come to a full understanding of *li* as well as an understanding of the complete *li* of all things. This also suggests that the important matter of *ko-wu* is knowledge in quality, not knowledge in quantity, and that the quantity in knowledge in due course with due background will lead to quality in knowledge so that one can reach a point of full understanding of *li*. The possibility of this integration apparently is conditional on two considerations: All *li* are interrelated in an organic unity; by understanding more and more of *li* in things, one will naturally reach a point of understanding the underlying organic unity of *li* for all things; furthermore, the mind with its latent structure of *li* can be said to be inclined to a holistic understanding of things, and therefore empirical and particular investigations will force a dawning on the mind. In this sense the latent structure of *li* will become awakened to mind; mind can be said to present an integrated picture of the *li*.

Apart from the first organic and the second aprioristic interpretation of this notion of sudden integration of *li*, we may also take a third view—a conservative scientific interpretation. The sudden integration of *li* can be considered as a natural theoretical systemization on generalized data one has collected and studied in the process of inquiry, and this systematization will not only have the explanatory power to relate all scattered observations, but will project a pervasive explanation of all things under intended survey. In either of these interpretations, what is clear is that sudden integration of *li* is a deep experience of mind, as well as deep experience of all things, for Chu Hsi. For in light of this experience, not only are the subtleties of *li* fully grasped, but the great function of mind is fully realized. There is a sense of self-content and self-satisfaction for this experience of sudden integration. For this reason I would consider this experience as resulting from the full interplay between the *li* of things and the *li* innate in mind or as at least contributing to such an interplay. Thus insofar as this experience gives rise to the knowledge that integrates all *li* of things, it also gives rise to an understanding of mind that illuminates the mind. Therefore I would call this knowledge not only integrational but illuminational. When knowledge is fully integrated, and thus illuminating, knowledge would be complete. Since this completeness cannot be understood in a quantitative sense, it must be understood in a highly qualitative sense. It is no longer empirical knowledge or scientific knowledge, but knowledge of the Great Ultimate or the dialectical knowledge of the real as the dialectics of unity and division suggests. It is the ontological knowledge of *li* and *li* is the ontological *li* of things. The sudden integration of *li* in mind may be said to represent a dialectical jump and dialectical transformation of both the *li* of things and the understanding of it. Onto-hermeneutically speaking, one may suggest that the "sudden integration in mind" is a dialectical integration of mind and things in light of their unity and division as rooted in understanding of the Great Ultimate.

In view of the above analysis of the doctrine of *ko-wu* of Chu Hsi, we can see that *ko-wu* as a rational activity of mind acts as a link between the *li* of things and the *li* of mind, which makes understanding possible by bringing the *li* of things to uncovering the *li* of mind and bringing the *li* of mind to illuminating the *li* of things. This activity of mind therefore creates an onto-hermeneutical circle between mind and things that in the continuing activity of mind will eventually grow and mature to a full objective integration of *li* of things and a full subjective integration of *li* in things, and consequently a full ontological integration of *li* in things and *li* in mind. This is the ultimate point when the *ko-wu* returns to the ontological understanding of the total and ultimate truth—the truth of the Great Ultimate. As it is the Great Ultimate that gives rise to the *ko-wu* activity of mind,[14] the *ko-wu* of mind and the potential influence of the Great Ultimate also form a relation that can be only understood as the onto-hermeneutical circle of understanding. In this view, *ko-wu* has as its goal the realization of the ontological understanding of the Great Ultimate by way of the integration of knowledge generated by the onto-hermeneutical circle between mind and things, which is rooted dialectically in the Great Ultimate. Thus if we call the Great Ultimate the original substance (*pen-t'i*[x]), and *li* the substance of things (*wu-t'i*[y] or *shih-t'i*[z]), and the *li* of mind the substance of mind (*hsin-t'i*[aa]), then *ko-wu* is the ontologically rooted logos of mind, which leads to a full integration between substance of things and substance of mind in the full awareness and illumination of the original substance. All relations among them become onto-hermeneutical circles. We can then represent this ontological structure of *ko-wu* and this onto-hermeneutical activity of mind as shown in Figure 1 below.

My analysis of the methodology of *ko-wu* in Chu Hsi is obviously based on my understanding of the structure of the *ko-wu* situation and the relation of mind to things: it need not be what Chu Hsi actually has in mind. My analysis is therefore inevitably onto-hermeneutical and dialectical, but this is nevertheless what a close and intimate understanding cannot avoid being. Furthermore, my analysis can be said to illuminate what Chu Hsi says on *ko-wu*, as his statements on *ko-wu* equally exemplify my full analysis of *ko-wu*.

Throughout the *Chu Tzu yü-lei*[ab] (Classified conversations of Master Chu) Chu Hsi stresses the organic unity of all *li*, which are scattered over all things. For example, he says that "For all thousands of affairs, they all belong to one

FIGURE I

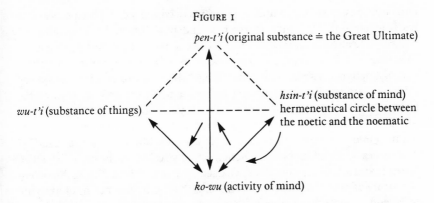

pen-t'i (original substance ≒ the Great Ultimate)

wu-t'i (substance of things)

hsin-t'i (substance of mind)
hermeneutical circle between
the noetic and the noematic

ko-wu (activity of mind)

li."[15] He also points out that for all things in the world one should try to first understand the *li* of them, and then one will understand the unity of *li*.[16] He uses the term *"li-hui"*[ac] for understanding the *li* of differentiated things and uses the term *"hui-t'ung"*[ad] for understanding the organic unity and interrelatedness of *li* in things.[17] He stresses the former as requiring great efforts,[18] but considers the latter as naturally taking place after great efforts are made and accumulated for individual investigations of things. In this manner, Chu Hsi follows the Confucian ideal of "broad scholarship first and simple ideas later" (*hsien-po hou-yüeh*[ae]) and the Confucian motto of learning from below so that one will reach the "*Tao* above" (*hsia-hsüeh shang-ta*[af]). The stress Chu Hsi puts on investigation of external things is truly remarkable. He urges students to see the "actual substance of things" *(shih-t'i),* and this means to see lights in terms of things; he even suggests experimenting with boats and carriages in order to understand how boats may not move on land.[19] Following this line, Chu Hsi's *ko-wu* notion might be said to embody some germic seeds of scientific experimentalism and positive empiricism from which a rigorous objective methodology of science can be developed. In providing his empirical explanation of natural phenomena (such as eclipses, fossilization, thundering rain),[20] Chu Hsi has demonstrated a naturalistic mind. He is able to use dialectical thinking on things in general to draw inferences and hypotheses regarding the possibility of the movement of the earth according to the movement of heaven.[21] He conceives the movement of heaven as similar to the turning of a grinder (*mo*[ag]) and renders a naturalistic picture of the relation between heaven and earth.[22] Most frequently, however, Chu Hsi seems to stress understanding *li* in a logical and mentalistic sense. He says that "Regarding general things in the world, there are infinite subtle meanings and reasons (*i-li*[ah]); it is hard to make a judgment of their beginnings and endings in one statement; one should see them crystal clear as not obstructing each other. This is the test of investigating things."[23]

Apparently, Chu Hsi speaks like a logician. He wishes to see truths as a system both consistent and complete. He wants to consider *li* in all aspects and to reach a state of "centrality, correctness and peacefulness" (*chung-cheng ho-p'ing*[ai]).[24] He also gives more examples of *ko-wu* in terms of learning moral virtues such as benevolence, righteousness,[25] love for one's parents, propriety, and distinction between right and wrong.[26] In terms of reading books, the things investigated become mental feelings and natural promptings of the heart—they are internal things of the mind-substance, not the more external things of the world. In this spirit, *ko-wu* is eventually conceived as "illuminating the mind" (*ming-hsin*[aj]). He says, "*Ko-wu* is for illuminating this mind."[27] "*Li* resides in things, but their function actually resides in the mind."[28] Thus, *ko-wu* leads to an extension of knowledge in the sense of "fulfilling the potential nature of mind" (*chin-hsin*[ak]) of Mencius.[29] It becomes a means of unifying mind and *li*, and *li* in the mind becomes "the moon which projects its image into all things."[30] This is the state of the integration of *li* which is a total mental experience. That Chu Hsi follows this line of thought (particularly in his later life) perhaps is due to his efforts to avoid the externalizing tendency of *ko-wu*. This is perhaps a result of his encounter with Lu Hsiang-shan (Lu Chiu-yüan,[al] 1139–1193). But he forgets that in doing so *li* also becomes internalized and the study of the *li* in things becomes a study of the *li* in mind. A rational system of logic and science cannot be developed on this ground. This means that the curtailment of the externalizing tendency in *ko-wu* and the rationalizing tendency in fully understanding *li (ch'iung-li)* has prevented Chu Hsi from evolving science and logic on the basis of the total methodology of *ko-wu*. Yet this methodology contains the seeds for such an evolution.[31]

Methodologically speaking, two more observations can be made on Chu Hsi's theory of *ko-wu* as a method for reaching truth and understanding *li*. First, Chu Hsi stresses the importance of the priority of investigating things close at hand. He says, "*Ko-wu* must begin with understanding things close at hand (*ts'ung ch'ieh-chi-ch'u li-hui-chü*[am]). Once one has settled on things close at hand, then one can gradually extend over other things. This is the *ko-wu*."[32] He also stresses "seeing the outline (*ta-kang*[an]) and seeing the large model (*ta-p'ei-t'ai*[ao]) and then going to the details. Thus, not losing sight of the outline, understanding moves on layer by layer, layer by layer."[33] This suggests, no doubt, an implicit working of the hermeneutical circle—the circle between the large and the small.

Second, like all Confucian philosophers, Chu Hsi is very much concerned with correct understanding of the right and wrong things. He says, "Confucian doctrine is such that in reading one finds gains and losses; in managing affairs one discerns right and wrongs. This is the matter of *ko-wu* and the extension of knowledge."[34] He also says, "Not separated from daily activities, one's *ko-wu* enables one to discern right from wrong and examine oughts and ought-nots; thus, understanding fully the subtleties of meanings of things one will extend their application to life and practice."[35] For Chu Hsi, one of the great purposes of *ko-wu* is to understand the moral relationships of men so that one may act correctly. But in the context of investigating things together with one's feelings, one may suggest that Chu Hsi has succeeded in putting moral value distinctions on an objective basis—namely, on the basis of knowing *li* or understanding *li*. But one may also suggest that Chu Hsi does both, which need not be considered incompatible. In light of our onto-hermeneutical analysis of Chu Hsi, we see that he wants to integrate knowledge of external things with knowledge of internal feelings in order to gain insight into the ontological understanding of *Tao* and in order to reach judgments of right and wrong as guidance for life and practice. In fact, it is in an effort to strengthen the possibility of fulfilling this goal that he suggests and works on other supplementary aspects of mind-activity beside the *ko-wu* activity. This is the doctrine of *han-yang*[ap] (immersive nourishing) and *ch'ih-ching*[aq] (holding steadfast to mind, a serious-mindedness, central-mindedness, mastery of mind). We may regard this as a move of mind to reach pragmatic or practical wisdom of life and action, and thus complete *ko-wu* in a general way.

Methodology of "Immersive Nourishing" and "Mind-mastering"

Perhaps under the influence of Taoist-Buddhist philosophy, the Neo-Confucianists stress the importance of tranquillity (*ching*[ar]) and the ontological priority of mind. Thus, Chou Tun-i[as] (1017–1073) speaks of concentrating on tranquillity in the *T'ai-chi t'u shuo*[at] (Discourse on the diagram of the Great Ultimate) and Shao Yung[au] (1011–1077) speaks of mind as the *T'ai-chi*, that is, as the source from which all things come, in the *Huang-chi ching-shih*[av] (The great norm for regulating world affairs).[36] They consider that it is through the concentration of mind in tranquillity that one will both have knowledge of reality and transform oneself into sagehood. Shao Yung speaks of the sage as capable of "unifying (reflecting) the truths of all things," because he is able to see things as things themselves (*i-wu kuan-wu*[aw])[37] and see things with *li* in one's mind.[38]

Chou Tun-i explains tranquillity as desireless, and in speaking of oneness as the key to the learning of sagehood, explains oneness also as desirelessness. He says, "Desireless, one will remain void when at rest, and upright, when in motion; if void at rest, one will be clear; being clear, one will understand the ultimate truth; if upright in motion, one will be public-minded (non-selfish), and being public-minded, one will be comprehensive in one's understanding."[39] Although Chang Tsai[ax] (1020–1077) does not stress mind and tranquillity, he still conceives mind as having its own innate knowledge (knowledge from virtuous nature, *te-hsing chih chih*[ay]), independent of experience (knowledge from seeing and hearing). He says, "What the virtuous nature knows is not rooted in seeing and hearing, but rooted in the nature of Heaven and Earth."[40] To become a sage, one has to uncover one's nature of Heaven and Earth and cultivate the knowledge from virtuous nature.

In response to Chang Tsai's query on how to "settle on one's nature" (*ting-hsing*[az]), Ch'eng Hao[ba] (1032–1085) speaks of being "not selfishly concerned with things" as a key to "settle on one's nature." He gives the motto: "Open oneself and be not selfish, respond naturally to things when they happen."[41] There is a strong tendency to apply the Taoist vision of removing feelings and artificial knowledge in this ideal of cultivating one's nature and mind. When we come to Ch'eng I, the same tradition of concentrating on one's nature and mind continues. He proposes the idea of residing in *ching*[bb] (mind-mastery, as we shall see). He says, "The so-called *ching* is to have mastery of oneself in oneness (*chu-i*[bc])." Oneness is defined as "no particular learning" (*wu-shih*[bd]).[42] With this, Ch'eng I suggests that "if one holds this and nourishes and preserves *(han-yang)* it, in due time the *li* of Heaven will become clear."[43] This, no doubt, is the answer for Ch'eng I on how to reach sagehood: it is the method of cultivating sagehood, that is, for reaching the ultimate truth and transforming oneself into correct conduct. Although he points out the parallel importance of immersive nourishing and fully understanding the *li (han-yang* and *ch'iung-li),*[44] the emphasis, nevertheless, falls on immersive nourishing, as indicated in his early discussion on "what Yen Tzu[be] likes to study."[45] He says there, "All learning has its way in rectifying one's mind and nourishing one's nature, so that one will remain central and correct and sincere and thus become sagely."[46] He points out that one "has understanding in one's mind and knows how to nourish, then makes the effort to practice and accomplish (one's virtues), and this is to reach sincerity from understanding."[47] In short, to cultivate sagehood, one needs to cultivate knowledge of one's true nature (*chih-hsing*[bf]) and fulfilling one's mind *(chin-hsin),* which are notions from Mencius and the *Doctrine of the Mean.*[48]

Given the above background, a Neo-Confucianist believes that a person's methodological task is to envision how one may reach the substance of mind so that one may have full knowledge of the Great Ultimate or Tao and the full ability to respond correctly to anything in the world. Chu Hsi confronted this problem when he became a disciple of Li Yen-p'ing (Li T'ung,[bg] 1093–1163) in his early years. For Yen-p'ing, the solution to the problem is to experience the substance of mind and, therefore, the original substance in meditating on one's mind. Although none of the Neo-Confucian thinkers mentioned above specifically mentions meditation (*ching-tso*[bh] or *mo-tso*[bi]) as the method for understanding the substance of mind,[49] it nevertheless appears natural to suggest meditation as a formal procedure to reach tranquillity of mind and to come to "settling on one's nature or mind." The important thing about meditation is not that one must sit in quietness, but that by sitting in quietness one will make efforts to clarify one's mind by clearing selfish desires and prejudicial thoughts (following the doctrines of the Ch'eng brothers). It is assumed that in this way, one will not only clarify one's mind, but will come to a full recognition on the substance of mind.

Of course, there are more difficult questions concerning this procedure. How is it possible to recognize the true nature of mind if mind is ontologically void and tranquil? If mind is active and moved with feelings and desires, how can one discover the true nature of mind amidst its activities? These questions are philosophically most serious. For they require an examination not only of the nature of mind, but of the methods needed to ascertain the true nature of mind. The difficulty of any such examination is that one has to use mind to do the examining, and therefore, to activate mind for seeing (which is a form of activity of mind), yet seek tranquillity of the mind-substance. The difficulty is a paradoxical situation: If mind is active, then it cannot be seen as inactive; and if the mind-substance is inactive, one has to see mind before activity. One cannot see it when mind activates itself, and therefore one cannot see it with the mind.

Chu Hsi was aware of the radically idealistic Buddhist doctrine of consciousness and specifically the Ch'an philosophy of enlightenment through understanding nature or mind (*chien-hsing*[bj] or *chien-hsin*[bk]). He wanted to avoid this doctrine for the reason that it is guided by the selfish desire of tranquillity. He also argued that there is no way that mind can observe mind, for there is no static mind to be observed or to contemplate.[50] Thus, how to know substance of mind becomes a real methodological puzzle to him—a puzzle with ominous metaphysical significance.

This problem has been known as "the problem of seeking the centrality (*chung*[bl]) of mind before the activation of mind"; this problem has been more exactly formulated and discussed in terms of the doctrine of centrality and harmony (*ho*[bm]) of mind in the *Doctrine of the Mean*. The *Doctrine of the Mean* defines the state of mind before feelings arise as centrality and the state of mind when all aroused feelings meet right occasions as harmony. Then the *Doctrine of the Mean* says, "Centrality is the great root of the world and harmony is the great attained way of the world. Once centrality and harmony are reached, heaven and earth will be in order and all things will grow."[51] There is no indication that the *Doctrine of the Mean* regards centrality and harmony as merely a state of mind. In fact, the state of mind known as *chung* and *ho* may only be understood in an ontological sense, since *chung-ho* may be regarded as having ontological, rather than simply psychological, properties. In this light, to reach centrality and harmony need not mean to reach them in the mind or through the mind. It can be a descriptive statement of how Heaven and Earth and all things are oriented in being. In other words, one can take the well-ordering of Heaven and Earth and the growth of all things as the sign of centrality and harmony of world-reality or even as meaning the centrality and harmony of the world-reality. When this consideration applies to an individual, the individual will lead an orderly life and act with a sense of order, and his life will have well-being. No doubt this explanation of centrality and harmony is not what Ch'eng I and Chu Hsi seek in their search and query for the ontological understanding of mind. Nor will this explanation satisfy an onto-hermeneutical analysis of mind with regard to the dialectical conception of *T'ai-chi*. Therefore, the problem of understanding the centrality of mind before its activation is not an original problem for the *Doctrine of the Mean* text, nor can it be directly answered in the context of the *Doctrine of the Mean*. It has to be answered in light of the Neo-Confucian metaphysical framework, where the structure of the *Tao* becomes more articulated.

If we survey Chu Hsi's writings on this problem, it is apparent that Chu struggled a great deal with this problem at the height of his career. According to a detailed documentation in Ch'ien Mu's[bn] *Chu Tzu hsin hsüeh-an*[bo] (A new study on Chu Hsi),[52] Chu Hsi does not follow the solution of his teacher, Yen-p'ing, to this problem: Meditate on mind in tranquillity so that one can grasp the centrality of mind before the mind is activated. The rationale for the possible rejection of Yen-p'ing's view seems to be the epistemological difficulty that one can only observe the mind when the mind is activated: there is no way for the mind to actively see mind in its unactivated state. If one can, indeed, see the mind-substance (not its functioning) by introspection, one has to admit the necessary priority of inspection over a postinspective orientation of mind toward "preserving and nourishing the substance of mind." Evidence seems to point to the latter, rather than the former, as the conclusion of Chu Hsi reached, in dealing with the problem of seeking centrality before mind-activation. This leads him to the position of Chang Nan-hsüan (Chang Shih[bp], 1133–1180). Chang Shih holds that one must see (experience) tranquillity in motion and, thus, recognize the mind-substance.[53] But this position does not satisfy Chu Hsi, for this position leaves the relation between tranquillity and motion only partially explained. If one can see or experience tranquillity in motion, why cannot one see or experience motion in tranquillity, as is evident from the dialectical relation of motion and rest in *T'ai-chi?*

Second, if "perceptive inspection" (*hsing-ch'a*[bq]) is the only way by which one may detect the activity of mind and the background substance, then one cannot "preserve and nourish" (*han-yang*) the mind-substance (not mind-functioning) where there is no such activity. If, on the other hand, one can indeed "preserve and nourish" mind-substance, and "preserving and nourishing" is a different form of experiencing and realizing the mind-substance than perceptive-inspection, then why does one need to preceptively inspect before preserving and nourishing the mind? That is, could not one simply preserve and nourish the mind-substance independently of the preceptive inspection of the mind-functioning whether before or after? The pressing problem, hence, becomes one of defining and recognizing another mode of experiencing the mind—the experiencing of mind by understanding or grasping the mind-substance. It also becomes a matter of defining and recognizing the nature of the mind-substance. The following consequence for such a query seems natural and obvious: one has to see "preserving and nourishing" as a distinctive and independent mode of experiencing,[54] by which the mind-substance will be experienced and seen. Mind-substance can be regarded as precisely the result of such a mode of perceiving. Unfortunately, Chu Hsi does not give any logical or metaphysical reason for drawing this conclusion; but he does seem to reach this conclusion, perhaps, as a result of reflecting on the parallelism of the activity of extending knowledge and the effort of preserving and nourishing as in Ch'eng I's motto: "To learn, one has to extend knowledge; to preserve and nourish mind, one has to reside in central-mindedness *(ching)*."[55]

According to the *Chu Tzu yü-lei*,[56] in the year of 1171, when Chu Hsi was forty-one years old, he said that when he adopted the Chang Shih position years before, he was unaware that there is tranquillity when there is no specific thought *(nien-lü*[br]*)*, and there is motion when one's mind responds to things. He says, "When in tranquillity, if there is feeling for the *li*, then there is motion; when in motion, if the *li* is at rest *(an*[bs]*)*, then there is tranquillity."[57] This, of course, shows a subtle appreciation of the interaction and interdependence of motion and rest. This constitutes a more advanced phenomenological observation of mind, for it can be said that the beginning of motion is in the midst of tranquillity and the beginning of tranquillity is rooted in motion. As there cannot be absolute motion or absolute tranquillity, one must be able to recognize a point where the tranquillity begins in motion and where the motion begins in tranquillity. To recognize this is to recognize a tendency and a direction relative to the functioning of mind as a whole in which motion and tranquillity interact and interplay. This is to recognize the mind as a substance and as a function as the same time. It is as substance that the mind is capable of beginning tranquillity in motin or beginning motion in tranquillity. In thus recognizing mind as a substance, one also recognizes the function of mind. These two recognitions define and determine each other as the dialectical methodology dictates. With this recognition of mind as substance, one will see and experience the source of the interplay and interaction of motion and tranquillity in the interplay between *li* and *ch'i* or yin and yang of the Ultimate Reality. Finally, one comes to the recognition that the metaphysical ground of experience of mind-substance is the original substance. In this light, the mind-substance can be seen to derive its significance and existence from the original substance. Mind is a vehicle for realizing the ultimate truth of the original substance, and hence the term "mind-substance" merely indicates how original substance becomes understood and experienced through mind functioning in tranquillity and in motion.

With the above analytical understanding of the mode of experiencing *(han-yang)* the mind-substance, we can better understand Chu Hsi's development of the methodology of *han-yang* (preserving and nourishing) or *ts'ao-ts'un*[bt] (holding and preserving) in terms of a phenomenology of mind. We may explicate this methodology on the following major points: First, to preserve and nourish is to seek centrality or the source of activity before activity of mind takes place. This requires both inspection by the mind and experience of mind. Chu Hsi, following Li Yen-p'ing, has used the term *t'i-jen*[bu] (experience intimately and recognize) to indicate this. What is intimately experienced and recognized is the general feeling of a totality called *ch'i-hsiang*[bv] (likeness of *ch'i*). One may say that this is a feeling or a state of mind free from any specific intentional and referential involvement; it can be further identified as a state of self-identity of mind. It is believed that when this state is well-preserved, the mind will be able to exercise clarity over its perceptions and, therefore, recognize *li* in clarity. In this sense, the unactivated state of mind is truly important. It is the source of adequate understanding and the source of the power for discovery of *li* and knowledge of things.

Second, this state of mind not only has epistemological importance but is ontologically significant as well. I have already indicated that to experience this state of mind is to lead to the experience of the original substance of reality. As the original substance is the source of inexhaustible creativity, to experience the mind-substance will lead to the experience of creativity of the ontological ultimate, which can be, nevertheless, experienced from the observation of the things or thing-substances. Chu Hsi, in failing to identify the unactivated conscious perception or perceptions of mind, tries to seek the unperturbed centrality (*wei-fa chih chung*[bw]) and the tranquil (*chi-jan pu-tung*[bx]) in daily goings-on. He says, "Amidst all those instances of feelings, understandings and perceptions, there is something remaining as a whole which responds to infinite things. This is the source of flow of heavenly nature (*t'ien-ming liu-hsing*[by] and the enduring life-creativity (*sheng-sheng pu-i*[bz]). Even within one day infinite responses arise and subside, the quiet original substance remains always quiet. The so-called centrality is just this. Is there another thing confined to one time and one place which can be called the centrality?"[58] Although in the later stage of his thought Chu Hsi himself rejected this early view, there is nevertheless a lesson to learn from this description of the centrality: If centrality is universal, unifying, and a source for all, then the understanding of centrality among all things is nevertheless the same understanding of the same centrality. This implies that the mind-substance and thing-substance should ultimately coincide, and that there should not be a unique way to understand centrality. What marks out Chu Hsi's mature position is that if one seeks centrality in mind, one should seek through mind, and thus seek through the procedure of preserving and nourishing.

In characterizing the mind-substance through preserving and nourishing, one has to experience mind-substance in the way one experiences the original substance. Tao or the Great Ultimate can be described: as a totality, as a harmony (consistency), as a process of creative transformation, as the ultimate grounding, and as the consummating and initiating value. To preserve and nourish mind is to recognize and experience and strengthen the feelings of harmony, totality, creativity, well-groundedness, and presence of value. With this experience of the mind-substance, one will be able to relate to things in a totality, one will be able to relate knowledge to practice, one will devote oneself to creative efforts in life, and one will not stop at one point of seeking and improving but will seek and improve to the utmost, for one will realize value in everything—one understands and acts. This would be the ideal way of preserving and nourishing the mind-substance and the ideal state of holding and preserving the mind-substance of a person.

In light of this phenomenological description of the methodology of preserving and nourishing, it is obvious that the unactivated state of mind-substance and the activated state of mind-functioning cannot be separated: there is an intimate unity and natural opposition between them. Their difference can be regarded as that between the inner and outer, and that between *li* and *ch'i*. With this onto-hermeneutical understanding, the dialectical unity of complementary opposites applies, and the understanding of mind-substance together with the understanding of the preserving and nourishing as a way for understanding of mind-substance can be seen as derived from the ontological insight into reality in general as well as from the ontological reflection on mind as a whole and as a unity. To preserve and nourish is therefore not just to experience mind-substance but to realize the truth of the way of heaven, the harmony and goodness of nature, and to realize them as foundations of one's behavior and source of values. To preserve and nourish, in this sense, is to cultivate both motion and tranquillity—the inner and the outer—at the same time without being misguided by the priority problem. By this method one will come to fully understand the mind as the unifying, commanding nature (as mind-substance) and feelings (as mind-functioning) as Chang Tsai's doctrine of *hsin-t'ung hsing-ch'ing*[a] (mind commands and unifies the nature and the feelings) suggests.[59] This means there is no need to begin with perceptive inspection in conducting preserving and nourishing, just as there is no need to begin with preserving and nourishing in rational perception of the *li*. Yet in light of the internal relationship between the two, it is clear that perceptive inspection will become unobstructed and efficient because of the preserving and nourishing, and preserving and nourishing will become effortless, stable, and profound in virtue of the perceptive inspection. One may even regard preserving and nourishing as providing a natural context for more perceptive inspection for reinforcing the motive and directive force for more preserving and nourishing. This mutual organic interdependence of the two has its great merit in "fulfilling the nature of mind," "realizing one's place among all things," and "fully understanding the *li*," which are ultimate goals of life. But viewing the two the ontologically inseparable leads to stressing human affairs and moral life at the expense of the external physical universe and stressing values at the expense of independent knowledge of physical things. The dialectical unity of preserving and nourishing and perceptive inspection may be said to deter the autonomy of a pure rational science from growing as it prevents the independence of perceptive inspection from preserving and nourishing.

This leads to a final observation of the understanding of the mind-substance by way of preserving and nourishing. The mind-substance as realized by preserving and nourishing is one in which moral distinctions originate and moral values reside. The recognition of mind as the source of moral values and moral distinctions can be traced to Mencius.[60] But in the Neo-Confucian writings, as we have seen, moral values and moral distinctions acquire an ontological significance. They are derived from the natural activities of the *Tao*. They are the manifestation of the fundamental nature of heaven. Thus *jen*,^{cb} the ultimate and ideal virtue of both Classical and Neo-Confucianism, becomes universalized and ontologized as the source of life and creativity; *jen* becomes the *jen*-substance, the original substance perceived under *jen* or universal life and creativity. This ontological transformation may be also seen as an onto-hermeneutical search for unity and totality in reality—therefore a methodological accomplishment. It may also be ontologically regarded as a reflection of the deeper understanding of mind-substance and mind-functioning. In both these senses Chu Hsi has made great contribution and has defined *jen* as "the principle *(li)* of love" and "virtue *(te*^{cc}*)* of mind."[61] With this understanding, it becomes also onto-hermeneutically clear that as *jen* is ontologically understandable, we may speak of the "mind of Heaven and Earth" to accentuate the *jen*-nature of the original substance.

Once mind is recognized as the source of moral distinctions and moral values, all procedures and methods for cultivating moral distinctions, moral values, moral visions, and moral practice and behavior become methods and procedures for preserving and nourishing. In this light we can see that the efforts and techniques for preserving and nourishing the mind-substance (an original mind) are described by Chu Hsi in terms of the Classical Confucian method of "disciplining oneself" *(k'o-chi*^{cd}*)* and Ch'eng I's Neo-Confucian procedure and formula called "residing in single-mindedness" *(chü-ching*^{ce}*)*.[62] In a retrospective view, this is how Wang Yang-ming (1472–1529) wishes to recover the mind-substance by fulfilling the innate knowledge of goodness in mind. The difference between Chu Hsi and Wang Yang-ming, however, is a difference of recognizing different methods for recovering mind-substance, and this difference is rooted in a description of the dialectical understanding of the ontology of mind. Chu Hsi has more of an awareness of dialectical understanding than Wang Yang-ming. It is clear that the understanding of mind-substance in terms of moral understanding and the consequent ontological integration of mind via moral cultivation indicates an important insight into the nature of mind, namely, mind can be seen from at least two points of view: an inner ontological point of view and an outer moral conduct point of view. Mind reveals the Great Ultimate from the first point of view and issues in moral behavior from the second. This means that the preserving and nourishing procedure for revealing and structuring (in an epistemological sense) the mind-substance has two dimensions: the dimension of ontological understanding of the Great Ultimate via mind and the dimension of the moral application of mind to conduct and life via mind. We may describe the first dimension as understanding and discovering the ultimate grounding of mind, that is, as discovering the *tao* and internally harmonizing mind with the *tao*. We may describe the second dimension as the discovery of applicable norms in practical life, thereby externally harmonizing mind with things and people.

The methodological structure of preserving and nourishing is represented

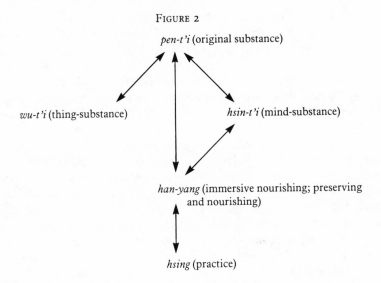

FIGURE 2

pen-t'i (original substance)

wu-t'i (thing-substance)   *hsin-t'i* (mind-substance)

han-yang (immersive nourishing; preserving
and nourishing)

hsing (practice)

in Figure 2. Preserving and nourishing produces an onto-hermeneutical circle between mind and the original substance on the one hand and an onto-hermeneutical circle between mind and the conduct or practice on the other.

Concluding Remarks

Chu Hsi's philosophy of *li* and *ch'i* is directed toward understanding Tao and embodying the activated Tao within the individual. In this sense this understanding is practical and transformative, that is, it fulfills the mind-substance and entails correct action and a fulfilling sense of creativity and attainment. This ultimate goal is called sagehood. Relative to this goal all learning and thinking are methodological; they can be conceived as methods toward the creative understanding of sagehood and creative transformation of the individual. This goal has been described by Chou Tun-i aptly as follows: "The sage identifies himself with Heaven and Earth in virtue and identifies himself with sun and moon in their brightness."[63] This view is complemented by Chang Tsai: "Establish mind for Heaven and Earth, represent the way of the people, continue the lost learning of sages, and open the path of peace for ten thousand years."[64] Chang Tsai's statement differs from Chou Tun-i's statement in one important aspect: Chang Tsai explicitly speaks of an individual's benefitting people and the world by sagely learning, whereas Chou Tun-i speaks of the embodiment of Tao in an individual, which could, but need not, be given a moral-political meaning as well as an ontological meaning. Together they define the ultimate goal of learning as attainment of "sageliness inside and kingliness outside" (*nei-sheng wai-wang*[cf])—an ideal state which all Confucianists have aspired to achieve since Confucius.

Both the *Great Learning* and the *Doctrine of the Mean* may be said to elaborate on this goal by presenting a system of ideas explaining this goal and their methods for attaining it. In this sense, everything is a method relative to this ultimate goal. Since the *Great Learning* and the *Doctrine of the Mean* are different in their approaches, having originated from different backgrounds, methodological differences reflect different emphases. It might be said that the *Great Learning* stresses the external side of the goal—the attainment of "kingliness outside," whereas the *Doctrine of the Mean* stresses the internal side of the goal—the attainment of "sageliness inside." With this understanding, we may say that Chu Hsi's philosophy is an attempt to combine both. But in light of the Neo-Confucian development, he succeeds more in the art of cultivating sageliness inside than in cultivating kingliness outside. In this respect he follows his predecessors Chou Tun-i, Chang Tsai, and the two Ch'engs. Chu Hsi's supplementary commentary on *ko-wu* bespeaks this emphasis. But this commentary is also important in providing an ontological link between the *Doctrine of the Mean* and the *Great Learning*, as it is intended to provide a link between internal cultivation and external cultivation of a person. As we have shown in our analysis, knowledge and full understanding of *li* enables a person to act rightly and to transform himself into a morally right and politically right person. Chu Hsi has provided an ontological basis for morality and an ontological-moral basis for family, society, and government.

In Chu Hsi's system everything is a methodology or has methodological significance for the ultimate end. Indeed, in so far as there is a goal, there is a method. In light of what is said in the *Doctrine of the Mean* and the *Great Learning* one begins with something very basic and moves on to a higher stage of cultivation. There are basic methods to higher ends or goals which, when cultivated, become methods to a still higher end. In so far as all goals and ends are hierarchically structured and processed, methods relative to them are analogically structured and processed. Thus as the investigation of things is the method to the extension of knowledge, the latter is the method to the authentification of intentions. In one sense, as we have seen, investigation of things and mastery of mind *(ch'ih-ching)* in Chu Hsi seem to be directly related to the ultimate goal of sageliness inside and kingliness outside and thus acquire a significance outreaching all other steps in the *Great Learning*. But we must nevertheless recognize the potential hierarchical structure of Chu Hsi's metaphysical and methodological thinking. After we recognize investigating things as an outstanding method for reaching sageliness inside, we may raise the question: What is the method for the investigation? Or what does investigating things presuppose as a methodological basis? As we have seen, Chu Hsi makes the investigation rely on learning from daily life and experience, on reflections, on inner promptings of heart and mind, on historical experiences of the past, and on words of sages from the past. This means we must presuppose a wide range of experience and cognition—an open range of individual, social, political, and historical experiences for doing the investigation. The

FIGURE 3

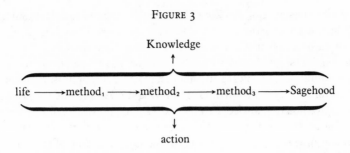

concepts of *li* and *ch'i* come from this wide range of experiences and become refined when we see their integrating, explanatory, organizing, and critical significance. In this way, these experiences lead to more refined appreciation of what is basic to the investigation of things, which in turn refines the methodology of the investigation toward extension of knowledge. Inevitably, there is hermeneutical interplay between elementary informal experiences and gradual formation of methodology. This hermeneutical interplay occurs on every level, and a chain of hermeneutical interplays finally take place between the elementary experiences of life and the understanding of the ultimate goal of sageliness inside and kingliness outside, which is also the ultimate method.

In light of this analysis, we can conclude that the methodology implicit in Chu Hsi's philosophy is always a structure and a process which heralds one method posterior to it and derives from another method prior to it. It serves the purposes of knowing and acting, as elementary experience of life is a combination of knowing and acting, knowing and believing, knowing and valuing, or deciding, as shown in Figure 3.

Since in the view of this ontological understanding the ultimate goal and the ultimate method require and reveal an ontological understanding of the Great Ultimate, all methods are given meaning.[65] Thus the hermeneutical understanding of a method in reference to another, like understanding one idea in reference to another, is onto-hermeneutical, that is, understandable in light of an ontology, and therefore constituting an explanation of the presupposed ultimate ontology, which is the ultimate goal. The hermeneutical circle or interplay between experiences and ontology, as between their methodological dimensions, is essentially an interpretation of the underlying ontology, and thus onto-hermeneutical. This is an meta-methodological observation on the methodologizing process and methodological structure in Chu Hsi.

The onto-hermeneutical methodology in fact is clearly reflected in Chu Hsi's own (together with Lü Tsu-ch'ien's,[cg] 1137–1181) compilation and commentary on the earlier Neo-Confucian writings, the *Chin-ssu-lu*.[ch66] The order and arrangement of the topics and titles for chapters in this book exhibit the methodological order of learning toward sageliness and kingliness, which is onto-hermeneutically meaningful. The book begins with the chapter on the

Tao-t'i[ci] (the substance of the Way). Because this is the ontological foundation for all learning and acting, one has to have some understanding of it before one can employ any method for perfecting the understanding. The second chapter on the essentials of learning (*wei-hsüeh*[cj]) may be said to lay the ground for orientating oneself toward the understanding and application of the Tao, and therefore serves as the method of knowing the *Tao-t'i*. The next two chapters, on extension of knowledge (*chih-chih*[ck]) and on preserving mind and nourishing nature *(ts'un-yang),* are no doubt the cardinal methodologies toward refinement of learning and perfection of the understanding of the way. They are nevertheless also methodologically essential for such later steps as self-cultivation, family-regulation, political service, and government-administration. These two steps are also closely related, and their relationship is made clear by an improved understanding of the *Tao-t'i* and hence by the improved understanding of the mind-substance and thing-substance. Chu Hsi's own philosophy of *li* and *ch'i, ch'iung-li* and *ch'ih-ching* explicates all this. The fifth chapter on self-discipline and self-improvement and return to propriety (*k'o-chih*[cl]) is a natural consequence of the improved understanding of mind, which in Chu Hsi has produced independent discussion of self-discipline. This reflects the methodological stage of "rectifying one's mind" (*cheng-hsin*[cm]) and "cultivating one's person" in the *Great Learning* scheme. Hence, it is a methodological basis for family-regulation and a methodological sequel and complement to the procedure of *ts'un-yang* and *ko-wu*.

After Chapter 5, all the remaining chapters are either methodological sequels to the earlier methodological procedures or are their applications. In this regard, the paradigm of substance and function (*t'i-yung*[cn]) is fully employed. A prior methodology is always a substance to the succeeding methodology, which is a function of the substance. Thus, *ko-wu* and *ts'un-yang* can be regarded as the functioning or cofunctioning of the substance of the way, whereas correcting one's mind and cultivating one's person can be regarded as the extension or complementation (also a matter of functioning) of *ko-wu* and *ts'un-yang*. Along this line, it is clear that such matters as how to regulate family and how to govern a state become matters of how to function according to the Way in qualitatively and quantitatively different contexts. Since the substance of the Way penetrates all levels and contexts of life, society, and the world, and since experiences and actions on all levels and on all contexts of life, society, and the world require particular attention in *ko-wu* and *ts'un-yang,* and make particular contributions toward fuller and fuller understanding of the substance of the Way, methodologically speaking, there is obviously an hermeneutical circle and interplay throughout the development and integration of the concept of the *Tao-t'i* and all the life activities of an individual from the first chapter to the last chapter of the *Chin-ssu-lu*.

The philosophical implications of Chu Hsi's onto-hermeneutical methodology in his philosophy of *li-ch'i* and philosophy of mind are many. We may limit our observations to three major implications. First, we cannot understand the ontological truth embodied in the philosophy of *li-ch'i* in any narrow sense of truth. One might say that Chu Hsi's philosophy and methodology have provided a new view of truth in virtue of its onto-hermeneutical understanding of the way in all human contexts. Truth is a primitive relation, which logic has shown to be not completely definable. This means that no complete conceptualization and formalization of truth are possible. Truth must be therefore illuminated rather than defined. The illumination may be conceived as a noetic awareness of a sense of completion and integration. The ontological understanding of the substance of the Way in Chu Hsi provides an illuminational theory of truth, rather than a definitional theory of truth. In light of Chu Hsi's onto-hermeneutical methodology of *ko-wu*, we may consider any relation between subject and object to constitute a truth relation in so far as a distinction between subject and object can be made. Then truth could be conceived as a relation of integration, illumination, and harmonization.[67] It is to be experienced and will be pragmatically effective in making a harmonization of actions and things, an integration of personality, and an illumination of mind. This seems to be precisely what the doctrine of *ko-wu* and *ts'un-yang* suggests.

Second, based on the conception of ontological truth above, Chu Hsi may be said to suggest a notion of knowledge that is integrative, dialectical, and highly pragmatic. For Chu Hsi knowledge is understanding of experience and principle. It always involves a reference to the ontological truth and the overall understanding and perception of truth. Centering on this perception of truth, knowledge integrates experience and grows with experience in scope, and becomes more applicable. This is a dialectical process to be understood again onto-hermeneutically as we have seen in the dialectical model of unity and division. The applicability of knowledge means that knowledge generates redistribution of values and requires axiological evaluation. This means that what we know raises questions as to what we ought to do and how we undertake to do it. For knowledge creates not only new views on things but new obligations, new rights, and new values, and thus makes a difference to social and political life. Yet knowledge should not become simply relative and temporalizing; it must instead be integrated with our perception of the ontological truth for generating guidelines for determination of values and guidance of actions. This implies of course that the ontological truth has an axiological dimension, which produces standards of good and right. Chu Hsi's view on the mind of heaven and earth and the virtue of benevolence as life-creativity provides both a metaphysical foundation for life-ends and moral distinctions and a moral foundation for metaphysical understanding. This is the best exemplification of the Confucian-Mencian tradition of regarding moral mind as ontological mind and vice versa.

On the basis of this observation, we may say that Chu Hsi has developed an integrational notion of knowledge through his doctrines of *ching*, which satisfies the following conditions: There is a total interrelation of all elements without conflict; there is an ontological perception of the Way and a constant reference to it in knowing; there is an illumination of mind; there is a practical applicability to action and life; there is an axiological evaluation implicit in each item of knowledge; and there is a fulfilling sense of growth and completion. Knowledge in this sense remains dialectical and requires active participation of the knowing individual in his life. In Western philosophy, only Spinoza's notion of the intellectual love of God seems to come close to this Neo-Confucian notion of knowledge.

Finally, in modern hermeneutics, understanding and knowledge are ontologically understood. This means that understanding and knowledge, which may be said to have an ontological rooting, are no better than our experience of daily life and our position in daily life. One may therefore say that our understanding of truth and knowledge begins with our positional understanding of life, which can be called preunderstanding or preknowledge of truth. With this beginning and rooting knowledge and understanding will grow and develop by the principle of the hermeneutical circle. It is clear that in Chu Hsi we have precisely this affirmation of preunderstanding and preknowledge. But Chu Hsi points to something even deeper: the preunderstanding and preknowledge is not simply of daily life but involves a perception of ontological truth of the *Tao*. This can be made clear by looking into not just things, but one's own mind and nature. From this, an onto-hermeneutical (not merely a hermeneutical) process begins between the inner mind and the outer things, eventually leading to a full understanding of and a full disclosure of truth. In fact, it is because of an interplay between a preunderstanding of the total truth and a preunderstanding of daily life that possibilities are created for a full understanding and a full integration of truth and experiences. The onto-hermeneutical principle works together with the principle of preunderstanding to achieve the illumination of mind and the transformation of an individual into acquiring sageliness. The pragmatic relevance cannot be ignored here. Preunderstanding is rooted in practice and practical experience of life; so is the onto-hermeneutical understanding, which permits mutual illumination between theory and practice. Hence, we may speak of the principle of transformation as part of the onto-hermeneutical methodology exemplified in Chu Hsi.

Notes

1. As versus purely scientific, objective discoveries.

2. See the *Chu Tzu yü-lei* [Classified conversations of Master Chu], (Taipei: Cheng-chung[co] Book Co., 1970), ch. 1, p. 2.

3. *Ibid.*, ch. 18, p. 640; cf. also ch. 6, pp. 156–160.

4. *Ibid.*, ch. 18, p. 640.

5. *Ibid.*, ch. 94, p. 3765.

6. *Ibid.*

7. See the *Erh-Ch'eng chi*[cp] [Collected works of the two Ch'engs], (Taipei: Li-jen[cq] Book Co., 1982), Bk. I, *Ho-nan Ch'eng-shih ching-shou*[cr] [Explanations of the Classics by the Ch'engs of Ho-nan], ch. 1, "I-shou"[cs] [Explanations of the *Book of Changes*], p. 1029.

8. See Hans-Georg Gadamer, *Philosophical Hermeneutics* (Berkeley and Los Angeles: University of California Press, 1972). Cf. also Martin Heidegger, *Discourse on Thinking* (translation of *Gelassenheit*), (New York: Harper & Row, 1961).

9. The term is used in the sense of Schleirmacher and Dilthey to indicate the mutual determining of meaning and value of part and whole in an ever-enlarging process of evolution and development.

10. See the *Erh-Ch'eng chi*, ch. 25, p. 316.

11. This is of course the strongest sense of *ch'iung-li*.

12. This is also the point of view of Ch'eng I, for Ch'eng I also suggests that one has to investigate one thing one day and another the next day, so that when one accumulates more investigations, one will quickly come to have integration of all *li*. Cf. the *Erh-Cheng chi*, ch. 18, p. 188.

13. Again this notion is originally suggested by Ch'eng I. See above, n. 12.

14. Although Chu Hsi does not regard *li* as moving and creative, he does say that "having this *li*, this *ch'i* is created," "there is no *li* without *ch'i* and there is no *ch'i* without *li*," and "before there is heaven-and-earth, there is this *li*. When moving yang is created, it is only due to this *li*. When being at rest, yin is created, it is only due to this *li*" (*Chu Tzu yü-lei*, ch. 1, p. 2). From these and other similar statements, it seems clear that Chu Hsi does not exclude a dynamic element from his concept of primary *li*, which apparently he identifies with the concept of the *T'ai-chi*, which must be considered the creative source of heaven-and-earth or yin-and-yang. He says, "If there is no *T'ai-chi*, there would be no heaven-and-earth" (*ibid.*, p. 2).

15. *Chu Tzu yü-lei*, ch. 41, p. 1673.

16. *Ibid.*, ch. 117, pp. 4502 and 4512; ch. 27, pp. 1086–1087, 1089.

17. *Ibid.*, ch. 27, pp. 1086–1087, 1089; ch. 46, p. 1863.

18. *Ibid.*, ch. 46, p. 1863.

19. *Ibid.*, ch. 15, p. 462. Of course Chu Hsi did not really experiment with boats and carriages, but he merely suggested that one can imaginatively experiment with boats and carriages in order to know and see the nature of boats and carriages.

20. *Ibid.*, ch. 2, pp. 34–39.

21. For all these see the *Chu Tzu yü-lei*, ch. 1, pp. 8–10; Ch'ien Mu, *Chu Tzu hsin hsüeh-an*, 5 vols. (Taipei: San-min[ct] Book Co., 1971), Bk. 1, pp. 215–219; and Yung Sik Kim,[cu] "The Worldview of Chu Hsi (1130–1200): Knowledge about Natural World in *Chu Tzu Ch'üan-shu*" (Ph.D. dissertation, Princeton University, 1979).

22. *Chu Tzu yü-lei*, ch. 1, p. 11.

23. See *Chu Wen Kung wen-chi*[cv] [Collection of literary works of Chu Hsi], (SPPY ed.), ch. 44, p. 746, answer to Ts'ai Chi-t'ung.[cw]

24. *Chu Tzu yü-lei*, ch. 8, p. 208.

25. *Chu Wen Kung wen-chi*, ch. 39, p. 648, answer to Ch'en Ch'i-chung.[cx]

26. *Chu Tzu yü-lei*, ch. 15, pp. 494–496. Cf. also Ch'ien Mu, *Chu Tzu hsin hsüeh-an*, Bk. II, p. 514.

27. *Ibid.*, ch. 118, p. 4561.

28. *Ibid.*, ch. 18, p. 669; ch. 60, p. 2323.

29. See the *Ssu-shu chi-chu*[cy] [Collected commentaries on the Four Books], (Taipei: World Book Co., 1977), the *Book of Mencius*, ch. 7, p. 187.

30. *Chu Tzu yü-lei*, ch. 18, p. 640.

31. A fair picture of Chu Hsi's doctrine of *ko-wu* can be obtained by examining his detailed and incisive criticisms of various other positions of *ko-wu*. For this see Ch'ien Mu, *Chu Tzu hsin hsüen-an*, Bk. II, pp. 521–534; also Bk. I, pp. 130–132.

32. *Chu Tzu yü-lei*, ch. 15, p. 454.

33. *Ibid.*, pp. 456–457, p. 480.

34. *Chu Wen Kung wen-chi*, ch. 72, p. 1333, on Lü's[cz] explanation of the *Great Learning;* also ch. 77, p. 1426, *Nan-chien-chou Yu-hsi hsien-shüeh chi*[da] [Record of the founding of a school in the Yu-hsi County of Nan-chien Prefecture].

35. *Ibid.*, ch. 38, p. 628, answer to Chiang Yüan-shih.[db]

36. See the following passages in the *Chu Tzu yü-lei* for Chu Hsi's discussion of tranquillity *(ching)* and quiet sitting: ch. 12, pp. 325, 345–351. In the first place, Chu Hsi is not opposed to quiet sitting; rather, he considered quiet sitting as "holding back" *(shou-lien*[dc]*)* one's mind, not as falling into a Ch'anist state of thoughtlessness (see pp. 347–348). He also regards tranquillity as the source of nourishing movement *(ching-che, yang-tung-chih-ken*[dd]*)* and movement as acting out one's tranquillity *(so-i hsing ch'i ching*[de]*)* (see p. 349).

37. *Huang-chi ching-shih* (Taipei: Chung-kuo tzu hsüeh ming chu chi-ch'eng pien-yin chi-chin hui,[df] reprint of 1606 ed.), ch. 12, "On the observation of things," p. 277.

38. *Ibid.*, p. 275.

39. See Chou Tun-i, *Chou Tzu ch'üan-shu* [Complete works of Master Chou], *T'ung-shu* [The comprehensive book on the *Book of the Changes*] (Taipei: Commercial Press, 1978), ch. 20, p. 165.

40. *Chang Tzu ch'üan-shu*[dg] [Complete works of Master Chang], *Cheng-meng*[dh] [Correcting youthful ignorance], (Taipei: Commercial Press, 1979), ch. 2, treatise 7, "Ta-hsin*[di] [Widening the mind], p. 45.

41. *Erh-Ch'eng chi*, Bk. I, *Ho-nan Ch'eng-shih wen-chi*[dj] [Collection of literary works by the Ch'engs], *Ming-tao Hsien-sheng wen-chi*[dk] [Collection of literary works by Master Ming-tao], ch. 2, p. 460, answer to Heng-ch'ü.[dl]

42. *Ibid.*; *Ch'eng-shih i-shu*[dm] [Surviving works of the Ch'engs], ch. 15, p. 143.

43. *Ibid.*

44. *Ibid.*, ch. 18, p. 118.

45. See *Ssu-shu chi-chu*, comment on the *Analects*, 6:11. Cf. n. 46.

46. *Erh-Ch'eng chi*, Bk. I, *Ho-nan Ch'eng-shih wen-chi*, *I-ch'uan Hsien-sheng wen-chi*[dn] [Collection of literary works by Master I-ch'uan], ch. 8, p. 577.

47. *Ibid.*

48. See *Ssu-shu chi-chu*, the *Book of Mencius*, *op. cit.*, pp. 187–188 (for Mencius), pp. 20–21 (for the *Doctrine of the Mean*).

49. Of course they did mention and discuss quiet sitting, as we have seen in the case of Chu Hsi (see above, n. 36). But they did not specifically assign an ontological significance to it.

50. See *Chu Tzu ta-ch'üan* [Complete literary works of Master Chu], (Taipei: Chung-hua*[do] Book Co., 1969), ch. 67, "Discourse on Meditating on Mind," pp. 19–20.

51. *Doctrine of the Mean*, ch. 1.

52. Ch'ien Mu, *Chu Tzu hsin hsüeh-an*, Bk. II, pp. 23–82.

53. Cf. Mou Tsung-san,[dp] *Hsin-t'i yü hsing-t'i*[dq] [Mind-substance and nature-substance], (Taipei: Cheng-chung Book Co., 1968), for a detailed study of the mind-substance in Neo-Confucianism.

54. *Chu Tzu yü-lei,* ch. 103, pp. 4191–4192.

55. *Erh-Ch'eng chi, Ch'eng-shih i-shu,* ch. 18, p. 188.

56. In this I follow Ch'ien Mu.

57. As we shall see, it in fact forms a relationship of interdependence with the perceptive inspection of the mind-functioning just as the function of mind and substance of mind forms such a relationship.

58. See *Yü-lei,* ch. 62, pp. 2411–2412.

59. See the *Chin-ssu-lu chi-chieh*[dr] [Collected explanations of the *Reflections on Things at Hand*], comp. by Chang Po-hsing[ds] (Taipei: Commercial Press, 1967), ch. 1, p. 28. Cf. also *Chang Tzu ch'üan-shu,* ch. 14, p. 290.

60. *Book of Mencius,* 2A:6. Mencius thinks that basic virtues of morality are rooted in the inceptive movements of human nature, which is innately good. Thus Mencius says, "The feeling of sympathy is the beginning of benevolence *(jen);* the feeling of shame and hating evil is the beginning of righteousness *(i*[dt]); the feeling of modesty is the beginning of propriety *(li*[du]); the feeling of distinctions between right and wrong is the beginning of moral wisdom *(chih*[dv])."

61. See *Lun-yü chi-chu*[dw] [Collected commentaries on the *Analects*], in the *Ssu-shu chi-chu,* ch. 6, p. 77.

62. *I-ch'uan Hsien-sheng wen-chi,* ch. 71, p. 1245.

63. See Chou Tun-i, "T'ai-chi-t'u shuo," p. 23.

64. *Chang Tzu ch'üan-shu,* ch. 14, p. 292.

65. As we have seen, this ontological understanding is methodologically formulated as dialectics of unity and division.

66. Translated as *Reflections on Things at Hand* by Wing-tsit Chan,[dx] (New York: Columbia University Press, 1967).

67. More can be said about truth. Any relation between subject and object in so far as the distinction is made constitutes a truth relation, which is a relation of harmonizing, corresponding, and cohering. Truth can be understood in two different senses. In the objective sense it is a relation only to be characterized in a reflective mood of mind in the meta-meta-language. It is an object of an order higher than objects of any recognized reality of objects. In the subjective sense it is the consciousness and acknowledgment of the truth relation. It is affirmative gesture of mind with regard to the relation existing between object and subject. It is a feeling of authenticity, sophistication, and stability. In both senses truth is freedom from conflict and contradiction. It is integration of a comprehensive scope. Understanding can be defined to be acknowledgement of truth in both the objective and subjective senses: to be given and experienced rather than defined. There are six idealized forms of truth and knowledge: total integration of elements, total illumination of mind, total grasp of ontological root, total applicability—practical meaningfulness, total axiological evaluation, and total guidance on life and contribution to life fulfillment.

Glossary

a 理學	c 本體之學	e 理氣
b 道	d 理	f 性

13

Chu Hsi and Wisdom
as Hidden and Stored

OKADA TAKEHIKO

I

AS IS UNIVERSALLY KNOWN, Confucianism in the Han (206 B.C.–A.D. 220) and
T'ang (618–907) periods deteriorated into a mere learning of comments and
recitations. Furthermore, after the Wei (220–265) and Chin (265–420)
periods, the thought of Taoists and Buddhists came to be dominant. Confucianism had to undergo a period of spiritual vacuum for a considerably long
time. However, the will of Heaven circles, and never passes without returning. Fortunately, during the Sung period (960–1279), Sacred Learning, once
considered to be extinct with the death of Mencius (372–289 B.C.?), was taken
up again by thinkers and it sublimated old Confucianism by way of transcending the thought of the Buddhists and Taoists. Thus, the defect which had long
been left uncorrected was finally rectified.

This Neo-Confucianism was advocated by Confucians of the Northern
Sung (960–1126). By comprehensively organizing their thoughts, Chu Hsi
established a grand philosophical system that is infinite in significance and
profound in depth. The appearance of Chu Hsi marked, finally, a sharp
change of direction in the world of thought, which had long been dominated
by the Buddhists and Taoists. From this period on, Confucianism was at the
center of the world of thought for a long time, eventually spreading to
neighboring Korea and Japan. We may reasonably aver that Chu Hsi's contribution to and accomplishment in the world of thought was as great as that of
Mencius.

Neo-Confucianism came into being not suddenly or abruptly but as a result
of historical developments in thought and against the background of the spirit
of the time. Hermits and Ch'an[a] masters who had long clung to empty learning (hsü-hsüeh[b]), advocating either the Way of hermits or a transcendental and
natural way of no practical use in the world, began to concern themselves with
Confucianism, for it emphasized practical learning (shih-hsüeh[c]) which, based
on human ethics, prescribed the way by which to support community life.
They also started to show a tendency to be involved and concerned with politics and economy.

Confucians came to regard as their aim and goal of learning an inclination and wish toward becoming sagely because they held that the learning of human ethical relations was the true orthodox learning. In addition, such learning returned to the study of mind and nature. To acquire the purity and absoluteness of one's mind and nature so as to realize the substance and function of the Way is the only way to become a sage after having mastered sacred learning.

At this time, corresponding changes took place in the literary circles as well. The idea that things had a value by dint of their mere existence came under criticism. It was asserted that things do not have a value until they have secured their origin or root that helps make their existence real. Consequently, the inclination toward the sensual and the superficial was spurned, with the logical result that men of letters became concerned with the spiritual and inner richness, and were accorded more value and significance. As a result, men of letters began to return to Classical styles.

Likewise, ceramic artists produced plain, monochromatic objects. Painters also began to draw wash drawings, which were more spiritual in terms of significance than sensual in terms of aesthetic effects. In other words, any outward expressiveness was avoided. That is, an attempt to suppress overt expressiveness and to imply covert richness through simplicity was thought of highly, and "unrevealed significance" was ardently sought after by those involved in artistic activities in many different fields.[1]

In this historical context, it should be noted, "wisdom as hidden and stored" (*chih-ts'ang*[d]), which Chu Hsi advocated, had an impact on and was influenced by the spirit of his time.

II

In recent years, Chu Hsi's learning has been vigorously studied in detail in quite a few fields of intellectual pursuit. Not only scholars of Confucianism, Buddhism, and Taoism, but also those of the humanities and natural sciences engage in research related to Chu Hsi's learning. The reasons for such revival of research interest and activities may be ascribed not only to the fact that Chu Hsi, who stands second only to Confucius (551–479 B.C.), is a great man of thought who was successful in building up a profound and comprehensive philosophical system, but also to the fact that scholars in one field alone can hardly manage to compile a whole and exact picture of Chu Hsi's philosophy and its implications.

In spite of all such activity, however, in my opinion research on Chu Hsi's learning seems to have overlooked two important points: "total substance and great functioning" (*ch'üan-t'i ta-yung*[e]) and "wisdom as hidden and stored." Although the former was studied in detail in reference to its essence by Kusumoto Masatsugu,[2] the latter has rarely been as often discussed and studied in depth as it should have been.

Chu Hsi's "total substance and great functioning," which deals with the functioning of the mind, is a comprehensive summary of substance and function as advocated by Confucians in the Northern Sung period. According to Chu, the substance of the mind is empty in itself but possessed of many principles. And, precisely because the substance is empty, it is of unmeasurable use; it controls principles of the world, and is, consequently, capable of judging happenings in the world. Therefore, Chu Hsi said, the substance is complete and the functioning is of great use.[3] If Chu Hsi's treatise ended here, it would not be so different from Wang Yang-ming's (Wang Shou-jen,[g] 1472–1529) substance and functioning.[4] The differences lie in the different efforts proposed. According to Chu Hsi, the principle of the mind is not different from the principle of things, and the principle of things is the principle of the mind.

The principle has neither such distinctions as being in the inside or on the outside nor such distinctions as being intricate or coarse. Unless effort is made to preserve the mind, it will become unintelligible and chaotic. If subtleties of many principles have not been investigated, the mind will become insulated and inflexible, and one will not be able to realize the wholeness of the mind.

The preservation of the mind, therefore, should be regarded as the basis of the investigation of principle to the utmost, and the investigation of things and principle to the utmost should be regarded as effort for a full development of the mind. And if one accumulates his efforts in the concomitant use of them, one will "awaken all of a sudden" to what is harmonious and unified. The total substance and great functioning of the mind will manifest itself.[5] Saying that there was neither any principle nor any matter outside the mind, Wang Yang-ming considered the effort devoted to the mind to be the root,[6] and came to think that the intelligence of the mind or the extension of knowledge was the basis of learning. Everything would, he thought, be settled if one devoted himself to the extension of knowledge.[7]

In contrast to this stand, Chu Hsi maintained that the extension of knowledge would deteriorate into the empty learning of Ch'an masters or useless learning if the extension of knowledge were not preceded by the investigation of things and mind. Unlike Wang Yang-ming, Chu Hsi considered the investigation of things to be the basis of learning.[8] A marked feature of Chu Hsi's thought of total substance and great functioning is that it extended to and involved politics and economy. Ideas in scientific technologies in later ages are in a sense a development out of this concept of Chu Hsi's philosophy. Thus the special character that differentiates Chu Hsi's learning from that of Yang-ming becomes obvious.

If knowledge is fully investigated, everything in the world will resolve itself as if by the touch of a sword,[9] for knowledge, being spiritual intelligence of the mind, is the most lively work of the mind. But it must be admitted that there exist some differences in regard to knowledge between Chu Hsi and Wang Yang-ming. Knowledge is an operation of the mind, and Chu Hsi regarded knowledge as a functioning of wisdom and the mind as that of principle. Thus he considered wisdom inseparable from knowledge, although he had to admit that there was some subtle difference between the two.[10] He always mentioned principle in discussing knowledge. As Asami Keisai[h] (1652–1711) has described it, knowledge for Chu Hsi is "an activity of principle," that is "a living principle."[11]

Furthermore, Chu Hsi's concept of knowledge may be said to be different from Wang Yang-ming's, which did not point to principle in particular. Chu Hsi's ideas on wisdom as hidden and stored especially put his concept of knowledge in sharp contrast to Wang's idea on innate knowledge of the good. For this reason, it is appropriate to agree with Miyake Shosai's[i] (1662–1741) assertion that Wang's concept of knowledge seems to be similar to Chu Hsi's but is actually different.[12]

Chu Hsi's principle comprises both "the norm governing things as they should be" (*so-tang-jan chih tse*[j]) and "the reason for things being as they are" (*so-i-jan chih ku*[k]). Knowledge is the mind-and-heart of principle, because it is the spiritual intelligence of the mind. It embodies many principles and responds to all things. If it is shown that for Chu Hsi knowledge has these features, then it becomes clear that its similarity to the knowledge of the Buddhists and Taoists is also only apparent, because, as Asami Keisai maintained, their concept of knowledge does not include the essence of principle.[13]

Chu Hsi's idea of wisdom as hidden and stored is a comprehensive synthesis not only of ideas on it before the Ch'in period (221–206 B.C.) and those handed down through the Han and T'ang periods, but also of opinions of Northern Sung Confucian scholars in regard to wisdom. He examined all of these ideas in detail and clarified the essence of wisdom. His "wisdom," which is based on realization through personal experience, should be differentiated from the literal and philological interpretations of the Han and T'ang scholars. By rejecting the Buddhist and Taoist ideas of wisdom, Chu Hsi raised the traditional understanding of wisdom to a higher level.

Unlike his theory of total substance and great functioning, which continued to develop because of its transmission and discussion by his successors, his "wisdom as hidden and stored" was appreciated by only a couple of his disciples. Not only in Yüan (1277–1368), Ming (1368–1644), and Ch'ing (1644–1912) China, but in Korea and Japan as well, only a few scholars have really understood its great significance. One of those scholars was Yamazaki Ansai[l] (1618–1682), who understood Chu Hsi's idea of wisdom as hidden and stored and appreciated its full implications. Thanks to him, Confucian scholars of the Kimon[m] School of Learning showed great interest in this part of Chu Hsi's philosophy and handed it down from generation to generation.

The idea of wisdom as hidden and stored originated in the *Book of Changes*. Being a book of great wisdom, with a grand and profound world-view, it has been valued highly in China since ancient times. It may be said to constitute the nucleus of Chinese thought. As the theory of wisdom as hidden and stored has been handed down from generation to generation, it has occupied an important position in the history of Chinese thought. Chu Hsi deserves the credit for comprehensively organizing all related ideas on the subject into a grand system and by identifying its essence. It was not, however, until his thought as a whole came to full maturity in his old age that Chu Hsi began to deal with wisdom as hidden and stored; he touched upon it for the first time in his lectures at Yü-shan[n14] at the age of sixty-five. Concisely he clarified the essential characteristics of wisdom as hidden and stored in a letter[15] in response to questions raised by Ch'en Ch'i-chih[o] about the Yü-shan lecture. More detailed discussions are found in the *Chu Tzu wen-chi*[p] (Collection of literary works of Master Chu) and, in particular, in the *Chu Tzu yü-lei*[q] (Classified conversations of Master Chu).

III

The *Book of Changes* gives an account of all the phenomena involved in human affairs and the natural order in terms of circulation, coming and going, and growth and decline. According to the book the singular material force (*ch'i*) alternates between yin,[s] the passive and static principle, and yang,[t] the active and dynamic principle. Such an alteration penetrates sharply into man's life and destiny and reveals ways to cope with them. In due time people increasingly realized the importance of an ethical stance in society. The *Book of Changes* did not merely proclaim a mechanistic world-view on the basis of Nature and its inevitability, but propounded a teleological world-view by which one can attain one's goal in life and in nature in conformity to, and not in separation from, a mechanistic world-view.

In the "Appended Remarks" in the *Book of Changes* it is said, "The successive movement of yin and yang constitutes the Way."[16] It is also said, "The great virtue of Heaven and Earth is called life,"[17] and "The endless production of things is called Change."[18] It was through the alteration of yin and yang that the *Book of Changes* saw the will of Heaven and Earth to produce things. Similarly, it accounts for all the phenomena in the world in terms of such an alteration. However, what is called yin or yang is not a fixed thing. The root of the negative principle is positive, and the root of the positive principle is negative. Accordingly, the negative contains the positive and vice versa. In other words, the negative produced the positive, and the positive produced the negative. The phenomena in the world are thus a facet of constant alternations between the negative and the positive principles. The *Book of Changes* clarified its overall content in terms of sixty-four signs of divination, which are synthesized in the *ch'ien*[u] or Heavenly Hexagram of pure yang, and the *kun*,[v] or Earthly Hexagram of pure yin.

The virtue of the Heavenly Hexagram is to produce things, and that of the Earthly Hexagram is to be obedient and thereby to help things to completion.[19] The former is yang, whose virtue functions externally. The latter is yin, whose virtue is "laid up in store."[20] Thus the *Book of Changes* saw a will for preservation in the Earthly Hexagram.[21] It equates the active virtue of the Heavenly Hexagram to produce things with the human virtue of humanity and the passive virtue of the Earthly Hexagram with wisdom.[22] On the basis of this, humanity is regarded as the rise of the will for life, and wisdom the completion of the will for life. But since yin and yang and their activity and tranquillity rotate endlessly, wisdom is the root of the will for life after all.

Chou Tun-i[w] (1017–1073) did not cut the grass outside his window[23] because he saw in the grass a will to live. It may be said that he saw in it the meaning of benevolence or the meaning of wisdom. Also, as Master Ch'eng (Ch'eng I,[x] 1033–1107) said, "Activity and tranquillity have no beginning and have no starting point."[24] Although the *Book of Changes* values the active principle more highly than the passive, we must wait for the nourishing of tranquillity, which constitutes the root, in order to anticipate the pure operation of activity. In order for *che-hu*[y] or a spanworm to stretch itself, it needs first to bend.[25] Collecting is impossible without scattering.

The *Book of Changes* calls for discretion and recuperation on the winter solstice when the active principle is on the verge of getting into motion and the passive principle reaches its limit.[26] According to it, heavenly duty is fullfilled by means of clarifying the period between motion and quietude, or, in other words, by means of clarifying subtleties which are about to move but have not yet begun. Such a rest puts in motion a profound meaning of Heaven and thus helps achieve a great task.[27] In his "Poem on the Winter Solstice," Shao Yung[z] (1011–1077) saw this revelation;[28] and in his valuing of *chi*[aa] (incipient force), Chou Tun-i showed perfect understanding of this process.[29]

"Wisdom as hidden and stored" in the *Book of Changes* is made clearer by equating *chen*[ab] or firmness, a heavenly virtue, with wisdom, a human virtue. Since the *Book of Changes* is a book of divination, the commentary on the Heavenly Hexagrams, as Chu Hsi said, must originally have read, "If one observes what is just, everything will work out to one's advantage."[30]

In the commentary on the texts of the *chien* hexagram, divination is interpreted in terms of morality, and origination, flourish, advantage, and firmness (*yüan heng li chen*[ac]) are regarded as the Four Virtues of Heaven. These are respectively assigned to humanity, righteousness, propriety, and wisdom (*jen i li chih*[ad]). Consequently, origination and flourish act toward the outside when a heavenly will for life goes in motion, and advantage and firmness hide and store themselves within the will for life. At the same time, advantage and firmness are thought of as virtues completing the will for life because the will for life repeats itself and circulates incessantly. Also, they are thought of as physical qualities of the will or the substance of origination and flourish.

Ch'eng I, therefore, thought that it was by virtue of the power of advantage and firmness that the will for life of origination and flourish never stops for a moment.[31] This shows that Ch'eng I comprehended that origination was based on firmness.[32] It is clear that the *Book of Changes* holds that firmness is hidden and stored, and, since wisdom corresponds to firmness, it is hidden and stored. As Chu Hsi said, there clearly lies a will for the cycle of beginning and end in the storage of firmness because firmness is a virtue with attains an ending of things, and is, at the same time, the root from which things are produced. The same is true of wisdom. Of course the *Book of Changes* does not clearly state that there is the cycle of beginning and end in firmness or in wisdom; it merely mentions the meaning of the cycle in connection with humanity.[33]

Originally, the authors of the *Book of Changes* witnessed such natural phenomena as the circulations of time and tide, rotation of the sun and the moon, alterations of nights and days, and changes of the four seasons, and they came to realize that the natural phenomena were nothing but the cycle of rise and fall of yin and yang. They applied such principles as were deduced from natural phenomena to human affairs, by which principles they attempted to predict the fate of mankind. Therefore, it seems justifiable that they began to assign the Four Virtues of Heaven and man to the four seasons, the four directions, and the Five Elements.[34]

Similar views are readily found in the *Book of Rites* and the *Kuan Tzu.*[ac][35] Li Ting-tso[af] of the T'ang period claimed that firmness was an evidence of wisdom. He equated the virtue of humanity, which is the spirit of life in the spring, with the east and Wood; the virtue of propriety, which governs nourishment of things in the summer, with the south and Fire; the virtue of righteousness, which governs the maturing of things in the autumn, with the west and Metal; and the virtue of wisdom, which governs the preserving of life in the winter, with the north and Water. He also quoted Confucius' saying,[36] "The man of humanity enjoys the mountain while the man of wisdom enjoys water."[37]

When winter comes, things contract themselves into storage and preservation and, as a result, become quiet. Likewise, a will for life also contracts itself into such preservation that it leaves hardly any traces on the surface. But the will of Heaven and Earth for life, which is ready to activate itself limitlessly, can be seen lying deep there. The nature of wisdom as hidden and stored is easy to understand in terms of the preservation of life in the winter.

IV

As it is known, Chu Hsi equated nature with principle, regarded principle as laws and norms governing things and their root, and looked upon the root as the Great Ultimate (*T'ai-chi*[ag]). The nature is complete in the mind, through which it works wonderfully. Before the feelings are aroused, the nature is undifferentiated and has no form but possesses many principles. It has regularities when it functions. The general features of such nature were described by Chu Hsi, following Mencius, as the four virtues of humanity, righteousness, propriety, and wisdom. Mencius had described the Four Beginnings as the feeling of commiseration, the feeling of shame and dislike, the feeling of modesty and complaisance, and the feeling of right and wrong.[38] But Chu Hsi identified the Four Beginnings as functions of nature. Thus, Chu Hsi differentiated nature from feelings, and substance from function. By doing so, he thought that the substance of undifferentiated unity could be appreciated. He distinguished between nature and feelings, and substance and function, because he felt that there were defects and drawbacks in Buddhist learning which, in dealing only with undifferentiated substance, had deteriorated into vacuity. Since the Han dynasty, the Five Constant Virtues, namely, humanity, righteousness, propriety, wisdom, and truthfulness, had been presented as elements of nature; Chu Hsi, however, considered that humanity, righteousness, propriety, and wisdom were all true and declared that it was unnecessary to include truthfulness in particular. He followed Mencius in this respect and expounded the Four Virtues of humanity, righteousness, propriety, and wisdom.[39]

Unlike former Confucian scholars, Chu Hsi considered that the Four Virtues of humanity, propriety, righteousness, and wisdom, and the Four Beginnings of the feeling of commiseration, the feeling of modesty and complaisance, the feeling of shame and dislike, and the feeling of right and wrong were the results of growth and decline in the cycle of the passive and the active principles just as origination, flourish, advantage, and firmness were. As a result, Chu Hsi said that wisdom was deeply hidden and profoundly stored moral principle, and that Mencius was the first to advocate wisdom as hidden and stored.[40] According to Chu Hsi, as humanity, propriety, and righteousness are manifested as the feelings of commiseration, complaisance, and shame and dislike, respectively, their operation in affairs can be seen. Wisdom, on the other hand, merely has the power of discretion between right and wrong and is devoid of such operation in human affairs. Thus it is hidden and stored.[41]

From the point of view of principle, with reference to its will for life, humanity is the creation of life, propriety is the growth of life, righteousness is the maturity of life, and wisdom is the storing of life.[42] Wisdom is, therefore symbolized as winter in terms of the four seasons, the limit of quietude of yin in terms of the activity and tranquillity of yin and yang, or the hour of *tzu*[ah] at midnight in terms of a day. It is in wisdom as hidden and stored that all things are stored and preserved and all forms or phenomena hide themselves.[43] Thus it becomes clear that for Chu Hsi, wisdom has the meaning of "being laid up in store and preservation." But viewed in terms of the principle of circulation in the *Book of Changes*, wisdom for Mencius has the meaning not only of "being laid up in store and preservation," but also of "embracing the storage and preservation" and of the cycle of beginning and end.

From the viewpoint of the will for life of principle, Chu Hsi elucidated Mencius' doctrine of the Four Virtues and characterized humanity as being mild, propriety as being outwardly functional, righteousness as being strict and judgmental, and wisdom as contracting. This is explained in terms of birth in the spring, growth in the summer, collecting in the autumn, and preservation in the winter. According to Chu Hsi, though the will for life may rise or fall in the spring, the summer, the autumn, and the winter, it penetrates through humanity, propriety, righteousness, and wisdom just as it penetrates through everything. Even in severe frost or snow during autumn or winter, there is the will of life, which never stops.

In light of the growth and decline of the will for life, Chu Hsi regarded humanity as the rise of the will for life, propriety as its growth, righteousness as its maturity, and wisdom as its preservation.[44] Also, from the standpoint of the rise and decline of the will for life, humanity is its beginning, and without it, the growth of propriety, the maturity of righteousness, and the preservation of wisdom would be impossible. Hence humanity is the most important of the Four Virtues. In terms of the Four Beginnings, humanity, being the feeling of gentleness and kindness, results in the feeling of commiseration, and when it expresses itself, gives rise to the feelings of complaisance, shame and dislike, and right and wrong when it operates, and this operation brings things to completion. Even after things have been brought to completion, gentleness and kindness remain unchanged. Therefore, the feeling of commiseration embraces the feelings of modesty and complaisance, shame and dislike, and right and wrong.

Thus, Chu Hsi decided that humanity includes propriety, righteousness, and wisdom. Like Ch'eng I, he thought that humanity, spoken of separately, stood in parallel with propriety, righteousness, and wisdom, but spoken of collectively embraces all four.[45] Confucius' humanity, according to Chu Hsi, was humanity in collective terms; and when Mencius talked about propriety, righteousness, and wisdom in addition to humanity, he did not set up another humanity aside from that of Confucius.[46] Chu Hsi gave humanity top priority over the other three virtues[47] and said that the School of the Sage was anxious to seek humanity.[48]

Because he fathomed the principle of rise and fall in the *Book of Changes* and in Mencius' teaching of humanity and wisdom, Chu Hsi not only attached great importance to humanity among the Four Virtues, but he also regarded wisdom as a vital virtue and said in analogy that humanity was the head of the Four Virtues and wisdom their tail. He considered the head and tail to be equally essential, and attached as much importance to wisdom as to humanity. His motive for discussing wisdom as hidden and stored may have originated in his desire to clarify its importance.

Chu Hsi called humanity and wisdom the greatest among the Four Virtues and said that it is just as impossible to expect origination without firmness as to expect humanity without wisdom.[49] As origination rises from firmness, not from origination itself,[50] so humanity rises from wisdom, not from humanity itself. For this reason, he also thought that humanity and wisdom, origination and firmness, being the beginning and end of the cycle, were of special importance.[51] In light of the principle of the will for life, humanity is the virtue in which the will for life begins, and it should be given great importance. Wisdom is the virtue in which the will for life brings itself to perfection; without wisdom it will be impossible for humanity, propriety, and righteousness to bring their task to completion. Just as humanity embraces the three other virtues and enables the cycle to complete, so wisdom constitutes a virtue that embraces the three other virtues, and enables the process of beginning and ending to complete. Thus wisdom can be spoken of separately and collectively.

Chu Hsi took special note of the fact that wisdom has a meaning of the beginning and ending, and tried to explain it by comparing it to storage and preservation in winter, which, in turn, possess the meaning of the beginning and ending. According to him, wisdom belongs to winter. It is a season when the will for life is finally fulfilled. Because it contains the force of activation, wisdom therefore has the meaning of the beginning and ending.[52]

Kusumoto Tanzan[ai] (1828–1883) said, "Knowledge belongs to both winter and firmness. It is wonderful because its substance is tranquil, in which the past is contained, and when its function becomes active, helps us to predict the future. It is a principle which generates all things and controls their beginning and ending."[53] This statement may be said to have clarified Chu Hsi's meaning of embracement, preservation, and beginning and end. Chu Hsi, who had discerned that wisdom possessed the meaning of the beginning and end, understood that in wisdom lies latent a great function that gives rise to the transformation of all things. He said, "The transformations cannot disperse unless they have been collected. That is a natural principle. The point of all transformations lies in the contact between humanity and wisdom."[54] Chu Hsi saw the mind of Heaven and Earth producing things in the interaction between humanity and wisdom.

According to Chu Hsi, humanity, propriety, righteousness, and wisdom, being virtues of the nature and also of Heavenly Principle are all metaphysical realities. They function through the mind, and, accordingly, nature and virtues can be known only through it. Therefore, wisdom as hidden and stored should have been considered through the medium of the feeling of discrete approval and disapproval, in which wisdom acts upon the mind. In a sense, this feeling is a perception of principle. It leaves no traces of any actual operation, but it has the function that helps the myriad principles to perform wonderfully and cause all things to grow and transform.

In this way wisdom becomes the fundamental principle that embraces the myriad principles and helps them to function well. For this reason, wisdom as hidden and stored may be said to be the Great Ultimate, because Chu Hsi held that the myriad principles are laid up in preservation in the Great Ultimate.[55]

Asami Keisai may be said to have expressed the true meaning of Chu Hsi's concept of wisdom as hidden and stored when he called it a living principle. He said that the illustrious virtue in the *Great Learning* is also wisdom, and that the Great Ultimate is where wisdom is stored.[56] Wisdom as hidden and stored, if viewed in terms of "being quiet and acted upon," is the critical juncture of being and action. In the analogy of the four seasons, it is the hour of *tzu* of the winter solstice, which is the time when wisdom as hidden and stored is most quiet and its wonderful function is on the verge of going into action. Just as all things remain in complete quietude in the winter, wisdom is laid up in preservation and has no outward traces. It has neither sound nor smell.

However, within wisdom as hidden and stored the mind of Heaven and Earth to produce things is active. It is nothing but the Great Ultimate and the substance of the Way because it exists in silence. As it is the Great Ultimate and the substance of the Way, it is also the nature mandated by Heaven described in the *Doctrine of the Mean*. Therefore, Chu Hsi said that the *Doctrine of the Mean* deals essentially with wisdom.[57] It was Yamazaki Ansai who showed a perfect understanding of the implications of this statement by Chu Hsi.[58] According to Kusumoto Tanzan, this is an unprecedentedly clear-sighted view, and very few Confucian scholars in the Yüan and Ming dynasties had been conscious of its significance.[59]

If we fully realize the meaning of wisdom as hidden and stored, we can appreciate why Chu Hsi attached great importance to the extension of knowledge. When we have reached this profound wisdom after our persistent quest for it, we will be able to solve anything.[60] Chu Hsi considers the investigation of things to be essential for the extension of knowledge and thinks that one will find all principles suddenly unfold before one's eyes if one perseveres in his quest. Obviously, it will not be necessary to talk about being awakened all of a sudden if one cultivates this profound wisdom with the understanding of it as hidden and stored. In discussing the meaning of the beginning and end of wisdom as hidden and stored Chu Hsi said, "How can there be a beginning without an end?" And he emphasized the importance of the effort to cultivate the subtle positive principle in quietude, citing the commentary on the *fu*[ai] (to return) hexagram in the *Book of Changes*.[61]

The more profound wisdom becomes, the fewer traces will be left, just as in the winter all things withdraw themselves in storage and leave no mark of actual operation. While wisdom remains quiet and silent, it contains infinite possibilities of movements and activities. All the activities will be able to show their real feature only if they are supported by the effort at quietude. For this purpose, therefore, one's self-cultivation by means of quiet sitting becomes indispensable. If, by doing so, the mind is intensely concentrated and becomes clear, wisdom will deepen and become profound. And if wisdom becomes more and more profound, what is laid up in preservation will expand its extent and dimensions. One will then reach a clear understanding of the reason for things being as they are. All the affairs that have arisen in front of one's eyes will resolve themselves as if by the power of a sword. If this is the case, it will not be necessary to stress the need of "being awakened all of a sudden."

Liu Tzu-hui (Liu P'ing-shan,[ak] 1101–1147) said,

> Trees dig into the darkness of the earth
> To bring forth the splendor of spring growth.
> Man digs into the darkness of his self
> To bring forth the pure light of mature wisdom.[62]

This is what Chu Hsi called "The Teaching of the Tree" (*mu-hui*[al]). Later, Li Yung (Li Erh-chu,[am] 1627–1705) said,

> Without enduring the chilling cold of winter
> How could the plum blossoms release their fragrance?[63]

If we follow the precepts and lessons set forth by them and bear in mind the investigation of things and the extension of knowledge, we may rest assured that we will certainly get to the core and essence of "wisdom as hidden and stored."

Here we have outlined the essence of Chu Hsi's concept of "wisdom as hidden and stored" and its implications. His "wisdom" sublimated the wisdom of ancient Confucianism by negating the "light" of the Taoists and the "enlightenment" of the Buddhists; it is an important concept comparable to Wang Yang-ming's "the innate knowledge of the good." It is my earnest hope that Chu Hsi's wisdom as hidden and stored will be reexamined from the global point of view by scholars whose academic concern relates to Confucianism.

Translated by Yoshitake Toshikazu[an]

Notes

1. Okada Takehiko, *So-min tetsugaku josetsu*[ao] [Introduction to Sung-Ming philosophy], (Tokyo: Bengensha,[ap] 1977), ch. 3.

2. Kusumoto Masatsugu, "Zentai taiyo no shiso" [The philosophy of total substance and great functioning], in the *Chugoku tetsugaku kenkyu*[aq] [Studies on Chinese thought], (Tokyo: Kokushikan[ar] University Library, 1975), pp. 353–391.

3. *Ta-hsüeh chang-chü*[as] [Commentary on the *Great Learning*], comment on the text.

4. See the *Ch'uan-hsi lu*[at] [Instructions for practical living], sec. 108, 112, 212, and Sato Issai,[au] *Denshu roku rangai sho*[av] [Notes and comments on the *Ch'uan-hsi lu*], (Tokyo: Keishin Shoin,[aw] 1905), pt. 1, p. 14a.

5. *Ta-hsüeh huo-wen*[ax] [Questions and answers on the *Great Learning*], (Japanese ed. printed by Yamazaki Ansai, 1647), comment on the "Amended Commentary" on the fifth chapter, pp. 20a–21b.

6. *Ch'uan-hsi lu,* pt. 1, p. 14a.

7. *Wang Wen-ch'eng Kung ch'üan-shu*[ay] [Complete works of Wang Yang-ming], ch. 7, "Preface to the ancient text of the *Great Learning.*"

8. *Chu Tzu yü-lei* [Classified conversations of Master Chu], (Kyoto: Yamagataya,[az] 1688), 126:13b; Kusumoto Masatsugu, *So-Min jidai Jugaku shiso no kenkyu*[ba] [Studies on Confucian thought in the Sung-Ming period], (Chiba[bb]: Hiroike gakuen,[bc] 1962), pp. 5–6.

9. *Chu Tzu yü-lei,* 19:16b.

10. *Chu Tzu wen-chi* [Collection of literary works of Master Chu], (Junbundo[bd] ed.), 55:1a, letter in reply to P'an Ch'ien-chih.[be]

11. Miyake Shosai, *Chizo ron hitsusatsu*[bf] [Notes on the theory of wisdom as hidden and stored], manuscript.

12. *Ibid.*

13. *Ibid.*

14. *Chu Tzu wen-chi,* 74:18a–22a, "Lecture at Yü-shan."

15. *Ibid.,* 58:21a–23a second letter to Ch'en Ch'i-chih on the lecture at Yü-shan.

16. *Book of Changes,* "Appended Remarks," pt. 1, ch. 5.

17. *Ibid.,* pt. 2, ch. 1.

18. *Ibid.,* pt. 1, ch. 5.

19. *Ibid.,* pt. 2, ch. 12.

20. *Ibid.,* pt. 1, ch. 5; "Remarks on the Hexagrams," ch. 3.

21. *Ibid.*

22. *Ibid.*

23. *I-shu*[bg] [Surviving works], in the *Erh-Ch'eng ch'üan-shu*[bh] [Complete works of the two Ch'engs], (1670 ed.) 3:2b.

24. Ch'eng I, *Ching-shuo*[bi] [Explanations of the Classics], in the *Erh-Ch'eng ch'üan-shu,* 40:15b.

25. *Book of Changes,* "Appended Remarks," pt. 2, ch. 5.

26. *Ibid.,* commentary on the *fu* (to return) hexagram.

27. *Ibid.,* "Appended Remarks," pt. 1, ch. 10; pt. 2, ch. 5.

28. *Chi-jan chi*[bj] [Poems of striking an earthen instrument], (1969 ed.), 5:33b.

29. *T'ung-shu*[bk] [Penetrating the *Book of Changes*], ch. 3.

30. *Chu Tzu yü-lei,* 68:6b.

31. *I-chuan*[bl] [Commentary on the *Book of Changes*], ch. 1, comment on the commentary on the *ch'ien* hexagram.

32. *Chizo ron hitsusatsu.*

33. *I-chuan,* ch. 1, comment on the commentary on the first hexagram.

34. Metal, Wood, Water, Fire, and Earth, Earth being in the center.

35. *Book of Rites,* ch. 19, "Record of Music"; ch. 49, "Four Systems of Funeral Dresses"; ch. 45, "Community Drinking Feast"; *Kuan Tzu,* second treatise, "Conditions and Circumstances."

36. *Analects,* 6:21.

37. Li Ting-tso, *Chou-i chi-chieh*[bm] [Collected explanations of the *Book of Changes*].

38. *Book of Mencius,* 2A:6.

39. *Chu Tzu wen-chi,* ch. 74, "Lecture at Yü-shan," 58:21a–23a, second letter to Ch'en Ch'i-chih on the lecture at Yü-shan.

40. *Chu Tzu yü-lei,* 32:11b.

41. *Chu Tzu wen-chi*, 45:23a–b, fifth reply to Liao Tzu-hui;[bn] supplementary collection, 10:6a–7a, letter in reply to Li Chi-shan's[bo] questions.

42. *Ibid.*, ch. 67, "Treatise on origination, flourish, advantage, and firmness."

43. *Chu Tzu yü-lei*, 6:13b. See also above, n. 15.

44. *Chu Tzu wen-chi*, 74:18a–22a, lecture at Yü-shan; 38:12b, fifth reply to Yüan Chi-chung;[bp] *Chu Tzu yü-lei*, 6:7a, 8a, 11b.

45. Ch'eng I, *I-chuan*, ch. 1, comment on the first hexagram, *ch'ien*.

46. See above, n. 15.

47. *Chu Tzu yü-lei*, 6:9a.

48. *Ibid.*, 6:13a.

49. *Ibid.*, 60:2b.

50. *Ibid.*, 6:11b. See also above, n. 15.

51. *Ibid.*, 6:10a.

52. *Ibid.*, 68:18a. See also above, n. 15.

53. *Kusumoto Tanzan isho*[bq] [Surviving works of Kusumoto Tanzan], ch. 6, "Gakushu roku"[br] [Records of learning and practice], pt. 1, p. 17a.

54. See above, n. 15.

55. *Chu Tzu yü-lei*, 94:8b.

56. See above, n. 11.

57. *Chu Tzu yü-lei*, 6:11b. The reference to the *Doctrine of the Mean* is to ch. 1.

58. *Yamazaki Ansai zenshu*[bs] [Complete works of Yamazaki Ansai], pt. 2, "Bunkai hitsuroku"[bt] [Records of a literary gathering], p. 504.

59. *Kusumoto Tanzan isho*, ch. 6, "Gakushu roku," pt. 2, p. 27b.

60. *Chu Tzu yü-lei*, 19:16b, 53:14b.

61. *Ibid.*, 53:15a–b.

62. *P'ing-shan chi*[bu] [Collected works of Liu Tzu-hui], (1901 ed.), 6:1b.

63. *Li Erh-ch'u ch'üan-chi*[bv] [Complete collection of Li Yung], (Hsien-feng,[bw] 1851–1861, ed.), 6:1b, "Self-reflection on reading the Four Books."

Glossary

a	禪	r	氣	ai	楠本端山
b	虛學	s	陰	aj	復
c	實學	t	陽	ak	劉子翬屏山
d	智藏	u	乾	al	木誨
e	全體大用	v	坤	am	李顒二曲
f	楠本正繼	w	周敦頤	an	吉武利和
g	王陽明守仁	x	程頤	ao	宋明哲學序説
h	淺見絅齋	y	尺蠖	ap	文言社
i	三宅尚齋	z	邵雍	aq	中國哲學研究
j	所當然之則	aa	幾	ar	國士館
k	所以然之故	ab	貞	as	大學章句
l	山崎闇齋	ac	元亨利貞	at	傳習錄
m	崎門	ad	仁義禮智	au	佐藤一齋
n	玉山	ae	管子	av	傳習錄欄外書
o	陳器之	af	李鼎祚	aw	啓新書院
p	朱子文集	ag	太極	ax	大學或問
q	朱子語類	ah	子	ay	王文成公全書

az 山形屋
ba 宋明時代儒学思想の
　研究
bb 千葉
bc 廣池學園
bd 壽文堂
be 潘謙之
bf 智藏論筆笥
bg 遺書

bh 二程全書
bi 經說
bj 擊壤集
bk 通書
bl 易傳
bm 周易集解
bn 廖子晦
bo 李繼善

bp 袁機仲
bq 楠本端山遺書
br 學習錄
bs 山崎闇齋全書
bt 文會筆錄
bu 屏山集
bv 李二曲全集
bw 咸豐

14

Chu Hsi's "Treatise on Jen*"*

SATO HITOSHI

THE ISSUES most actively discussed by scholars in recent years concerning Chu Hsi's thought, in particular his *weltanschauung*, are his views on *t'ai-chi*[a] (Supreme Ultimate), which explore the original substance of the cosmos, and on *li-ch'i*[b] (principle and material force), which explain the overall structure of the cosmos. These issues have generally been regarded as the most philosophical aspect of Chu Hsi's thinking. Yet there is, in the traditional thinking of the Chinese people, the notion of the unity of Heaven and man (*t'ien-jen he-i*[c]). In the long history of Chinese thought, this idea has manifested itself in various forms. This is a concept that asserts the continuity between nature and man as well as the identity between the principles of the natural world and that of the human world. Furthermore, it is a concept that maintains that if something spiritual does exist in the natural world, this spirituality is best manifested in the human mind. The Mencian statement that "when the original nature of man is understood, then Heaven will also be understood"[1] is premised upon this idea of *t'ien-jen he-i*. Concerning this statement, Chu Hsi offers the following explanation:

> Nature (*hsing*[d]) is the allotment that is endowed to man. Heaven (*t'ien*[e]) is the principle that is shared in common by the myriad things. Heaven is thus an enlarged version of man, while man is a miniaturized version of Heaven. The Four Moral Qualities of Humanity (*jen*[f]), Righteousness (*i*[g]), Propriety (*li*[h]), and Wisdom (*chih*[i]) inherent in human nature are identical with the Four Qualities of Origination (*yüan*[j]), Flourish (*heng*[k]), Advantage (*li*[l]), and Firmness (*chen*[m]) intrinsic to Heaven. All things possessed by human beings come from Heaven. Thus if we understand our own nature, we will understand Heaven as well.[2]

According to Chu Hsi, therefore, even though there may be a vast disparity between Heaven and man, their basic structures are essentially identical. This being the case, it follows that when man is understood, so will be Heaven. Indeed, there were thinkers who argued precisely from this standpoint. Ch'eng I-ch'uan (Ch'eng I,[n] 1033–1107) made the following observation:

"Formerly Yang Hsiung[o] [53 B.C.–A.D. 18] remarked that when Heaven and Earth are observed, the sage will be known. I disagree. Rather, I think it is more accurate to state that when the sage is observed, Heaven and Earth will be understood."[3]

As the quotation indicates, this priority given to the understanding of man represents the main line of Confucian thinking. Consequently, in order to analyze the characteristics of Chu Hsi's ideas, it is of primary importance to focus on his views of man. In Chu Hsi's views of man, nothing is more significant than his theory on mind and nature (*hsin-hsing*[p]). This theory illustrates Chu's conception of the overall structure of the mind; and this mind has been fondly referred to by him as "the master of the self and the root of all affairs."[4] The cornerstone of Chu Hsi's theory of mind and nature is none other than his celebrated *Jen-shuo*[q] (Treatise on *jen*).

It is common knowledge that *jen* is the highest ideal in Confucianism. As the source of morality and the basis of all moral deeds, it has been regarded as at once the root and the stem of all ethical virtues. Consequently, it will not be an overstatement to note that for all Confucianists, the greatest mission in life is the pursuit of *jen* in both the cognitive and the practical sense. Chu Hsi has made it clear.

> In the pursuit of knowledge, it is impossible to learn exhaustively about the Five Constant Virtues (*wu-ch'ang*[r]) and the hundred moral deeds. In man's original nature, the Five Constant Virtues of Humanity, Righteousness, Propriety, Wisdom, and Faithfulness (*hsin*[s]) are most basic. Of the five, *jen* is the most fundamental. In the cultivation of the way of *jen*, holding on to seriousness (*ch'ih-ching*[t]) is the most important. When one is ever watchful and alert in the pursuit of the lost mind, without a moment of laxness, then even when one is incapable of knowing exhaustively the myriad principles, the virtues of righteousness, propriety, wisdom, and faithfulness will naturally become manifested in one's handling of affairs. It is imperative that we take note of this fact. The pursuit of *jen* through seriousness is the key to learning. All followers of Confucius are given this principle instruction in the pursuit of *jen*.[5]

In what follows, I shall focus my discussion on Chu Hsi's view on *jen* as an integral part of his thinking. Before doing so, however, I shall provide a brief history of the various views on *jen* propounded by scholars before Chu Hsi.

According to the latest interpretation by etymologists, the Chinese character of *jen* symbolizes a person carrying a heavy burden and walking bent-backed under the load. Thus originally *jen* is a word that signifies "bearing and enduring."[6] It was Confucius who attached a profound philosophic implication to this word. In Confucius' view, one attains maturity in one's social interaction with others when one can actually master or conquer oneself. In *Analects*, 12:1, it is stated that "to master oneself and return to propriety is jen." This assertion confirms that even though self-mastery or self-conquest is not the attainment of *jen* itself, it is certainly an important condition in the realization of it. Mencius has also noted that "all men have the mind which cannot bear to witness the sufferings of others."[7] This shows that the mind which cannot bear to see the misery of others, namely the feeling of sympathy, as well as the mind that harbors fondness for others, namely the feeling of love, are also important dimensions of *jen*. The mastery of the self on the one hand and the love for others on the other thus form, respectively, the inner and outer aspects of *jen*. Regrettably, Confucius himself did not provide a clear and unequivocal explanation of the meaning or content of *jen*. The majority of the references to *jen* in the *Analects* offer only an indirect explanation. In response to a disciple's complaint that while Mencius was clear in his exposition of *jen*, Confucius was decidedly not, Chu Hsi answers, "Confucius also explains with clarity. It is only that you have failed to understand it. Take the case of sugar, for instance. Mencius points out that sugar is sweet. Yet Confucius directly instructs people to taste it themselves. When they do taste it, they know that sugar is indeed sweet, without any explanation at all!"[8] Elsewhere Chu Hsi further observes, "In educating his disciples, Confucius elucidates variously on *jen*. Yet he does not offer a clear definition of the term. This is probably because the principle of *jen* cannot easily be conveyed with words. If a fixed definition is given, then violence might be done to the all-encompassing nature of *jen* itself. If one exerts oneself to experience *jen*, its true meaning will naturally be grasped."[9] Thus, according to Chu, the reasons for Confucius' failure to provide a clear-cut exposition of *jen* are two-fold. The first is that *jen* should be ultimately appreciated experientially, not cognitively. The second is that it is difficult to provide a rigid definition of *jen*. Such a rigid definition will freeze the meaning of *jen* in a narrow sense, thus doing violence to the all-inclusiveness and totality of *jen*. Leaving aside the question whether Chu Hsi's comments are accurate or not, it is evident that scholars through the ages were very much frustrated by Confucius' lack of a clear-cut explanation of *jen*. The reticence on the part of Confucius was also responsible for the proliferation of interpretations of *jen* in later times.

These various interpretations of *jen* have been painstakingly collected into numerous volumes, one of which is entitled *Jinsetsu yōgi*[u] (Essentials of the theories on *jen*), a work compiled by Ōta Kinjo[v] (1765–1825). Ōta was, to be sure, a scholar with an anti–Sung Learning, anti–Chu Hsi bent. This fact notwithstanding, his *Jinsetsu yōgi* provides a comprehensive account of the various ways in which *jen* was understood by generations of scholars. Its content is too detailed and tedious to be recounted here. Stated briefly, however, it shows that *jen* has been generally understood by Confucianists before Sung to be the love that is extended toward others as well as the deeds that are based on such love. The object of one's extension of *jen* can be one's blood relatives or total strangers, or it can be the monarch or the subject, the common people or the animals and plants. As will be demonstrated later, Sung (960–1279) scholars, Chu Hsi included, were generally dissatisfied with this interpretation of *jen* as love. It was their dissatisfaction with this interpretation, which was dominant since the Han period (206B.C.–A.D.220), that prompted them to offer a different understanding of *jen*.

The Sung period was an era in which the ideals of ancient China were revived. From among the literati there emerged the belief that the way of the ancient sages, the so-called principles of "monarch/subject, father/son, humanity, righteousness, propriety, and music" were ultimately immutable.[10] This new thinking, known as Sung Learning, represented a restorative movement that attempted to revive the spirit of ancient times. These Sung scholars took it upon themselves to reexamine the traditional understanding of *jen* as love and to propose a new interpretation befitting this noblest ideal in Confucianism. In what follows I shall try to discuss the various views of *jen* espoused by the Sung scholars before Chu Hsi.

We start with Chou Tun-i[w] (1017–1073), who was accorded the highest respect by Chu Hsi as the precursor of Sung Learning. Chou places the fundamentals of humanity on the principles of "centrality, rectitude, benevolence, and righteousness (*chung-cheng jen-i*[x])."[11] Furthermore, he asserts that the virtue of love is *jen*.[12] At the same time, he regards as *jen* the production of the myriad things by Heaven through the breath of *yang*[y] (male, active principle), and maintains that it is the task of the sage to cultivate and nourish the people through the Heavenly way of *jen*.[13] The famous episode of his refusal to cut the grass outside his window so as to let it grow luxuriantly is reflective of his acute appreciation for, and total identification with, the life-sustaining and life-nurturing capacity of nature.[14] It is clearly indicative of the Sung scholars' preoccupation with production and growth in their explanation of *jen*.

The "Western Inscription" of Chang Tsai[z] (1020–1077), a text exemplifying the boundless spirit of the fellowship of humanity as a whole, has been given the highest accolade by Ch'eng Hao[aa] (1032–1085), who hails it as one "complete with the principles of *jen* and filial piety."[15] This essay, long honored by generations of Confucianists as the best expression of the fundamental essence of Confucian morality, provides clear elucidation on the twin aspects of *jen*. They are the boundless love with which Heaven, Earth, and our parents endow us with life, and filial piety, the absolute sense of attachment and belonging with which we reciprocate and repay their love.

Ch'eng Hao also interprets *jen* as the life-giving quality of nature,[16] and argues that the man of *jen* forms one body with the universe and the myriad things.[17] His younger brother Ch'eng I likens the human mind to a seed of grain. The quality of life and growth inherent in the seed, he declares, is the *jen* in human beings.[18] Moreover, since he agrees that the way of *jen* cannot be adequately conveyed with words, he proposes the way of the public good (*kung-tao*[ab]) to be an approximation of it.[19] All these views of *jen*, from Chou

Tun-i to Ch'eng I, contribute to Chu Hsi's formulation of his own idea on the subject. The following statement by Ch'eng I is particularly significant:

> Because Mencius said that "the feeling of commiseration is *jen*," later scholars have regarded love as *jen*. But love is feeling (*ch'ing*[ac]), whereas jen is nature (*hsing*[ad]). It is therefore erroneous to consider love as *jen*. It is wrong for Han Yü[ae] [768–824] to have said that universal love is *jen*. The man of *jen* of course loves universally, yet one may not therefore confuse *jen* with universal love.[20]

This argument is characteristic of all Sung scholars' interpretation of *jen* and largely determines the direction of later debates on the subject. Ch'en Ch'un[af] (1159–1223), one of the most prominent disciples of Chu Hsi, clearly displays the influence of Ch'eng I in the following remark:

> After Confucius, no one correctly comprehended the true meaning of *jen*. Scholars in the Han period used *jen* to mean favor or benefit. *Jen* was deeply entangled with the feeling of love. As a result, it was believed that something loftier and nobler than *jen* existed. In turn *jen* became an inferior and crude concept. In the T'ang dynasty (618–907), Han Yü upheld *jen* as universal love, yet basically he still followed the traditional understanding of the term. It was starting with Master Ch'eng [Ch'eng I] that *jen* came to be understood as nature, while love was interpreted as feeling. *Jen* and love thus became clearly differentiated. Unfortunately, the disciples of Master Ch'eng went overboard in this differentiation and forgot about love altogether. In their attempt to look for something vast and lofty, they lost sight of the fact that *jen* is the nature of love, and love is the feeling of *jen*. Even though we may not regard love as the correct label for *jen*, the two must never be completely separated from each other.[21]

Ch'en Ch'un further addresses himself to Hsieh Shang-ts'ai's (Hsieh Liang-tso,[ag] 1050–c.1120) view of *jen* as consciousness,[22] Yang Kuei-shan's (Yang Shih,[ah] 1053–1135) interpretation of the substance of *jen* as the unity of the self with all things,[23] and Lü Yü-shu's (Lü Ta-lin,[ai] 1046–1092) explanation of *jen* as set forth in his "Inscription on Self-mastery,"[24] and criticizes each of them for having totally separated love from *jen*.

Chu Hsi shares his disciple's assessment that after Ch'eng I defined love as feeling and *jen* as nature, some of Ch'eng's students discoursed on *jen* without mentioning love. This rigid differentiation of the two is, in Chu's opinion, the cause that has made their scholarship empty pursuits without authenticity and genuineness. Chu Hsi comments,

> The scholars before Master Ch'eng [Ch'eng I] showed no concern for *jen*. Where the ancient sages used the word *jen*, they read as love. After Master Ch'eng, scholars finally came to see the importance of *jen* and stopped interpreting it as love. But there arose abuses among some later followers of the Master. Preoccupied only with the exposition of *jen*, they were remiss in the effort to hold onto the essentials and to immerse themselves in comprehensiveness. For this reason,

they missed the joy of the relaxed appreciation of things, and failed to accomplish any concrete results in mastering the self and returning to propriety. They not only suffered the ills of ignorance produced by what the *Analects* has referred to as the result of being fond of *jen* but not of learning; they also removed their pursuits entirely away from love. They engaged themselves only in empty principles and empty discourses, and failed to arrive at any true understanding. Their scholarship consequently lacked clarity and common sense, and their shortcomings were most noticeable. They ended up not having any comprehension of *jen* at all. This situation was worse than the earlier case of treating *jen* only as love. In my opinion, when one really focuses one's mind on the pursuit of *jen*, the most effective way is of course to put it into practice. But unless one establishes a definite idea on the meaning and content of *jen* through learning, one encounters the danger of being mired in aimless confusion. The defect of the lack of learning is ignorance. If one can exert the effort of dwelling on seriousness and extending knowledge, and make them complement each other, then this defect will be eliminated. When one wants to gain a clear understanding of the meaning and content of *jen*, one will do well if one uses the concept of love as aid. When one realizes that *jen* is the source of love, and that love can never exhaust *jen*, then one has gained a definite comprehension of *jen*. Thus it is absolutely not necessary to search for *jen* in obscure places.[25]

When one reads the above passage with close attention, one should be able to detect all the essential points of Chu Hsi's view on *jen*. In his critique of some disciples of Ch'eng I, Chu clearly shows that they have deviated into the side tracks. He criticizes them where he sees fit, but retains what he deems valuable, and arrives at his own perception of *jen*, one that he regards as the most appropriate understanding of the noblest ideal in Confucianism. His perception of *jen* can be summarized as "the principle of love, and the character of the mind (*ai chih li, hsin chih te*[ai])."[26]

It is common knowledge that Chu Hsi's thinking is the culmination of the philosophic inquiries undertaken by the five Northern Sung (960–1126) masters—Chou Tun-i, Chang Tsai, Ch'eng Hao, Ch'eng I, and Shao Yung[ak] (1011–1077). It is also well known that scholars such as Chang Nan-hsüan (Chang Shih,[al] 1133–1180) and Lü Tsu-ch'ien[am] (1137–1181) have played an important role in the formulation of Chu Hsi's ideas. Of course, the contribution of Li T'ung[an] (1093–1163) in guiding Chu onto the orthodox line of Confucian tradition must also be mentioned. It is only natural that in the formation of Chu's view on *jen*, the same kind of influences are at work. In particular, Chu's discussions with Chang Nan-hsüan on the nature of *jen* provide the finishing touch to his thinking on the subject. Furthermore, they also enable Chu to brush off an earlier influence exerted on him by the Hunan School through Chang. The scope and points of contention of these debates are fully revealed in the correspondence between the two men.

These details of the discussions aside, it suffices to point out that the most intense period of discussion is believed to have taken place around 1172, when Chu Hsi was forty-three years old. The heated exchange took the format of each man composing his own "Treatise on *Jen*" and sending it to the other for comment and criticism. After numerous revisions, Chu Hsi's own "Treatise on *Jen*" was completed and included in ch. 67 of his *Collected works*. Since there are indications that Chu Hsi revised his "Treatise on *Jen*" at least one more time at age forty-four—apparently around the same time he finished another essay entitled "K'e-chai chi"[ao] (Record of the studio of self-mastery)[27] —the completion of the "Treatise" must have been accomplished slightly after then.[28]

In Japan, a book compiled by Yamazaki Ansai[ap] (1618–1682) entitled *Jinsetsu mondō*[aq] (Questions and answers on the "Treatise on *jen*")[29] constitutes an important collection of materials on the debate, seen from Chu Hsi's point of view. Asami Keisai,[ar] a leading disciple of Yamazaki, later lectured on this *Jinsetsu mondō*, and the record of his lectures formed the basis for his *Jinsetsu mondō shisetsu*[as] (The Master's views on *Jinsetsu mondō*).[30] Together these two works greatly enhance our understanding of the content of *jen* as conceived by Chu Hsi.

Chang Nan-hsüan's own "Treatise on *Jen*" is collected in ch. 18 of his *Nan-hsüan wen-chi*[at] (Collected literary works of Chang Shih). As a result of Chu Hsi's relentless assault, this essay reveals the unqualified defeat of Chang's Hunan scholarship as well as his total submission to Chu's views. This work furthermore shows that Chang's notion of *jen* remarkably resembles that held by Chu. A note by the editors attached to Chu Hsi's "Treatise on *Jen*" actually concedes a startling point: "In the Chekiang edition, the 'Treatise on *Jen*' by Chang Nan-hsüan is erroneously considered to be by Master Chu and Master Chu's 'Treatise' is considered to be a preface to Chang's essay." This clearly indicates that the two essays are so similar in tone that they are easily confused. Even Chu Hsi's disciple Ch'en Ch'un is not immune from such confusion. At one point he states that "my late Master composed two treatises on *jen*. One was mistakenly included in the *Collected literary works of Chang Shih*."[31] Hsiung Chieh[au] (1199 cs), another follower of Chu, is the author of *Hsing-li ch'ün-shu chü-chieh*[av] (Punctuation and annotation on the various books on nature and principle) and collects in this work the "Treatise on *Jen*" that appears in the *Nan-hsüan wen-chi*, treating it as his master's own essay. It is thus apparent that even among Chu Hsi's disciples, confusion about the authorship of the two treatises does occur. It is most definitely caused by the almost identical nature of the two essays.

Of particular interest to us, of course, is the content of the discussion between the two men. Among the several points of contention, one is especially significant. It is Chang Nan-hsüan's critique of the first sentence in Chu Hsi's "Treatise on *Jen*" and Chu's rebuttal. The sentence in question is: "Heaven and Earth treat the production of things as their mind." This sentence is originally a statement made by one of the Ch'eng brothers to explain the phrase "through 'return' one understands the mind of Heaven and

Earth," which is taken from Ch'eng I's commentary on the *fu*[aw] (return) hexagram in the *Book of Changes*.[32] In his essay Chu Hsi simply adopts this statement without modification. Nan-hsüan, however, disagrees with it. He does,
however, approve of another phrase, which first appears in the *Ch'eng
Brothers' Commentary on the Book of Changes* and is adopted by Chu Hsi in
his "Record of the Studio of Self-mastery." The phrase is: "the mind of
Heaven and Earth that produces things."

In his rebuttal Chu Hsi argues that both statements express an identical
meaning, and that the apparent trivial difference is only one of sentence structure in composition.[33] But the reason behind Chang Nan-hsüan's making this
a major issue lies in the particular thinking of the Hunan philosophic tradition, to which Chang himself belongs. To begin with, the Hunan school has
the tendency to emphasize the wondrous workings of the mind, which is
regarded as one that "comprehends all under Heaven, and has dominion over
all the myriad things."[34] Hu Wu-feng's (Hu Hung,[ax] 1106–1161) notion of *jen*
as "the mind of Heaven and Earth"[35] clearly reflects this propensity to understand *jen* as the wondrous mind, at once mobile and complete, broad and inexhaustible. Consequently, Chu Hsi's view of the mind of Heaven and Earth as
one that produces things is seen by the Hunan scholars as a narrow view that
limits and undermines the all-pervasiveness of the substance of *jen*. This line
of reasoning is similar to Chu Hsi's critique of Chou Tun-i's "Explanation of
the Diagram of the Supreme Ultimate," in which Chu maintains that "since
jen is the unified substance, it is wrong to regard it only as the movement of
the yang force."[36]

In response to this Hunan challenge, Chu Hsi comments,

> Scholars of late do not use love to define *jen*. They therefore feel dissatisfied with
> the ancient scholars' effort to interpret the mind of Heaven and Earth through
> the workings of the single yang to produce the myriad things. They establish
> theories different from those of the ancients and portray the mind of Heaven and
> Earth as something transcendental and lofty. They do not understand that what
> Heaven and Earth focus on as their mind is none other than the production of
> things, that if one interprets this mind any other way, one will invariably be
> drowned in emptiness and submerged in quietude, and will fail to attain the
> proper connection between substance and function, root and branch.[37]

In other words, Chu firmly believes that the mind of Heaven and Earth rests
precisely on the production of things. Any interpretation of this mind without
this focus on productiveness will be similar to Wang Pi's[ay] (226–249) interpretation of the *fu* hexagram, which perceives the mind as an entity of quietude
and emptiness,[38] thus degenerating into the transcendentalism of Lao Tzu[az]
(6th or 4th century B.C.) and Chuang Tzu[ba] (c. 369–286 B.C.). It will further
jeopardize one's ability to attain proper connections between substance and
function, root and branch. What Chu Hsi attempts to accomplish is the resto-

ration of love in the understanding of *jen*. This is unequivocally illustrated in
the following two passages. The first reads:

> When Heaven and Earth produce things, that which is warm and gentle is *jen*.
> Hence all human beings and things, which inherit the mind of Heaven and
> Earth when they come into being, are endowed with the mind of compassion,
> love, and commiseration.[39]

The second is cited from his "Treatise on *Jen*":

> What is the mind of *jen?* In Heaven and Earth it is the mind to produce things in
> abundance. In human beings it is to love others warmly and to provide them
> with benefits.

As mentioned above, Chang Nan-hsüan's disapproval of Chu Hsi's assertion that "Heaven and Earth regard as its own mind the production of things"
can be attributed to the Hunan School of scholarship. Yet Chang agrees with
another statement made by Chu, which reads, "When Heaven and Earth
endow human beings and things with the mind of productiveness, this
becomes the mind of human beings and things as well."[40] This agreement,
however, does not mask the fact that Chang's understanding is totally different from Chu Hsi's. In contrast to Chu Hsi's focus on the mind of Heaven
and Earth as being warm and gentle, Chang chooses to concentrate more on
its being universally possessed by human beings and things alike. Taking the
position, which transcends the contrast between the self and other things,
namely, the view which sees Heaven and Earth, the self and the myriad things
as forming one body, Chang contends that this is the substance of *jen*. In his
understanding of love as well, Chang seems to put emphasis on the all-perva-
sive, indiscriminatory universality of its extension rather than its empathizing
and commiserating quality.[41] In this case also the Hunan School's perception
of *jen* as an all-encompassing, all-inclusive entity is made manifest. Incidentally, the Hunan tradition was influenced significantly by the thinking of
Hsieh Shang-ts'ai and Yang Kuei-shan. The idea that the unity of man with
the myriad things represents the substance of *jen* is characteristic of Yang
Kuei-shan's view of *jen*.[42] To Chu Hsi, such a view is plausible when one
explains the universality of *jen*, that is, when the spread of love encompasses
all things. But this, according to him, recalls Confucius' statement in his
reply to his disciple Tzu-kung's inquiry, which maintains that "spreading
charity widely to save the multitudes"[43] is not *jen*. Love and compassion represent the effect, not the actual substance, of *jen*. Furthermore, according to
Chu, the theory of the unity of all things shackles human beings to an
unenlightened, ignorant state, and discourages them from keeping a persistent
and vigilant watch over themselves. The defect of this view, in short, is to
"treat things as the self."[44] Treating things as oneself implies the Buddhist

notion of universal identity, which sees the entire cosmos as being identical with oneself. To be sure, such a view is breathtakingly broad and noble, yet when one considers its negative aspect, one realizes that it may lead to a contemptuous attitude toward affairs that pertain to the self. In other words, it carries a dangerous potentiality of degenerating into self-negation. The Buddhist tradition abounds with references to "give up oneself to feed the starving tiger" and to practice "compassion with no origination." In all these references the body bestowed upon oneself by one's parents is carelessly and contemptuously abused.[45] These actions, which may indicate a lofty religious conviction or ideal, are nevertheless regarded by Confucianists concerned with human ethics as incomprehensible and nonsensical behavior that destroys the communal bond of social interaction. An anecdote about Ch'eng I tells that the master was once questioned by a certain Ch'en Ching-cheng,[bb] who claimed that true self-liberation was possible through the Buddhist ideal of the unity of all things. Ch'eng I's terse response was: "When other peoples' stomachs are full, can you do without eating (since you are identical with them?"[46] This is a sharp observation which incisively warns how easy it is for the concept of the unity of things to fall into empty, delusive ideation and self-contempt.

On the question of Chu Hsi's definition of *jen* as "the principle of love," numerous theories have been proposed to determine its origin. But ultimately they all agree that Chu Hsi himself was probably the inventor of this definition.[47] When Chu Hsi and Chang Nan-hsüan were engaged in debate, the latter, who conceived of *jen* as an all-encompassing entity, was initially opposed to this definition. As a result of Chu's persistent argumentation, Chang's opposition gradually softened and he ended up embracing his rival's definition. Before he reached full agreement with Chu, however, his appreciation of the phrase "principle of love" was somewhat different. When addressing the issue why human beings must love others, Chang initially sought for an explanation in the theory of the unity of all things. He thus emphasized the universal extension of love towards all things. In contrast, Chu Hsi's "principle of love" is not a definition of *jen* predicated on the assumption of the unity of all things, nor does it emphasize only the universalistic extension of *jen*'s loving quality. Chu explains,

> Naturally we should not label love as *jen*. Yet this does not mean that love should be separated from *jen* either, for the substance of *jen* is the principle of love. That there is unity between the self and the myriad things is the reason for loving all things. However, this principle of love does not exist for, or is premised upon, the theory of the unity of all things. *Jen, i, li,* and *chih*—these four are the character of nature and the a priori principles. It is not for the sake of anything that they come into existence. This fact must be understood. Among the four, *jen* is the principle of love and the way of life. Thus by dwelling on *jen* all four virtues will be covered. This is why the pursuit of *jen* is the principal task in scholarship.[48]

The concrete basis that forms the source of love is the a priori principles, or the intrinsic nature, which exist in the depth of one's mind. This is the principle of love, and this is *jen*. Hence love is a true feeling which is irrepressively issued forth from the basic nature of human beings. The range of its extension is, in the final analysis, only a secondary consideration.

As indicated in the second half of the above quotation, Chu Hsi's idea of human nature on the one hand regards *jen, i, li,* and *chih* as four equally important characteristics of nature and a priori principles. On the other hand, however, it considers *jen* alone as inclusive of all four. Such a view of *jen* and human nature is also adumbrated in the first part of Chu Hsi's "Treatise on *Jen*." This view, by the way, has been transmitted from Ch'eng I to Chu Hsi.[49] We must keep these things in mind when we study the characteristics of the Sung scholars' views of *jen*. Because of the limitation of space, the details of this subject will not be discussed. But if I were to offer one short summary on this subject, I would point out that Chu Hsi insists upon the clear distinction between *jen, i, li,* and *chih* as a precondition for any discussion of the inclusiveness of *jen*.[50] This distinction, together with the emphasis on self-mastery, is considered by Chu to be the most crucial aspect of learning. The methodology he advances in the pursuit of *jen* is prompted by his desire to eschew what the *Analects* has labelled the mistake of "ignorance created by a fondness for *jen* but dislike for learning."[51] His interpretation of *jen* also reveals fully the rational and analytical aspects of his thinking.

The characteristics of Chu Hsi's idea of *jen* can be further illustrated by another contrast with the Hunan School. This is his objection to the definition of *jen* as consciousness, a view held by the Hunan scholars. The immediate motivation for his critique of such a view is his desire to surpass the Hunan School's own highly emphasized method of pursuing *jen*, which first aims at "the detection of the seed of conscience amidst profit and desire, then moves on toward its careful preservation, nourishment, and extension."[52] As an example of this divergence in opinion between Chu Hsi and the Hunan School, let me cite a Hunanese interpretation of one sentence in the *Analects* and Chu's critique of this interpretation. The sentence in question is taken from *Analects,* 4:7, and reads: "By observing the faults, *jen* may be made known." Numerous meanings have been proposed for this sentence. Chu Hsi, following Ch'eng I's example, reads it as "observing a man's faults, one can determine whether or not he is a man of *jen*."[53] The Hunan scholars disagree with this reading and argue that this sentence is ultimately directed toward the self. They maintain that through the awareness of the mistakes committed by oneself, one realizes the wondrous, ingenious, and active functions of the mind.[54] This is to them the correct interpretation of the sentence. It is evident that this point of view is derived from Hsieh Shang-ts'ai's theory of consciousness which regards the incipient, active, and lively functions of the mind as *jen*.[55]

Chu Hsi, however, criticizes this interpretation as an error analogous to mistaking the unicorn for the lion.[56] According to him, there was a certain Wang Jih-hsiu[bc] who lived during the transitional period between Northern and Southern Sung (1127–1279). Commenting on a passage in *Mencius* 2A:2 which proclaims that "the unicorn is the most superior among all beasts," Wang asserted that the unicorn was but a different name for the lion. Though there is no apparent relationship between Wang Jih-hsiu and the Hunan scholars, Chu is here using the obvious blunder of the former to ridicule what appears to him to be an analogous mistake of the latter. The unicorn has been known as the animal of *jen* since ancient times, and has been idealized by the Chinese people as an animal with a sentient spirit as well as a messenger of peace. That it is called the animal of *jen* and the king among beasts is due to the belief that it never steps on growing grass and never eats living things, and that it is a noncombative, gentle, and tranquil animal. It is definitely not a fierce, wild, and threatening beast like the lion. As recited in the "Airs of the States" section of the *Book of Odes*, the gentle and harmonious disposition of the unicorn is symbolic of the original nature of *jen*. In Chu Hsi's opinion, if *jen* is indeed as fearsome and awe-inspiring as the lion, then the ancient sages and worthies would not have felt the need to contrast *jen* with *i*, the latter concept being likened to a sharp sword that dispels the deviant and makes manifest what is proper.

Both Hsieh Shang-ts'ai's theory of *jen* as consciousness and the Hunan School's prescribed method of detecting *jen* as conscience share a common tendency. This tendency, simply stated, is to use the mind in pursuit of the mind. The result, according to Chu Hsi, is the loss of a sense of ease and composure among the scholars. His criticism is bitingly incisive. Concerning the Hunan scholars' reading of the sentence in *Analects,* 4:7 discussed above, Chu Hsi notes that while it is nice to consider the sentence as an injunction to master the self, this interpretation leaves the mind in a constant state of anxiety and tension, with no room for repose and relaxation. Furthermore, this interpretation tends to drift into empty, lofty tones and drives people to fall far short of the serene, tranquil state of mind that belongs to what the *Analects* describes as "the man of *jen* who delights in mountains."[57] Chu further argues that if indeed this view of the Hunan School is tenable, then it implies that the mind, which originally is one single entity, has to perform three different functions in a split second, namely, to commit a mistake, to observe the mistake being committed, and to realize that it is *jen* which observes this mistake.[58]

In this manner Chu Hsi chastises the Hunan School's pursuit of *jen* as a method that employs the mind to search for the mind, which invariably results in its being rushed, pressed, vexed, and confounded. Such a chastisement is subtly reminiscent of Chu Hsi's own ideas about the mind and seriousness. It is also related to his critique of Ch'an[bd] Buddhism and the philosophy of Lu Hsiang-shan (Lu Chiu-yüan,[be] 1139–1193). But because of the constraint of space, I shall refrain from probing this relationship further.

In the preceding paragraphs I have highlighted the major points of Chu Hsi's criticism of the Hunan School, in particular its perception of *jen* as a separate entity from love. His definition of *jen* as "the principle of love" is precisely the product of this critical view. From the four virtues of *jen, i, li,* and *chih,* and from the Four Beginnings of commiseration, shame and dislike, respect and reverence, and right and wrong, Chu Hsi's definition of *jen* singles out *jen* and commiseration and treats their relationship as one between nature and feeling, or substance and function. This is *jen* spoken of separately (*p'ien-yen*[bf]).[59] In this connection love assumes an even more genuine and stable status, and its former exalted position is restored.

Chu Hsi has another definition of *jen,* which is "the character of the mind." *Jen* is understood to be "the principle of love" because of its embodiment of the four virtues of *jen, i, li,* and *chih.* Yet there are times when *jen* is referred to as "the complete character of the mind," "the complete character of the human mind," and "the complete character of the original mind."[60] This is because *jen,* the "principle of love," is at the same time "the source of all morality and the root of all moral deeds."[61] In this connection *jen*'s inclusiveness and comprehensiveness are emphasized. This view of *jen* is what Ch'eng I has pointed out as *jen* spoken of collectively (*chuan-yen*[bg]).[62] It is reminiscent of Confucius' own discussion of *jen.* In explaining *jen* as the "character of the mind," Chu Hsi likens his understanding to Ch'eng I's metaphor of the seed of grain.[63] It "compares the mind to a seed, for the nature of life and growth inherent in this seed is its *jen.*"[64] This intrinsic quality for growth that lies latent in the inner core of a seed forms the basis for its future germination and luxuriant growth. Likewise, when human beings grasp the mind of Heaven and Earth to produce things and regard it as their own mind, what lies inherent in it (that which is known as the way of life, or the potential for growth, or the principle of life's dynamic activity) is precisely Chu Hsi's idea of *jen.* Because of the presence of this *jen,* the virtues of *jen, i, li,* and *chih* are able to activate themselves and become respectively the feelings of commiseration, shame and dislike, respect and reverence, and right and wrong, and develop further into all morality and moral deeds.[65] Chu Hsi's definition of *jen* as the character of the mind is derived primarily from this unimpeded potential for growth inherent in all human beings and things.[66] His understanding of *jen* as the principle of life is, in the final analysis, not very different from the view of *jen* as the growth potential in all things, a view that has been passed down from the Ch'eng brothers through Hsieh Shang-ts'ai to the Hunan scholars.

Translated by Richard Shek[bh]

Notes

1. *Book of Mencius,* 7A:1.
2. *Chu Tzu yü-lei*[bi] [Classified conversations of Master Chu], (Tokyo: Chubnun[bj]

Press reprint of the Ch'eng-hua[bk] period, 1465–1487, of the Ming dynasty ed.), 60:4b. The Four Moral Qualities are those in the *Book of Mencius*, 2A:6, and the Four Qualities are those of the first hexagram, *ch'ien*[bl] (heaven, male), in the *Book of Changes*.

3. *Wai-shu*[bm] [Additional works], ch. 11, in the *Erh-Ch'eng chi*[bn] [Collected works of the two Ch'engs], (Taipei: Chung-hua[bo] Book Co., 1981), p. 414.

4. *Ta-hsüeh huo-wen*[bp] [Questions and answers on the *Great Learning*], (Tokyo: Chubun Press, 1977), 20b.

5. *Chu Tzu yü-lei*, 121:17a, 6:13a.

6. Kato Jōken,[bq] *Kanji no kigen*[br] [Origin of Chinese characters], (Tokyo: Kadokawa[bs] Book Co., 1970), p. 40.

7. *Book of Mencius*, 2A:6.

8. *Chu Tzu yü-lei*, 19:3b.

9. *Ibid.*, 20:21b.

10. *Wu-ch'ao ming-ch'en yen-hsing lu*[bt] [Records of the words and deeds of prominent ministers of the five reigns], (SPTK ed.), 10B:3a.

11. Chou Tun-i, *T'ai-chi-t'u shuo*[bu] [Explanation of the diagram of the Supreme Ultimate], in the *Chou Tzu ch'üan-shu*[bv] [Complete works of Master Chou], (Shanghai: Commercial Press, 1937), 2:23.

12. Chou Tun-i, *T'ung-shu*[bw] [Penetrating the *Book of Changes*], ch. 3, in the *Chou Tzu ch'üan-shu*, 7:127.

13. *Ibid.*, ch. 11, in the *Chou Tzu ch'üan-shu*, 8:150.

14. *I-shu*[bx] [Inherited works], ch. 3, in the *Erh-Ch'eng chi*, p. 60.

15. *I-shu*, ch. 2A, in the *Erh-Ch'eng chi*, p. 39.

16. *Ibid.*, ch. 11, in the *Erh-Ch'eng chi*, p. 120.

17. *Ibid.*, ch. 2A, in the *Erh-Ch'eng chi*, p. 15.

18. *Ibid.*, ch. 18, in the *Erh-Ch'eng chi*, p. 184.

19. *Ibid.*, ch. 3, in the *Erh-Ch'eng chi*, p. 63.

20. *Ibid.*, ch. 18, in the *Erh-Ch'eng chi*, p. 182. For Han Yü's theory, see the *Han Ch'ang-li ch'üan-chi*[by] [Complete works of Han Yü], ch. 11.

21. Ch'en Ch'un, *Pei-hsi tzu-i*[bz] [Meaning of words], pt. 1, 30a, in the *Pei-hsi ch'üan-chi*[ca] [Complete works of Ch'en Ch'un], (1831 ed.).

22. Hsieh Liang-tso, *Shang-ts'ai yü-lu*[cb] [Recorded sayings of Hsieh Liang-tso], (1756 Japanese ed.), pt. 1, 2b, 7b, 12b; pt. 2, 1a.

23. Yang Shih, *Yang Kuei-shan Hsien-sheng ch'üan-chi*[cc] [Complete works of Master Yang Shih], (1883 ed.), 11:1b.

24. *Hsing-li ch'ün-shu chü-chieh* (1668 Japanese ed.), 3:5b.

25. *Chu Wen Kung wen-chi*[cd] [Collected literary works of Master Chu], (SPTK ed.), 31:5a, sixth letter in answer to Chang Ching-fu.[ce]

26. *Lun-yü chi-chu*[cf] [Commentary on the *Analects*], comment on the *Analects*, 1:2.

27. *Chu Wen Kung wen-chi*, 77:16a.

28. *Ibid.*, separate collection, 6:9a, letter to Lin Tse-chih.[cg]

29. *Nippon shisō taikei*[ch] [Compendium of Japanese thought], (Tokyo: Iwanami shoten,[ci] 1980), vol. 31, pp. 244–252.

30. *Ibid.*, pp. 253–304.

31. *Pei-hsi ch'üan-chi*, 14:4b, fifth letter in answer to Ch'en Po-tsao.[cj]

32. *Wai-shu*, ch. 3, in the *Erh-Ch'eng chi*, p. 366.

33. *Chu Tzu yü-lei*, 53:3b.

34. *Chih-yen*[ck] [Knowing words], (*Ssu-k'u ch'üan-shu chen-pen*[cl] ed.), 1:1a; *Nan-hsüan*

wen-chi (Tao-kuang[cm] period, 1821–1850, ed.), 9:7b, an account of the Kuei-yang[cn] Prefectural School; 10:1a, an account of the remodelling of the Yüeh-lu[co] Academy at T'an-chou;[cp] 15:6a, farewell to Tseng Ch'iu-fu.[cq]

35. *Chih-yen,* 1:8a.

36. *Chou Tzu ch'üan-shu,* 2:33–36, interpretation of the *T'ai-chi-t'u shuo* with rebuttal.

37. *Chu Wen Kung wen-chi,* 42:19b, tenth letter in answer to Wu Hui-shu.[cr]

38. *Wang Pi chi chiao-shih*[cs] [Explanation of the *Collected Works of Wang Pi*], (Taipei: Chung-hua Book Co., 1980), pp. 336–337, commentary on the *fu* hexagram of the *Book of Changes.*

39. *Chu Tzu yü-lei,* 53:3b.

40. *Nan-hsüan wen-chi,* 21:5a, eighth letter in answer to Chu Yüan-hui;[ct] *Chu Wen Kung wen-chi,* 32:18a, first letter in answer to Chang Ching-fu on *jen;* 32:22b, fourth letter to Chang on *jen.*

41. *Ibid.*

42. See above, n. 23.

43. *Analects,* 6:28.

44. *Chu Wen Kung wen-chi,* 67:21b–23a, treatise on *jen.*

45. *Chu Wen Kung wen-chi,* 43:24a, twelfth letter in answer to Lin Tse-chih; *Chu Tzu yü-lei,* 126:21b; *Nippon shiso taikei,* vol. 31, p. 270. See also *Chih-yen,* 2:4a.

46. *Wai-shu,* ch. 11, in the *Erh-Ch'eng chi,* p. 413.

47. Tomoeda Ryūtarō,[cu] *Shushi no shisō keisei*[cv] [Formation of Chu Hsi's thinking], (Tokyo: Shunjusha,[cw] 1969), pp. 119–120.

48. *Chu Wen Kung wen-chi,* 42:9a, fifth letter in answer to Hu Kuang-chung.[cx]

49. Ch'eng I, *I-chuan*[cy] [Commentary on the *Book of Changes*], ch. 1, in the *Erh-Ch'eng chi,* p. 697, commentary on the *ch'ien* hexagram.

50. *Chu Wen Kung wen-chi,* 42:38b, twelfth letter in answer to Shih Tzu-chung;[cz] 56:14a, third letter in answer to Fang Pin-wang.[da]

51. *Analects,* 17:8.

52. *Chih-yen,* 4:7b; *Nan-hsüan wen-chi,* 9:7b, an account of the Kuei-yang Prefectural School; 10:1a, an account of the remodelling of the Yüeh-lu Academy at T'an-chou.

53. *Lun-yü chi-chu,* Chu Hsi's comment on the *Analects,* 4:7; *Chu Wen Kung wen-chi,* 42:15a, sixth letter in answer to Wu Hui-shu.

54. *Chu Wen Kung wen-chi,* 42:15a, sixth letter in answer to Wu Hui-shu.

55. See above, n. 22.

56. *Chu Tzu yü-lei,* 6:12b–18a; 26:14b–15a.

57. *Chu Wen Kung wen-chi,* 67:23a, treatise on *jen;* 42:15a, sixth letter in answer to Wu Hui-shu.

58. *Ibid.,* 42:15a, sixth letter in answer to Wu Hui-shu.

59. *Chu Tzu yü-lei,* 20:15b–17b.

60. *Lun-yü chi-chu,* Chu Hsi's commentary on the *Analects,* 7:5, 8:7, 12:1.

61. *Chu Wen Kung wen-chi,* 67:22a, treatise on *jen.*

62. See above, n. 49.

63. *Chu Tzu yü-lei,* 20:20b.

64. See above, n. 18.

65. See above, n. 61.

66. *Chu Tzu yü-lei,* 20:17a.

Glossary

a 太極
b 理氣
c 天人合一
d 性
e 天
f 仁
g 義
h 禮
i 智
j 元
k 亨
l 利
m 貞
n 程伊川頤
o 揚雄
p 心性
q 仁說
r 五常
s 信
t 持敬
u 仁說要義
v 太田錦城
w 周敦頤
x 中正仁義
y 陽
z 張載
aa 程顥
ab 公道
ac 情
ad 性
ae 韓愈
af 陳淳
ag 謝上蔡良佐
ah 楊龜山時
ai 呂與叔大臨
aj 愛之理心之德
ak 邵雍
al 張南軒栻
am 呂祖謙
an 李侗
ao 克齋記
ap 山崎闇齋
aq 仁說問答
ar 淺見絅齋
as 仁說問答師說
at 南軒文集
au 熊節
av 性理羣書句解
aw 復
ax 胡五峯宏
ay 王弼
az 老子
ba 莊子
bb 陳經正
bc 王日體
bd 禪
be 陸象山九淵
bf 偏言
bg 專言
bh 石漢椿
bi 朱子語類
bj 中文
bk 成化
bl 乾
bm 外書
bn 二程集
bo 中華
bp 大學或問
bq 加藤常賢
br 漢字の起源
bs 角川
bt 五朝名臣言行錄
bu 太極圖說
bv 周子全書
bw 通書
bx 遺書
by 韓昌黎全集
bz 北溪字義
ca 北溪全集
cb 上蔡語錄
cc 楊龜山先生全集
cd 朱文公文集
ce 張敬夫
cf 論語集註
cg 林擇之
ch 日本思想大系
ci 岩波書店
cj 陳伯澡
ck 知言
cl 四庫全書珍本
cm 道光
cn 桂陽
co 嶽麓
cp 潭州
cq 曾裘父
cr 吳晦叔
cs 王弼集校釋
ct 朱元晦
cu 友枝龍太郎
cv 朱子の思想形成
cw 春秋社
cx 胡廣仲
cy 易傳
cz 石子重
da 方賓王

15

Morality and Knowledge in Chu Hsi's Philosophical System

YING-SHIH YÜ

Moral Nature versus Inquiry and Study

IN A LETTER to Hsiang An-shih (Hsiang P'ing-fu,[a] 1153–1208), Chu Hsi says,

> Generally speaking, since the time of Tzu-ssu[b] "honoring the moral nature"
> (*tsun te-hsing*[c]) and "following the path of inquiry and study" (*tao wen-hsüeh*[d])
> have been the two basic methods of instruction according to which people are
> taught to exert themselves.[1] Now, what Tzu-ching [Lu Hsiang-shan,[e] 1139–
> 1193] talks about are matters pertaining exclusively to "honoring the moral
> nature" whereas in my daily discussions I have placed a greater emphasis on
> "inquiry and study" . . . From now on I ought to turn my attention inwardly to
> self-cultivation. Thus by removing weakness on the one hand and gathering
> strength on the other, I probably would be able to prevent myself from falling
> into one-sidedness.[2]

This letter was written in 1183 in response to a criticism made by Lu Hsiang-
shan. However, when Lu later learned about the letter, he remarked pointedly, saying,

> Chu Yüan-hui[f] [Chu Hsi] wanted to get rid of the defects and combine the merits
> of both sides. But I do not think this is possible. If one does not know anything
> about honoring the moral nature, how can there be inquiry and study in the first
> place?[3]

These exchanges have led later scholars to believe that the basic difference
between Chu and Lu lies in the fact that the former stressed the importance of
inquiry and study *(tao wen-hsüeh)* whereas the latter that of moral nature *(tsun
te-hsing)*. Wu Ch'eng[g] (1249–1333) was probably more responsible than anybody else for the initial dissemination of this view.[4] By the time of the Ming
dynasty (1368–1644), this view had become so firmly established that even
Wang Yang-ming[h] (1472–1529) found it difficult to alter.[5] Although Wang
Yang-ming's powerful refutation was generally accepted by his followers with-

out question,[6] it nevertheless failed to eradicate this popular view completely. Thus we find the very same distinction perpetuated in the *Sung-Yüan hsüeh-an*[i] (Scholarly records of Confucians of the Sung and Yüan dynasties) where Huang Tsung-hsi[j] (1610–1695) explicitly remarks that Lu Hsiang-shan's teaching was focused on *tsun te-hsing* and Chu Hsi's was on *tao wen-hsüeh*. While neither side completely ignored the emphasis of the other, the difference between the two in terms of priority was nevertheless a real one.[7]

However, my purpose here is not to discuss the philosophical differences between Chu and Lu. Instead, I set as my central task in this study to examine the relationship between morality and knowledge in Chu Hsi's philosophical system. Like *li*[k] (principle) and *ch'i*[l] (material force), *T'ien-li*[m] (Heavenly Principle) and *jen-yü*[n] (human desire), or yin and yang[o] (passive and active cosmic forces), morality and knowledge form a polarity in Chu Hsi's thought.[8] Because of its central position in his system, Chu Hsi used many different paired concepts in the Confucian tradition to express this polarity. Apart from *tsun te-hsing* and *tao wen-hsüeh*, which are clearly an overarching pair in this category, there are also other polarized pairs such as "seriousness" (*ching*[p]) and "learning" (*hsüeh*[q]), "self-cultivation" (*han-yang*[r]) and "extension of knowledge" (*chih-chih*[s]), "exercise of seriousness" (*chü-ching*[t]) and "exhaustive investigation of principles" (*ch'iung-li*[u]), "essentialism" (*yüeh*[v]) and "erudition" (*po*[w]), "a single thread" (*i-kuan*[x]) and "extensive knowledge" (*to-shih*[y]). Each and every one of these pairs of polarized concepts describes in its own way the relationship between morality and knowledge. It is therefore necessary to treat them below as, in the terminology of Arthur O. Lovejoy, unit-ideas.

To begin with, we must try to understand Chu Hsi's statement, quoted above, about his emphasis on "inquiry and study." Does this mean that he assigned a greater importance to knowledge than to morality? Needless to say, this could not possibly have been the case. "Honoring the moral nature" was a central and fundamental assumption in Neo-Confucianism shared by all individual thinkers irrespective of their different views on other matters. Chu Hsi was certainly no exception. Like Lu Hsiang-shan, he also took "honoring the moral nature" to be the primary and ultimate goal toward which all "inquiry and study" must be directed. Morality not only takes precedence over, but also gives meaning to knowledge.[9]

The question then inevitably arises: If this is the case, why did Chu Hsi, by his own admission, place a greater emphasis on "inquiry and study"? First of all, it is important to point out that in the letter to Hsiang An-shih quoted above, Chu Hsi is not talking about the relative importance of knowledge vis-à-vis morality in Confucian learning as a whole. There, it may be recalled, he is merely referring to "honoring the moral nature" and "following the paths of inquiry and study" as two "methods of instruction." In other words, his emphasis on "inquiry and study" was made, not on the general theoretical level, but on the practical, pedagogic level.[10] I am not suggesting, however, that their overall differences are reducible to a pedagogic one. As we shall see below, Chu Hsi's emphasis on "inquiry and study" is very much a reflection of his philosophical views on such key concepts as "principle" *(li)* and "mind" *(hsin²)*. All I am saying is that the traditional distinction between Chu and Lu in terms of *tsun te-hsing* versus *tao wen-hsüeh* is more apparent than real; its validity is rather limited in scope.

Having clarified this point, the above question must be modified as follows: Why was it necessary for Chu Hsi to say a great deal about "inquiry and study" but relatively less about "honoring the moral nature" in his instructions? The answer is provided by Chu Hsi himself. He says,

> The actual work in the realm of inquiry and study involves many items, but that in the realm of "honoring the moral nature" is rather simple. For instance, I-ch'uan [Ch'eng I,[aa] 1033–1107] only said: "To be serious is to concentrate on one" and "to concentrate on one means not to go away from it." That is all ["honoring the moral nature"] is about and there is nothing else. However, in the past my discussions on the side of "honoring the moral nature" have been rather light. Now I feel this to be a mistake. The first part of the phrase ["honoring the moral nature"] provides a general framework so that the work of "inquiry and study" can be carried out meaningfully.[11]

So, according to him, while "honoring the moral nature" is a matter of the first order, there is nevertheless very little that can be directly said about the former. For, in his view, the so-called honoring the moral nature involves mainly establishing as well as maintaining a moral state of mind, which is identifiable with Ch'eng I's "seriousness" or "reverence" *(ching)*. This brings us naturally to Ch'eng I's best-known formula, "Self-cultivation requires seriousness; the pursuit of learning depends on the extension of knowledge."[12]

Self-cultivation versus Extension of Knowledge— Struggle with Ch'eng I's Formula

As we know, throughout his long intellectual life Chu Hsi placed this formula at the very center of his teaching. As a matter of fact, he regarded this formula as a most satisfactory reformulation of the polarity of *tsun te-hsing* and *tao wen-hsüeh*.[13] Although he discussed a great deal more about "seriousness" or "reverence" than about "honoring the moral nature," his conception of the relationship between "seriousness" and "extension of knowledge" bears a remarkable resemblance to that between *tsun te-hsing* and *tao wen-hsüeh:* "Seriousness" is not a separate task to be accomplished before everything else can be carried out. Rather, it is a state of mind or mental attitude under which knowledge can be effectively extended.[14] In other words, "exercise of seriousness" and "extension of knowledge" must begin simultaneously.[15] It is in this reformulation that his views of the relationship between morality and knowledge are most fully revealed.

There can be no doubt that the first part of Ch'eng I's formula, "self-culti-vation requires seriousness," falls exclusively into the category of morality and therefore constitutes the key to Confucian learning.[16] But the second part, "the pursuit of learning depends on the extension of knowledge," requires a word of explanation. Chu Hsi says,

> "The investigation of things" simply means that in regard to a thing that comes to our attention, we make an exhaustive study of all its principles. "The exten-sion of knowledge," on the other hand, means that after we have studied exhaus-tively the principles of a thing, our knowledge of it becomes complete. We obtain this knowledge as if we have extended it [from our minds].[17]

"The investigation of things" (ko-wu[ab]) and "the extension of knowledge" (chih-chih) are, in this case, taken as two different descriptions of the same operation seeking to discover the "principles" of things: We use the term ko-wu when we speak of this operation from the point of view of the object of investigation and the term chih-chih when we speak of it from the point of view of the knowing subject. In the light of the above discussion, Ch'eng I's formula as understood and interpreted by Chu Hsi may be seen as involving altogether three aspects: First, a moral attitude of "seriousness" or "rever-ence" must be established and maintained at all times; second, an intellectual activity of ko-wu or chih-chih must be pursued in a spiritual state of "serious-ness" or "reverence"; third, as a result, "principles" (li) of things become known. In Chu Hsi's view this operation is an endless, ever ongoing process in the life of every truly confirmed Confucianist. It is through this spiritual journey that a Confucianist seeks to bring his moral nature to perfection. Thus, taken as a whole, these three aspects constitute a total system of moral practice. But even in such a system of primarily moral character, we find that the role assigned to knowledge by Chu Hsi is essential even though it is, para-doxically, also secondary at the same time.

On the surface, it is true that "seriousness" and "reverence" are moral lan-guage and that "principles" are also primarily principles of the moral kind. A closer examination shows, however, that "investigation of things" or "exten-sion of knowledge," the central and operative part of the entire system, is clearly a reference to an intellectual process by which knowledge is gained about "principles of things." That this process is necessarily intellectual can be explained by the fact that in Chu Hsi's conception the mind (hsin) is identi-fied with material force (ch'i), though the most intelligent and sensitive of all the material forces.[18] In investigating things, internal or external, the mind only seeks to know their constitutive principles in an objective way; it does not engage in moral activities of any kind on this level. Even though the initial decision to investigate a thing is a moral one and the knowledge thus gained is only to serve moral ends, there is nevertheless no indication that in Chu Hsi's system morality is ever allowed to interfere directly with the intellectual oper-

ation of *ko-wu* or *chih-chih*. Moral considerations always take place on a different (from the Neo-Confucian point of view, however, higher) level.

Throughout his life Chu Hsi never swerved from the view that knowledge
must precede practice or action (*hsing*[ac]). While this cannot be taken to mean
that he valued knowledge above everything else in life, it does reveal nonetheless his central concern with the intellectual foundation of morality. He says,

> Knowledge and practice always require each other like the eyes and legs of a
> man. Without legs a man cannot walk although he has eyes, but without eyes he
> cannot see although he has legs. With respect to order, knowledge comes first;
> with respect to importance, however, a greater weight must be attached to prac-
> tice.[19]

Here Chu Hsi is clearly talking about the relationship between knowledge
and morality. By "knowledge" he is referring to "extension of knowledge"
which, as explained above, is basically an intellectual operation; by "practice"
or "action" he is referring to moral practice—practice based on the "principles" obtained from the "extension of knowledge." Since, according to him,
the pursuit of knowledge can be justified not on its own ground but only on
the ground of its relevance to moral life, it is therefore natural that between
knowledge and morality his emphasis lay ultimately on the latter. However,
his insistence that "knowledge must precede practice" reveals unmistakably
the crucial role that knowledge plays in his total system.

In response to a questioner Chu Hsi says,

> With regard to the question you raised yesterday about the order of self-cultiva-
> tion, extension of knowledge and practice, I think self-cultivation should come
> first, extension of knowledge next, and practice still next. Without self-cultiva-
> tion you cannot become your own master. . . . Having cultivated yourself you
> must extend your knowledge and having extended your knowledge you must put
> it into practice. Knowledge without practice is no different from having no
> knowledge. But all the three things must be done simultaneously. The order
> should not be taken to mean that you cultivate yourself today, extend your
> knowledge tomorrow and then practice it day after tomorrow.[20]

We can sense that he was at pains trying to establish the order of this triad.
Clearly, the order here is conceived more as a logical one than a temporal one.
In the actual temporal order, he always took the "extension of knowledge" to
be the starting point of Confucian learning. Thus, when really hard pressed
he would not even hesitate to reverse the original order in Ch'eng I's formula
by placing the "extension of knowledge" before "self-cultivation."[21] From his
point of view this is necessary because self-cultivation, like practice, must also
be predicated on principles of the right kind. Without a correct knowledge of
the principles involved, cultivation or practice would be blind.[22]

The Role of Book-learning

The above analysis shows that although Chu Hsi used Ch'eng I's formula as a heuristic principle throughout his long teaching career and always spoke of it with worshipful reverence, in practice he reinterpreted it in such a way that the role played by knowledge was clearly more active and central than in the original formulation. In order to clarify Chu Hsi's conception of knowledge, it is desirable that we now turn to his views on book-learning and its relation to morality. Of all the Sung (960–1279) Neo-Confucian philosophers, Chu Hsi alone emphasized the importance of book-learning to the attainment of the Way and, moreover, developed a systematic methodology about it. It was this aspect of his thought that led to the criticism of a seventeenth-century thinker that "Master Chu's learning consists wholly of book-learning and nothing else."[23] While this is undoubtedly an over-statement, it nevertheless serves well as an illustration of the influence that his emphasis on book-learning exerted on the subsequent development of Neo-Confucianism. Even his admirers characterized a central part of his teaching as "Study the principles thoroughly through book-learning so that one's knowledge may be extended."[24]

To be fair to Chu Hsi, we must begin by pointing out that he never advocated the primacy of scholarship in Confucian learning. On the contrary, he made it very clear in his instructions that "book-learning is only a matter of the second order."[25] But it is nevertheless true that on the whole he was convinced that to be a good Confucian does commit one to a basic understanding of the original Confucian teaching and its tradition. In a memorial presented to the throne in 1194, he said,

> With regard to the way of learning, nothing is more urgent than a thorough study of principles; and a thorough study of principles must of necessity consist in book-learning. . . . All principles in the world are wondrous and subtle, each perfect in its own way, and eternally valid. However, only ancient sages had been able to grasp them in their entirety. As a result, the words and the deeds [of the ancient sages] have all become permanent and fundamental exemplars for the later generations to emulate. Those who followed them were gentlemen and blessed; those who contradicted them were small men and accursed. The most blessed can preserve the empire and therefore serve as a positive example; the most accursed cannot even preserve his own person and would therefore serve as a negative example. These visible traces and necessary results are all contained in the classics and histories. A person who wishes to have a thorough knowledge of the principles in the world without first seeking for them [in the classics and histories] is one who wishes to go forward but ends up standing right in front of a wall. This is why we say "a thorough study of principles must of necessity consist in book-learning."[26]

In this connection, two related observations may be made about Chu Hsi's theory of book-learning. First, it appears that he honestly believed that the ancient sages had not only discovered most, if not all, of the principles but also embodied them in what they said and what they did. Since the words and the deeds of the sages are preserved in books, book-learning naturally provides "the study of principles" with a most logical starting point. Little wonder that he identified book-learning as a matter of "investigation of things."[27] In fact, it forms the most substantial part of his teaching of "investigation of things." In his famous "emendation" to the text of the *Great Learning*, he says, "The first step in the education of the adult is to instruct the learner, in regard to all things in the world, to proceed from what knowledge he has of their principles, and investigate further until he reaches the limit."[28] There can be little doubt here he is primarily talking about knowledge derived initially from book-learning as a basis for further study.

Second, book-learning in his system is always morality-oriented. He never advocated book-learning for its own sake and without a moral focus. He specifically singled out, in the above memorial, classics and histories as the two kinds of books for study. This is because he believed that moral principles discovered by the sages are clearly recorded in the Confucian Classics and their actualization in the past is amply illustrated in historical works. According to his disciple Yang Chi,[ad] Chu Hsi's general educational program runs in the following order: The Four Books, the Six Classics, and histories. As to the literary art of the post-Ch'in and Han period (221 B.C.–A.D. 220), he discussed it with students only in his spare time.[29] This testimony concerning the order of book-learning not only agrees with the above memorial but is also corroborated by Chu Hsi's conversations. For instance, he once gave the following instruction to a student: "You should first read the *Analects, Mencius,* and the *Doctrine of the Mean.* Then you turn to study one of the Confucian Classics. Finally, you should read histories. You will find [this order of book-learning] easy to follow."[30] The criterion according to which Chu Hsi established his order of priority in book-learning was knowledge of moral principles. Study of the *Analects* and the *Book of Mencius* should precede that of the Six Classics because, in his view, the former takes less time but yields more results while in the case of the latter the contrary is true.[31] Historical works, on the other hand, report moral principles in actual operation.[32] However, history can only reveal the changes of the past and the present as well as teach moral and practical lessons. It is quite irrelevant as far as moral cultivation of the self is concerned.[33] So, while Chu Hsi fully recognized the importance of history as a subject of study in Confucian learning, he nevertheless assigned it a low priority.

In a letter to his friend Lü Tsu-ch'ien[ae] (1137–1181), Chu Hsi attributed the establishment of this order of study—the Four Books, Classics, histories—to Ch'eng I.[34] This may well have been the case. However, a close look at the recorded sayings of the two Ch'eng brothers does not exactly bear out Chu

Hsi's statement.[35] It was in the hands of Chu Hsi that the scope of book-learning was greatly enlarged. Moreover, as we shall see, he also developed a comprehensive methodology to cope with the problem of how to understand the meaning of a Confucian text on all levels. The intellectual foundation of morality thus became firmly established in the Neo-Confucian tradition.

Chu Hsi further justified book-learning on the ground that the moral mind is constantly in need of the support of knowledge obtained from the study of Confucian texts. In this respect, he actually followed a line of thinking first developed by Chang Tsai[af] (1020–1077). Chang says,

> If one does not read enough, one will not be able to investigate and examine moral principles to the minutest details. Book-learning can always give support to one's mind. The moment one stops reading is the moment one's moral nature lapses into laxity. As one reads, one's mind is always on the alert. But one is surely not to see any moral principles without engaging in book-learning.[36]

Chu Hsi often quoted this passage with approval in preaching his gospel of book-learning. On one occasion he offered the following remark:

> The expression "to give support to" is extremely well said. As is usually the case, when the mind is not occupied with book-learning, it has no place to apply itself. Nowadays there are people who are unwilling to pursue principles of things with thoroughness once they have caught a glimpse [of the Way]. As a result, they indulge their minds in empty speculation.[37]

But what exactly did he mean when he praised Chang Tsai's expression "book-learning gives support to the mind?" The answer may be found in the following statement:

> In learning one cannot afford not to learn from books. As for the method of book-learning, it ought to include intimate familiarity with, deep reflection on, and total immersion in [the text]. As [knowledge] accumulates inch by inch, the effort will eventually come to fruition. In the end not only the principles become clear but the mind also naturally gets settled.[38]

Clearly, in his view, a profound intellectual understanding of principles can keep the mind in a moral state thereby preventing it from being disturbed by selfish desires. On this problem, however, Chu Hsi must not be regarded as a slavish follower of Chang Tsai. As a matter of fact, he took a further step by giving knowledge a more positive role to play in the cultivation of moral nature. Chang Tsai's view in terms of "support" implies that the function of knowledge is passive: It only "supports" moral nature from collapse but does not add anything to it. Chu Hsi, on the other hand, relates knowledge to morality in terms of growth. In one place he speaks of book-learning as capable of cultivating the root of moral nature.[39] In another context he is even more explicit, saying, "A thorough study of the principles enunciated by the sages and the worthies can nourish the root so that the branches and the leaves may grow luxuriantly by themselves."[40] Here his organistic language contrasts vividly with Chang Tsai's mechanistic language. In Chu Hsi's deep consciousness, knowledge does more than just "give support to" morality; it provides morality with nourishment for its continuous growth.[41]

In his discussion of the polarity of "erudition" *(po)* and "essentialism" *(yüeh),* he says,

> In learning we must first establish a base. Its beginning is rather simple, starting with what is essential [to moral practice]. The middle part is very broad. In the end, however, it returns to what is essential. Scholars nowadays are fond of the essentialist approach and do not pursue broad knowledge. The problem is: without an extensive knowledge how can we test [the authenticity or falsity] of what we hold to be essential . . . There are other scholars who are only after erudition but never return to what is essential. They study one institution today and another institution tomorrow, exerting themselves only in the investigation of the functional aspects [of the Way]. They are even worse than the essentialists.[42]

Obviously, Chu Hsi was fighting on two different fronts at the same time. Moral essentialism without intellectual base and erudition without moral focus were both detestable to him. His own position may be described as a centrist one, always seeking to combine "essentialism" and "erudition" in a most creative way. In the realm of knowledge, as he once remarked, "essentials come entirely from erudition."[43] This conception of the relationship between *po* and *yüeh,* it must be emphatically pointed out, presupposes the autonomy of book-learning.

In the above-quoted passage, Chu Hsi speaks of a moral beginning as well as a moral end in learning, but his emphasis is clearly placed on the broad "middle part," which is an autonomous intellectual realm. It is very revealing that, with all his admiration for Ch'eng I, he was nevertheless profoundly dissatisfied with the latter's *Commentary on the Book of Changes* precisely for its disregard for the autonomy of the original text. He sharply criticized this work as follows: "I-ch'uan intended to give moral instructions [in the *Commentary*]. But he should have said them elsewhere, not in connection with the *Book of Changes.*"[44] This is clear evidence that he was very much conscious of the autonomy of the world of knowledge with which morality must not be allowed to interfere directly.

Chu Hsi also extended his respect for autonomy to the world of arts. The *Analects* contains the following statement of Confucius (551–479 B.C.): "I set my heart on the Way, base myself on virtue, lean upon benevolence for support and take my recreation in the arts."[45] Chang Shih[ag] (1133–1180) explained the meaning of the last phrase, "take my recreation in the arts," as follows: "The arts are only to nourish our moral nature." To this explanation Chu Hsi raised a strong objection, pointing out that this statement is especially fallacious. Although the arts occupy the lowest place [in the Confucian scheme of things], they nevertheless have a *raison d'être* all their own and each follows its own natural pattern. The expression "take recreation in the arts" shows that [Confucius] only intended, in each and every case, to respond to things without going contrary to their principles. By not going contrary to principles our moral nature is naturally nourished. But we do not, in the beginning, count on the arts for the cultivation of our moral nature. Your explanation also has its origin in a contemptuous attitude toward the arts because of their low place. It is probably because you regard it as shameful to "take recreation in the arts" that you offer this interpretation to justify your point of view. . . . But the arts are entitled to their own right of existence. We take recreation in them not necessarily because they can nourish our moral nature.[46]

The importance of this passage can hardly be overstated. Here Chu Hsi comes very close to the view of "art for art's sake." Each of the Six Arts (ceremonies, music, archery, carriage-driving, writing, and mathematics), in this view, follows its own "natural pattern" or "principle" and each is to be played according to its own rules. Altogether they constitute an autonomous realm which tolerates no external interference, not even moral interference. They may very well produce moral effects and serve moral ends, but their existence needs no moral justification. Clearly, Chu Hsi's conception of human culture is pluralistic and hierarchical at the same time. It is pluralistic because morality, knowledge, and arts all have their separate realms; it is hierarchical because the Way (Tao[ah]) holds all these realms together with the highest one reserved for morality.

Interpretation and Objectivity— Chu Hsi's Neo-Confucian Hermeneutics

In Chu Hsi's cultural order, knowledge is next only to morality. Since, we have seen above, knowledge for him is primarily knowledge gained through book-learning, especially the Confucian Classics, it requires a comprehensive and systematic methodology for the interpretation and understanding of texts. This is precisely the area wherein lies one of his monumental contributions to Neo-Confucian learning. The autonomy of knowledge, in his case, depends almost entirely on his methodology of book-learning; this methodology led to a full-blown development of what may be called Neo-Confucian hermeneutics.

Chu Hsi's hermeneutics covers practically all levels of interpretation ranging from the philological, the historical, the literal, the reconstructive, to the existential. To interpret a Classical text, according to him, it is necessary to begin with the philological and historical explications of early exegetes. In addition to the text, he says, a student must also be able to familiarize himself with the commentary to such an extent that he can grasp all the details in the commentary that bear directly on the meaning of the text.[47] What is even

more important on this level is to compare closely all the different interpretations of a text offered by various exegetes through the ages. Truth will emerge
only through cross-examination and comparison of all these differences.[48] But
philological interpretation in his hermeneutical system is only the first step.
Although it cannot be bypassed it must be transcended. At the end of this
stage one sees no commentaries at all, only the text.[49]

According to Chu Hsi, reading a text usually requires a person to undergo
three stages: In the beginning he learns how to set his mind attentively on the
text. In the second stage he penetrates into the text by following correct rules
of textual analysis. Being bound by these rules, he can describe the text in its
general outlines, but the description is lifeless. Only when he reaches the final
stage can he bring the text to life.[50] We can ignore the beginning stage and
proceed directly to say a word about the second and final stages.

The second stage involves at least two levels of understanding, namely, the
literal significance of the text and the original intention of the author. The literal level of understanding is relatively simple; it consists mainly of a grasp of
the language of the text.[51] But the line between the literal and the intentional
levels of understanding is by no means clear-cut. As is often the case, our
determination of the literal significance of a text very much depends on our
understanding of the intentional meaning of its author and vice versa.
Throughout his numerous discussions on the problem of textual interpretation, Chu Hsi's central concern is always with how to understand the "original intention" (pen-i[ai]) of the author of a Classical text, in his case the author
being either a sage or a worthy. In a letter to a friend he says, "To study a text
requires the interpreter to be open-minded and cool-headed. His understanding follows closely the literal meaning of the text. He must not come to the
text with his preconceived ideas . . . which prevent him from seeing the original intentions of the sages and the worthies."[52] Here what he is actually saying
is that the reader cannot reach the intentional level without first going
through the literal level. On the other hand, he was also quite aware that the
latter is no absolute guarantee of the former. Otherwise he would not have
criticized his disciples for engaging only in literal interpretation but neglecting the intention of the sages.[53]

Special attention must be paid to both his plea for "open-mindedness" and
his warning against "preconceived ideas" in the understanding of a classical
text. A basic principle in his theory of interpretation is formulated as follow:
"To read a text one must not forcibly impose one's own view on it. Instead
one must remove one's ideas and find out the meaning in it exactly as the
ancients intended."[54] In this regard, Chu Hsi is indeed very close to some of
the modern theorists of interpretation, especially Emilio Betti. For Chu Hsi,
like Betti, was also centrally concerned with the autonomy of the object of
interpretation (text) as well as the possibility of objective knowledge derived
from textual interpretation.[55] Because of the unique nature of his object of
interpretation—the Confucian text—Chu Hsi always took the problem of the

author's original intention very seriously. This does not mean, however, that he was totally unaware of what Paul Ricouer calls the problem of "distanciation." On the contrary, his great emphasis on the necessity to compare and contrast all the different interpretations of a classical text and, indeed, his lifetime work in the realm of exegesis fully testify to the fact that he had all along been grappling with the difficulties arising from the distance between the autonomy of the text and the original intention of the author.[56]

Chu Hsi's concern with the objectivity of textual interpretation also led him to stress the importance of doubt in book-learning. This is equivalent to what Betti calls the "critical moment" within the process of interpretation—a moment that "is called upon in cases requiring a questioning attitude, such as the emergence of incongruences, illogical statements or gaps in a line of argument."[57] Chu Hsi says,

> I used to tell friends that in book-learning one ought to think and seek points of doubt. However, I have now come to realize that it is better to study with an open mind. After working closely at a text for a long time, you will naturally benefit by it, but at the same time you will also encounter points where doubt naturally arises. For a close reading will inevitably lead to places that block your path and cause you perplexity. Thus doubts will come to your consciousness and require you to compare, to weigh, to ponder over. It is not fruitful to start out with the intention of finding things to doubt . . . When I studied the *Analects* in my early years, my doubts were immediately raised. The simple fact that the same passage had been given widely different explanations by various commentators led me to doubt.[58]

The late Dr. Hu Shih[aj] (1891–1962) may have somewhat exaggerated his case when he said that Chu Hsi's "doubt with an open mind" has led to the growth of a "scientific tradition" in China.[59] However, it may not be too farfetched to suggest that Chu Hsi's emphasis on the importance of openmindedness, removal of "preconceived ideas," and, above all, the critical spirit of doubt in textual interpretation did lead him to establish a methodology of Chinese *Geisteswissenschaften* with which objective knowledge of the Confucian message may be fruitfully pursued.

Now let us turn to Chu Hsi's final stage of interpretation in which the text comes to life. "Once we obtain principles," he says, "we also have no need of the Classics."[60] This clearly means that the Classical text itself is also eventually to be transcended. It is at this point that the text comes to life in the sense that what is interpreted is transformed into an organic part, so to speak, of the interpreter's spiritual life. He points out, "The reason that we have to learn from books is to discover moral principles. However, once we have understood these principles, we will find that they are originally inherent in our own nature, not imposed on us from the outside."[61] He further clarifies the meaning of this statement as follows: "In book-learning we must not only seek moral principles from the text. Instead we must also reverse the process by seeking them in ourselves. There are [principles] that had already been clearly stated by the sages but of which we are still ignorant. In the light of the words of the sages we will be able to acquire them by examining ourselves."[62] What he is saying here is that not only do we interpret the Classics but, more importantly, the Classics interpret us. In this regard, he is no different from his philosophical opponent Lu Hsiang-shan, who has been particularly known for the statement "All the Six Classics are my footnotes."[63] Thus Chu Hsi reaches the level of existential interpretation, which presupposes some kind of preunderstanding. In his terminology, it is an "inner experience relevant to the self" (ch'ieh-chi t'i-yen[ak]). Ultimately, as he repeatedly stressed, all the Classical texts must be understood beyond literalism and as an inner experience relevant to the interpreter's self.[64] He testified that this was exactly how he had studied the Confucian text all along.[65] What is actually involved here is, to borrow Bultmann, "a preceding living relationship to the subject matter which finds expression in a text either directly or indirectly." It is a kind of inquiry that "is always guided by a pre-existing and preliminary understanding of human existence, i.e., a definite existential understanding."[66] However, I must hasten to add that, in the case of Chu Hsi, "human existence" can only be understood in a moral sense of the Confucian type. For him what is "relevant to the self" is always morally relevant. Although his "inner experience relevant to the self" involves preunderstanding of a moral kind, there is no reason to believe that this moral element interferes directly with the objective interpretation of a text. What it actually affects is rather the decision to select and order texts for interpretation. His order of book-learning—the Four Books, the Five Classics, and histories, for example, was established precisely on the basis of "moral relevance to the self." But once the interpreter sets out to work on his text, he must follow strictly the methodological rules of textual interpretation and relegate all moral considerations to the background. It is only at the very end of the investigations of a text that moral relevance to the self of the interpreter comes into full play. He must then be able to rise above the text in order to seek existential understanding, which alone can give meaning to his moral existence. It is precisely at this point that tao wen-hsüeh returns to tsun te-hsing, po to yüeh, and chih-chih to ching. In a word, knowledge is transformed into moral practice. The transformation undoubtedly involves a "leap" in understanding—a "leap" from the intellectual level to the moral level. Such a "leap" is possible only if the desire to understand arises from the actual moral needs of the interpreter. Thus Chu Hsi's view of the role of knowledge in life may be seen as necessarily presupposing spiritual cultivation at the same time. Without self-cultivation how can one possibly distinguish authentic moral needs from disguised selfish desires? Intellectual progress and spiritual progress must go side by side to reach the meeting-ground on which the "leap" finally takes place. Here, I believe, lies the central significance of Chu Hsi's lifetime efforts to reinterpret Ch'eng I's formula, "self-cultivation requires seriousness; the pursuit of learning depends on the extension of knowledge."

Knowledge as the Foundation of Morality— A Philosophical Overview

As indicated earlier, Chu Hsi's emphasis on "inquiry and study" in his debate with Lu Hsiang-shan is deeply rooted in his philosophical system. In this concluding section I propose to discuss, briefly, a few of his philosophical ideas directly related to the central thesis of this study.

The logical place to begin is Chu Hsi's view of the function of "intelligence" (or "wisdom" *chih*[al]) in human nature. Of the four cardinal virtues inborn in man according to Mencius (372–289 B.C.)—humanity (*jen*[am]), righteousness (*i*[an]), propriety (*li*[ao]), and intelligence *(chih)*—it is noteworthy that Chu Hsi considered "humanity" and "intelligence" to be the more active pair. While "humanity" is undoubtedly an all-embracing virtue, "intelligence," by virtue of its power to "accomplish things from beginning to end," is no less important.[67] When a student asked him why Mencius placed "intelligence" at the end of the list, he answered thus: "Mencius was actually talking about a circle. In fact, humanity, righteousness, and propriety are all stored in intelligence. You can act in a certain way only when you know it."[68] Elsewhere he further pointed out, "[Like humanity] intelligence also includes all [the four virtues] because knowledge comes first"[69] and "Humanity and intelligence are inclusive while righteousness and propriety are not."[70] To say that Mencius' list is actually a "circle" is to refute in a subtle way the traditional interpretation that "intelligence" is the last of the four cardinal virtues. His description of "intelligence" in terms of its "power to accomplish things" and "inclusiveness" refers primarily to its active and dynamic character, which alone can set the other three virtues in motion. For example, he explicitly stated, "Consciousness is clearly something arising from intelligence . . . The reason that intelligence is close to humanity is that it is the point at which the circle of the 'Four Beginnings' starts to move. Without intelligence, humanity cannot be set in motion."[71] This also explains why he defined, elsewhere, "intelligence" as the "masculine way" (*ch'ien-tao*[ap]), that is, possessing active, vigorous, aggressive, productive qualities.[72] For this reason, he held the view that sagehood (*sheng*[aq]) must also require "intelligence" for completion.[73] "Without intelligence sagehood gets nowhere."[74]

With his emphasis on the importance of "intelligence" (better, in his case, "intellect"), it is only natural that his philosophical system admits of no such distinction as moral knowledge (*te-hsing chih chih*[ar]) versus sense knowledge (*wen-chien chih chih*[as]). In the history of Neo-Confucianism, this distinction was first proposed by Chang Tsai;[75] it received the following reformulation in the hands of Ch'eng I: "The knowledge obtained through hearing and seeing is not the knowledge through moral nature. When a thing (the body) comes into contact with things, the knowledge so obtained is not from within. This is what is meant by extensive learning and much ability today. The knowledge obtained from moral nature does not depend on seeing and hearing."[76] The language suggests Mencius' distinction between the function of the senses and that of the mind.[77] But Mencius did not distinguish two types of knowledge. In a different place, Chang Tsai speaks of the two types of knowledge in a slightly different way: "Knowledge gained through enlightenment that is the result of sincerity is the innate knowledge of one's natural character. It is not the small knowledge of what is heard or what is seen."[78] The term of "small knowledge" is obviously a borrowing from Chuang Tzu[at] (369?–286? B.C.). Although Chuang Tzu contrasts "small knowledge" with "great knowledge," the difference between the two is most likely one of degree rather than kind.[79] Clearly, the distinction must be credited to Chang Tsai and Ch'eng I.

According to this distinction, then, moral knowledge lies in a higher realm, to which human intellect has no access. This is even more so with Ch'eng I than with Chang Tsai, for while the latter only said that moral knowledge does not originate from senses, the former held that moral knowledge does not depend on the senses. If this is the case, then all Chu Hsi's talk about "investigation of things," "extension of knowledge," book-learning, would be pure nonsense. Therefore, from Chu Hsi's philosophical point of view, this distinction is false and must be rejected. When a student asked him whether there is something called sense knowledge, he replied with a contemptuous tone,

> There is only one kind of knowledge! What is at issue is whether our knowledge is true or not true. Why should we argue on such a matter? It is definitely not the case that [after we have acquired sense knowledge] we later obtain another kind of knowledge.[80]

Discussing Chang Tsai's conception of sense knowledge, he further remarked,

> In order to be able to learn, we must possess senses of seeing and hearing (chien-wen[au]). How can we possibly do without them? We work hard with our senses until we achieve a wide and far-reaching penetration. Ordinarily, when we study something by relying on senses, the knowledge obtained is only limited to a single principle. However, when we reach the stage of a general penetration, all the principles become one.[81]

In his view even if we call knowledge arrived at in the final stage "moral knowledge," it differs from sense knowledge only in degree. In his terminology, it is rather a difference between shallowness and depth as well as between coarseness and refinement.[82] Moreover, moral knowledge, a term he never really adopted, can only be developed out of sense knowledge. What is even more revealing is his sharp criticism of Chang Tsai with respect to this distinction:

> *Question:* What about Heng-ch'ü's[av] [Chang Tsai] distinction between sense knowledge and moral knowledge?
> *Answer:* It is fallacious. Sense knowledge is also after the same principle. I do not understand, given such an extraordinary intelligence as his, how he could possibly make so glaring a mistake.[83]

He knew very well that Ch'eng I not only had subscribed to the same view but even developed it to a more rigid form. So his criticism of Chang Tsai was equally applicable to Ch'eng I. However, because of his great respect for the latter, he purposely omitted the latter's name in his discussions. This is clear evidence that although he basically followed Ch'eng I's teaching, he nevertheless consciously went beyond him in the intellectualization of the Confucian Way.[84] It was largely because of his great influence that the distinction between moral knowledge and sense knowledge had fallen into almost complete oblivion until Wang Yang-ming arrived on the scene.

Chu Hsi's emphasis on knowledge as a foundation of morality must also be understood in light of his views of *li* (principle) and mind. To begin with, it is necessary to clarify a common misunderstanding concerning one aspect of the relationship between principle and mind in his system. Chu Hsi often makes such statements as "the mind possesses a multitude of principles and responds to the myriad affairs," "the mind embraces all the principles," "the myriad principles are completely embodied in a mind," and "all the principles are originally within the mind, not obtained from the outside."[85] These statements have given rise to the interpretation that he was not really interested in objective knowledge of the external world. His "investigation of things," according to this interpretation, is therefore nothing but seeking confirmation of the knowledge of "principles" already contained in one's own mind. Tai Chen's[aw] (1724–1777) sharp criticism of his view that "principle is received from Heaven and completely embodied in the mind,"[86] for example, is based on such an interpretation. This is not the place to go into details concerning this important matter. I merely wish to point out that, despite his sometimes loose and therefore misleading language, Chu Hsi did not hold that the mind possesses knowledge of principles before the "investigation of things." As he makes clear in his famous "emendation" to the *Great Learning*, the mind is only "formed to know." He also states unequivocally, "Although the myriad principles are embodied in our minds the mind must still be made to know them."[87] I believe it would make much better sense if we took his "principles embodied in the mind" as a priori forms of understanding—something akin to, though not the same as, "categories" in the Kantian spirit. He seems to think that for each and every "principle" of a thing or event there is corresponding a priori form in the mind. Apparently he also believes that eventually all the principles can be shown to be differentiations from a single unitary principle. This is clearly expressed in the celebrated dictum he inherited from Ch'eng I, "The principle is one, but manifestations are many" (*li-i fen-shu*[ax]).[88] However, these a priori forms in the mind are empirically empty. The postulation of a priori forms corresponding to principles of things and events in the external world is necessary because, from his point of view, it alone can explain how our minds are "formed to know" the latter. But, on the other hand, as amply shown in his conversations as well as writings, no positive knowledge of principles is possible without the "investigation of things." Seen in this way, not only was he genuinely interested in objective knowledge of the external world but his whole philosophical system also required it. It is true, as we have already noted, that he was much more concerned with knowledge of the human world than that of the natural world. Nevertheless, his objective curiosity about and keen observation of natural phenomena were clearly without match among the Neo-Confucianists.[89] This sustained interest in the natural world came partly from his intellectual temper; his earliest wonder, which occurred at the age of five or six (Chinese counting), was about heavenly bodies.[90] But it was undoubtedly also closely related to his firm belief that principles are inherent in things in the external world including "a blade of grass or a tree." He once told his students,

> Principles are universally inherent in all things in the world. But it is the mind that takes charge of them. Being in charge, the mind therefore makes use of them. It may be said that the substance of principles is in things themselves while their functions depend on the mind.

But the next morning he added the following:

> I stated the case in this way because I was taking myself as the [knowing] subject and things as objects [of knowledge]. However, the important truth is that there is really no difference between saying that principles exist in things and that they exist in us [i.e., mind].[91]

Both the original statement and the afterthought are highly illuminating. The original statement shows that he fully recognized the objectivity of principles. In terms of substance, they exist in things and are independent of the mind. By saying that "the mind takes charge of principles," he obviously refers to the fact that the mind can discover, order, and apply them. The afterthought shows, on the other hand, that he became aware of the possibility that the original statement might mislead his students to question the validity of his postulation about a priori forms in the mind which correspond to principles inherent in things of the external world. To say that "there is really no difference between saying that principles exist in things and that they exist in us" is to stress the point that in the actual practice of "investigation of things" and "extension of knowledge," the subjectivity of a priori forms and the objectivity of principles are ultimately to become unified.[92]

In a letter to Chang Shih, Chu Hsi says,

> Confucian learning on the whole begins with a thorough study of principles. Each individual thing has its own principle. Only when a person has a clear knowledge of principles can he get hold of an exact standard (*chun-tse*[ay]), as of weight and measurement, for his mind to follow in its functioning. If he does not extend his knowledge in this [realm of principles] thereby being left, generally, without an exact standard, and is rather content with the sole claim that he has obtained such and such a knowledge and understanding of the mind, then how would it be possible for what is preserved in and issued from his mind to conform unerringly to principles?[93]

Nowhere is the necessity of "the investigation of things" and "the extension of knowledge" in Chu Hsi's philosophical system more clearly explained than in this letter. Because his trust of the material and fallible human mind was always less than total, he therefore wanted to find an objective standard for the mind to follow so that it may not mistake selfish desires for moral principles. This exact standard, in his view, can only be established on the basis of a thorough knowledge of principles which exist objectively in things and events of the external world. Thus we see that at least in theory, knowledge of the natural world and knowledge of the human world are equally important as far as the objectivity of principles is concerned. As he emphatically pointed out, "Principles of things are identical with moral principles. The world does not possess two kinds of principles."[94] This is a logical conclusion easily derivable from his fundamental presupposition that all the individual principles in the world are but differentiations from a single unitary one which is none other than what he calls the Great Ultimate (*T'ai-chi*[az]). So, in the final analysis, the cosmic order and the moral order follow the same pattern; law for things and moral law are of the same kind.[95] Through "inquiry and study," an objective standard can be discovered in either world which, from his point of view, would guarantee the objectivity as well as the stability of moral truth.

It was also his distrust of the ordinary human mind and his search for an exact standard that led him to see the necessity of book-learning. He says,

> As I see it, the reason that we have to study is because our minds are not yet as [purified as] the sages' minds. Since our minds are not yet as purified, we therefore cannot see principles clearly and do not have an exact standard to conform to. As a result, we often follow our personal inclinations, which generally fail to meet the standard by either going beyond or falling below it. But we are usually unaware of our excesses of deficiencies. If our minds are from the very beginning not at all different from the sages' minds or the cosmic mind, then what do we need study for? For this reason it is necessary that we as learners first seek to understand the ideas or intentions of the sages through early commentaries and

then search for universal principles in the light of the ideas or intentions of the sages. Our search proceeds from the superficial to the profound as well as from what is at hand to what is far-reaching. We do this by following a step-by-step order, not by jumping to the conclusion with burning impatience . . . Once we have reached the ultimate limit, our minds will become naturally rectified. By then even the sages' minds or the cosmic mind cannot be very different from ours. But I do not mean to suggest that we be satisfied with what is superficial and at hand [book-learning] and forget about what is profound and far-reaching [moral principles]. Nor do I mean that we simply go after the minds of the sages at the expense of our own minds and follow uncritically the interpretations of early commentators at the expense of our own interpretations.[96]

This letter speaks remarkably well for itself. I only want to call attention to a few important points. First, the "exact standard" he was seeking to establish is ultimately to be found in the objectivity of principles of things and events of the external world, not in the subjectivity of the sages' minds. For the search must eventually go beyond "the ideas or intentions of the sages." This is entirely consistent with his hermeneutical principle that in the end our under-standing must be able to transcend the classical text. Second, it was never his idea that we must follow the sages blindly. As a matter of fact, his critical spirit of "doubt" led him to the contrary. As he explicitly stated elsewhere, "We should always read a text with open mind and fair spirit in order to scru-tinize the principles enunciated in it. If there is a valid point, we do not cast it aside simply because it is made by a common man. On the other hand, if there is a doubtful point, we must examine it carefully even though it is attributed to a sage or worthy."[97] Third, it is true that book-learning is central to his teaching at the methodological level. However, his insistence on learning from the sages and the worthies of the past can by no means be construed as arising out of an uncritical and idolatrous attitude on his part. Nor is it a result of sheer antiquarianism. It is rather based on his belief that the past sages had bequeathed to us numerous objective principles that they had dis-covered through "investigation of things." They can serve as our models because their minds had been extremely well cultivated (or purified) through "inquiry and study." As learners we must also cultivate our minds in the same way. We do this not only by following their examples but, more importantly, by also standing on their shoulders. This is precisely why he says, in his "emendation" to the *Great Learning*, that the learner, in regard to all things in the world, must "proceed from what knowledge he has of their principles, and investigate further until he reaches the limit." The knowledge of princi-ples of things and events now at our disposal is the richest and the most valu-able legacy we have inherited from the past sages and worthies. It must of necessity serve as the starting-point of our new investigations. He says,

It is of course true that in high antiquity, before the writing system had been invented, the learners had no books to read. Moreover, it is also true that people with above-average intelligence sometimes can attain to the Way through self-realization and without book-learning. However, ever since the sages and worthies began their creative work, a good deal of the Way has been preserved in the Classics. Therefore, even a sage like Confucius could not have possibly pursued learning apart from them.[98]

There cannot be the slightest doubt, as Professor Ch'ien Mu[ba] points out, that he must have written this passage with the question posed by Lu Hsiang-shan during their Goose Lake Temple meeting in mind: "Before the time of Yao[bb] and Shun[bc] what books were there for people to read?"[99] From his point of view, this is asking a wrong question, one which borders on sophistry. The historical situation between now and "the time before Yao and Shun" has been fundamentally changed. The simple truth is that we now do have the Confucian Classics which define the Way in its main outlines as well as in its minute details. If we are in quest of the very same Way, as Lu Hsiang-shan apparently was, then what possible justification do we have for our refusal to start the search with the Classics? Chu Hsi's keen historical consciousness naturally led him to emphasize the importance of the tradition of Confucian scholarship. For him, knowledge of principles of things and events is always an accumulative enterprise.

Lastly, Chu Hsi's statement in the above passage, "Nor do I mean that we simply go after the minds of the sages at the expense of our own minds," is an outright rejection of the idea of "transmission of mind," then in wide currency. In his view, what can be transmitted is not the mind but the Way, which consists of the principles objectively discovered by the sages' minds in things and events.[100] Since the mind is essentially a knowing mind, the best a person can hope to accomplish is to raise his mind to the level of purification as high as the sages' minds. But there is no way he can take the sage's mind as his own. He is convinced that only the sage's words exhibit the sage's mind, which is nothing but the embodiment of the principles in the world. Only by studying, carefully and step by step, the sage's words can one expect to grasp these principles. But Lu Hsiang-shan believes, according to Chu Hsi, that a person can obtain the principles by relying only on his own mind without the help of the sages' words. It is indeed excellent, says Chu Hsi, if a person is able to get hold, all by himself, of the right kind of principles. But what if the principles he gets turn out to be of the wrong kind?[101] Here again Chu Hsi displays his deep distrust of the subjectivity of mind on the one hand and his basic concern with the objective validity of moral principles on the other. Seen in this light, the roots of his differences with Lu Hsiang-shan on the pedagogic level indeed strike deep in their different conceptions of such key Neo-Confucian ideas as "principle" *(li)* and "mind" *(hsin)*.

Unlike Chu Hsi, Lu Hsiang-shan's concern is not with the objectivity of principles but rather with the subjectivity of mind. Needless to say, I cannot deal with his theory of mind here.[102] All I need to say is that his trust of the subjectivity of mind is unlimited.[103] His well-known proposition, "Mind is Principle," his identification of the mind with the (spatio-temporal) cosmos, his emphasis on the "recovery of the original mind," and many other similar formulations all point in the same direction. "Mind" conceived in this way cannot possibly be identified with that as understood by Chu Hsi which, as we have seen, is essentially "formed to know." It makes sense only if interpreted as the absolute moral mind.[104] With regard to this mind, there cannot be principles external to it; all objectivity is absorbed into subjectivity. Chu Hsi's question of an "objective standard," therefore, will never arise in the context of Lu Hsiang-shan's philosophy. Moreover, according to Lu Hsiang-shan, this absolute moral mind which is shared by everyone does not change with time. History, therefore, makes little difference, and tradition is of no fundamental importance. The "recovery of the original mind" depends entirely on everyone's own effort; it cannot count on the words or minds of the sages and the worthies for help in an essential way. Lu once reminisced that his understanding of Confucian learning was self-attained on the occasion of reading the *Book of Mencius*.[105] Obviously, he here placed the emphasis more on self-attainment than on the book, which only provided the occasion for his enlightenment. It is also very interesting to note that he reached the same conclusion as Chu Hsi did with regard to the problem of "transmission of mind," but for completely different reasons. In the Goose Lake Temple meeting, he was dissatisfied with the second line of his brother Chiu-ling's[bd] poem composed specifically for the occasion. It reads: "Ancient sages pass on this mind." In response the same line of his own poem says: " 'Tis man's indestructible mind through all ages."[106] Clearly, in his view, recovery of the original mind depends primarily on everyone's "self-attainment" whereas "transmission of mind" implies a dependence on the minds, and consequently also the words, of the sages.[107] It was in this way that Lu Hsiang-shan's view of mind led, by its inner logic, to an attitude toward book-learning diametrically opposed to Chu Hsi's.

Notes

1. This is a reference to the *Chung yung*[be] [Doctrine of the Mean] which provides the *locus classicus* of *tsun te-hsing* and *tao wen-hsüeh*. The *Chung yung* has been traditionally ascribed to Tzu-ssu (483–402 B.C.?), Confucius' grandson.

2. *Chu Wen-kung wen-chi*[bf] [Collected literary works of Chu Hsi, hereafter *wen-chi*] (SPTK ed.), ch. 54, p. 962, "Reply to Hsiang P'ing fu."

3. See Lu Hsiang-shan's "Nien-p'u"[bg] [Chronological biography] in the *Hsiang-shan Hsien-sheng ch'üan-chi*[bh] [Complete works of Lu Hsiang-shan], (SPTK ed.), ch. 36, p. 321; and *Yü-lu*[bi] [Recorded conversations] in ch. 34, p. 261. I have followed Lu's *nien-p'u* in dating Chu's letter to Hsiang An-shih. Wang Mao-hung[bj] (1668–1741) is clearly wrong in assigning this letter to 1181, for this was the year that Hsiang An-shih first came to know Lu Hsiang-shan. See Wang Mao-hung's *Chu Tzu nien-p'u*[bk] [Chronological biography of Master Chu], (Kuo-hsüeh chi-pen ts'ung-shu[bl] [Basic Sociological Series] ed.), p. 100.

4. See Yü Chi's[bm] (1272–1348) "Hsing-chuang"[bn] [Career biography] of Wu Ch'eng in *Tao-yüan hsüeh-ku lu*[bo] [Records of learning from antiquity in the Garden of Way], (SPTK ed.), ch. 44, pp. 386–387.

5. See Wang Yang-ming's two letters to Hsü Ch'eng-chih,[bp] written in 1522, in the *Yang-ming ch'üan-shu*[bq] [Complete works of Wang Yang-ming] (SPPY ed.), 21: 5a–8b.

6. For example, see Hsü Chieh's[br] (1503–1583) "Hsüeh-tse pien"[bs] [A discussion of methods of learning] in *Hsiang-shan Hsien-sheng ch'üan-chi*, "Fu-lu"[bt] [Appendix], pp. 14–15.

7. See *Sung-Yüan hsüeh-an* (Wan-yu wen-k'u[bu] [Universal Library] ed.), ch. 58, pp. 6–8. Huang Tsung-hsi's view was also followed by his son Po-chia[bv] (*ibid.*, p. 8) and Ch'üan Tsu-wang[bw] (1705–1755) in *Chi-ch'i t'ing chi wai-pien*[bx] [Collected works of Ch'üan Tsu-wang, outer chapters], (SPTK ed.), ch. 44, pp. 656–657.

8. For the term "polarity" see B. I. Schwartz, "Some Polarities in Confucian Thought," in David S. Nivison and Arthur F. Wright, eds., *Confucianism in Action* (Stanford, Calif: Stanford University Press, 1959), pp. 51–52.

9. *Chu Tzu yü-lei*[by] [Classified conversations of Master Chu], (hereafter *yü-lei*), (Taipei: Cheng-chung[bz] Book Co., 1973), ch. 64, p. 2524.

10. See Chu Heng-tao's[ca] letter quoted in *Hsiang-shan Hsien-sheng ch'üan-chi*, ch. 36, p. 319.

11. *Yü-lei*, ch. 64, pp. 2521–2522. Similar discussions on the relationship between *tsun te-hsing* and *tao wen-hsüeh* may also be found in ch. 117, pp. 4504–4505 and ch. 118, pp. 4568–4569. For the quoted saying of Ch'eng I, see *I-shu*[cb] [Surviving works] in the *Erh-Ch'eng ch'üan-shu*[cc] [Complete works of the two Ch'engs], (SPPY ed.), 15:20a.

12. See *I-shu*, 18:5b; English translation in Wing-tsit Chan,[cd] *A Source Book in Chinese Philosophy* (Princeton, N.J.: Princeton University Press, 1963), p. 562.

13. For instance, see *yü-lei*, ch. 64, pp. 2522–2523.

14. *Ibid.*, ch. 115, p. 4425.

15. *Ibid.*, p. 4415.

16. For instance, he says, "The concept 'seriousness' truly constitutes the key link (*kang-ling*[ce]) in the teachings of the sages. It is also the chief method for moral cultivation." *Ibid.*, ch. 12, p. 335.

17. *Wen-chi*, ch. 51, p. 897, "Reply to Huang Tzu-keng."[cf]

18. For instance, Chu Hsi says, "The mind is the refined essence of material force." *Yü-lei*, ch. 5, p. 138.

19. *Ibid.*, ch. 9, p. 235. Similar views may also be found in his writings. See *wen-chi*, ch. 50, p. 875, "Reply to Ch'eng Cheng-ssu,"[cg] and ch. 54, p. 972, "Reply to Kuo Hsi-lü."[ch]

20. *Ibid.*, ch. 115, p. 4425.

21. *Yü-lei*, ch. 9, p. 241.

22. *Ibid.*, ch. 9, pp. 241–242.

23. Yen Yüan[ci] (1635–1704), *Ssu-ts'un pien*[cj] [Four preservations], (Shanghai: Ku-chi[ck] Press, 1957), p. 104.

24. Ch'en Chien,[cl] *Hsüeh-pu t'ung-pien*[cm] [A general discussion of defects of learning], (Ts'ung-shu chi-ch'eng[cn] [Collection of series] ed.), "T'i-kang"[co] [outline], p. 102; Ch'en's view is quoted with approval in Ku Yen-wu,[cp] *Jih-chih lu*[cq] [Record of daily knowledge], (Wan-yu wen-k'u ed.), ch. 18, p. 118.

25. *Yü-lei*, ch. 10, p. 255.

26. *Wen-chi,* ch. 14, p. 204. For the dating of this memorial, see Wang Mao-hung, *Chu Tzu nien-p'u,* ch. 2, pp. 197–200.

27. *Yü-lei,* ch. 10, p. 264.

28. Chan, *Source Book,* p. 89.

29. Wang Mao-hung, *Chu Tzu nien-p'u,* ch. 4, pp. 340–341. The Four Books are: the *Great Learning,* the *Doctrine of the Mean,* the *Analects,* and the *Mencius.* The Six Classics are: the *Poetry,* the *History,* the *Book of Changes,* the *Rites,* the *Spring and Autumn Annals,* and the *Music.* Since, however, the *Music* has long been lost, the Six Classics are also referred to as the Five Classics.

30. *Yü-lei,* ch. 11, p. 309. See also pp. 298, 200–201.

31. *Ibid.,* ch. 19, p. 689. His discussions throughout this chapter make it clear that his emphasis in classical studies is placed on knowledge of moral principles.

32. *Ibid.,* ch. 11, p. 301.

33. *Wen-chi,* ch. 46, p. 800, "Reply to P'an Shu-ch'ang."[cr]

34. *Ibid.,* ch. 35, p. 558, "Reply to Lü Po-kung."[cs]

35. For Ch'eng Hao's[ct] (1032–1085) rather negative attitude toward book-learning, see *I-shu,* 3:1b and 2a; *Shang-ts'ai yü-lu*[cu] [Sayings of Hsieh Liang-tso,[cv] 1050–c. 1120], (Cheng-i t'ang ch'üan-shu[cw] [Complete library of the Hall of Rectifying Moral Principles] ed.), 2:11b. For Ch'eng I's limited approval of study of the Classics, see *I-shu,* 15:12a; 16a; *Ts'ui-yen*[cx] [Pure words] in the *Erh-Ch'eng ch'üan-shu,* 1:25a. On this problem, see Ichikawa Yasuji,[cy] *Tei I-sen no tetsugaku no kenkyu*[cz] [Study of Ch'eng I's philosophy] (Tokyo: Tokyo University Press, 1964), pp. 137–140. Professor Ch'ien Mu is right in saying that it was Chu Hsi who introduced history into the Ch'eng-Chu curriculum of Neo-Confucian learning. See his *Chu Tzu hsin hsüeh-an*[da] [A new scholarly record of Master Chu], (Taipei: San-min[db] Book Co., 1971), Bk. V, p. 113.

36. *Chang Tzu ch'üan-shu*[dc] [Complete works of Master Chang], (Kuo-hsüeh chi-pen ts'ung-shu ed.), ch. 6, p. 108.

37. *Yü-lei,* ch. 119, p. 4584. See also ch. 114, pp. 4399–4400 where he says, "Only by a constant engagement in book-learning can the functioning of one's mind be prevented from being interrupted."

38. *Wen-chi,* ch. 64, p. 1188, "Reply to Chiang Tuan-po."[dd]

39. *Ibid.,* ch. 44, p. 764, "Reply to Chiang Te-kung."[de]

40. *Ibid.,* ch. 49, p. 855, "Reply to Ch'en Fu-chung."[df]

41. This idea comes from a passage in the *Book of Changes;* see James Legge, trans., *Yi King*[dg] (Sacred Books of the East ed.), p. 300. Chu Hsi actually quoted it in another conversation. See *Yü-lei,* ch. 120, p. 4639.

42. *Yü-lei,* ch. 11, pp. 298–299. Here he referred, respectively, to the essentialists of the Lu Hsiang-shan School and the many-angled scholars of the Lü Tsu-ch'ien School. See Ch'ien Mu, *Chu Tzu hsin hsüeh-an,* Bk. III, p. 676.

43. *Yü-lei,* ch. 33, p. 1336.

44. *Ibid.,* ch. 69, p. 2767.

45. *The Analects of Confucius,* trans. by D. C. Lau[dh] (Penguin Classics ed., 1979) 7:6.

46. *Wen-chi,* ch. 31, p. 494, "Comments on Chang Shih's 'Interpretations of the Analects' of 1173."

47. *Yü-lei,* ch. 11, p. 304. However, he also points out that if the names of things and institutions in a text are not central to our understanding of its meaning, we may be satisfied with a general knowledge of them. See *ibid.,* p. 301.

48. *Ibid.*, p. 305.

49. *Ibid.*

50. *Ibid.*, p. 282.

51. *Ibid.*, pp. 292, 306.

52. *Wen-chi*, ch. 53, p. 943, "Reply to Liu Chi-chang."[di]

53. *Yü-lei*, ch. 36, p. 1581.

54. *Ibid.*, p. 293. This compares well with the following maxim in contemporary Western hermeneutics: "Meaning has to be derived from the text and not imputed to it." See Josef Bleicher, *Contemporary Hermeneutics* (London: Routledge and Kegan Paul, and Boston: Henley, 1980), p. 36.

55. See Emilio Betti's discussion of the need of an "intellectual open-mindedness" for interpretations in his "Hermeneutics as the General Methodology of the *Geistewissenschaften*," translated by Bleicher in *Contemporary Hermeneutics*, p. 85.

56. Paul Ricoeur, "The Hermeneutical Function of Distanciation," in his *Hermeneutics and the Human Sciences*, ed. and trans. John B. Thompson (Cambridge: Cambridge University Press, 1981), pp. 131–144.

57. Bleicher, *Contemporary Hermeneutics*, p. 40.

58. *Yü-lei*, ch. 11, p. 295.

59. Hu Shih, "The Scientific Spirit and Method in Chinese Philosophy," in Charles A. Moore, ed., *The Chinese Mind* (Honolulu: East West Center Press, 1967), pp. 104–131.

60. *Yü-lei*, ch. 11, p. 305.

61. *Ibid.*, ch. 10, p. 255.

62. *Ibid.*, p. 287.

63. *Hsiang-shan Hsien-sheng ch'üan-chi*, ch. 34, pp. 256–261.

64. *Yü-lei*, ch. 11, pp. 286–288.

65. *Ibid.*, ch. 30, pp. 1235–1236.

66. Quoted in Bleicher, *Contemporary Hermeneutics*, pp. 105–106.

67. *Yü-lei*, ch. 6, p. 175. The *locus classicus* of these four virtues is the *Book of Mencius*, 6A:6 and 7A:21.

68. *Ibid.*, ch. 53, p. 2048.

69. *Ibid.*, ch. 20, p. 766.

70. *Ibid.*, ch. 6, p. 172.

71. *Ibid.*, ch. 20, p. 771. As taught in the *Book of Mencius*, 2A:6, the Four Beginnings are: the sense of compassion is the beginning of humanity, the sense of shame and dislike is the beginning of righteousness, the sense of deference is the beginning of propriety, and the sense of right and wrong is the beginning of intelligence.

72. *Ibid.*, ch. 42, p. 1719; ch. 104, p. 4162.

73. *Ibid.*, ch. 58, p. 2173.

74. *Wen-chi*, ch. 58, p. 1062, "Reply to Chang Ching-fu."[dj]

75. *Chang Tzu ch'üan-shu*, ch. 2, p. 45. English translation by Chan, *Source Book*, p. 515.

76. *I-shu*, 25:2a; English translation by Chan, *Source Book*, p. 570. On the connection between Chang Tsai and Ch'eng I, see A. C. Graham, *Two Chinese Philosophers, Ch'eng Ming-tao[dk] and Ch'eng Yi-ch'uan[dl]* (London: Lund Humphries, 1958), pp. 176–178.

77. *Book of Mencius*, 6A:15.

78. *Chang Tzu ch'üan-shu*, ch. 2, p. 40; Chan, *Source Book*, p. 507.

79. Kuo Ch'ing-fan[dm] (1844–1897), *Chuang Tzu chi-shih*[dn] [Collected interpretations of the *Chuang Tzu*] (Peking: Chung-hua[do] Book Co., 1961), ch. 1, pp. 11 and 51.

80. *Yü-lei*, ch. 34, p. 1440.

81. *Ibid.*, ch. 98, p. 4002.

82. On this point, see also Ch'ien Mu, *Chu Tzu hsin hsüeh-an*, Bk. II, pp. 388–389, and Chang Li-wen,[dp] *Chu Hsi ssu-hsiang yen-chiu*[dq] [A study of Chu Hsi's thought], (Peking: Chinese Academy of Social Science Press, 1981), pp. 411–416.

83. *Yü-lei*, ch. 99, p. 4031.

84. Chu Hsi's intellectualism also led him to distinguish two types of approach to the Confucian Way. He said that among Confucius' leading disciples, Tzu-kung[dr] took the "intellectual approach" (*chih-shih*[ds]) whereas Tseng Ts'an[dt] took the "practical approach" (*chien-lü*[du]). By the former he meant inquiry and study and by the latter he meant practicing filial devotion and other moral virtues in daily life (*Yü-lei*, ch. 27, pp. 1088–1089). This distinction is interesting in two ways: On the one hand, the very idea that there is an "intellectual approach" to the Way reveals his emphasis on the role of knowledge in Confucian teaching as a whole. On the other hand, the idea of a "practical approach" to the Way suggests that he was very much conscious of the problem of how to relate Confucianism to the life of the common (and in most cases also unlettered) man. This is an important subject needing further investigation. His view contrasts sharply with that held by both Lu Hsiang-shan and Wang Yang-ming. Both philosophers spoke highly of Tseng Ts'an and slighted Tzu-kung precisely because of the latter's "intelligence" and pursuit of many-sided "knowledge." See *Hsiang-shan Hsien-sheng ch'üan-chi*, ch. 1, p. 20, "Letter to Hu Chi-sui";[dv] *Yang-ming ch'üan-shu*, 1:24b; and Wang Yang-ming, trans. by Wing-tsit Chan, *Instructions for Practical Living and Other Neo-Confucian Writings* (New York: Columbia University Press, 1963), pp. 71–72. It may be further noted that Chu Hsi's distinction continued to provoke strong reactions among scholars as late as the Ch'ing period (1644–1912). For example, Ch'eng T'ing-tso[dw] (1691–1767), a great admirer of Yen Yüan, understandably rejected the distinction of two types as nonsense. See Tai Wang[dx] (1837–1873), *Yen-shih hsüeh-chi*[dy] [Record of the Yen School], (Wan-yu wen-k'u ed.), ch. 9, p. 115. But Ch'üan Tsu-wang, in his *Ching-shih wen-ta*[dz] [Questions and answers on the classics and histories], ch. 6, *Chi-ch'i t'ing chi*, p. 451; and Tai Chen, in *Meng Tzu tzu-i shu-cheng*[ea] [Commentaries on the meanings of terms in the *Book of Mencius*], (Peking: Chung-hua Book Co., 1961), p. 56, accepted it as valid.

85. See the examples conveniently collected together in Ch'ien Mu, *Chu Tzu hsin hsüeh-an*, Bk. II, pp. 1–24.

86. See Tai Chen's criticism translated in Chan, *Source Book*, pp. 715–717. For further analysis see Yü Ying-shih, "Tai Chen and the Chu Hsi Tradition," in Chan Ping-leung[eb] et al., eds., *Essays in Commemoration of the Golden Jubilee of the Fung Ping Shan*[ec] *Library* (Hong Kong: Fung Ping Shan Library, Hong Kong University, 1982), pp. 390–391.

87. *Yü-lei*, ch. 60, p. 2263.

88. *Ibid.*, ch. 1, p. 2; cf. Chan, *Source Book*, p. 639.

89. This area of Chu Hsi's thought has been extensively explored in a monographic study by Yamada Keiji;[ed] see his *Shushi no shizenkaku*[ee] [Master Chu's study of nature], (Tokyo: Iwanami[ef] Book Co., 1978).

90. Wang Mao-hung, *Chu Tzu nien-p'u*, ch. 1, pp. 1–2.

91. *Yü-lei*, ch. 18, p. 669.

92. On this point, a roughly similar interpretation may also be found in Takahashi Susumu,[eg] *Shu Ki to Ō Yōmei*[ch] [Chu Hsi and Wang Yang-ming], (Tokyo: Kakusho kankōkai,[ci] 1977), pp. 108–117 and 225–236.

93. *Wen-chi*, ch. 30, p. 473, "Reply to Chang Ching-fu."

94. *Yü-lei*, ch. 15, p. 471.

95. On this problem, see also the analysis by Tomoeda Ryūtarō,[ej] in his *Shushi no shisō keisei*[ck] [The formation of Chu Hsi's thought], (Tokyo: Shun-ju-sha,[cl] 1969), esp. pp. 354–366.

96. *Wen-chi*, ch. 42, pp. 712–713, "Reply to Shih Tzu-chung."[em]

97. *Ibid.*, ch. 31, p. 484, "Reply to Chang Ching-fu."

98. *Ibid.*, ch. 43, p. 724, "Reply to Ch'en Ming-chung."[en]

99. Chien Mu, *Chu Tzu hsin hsüeh-an*, Bk. III, p. 616. Yao and Shun were legendary sage-emperors.

100. *Wen-chi*, ch. 70, p. 1291, "Notes on Some Doubtful Points."

101. *Yü-lei*, ch. 120, p. 4657.

102. For general discussions of Lu Hsiang-shan's theory of mind the reader is referred to T'ang Chün-i,[co] *Chung-kuo che-hsüeh yüan-lun, yüan hsing p'ien*[cp] [Fundamentals of Chinese philosophy: inquiry into human nature], (Hong Kong: New Asia Institute, 1968), esp. pp. 538–552; and Kusumoto Masatsugu,[cq] *Sō-Min jidai jugaku shisō no kenkyū*[er] [Studies on Confucian thought in the Sung and Ming times], (Tokyo: Hiroike gakuen[es] Press, 1972), pp. 341–367.

103. See a saying of Lu Hsiang-shan ("I only trust this mind of mine") preserved in *Sung-Yüan hsüeh-an*, ch. 77, p. 27.

104. Professor Fung Yu-lan[et] in his *History of Chinese Philosophy* holds that both Chu Hsi and Lu Hsiang-shan shared the same view of "mind" (trans. by Derk Bodde, Princeton, N.J.: Princeton University Press, 1953, vol. 2, pp. 587–588). Recent studies, however, suggest that the contrary is true. See Mou Tsung-san,[eu] *Ts'ung Lu Hsiang-shan tao Liu Chi-shan*[ev] [From Lu Hsiang-shan to Liu Tsung-chou], (Taipei: Student Book Co., 1979), ch. 2; and Lao Ssu-kuang,[ew] *Chung-kuo che-hsüeh shih*[ex] [A history of Chinese philosophy], (Taipei: San-min Book Co., 1980), Bk. III, pt. 1, pp. 409–414.

105. *Hsiang-shan Hsien-sheng ch'üan-chi*, ch. 35, p. 307.

106. *Ibid.*, ch. 34, p. 279. For a complete English translation of the two poems see Julia Ching,[ey] "The Goose Lake Monastery Debate (1175)," *Journal of Chinese Philosophy* I (1974), p. 165.

107. Ch'ien Mu, *Chu Tzu hsin hsüeh-an*, Bk. III, pp. 299–301.

Glossary

a 項安世平父	j 黃宗羲	s 致知
b 子思	k 理	t 居敬
c 尊德性	l 氣	u 窮理
d 道問學	m 天理	v 約
e 子靜陸象山	n 人欲	w 博
f 朱元晦	o 陰陽	x 一貫
g 吳澄	p 敬	y 多識
h 王陽明	q 學	z 心
i 宋元學案	r 涵養	aa 伊川程頤

ab 格致	bs 學則辨	dj 張敬夫
ac 行	bt 附錄	dk 程明道
ad 楊楫	bu 萬有文庫	dl 程伊川
ae 呂祖謙	bv 百家	dm 郭慶藩
af 張載	bw 全祖望	dn 莊子集釋
ag 張栻	bx 鮚埼亭集	do 中華
ah 道	by 朱子語類	dp 張立文
ai 本意	bz 正中	dq 朱熹思想研究
aj 胡適	ca 朱亨道	dr 子貢
ak 切己體驗	cb 遺書	ds 知識
al 智	cc 二程全書	dt 曾參
am 仁	cd 陳榮捷	du 踐履
an 義	ce 綱領	dv 胡季隨
ao 禮	cf 黃子耕	dw 程廷祚
ap 乾道	cg 程正思	dx 戴望
aq 聖	ch 郭希呂	dy 顏氏學記
ar 德性之知	ci 顏元	dz 經史問答
as 聞見之知	cj 四存編	ea 孟子字義疏證
at 莊子	ck 古籍	eb 陳炳良
au 見聞	cl 陳建	ec 馮平山
av 橫渠	cm 學蔀通辨	ed 山田慶兒
aw 戴震	cn 叢書集成	ee 朱子の自然学
ax 理一分殊	co 提綱	ef 岩波
ay 準則	cp 顧炎武	eg 高橋進
az 太極	cq 日知錄	eh 朱熹と王陽明
ba 錢穆	cr 潘叔昌	ei 國書刊行會
bb 堯舜	cs 呂伯恭	ej 友枝龍太郎
bc 舜	ct 程顥	ek 朱子の思想形成
bd 九齡	cu 上蔡語錄	el 春秋社
be 中庸	cv 謝良佐	em 石子重
bf 朱文公文集	cw 正誼堂全書	en 陳明仲
bg 年譜	cx 粹言	eo 唐君毅
bh 象山先生全集	cy 市川安司	ep 中國哲學原論原性篇
bi 語錄	cz 程伊川哲学の研究	eq 楠本正繼
bj 王懋竑	da 朱子新學案	er 宋明時代儒学思想の研究
bk 朱子年譜	db 三民	es 廣池學園
bl 國學基本叢書	dc 張子全書	et 馮友蘭
bm 虞集	dd 江端伯	eu 牟宗三
bn 行狀	de 江德功	ev 從陸象山到劉蕺山
bo 道園學古錄	df 陳膚仲	ew 勞思光
bp 徐成之	dg 易經	ex 中國哲學史
bq 陽明全書	dh 劉殿爵	ey 秦家懿
br 徐階	di 劉季章	

16

Chu Hsi on the Standard
and the Expedient

WEI CHENG-T'UNG

IN CHU HSI'S DIALOGUES with his students, the question of the standard (*ching*[a]) and the expedient (*ch'üan*[b]) was repeatedly raised. There are two reasons why his disciples unceasingly asked this question: Considerable debate by later Confucian scholars, each advocating his own interpretation, had arisen over what Confucius (551–479 B.C.) had meant by the term the "expedient" as mentioned in the *Analects*,[1] and Chu Hsi's students wanted to know whose interpretation was the correct one; and, while all the numerous debaters[2] of the standard and the expedient agreed that the two concepts are closely related, they are after all two different concepts. Ch'eng I[c] (1033–1107) alone maintained that the expedient is the same as the standard, a view which Chu Hsi's students found impossible to understand.

These questions both originate from the same source—just what did Confucius mean by the expedient? Chu Hsi in his work *Lun-yü chi-chu*[d3] (Collected commentaries on the *Analects*) which he finished, after repeated revisions, at the age of forty-eight, emphasized Ch'eng I's rendering of the term "expedient," but he cited Mencius' (372–279 B.C.?) remark that "He who extends his hand to save his drowning sister-in-law, is exercising the expedient," thus inferring that the expedient and the standard should be considered as two separate concepts. In the *Collected Commentaries on the Analects*, Chu Hsi was favorable toward Ch'eng I's interpretation. If he occasionally took exceptions, the dissenting views were indicated as derived from Mencius' teaching.

His posture in regard to this question in his dialogues with his students is different, however. In his dialogues, Chu Hsi made many overt criticisms of Ch'eng I's theory. On the twenty-eight occasions in which the problem of the standard and the expedient is discussed, Ch'eng I is mentioned sixteen times; ten of those times Chu Hsi disagrees with him. The basic difference between Chu Hsi and Ch'eng I is that while Ch'eng I's view that "The expedient is the same as the standard" was originally set up to refute the argument of the Han (206 B.C.–A.D. 220) scholars that "That which is at variance with the standard and complies with the Way is the expedient,"[4] Chu Hsi repeatedly indicated his approval of the Han scholars' view. To be sure, Chu Hsi was greatly influenced by Ch'eng I, whom he always deeply respected and revered. On the one hand, Chu Hsi, being faithful to himself, was unable to conform fully to Ch'eng I's view. On the other hand, he made several attempts to defend Ch'eng I, lest his intentions be misunderstood by his disciples.

Chu Hsi, having firmly grasped the distinction between "rites" (*li*) and the "expedient" made by Mencius, was able to have sympathetic understanding of the Han scholars' thesis of "being at variance with the standard" (*fan-ching*). In his dialogues and other works, Chu Hsi repeatedly centered upon the problem of the standard and the expedient, in the end making it an independent and significant topic.

The purpose of this paper is to resurrect this age-old problem and, by assembling the relevant material and using new methods and format, to present the topic in a new light. As far as I know, the problem has not been sufficiently attended to by contemporary Chu Hsi scholars. What I do here may, I hope, help to clarify an important aspect of Chu Hsi's complex philosophical system.

The Standard and the Expedient

If we consider Ch'eng I's definition that the expedient is the standard, we therefore ought to reject the term the "expedient." This is what Chu Hsi regards as the fundamental problem of the twin concepts.[5] It is just because the standard and the expedient are two different concepts that we may speak of the relationship between them. The discussion of this relationship demonstrates a key advancement in the development of Confucian moral philosophy. Not only does it enrich the content of the Confucian ethical theory, but also it enables the Confucians to deal more satisfactorily with changing situations. In Chinese intellectual history, Mencius was the first to relate the two ideas,[6] and while several later thinkers discussed the problem, none of them were able to leave behind a discussion as rich and brilliant as Chu Hsi's.

That Chu Hsi's interpretation of the standard and the expedient differs from that of Ch'eng I does not mean that Chu Hsi is opposed to Ch'eng I. Ch'eng I's arguments emphasize the absoluteness of morality. If Chu Hsi were to oppose Ch'eng I, then Chu Hsi would have had to advocate a doctrine of the relativity of morality, when in actuality he did not. Their propositions shared the same basis, and as such we see Chu Hsi on the one hand criticizing Ch'eng I and yet on the other repeatedly defending him. Chu Hsi differs from Ch'eng I because Chu Hsi was stimulated by Mencius, thus causing him to focus on how an individual puts his ethical principles into practice in a particular situation, where he might have to make a decision in clear opposition to regular moral rules. From this he was able to see that the theory of the Han scholars, "That which is at variance with the standard and complies with the

Way is called the expedient," not only does not contradict Mencius' view, but rather is a most accurate explication of what Mencius meant by the term the "expedient." Thus the question for Chu Hsi was how to eliminate the contradiction between Ch'eng I and the Han scholars. Upon close examination of Chu Hsi's ideas, we find that this contradiction is not difficult to resolve.

Chu Hsi said, "The standard is the constant principle and the expedient is the varying principle when the constant principle won't work and there is no other choice."[7] According to this explanation, Chu Hsi has transformed the relationship between the standard and the expedient into that between the constant (*ch'ang*[g]) and the varying (*pien*[h]); in other words, "The constant is called the standard; that which varies is called the expedient."[8] The earliest appearance of this statement, supposedly made by Mencius, is recorded in the *Han-shih wai-chuan*[i] (Moral discourses illustrating the Han text of the *Book of Odes*). Examples of when "the standard is the constant principle" are lords who are benevolent and ministers loyal, and fathers who are loving and sons filial.[9] When the constant principle cannot be practiced and the situation leaves no alternatives, a need to allow for change or variation arises. In allowing change one may pursue several different strategies. For example, one may choose some clever pragmatic maneuver, a choice that Ch'eng I opposed. If the expedient was to be regarded as being no more than this, then Chu Hsi would oppose it as well. According to Chu Hsi's analysis, "change" is equivalent to what the Han scholars called "to vary" (*fan*[j]), namely, "to be at variance with the standard."[10] From this explanation we may infer that the Han scholars' view of "being at variance with the standard" can be included in the relationship between the standard and the expedient. But from another point of view, Chu Hsi repeatedly emphasized that although the standard and the expedient are different, yet the expedient that varies is not necessarily separate from the standard.[11] He even went so far as to say, "Complying with the expedient means that the standard is found in it."[12] According to this, while the outward forms of the standard and the expedient may vary, their essential qualities are the same. Thus, his view and the theory of "being at variance with the standard" produce an obvious contradiction. To be at variance with the standard is, in either form or substance, to contradict or oppose the standard itself. Mencius' example,[13] that according to rites, unmarried or unrelated members of the opposite sex are forbidden to touch each other, represents a kind of social norm or custom that may be considered to be a "standard." Now if a man were to be in the special situation of the "drowning sister-in-law" and were to adhere to the rite, then he would have to watch someone die without lifting a finger. While it is not in accord with social custom, to extend a hand to save the drowning sister-in-law is still a moral decision founded upon basic humanitarian principles. Mencius called this manner of decision exercising the expedient. The expedient thus is in clear contradiction to the above definition of the standard as rite. How may we resolve this contradiction whereby one may in adapting oneself to the changing situation be at variance with the standard, and yet, while carrying out the expedient be still in accord with the standard? This problem as well as that between Ch'eng I and the Han scholars can be solved simultaneously.

It is possible that Ch'eng I and Chu Hsi have different reactions to the thesis "That which is at variance with the standard and yet complies with the Way is called the expedient" because Ch'eng I resents the theory of "being at variance with the standard"; in addition his understanding of what the term the "standard" means is perhaps different from that of the Han scholars. The Han scholars' concept of the term is the same as the above-mentioned definition as rite, while Ch'eng I's concept of the standard is something similar to the "Way" (Tao^k).[14] If we accept Ch'eng I's definition, then how may we speak of being at variance with the Way and complying with the Way at the same time? The apparent contradiction can, perhaps, be resolved by the explanation that Ch'eng I subjectively assumed that the standard is similar to the Way; since he believed that the Way is the universally valid principle, he considered all the doctrines of change and variation to be false, and totally rejected the Han scholars' view. He logically concluded that "The expedient is the same as the standard."[15]

Chu Hsi had a different idea. He realized that the Way and the standard in the statement "being at variance with the standard and yet complying with the Way" are not of the same level. He said, "As for the phrase 'that which is at variance with the standard and complies with the Way,' upon careful consideration it is reasonable because the expedient is correlative to the standard. As soon as the term the 'expedient' is mentioned, then a kind of change is suggested, and we may call it a variation. And yet, though it is at variance with the standard, it does not contradict the Way. Although it is different from the standard, it is in accord with the Way."[16] In another dialogue he said, "The Way is an integrated entity which penetrates the standard and the expedient."[17] The so-called integrated entity is the highest original substance which comprises all the things in the world. It is the reality which is higher and more fundamental than the standard and the expedient. From the Confucian point of view, reality is not merely an object of purely intellectual consideration, but also the principle of both existence and action. Therefore the Way can "penetrate" (kuan^l). The Way penetrates all the things in the world and completes them. It penetrates the standard and the expedient, providing a ground for standard and expedient activities. Because the Way penetrates both the standard and the expedient, both of them partake of the Way. Thus we may say that the expedient is the same as the standard; yet because the standard and the expedient are not on the same level as the Way, when the expedient varies from the standard, it does not necessarily contradict the Way. Seen thus, there would be no conflict between Ch'eng I and the Han scholars. Through Chu Hsi's interpretation, the views of Mencius, the Han scholars, and Ch'eng I are unified. Furthermore, with the introduction of the concept of the

"Way," Chu Hsi's position becomes consistent with Ch'eng I's in regard to the absoluteness of morality.

As for Chu Hsi's remark, "Though at variance with the standard, yet not contradicting the Way," we can see that there is no inconsistency in Chu Hsi's thought, but merely confusion in the use of terms. When he said that in dealing with changing circumstances one may be at variance with the standard, he referred to the standard as relative to the expedient, which is one level below the Way. When he said that one may use the expedient and yet not depart from the standard, his concept of the term "standard" is different from the "standard" in "That which is at variance with the standard," and is quite close to the term the "Way" in the phrase "not contradicting the Way." Therefore once we understand the term the "standard" in "The expedient in reality does not depart from the standard,"[18] to be the same as the "Way," the confusion will be clarified.

In Chu Hsi's usage, the term the "standard" is sometimes called "the great norm" (*ta-fa*[m])[19] and sometimes "the permanent principle for all ages" (*wan-shih ch'ang-hsing chih tao*[n]).[20] The standard and the Way were originally indistinguishable. In regard to Chu Hsi's statement that "Complying with the expedient means that the standard is found in it,"[21] we can be sure that the "standard" here is the same as the "Way."

The Expedient, Righteousness, and Timely Equilibrium

When one is confronted by a certain situation that can't be resolved by normal principles, one must use an expedient. In exercising the expedient, one is hoping to adapt oneself to the changing situation; but while attempting to change and adapt, one may be forced to deviate from social norms and precepts. This is not only a very serious problem for the individual but for society as well. Regarding this issue, the Han scholars insisted that while one may be at variance with the standard, one must aim to "comply with the Way." Chu Hsi also repeatedly emphasized this point, for he feared that if one is allowed to be at variance with the standard without having to comply with the Way, one would exhibit behavior in obvious opposition to social norms; thus in becoming indulgent and reckless, one would commit chicanery and deceit, and yet claim that one was merely exercising the expedient. Such would be what Chu Hsi called "using the expedient for self-rationalization" (*chieh-ch'uan i tzu-shih*[o]).[22] It is certainly not the original meaning of exercising the expedient. The requirement "to comply with the Way" is intended to prevent such abuses from taking place.

Now the question is: How can one both be at variance with the standard and at the same time comply with the Way? Chu Hsi introduced the ideas of righteousness (*i*[p]), equilibrium (*chung*[q]), or timely equilibrium (*shih-chung*[r]) and interlocked them with the idea of the expedient to arrive at a new line of thought that enabled him to solve this question.

While being at variance with the standard is a kind of deviant behavior, deviation is only a step in the process of carrying out the expedient. It has not yet touched on the essence of exercising the expedient. The main idea of exercising the expedient is that once an individual is forced to depart from the normal order, he must, in order to resolve the particular difficulties of his particular circumstances, come up with a new moral decision that does not contradict ultimate moral principles. Thus exercising the expedient is not meant to corrupt the concept of morality but is instead a way of overcoming moral difficulties. We see at once that the content of moral life is enriched and the application of moral principles is expanded—a difficult task indeed! This was perhaps why Confucius on this point felt "using the expedient" to be more difficult than "learning together" (*kung-hsüeh*[s]), "aspiring to the Way" (*shih-tao*[t]), and "getting established" (*li*[u]).[23]

Chu Hsi understood "being able to adopt the expedient" to mean "when one meets a varying situation and knows the appropriate measure."[24] In other words, when one meets up with the difficulty of a peculiar situation, one must then assess what is appropriate and inappropriate according to the concept of righteousness. Chu Hsi's theory of the expedient is something that "must by necessity comply with the righteousness."[25] We may say that to comply with righteousness is to know appropriateness. When a situation changes suddenly while one is unprepared, it is only by applying the concept of righteousness that one may determine what conduct is morally suitable. Righteousness as the ground for assessing a situation is not an objectively existing norm ready to be followed. Righteousness means appropriateness. It is something that must be decided through one's innate knowledge (*liang-chih*[v]). Whether the application of innate knowledge is appropriate or not depends on the individual's level of personal cultivation. Those who are not thoroughly familiar with the principles of humanity and righteousness cannot, then, exercise the expedient. Chu Hsi therefore insisted that those who were not sages could not casually appeal to the expedient.

Righteousness can be linked up with the concept of the varying expedient because righteousness itself has the special characteristic of being able to adapt to temporal change; hence righteousness is appropriateness and not a fixed or unchanging entity. What is appropriate with regard to one particular event may not necessarily be appropriate with regard to another event. To determine whether something is appropriate or not, we must look at the concrete situation. To do otherwise, that is, to be obstinate and stubborn, was a position strongly opposed by Confucius, who also disapproved of the idea that once something is deemed appropriate, it is always appropriate.[26] This is why he condemned "obstinacy" (*ku*[w]). Confucius also pointed out that nothing in the world could always be right or always wrong. One only had to comply with righteousness (recognized by innate knowledge) and thus "what is right, one would follow."[27] What is appropriate and what is expedient, these two ideas, must both be based upon the principle of righteousness before they are accepted. This is what Chu Hsi meant by saying that the expedient must comply with righteousness.

Now that the relationship between the expedient and righteousness is clarified, what then is the relationship between the two and equilibrium? Chu Hsi explains with an analogy: "One must use righteousness to assess situations before one will be able to attain equilibrium. Righteousness is like a balance, and to exercise the expedient is to weigh something with this very scale. Equilibrium occurs when the thing attains its balance."[28] Encountering a change in circumstances with a moral decision to make, one actively weighs whether to accept or reject a certain course of action, basing the decision on righteousness. Therefore it is said, "One uses righteousness to assess situations." This mental activity of assessing a situation must be fully thought out before the process of carrying out the expedient can be considered achieved; when it is finally achieved, the final conclusion is called equilibrium. "When things attain their balance" is to say that the conclusion was neither biased nor odd. It must be appropriate and must comply with the principle of equilibrium (*chung-tao*[x]). If the behavior of assessing how to be in accord with change cannot attain equilibrium, then it cannot be called the expedient. Therefore Chu Hsi said, "The expedient is timely equilibrium. Without equilibrium, one will have no way to use the expedient."[29]

"The expedient is timely equilibrium" means that in situations of assessing change, one must be able to "reside in the equilibrium" at all times. Timing is a specific factor; that which may be appropriate at one time may be inappropriate in another. This is what is meant when it is said that equilibrium "is without fixed form, yet it exists in all different temporal situations."[30] Chu Hsi also said that the expedient is "the equilibrium of one particular instant" (*i-shih chih chung*[y]),[31] thus explaining that both the process of exercising the expedient and the result of it are in regard to particular situations and are carried out when there is no alternative. One may adapt the expedient once, but not twice, for "It is provisional and not constant."[32] We cannot arbitrarily extend the meaning of the expedient and utilize it for self-rationalization.

In the case of "Tzu-mo always grasping equilibrium" (*Tzu-mo chih-chung*[z]), Mencius criticized him as being "without the expedient while grasping equilibrium."[33] Because Tzu-mo considered change to be the norm, he was harming the Way. Hence, Chu Hsi has a theory of the "living" and the "dead aspects of equilibrium."[34] The dead aspect of equilibrium is like Tzu-mo's manner of grasping equilibrium. The living aspect of equilibrium is the timely equilibrium, which is in accordance with changing temporal reality.

These ideas of righteousness, equilibrium, and timely equilibrium are all to be found in the ancient Classics. They all have complex significance.[35] Chu Hsi has taken them and applied them to the problem of the standard and the expedient, therefore leading not only to the creation of a framework for the examination of expedient conduct, but also to an effective means for resolving the problem of the standard and the expedient.

Practicing the Expedient

Chu Hsi raised three questions regarding this topic: (1) What kind of person can put the expedient into practice? (2) In what kind of situations can the expedient be put into practice? (3) What events can be considered to be acts of exercising the expedient? The first two questions deal with conditions for exercising the expedient, while the last problem incorporates concrete situations that will be useful in determining the nature of the conduct of exercising the expedient.

What kind of person can put the expedient into practice? This question was originally asked by Confucius. He felt that "using the expedient" was more difficult than "getting established." Therefore Chu Hsi said that only a sage could use the expedient.[36] This is a reasonable surmise, but Chu Hsi also said, "In examining the intention of the Sage (Confucius), he does not allow ordinary people to utilize the expedient."[37] This is not necessarily Confucius' intention; considering something to be difficult is different from not permitting it. Looking at Chu Hsi's statements that "the expedient is applied only if there is no other way out" and "the standard is a principle that cannot always be carried out,"[38] we may speculate as to Chu Hsi's true intention. It isn't that we are not permitted to utilize the expedient, but that Chu Hsi is highly alarmed by the act of employing the expedient. He was deeply worried that ordinary people might casually utilize the expedient for their own convenience.

Why is putting the expedient into practice so difficult? We may use Wang Pi's[aa] (226–249) words to explain. He said, "The expedient is a variation of the Way and variation is without fixed entity. Illuminating it spiritually lies in the right person. Not being able to set it up beforehand is the most difficult part of it."[39] That is, in exercising the expedient, there are no de facto rules that can be followed. A change in circumstances is a special situation. It is extremely difficult for an individual to anticipate it; and while in the midst of change, it is even more difficult for that individual to be able within the flicker of an eye to determine what his future conduct ought to be. In such a situation one can only rely upon his own spiritual instinct. As for "illuminating it spiritually lies in the right person," we may quote Chu Hsi's statement that "one's being able carefully to assess a situation depends on one's daily cultivation of the root—this very mind is unobstructed, pure, integrated and natural."[40] While Chu Hsi is pointing to a high level of moral cultivation, Wang Pi's expression, "illuminating it spiritually" (*shen erh ming chih*[ab]), does not necessarily have moral connotations. Chu Hsi also said, "Only those who have thoroughly examined and are perfectly familiar with moral principles can talk about the expedient."[41] Obviously, only those who have the same level of cultivation as sages and worthies will be able to put the expedient into practice. From the modern point of view, Chu Hsi's assertion that only sages could exercise the expedient amounts to forbidding the expedient, for the ideal of sagehood is totally beyond the reach of modern men. Yet the problem of the standard and the expedient is a concrete one that anyone may have to confront.

In regards to the above question, if we won't be tied down by a literary reading of his statement, it seems that Chu Hsi's conclusion is this: Only good means will produce good results; evil means will not lead to desirable ends. This is the case not only in normal situations but also under exceptional circumstances.

The next question is: In what kinds of situations may the expedient be practiced? Feng Yung-chih[ac] of the T'ang dynasty (618–907) once said, "As for the expedient, it is merely appropriate to a varying situation temporarily; it isn't a long-term practice. . . . The Sage knew that moral principles are sometimes powerless, that rite and righteousness sometimes cannot be applied, and that laws and punishment sometimes cannot be enforced. Under these circumstances we should use the expedient as a remedy."[42]

It is not difficult to supply examples for the three kinds of situations mentioned here. The case of extending a hand to save the drowning sister-in-law is a good example of a situation in which rite and righteousness cannot be applied. Mencius cited the case of Shun's[ad43] father murdering a man[44] and suggested that Shun carry his father on his back and flee. This is an example of a situation in which law and punishment cannot be enforced. Many stories of the conflict between loyalty and filial piety[45] are examples of situations in which moral principles are powerless. Extending a hand to save a drowning sister-in-law is undoubtedly an excellent example of exercising the expedient. Carrying one's father and fleeing may also be called exercising the expedient. This second action, however, might be controversial because it involves conflicts between personal feelings and law and order. The conflict between loyalty and filial piety is a serious moral dilemma. Whether one chooses to be a loyal subject or a dutiful son, either choice may be considered right or wrong. Thus when we consider these two examples, the circumstances in which one may use the expedient are difficult to determine indeed.

Chu Hsi's discussion of the problem tends to be too general. On the one hand he said, "As for the constant principle, how can we obtain the right application in every action? Sometimes there might be a situation that can't be covered. Then we must adopt the expedient."[46] On the other hand he said, "There might be events that are without other choices and the standard can't be applied. One can then merely carry through by being at variance with the standard."[47] Yet he also said, "There are occasions when events require variation of the standard."[48] These three statements all have the same meaning. When one is following the usual practice of the Way, and then a dilemma offering no alternative arises, one has to be at variance with the standard. The problem is that there is no objective way of deciding whether a situation is really without alternatives. Although one person may consider a situation to be without alternatives, another person might think otherwise. In the case of a widowed woman remarrying, for example, even if the widow has no one to depend on and thinks she has no other alternatives, others will still feel that she is commiting adultery when she remarries. It is in such situations—in which there is no one, certain, acceptable decision—that the problem of exercising the expedient is created.

The third question is: What kind of measures can be considered to be cases of the expedient? This question puts Chu Hsi's two theories of "that which is at variance with the standard and complies with the Way" and "by using righteousness to make an assessment, one then attains equilibrium" in a position where they must be tested against actual situations. The situations referred to by Chu Hsi may be divided into two categories: how the sages exercised the expedient, and the incidents that Chu Hsi provided from his own experience. Both these categories can be considered as practical applications of the theory of the standard and the expedient.

Among the cases belonging to the first category, Chu Hsi mentioned the voluntary abdications of emperors Yao[ae] and Shun,[49] King T'ang's[af] banishing Chieh,[ag][50] King Wu's[ah] punishing Chou,[ai][51] I-yin's[aj] expelling T'ai-chia,[ak][52] and the Duke of Chou's[al] execution of Kuan-shu[am] and Ts'ai-shu.[an][53] Chu Hsi considered all of the above to be examples of ancient sages exercising the expedient.

> The standard is the Way that is carried out constantly generation after generation, while the expedient is applied only if there is no other choice and the expedient complies with righteousness, such as King T'ang's banishing Chieh, King Wu's punishing Chou, and I-yin's expelling T'ai-chia. These are all practices of the expedient. If they are often applied, what kind of world will it be? . . . But it was 600–700 years after emperors Yao and Shun before there was King T'ang, another 600–700 years before there was King Wu. Accordingly, the application of the expedient is really difficult to speak of.[54]

> Furthermore, in the cases of the Duke of Chou's executing Kuan-shu and Ts'ai-shu, and T'ang T'ai-tsung's[ao] killing Ch'ien-ch'eng[ap] and Yüan-chi[aq] (his elder and younger brothers),[55] their applying the sword to siblings was the same, but their reasons were different. Kuan-shu and Ts'ai-shu plotted together with the descendants of Shang to endanger the Chou court. This is a case of committing a crime against the empire as well as against the ancestral temple. It could be said that the Duke of Chou had no choice but to execute them. T'ang T'ai-tsung's case was obviously for the sake of rivalry for the throne. Hence the Duke of Chou's case could be called an application of the expedient, while T'ang T'ai-tsung's is not.[56]

When ministers are loyal to their lords, they are following the standard, but when ministers commit regicide, they are at variance with the standard. As a result of these slayings there were power struggles aimed at the establishing of a new order. This interplay between rival forces is a common historical occurrence. Chu Hsi, however, singularly feels that they may be considered as cases of the sages exercising the expedient. This is because T'ang and Wu had long since been idealized by the Confucian tradition. In other words, "The revolution carried out by kings T'ang and Wu complied with the Mandate and were supported by the people."[57] Because both T'ang and Wu were already idealized as sages, it can be said that the regicides they performed were cases of the expedient in compliance with the principle of righteousness. To those who do not accept the Confucian position, Chu Hsi's argument is hardly convincing. Historically speaking, it appears that success is the only criterion for judgment, and thus anything that is conducive to success is thereby also judged to be justified. If this is to be considered as exercising the expedient, then it must be said that the end justifies the means. Clearly, this is not consistent with Chu Hsi's intentions. Such examples of idealization are not really applicable. Therefore, whether from the historical or idealized point of view, Chu Hsi's theory of the standard and the expedient is very difficult to apply in such situations as King T'ang's banishing Chieh. In other words, these kinds of events cannot at all be tested by Chu Hsi's theory of the standard and the expedient.

Chu Hsi felt that it was for the throne and not the expedient that T'ang T'ai-tsung murdered his elder brother. This judgment conforms to the requirements of Chu Hsi's theory, but what of the Duke of Chou's case? The Duke was a sage and Chu Hsi pointed out that only sages may exercise the expedient. Hence, although he murdered his own brothers—no matter what the real reason was—his act must be regarded as exercising the expedient. Either the Duke of Chou's situation is different from those of King T'ang, King Wu, and T'ai-tsung or it is in accord with Chu Hsi's words that "There might be events that are without other choices." Even though the Duke of Chou murdered his own brothers, the action can still be looked upon as a case of using the expedient.

Regardless of how we evaluate the individual situations, they all appear to be using the ends to justify the means. According to Chu Hsi's theory, the conduct of being at variance with the standard can only permit opposition to such kinds of customs as the avoidance of physical contact between members of the opposite sex who are neither married nor related. Such crimes as the slaying of one's brother definitely cannot be permitted. According to Chu's theories, an ordinary person's murder of his brother is a crime, while the Duke of Chou's murder of his brother is a case of exercising the expedient. This is absurd. Even if the Duke of Chou's acts were meant to serve the throne and save the people, we must still employ another criterion in order to justify his conduct. In this case, Chu Hsi's purely moralistic theory of the standard and the expedient cannot be applied.

Next, we will consider Chu Hsi's personal reflections of how to deal with the problem of the standard and the expedient.

Question: What if one is observing the rite of mourning and one's elders compel one to drink wine?

Answer: If one cannot obtain permission to abstain, then no harm is done if one reluctantly complies with the elders' intention. But one cannot willingly get drunk. After drinking, one may return to his initial state.[58]

According to ancient rites, one cannot drink during the mourning period. This is the "standard." "The elders compelling one to drink" is "to be at variance with the standard." Under these circumstances, should the individual obey the ancient rites and not the elders' intentions, or should he do the opposite? Although this isn't a serious situation, it is still a difficult moral predicament. One has to make a choice between obeying the rites and respecting the elders.

Chu Hsi has pondered over this question rather thoroughly, as we can see from his reply. The phrase "If one cannot obtain permission to abstain," indicates that one, when forced to drink, must first decline. To decline is to show that one knows that the ancient rites should be observed. If one is not permitted to abstain after repeated pleadings, which means that one has no other alternatives, then it is all right to follow the expedient. "The expedient must be in accord with righteousness," and righteousness (appropriateness) varies with varying situations. "To reluctantly comply with the elders' intentions" means that one provisionally replaces the appropriateness of obeying the rites with that of respecting the elders, thereby resolving the present dilemma. However, there are still further conditions to be fulfilled: One must not get drunk and one must return to the original state after drinking. Getting drunk is contrary not only to the rites but also to the idea of respecting the elders. To say that "one must return to the original state after drinking" is to insist that the expedient is used only when one has no choice. It is not to be considered as a precedent that might be lightly invoked later on.

Question: Suppose one's parent has died and has willed that Buddhist and Taoist monks be employed to chant at services. What should the son do?
Answer: This is a difficult problem to deal with.
Question: May he disregard these instructions?
Answer: The dead one's descendant naturally has an affection that cannot bear to violate the will. This matter must be carefully studied.[59]

The difficulty of this problem is due to the difference in religious beliefs of the two generations. If the son is a Confucian disciple, he would obviously hope to adhere to the mourning rites of the Confucians, even if the deceased parent is Buddhist. But this would be in contradiction to the instructions of the dying parent, and to oppose the parent's will is to be unfilial. Thus the issue is a controversial one. For a Confucian, filial piety is the most important moral virtue. Therefore when the enquirer asked, "May he disregard these instructions?" Chu Hsi replied that if so the conscience of the son would be disturbed. Yet Chu Hsi was troubled by the combining of the concept of filial piety with Buddhist rituals. Deducing from the dialogue's content, if the son would want to use the expedient by carrying out the will's instructions to hire the monks, Chu Hsi would not be opposed. After all, it does not conflict with Chu Hsi's theory.

> *Disciple:* What if there is an occasion that the mother is dead and the father is still alive, and the father wishes to follow the common customs for mourning by wearing mourning dress, hiring monks, and cremating the remains?
> *Chu Hsi:* What will you do?
> *Disciple:* I will not obey.
> *Chu Hsi:* These are just trifling matters. If you had decided to obey, it would not harm anything. But cremation is certainly forbidden.
> *Disciple:* Cremation would destroy the parent's remains.
> *Chu Hsi:* If you group the question of cremation together with that of mourning dress and hiring monks, then you still have not been able to discriminate between light and serious matters.[60]

Chu Hsi was able to reach a conclusion because Buddhist mourning rites include mourning dress and cremation, and this is helpful in avoiding the situation where both filial piety and Buddhist rituals are called for. If the father had only wanted the son to follow traditional custom by employing monks and wearing mourning dress, then one might use the expedient because these are only "trifling matters." But cremation cannot be allowed because it would "destroy the parent's remains," which is something far more serious than not following Confucian rituals. While it is hard to ease the mind of the son, this decision would still be acceptable to the father. Chu Hsi's manner of handling the situation not only maintains the Confucian viewpoint but also resolves the conflict between father and son. This can be called settling the accounts of both parties. Chu Hsi in this instance of resolving the conflict between the standard and the expedient has left behind for later generations an important revelation. If one has grasped the major principle of ethics (that is, the standard), then when in the midst of difficulties one may provisionally apply the secondary principle (that is, the expedient) to assess the situation.[61]

Conclusion

Historically speaking, the question of the standard and the expedient began with Confucius. Although many scholars debated the problem afterwards, it is not until we read Chu Hsi that we find a well-developed analysis. Stimulated by Ch'eng I's dissatisfaction with the thesis of Han scholars that "That which is at variance with the standard and complies with the Way is called the expedient," Chu Hsi made a deep and thorough analysis of the twin concepts. While both respecting Ch'eng I and sympathizing with the standpoint of the Han scholars, Chu Hsi felt compelled to confront the problem and to search for a reasonable solution. He must have been troubled by the problem, as witness his wavering comments on Ch'eng I. In the end, however, he found the key to the solution in the distinction between the standard and the Way.

Since the idea of the constant principle can be found both in the standard and the Way, one concept is easily mistaken for the other. Ch'eng I interpreted "that which is at variance with the standard" to be one and the same as "that which opposes the Way of the standard." Here we can see that he has evidently confused the standard to be something equivalent to the Way. Thus, Ch'eng I's understanding of the term "standard" is very different from that of the Han scholars. According to Chu Hsi's point of view, while the standard and the expedient are relative concepts, they are transcended by the Way, and the Way is contained by them. Because the Way is transcendent, the expedient may be at variance with the standard, but not opposed to the Way. As to the Way being contained in the standard and the expedient, we may say that the expedient is the same as the standard: both are in accord with the Way. With this formulation Chu Hsi offered a reasonable solution to the contradictions between the positions of Ch'eng I and the Han scholars while at the same time he advanced considerably the theory of the latter.

The Han scholars only claimed that "That which is at variance with the standard and complies with the Way is the expedient." Chu Hsi attempted to show how this is possible. His statement "The Way is an integrated entity which penetrates the standard and the expedient" is not alone enough to provide an adequate explanation of the concept of the expedient conduct. His theory became effective when he added the concepts of righteousness, equilibrium, or timely equilibrium, and explained their relationship to the expedient. These ideas were originally scattered throughout the various Classics; it was not until after Chu Hsi gathered and analyzed them that they became the core of the solution to the problem of the standard and the expedient.

A theory of the relationship between the standard and the expedient must not merely be a play of ideas. It must be able to direct how the expedient is to be carried out and how one is to find effective solutions to the numerous particular moral questions that arise. Therefore I have sought to examine Chu Hsi's view by reviewing his theoretical treatment of the subject and his observations on practical issues. Upon examination I discover that Chu Hsi's moralistic theory of the standard and the expedient is not necessarily applicable in such cases as King T'ang banishing Chieh and King Wu punishing Chou. If these activities are considered to be expedient and appropriate, the criterion of expediency and appropriateness is something other than a moralistic one. On the other hand, I find Chu Hsi's practical observations extremely effective in solving complex ethical problems within the boundary of rites and social customs.

The problem of the standard and the expedient is an important issue in ethics. Man's situation is always changing and growing increasingly more complex, thus endlessly producing new and difficult problems requiring fresh solutions. Chu Hsi was born eight hundred years ago, and while it is true that some of the moral problems to which he referred have naturally disappeared because of changes in society, yet his theories and teachings have touched upon some of the central issues in contemporary situational ethics. How to reexamine Chu Hsi's theory and to improve or reconstruct it in light of our new experience and knowledge is a new challenge that must be taken up by the moral philosophers of this generation.

Translated by Roseanne E. Freese[ar]

Notes

1. *Analects*, 9:29.

2. Cf. Ch'ien Chung-shu,[as] *Kuan-chui p'ien*[at] [Notes of small discoveries], (Beijing: Zhong-hua[au] Book Co., 1979); "Tso-chuan"[av] in the *Tso-chuan* [Tso's commentary on the *Spring and Autumn Annals*], sec. 30, fifteenth year of Duke Ch'eng,[aw] pp. 206–209; and Wei Cheng-t'ung, *Chung-kuo che-hsüeh tz'u-tien*[ax] [Dictionary of Chinese philosophy], (Taipei: Ta-lin[ay] Publishing Co., 1977), pp. 803–805, on the term *ch'üan*.

3. Chu Hsi's comments on the *Analects*, 9:29. For Mencius' remarks see the *Book of Mencius*, 4A:17.

4. The actual text reads, "The Han scholars considered being at variance with the standard and in compliance with the Way to be the expedient. Hence they talked about expedient variations and tactics, which are all false. The expedient is the same as the standard. No one has understood the meaning of the term 'expedient' since the Han dynasty." Quoted in the *Lun-yü chi-chu*. The theories of the Han scholars are found in Tung Chung-shu[az] (176–104 B.C.), *Ch'un-ch'iu fan-lu*[ba] [String of pearls on the *Spring and Autumn Annals*], ch. 3, sec. 4: "Although the expedient is at variance with the standard, it must be within the scope of what can be allowed. . . . The expedient is a tactful measure. It would be better if we can return to the great standard"; *Kung-yang chuan*[bb] [The Kung-yang commentary on the *Spring and Autumn Annals*], eleventh year of Duke Huan:[bc] "What does the expedient mean? It means to deviate from the standard with good results"; Chao Ch'i[bd] (?–201 A.D.), *Commentary on the Book of Mencius* [*Meng Tzu chu*[be]]: "The expedient is that which is at variance with the standard but is still good."

5. *Chu Tzu yü-lei*[bf] [Classified conversations of Master Chu], (Taipei: Cheng-chung[bg] Book Co., 1960), ch. 37, p. 1646.

6. *Book of Mencius*, 4A:17.

7. *Chu Tzu yü-lei*, ch. 37, p. 1639.

8. *Han-Wei ts'ung-shu*[bh] [Library of Han and Wei dynasties], (Taipei: Hsin-hsing[bi] Publishing Co., 1959), 1:76b.

9. *Chu Tzu yü-lei*, ch. 37, p. 1642.

10. *Ibid.*, ch. 37, p. 1647.

11. *Ibid.*, ch. 37, p. 1642.

12. *Ibid.*, ch. 37, p. 1639.

13. *Book of Mencius*, 4A:17.

14. For example, Ch'eng I said, "In confronting a certain event, one deals with it by assessing it in order to have it comply with righteousness. This is called the expedient. How could it be contradictory to the Way of the standard?" See the *Erh-Ch'eng*

ch'üan-shu[bj] [Complete works of the two Ch'engs], (SPPY ed.), *Ts'ui-yen*[bk] [Pure words], pt. 1, p. 6a.

15. Quoted in Chu Hsi, *Lun-yü chi-chu,* comment on the *Analects,* 9:29.
16. *Chu Tzu yü-lei,* ch. 37, p. 1647.
17. *Ibid.,* ch. 37, p. 1638.
18. *Ibid.,* ch. 37, p. 1642.
19. *Ibid.,* ch. 37, p. 1643.
20. *Ibid.,* ch. 37, p. 1638.
21. *Ibid.,* ch. 37, p. 1639.
22. *Ibid.,* ch. 37, p. 1637.
23. *Analects,* 9:29.
24. *Chu Tzu yü-lei,* ch. 37, p. 1633.
25. *Ibid.,* ch. 37, p. 1638.
26. Ch'en Ta-ch'i,[bl] *K'ung Tzu hsüeh-shuo lun-chi*[bm] [Essays on Confucius' doctrines], (Taipei: Cheng-chung Book Co., 1958), p. 61.
27. *Analects,* 4:10.
28. *Chu Tzu yü-lei,* ch. 37, p. 1633.
29. *Ibid.,* ch. 37, p. 1637.
30. Chu Hsi, *Chung-yung chang-chü*[bn] [Commentary on the *Doctrine of the Mean*], comment on ch. 2.
31. *Chu Tzu yü-lei,* ch. 37, p. 1638.
32. *Ibid.,* ch. 37, p. 1640.
33. *Book of Mencius,* 7A:26.
34. *Chu Tzu wen-chi*[bo] [Collection of literary works of Master Chu], (SPPY ed. entitled *Chu Tzu ta-ch'üan*[bp] [Complete literary works of Master Chu], 58:15b.
35. Cf. Wei Cheng-t'ung, *Dictionary of Chinese Philosophy,* the terms *i,* p. 678; *chung,* p. 210; and *shih-chung,* p. 512.
36. *Chu Tzu yü-lei,* ch. 37, pp. 1634, 1638.
37. *Ibid.,* p. 1640.
38. *Ibid.,* pp. 1637, 1640.
39. Quoted in Huang K'an[bq] (488–545), *Lun-yü chi-chieh i-shu*[br] [Exegesis of collected commentaries on the *Analects*], on the *Analects,* 9:29.
40. *Chu Tzu yü-lei,* ch. 37, p. 1635.
41. *Ibid.,* ch. 37, p. 1643.
42. Feng Yung-chih, *Ch'üan lun*[bs] [On the expedient] in the *Ch'üan T'ang wen*[bt] [Complete essays of T'ang authors], vol. 404, p. 5216.
43. Shun, the legendary ruler of ancient China c. 2255–2206 B.C., was known as a sage-emperor, based on the *Book of History,* ch. 2, "Canon of Shun."
44. *Book of Mencius,* 7A:35.
45. Ch'ien Chung-shu, *Kuan-chui p'ien,* "Sixty Notes on the *Mao Shih cheng'i*"[bu] [Commentaries on Mao's *Book of Odes*], note no. 49, pp. 134–136.
46. *Chu Tzu yü-lei,* ch. 37, p. 1642.
47. *Ibid.,* ch. 37, p. 1643.
48. *Ibid.*
49. Yao, a legendary sage-emperor (c. 2357–2256 B.C.), abdicated the throne in favor of Shun instead of his son. The story was first mentioned in the *Mo Tzu,*[bv] ch. 93. Shun passed on his throne to Yü the Great instead of his own son. See above, n. 43.

50. King T'ang founded the Yin[bw] (or Shang) dynasty (c. 1766–1123 B.C.) by banishing the tyrant Chieh (c. 1818–1766 B.C.), the last emperor of the Hsia dynasty (c. 2183–1752 B.C.). Cf. the *Shih-chi*[bx] (Historical records), ch. 2, "Record of Hsia."

51. King Wu (1121–1116 B.C.) was the founder of the Chou dynasty (1111–249 B.C.) after his successful revolt against the tyrant Chou of the Shang dynasty. Cf. the *Shih-chi*, ch. 3, "Record of Yin."

52. I-yin, the prime minister appointed by King T'ang, expelled T'ai-chia, the grandson of King T'ang. Cf. the *Shih-chi*, ch. 3, "Record of Yin."

53. The Duke of Chou, the younger brother of King Wu, executed Kuan-shu and Ts'ai-shu, his elder and younger brothers. Cf. the *Shih-chi*, ch. 3, "Record of Yin."

54. *Chu Tzu yü-lei*, ch. 37, p. 1638.

55. T'ai-tsung, the second emperor of the T'ang dynasty, killed his brothers Ch'ien-ch'eng and Yüan-chi. Cf. the *Chiu T'ang-shu*[by] [The earlier history of the T'ang dynasty], ch. 64, "Biographies no. 14."

56. *Chu Tzu yü-lei*, ch. 37, p. 1641.

57. The *Book of Changes*, explanation of the remarks on the forty-ninth hexagram *ke*[bz] (to change).

58. *Chu Tzu yü-lei*, ch. 89, p. 3676.

59. *Ibid.*

60. *Ibid.*

61. Cf. Yang Hui-chieh,[ca] *Chu Hsi lun-li hsüeh*[cb] [Chu Hsi's ethics], (Taipei: Cowboy Publishing Co., 1978), p. 149.

Glossary

a 經
b 權
c 程頤
d 論語集註
e 禮
f 反經
g 常
h 變
i 韓詩外傳
j 反
k 道
l 貫
m 大法
n 萬世常行之道
o 藉權以自飾
p 義
q 中
r 時中
s 共學
t 適道
u 立
v 良知

w 固
x 中道
y 一時之中
z 子莫執中
aa 王弼
ab 神而明之
ac 馮用之
ad 舜
ae 堯
af 湯
ag 桀
ah 武
ai 紂
aj 伊尹
ak 太甲
al 周
am 管叔
an 蔡叔
ao 唐太宗
ap 建成
aq 元吉
ar 費如安

as 錢鍾書
at 管錐編
au 中華
av 左傳
aw 成
ax 中國哲學辭典
ay 大林
az 董仲舒
ba 春秋繁露
bb 公羊傳
bc 桓
bd 趙岐
be 孟子註
bf 朱子語類
bg 正中
bh 漢魏叢書
bi 新興
bj 二程全書
bk 粹言
bl 陳大齊
bm 孔子學說論集
bn 中庸章句

bo 朱子文集
bp 朱子大全
bq 皇侃
br 論語集解義疏
bs 權論

bt 全唐文
bu 毛詩正義
bv 墨子
bw 殷
bx 史記

by 舊唐書
bz 革
ca 楊慧傑
cb 朱熹倫理學

17

Chu Hsi on Personal Cultivation

JULIA CHING

CHU HSI IS HEIR to a tradition, the Confucian tradition as transmitted and interpreted by Mencius (372–289 B.C.?) and others. In this tradition, a key doctrine concerns universal human perfectibility—that every person can become a sage like the ancients Yao and Shun.[a1] This is an optimistic teaching, which claims to see the unity of humankind in the universally accessible goal of sagehood. This teaching is grounded in the belief that human nature is originally good and can be made perfect by personal cultivation. Indeed, the affirmation that human nature is perfectible, that the human being possesses naturally a desire to transcend the narrow goals of self-survival and self-satisfaction, implies the affirmation that this desire is somehow possible of fulfillment. But how? There is need to show a way by which such fulfillment is to be realized. For, without praxis, there is no assurance that theory can be tested, and without testing, theory remains empty—a powerless wish, or rather, a wish capable of destroying the person through frustration, but incapable of its own fulfillment.

When we turn from Chu Hsi's cosmology and metaphysics of human nature to his practical moral philosophy, we shall find a certain continuity of both language and thought. In his ethics and theory of cultivation, Chu Hsi continues to speak of T'ai-chi[b] (Great Ultimate), of li[c] (principle), and of ch'i[d] (matter, energy). He does not abandon one realm, that of speculative thought, in order to enter another, that of moral action and spiritual cultivation. He integrates the two in a philosophy that is, on every level, both theoretical and practical.

As we examine at closer range Chu Hsi's practical doctrines, we shall discover further evidence against accepting a widespread, conventional image of him as a model of rigid moral propriety and a dispenser of prescriptions and proscriptions regarding the correctness of human relationships. True, Chu Hsi does speak of the Three Bonds and the Five Relationships[2]—the warp and woof of Confucian social morality. He was himself a model of correct living, by his own account watchful over the least movements of his mind and heart.

But he does not devote his principal attention to questions pertaining to duties and obligations, virtues and vices. He appears rather to have set his mind on higher things.

It is my belief that Chu Hsi's doctrine of personal cultivation belongs to the realm of practical moral philosophy while also going beyond it to embrace a spiritual and ascetic doctrine with mystical implications. It is also firmly grounded in the more speculative parts of his philosophy, namely, in his metaphysics of human nature, in his view of man as the microcosm of the universe, participating in the cosmic process and assisting in the perfection of the universe through his efforts toward self-perfection. I do not deny that there can be problems with Chu's teachings—problems of consistency, either internally within his own philosophical system, or externally with the teachings handed down by Confucius (551–479 B.C.) and Mencius. He certainly shows signs of having been influenced by Buddhism and Taoism although he also consciously rejects them, in the sense that his commitment is to the Confucian vision of moral and social responsibility. Besides, it seems to me that problems of internal consistency are minor, within a highly integrated and well-balanced thought structure, while problems of external consistency with the entire Confucian tradition deserve somewhat more attention and scrutiny, especially for those whose concern is doctrinal orthodoxy. My own plan is to move from a review of Chu's teachings on human nature to discussions of human emotions—whether these be good or neutral—then to his views of the human mind and heart (*hsin*[c]) and the problems of "preserving the mind and nurturing nature" (*ts'un-hsin yang-hsing*[f]), that is, to his practical teachings on personal cultivation. Thus, I wish to examine his teachings of reverence and knowledge, to see the exact place given to meditation or quiet-sitting, to evaluate the importance of the pursuit of knowledge in his whole formula of self-cultivation, before making some concluding observations.

The Background: Chu Hsi on Human Nature

Chu Hsi's greatness consists less in originality of thought than in his remarkable ability to adapt and fuse together in one philosophical system the individual contributions of the thinkers who preceded him,[3] who had made serious efforts to inherit and transform the Confucian legacy of the past according to new needs and with the help of new insights derived from Taoism and Buddhism. From Chou Tun-yi[g] (1017–1073), Chu Hsi derives an understanding of the world of things and of men as the spontaneous reproduction of the interaction between the Five Agents (Metal, Wood, Water, Fire, and Earth) and the principles of yin[h] and yang[i] which, in turn, came from the Great Ultimate, a notion, traced to the *Book of Changes,* referring to that which holds the universe together.[4] Chou also describes it as the *wu-chi*[j] (literally, "limitless"), thereby giving rise to later debates about its intended meaning. But his effort is generally directed toward the construction of a world view that explains the countless phenomena of existence as having come from an original source, pure and undifferentiated, the totality of reality.[5] In this way, he affirms the idea that reality is both "one" and "many," an idea that has become basic to the Sung (960–1279) philosophical synthesis.

Also from Chou Tun-yi, Chu Hsi derives the belief that man participates in the excellence of the *T'ai-chi*, possessing a moral nature of *li* that comes to him through the cosmic transformations. Contact with external things provided the occasion for evil, as deflection from the good rather than a positive presence. The perfect man, the sage, is completely sincere (*ch'eng*[k]). His mind and heart is like a mirror, quiet when passive, upright when active or moved by emotions. Chu Hsi recognizes Chou's *T'ai-chi* as the source and fullness of all being and perfection. He calls it *T'ien-li*[l] (Heavenly Principle), using a term found in Ch'eng Hao[m] (1032–1085) and Ch'eng Yi[n] (1033–1107). Ch'eng Yi's distinction between *li* (principle, goodness, being) as that which belongs to the realm "above shapes" (*hsing-erh-shang*[o]) which gives form and identity to *ch'i* (matter, energy), the basic stuff that makes up all things, and which belongs to the realm "within shapes" (*hsing-erh-hsia*[p]), provides a basis for a new explanation of human nature and its capacity (*ts'ai*[q]) for good and evil. Chu insists on the original goodness of human nature, which he attributes to *li*, while explaining the capacity for evil, ascribing it to the quality of *ch'i* or man's physical endowment. In so doing, he incorporates as well the teachings of Chang Tsai[r] (1028–1077) concerning *ch'i*. According to this view, emotions (*ch'ing*[s]), which are manifestations of *ch'i*, become occasions for evil whenever they show excess. As a method of self-perfection, and for control of emotions, Chu proposes the cultivation of a disposition of reverence (*ching*[t]) through quiet-sitting (*ching-tso*[u]), a form of meditation and self-examination, and correct behavior, as well as the investigation of things through assiduous study. He claims that this dual formula can contribute toward the state of psychic harmony (*ho*[v]) characterizing the due proportion of emotions described in the *Doctrine of the Mean*.[6]

We have spent some time discussing the Great Ultimate in a cosmic context. According to Chu Hsi, it is also present within us. "Every human being has a *T'ai-chi*. Every thing has a *T'ai-chi*."[7] Thus the transcendent, the absolute, is also immanent not only in the totality of the universe but also in every individual human being, indeed, also in every individual thing (*wu*[w]). But this immanence appears to remain latent in most people. It has to be made manifest, to become actualized, by self-cultivation.

A problem here is that of the relationship between the Great Ultimate, which is immanent in human nature, and the *li*, which constitutes human nature. Are they one and the same, all the more as the *li* is frequently described as having come from Heaven, indeed, as the "Heavenly Principle" (*T'ien-li*)?

There is much ambiguity in this area. The language Chu Hsi uses may lead us to think that the Great Ultimate in human nature is also the *li* constituting human nature. Indeed, Chu Hsi seems to say as much. But Fung Yu-lan[x] is of the opinion that they are different, that whereas the *li* constituting human nature is usually manifest, through *ch'i,* the Great Ultimate requires personal cultivation and liberation to become manifest.[8] On the other hand, I think it may be useful to see the immanent Great Ultimate as the fullness of *li* in man, a fullness that is usually not manifest, except in the persons of the sages. In other words, the identity between the Great Ultimate and *li* in the nature of sages is not true in ordinary humans. It can, however, be made so by a process of cultivation.

Here we touch upon another problem: that of inequality in human endowments notwithstanding original goodness and universal perfectibility. Chu Hsi explains this in terms of the differences in physical endowment of *ch'i* (*ch'i-chih chih hsing.*[y]) He agrees with Han Yü[z] (768–824) that there are different grades in human nature[9] but praises Ch'eng Yi and Chang Tsai[10] for the philosophical explanation for such differences. He admits, with them, that some men have a purer endowment of *ch'i* and others a more turbid. "Human nature is always good, yet some men are good from their births on, and others are evil from their births on. This is due to differences in physical endowment. . . . The goal of education is to transform physical endowment. But such transformation is very difficult."[11] Chu Hsi therefore tempers his optimism regarding human nature with a touch of realism regarding the existential differences between human beings, as well as the difficulties of changing the given physical endowment.

Chu Hsi's construction of a new philosophical synthesis brings with it the definitive acceptance of a certain formulation of the new Confucian message, a terse formula supposedly containing the essentials of the doctrine of the sages. This is taken not from the Four Books[12] but from the *Book of Documents,* considered to be one of the earlier Classics. Actually, it is taken out of a chapter allegedly transmitted to posterity in the old pre-Ch'in script: the "Counsels of Great Yü"[aa]—even though the authenticity of this chapter is subject to doubt, and Chu Hsi himself acknowledges it. All complete in sixteen Chinese characters, this cryptic formula may be translated as

> The human mind (*jen-hsin*[ab]) is prone to error,
> But the moral mind (*Tao-hsin*[ac]) is subtle (*wei*[ad]).
> Remain discerning and single-minded:
> Keep steadfastly to the Mean Equilibrium (*chung*[ae]). [13]

In his preface to the annotated edition of the *Doctrine of the Mean (Chung-yung chang-chü*[af]), Chu Hsi refers to this formula as the eternal message of the ancient sages, associating the *Tao-hsin* with *T'ien-li* and the *jen-hsin* with *jen-yü*[ag] (human passions), and emphasizing the need of the one dominating the other. According to him, this is to be done by adherence to the Mean, or the state of psychic equilibrium prior to the rise of emotions (*wei-fa*[ah]). Therefore, for him, the Confucian Way (Tao^a^) may be described as this psychic equilibrium, a state of mind and heart that reflects man's original goodness and enables him to pursue and acquire sagehood.[14]

Chu Hsi tends to portray the sage in cosmic and metaphysical terms, following closely the language and teachings of the *Doctrine of the Mean* and of the *Book of Changes*. He speaks of the importance of having, or repossessing, psychic equilibrium and harmony, so that the mind and heart become like a bright mirror, reflecting all things.[15] While these statements also affirm Mencius' teaching of man's original goodness and perfectibility, Chu Hsi's distinctions between *li* and *ch'i*, his association of the former with goodness and the latter with emotions, lead also to another question, that of the emotions themselves: are they good or evil, are they a help or a hindrance to the goal of sagehood?

Emotions: Good or Evil?

I suggest that we examine the discussions of emotions given in the classical texts, as well as Chu Hsi's commentaries on this subject. I refer here to Mencius' teachings of the beginnings of virtue in human nature; I refer also to the discussion of the emotions—of pleasure, anger, sorrow, and joy—in the *Doctrine of the Mean,* of the state prior and posterior to the rise of these emotions.[16] These are the pivotal texts that Chu Hsi accepts and incorporates into his own theory of human nature and his doctrines of sagehood and self-cultivation.

Emotions as Good

The philosophical tradition coming from Mencius, with its emphasis of human perfectibility based on the doctrine of man's original goodness, offers an important foundation for the positive evaluation of human emotions. For the doctrine of the original goodness of human nature is grounded in that of the morality and goodness of certain human emotions. In the words of Mencius, the "Four Beginnings of virtue"—compassion, shame, modesty, and the discernment between right and wrong—"are not welded on to me from the outside; they are in me originally."[17]

Mencius uses the word *hsin* (mind or heart) to discuss these basic feelings or emotions. It is the same word Chu Hsi uses in his references to "mind" *(hsin)* as that which controls nature and the emotions. We may note here that the Mencian context in which this word occurs is a broader, almost "naturalistic" one when compared to the Neo-Confucian context in which Ch'eng Yi, Chang Tsai, and Chu Hsi make use of the same word, which, by their time, had gathered certain metaphysical connotations from Buddhist philosophy. All the same, for both Mencius and Chu Hsi, the "mind" or "heart" of man is the seat of his emotions as well as of his intelligence and volitions.

Let us now turn to an examination of Mencius' words:

Mencius said: "No man is devoid of a heart sensitive to the sufferings of others.
. . . The heart *(hsin)* of compassion is the germ of humanity *(jen*[ai]*)*; the heart of
shame, of dutifulness or righteousness *(yi*[ak]*)*, the heart of courtesy and modesty,
of propriety *(li*[al]*)* or the observance of rites; the heart of right and wrong, of wisdom *(chih*[am]*)*. Man has these four germs ('beginnings') just as he has four
limbs."[18]

The word *hsin* (heart) refers obviously to certain sentiments of the heart: that
by which a person, for example, forgets his own interests and rushes to the
rescue of a drowning child. And we may especially wonder at the inclusion of
a sense of right and wrong among these basic sentiments, these "emotions" of
the heart. In Kantian terms,[19] Mencius offers an empirical ground for morality: that of moral feeling, based on human nature and its spontaneous, even
instinctive choice of the good in moments of crisis calling for altruism. He has
built his entire doctrine of human perfectibility, of the possibility of attaining
the highest ideals of sagehood and virtue, upon this foundation of moral feeling.   And Chu Hsi has accepted this foundation without any question. He
has, indeed, used it as a starting point in the elaboration of his own views on
human nature and the emotions. To quote him here:

> Where mind, nature, and emotions are concerned, Mencius and Chang Tsai
> have given the best explanations. [Mencius says], "The heart of compassion is
> the beginning of humanity."[20] Now humanity is nature *(hsing*[an]*)*, and compassion
> is emotion *(ch'ing)*, which arises necessarily from the mind and heart *(hsin)*.
> "The mind unifies nature and the emotions."[21] As to nature, it is just principle
> *(li)* . . . and not a physical thing. . . . That is why it is entirely good.[22]

And so, in commenting upon Mencius, Chu Hsi continues to develop the
teachings of his immediate predecessors, especially here of Chang Tsai and
the Ch'eng brothers. He has done so without violating the intentions of Mencius. But he has also gone beyond Mencius, for he has made his own contribution as well, clarifying the relationship between nature and the emotions,
while accepting mind *(hsin)* as the unifying agent between the two, indeed, as
the determining agent for good and evil actions.

But the *Book of Mencius* is not the only important Confucian text discussing the role of emotions. There is also the *Doctrine of the Mean* with its enu-
meration of pleasure, anger, sorrow, and joy, with its distinction between the
state of consciousness that prevails before and after the stirring of these emotions. It is to an examination of this second text that I shall now turn.

Emotions as Neutral

The *Doctrine of the Mean* begins with certain definitions of nature *(hsing)*, of
the Way (Tao), and of instruction *(chiao*[ao]*)*. It sets these definitions in a cosmic
context.

What Heaven has conferred is called nature; exercising this nature is called the Way; cultivating the Way is called instruction. The Way is that which may not be left for an instant. . . . Therefore the gentleman is watchful over himself when he is alone.[23]

And then, immediately following the above preface comes this passage about the emotions.

Before the rise *(wei-fa)* of joy, anger, sorrow, and pleasure, [the mind-and-heart] may be said to be in the state of equilibrium *(chung)*. When they are arisen and reach due proportion, there is what may be called the state of harmony *(ho)*. This equilibrium is the great root of all under heaven; this harmony is the universal Way of all under heaven. Let the states of equilibrium and harmony prevail, and a happy order will reign throughout heaven and earth, and the myriad things will all be nourished.[24]

The praise is of equilibrium, the "Mean," the state of consciousness that prevails before the rise of emotions, as well as of harmony, the state of consciousness that prevails when emotions are maintained in proper balance. The obvious warning is to keep emotions from going to excess. In other words, emotions in themselves are neither good nor evil. But because they possess a power of disruption, they should be kept under control.

Chu Hsi has given much attention to this passage, focusing especially on the method of achieving emotional harmony. In distinguishing between the two states of consciousness, that before and that after the rise of emotions, he uses the words "substance" *(t'i*[ap]*)* and "function" *(yung*[aq]*)*.

The state before the emotions of pleasure, anger, sorrow, and joy arise . . . is identical with the "substance" of the mind, which is absolutely quiet and inactive, and the nature conferred by Heaven should be completely embodied in it. . . . When it is acted upon . . . the emotions are then stirred. In this state the "functioning" of the mind can be seen.[25]

The analysis of these two states of consciousness remains cool and dispassionate. There is no attempt to disparage the emotions as such.

In discussing the problem of evil, however, Chu Hsi makes use of another word, passion *(jen-yü*, literally, "human desires"), which he associates with emotions and to which he attaches an ambiguous connotation.

The mind is like water; nature is like the tranquillity of still water; emotions are like the flow of [moving] water, and passions are the waves. Just as there are good and bad waves, so too there are good passions . . . and bad passions which rush out like wild and violent waves. . . . When Mencius said that emotions can help people to do good, he meant that the correct emotions flowing from our nature are originally all good.[26]

Chu Hsi does not condemn passions in themselves. He does, however, condemn wild and violent passions—what he calls "bad" waves—and he has devoted much of his philosophy to a theory of moral and spiritual cultivation by which such passions can be controlled and the goodness of the Heavenly Principle (T'ien-li) may be recovered.

All the same, the caution against emotional excess and the exhortation to maintain constant control and balance spell out a certain distrust of human nature itself, which makes an imperative of self-conquest in moral striving. In themselves, some emotions may be good, others neutral, while excessive and violent emotions are definitely dangerous. Besides, the power of emotions is such that they require constant checking. "Therefore the gentleman is watchful over himself when he is alone."[27] Such vigilance in solitude (shen-tu[ar]) lies at the core of Chu Hsi's teachings on self-cultivation. Chu Hsi, after all, is an optimist regarding human nature. As such, he believes that sagehood may be attained. At the same time as a realist who is aware of the need for control he has formulated a theory of personal cultivation that puts man on guard against his own excesses and facilitates the cultivation of the beginnings of goodness in human nature.

The Doctrine of Reverence

The word ching figures prominently in Chu Hsi's doctrine of cultivation. The fact that different scholars have translated the term differently (reverence, seriousness, composure) shows the difficulty of explaining its Chinese usage in general and Chu's intended meaning in particular. The usage of the word can be traced to various Confucian texts, including the Book of Documents, where the ancient sage kings are described frequently as being "reverentially obedient" to the Lord-on-high or Heaven, while their descendants are exhorted to imitate such reverence.[28] With Confucius the word is used more with regard to oneself than to a higher being: "In retirement, to be sedately gracious; in doing things, to be reverently attentive (ching); in contact with others, to be very sincere."[29] The Book of Changes continues in the same direction when it says, "The gentleman practices reverence to maintain inner rectitude and righteousness to assure exterior correctness."[30]

The first text counsels "reverence" in action where the second text refers to a more interior vigilance. For both Ch'eng Yi and Chu Hsi, "reverence" points to the process by which the original unity of the mind is preserved and made manifest in one's activity.[31] Chu speaks of abiding in reverence (chü-ching[as]), defining it in terms of single-mindedness and freedom from distraction (chu-yi wu-shih[at]) and comparing it to the Buddhist practice of mindful alertness (hsing-hsing[au]).[32] He also associates it specifically with the teaching of "vigilance in solitude" of the Doctrine of the Mean. And he is careful to guard his disciples against a "dead" reverence which merely keeps the mind alert without also attending to moral practice.[33] Following in Ch'eng Yi's footsteps, Chu Hsi informs the word with a depth that transforms it from the earlier, occasional usage in Confucian thought to a doctrine of personal and spiritual cultivation. In Chu Hsi's words:

> Reverence does not mean one has to sit stiffly in solitude, the ears hearing nothing, the eyes seeing nothing, and the mind thinking of nothing, . . . It means rather keeping a sense of caution and vigilance, and not daring to become permissive . . . [with oneself].[34]

Chu Hsi does not overlook Mencius' teaching. He agrees that reverence also means "preserving the mind" *(ts'un-hsin)* without allowing it to get dissipated:

> When our mind-and-heart is "outside," it should be drawn inward; when it is "inside," it should be pushed outward. This is the meaning of the *Book of Mencius*.[35]

However, he expresses preference for *Analects* 13:19,[36] explaining that such a discipline of vigilance over the mind is helpful when the mind already understands all the principles *(li)*. On the other hand, "what use is there in merely keeping watch over an empty mind . . . ?"[37] Elsewhere, he clearly says that reverence refers to keeping the Principle of Heaven and getting rid of human passions.[38] Reverence is obviously part and parcel of his philosophy of *li* and *ch'i*, pointing to the constant need of growing in virtue and keeping the passions under control. As Ch'eng Yi says, "Cultivation *(han-yang*[av]*)* requires the practice of reverence."[39] The term *han-yang* includes the meaning of nurturing. The aspirant to sagehood needs to nurture the seeds of goodness in his mind and heart, and reverence refers to this process of nurturing as well as to the goal of harmony of the emotions—an abiding state of mind characteristic of the sage.

The practice of reverence is very like that of "recollection" in Western Christian spirituality.[40] The English word "recollection" is usually understood in terms of "remembrance." It is, however, a technical term in spirituality referring to the "collecting" or "gathering" of one's interior faculties, keeping them silent and "recollected" in an atmosphere of peace and calm, in preparation for formal prayer or in an effort to prolong the effects of such prayer. In a work on Christian spirituality, Canon Jacques Leclerq says,

> The word recollection has no meaning for many worldly people. . . . Yet recollection is the chief disposition required for the interior life. It is not itself interior life but it is so much a condition for it and prepares us for it to such an extent that it almost necessarily develops it. . . . It is simply the calm which is born into the soul through solitude and silence. . . . Man has need of it to find himself as well as to find God.[41]

The proper Chinese term for "recollection," however, is *shou-lien*[aw] (literally, "collecting together"). It has also the practical meaning of "gathering" a harvest, but its usage in Neo-Confucian writings made it a technical term. Chu Hsi talks about the need for scholars to "keep always recollected *(shou-lien)* without allowing oneself to become dispersed."[42] If, however, the immediate goal of Neo-Confucian *shou-lien* is similar to that of Christian recollection, the ultimate end is not necessarily the same. In the Chinese context, there is no specific reference to finding God, even if one may argue the similarity in the quest for the absolute.

The Role of Meditation

The Confucian term for meditation is quiet-sitting *(ching-tso)*. It suggests strong Taoist and Buddhist influences, calling to mind Chuang Tzu's[ax] (c. 369–c. 286 B.C) "sitting and forgetting" *(tso-wang*[ay]*)*[43] and the Buddhist practice of *dhyāna* (meditation) from which the name *Ch'an* or Zen[az] is derived. As many other Neo-Confucian thinkers, Chu Hsi had experience of Taoist and Buddhist meditation. His biography reveals his fondness for conversations with Buddhist monks at a time when he was still preparing for civil examinations.[44] In his writings we can find an essay on using breath control as a form of Taoist meditation.[45] Chou Tun-yi and the Ch'eng brothers all appeared to have practiced quiet-sitting. But Chu Hsi would make a special effort to show the distinctiveness of Confucian quiet-sitting and its difference from Taoist and Buddhist meditation.

For the Buddhist, quiet-sitting is an exercise by which the mind concentrates upon itself to the exclusion of all distracting thoughts and for the sake of attaining unity and harmony with one's innermost self. For the Taoist, the same usually applies, frequently with an additional motive of preserving health and prolonging life. For the Confucian, unity and harmony are sought, together with the knowledge of the moral self, of one's own strengths and weaknesses, in view of achieving self-improvement, of becoming more perfect in the practice of virtues and the elimination of vices, and therefore in the fulfillment of one's responsibilities in the family as well as in society at large.

Chu Hsi gives some importance to quiet-sitting also for making possible a fuller manifestation of the "Heavenly Principle" within. What is implied is a cyclical movement: the return to one's original nature, the recapture of the springs of one's being, and the enabling of this state of original equilibrium of nature and the emotions to permeate one's daily living. It is, however, different from the Buddhist practice of "introspection," which has reference only to oneself and not to the larger world.

> According to the Buddhist teaching, one is to seek the mind with the mind, deploy the mind with the mind. This is like the mouth gnawing the mouth or the eye looking into the eye. Such a course of action is precarious and oppressive, such a path is dangerous and obstructed, such a practice is empty of princi-

ples *(li)* and frustrating. If they sound like us [Confucians], they are really quite different.[46]

For Chu Hsi, duty and common sense are always more important than the search for quietude.

> Although we speak of focusing on tranquillity, we are not about to abandon things and affairs to find it. As human beings, we also need to serve our rulers and parents, relate to friends and spouses, govern servants and subordinates. We cannot leave everything in order to do quiet-sitting behind closed doors, refusing to attend to things and affairs.[47]

Chu Hsi has been taken to task, especially by Yen Yüan[ba] (1635–1704), for exaggerating the importance of quiet-sitting, for recommending the practice of spending half a day in quiet-sitting and half a day reading books.[48] Although this recommendation made a deep impression on some later thinkers,[49] it comes up only once in Chu's recorded conversations in a specific context with a single disciple.[50] Chu Hsi guarded against excessive emphasis on quietude. He is reported to have said that "The teaching of quietude is close to Buddhist and Taoist teachings. Our sages have not taught it."[51] Also: "Today, scholars sometimes say that they should spend half a day daily in the practice of quiet-sitting. I find it a mistake."[52] He corrects Chou Tun-yi by saying, "Chou emphasizes quietude and tranquillity *(ching)*. But the word *ching* should only be interpreted as reverence *(ching)*. That is why he says desirelessness *(wu-yü[bb])* is tranquillity. If he means empty quietude, I fear it would turn him into a Buddhist or Taoist."[53]

In answering questions about quiet-sitting, Chu Hsi is insistent that one need not sit like the Ch'an Buddhists, seeking to stop all thought. According to him, all one needs to do is to recollect the mind, prevent it from dissipation, and thus permit its natural brightness to radiate in a state of peace and concentration. Repeatedly, Chu associates tranquillity with moral behavior, which is made easy by a disposition of reverence. "As the mind is master of the self, without distinguishing between activity and tranquillity, speech and silence, so too the gentleman practices reverence without distinguishing between activity and tranquillity, speech and silence."[54] Meditation, therefore, is a time when the person gathers himself together inwardly, calms his emotions, examines his conscience, and fills his mind and heart with principles of right action in order that a disposition of reverence may permeate his entire life.

Expressing his ideas through metaphors, Chu Hsi discusses self-cultivation in terms of cleaning or polishing a mirror. The human mind is like a mirror. It is originally pure, capable of reflecting all things. Cultivation requires the practice of "keeping still" *(ching)*, which permits one to restore and maintain the original purity of the mirror by removing from the mind all selfish desires.

When this is accomplished it will function as a clear mirror, quiet and still when passive, straight and upright when active, that is, when stirred up by emotion.[55]

On Self-conquest

Chu Hsi derived his dual formula of reverence and extension of knowledge from Ch'eng Yi.[56] However, he also made his own contribution by emphasizing self-conquest (*k'o-chi*[bc]) as an integral part of cultivation. The term *k'o-chi* comes from *Analects 12:1* where Confucius explains the meaning of *jen* to his favorite disciple Yen Hui[bd] in terms of *k'o-chi fu-li:*[be] to subdue one's self and recover the virtue of propriety. To quote the *Analects* on the specific duties of self-conquest: "Look not at what is contrary to propriety; listen not to what is contrary to propriety; seek not what is contrary to propriety; make no movement that is contrary to propriety."[57] Seen in this light, self-conquest is the negative side of the positive effort of seeking self-perfection and a necessary corollary in any doctrine of personal cultivation based on a realistic evaluation of human nature. Where Ch'eng Yi makes occasional mention of *k'o-chi*, Chu Hsi integrates it into his system, speaking of it much more, as in connection with reverence and the extension of knowledge in this vivid parable:

> To use the example of a house: reverence represents the watchman who keeps guard at the door, self-conquest refers to resisting thieves, and the extension of knowledge refers to the investigation of things and affairs pertaining to one's own house as well as what comes from outside.[58]

Elsewhere, Chu Hsi compares self-conquest to irrigating the fields,[59] to keeping the room clean and the mirror shining.[60]

For Chu Hsi, the goal of self-conquest is to nurture the Heavenly Principle by overcoming human passions not only at the moment of the awakening of selfish desires but also through the practice of caution before the rise of emotions. Indeed, Chu Hsi became increasingly emphatic about the need for thoroughness in the work of self-conquest, using such language as "uprooting" weeds and "killing" thieves or rebels.[61]

Chu Hsi recognizes that self-conquest, instead of adding a third dimension to his doctrine of personal cultivation, merely assists the task of reverence. He acknowledges that the "highest" degree of reverence eliminates the need for self-conquest, but he takes care to add that such an achievement may only be assumed to have been attained by sages, while ordinary persons must continually attend to self-conquest.[62]

Extending Knowledge

For Chu Hsi, knowledge refers primarily to moral knowledge—the knowledge of the good—as discovered in life itself and in Confucian classical texts, particularly the Four Books. Chu gives a place of honor to intellectual pursuit, while teaching an all-encompassing theory of knowledge based on his philosophy of principles—that all things are made of *li* and *ch'i* and that the human mind is ordained to seek and possess the *li* of things. In his commentary on the *Great Learning*, Chu offers an expansion of the meaning of the sentence in the text "The investigation of things consists in the extension of knowledge."

> If we wish to extend our knowledge to the utmost, we must investigate the principles of all things with which we come into contact. For the mind and spirit of man are formed to know, and the things of the world all contain principles. So long as principles are not exhausted, knowledge is not yet complete.[63]

Where praxis is concerned, Chu Hsi says that the student is to move from the known to the unknown, proceeding from the knowledge he already possesses of the principles of things and continuing his investigation until the task is finished. This happens as a sudden breakthrough, an experience of inner enlightenment, at the end of a long and arduous process of search and exertion.

> After exerting himself in this way for a long time, he will suddenly find himself possessed of a wide and far-reaching penetration. The qualities of all things, both internal and external, subtle and coarse, will all then be apprehended, and the mind, in its entire substance *(t'i)* and in its relation to things *(yung)*, will become completely manifest. This is called the investigation of things; this is called the perfection of knowledge.[64]

Thus, if the mind is ordained to know the truth of principles, truth itself also modifies the mind, making it manifest and radiant *(ming*[bf]*)*. Here we observe a circular motion, from the mind to things and then back to the mind —but not just from the mind to the mind. For Chu Hsi regards the mind as embracing all principles, and all principles as being complete in this mind. If a person cannot "preserve" his mind *(ts'un-hsin)*, neither will he be able to investigate principles to the utmost. We see here the interdependence of the doctrine of reverence and the need of concentration with the teaching of the extension of knowledge and the investigation of principles. Together, indeed, they make up Chu's complete formula for self-cultivation, a formula he learned from Ch'eng Yi and carefully developed, making it a necessary part of his entire system.

Chu Hsi also relates this pursuit of principles, which came from Ch'eng Yi, to the doctrine of self-cultivation found in the *Book of Mencius*. He identifies the task of extending knowledge and investigating things to "developing the mind to the utmost, knowing one's nature and knowing Heaven,"[65] a doctrine of introvertive, philosophical mysticism which he seeks to explain in terms of his own metaphysics of mind and nature, the principles of things and the

Principle of Heaven. And he sees a certain sequential order in which this self-cultivation is to be organized, with the extension of knowledge as the first step to take in the long search for sagehood, preceding the work of "making the intention sincere, rectifying the mind, and cultivating the person" of the *Great Learning*.[66] Thus he envisages perfect virtue (*jen*) as the crowning achievement of a long life of investigating principles and extending knowledge, the fruition of a life of diligent scholarship and careful moral cultivation.

A problem arises here in the case of personal cultivation, of which the ultimate goal is sagehood. Mencius asserts that every person can become a sage;[67] Chu Hsi accepts this assertion. But how can sagehood be in practice universally accessible if everyone must first study the principles of morality as these are laid down in the Confucian texts? Even if we regard Chu's own times, much of the population then remained illiterate, deprived of the opportunity of receiving a formal education and book learning. How many of them could have been considered potential sages? Is not Chu Hsi, the scholar, speaking to other scholars about a goal of scholarship, rather than of life itself?

We reach here a most controversial aspect of Chu's teachings, disputed by his contemporary and rival thinker, Lu Chiu-yüan (Lu Hsiang-shan,[bg] 1139–1192), as well as by Lu's spiritual heir Wang Yang-ming (Wang Shou-jen,[bh] 1472–1529).[68] These two point out the problem in any doctrine of cultivation that makes of intellectual pursuit the cornerstone of moral and spiritual striving: that it necessarily makes intellectuals of all sages and makes those deprived of intellectual development the underprivileged in the quest of sagehood as well.

Here we discover the elitist character of Chu Hsi's philosophy. This does not mean necessarily that Chu denies the universal accessibility of sagehood. Rather, it means that Chu sees himself as a scholar and a teacher of scholars, indeed, a guardian of the Confucian tradition of scholarship. Of course, Mencius' teaching of the universal possibility of sagehood made relative the importance of particular traditions, whether Confucian, Taoist, or Buddhist. Chu Hsi must have been aware of this fact, given his youthful interest in Buddhism and his life-long interest in Taoism. In mature life, however, he made a definite choice for himself, consciously becoming a follower of the Confucian School and committing himself also to the task of redefining and upholding the Confucian mission. In this context, he sees the need of making clear distinctions. For him, a Confucian (*ju*[bi]) is not simply any well-meaning person who respects the moral law governing human relationships. He must also possess a penetrating understanding of the principles of this moral law itself. Indeed, he must be more than a scholar (*ju*); he must also be committed to the Confucian way (Tao). In this light, we may also understand how the Confucian School became transformed in the Sung dynasty to the School of the Way (*Tao-hsüeh*[bj]).

Chu Hsi puts special emphasis on book learning because he sees a special mission for the teacher of the Way, who must instruct others. He discerns a clear danger in relativizing completely the need of book learning in the case of those who are able to acquire it. The danger lies in subjectivizing the moral law, in making of every man a law unto himself. The danger lies in forgetting the wisdom of the ancients, in giving up an entire tradition, with its insights and merits, as well as its limitations. This could create a vacuum, an emptiness (*k'ung*^(bk)) and listlessness, an intellectual iconoclasm. It is in these terms that Chu Hsi criticizes Buddhism and Buddhist meditation: a quest of inner enlightenment, for the sake of pure experience. Ultimately, this might mean the abandonment of the Confucian cause and its commitment to the renewal of society.

What about Enlightenment?

Chu Hsi does not reject the enlightenment experience in itself. Rather, he regards it positively. He sees the attainment of sagehood as an arduous task, requiring much effort—a lifetime of cultivation, including possibly the accumulation of encyclopedic knowledge, which may prepare the person for an experience of inner enlightenment. But unlike the Buddhist or Taoist, Chu Hsi seeks this experience not for its own sake, but only as an aid in achieving the higher ideal of sagehood. True, there is a mystical dimension to his understanding of sagehood itself. It refers also to a state of consciousness in which the true meaning of man's oneness with Heaven and Earth and all things is perceived. However, this is achieved through spiritual and moral cultivation, including intellectual pursuit, rather than in mystical experience alone. For Chu, as for other Neo-Confucian philosophers, the scholar transcends the difference between the self and others by extending his practice of *jen*, of love, from himself and those near him to all others in the universe. This kind of mystique is open to others and supports ethical values, whereas the focus on an enlightenment experience might obliterate the need for any personal cultivation. Chu Hsi maintains that the human mind *(jen-hsin)* and the moral mind (*Tao-hsin*, 'the mind of the sage') represents two different orders, that of human passion and that of Heavenly Principle. His emphasis is on the constant struggle to allow the "moral mind" to triumph over the "human mind." That is why a doctrine of cultivation is so important in Chu Hsi's thought.

Conclusion

Chu Hsi tempers his optimism about human nature with his realism about human nature. He acknowledges both the accessibility of sagehood and the difficulty of achieving it. He offers a dual formula for personal cultivation, knowing well that it cannot serve all, especially the uneducated. But he does not say that they are deprived from achieving the ultimate goal. He seems to think that some are called only to a life of practical morality, which is admirable in itself. However, to those others, fortunate enough to be his students—

whether in his own days or much later, through his writings—his constant urge is to a sense of striving, to the cultivation of that which is precious within us, against all the difficulties that threaten us.

Man's nature is originally clear, but it is like a precious pearl immersed in impure water, where its lustre cannot be seen. After being removed from the water, [the precious pearl] becomes lustrous of itself as before. If one should only realize himself that passions *(jen-yü)* are what obscure [his nature], [he should be able] to find illumination.[69]

A mirror to polish, a pearl to be rescued from impure water, so that each should shine. Such are the metaphors Chu Hsi delighted in using, to represent the task of personal cultivation as he sees it: an arduous task, but not without its reward.

Notes

1. Yao and Shun are legendary sage-kings, especially venerated by Confucian scholars.

2. The Three Bonds refer to the special relationships between father and son (parent and child), husband and wife, ruler and subject, with their corollary duties of affection and loyalty, while the Five Relationships include as well the older and younger brothers and the relationship between friends. Sometimes, the Three Bonds are mentioned together with the Five Constant Virtues, that is, the virtues of humanity *(jen)*, righteousness *(yi)*, propriety *(li)*, wisdom *(chih)*, and faithfulness *(hsin*[bl]*)*. The Confucian school has always emphasized the moral character of human relationships.

3. See Julia Ching, *To Acquire Wisdom: The Way of Wang Yang-ming* (New York: Columbia University Press, 1976), Introduction. See also Julia Ching, "Chu Hsi's Theory of Human Nature," *Humanitas* 1B (1979), pp. 77–100.

4. *Book of Changes*, "Appended Remarks," pt. 1, ch. 11.

5. *Chu Tzu yü-lei*[bm] [Classified conversations of Master Chu (hereafter cited as *Yü-lei*)], (Taipei: Cheng-chung[bn] Book Co., 1973 reprint), 1:1a–b, 94:4a–6b, 12a, 20b, 35a–b. See also Ch'ien Mu,[bo] *Chu Tzu hsin hsüeh-an*[bp] [A new record of Chu Hsi's thought], (Taipei: San-min Book Co., 1971), Bk. I, ch. 3.

6. *Yü-lei*, 4:2–3, 9–16; 12:5–18. See also Ch'ien Mu, *Chu Tzu hsin hsüeh-an*, Bk. I, ch. 9, 13, 23. Reference to the *Doctrine of the Mean* is to ch. 1.

7. *Ibid.*, 94:6a.

8. Fung Yu-lan, *A History of Chinese Philosophy*, trans. Derk Bodde (Princeton, N. J.: Princeton University Press, 1953), vol. 2, p. 541.

9. See Han Yü, "*Yüan-hsing*"[bq] [An inquiry into human nature] in *Han Ch'ang-li ch'üan-chi*[br] [Complete writings of Han Yü], (SPPY ed.). English translation in Wing-tsit Chan,[bs] *A Source Book in Chinese Philosophy* (Princeton, N. J.: Princeton University Press, 1963), pp. 451–452.

10. For Chang Tsai, see *Cheng-meng*[bt] [Correcting youthful ignorance] in *Chang Tzu ch'üan-shu*[bu] [Complete works of Chang Tsai], (SPPY ed.), ch. 6. English translation in Chan, *Source Book*, pp. 507–509; for Ch'eng Yi, see *Yi-shu*[bv] [Surviving writ-

ings], (SPPY ed.), 18:17b, 19:4b, in the *Erh-Ch'eng ch'üan-shu*[bw] [Complete works of the two Ch'engs]. English translation in Chan, *Source Book*, pp. 568–569. For Chu Hsi's comments on Chang's and Ch'eng's contributions, see *Yü-lei*, 4:12a–13b.

11. *Ibid.*, 4:11b.

12. The Four Books include the *Analects* of Confucius, the *Book of Mencius* (recorded conversations between the two Masters and their disciples), the *Great Learning*, and the *Doctrine of the Mean* (originally, two chapters taken from the *Book of Rites*, one of the Five Confucian Classics, the other four being the *Book of Changes*, the *Book of Documents*, the *Book of Poetry*, and the *Spring and Autumn Annals*).

13. *Book of Documents*, ch. 3. English translation adapted from James Legge, *The Chinese Classics* (Oxford: Clarendon Press, 1893), vol. 3, p. 61.

14. See *Ssu-shu chi-chu*[bx] [Collected commentaries on the Four Books], (SPPY ed.), *Chung-yung chang-chü*, p. 1.

15. *Yü-lei*, 60:3a–4b; Ch'ien Mu, *Chu-tzu hsin hsüeh-an*, Bk. 1, pp. 366–376.

16. *Doctrine of the Mean*, ch. 1.

17. *Book of Mencius*, 2A:6 and 6A:6; see Legge, *Chinese Classics*, vol. 3, pp. 202–203 and pp. 402–403.

18. *Book of Mencius*, 2A:6. English translation adapted from Legge, *Chinese Classics*, vol. 3, pp. 202–203.

19. Julia Ching, "Chinese Ethics and Kant," *Philosophy East and West* 28 (1978), pp. 161–172.

20. *Book of Mencius*, 2A:6.

21. Chang Tsai, *Chang Tzu ch'üan-shu*, 14:2a.

22. *Yü-lei*, 5:9a.

23. *Doctrine of the Mean*, ch. 1. English translation adapted from Legge, *Chinese Classics*, vol. 1, pp. 383–384.

24. *Ibid.*

25. First letter to the Gentlemen of Honan on Equilibrium and Harmony, in the *Chu Tzu wen-chi*[by] [Collection of literary works of Master Chu], (Taipei: Kuang-wen[bz] Book Co., 1972 reprint), 64:31a. English translation adapted from Chan, *Source Book*, p. 601.

26. *Yü-lei*, 5:10a–10b. English translation adapted from Chan, *Source Book*, p. 631.

27. *Doctrine of the Mean*, ch. 1, see Legge, *Chinese Classics*, vol. 1, p. 384.

28. See the *Book of Documents*, ch. 16 "*T'ai-chia*,"[ca] pt. 3; ch. 40, "Announcement of the Duke of Chao,"[cb] pts. 4–5. English translation in Legge, *Chinese Classics*, vol. 3, pp. 209–212, 426–427.

29. *Analects*, 13:19. English translation adapted from Legge, *Chinese Classics*, vol. 1, p. 271.

30. Commentary on second hexagram. English translation adapted from Legge, *Yi King*,[cc] Sacred Books of the East series, ed. Max Muller (Oxford: Clarendon Press, 1885), p. 420.

31. See A. C. Graham, *Two Chinese Philosophers* (London: Lund Humphries, 1958), p. 67.

32. See *Yü-lei*, 17:2–3, where Chu Hsi discusses Ch'eng Yi's teaching on reverence in these terms. See also *Yi-shu*, 15:1a. The term *hsing-hsing* was used by Hsieh Liang-tso[cd] (1050–c.1120) in explaining reverence. See *Shang-ts'ai yü-lu*[ce] [Recorded sayings of Hsieh Liang-tso], (Taipei: Kuang-wen Book Co., 1972 reprint), 2:13a.

33. *Yü-lei*, 12:14b.

34. *Ibid.*, 12:10b. English translation adapted from Chan, *Source Book*, p. 607.

35. *Ibid.*, 19:7b.

36. See above, n. 29.

37. *Yü-lei*, 59:29a–b.

38. *Ibid.*, 53:18a–21b.

39. *Yi-shu*, 18:5b.

40. I developed this point in a paper entitled "What is Confucian Spirituality?" which was presented at the Vitaly Rubin Memorial Colloquium held at The Hebrew University of Jerusalem, March 14–16, 1983.

41. See J. Leclerq, *The Interior Life*, trans. from French by F. Murphy (New York: P. J. Kennedy, 1961), p. 118.

42. *Yü-lei*, 12:2b.

43. See *Chuang Tzu*, ch. 6; Chan, *Source Book*, p. 201.

44. "Nien-p'u"[cf] [Chronological biography], in *Tai Hsien*[cg] (1496 cs), comp., *Chu Tzu shih-chi*[ch] [True records of Chu Hsi], (Taipei: 1972 reprint), 2:4–6.

45. *Chu Tzu wen-chi*, 85:6b.

46. "Kuan-hsin shuo"[ci] [On contemplating the mind], *Chu Tzu wen-chi*, 67:21b. English translation adapted from Chan, *Source Book*, p. 604.

47. *Yü-lei*, 45:11b.

48. *Chu Tzu yü-lei p'ing*[cj] [A critique of the *Classified Conversations of Master Chu*], p. 18b, in the *Yen-li ts'ung-shu*[ck] [Yen Yüan and Li Kung[cl] series] (1923).

49. I refer especially to Kao P'an-lung[cm] (1562–1626) who took this literally in his own cultivation. See his *K'un-hsüeh chi*[cn] [Records of painful study], 3:15, in the *Kao Tzu i-shu*[co] [Surviving works of Master Kao], (1631 ed.).

50. *Yü-lei*, 116:17b. This is pointed out in Ch'ien Mu, *Chu Tzu hsin hsüeh-an*, Bk. II, p. 293.

51. *Yü-lei*, 60:10b.

52. *Ibid.*, 62:25b.

53. *Ibid.*, 94:17a.

54. *Chu Tzu wen-chi*, letter to Chang Ch'in-fu,[cp] 37:27a.

55. *Chu Tzu wen-chi*. English translation in Chan, *Source Book*, p. 601.

56. *Yi-shu*, 18:5b.

57. *Analects*, 12:12. English translation in Legge, *Chinese Classics*, vol. 1, p. 250. Chu Hsi's teaching on self-conquest is especially developed in Ch'ien Mu, *Chu Tzu hsin hsüeh-an*, Bk. I, pp. 336–363.

58. *Yü-lei*, 9:3b.

59. *Ibid.*, 12:13a.

60. *Ibid.*, 41:21b. This gives a clear resonance of the Ch'an patriarch Hui-neng's[cq] (638–713) gatha. See *Liu-tsu ta-shih fa-pao t'an-ching*[cr] [The precious platform scripture of the Great Teacher, the Sixth Patriarch], *T'aishō shinshū daizōkyō*[cs] [Taishō edition of the Buddhist Canon], no. 2007, pp. 337–340.

61. *Yü-lei*, 42:4a.

62. *Ibid.*, 97:10b.

63. English translation adapted from Legge, *Chinese Classics*, vol. 1, p. 365.

64. *Ibid.*, pp. 365–366.

65. *Yü-lei*, 9:6a; *Book of Mencius*, 7A:1.

66. *Great Learning*, the text.

67. *Book of Mencius*, 6B:2.

68. Julia Ching, *To Acquire Wisdom: The Way of Wang Yang-ming*, ch. 7.
69. *Yü-lei*, 12:7a.

Glossary

a	堯舜	ah	未發	bn	正中
b	太極	ai	道	bo	錢穆
c	理	aj	仁	bp	朱子新學案
d	氣	ak	義	bq	原性
e	心	al	禮	br	韓昌黎全集
f	存心養性	am	智	bs	陳榮捷
g	周敦頤	an	性	bt	正蒙
h	陰	ao	教	bu	張子全書
i	陽	ap	體用	bv	遺書
j	無極	aq	用	bw	二程全書
k	誠	ar	慎獨	bx	四書集註
l	天理	as	居敬	by	朱子文集
m	程顥	at	主一無適	bz	廣文
n	程頤	au	惺惺	ca	太甲
o	形而上	av	涵養	cb	召
p	形而下	aw	收斂	cc	易經
q	才	ax	莊子	cd	謝良佐
r	張載	ay	坐忘	ce	上蔡語錄
s	情	az	禪	cf	年譜
t	敬	ba	顏元	cg	戴銑
u	靜坐	bb	無欲	ch	朱子實紀
v	和	bc	克己	ci	觀心說
w	物	bd	顏回	cj	朱子語類評
x	馮友蘭	be	克己復禮	ck	顏李叢書
y	氣質之性	bf	明	cl	李珙
z	韓愈	bg	陸九淵象山	cm	高攀龍
aa	禹	bh	王陽明守仁	cn	困學記
ab	人心	bi	儒	co	高子遺書
ac	道心	bj	道學	cp	張欽夫
ad	微	bk	空	cq	惠能
ae	中	bl	信	cr	六祖大師法寶壇經
af	中庸章句	bm	朱子語類	cs	大正新修大藏經
ag	人欲				

18

An Analysis of Chu Hsi's System of Thought of I

CHANG LIWEN

THE SUBSTANCE in the logical structure of Chu Hsi's philosophy is his system of thought of I^a (Changes). Delving into such categories as $T'ai-chi^b$ (supreme ultimate), yin-yang^c (passive and active cosmic forces), and $kang-rou^d$ (strength and weakness and fluctuation) of Chu Hsi's theory of Changes will facilitate not only an exposition of Chu Hsi's philosophy but also a search for the law of development in the history of Sung (960–1279)-Ming (1368–1644) Neo-Confucianism.

I

I-$ching^e$ (Book of changes) is a work which is simple and terse in its language but comprehensive and rich in its meaning, and so it is capable of being extended and developed. Scholars and philosophers of past ages have annotated the I-$ching$ in their respective lights and from their own views inconsistent with the original meaning of the classic. Several schools came into being. Since the Ch'in and Han dynasties (221 B.C.–A.D. 220), there have been the so-called Yin-$yang$-$chia^f$ (school that explained the I in terms of yin-yang doctrine), Tao-$chia^g$ (school that dealt with the I-$ching$ in a Taoist way), $Ch'an$-wei $chia^h$ (school that illustrated the I-$ching$ in a necromantic language), $Hsüan$-$hsüeh$-$chia^i$ (school that expressed the idea of Changes in an abstruse way), Li-$hsüeh$-$chia^j$ (school that expounded the I-$ching$ in accordance with Neo-Confucianism), and so on. Of these schools some held that the I-$ching$ should be interpreted by means of necromancy and others suggested that it should be explained in accordance with moral principles. Each of them had its own view in regard to how to interpret the I-$ching$. Chu Hsi commented on them thus, "Ever since the times of Ch'in and Han, those who devoted their study to the illustrations of the *Book of Changes* followed a bigoted course of emblems and numbers, failing to adopt an approach of comprehensiveness and simplicity, while those who talked about moral principles were confined to mere empty talk, far from being in consonance with the theme of humaneness, righteousness, moderation, and uprightness."[1] Obviously, Chu Hsi agrees neither with those who had belief in emblems and numbers nor with those who were merely high-sounding in empty talk. In criticism of Shao Yung's[k] (1011–1077) emblems and numbers and Ch'eng I's[l] (1033–1107) *I-chuan*[m] (Commentary on the *Book of Changes*), he himself wrote a book entitled *Chou-i pen-i*[n] (The original meaning of the *I-ching of Chou*); later he wrote the *I-hsüeh ch'i-meng*[o] (A guide to the study of *Changes*).[2] Having absorbed the essentials from the doctrines of Shao and Ch'eng, Chu Hsi in his works unifies both emblems and numbers and moral principles—a summation of the two approaches. Just as the School of Principle (*Li-hsüeh*[p]) was recognized as an official philosophy in the later period of the feudal society of China, so Chu Hsi's thought of *I* was also regarded as an orthodox school of learning.

About the nine diagrams Chu Hsi prefixed to his book *Chou-i pen-i*,[3] Wang Mao-hung[q] (1668–1741) was of the opinion that "the nine diagrams mentioned in the *Chou-i pen-i* were not Chu Hsi's. . . . Chu Hsi had written two books on the *I-ching*: one is the *Chou-i pen-i*, the other the *I-hsüeh ch'i-meng*. Besides, his thought of *I* is also expounded elaborately in his collected works, recorded sayings, and lectures. But nowhere in his writing could be found a reference to the nine diagrams, which are quite incongruous with the *Chou-i pen-i* and the *I-hsüeh ch'i-meng*."[4] This view of Wang's has encountered disagreements in the writings of recent scholars. In my opinion his view has both merits and demerits.

Concerning the record of *ho-t'u*[r] (the Yellow River map; the map, as legend goes, was sent forth from the Yellow River at the time when Yü[s] the Great of the Hsia dynasty [2183–1752 B.C.] ascended the throne), a reference to it was first seen in chapter 50, "Ku-ming"[t] (On contemplating the decree), of the *Book of History:* "[in a ceremony] five kinds of jades, a state-guarding gem, a red precious sword, records of deceased sage-kings' teachings and a big piece of jade should be exhibited before a table kept near the western wall opposite to the east. A big precious stone, a gem obtained from a frontier state, an armillary sphere and *ho-t'u* should be shown in front of a table placed near the eastern wall opposite to the west" (sec. 19). Ts'ai Shen's[u] (1167–1230) annotation on this is thus:

About the *ho-t'u*, it is said that during the time of the legendary emperor Fu-hsi,[v] a dragon and a horse came out from the Yellow River carrying a map on their backs. The map shows ten numbers, of which the numbers 1 and 6 are in its northern direction, the numbers 2 and 7 are in its southern direction, the numbers 3 and 8 are in its eastern direction, the numbers 4 and 9 are in its western direction, and the numbers 5 and 10 are in its center. This is the so-called *ho-ch'u-t'u*[w] (the river sends forth pictures) mentioned in the "Appended Remarks" of the *I-ching*.[5]

Confucius (551–479 B.C.) had also said, "The phoenix does not come; the river sends forth no map. It is all over with me!"[6]

About the *lo-shu*[x] (the book of the River Lo), a record in chapter 32, *"Hung-fan"*[y] (Great plan), of the *Book of History* says, "On the occasion when King Kun[z] was put to death and was succeeded by his son Yü the Great, Heaven bestowed on the latter a book teaching him how to rule in conformity with the *Hung-fan chiu-ch'ou*[aa] (Great plan and nine categories or ways to rule)" (sec. 3). Ts'ai Shen's explanatory note on this is: "Yü the Great followed the nature of water and succeeded in regulating the rivers and watercourses. Therefore, Heaven favored him with a book which was sent forth from the River Lo, which Yü identified as the *Hung-fan chiu-ch'ou*. Yü governed the people and rule the state in accordance with the moral laws taught in the book."[7] Before the Sung dynasty, books like *Ch'un-ch'iu-wei*[ab] (Apocryphal explanations of the *Spring and Autumn Annals*), the *Chou-pi ching-chi*[ac] (Illustrations of the book of astronomy), and the "Ming-t'ang"[ad] (Imperial ancestral hall) chapter of the *Ta-tai li-chi*[ae] *(The elder Tai's Book of Rites)* all referred to the record of the *ho-t'u lo-shu*. This shows that the record was not created by Chu Hsi. Nevertheless, it would contradict the facts if one were to think that no mention of the nine diagrams was ever made in Chu Hsi's collected essays and recorded sayings. In fact, he made the items of *ho-t'u, lo-shu*, Fu-hsi's eight trigrams, numbers, and so on, special entries in his *Chu Tzu yü-lei*[af] (Classified conversations of Master Chu) in chapter 65 and has drawn an orderly table of Fu-hsi's eight trigrams in chapter 76. Also, in a letter "Reply to Yüan Chi-chung,"[ag] Chu Hsi in several places discussed the *ho-t'u lo-shu* and the question about each divination diagram in King Wen's eight trigrams.[8] The contention that there has not been found a single word referring to the *ho-t'u* and *lo-shu* in Chu Hsi's writings is clearly not a fact.

However, Chu Hsi was the first to make a definite correlation between the *I-ching* and the *ho-t'u lo-shu* and to put the *ho-t'u* and the *lo-shu* together with the other seven pictures at the head of the *I-ching*. The correlation between the *I-ching* and the *ho-t'u lo-shu* was expounded earlier in the "Appended Remarks" of the *Books of Changes*.[9] Later, Cheng Hsüan[ah] (127–200) in his annotations on the *Book of Changes* said, "During Fu-hsi's reign, the auspicious sign of the dragon was seen on the Yellow River, and Fu-hsi wrote his work on the eight trigrams according to the design he saw on the back of a tortoise that came forth from the River Lo."[10] K'ung An-kuo[ai] also said in his commentary on the "Contemplating the Degree" chapter of the *Book of History*, "When Fu-hsi ruled under Heaven, auspicious signs of dragon, horse, etc. appeared from the river. Fu-hsi drew the picture of eight trigrams in compliance with the signs he saw, and named it *ho-t'u*."[11] But the *ho-t'u* and the *lo-shu* had not been found prefixed to the *Book of Changes* by scholars and philosphers from Ching Fang[aj] (77–37 B.C.), Ch'iao Kan[ak] (fl. 13–50 B.C.), Hsün Shuang[al] (128–190), and Yü Fan[am] (164–233) of the Han dynasty (206 B.C.– A.D. 220) down to K'ung Ying-ta[an] (574–648) and Li Ting-tso[ao] of the T'ang dynasty (618–907).

And the work *Chou-i chi-chieh*[ap] (Collected explanations of the *I-ching of*

Chou) recorded in itself only the *kua-ch'i-t'u*[aq] (a table of diagrams being fitted in with the weather of four seasons), the *yao-ch'en-t'u*[ar] (a table showing a combination of yin-yang and lines of the trigrams with the twelve horary characters), *na-chia-t'u*[as] (a table of diagrams being fitted in with ten celestial stems and the twenty-four divination positions). Although there had been going on, during the Northern Sung period (960–1126), an endless controversy among Confucians over the question of how the *ho-t'u lo-shu* was handed down from ancient times and how it was taught and accepted, yet it was Chu Chen's (1072–1138)[at] work, the *Chou-i-t'u*[au] (The *I-ching* diagrams), which first made the entry of *ho-t'u lo-shu* in the *I-ching*, and which was presented to Emperor Kao-tsung[av] in 1136. Be that as it may, Hu Wei[aw] (1633–1714) still holds, "No item about the *ho-t'u lo-shu* has ever been found recorded in the opening pages of the ancient *I-ching*, or its various explanatory works. If there is any, it is Chu Hsi's *Chou-i pen-i* which initiated prefixing the *ho-t'u lo-shu* to the *I-ching*. Then, in his *I-hsüeh ch'i-meng*, of which the draft was prepared by Ts'ai Chi-t'ung (Ts'ai Yüan-ting,[ax] 1135–1198), the *ho-t'u lo-shu* appears as the first item in the book, and next comes the item of diagram-lines."[12] The *Chou-i pen-i* was completed in 1177 and the *I-hsüeh ch'i-meng* in 1186, about forty or fifty years after Chu Chen. There is a difference between Chu Hsi and Chu Chen: Chu Hsi prefixed seven pictures to the *I-ching* in addition to the two pictures *ho-t'u* and *lo-shu*. Also, while Chu Chen considers that there are nine numbers in the *ho-t'u* and ten numbers in the *lo-shu*, Chu Hsi, having accepted Shao Yung's theory, takes the *lo-shu* as having nine numbers and the *ho-t'u* as having ten. This latter view has become the final version.

As to the pseudonym *Yün-t'ai chen-i*[ay] (a true recluse of the Yün-t'ai Temple) Chu Hsi gave in the preface to his *I-hsüeh ch'i-meng*, when he held a sinecure as the superintendent of the Yün-t'ai Taoist Temple at Hua-chou,[13] he used the pseudonym just to show what he was and where he was then. His preface was written in the late spring of 1186, and on the seventh of July (according to the lunar calendar) of the same year he used a similar pseudonym, Yün-t'ai wai-shih[az] Chu Hsi (the Yün-t'ai retired historiographer Chu Hsi).[14] Chu Hsi was appointed superintendent of the Yün-t'ai Temple at Hua-chou[ba] in April 1188; from then on he adopted the name Yün-t'ai yin-li Chu Hsi Chung-hui-fu[bb] (the Yün-t'ai retired officer Chu Hsi Chung-hui-fu).[15] Even in the year 1197, twelve years after his term at the temple, Chu Hsi still used the name Yün-t'ai-tzu[bc] (Master of the Yün-t'ai Temple).[16] There is, therefore, nothing surprising at Chu Hsi's adoption of the pseudonym Yün-t'ai chen-i; in fact, Chu Hsi has thus indicated that he himself wrote the book *I-hsüeh ch'i-meng*.

II

In the logical structure of Chu Hsi's philosophy, principle (*li*[bd]) is the highest category, while the Supreme Ultimate, Tao, and Heavenly Principle (*T'ien-li*[be]) are the categories equivalent to that of principle, or the designations for principle under different conditions and circumstances. Chu Hsi says, "What is called the Supreme Ultimate is principle."[17] "The so-called Supreme Ultimate is, indeed, nothing but principle."[18] So, being principle, the Supreme Ultimate has its innate character similar to that of principle; it has no form, no symbol and no direction. "The Supreme Ultimate is an appellation for principle before all things appeared in forms and numbers. . . . This is what Master Shao Yung called 'Tao is the Supreme Ultimate'[19] and 'Mind is the Supreme Ultimate.'[20]"[21] The Supreme Ultimate is the principle of the two forms (*liang-i*[bf]), the four emblems (*ssu-hsiang*[bg]), and the eight diagrams. It cannot be spoken of as nothingness, but it has no form and no symbol to be described."[22] And yet, the Supreme Ultimate is not a thing; it has no spot where it may be placed. It is the Ultimate of the formless.[23] Since the Supreme Ultimate has no form and no place to rest in, it is not an object able to be perceived. Being without form or symbolic representation is, of course, not emptiness, but matter that exists without depending upon our perception. As the Supreme Ultimate has no direction and no place to stay in, so it transcends time and space; it is not a thing that objectively exists; it is but some sort of psyche, the manifestation of which becomes possible only through physical things.

With respect to the original substance of this spirituality, Chu Hsi says, "Master Chou Tun-i[bh] [1017–1073] . . . considers that it was prior to physical things, yet it has never ceased to stand even after such physical things came into being. He maintains that it lies beyond yin and yang, yet it never fails to operate within them. He maintains that it penetrates the whole universe and is omnipresent, and yet there was no sound, smell, reflection, or resonance that could be ascribed to it in the beginnng."[24] Describing the Supreme Ultimate as antedating any physical thing and standing outside yin and yang means that the Supreme Ultimate is the very principle that existed before all things of the universe were produced and is beyond the realm of matter. Viewing the Supreme Ultimate as remaining even after all things came into being and as moving between yin and yang means that there can be no separation of the Supreme Ultimate from yin and yang. This is to say that the relation between the Supreme Ultimate and yin-yang is that of nonseparation yet nonmingling as well, a unity of opposites. As Chu said,

> What is all-pervading in heaven and on earth is nothing but the mystery of the Supreme Ultimate and yin-yang. . . . Hence from the time when the two forms had not stood apart one from the other, there already existed the perfect wholeness of the Supreme Ultimate in which the principle of the two forms, the four emblems, and the sixty-four hexagrams was distinctly manifested. From the time when the separation of the Supreme Ultimate from the two forms happened, the Supreme Ultimate became the absolute one (as distinct from the two forms) and the two forms obviously became the two (as distinct from the Supreme Ultimate).[25]

That the principle of the Supreme Ultimate already exists within the state of nonseparation of the two forms, that is, before the separation of yin from yang, means that there exists an interdependence and a nonseparation between the Supreme Ultimate and the two forms; and that the Supreme Ultimate became the absolute one and the two forms distinctly became the two when the separation between the Supreme Ultimate and yin-yang happened means that there is no intermingling of the Supreme Ultimate with the two forms.

Obviously, the relation between the Supreme Ultimate and yin-yang resembles that between principle and ether (*ch'i*[bi]). The Supreme Ultimate occupies no resting place in itself, but takes yin and yang as a spot where it could rest itself. Because of the fluctuation between yin and yang, and between movement and quiescence, "Yin produces yang, yang produces yin, and so the mutual generation goes on to no end."[26] Thus, it produces the four emblems, such as spring, summer, autumn, and winter; metal, wood, water, and fire; east, west, south, and north. The four emblems in turn produce the eight trigrams representing heaven and earth, mountain and marsh, wind and thunder, and water and fire. In this way come into being the natural world and human society. In his *I-hsüeh ch'i-meng*, Chu Hsi quoted Shao Yung as saying,

> By Heaven it means that it created things in the beginning. Therefore yin appears above while yang appears below. This shows the significance of the alternating interplay between yin and yang. By Earth it means that it made things coming into actual existence. Therefore yang stands above, while yin comes below. This shows a relative rank in the social order. [According to the principle manifested in the eight trigrams] the diagrams of *ch'ien*[bj] (Heaven) and *kun*[bk] (Earth) are respectively fixed in the upper position and the lower position, while the diagrams of *k'an*[bl] (pit) and *li*[bm] (brightness and separateness) are respectively placed on the left side and the right side. In this way (from the same principle), the opening and closing movements of heaven and earth, the rising and setting of the sun and the moon, the four seasons of spring, summer, autumn, and winter, the darkness of the new moon and the brightness of the full moon, the longer and shorter duration of the day and night, and the law of waxing and waning of the sun and the moon have all been derived.[27]

Thus, Chu Hsi, starting from the logical structure of his philosophy, tries to illustrate the correlation and transformation between all natural phenomena and social phenomena as well as the formation of the universe and society. He describes a world pattern by means of an orderly sequence of the Supreme Ultimate, the two forms (yin and yang), the four emblems, and the eight trigrams.

Looking into it deeper, one would find that Chu Hsi's doctrine about the formation of the universe and society—the endless orderly sequence from the Supreme Ultimate to the two forms, the four emblems, the eight trigrams—is in accordance with such a law as "one divides into two." He says, "In its division, the Supreme Ultimate produces one odd number and one even number in the very beginning, which is marked by one stroke (in the eight trigrams). The two numbers (odd and even) signify the two forms, of which yang has one stroke ($—$) while yin has two broken strokes ($-\ -$). . . . What Master Shao called one dividing into two simply means this. Of the two forms marked by two strokes, each produces one odd number and one even number. These four numbers signify the four emblems. What Master Shao called two dividing into four precisely means this."[28] By inference from this analogy, one would see that of the four emblems marked by three strokes, each again produces one odd number and one even number, thus (the four emblems each having two numbers) making the eight trigrams. This is what Shao Yung called four dividing into eight. Again, of the eight trigrams marked by four strokes, each produces one odd and one even number (the eight trigrams each having two numbers), thus making eight dividing into sixteen. Again, of these sixteen numbers marked by five strokes, each produces one odd and one even number, thus making sixteen dividing into thirty-two. And again, of these thirty-two numbers marked by six strokes, each produces one odd and one even number, thus making thirty-two dividing into sixty-four.

Here, Chu Hsi applies the correlation and transformation of the emblems ($—$, $-\ -$) and numbers (odd and even) as mentioned in the *Book of Changes* to reveal and generalize the most complicated structure and contradictions in the universe and society. He further takes the unity of the two opposites of yin and yang and the law of odd and even numbers as the fundamental law of cosmogony. In the uninterrupted evolution of "one dividing into two" derived from the Supreme Ultimate, it is precisely because of the functioning of the unity of the two opposites of yin and yang and the law of odd and even numbers that the evolution of "one dividing into two" goes on without end. This may be shown by the following figures:

1	2	4	8	16	32	64	. . .
2^0	2^1	2^2	2^3	2^4	2^5	2^6	$. . . 2^n$

The Supreme Ultimate is marked by figure 1 or 2^0, and then divides into one yin and one yang. That is, it produces one odd number and one even number. This division is marked by figure 2^1, the so-called one stroke. Figure 2^1 each again produces one odd number and one even number. This is shown by figure 2^2, the so-called two strokes. Figure 2^2 each again produces one odd number and one even number. This is recorded by figure 2^3, the so-called three strokes. Figure 2^3 each again produces one odd number and one even number, and it is marked by figure 2^4, the so-called four strokes, and so on. Here, not only is every link in the evolution of "one dividing into two" formed by yin and yang and the odd and even, but the geometric progression of "one dividing into two"—0, 1, 2, 3, 4, 5, 6—is also made by one odd and one even number. In Chu Hsi's opinion, this "one dividing into two, two dividing into four" is a limitless course of evolution. "This is merely a law of 'one dividing into two' in operation, and it works in this way at every stage of the evolution and continues to no end. All this means only that everything produces two."[29]

Being a law of the constitution of the universe and society, this "one dividing into two" deeply reflects the phenomena of contradiction existing in the universe and society. Chu Hsi holds that in "one dividing into two" the one means an integrated object or a thing that existed long before heaven and earth were differentiated from each other in a state of great chaos. This integrated object contains in itself two opposite aspects. "One is one principle, and yet it has two aspects of which each has a different function. For example, regarding the relation between yin and yang, in yin there is yang, and in yang there is yin. When yang reaches its apogee, yin is produced and when yin reaches its apogee, yang is produced. Therefore the mysterious transformation of spirit knows no boundary."[30] This shows that in an integrated or identified entity there exist two mutually repelling and opposing aspects as yin and yang, each playing its respective role. "Yang comes first, and yin next. Yang indicates righteousness while yin means benefit."[31] However, "yang means generating while yin indicates killing. That is to say that there is a differentiation of the good from the bad."[32] At the same time, the two opposite sides are interdependent and mutually permeating, one opposite side taking the other as the condition for its own existence. "Yin is yang's mother, while yang is yin's father. . . . When yang is within yin, yang goes adversely, and when yin is within yang, yin goes adversely."[33] It is clear that the two opposites of yin and yang exist simultaneously within an integrated entity. This is the so-called oneness. Even though Chu Hsi, while dealing with the oneness, bypasses certain conditions under which the two opposite sides would undergo a mutual transformation, as far as his illustration of a mutual permeation between the two opposite sides is concerned, there are some reasonable elements in the viewpoint he strongly advocates.

On the one hand, Chu Hsi accepts the theory of two opposite aspects; on the other hand, he considers that the two opposites are in one integrated entity. Hence he takes the two opposites and the unity to be two phases of one thing. "What originally prevailed between heaven and earth was one ether which had movement and quiescence. . . . It was by the difference between its movement and quiescence that the difference between yin and yang, and between hardness and softness, appeared."[34] "So, not only yin and yang, as a pair, undergo alternately the fluctuation of increase (light) and decrease (darkness); but in everything, each of the pair acts to increase and decrease alternately."[35] Since yin and yang are two phases of one thing, the opposites are the opposites of a unity. The two opposite phases would exist no more if the integrated entity were cast away. Hence, "in terms of derivation, yin and yang are merely one, while in terms of opposition, they are two, just as the sun and moon, water and fire, and the like are two."[36] Here, the so-called one unified entity in view of its derivation means that "though yin and yang are two words, yet they are the fluctuation of one ether, . . . which from time immemorial down to date has been doing myriad of things between heaven and earth. So, it is right to say that yin and yang are one; it is also right to say that yin and yang are two."[37] Viewed as one, it means that ether undergoes fluctuation, and viewed as two it means that ether is divided to become yin and yang. Therefore, there is no unity that does not possess opposites, and there are no opposites that are not unified. In short, both opposites and unity never fall apart. This kind of relation of "one" with "two" in the universe is not an artificial, but a natural one. "Yin and yang are the very source of changes and cannot negate each other. Their fluctuation is regular and cannot be artificially enlarged or diminished."[38] This means that it was the Supreme Ultimate which created the boundless universe by means of the fluctuation between the movement and quiescence of the ether (yin and yang) by means of the formula of one dividing into two. "Between heaven and earth there existed one ether only which, when divided into two, produced yin and yang and the Five Elements [Metal, Wood Water, Fire, and Earth]. All the myriad things in the process of creation are governed forever by this only."[39] This is the very pattern of the universe constructed in accordance with the theory of Changes.

III

Let us proceed to discuss Chu Hsi's theory of movement (*tung*[bn]) and quiescence (*ching*[bo]).

Everything is subject to the law of unity of two contradictory aspects and of division of one into two, and by this are motivated the movement and transformation in all things. Chu Hsi says,

> In its division the Supreme Ultimate in the beginning produced one odd number and one even number. By the orderly sequence, yang stands as number 2. This is also described as odd and even numbers in the *lo-shu*. Master Chou says, "The Supreme Ultimate through movement produces yang. This movement having reached its limit, quiescence is produced, and by this quiescence it produces yin. When quiescence has reached its limit, there is a return to movement. Thus, movement and quiescence, in alternation, becomes each the source of the other, the distinction between yin and yang is determined, and their two forms stand revealed.[40]

This proves that it is the contradictory movement between yin and yang that makes things undergo ceaseless changes. "What appears everywhere between heaven and earth is nothing more than yin and yang. Hence movement and quiescence, speech and taciturnity, are all the principle of yin and yang."[41]

That is to say that movement and quiescence are the law of the fluctuation between yin and yang.

Based on the theory of movement and quiescence, Chu Hsi further deals with the movement that manifests itself in the form of relative steadiness and the form of obvious fluctuation. He calls this "change" (*hua*[bp]) and "transformation" (*pien*[bq]). The former means a gradual change and is equal to a quantitative change, while the latter means a sudden transformation and is equal to a qualitative change. The relation of movement-quiescence to change-transformation is this: "Transformation is a process of change from yin to yang and from quiescence to movement, whereas change is a process of change from yang to yin and from movement to quiescence. The process gradually reaches a state where no trace of change is detectable."[42] While transformation is a fluctuation from quiescence to movement and change a fluctuation from movement to quiescence, both are manifestations of things in different states and different forms in the process of fluctuation. Hence Chu Hsi says, "Movement means transformation and change."[43] And so, fluctuation contains two shapes: "gradual change" and "sudden transformation."

From Chu Hsi's viewpoint, the original meaning of "change" in the *Book of Changes* has two senses: one is transformation, which involves an operation; the other is exchange, which involves two opposites.[44] Transformation means the change from yang to yin, from yin to yang, from the greater yang to the lesser yin, and from the greater yin to the lesser yang. Exchange means that yang interacts with yin, yin interacts with yang, and there is interaction between the above and the below. "The myriad principles of the world are derived from movement and quiescence, the countless numbers of the world are derived from odd and even, and the multifarious emblems of the world are derived from square and round. However, all are derived from the two strokes, the *ch'ien* and *kun*."[45] If, in this view, it can be said that principles, numbers, and emblems constitute the very essence of change, then it is understood that change permeates through them all.

If we compare the *ho-t'u lo-shu* with the numbers and emblems of the *Book of Changes*, we would find that the emblems in the *ho-t'u* are round, while the emblems in the *lo-shu* are square. The *ho-t'u* and the *lo-shu* are, in fact, a plan of both square and round diagrams. According to the *ho-t'u*, "The heavenly numbers are the odd ones of yang, the earthly numbers are the even ones of yin; this is the so-called *ho-t'u* numbers."[46] Chu Hsi in his *Chou-i pen-i* and *I-hsüeh ch'i-meng* quoted from Yang Hsiung's[br] (53 B.C.–A.D. 18) work, the *T'ai-hsüan ching*[bs] (Classic of great mystery), *Hsüan-t'u pien*, a pithy oral formula, which says, "The numbers 1 and 6 are kin in the north, 2 and 7 are companions in the south, 3 and 8 are comrades in the east, 4 and 9 are friends in the west, and 5 and 10 protect each other in the center"[47] (see Figure 1).

By differentiation of numbers, "The numbers of yang, 1, 3, 5, 7 and 9, being odd, belong to Heaven. This is what is called the five heavenly num-

FIGURE I

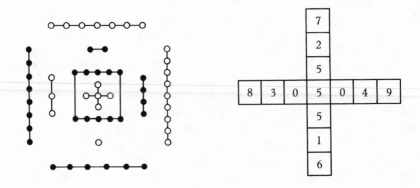

bers. The numbers of yin, 2, 4, 6, 8 and 10, being even, belong to Earth. This is what is called the five earthly numbers. The heavenly numbers and the earthly numbers mutually seek their respective partner-numbers. This means that one group of five is adapted to another group of five."[48] That is:

Heavenly Numbers (odd)	1	3	5	7	9	25
Earthly Numbers (even)	2	4	6	8	10	30

Here, "The addition of the five odd numbers makes 25, while the addition of the five even numbers makes 30. The two together make 55. This is the total number mentioned in the *ho-t'u*."[49]

As to the *lo-shu*, the chapter on the imperial ancestral hall in the *Elder Tai's Book of Rites* describes: "The imperial ancestral hall was already known in olden days. It consists of nine rooms—rooms 2, 9, and 4; rooms 7, 5, 3; and rooms 6, 1, and 8." Chen Luan,[bt] a mathematician of the Northern Dynasties (386–554) in his annotation of the *Shu-shu chi-i*[bu] (A mathematical memorandum) explained the passage, saying, "Of the nine rooms of the imperial ancestral hall, rooms 2 and 4 stand for one's shoulders, rooms 6 and 8 stand for one's feet, room 3 indicates one's left side, room 4 indicates one's right side, room 9 symbolizes one's hat, room 1 symbolizes one's shoes, and room 5 stands for one's central part." Ts'ai Yüan-ting adopted Chen's view in his commentary on the *I-hsüeh ch'i-meng* (see Figure 2).

In this magic square of nine numbers, the three numbers in any row—horizontal, vertical, or diagonal—add up to 15, a sum equal to that of the number 9 of the *yang-yao*[bv] (odd numbers) plus the number 6 of the *yin-yao*[bw] (even numbers), or equal to that of the number 8 of the *yin-yao* plus the number 7 of the *yang-yao*. A distinction between the *lo-shu* and the *ho-t'u* is that in the *lo-shu* the diagram numbers are made up of 1 to 9, while in the *ho-t'u* they are made up of 1 to 10.

FIGURE 2

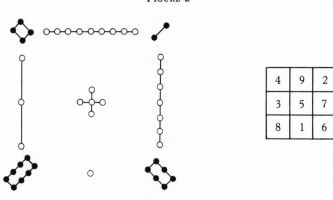

4	9	2
3	5	7
8	1	6

A great number of wise men in the past have devoted themselves to exploring the secret of the magic square. Chu Hsi, in an attempt to find an answer to this enigma, raises the question Why does the number 5 always stand at the center of the diagram, whether in the *ho-t'u* or in the *lo-shu*? He explains it thus: "Number begins with only one yin and one yang. The symbolic emblem of yang is circular, and the diameter of a circle is to its circumference as (roughly) 1 to 3. The symbolic emblem of yin is square, and one side of a square is in a ratio of 1 to 4."[50] If we explain the second and third tiers of the *ho-t'u* diagram in accordance with this answer that one side of a square is in a ratio of one to four, then as Chu Hsi says, "The four sides of a square are 2 made into 1," and at the same time, the diameter (of a square) becomes a square side-length (L), that is, the diameter being made 5 from 1. In the second tier, $A'B' + B'C' + C'D' + D'A' = 3 + 2 + 4 + 1 = 10$. In the third tier, $AB + DC = 5 + 5 = 10$ (see Figure 3).

If the first tier of the *ho-t'u* is illustrated according to the old theory that the diameter of a circle is to its circumference as 1 to 3, and the figure 5 in the center is taken as the radius of the circle, then the length of a circumference is $2 \times 3 \times 5 = 30 = 6 + 8 + 7 + 9$. The explanation corresponds to the notions that heaven is round and earth is square, that heaven covers and earth supports, and that the square is embraced by the circle.

If we explain the *lo-shu* that one side of a square is in a ratio of one to four, and assuming that the diameter is a square side-length, and the diameter is 5, then the circumference becomes $4L + AB + BC + CD + DA = 1 + 3 + 9 + 7 = 20$, the sum of the odd numbers, or $4L = A'B' + B'C' + C'D' + D'A' = 2 + 4 + 6 + 8 = 20$, the sum of the even numbers (see Figure 4).

Regarding how "transformation" and "change" operate, as expressed in the *ho-t'u* and the *lo-shu*, "One, the first number, produces Water by transformation while 6 forms it by change, 2 produces Fire by change while 7 forms it by transformation, 3 produces Wood by transformation while 8 forms it by

FIGURE 3

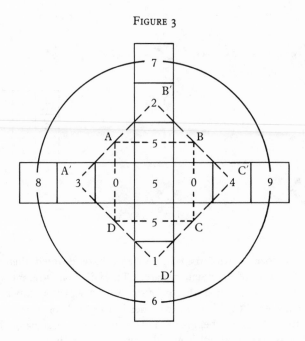

FIGURE 4

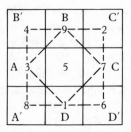

change, 4 produces Metal by change while 9 forms it by transformation, and 5 produces Earth by transformation while 10 forms it by change."[51] A distinction between the *ho-t'u* and *lo-shu* is obvious: "In the *ho-t'u*, 1, 2, 3, and 4 are all outside the inner square where the emblem or number 5 is, while 6, 7, 8, 9, and 10 all derive their numbers from the number 5, and at the same time, stand outside the number (5) that generates them. In the *lo-shu*, 1, 3, 7, and 9 are also outside the symbol 5 at the center of the square while 2, 4, 6, and 8 are beside the odd numbers because of their respective partner-numbers."[52] This kind of transformation and change described in the *ho-t'u* and *lo-shu* precisely constitutes the relationship of reciprocal production and reciprocal restraint between the Five Elements (see Figure 5).

FIGURE 5

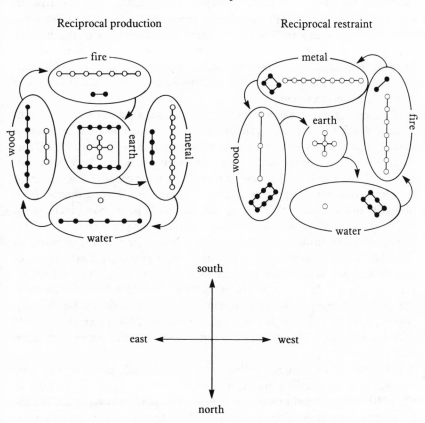

Reciprocal production   Reciprocal restraint

According to the *ho-t'u,* the reciprocal production among the Five Elements begins with Wood that produces Fire. Moving clockwise from the east, "After a complete round, it starts from the east again." According to the *lo-shu,* the reciprocal restraint among the Five Elements starts with Water that overcomes Fire. "After a complete round counter-clockwise, it makes a rotation moving to the right and coming to Earth overcomes Water again."[53] Both the mutual production and the mutual restraint are forms of transformation and change.

What do we mean by transformation and change? There are three characteristics of change. In the first place, "Change means a gradual and imperceptible melting-away."[54] "Things that undergo a gradual change do so not only by months, by days, but by hours also, but we are unaware of it."[55] Second, change means that things fade away by degree. "Change implies that things change from yang to yin and will gradually fade away. This is called change."[56] The third sense is that change leaves no trace. "Yang changes into softness, gradually melting away and leaving no trace whatsoever. This is the change."[57] Chu Hsi illustrates: "Change is not a sudden thing occurring in one day. The same is true of a man's advancement in virtues. 'At thirty, I had established my character'[58] does not mean that Confucius established his character suddenly when he reached thirty, but that he had his mind bent on learning from fifteen and constantly made a step-by-step conversion of himself into that state at thirty."[59] This is to say, change is a slow, gradual process of decreasing transformation.

If a change goes beyond a certain limit, it causes a discontinuous transformation, which Chu Hsi calls a sudden transformation. This transformation is described in three aspects. First, "Transformation is momentary."[60] "Transformation means a thing shifts from yin to yang and then becomes transformed all of a sudden. That is what transformation means."[61] That is a swift transformation, an abrupt leap. Second, "Transformation is a process from obscurity to obviousness."[62] "As transformation of yin into yang increases in intensity, it appears to us as sudden and as possessing a perceptible form. This is what we call transformation"[63]—that is, transformation that is obvious and traceable. Third, transformation indicates a break in a continuity. "Transformation means a sudden discontinuation which may be visible."[64] Change, then, is a gradual shift, whereas transformation is a sudden shift. For instance, the process of change takes place from the first day of a month. When it discontinues on the thirtieth day, it is called a month. This is transformation.[65] As the gradual shift discontinues at a certain point, change becomes transformation.

One may see from the above that transformation and change are mutually opposed, mutually differentiated, mutually linked and mutually permeated. Chu Hsi says, "Transformation is a slow process of change, while change indicates a completion of transformation."[66] Change permeates through transformation and in turn transformation permeates through change, that is, "transformation includes change in itself."[67] Because transformation arises from a change having reached a certain limit, and on this basis a new process of quantitative transformation appears, Chu Hsi calls change the completion of transformation. Chu Hsi thinks that transformation and change may be converted. He gives the relationship between hardness and softness as an example: "With regard to the transformation and change of hardness and softness, when a thing becomes hardened, it changes. As it changes, it becomes soft. Having become soft, it transforms. What is transformed is hardness, and thus it goes on round and round without stop."[68] Thus softness becoming hardness is analogous to change becoming transformation, hardness becoming softness to transformation becoming change. Softness having reached its apogee becomes hardened, change having reached its apogee becomes transformed; hardness having reached its apogee becomes softened, transformation having reached its apogee becomes changed. In this way the mutual conversion proceeds in endless cycles.

Chu Hsi's conception about transformation and change has, of course, its limitations. He accepts the notion that there exists something unchanged. He says, "[A hexagram consisting of six lines or *yaos* signifies changes. Accordingly] a change that begins at the lowest line, going upward, will stop or vanish when it reaches the top line, whereas a nonchange that remains at the lowest line becomes the origin of nonchange which should be, therefore, regarded as the primary essence."[69] Thus, Chu Hsi, having rejected change or transformation as a universal phenomenon, becomes inclined towards metaphysics.

We have so far analyzed Chu Hsi's system of thought of Changes, which was the result of how Chu Hsi followed, synthesized, and developed the doctrines of Changes expounded by Shao Yung and Ch'eng I; in so doing he inaugurated a new phase in this field of learning. If it can be said that it was Shao Yung who made clear the range of emblemology and numerology from the very beginning, then it was Ch'eng I who laid the foundations of the school of righteousness-and-principle. Chu Hsi, dissatisfied with these one-sided viewpoints, combined the theory of emblem-and-number and that of righteousness-and-principle, and synthesized them into a comprehensive whole. This led to the further development of the learning of Changes in the Sung, Ming, and Ch'ing (1644–1912) periods. Between the Ming and Ch'ing dynasties, Hu Wei, Huang Tsung-hsi[bx] (1610–1695), Huang Tsung-yen[by] (1616–1686), and Chu I-tsun (1629–1709) had criticized Shao Yung. They said, "The purpose of K'ang-chieh[bz] [Shao Yung] in writing his book was to sum up the calendars of all ages, ancient and modern and attribute them to the theory of Changes. But how could that be so? As a matter of fact, the theory of Changes has basically nothing in common with calendar. He made a forcible or unnatural combination of the Changes and calendar; and the more elaborate his doctrines, the more complicated his way of explanation. As a result his works became a kind of almanac full of confusion and of no use at all."[70] Shao Yung "picked up the Taoist heterodoxy to mislead the world."[71] In spite of these uncomplimentary comments, he still had a number of successors to carry on his doctrine of emblemology and numerology. After Chu Hsi's elucidation of Changes, however, only a few did not combine the theory of emblem-and-number and moral principles in their study of Changes. Although there is still some controversy over Chu Hsi's system of thought of Changes, yet it occupies a very important place in the history of Sung-Ming Neo-Confucianism and deserves our attention.

Translated by Wu Bai-hui[ca]

Notes

1. See "Shu I-ch'uan hsien-sheng *I-chuan* pan-pen hou"[cb] [A note appended to the edition of Master I-ch'uan's *Commentary on the Book of Changes*], in the *Chu Wen Kung wen-chi*[cc] [Collection of literary works of Master Chu], (abridged edition of the Four Libraries series), ch. 81, pp. 1474–1475.

2. About the author of the *I-hsüeh, ch'i-meng*, the *Sung-shih*[cd] [History of the Sung dynasty] records, "The *I-hsüeh ch'i-meng* was first drafted by Ts'ai Yüan-ting" (biography of Ts'ai Yüan-ting in ch. 434 [Chung-hua[ce] Book Co. ed.], p. 12876). But one can find from Chu Hsi's own words why he wrote the *I-hsüeh pen-i* and the *I-hsüeh ch'i-meng*: "What you have understood about the reading of the *Book of Changes* is very good. This work was originally written for the use of divination. What is described in it is simply forms and numbers by which to foretell one's good or evil fortune. Now, this traditional way of divination has been lost. Generally, those Confucians who talk about forms and numbers give strained interpretations and draw farfetched analogies, while those who preach righteousness and principle stray far from the subject. This is the reason why their books are too difficult to read, and this is also the reason why I wrote my *I-hsüeh pen-i* and *I-hsüeh ch'i-meng*" (reply to Liu Chun-fang[cf] in the *Collection of Literary works of Master Chu*, ch. 60 p. 1095). Hence, Chu Hsi prides himself upon the work *I-hsüeh ch'i-meng*. He says, "Insofar as the *Ta-hsüeh chang-chü*[cg] [Commentary on the *Great Learning*] and the *I-hsüeh ch'i-meng* are concerned, I have been observing throughout my life that only these two works have thrown light on what our predecessors had not yet touched" (*Chu Tzu yü-lei*, ch. 14). This is the proof that the *I-hsüeh ch'i-meng* is Chu Hsi's own work. Nevertheless, prior to its publication, Chu Hsi consulted with Ts'ai Yüan-ting (Ts'ai Chi-t'ung) again and again till the manuscript was finalized. Chu Hsi says in a reply to Ts'ai Chi-t'ung, "In the *I-hsüeh ch'i-meng*, there are several places that need revision. I am sending you herewith these parts as marked out. I hope you will examine them once more. It would be very nice if you could correct what should be corrected" (supplementary collection, *Chu Wen Kung wen-chi*, ch. 2, p. 7816). "Having perused the *I-hsüeh ch'i-meng*, I consider that it needs no more correction. It suffices only to correct the sentence as pointed out the other day" (*Ibid.*, p. 1817). One can tell from the aforesaid that Ts'ai Yüan-ting contributed a great deal to bring the work to completion. We cannot rule out the possibility that some portions of the work were actually written by Ts'ai Yüan-ting.

3. Nine diagrams: The *ho-t'u* diagram, the *lo-shu* diagram, the eight trigrams arranged in order according to legendary emperor Fu-hsi, the eight trigrams arranged in directions according to Fu-hsi, the sixty-four hexagrams arranged in order according to Fu-hsi, the sixty four hexagrams arranged in directions according to Fu-hsi, the eight trigrams arranged in order according to King Wen[ch] (r. 1171–1122 B.C.), the eight trigrams arranged in directions according to King Wen, the hexagrams arranged in their changes.

4. "I-pen-i chiu-t'u lun"[ci] [Discussion on the nine diagrams arranged according to *The Original Meaning of the Book of Changes*], in the *Pai-t'ien ts'ao-t'ang ts'un-kao*[cj] [The remaining drafts of the Grass Hut of Wang Mou-hung], (1752 ed.), ch. 1, p. 1.

5. *Book of Changes*, "Appended Remarks," pt. 1, ch. 11.

6. *Analects*, 9:8.

7. Quoted in the *Shu-ching chi-chuan*[ck] [Collected commentaries on the *Book of History*], ch. 4, p. 74.

8. *Chu Wen Kung wen-chi*, 38: 1a–b, 5a, first and third replies to Yüan Chi-chung.

9. "Appended Remarks," pt. 1, ch. 11.

10. Cheng Hsüan's commentary is found in the commentaries of the *Book of Changes* in the Thirteen Classics edition.

11. Kung An-kuo's commentary is found in the commentaries on the *Book of History* in the Thirteen Classics edition.

12. *I-t'u ming-pien*[cl] [Illustration of the diagrams in the *Book of Changes*], (1796 ed.), 1:17b.

13. In Shensi Province.

14. *Chu Wen Kung wen-chi*, ch. 82, p. 1486, "Compliments on Prefect Ku's[cm] Treatise on Archery."

15. *Ibid.*, ch. 82, p. 1484, "An Epilogue to a Piece of Writing by Chou Yüan-weng."[cn]

16. *Ibid.*, ch. 84, p. 1517, "An Epilogue to the Hand-written Copy of the *Tao-te ching* by Chu Hsi-chen."[co]

17. *Chou-i pen-i*, ch. 3, commentary on the *Book of Changes*, "Appended Remarks," pt. 2, ch. 11.

18. *Ch'u-tz'u chi-chu*[cp] [Assembled explanations of the *Book of Ch'u*], (Shanghai: Ku-chi[cq] Publishing Co., 1979), ch. 3, p. 50, "Essay on Questioning Heaven."

19. *Huang-chi ching-shih*[cr] [Supreme principles governing the world], 7:36.

20. *Ibid.*, 8:37.

21. *I-hsüeh ch'i-meng* (*Chu Tzu i-shu*[cs] [Surviving works of Master Chu] ed.), 2:2a.

22. *Chu Wen Kung wen-chi*, ch. 71, p. 1295, on Lin Huang-chung's[ct] discussion on the "Western Inscription."

23. *Chu Tzu yü-lei* (Ying-yüan[cu] Academy ed., 1872), 75:19.

24. *Chu Wen Kung wen-chi*, ch. 36, p. 573, reply to Lu Tzu-ching.[cv]

25. *I-hsüeh ch'i-meng*, 2:1a–b.

26. *Chou-i pen-i*, commentary on "Appended Remarks," pt. 1, ch. 5.

27. *I-hsüeh ch'i-meng*, 2:15a–b. Shao Yung's statements are found in the *Huang-chi ching-shih*, 7:40–41.

28. *I-hsüeh ch'i-meng*, 2:3a.

29. *Chu Tzu yü-lei*, 67:7.

30. *Ibid.*, 98:6.

31. *Chou-i pen-i*, ch. 1, commentary on the text of the second hexagram, *k'un* (female).

32. *Ibid.*, commentary on the lowest line of the *k'un* hexagram.

33. *I-hsüeh ch'i-meng*, 2:15a.

34. *Chou-i pen-i*, ch. 1, commentary on the text of the first hexagram, *ch'ien* (male).

35. *I-hsüeh ch'i-meng*, 3:7a.

36. *Chu Tzu yü-lei*, 65:1.

37. *Ibid.*, 74:5.

38. *Chou-i pen-i*, ch. 1, commentary on the lowest line of the *k'un* hexagram.

39. *I-hsüeh ch'i-meng*, 1:4b.

40. *Ibid.*, 2:b. For Chou Tun-i's statement, see the *Chou Tzu ch'uan-shu*[cw] [Complete works of Master Chou], (Wan-yu wen-k'u[cx] [Universal library] ed.), ch. 1, p. 6.

41. *Chu Tzu yü-lei*, 65:3.

42. *Ibid.*, 74:3.

43. *Chou-i pen-i*, ch. 3, commentary on "Appended Remarks," pt. 1, ch. 2.

44. *Chu Tzu yü-lei,* 65:1.

45. *Ibid.,* 65:8.

46. *Chou-i pen-i,* ch. 3, commentary on "Appended Remarks," pt. 1, ch. 9. The illustration suggested by Dr. Joseph Needham about the *ho-t'u* diagram seems somewhat different from its original meaning. See the Chinese version of *Science and Civilisation in China,* vol. III, on mathematics (Beijing: Science Publishing House, 1978), p. 127.

47. Yang Hsiung, *T'ai-hsüan ching* (Ch'ung-wen[cy] Book Co.: 1875 reprint), 10:3.

48. *I-hsüeh ch'i-meng,* 1: 1b–5b.

49. *Ibid.,* 1:5a.

50. *Ibid.,* 1:5a–b.

51. *Chou-i pen-i,* ch. 3, commentary on "Appended Remarks," pt. 1, ch. 9.

52. *I-hsüeh ch'i-meng,* 1:6a.

53. *Ibid.,* 1:6b.

54. *Chu Tzu yü-lei,* 74:3.

55. *Ibid.,* 71:8.

56. *Ibid.,* 74:12.

57. *Ibid.,* 74:11.

58. *Analects,* 2:4.

59. *Chu Tzu yü-lei,* 75:24.

60. *Ibid.,* 74:3.

61. *Ibid.,* 74:12.

62. *Ibid.,* 74:3.

63. *Ibid.,* 75:24.

64. *Ibid.,* 75:24.

65. *Ibid.,* 75:24.

66. *Chou-i pen-i,* ch. 1, commentary on the remarks on the text.

67. *Ibid.,* ch. 3, commentary on "Appended Remarks," pt. 1, ch. 2.

68. *Chu Tzu yü-lei,* 74:10–11.

69. *Ibid.,* 66:17.

70. Huang Tsung-hsi, *I-hsüeh hsiang-shu lun*[cz] [On emblems and numbers of the *Book of Changes*], (Kuang-ya[da] Book Co. ed.), ch. 5, p. 2.

71. Huang Tsung-yen, *Chou-i shen-men yü-lun*[db] [Complementary notes on the search for a way to understand the *Book of Changes*], (Chao-tai[dc] Series ed.), p. 9.

Glossary

a 易	k 邵雍	u 蔡沈
b 太極	l 程頤	v 伏羲
c 陰陽	m 易傳	w 河出圖
d 剛柔	n 周易本義	x 洛書
e 易經	o 易學啓蒙	y 洪範
f 陰陽家	p 理學	z 鯀
g 道家	q 王懋竑	aa 洪範九疇
h 讖緯家	r 河圖	ab 春秋緯
i 玄學家	s 禹	ac 周髀經解
j 理學家	t 顧命	ad 大戴禮記

ae 明堂
af 朱子語類
ag 袁機仲
ah 鄭玄
ai 孔安國
aj 京房
ak 焦贛
al 荀爽
am 虞翻
an 孔穎達
ao 李鼎祚
ap 周易集解
aq 卦氣圖
ar 爻辰圖
as 納甲圖
at 朱震
au 周易圖
av 高宗
aw 胡渭
ax 蔡季通元定
ay 雲台真逸
az 雲台外史
ba 華州
bb 朱熹仲晦父
bc 雲台子
bd 理

be 天理
bf 兩儀
bg 四象
bh 周敦頤
bi 氣
bj 乾
bk 坤
bl 坎
bm 離
bn 動
bo 靜
bp 化
bq 變
br 揚雄
bs 太玄經
bt 甄鸞
bu 數術記遺
bv 陽爻
bw 陰爻
bx 黃宗羲
by 黃宗炎
bz 康節
ca 巫伯慧
cb 書伊川先生易傳板本後
cc 朱文公文集

cd 宋史
ce 中華
cf 劉君房
cg 大學章句
ch 文
ci 易本義九圖論
cj 白田草堂存稿
ck 書經集傳
cl 易圖明辨
cm 顧
cn 周元翁
co 朱希真
cp 楚辭集註
cq 古籍
cr 皇極經世
cs 朱子遺書
ct 林黃中
cu 應元
cv 陸子靜
cw 周子全書
cx 萬有文庫
cy 崇文
cz 易學象數論
da 廣雅
db 周易尋門餘論
dc 昭代

19

Chu Hsi's Discipline of Propriety

Kao Ming

Contents of the Discipline of Propriety of Chu Hsi

The Discipline of Propriety is also called the Discipline of the Three Proprieties. It covers the following subjects.

1. The study of *Chou-li*,[a] (Ritual of Chou) or *Chou-kuan*[b] (Government organization of the Chou dynasty) deals with the state organization and systems of the Chou dynasty (1111–249 B.C.). The organization and institutions of a state vary greatly according to the specific requirements of different times. Nevertheless, the experiences and ideas of state organization of the Chou dynasty have been an important source of reference and inspiration for later dynasties since the Han (206 B.C.–A.D. 220). For instance, Cheng Hsüan[c] (127–200) of the Han dynasty compared the Han system with that of the Chou in his *Chou-li chu*[d] (Annotations of the *Chou-li*). Chia Kung-yen[e] (*fl.* 650) of the T'ang dynasty (618–907) compared the T'ang system with that of the Chou in his *Chou-li shu*[f] (Commentaries on the *Chou-li*), while Tu Yu[g] (735–812), also a scholar of the T'ang, did the same in his *T'ung-tien*[h] (Encyclopedia of institutions and customs). Scholars of the Sung dynasty (960–1279) were no exception. For instance, Ssu-ma Kuang[i] (1019–1086) cited passages of the *Chou-li* as supporting evidence in his "Lun ts'ai-li shu"[j] (Memorial to the throne on wealth and profit).[1] Similarly, Wang An-shih[k] (1021–1086) wrote the *Chou-kuan hsin-i*[l] (New meanings of the *Chou-kuan*) in support of his unprecedented political reform. After Wang's abortive attempt, Sung scholars seldom directed their efforts toward the study of the *Chou-li*. Nevertheless, Chu Hsi still considered the *Chou-li* "the key link of propriety" in his "Ch'i hsiu san-li ta-tzu"[m] (Memorial to the throne asking for renovation of the *Three Proprieties*).[2] He also wrote the "*Chou-li* san-te shuo"[n] (The three virtues of the *Chou-li*) and the "*Chou-li* t'ai-chu chiu-pai pien"[o] (Discussion on the Grand Player's nine salutes) as well as other similar treatises.[3] It is evident that he also has thoroughly studied the *Chou-li*, directing his main concern at the parts concerning principles and rules of propriety, in other words, the parts that could be associated with those in the *Li-chi*[p] (Book of propriety) and *I-li*[q] (Book of rituals).

2. The study of *I-li* deals with the codes of conduct of social life. Although society changes constantly, man still retains his basic nature and his relationship with other people. Therefore, the social rules of the Chou dynasty were still valuable in the eyes of the people of the Sung dynasty. Chu Hsi was a man with keen interest in social rules, believing that social unrest was caused by the decay of moral virtues in society, which was in turn attributable to the failure to assign sufficient authority to the rules of social life. Thus, he repeatedly asked the government to promulgate books of propriety as well as to revise and add to those already available. For instance, chapter 20 of the *Collection of Literary Works* contains the "Ch'i pan-chiang li-shu chuang"[r] (Memorial to the throne asking for promulgation of books on propriety) and "Ch'i tseng-hsiu li-shu chuang"[s] (Memorial to the throne asking for addition to books on propriety).[4] In his "Postface" to Chang Shih's[t] (1133–1180) *San-chia li-fan*[u] (Examples of propriety by three scholars), he greatly praised Ssu-ma Kuang's *Shu-i*[v] (Correspondence and etiquette).[5] He wrote the *Chia-li*[w] (Family etiquette) and the *I-li ching-chuan t'ung-chieh*[x] (Comprehensive exegesis of the text of and commentaries on the *I-li*). His *Family Etiquette* was intended for adoption by his contemporaries; the *Comprehensive Exegesis* annotates the *I-li* with original passages from the *Li-chi* and other Classics and historical writings, as well as with previous annotations and commentaries on the *I-li*, the *Chou-li*, and the *Li-chi* as cited in the *Annotations of and Commentaries on the Thirteen Classics*. The *Comprehensive Exegesis* is his attempt to associate the codes of conduct and rules of social life with moral principles and reasons that originate and support them, in order to provide the reader with an adequate understanding of these rules and codes that would in turn strengthen his willingness and determination to practice them. Moreover, the *Exegesis* divides its contents into such sections as "Family Rituals," "Country Rituals," "School Rituals," "State Rituals," and "Rituals of the King's Court," which cover all the rules of social life at all levels and on all occasions, such as the "auspicious, mourning, military, visiting and reception, and celebrating" protocol and ceremonies. This is considered the most important part of his *Discipline of propriety*.

3. The study of the *Li-chi* deals with the meaning and significance of state organization and institutions as well as with the rules of social life and certain related academic matters. The *Li-chi* is a collection of articles, authored or edited by Confucian scholars after the death of Confucius (551–479 B.C.) up to the early period of the Han dynasty and including writings by Confucius' disciples or later followers such as Yen Yen,[y] Pu Shang,[z] Tseng Shen,[aa] Tzu-ssu,[ab6] and others, which elucidate and expound the concepts and theories of Confucius. The influence of the *Li-chi* should be less prominent than that of the *Book of Mencius* and the *Hsün Tzu*.[ac] While the words and deeds of Confucius are recorded in the *Analects*, the *Li-chi* contains the concepts and theories of Confucianism as refined and developed after the passing away of the Master. Following the steps of Ch'eng Hao[ad] (1032–1085) and Ch'eng I[ae] (1033–

1107), Chu Hsi made energetic efforts to elucidate the *Great Learning* and the *Doctrine of the Mean*, which were originally two separate treatises in the *Li-chi*. In explaining the ultimate goal of learning, the *Great Learning* starts from "manifesting the illustrious virtue"—manifesting the virtuous nature endowed in oneself—then goes on to "enabling all the people to be intimate with each other," and finally to "resting in the highest excellence." It recommends that the steps for such an achievement should be "investigation of things," "achievement of knowledge," "sincerity of the will," "rectification of the heart," "cultivation of oneself," "regulation of the family," "government of the state," and finally, "making the whole world just and peaceful." All this offers a systematic, complete, and step-by-step elucidation of the philosophy of life and political philosophy upheld by Confucianism, which are centered on morality. It is indeed the most mature thought of Confucianism. Similar in nature, the *Doctrine of the Mean* expounds that in learning the truth of the universe and the path that man should take, one must follow, and bring into full play, the virtuous nature one is endowed with. The opening paragraph says: "What Heaven has conferred is called the nature; an accordance with this nature is called the path; the regulation of this path is called instruction." This is the truth and path that man must keep to without a moment of deviation. Even if he is all alone, out of the sight and hearing of others, he must still be "cautious and apprehensive." That is what may be called "being watchful over oneself when alone." The ultimate goal is to achieve a state of "equilibrium" without deviation, inclination, excess, or insufficiency. Thus, a man will be able to regulate his emotions and feelings such as pleasure, anger, sorrow, or joy, and arrive at the state of "harmony"—the harmony between nature and man and among men. Through what is called "achievement of equilibrium and harmony," all creatures in the universe can have their proper places and develop themselves. This lofty idea is expressed in the *Doctrine of the Mean* as "A happy order will prevail throughout heaven and earth, and all things will be nourished and flourish." The idea identifies man with nature in a harmonious oneness, in a state where "nature and man form one unity"—a moral state that is achieved through the utmost exertion of man's humaneness, wisdom, and the spirit of brave advancement. It is reasonable to assert that the most refined theory of Confucianism is very aptly defined therein. Chu Hsi analyzed and rearranged sentences and paragraphs of these two treatises, added ample commentaries to illustrate their significance, and compiled them into two books, *Ta-hsüeh chang-chu*[af] (Commentary on the *Great Learning*) and *Chung-yung chang-chü*[ag] (Commentary on the *Doctrine of the Mean*). Together with his *Lun-yü chi-chu*[ah] (Collected commentaries on the *Analects*) and *Meng Tzu chi-chu*[ai] (Collected commentaries on the *Book of Mencius*), they were placed under a single title, *Ssu-shu chi-chu*[aj] (Collected commentaries on the Four Books), which became the most cherished reference for the School of Principle in the Sung dynasty.

In "Chung-ni yen-chü"[ak] (Confucius at leisure) in the *Li-chi*, it is recorded that Confucius said that "propriety is the practice of principle"; in "Yüeh-chi"[al] (Record of music) in the *Li-chi,* Confucius is again quoted as saying that "propriety is the principle that cannot be altered."[7] Accordingly, since principle resides in propriety, then the School of Principle is derived from the "discipline of propriety." The reason that Chu Hsi became one of the most distinguished masters of the School of Principle is attributable to his profound study and understanding of propriety, especially the study of the *Li-chi.* It must be pointed out here that his study of the *Li-chi* is by no means limited to the *Great Learning* and the *Doctrine of the Mean.* For instance, in the "Table of Contents" of his *Comprehensive Exegesis,* he has emphasized: " 'Hsüeh-chi'[am] (Record of schooling) describes the schools' process of teaching, of transmitting the doctrine, and of providing knowledge as well as the causes of success and failure, merits and demerits of education. It should have covered both advanced and primary schooling. However, previous commentaries on it have mostly missed the point. Now, with reference to the viewpoints of Master Chang of Heng-ch'ü[an] (Chang Tsai, 1020–1177) and with ideas of my own, I have made additional annotations to it."[8] It is evident that Chu Hsi paid equal attention to the "Hsüeh-chi." As to other works contained in the *Li-chi,* he has as much as possible integrated their passages into the *Comprehensive Exegesis* to associate the theoretical sayings with rules, and principle with practice. This is the most significant achievement of his study of propriety.

Chu Hsi's Works on the Discipline of Propriety

The *Comprehensive Exegesis of the Text of the Commentaries on the I-li* can be regarded as the most important work of this kind produced by Chu Hsi, although it was not entirely completed by his own hands. In initial preparation, the book had been entitled *I-li chi chi-chuan chi-chu*[ao] (Collected commentaries on the annotations of the *I-li*). The present title was adopted after his revision in later years. It was not published until 1217 at Nan-k'ang[ap] after his death in 1200. This edition contains, under the present title, five chapters of "Family Rituals," three chapters of "Country Rituals," eleven chapters of "School Rituals," and four chapters of "State Rituals," totalling twenty-three chapters with forty-two articles listed in the table of contents. However, one article listed under "Writing and Mathematics" is missing, while eight articles from "Grand Archery" to "Mutual Visits Among State Princes" are unfinished. In the same edition but under the old title, there are eighteen articles contained in chapters 24–37. They are the "Rituals of the King's Court." Moreover, among the listed articles the one entitled "Prognostication and Divination" is missing, while in the table of contents, the forewords and remarks for the articles from chapter 31, which is entitled "Ascending the Throne," to the last are all missing. It is therefore evident that this edition is the unfinished one.

In fact, Chu Hsi had asked Huang Kan[aq] (1152–1221), one of his students, to revise drafts of the "Funeral Rites" and "Sacrificial Rites." In 1219, Huang Kan completed the revision of fifteen chapters of the "Funeral Rites"; he died of illness not long after. In 1222, four years after his death, Chang Fu[ar] (fl. 1222) published the revised "Funeral Rites" at Nan-k'ang. As a complete book planned by Chu Hsi, the job still was unfinished. Some time later, Yang Fu[as] (fl. 1222), another student of Chu Hsi, revised the drafts of fourteen chapters of "Sacrificial Rites" and published them. Together with the previously published works under the titles of *Comprehensive Exegesis* and the *Collected Commentaries on the Annotations of the I-li,* and both Huang Kan's and Yang Fu's revisions, the book as now available contains sixty-six chapters. Although the book was not entirely completed by Chu Hsi himself, Huang Kan and Yang Fu were his disciples and they followed the format and style of their master very closely. There should be no serious question about the editorship.

In the *Complete Collection of the Four Libraries* there is a five-chapter edition (with one chapter of "Supplements") of the *Chia-li.* Listed in both the *Chi-ku-ko chen-ts'ang mi-pen shu-mu*[at] (Bibliography of rare editions kept in the Chi-ku Pavilion) by Mao I[au] (1640–1686) and the *Hsiao-tz'u-t'ang shu-mu*[av] (Bibliography of Hsiao-tz'u Hall) by Wang Wen-yüan[aw] (1663–?), is the five-chapter Sung edition of Chu Hsi's *Family Etiquette.* In the collective bibliography of reprints of Sung originals compiled by Teng Chung-yüeh[ax] of the Ming dynasty (1368–1644), the *Family Etiquette* consists of five chapters plus one chapter of supplements. This might be the edition adopted by the compilers of the *Complete Collection of the Four Libraries.* For critical descriptions, see the *Ssu-shu ch'üan-shu tsung-mu t'i-yao*[ay] (Essential points about works in the *Complete Collection of the Four Libraries*), compiled by Chu Yün[az] (1794–1805) and others with supplement by Hu Yü-chin[ba] (1858–1940).[9]

However, listed in both the *T'ieh-ch'in t'ung-chien lou shu-mu*[bb] (Bibliography of the Iron-Lute Bronze-Sword Tower) by Ch'ü Yung[bc] (fl. 1850) and the *Tung-hu ts'ung-chi*[bd] (Collected notes of Tung-hu) by Chiang Kuang-hsü[be] (1813–1860) both of the Ch'ing dynasty (1644–1912), are copies of the ten-chapter Sung edition of the *Tsuan-t'u chi-chu Wen Kung Chia-li*[bf] (Chu Hsi's *Family Etiquette* with illustrations and collected annotations). Furthermore, this ten-chapter edition is marked with the words "With annotations supplemented by Yang Fu and additional annotations by later follower Liu Kai-sun[bg] [fl. 1222]." This edition contains one chapter of "Common Etiquette," one chapter of "Capping Ceremony," five chapters of "Funeral Rites," and two chapters of "Sacrificial Rites." The "Preface by the Author" therein is a reproduction of Chu Hsi's own handwriting. It is then evident that even in the Sung dynasty there were two different editions of the *Family Etiquette,* one in five chapters and one in ten. In his "Biographical Account" of Chu Hsi, Huang Kan pointed out that "the *Family Etiquette* authored by him has been widely adopted for practice in society. He made deletions and additions but was not able to make a final revision of the book in his lifetime."[10] It is obvious that Chu did write the *Family Etiquette*, which was circulated widely. He also made several additions and deletions but did not have time to complete a final version. Furthermore, the "Preface to the *Family Etiquette*" can also be found in the *Collection of Literary Works of Chu Hsi*,[11] with minor differences of wording from that published in the ten-chapter edition. Understandably, some minor changes might have been made between its preparation for the book and its later inclusion in the *Collection of Literary Works*. Moreover, the date of completion of the *Family Etiquette* is recorded in the *Chu Tzu nien-p'u*[bh] (Chronicle biography of Master Chu Hsi)[12] while the "Supplement" to the book explains how it was lost and recovered. Thus, there should be no doubt about its authenticity.

Nonetheless, Wang Mao-hung[bi] (1668–1741), a Ch'ing dynasty authority on the study of Chu Hsi's scholarship, produced a treatise entitled *"Chia-li k'ao"*[bj] (An investigation into the *Family Etiquette*). This work, collected in his *Pai-t'ien tsa-chu*[bk] (Miscellaneous works of Wang Mao-hung),[13] energetically argues that the *Family Etiquette* was not a work by Chu Hsi. Wang has expressed serious doubts about the book by pointing out the controversial sayings in the "Biographical Account," the *Chronicle Biography*, the "Preface to the *Family Etiquette*," and the "Supplement to the *Family Etiquette*" as well as by noting that the book was rarely mentioned in the *Collection of Literary Works* and the *Classified Conversations* of Chu Hsi. Wang has also written the *"Chia-li* hou-k'ao"[bl] (A further investigation into the *Family Etiquette*), which contains seventeen items, quoting the viewpoints in *"Chia-li* pien"[bm] (Disputing the *Family Etiquette*) by Mister Ying[bn] of the Yüan dynasty (1271–1368) and those of Ch'iu Chün[bo] (1418–1495) of the Ming dynasty in support of his own opinion. He then wrote the *"Chia-li* k'ao-wu"[bp] (An examination of the errors in the *Family Etiquette*) containing forty-six items, in which he cited ancient codes of ritual to debate the authenticity of Chu Hsi's work.

Let us look at the matter of authenticity another way. To begin with, the "Preface to the *Family Etiquette*" written by Chu Hsi was included in the *Collection of Literary Works of Master Chu Hsi*. This is beyond reasonable doubt. Because the "Biographical Account," the *Chronicle Biography*, and the "Supplement to the *Family Etiquette*" were produced by different authors, it is understandable that they contain some controversial points. These points, however, cannot negate the fact that Chu Hsi did write the book. As to the viewpoints of Ying and Ch'iu, Ch'iu also considered Ying's opinion incorrect. Moreover, even Wang himself criticized Ch'iu statements as "inaccurate and unreliable"; they cannot resolve the doubts in the mind of others." Therefore, "A Further Investigation into the *Family Etiquette*" cannot be regarded as plausible scholarship.

In fact, Chu Hsi pointedly emphasized in his "Preface to the *Family Etiquette*": In the time of the three ancient dynasties Hsia (2183–1752? B.C.), Shang (1751–1112? B.C.), and Chou, the codes of etiquette were complete. However, those extant today . . . are not suitable for contemporary society.

Although some acknowledged gentlemen have made rules for contemporary times by weighing the changes from ancient times to the present, such works still lack discrimination while being rather simple in content. . . . Therefore, I have consulted works of ancient and modern times and have come up with my own opinion by adopting those items that cannot be altered and making some minor deletions from and additions to them."[14] It is a fact that ancient etiquette is not suitable for later generations. Of course, in formulating his work with reference to the changes since ancient times, Chu Hsi did not stick to the institutions of ancient time. Thus, Wang citing ancient rules to debate the authenticity of the *Family Etiquette* can be considered as showing ignorance to the "changes from ancient times to the present." To reiterate, the *Family Etiquette* was written by Chu Hsi for adoption by his contemporaries, and is of a different nature from the "Family Etiquette" portion of the *Comprehensive Exegesis of the Text of the Commentaries on the I-li*, which inquires into ancient rituals. One should not lump them together as something identical. Therefore, it appears fair to say that Wang failed to build a plausible case for refutation.

A brief mention of the *Collection of Literary Works* of Master Chu Hsi might be appropriate because it contains numerous passages concerning the study of the *Chou-li*, the *I-li*, and the *Li-chi*. Besides the few that have been mentioned previously in this paper, there are more than a hundred single articles in the collection which research, examine, discuss, and elucidate the systems, details, principles, and significance of rituals of ancient and contemporary periods. His opinions appear to be well-balanced and feasible while at the same time meticulous and penetrating; and the insights are excellent. When studying his discipline of propriety, these materials should not be overlooked.[15]

Of the editions of Ch'u Hsi's dialogues, the 140-chapter *Chu Tzu yü-lei*[bq] (Classified conversations of Master Chu)[16] is of course the most complete. Ch'eng Ch'uan[br] of the Ch'ing dynasty selected from it the sayings related to the Five Classics and compiled them into a single book in eighty chapters entitled *Chu Tzu wu-ching yü-lei*[bs] (Classified conversations of Master Chu, concerning the Five Classics) that contains forty chapters of sayings on the *Book of Changes*, nine chapters on the *Book of History*, seven chapters on the *Book of Odes*, three chapters on the *Spring and Autumn Annuals*, and twenty-one chapters on *Li* (Propriety). Since one-fourth of the edition's contents are about propriety, it has an abundance of original material. It would be advisable for one studying Chu Hsi's discipline of propriety to pay attention to it.[17]

Li Kuang-ti[bt] (1642–1718) has also compiled a five-chapter *Chu Tzu li-tsuan*[bu] (Collection of Master Chu's sayings about propriety)[18] by gathering together such passages and sayings originally contained in Chu Hsi's *Collected Literary Works* and *Classified Conversations* but not in the *Comprehensive Exegesis* and *Family Etiquette*. The book is divided into the categories of "General," "Capping and Wedding," "Funeral," "Sacrificial," and "Miscellaneous Etiquette." It offers a rather systematic and itemized reference to researchers of Chu Hsi's discipline of propriety so that they do not have to spend too much time piecing together the scattered materials. The book is considered a very helpful reference. However, there still are a few omissions. Examples of these omissions are Chu Hsi's answer to P'an Kung-shu[bv] (*fl.* 1180), which discusses the style and format of integrating the *Li-chi* and the *I-li* and compiling it into a single book;[19] the "Shu Ch'eng Tzu's 'T'i-shuo' hou"[bw] (Postscript to Ch'eng I's "Discussion of the *T'i* Sacrifice";[20] the *"Chou-li san-te shuo,"* and the *"Yüeh-chi tung-ching shuo"*[bx] (Discussion of the dynamics and statics of the "Record of Music");[21] and certain other writings. Although Chu Hsi's letter to Wu Hui-shu,[by22] which expresses his opinion that the grand ancestral temple should have faced south while the ancestral tablets faced east, is quite similar in principle with his letter in answer to Wang Tzu-ho,[bz23] the former contains a much clearer and more detailed exposition of his views. Intentionally or otherwise, Li Kuang-ti has rejected the more detailed one in favor of the less useful one, which may have been an unwise decision. Things like these can be considered minor shortcomings of Li's edition. In our study of Chu Hsi's discipline of propriety, Li's work can save us a lot of trouble. One should not overlook his significant contributions despite these minor deficiencies.

Besides the works already mentioned, Liang Wan-fang[ca] of the Ch'ing dynasty has also published a sixty-nine–chapter edition of the *Ch'ung-k'an Chu Tzu I-li ching-chuan t'ung-chieh*[cb] (Reprint of Master Chu's *Comprehensive Exegesis of the Text of and Commentaries on the I-li*).[24] Although called a reprint, the edition is actually a revision that has altered the original beyond recognition. Whereas Ch'iu Chün of the Ming dynasty compiled an eight-chapter *Chia-li i-chieh*[cc] (Ceremonial usages from the *Family Etiquette*),[25] a book was also published under the same title and in the same number of chapters but with the compiler's name designated as Yang Shen[cd] (1488–1559). The latter is in fact a pirated copy of the former.[26] In the Ch'ing dynasty, Wang Fu-li[ce] also produced a ten-chapter edition of *Chia-li pien-ting*[cf] (*Family Etiquette* critically finalized).[27] In all, the works mentioned in this paragraph are actually rewritings based on Chu Hsi's works with deletions and additions. They are not useful as source materials because they deviate greatly from the original.

Evaluation of Chu Hsi's "Discipline of Propriety"

As mentioned previously, the most important achievement of Chu Hsi's study of propriety lies in his association and synthesis of, on the one hand, principles with rules, and, on the other, theories with practices. He was able to achieve this synthesis because of his thorough research into the annotations of and commentaries on the three Classics of propriety by previous eminent scholars such as Cheng Hsüan and Chia Kung-yen. In the Sung dynasty, many scholars of the School of Principle were inclined to neglect the annotations and commentaries by the scholars of the Han and T'ang periods while being fond of abstract discussions of principle. Some of them were even Confucianist in name while Buddhist Meditationist in nature; they ignored the Confucian Classics and sought instead an unclouded heart through meditation. Chu Hsi was different. Not only did he encourage others to read the necessary Classics, but also the annotations and commentaries by Han and T'ang scholars. He deplored those who ignored proper study and said, "The well-informed gentlemen of today do not read proper books and proper annotations and commentaries."[28] He also commented, "Since the beginning of the current dynasty, scholars have just stuck to annotations and commentaries and then talked about the Way. People like the two Su brothers [Su Shih,[cg] 1036–1101, and Su Ch'e,[ch] 1039–1112] just wanted to talk about the Way. But how can one reject the annotations and commentaries!"[29] In his letter to Chang Ching-fu (Chang Shih,[ci] 1133–1180) discussing doubtful sayings in the *Book of Mencius*, he said, "The book [the *Mencius*] has not been read again because of lack of time. But I have read once again the *Chou-li* and the *I-li*. Because there are annotations and commentaries, I do not find the reading exhausting."[30] Furthermore, in his letter in answer to Yü Cheng-fu,[cj] Chu Hsi has emphasized that "in the extant editions of classical propriety books, there are original missing parts. They must be supplemented with the annotations and commentaries by Han and T'ang scholars. One should not only rely on the Classical texts and simply reject those annotations and commentaries."[31] The evidence thus shows that Chu Hsi had not only studied the previous annotations and commentaries, but also advised others to do so while criticizing those who did not.

As a matter of fact, in preparing the *Comprehensive Exegesis of the Text of and Commentaries on the I-li*, Chu Hsi made meticulous references to the annotations and commentaries by both Han and T'ang scholars. Moreover, while having carefully investigated the *Annotations* by Cheng Hsüan of the Han dynasty and the *Commentaries* by Chia Kung-yen of the T'ang dynasty and thus obtained a profound understanding of their scholarship, he was also able to correct the errors and supplement the omissions in them. In editorial methodology, he adopted the excellent ways of Cheng, which were further developed by Chia. Thus, he was able to render the difficult *I-li* into an easier reading. In his letter in answer to Li Chi-chang[ck] he said, "For years I have had the desire to edit the *I-li* by separating the paragraphs and sentences therein as well as by attaching commentaries and other materials to it. Recently, I completed more than ten parts. That seems to be rather an achievement. I expect that the rest of the book can be finished before the end of the year. All the confused portions and textual mistakes in it have been pointed out by previous scholars. However, since the book is a conglomeration of words without division into paragraphs, it is a difficult thing to read. If I can make it clearer and better organized as something easier to read, it would be some kind of contribution."[32] This is what he has done. Chu Hsi's method was emulated by later scholars. For instance, in the Ch'ing dynasty, Chang Erh-ch'i[cl] (1612–1677) adopted it in his *I-li Cheng chu chü-tu*[cm] (The *I-li* annotated by Ch'eng Hsüan with division of sentences)[33] while Wu Chien-hua[cn] did the same in his *I-li chang-chü*[co] (The *I-li* with division of paragraphs and sentences).[34] The *Li-shu kang-mu*[cp] (General outline of *Books of Propriety*) by Chiang Yung[cq] (1681–1762)[35] of the same dynasty took the *Comprehensive Exegesis* as a basic reference and, quite naturally, Chiang also adopted Chu's method of editing. The same method was again adopted by Hsü Ch'ien-hsüeh[cr] (1631–1694) in his *Tu-li t'ung-k'ao*[cs] (General investigation into readings of propriety)[36] and by Ch'in Hui-t'ien[ct] (1702–1764) in his *Wu-li t'ung-k'ao*[cu] (General investigation into the five categories of propriety).[37] This shows the far-reaching influence of Chu's scholarly efforts.

The "directions to the reader" in Cheng Hsüan's annotations of the *I-li* guide the reader to items dealing with similar subjects that are scattered throughout the book. Chia Kung-yen provided the same in his commentaries to the *I-li* while adding some that Cheng had omitted.[38] Because of their profound understanding of the original editing rules of the *I-li*, Cheng and Chia were able to work out annotations and commentaries. By the same token, because of Chu Hsi's thorough knowledge of such annotations and commentaries, he likewise knew the value of the "directions to the reader." He began his letter in answer to Ch'en Ts'ai-ch'ing,[cv] "You know that there is a systematic way to read the *I-li*. That is very good! Although the book is difficult to read, many passages are simply repetitions. If one knows the categorical classification of it and makes cross reference to the following and preceeding passages so that these passages can elucidate each other, after some time he will come up with a comprehensive understanding."[39] What Chu Hsi calls "categorical classification" is identical with "directions to the reader." Chu Hsi was able to achieve a comprehensive understanding of this Classical work on propriety because of his mastery of the "directions to the reader" suggested in the annotations and commentaries of Cheng and Chia.

However, Chu Hsi was not a pedant staying in a rut. As mentioned before, he made corrections and additions to the work of previous eminent scholars such as Cheng and Chia.[40] All this clearly demonstrates his solid academic foundation and seriousness of attitude.

Chu Hsi's scholarly efforts notwithstanding, the *Comprehensive Exegesis of the I-li* cannot be considered a perfect work. On the one hand, Chu has taken passages of the *Li-chi* and used them to annotate passages in the *I-li*. On the other hand, he has excluded the "Meaning of Capping" and "Meaning of Wedding" of the *Li-chi* from his annotations of "Capping Ceremony for Scholar" and "Wedding Ceremony for Scholar" in the *I-li* by putting them under independent chapter titles. The "Domestic Mannerism," "Domestic Management," "Five Clans," and "Relatives" are chapters not originally contained in the *I-li*. One wonders why Chu Hsi should have taken the materials in the *Li-chi,* supplemented them with previous annotations and commentaries, and put them in the *Exegesis* as original "classic texts." Furthermore, in the *Comprehensive Exegesis* the sequence of chapters of the original *I-li* was rearranged, with some alteration of passages.[41] Such liberal alterations of the original text and commentaries are a matter of controversy. It appears that the editors of the *Complete Collection of Books in the Four Libraries* disagree with such rearrangements.[42] The book, however, was not completed by Chu Hsi himself; parts were revised by Huang Kan and Yang Fu. Although the editorial style of the book is consistent, shortcomings are inevitable.

Application of Chu Hsi's discipline of propriety in real life is mainly illustrated in the *Family Etiquette.* Life changes, and and so do the codes of conduct and propriety. It is said in the "Record of Music" of the *Li-chi* that "Kings of the Three Dynasties did not copy the rituals of the preceeding dynasty because of differences in society."[43] And it has also been emphasized in the "Ceremonial Objects" chapter of the *Li-chi* that "in propriety, timeliness is most important."[44] The *K'ai-yüan li*[cw] (Etiquette prepared in the K'ai-yüan period, 713–755) was not entirely practicable in the Sung dynasty, not to mention the rules established in the Classical *I-li.* For this reason, Ssu-ma Kuang wrote the *Correspondence and Etiquette* and Chu Hsi the *Family Etiquette* for the requirements of their contemporaries. Of course, whether their contemporaries would accept such codes of conduct is a question and, understandably, there must have been differences of opinion. Nevertheless, the principles adopted by Chu Hsi in creating such a work appear to be correct and sound.

In the first place, in formulating a code of etiquette one must grasp the fundamentals of propriety. In the opening of the "Preface to the *Family Etiquette*" Chu Hsi stated that "All things of propriety have fundamentals and expressions. As for those applicable in the family, attention to name and obligation as well as manifestation of love and respect is the fundamental." In the conclusion he reiterated, "In general, attention to name and obligation as well as manifestation of love and respect is considered the fundamental."[45] A family is organized by a couple—a husband and a wife. A man in the name of husband must perform the obligations of a husband, while the wife should perform her obligations. Furthermore, a genuine and complete agreement of name and obligation can only be attained by love and respect. Mutual love and respect between the husband and the wife will ensure a happy marriage as well as a harmonious family. When the couple have children, they become parents. Between the parents and the children are also certain obligations to be fulfilled in the name of "father," "mother," "son," and "daughter." While the parents should have parental love toward their chidren, the sons and daughters must also be filial and respectful to their parents. In such a family, there is also the relationship between brothers and sisters, since they are the offspring of the same parents and are being raised in the same family. Elder brothers and sisters should love and take care of the younger while the younger ones ought to respect and love their elder siblings. Thus will a large family be rendered more harmonious and happy. In a larger sense, the parents of a family have their own parents, grandparents, and so on. In tracing one's origin, one should love and venerate one's ancestors, however remote. Thus, Chu Hsi believed that in establishing a code for family life in the form of *Family Etiquette,* the fundamental principle should be a genuine fulfillment of the obligations attached to names through conscientious manifestation of love and respect. This is in fact a heritage of traditional Chinese culture.

  Secondly, it is Chu Hsi's conviction that ethical relations should be manifested in detail in a code of conduct. He emphasized this belief in the "Preface to the *Family Etiquette*" and said, "Capping, wedding, sacrifices, protocol, . . . are manifestations. . . . Such manifestations are for outlining and governing the deed and acts of humaneness from the beginning to the end of human life. They are to be practiced on certain occasions and at certain places. Unless one has been explicitly told how to do them and one has frequently practiced them, one will not be able to carry them out correctly when suddenly confronted with such occasions. Therefore, they should be frequently discussed and practiced." Such discussions and practice should be part of family life. People grow up under the care and education of their parents. In the families of ancient China, when a person reached maturity, a capping ceremony was held for males and a ceremony of binding up the hair of a girl at fifteen was held for females. Such ceremonies were intended to tell sons and daughters that they had become adults who must have the posture and virtues proper to adults as well as a sense of responsibility toward their ancestors, families, and country. At a wedding, a solemn ceremony was held to tell the young couple that this was the beginning of a new life for them as well as the beginning of more new lives, and each partner must fulfill the obligations attached to the names of "husband" and "wife," and later on "father" and "mother," so that the marriage might be happy and long-lasting and that the family could accomplish the role of succession to ancestors and initiation of posterity. There are other social obligations as well. A man cannot isolate himself from family, society, and country all his life, so there must also be etiquette governing contacts with other people. This was dealt with in the "etiquette for mutual contacts" of ancient times, which ensured harmony in relationships between individuals. Likewise, there were, in ancient times, the "etiquette for drinking in the community" praising the virtuous and talented, the "etiquette for community archery competition" promoting physical training, the "etiquette for entertainment" expressing gratitude, and the "etiquette for exchange of visits" describing proper conduct in formal dealings. In the same vein, there was solemn funeral etiquette for the end of a person's life, which enabled the bereaved, relatives, and friends to express their sorrow. Such a ceremony required mourning attire, mourning behavior, and rites. These rites included those to be performed in the death chamber such as shrouding and dressing the deceased, and those performed elsewhere such as encoffining, burying, *yü*ᶜˣ (the rite performed at the tomb to lead the spirit of the deceased to the ancestral temple), and *fu*ᶜʸ (the rite performed in the ancestral temple to initiate the union of the newly deceased with the ancestors). The funeral ceremony as a whole was intended to turn mourning into a wish —wishing that the spirit of the deceased would be immortal. A solemn funeral according to the description of Tseng Shen included a "careful attention of one's parents to the end of lives," while the placing of the tablet of the deceased in the ancestral temple in company with the forefathers and making reasonable sacrifices to express everlasting gratitude were described as "memory of ancestry." He said, "With careful attention to the end of one's parents' lives and memory of one's ancestry, the virtue of the people will reach its proper excellence."[46] It is understandable that when people can use funeral ceremonies and sacrificial services to reflect their everlasting love and reverence to their deceased parents, they should be virtuous. Therefore, in his *Family Etiquette* Chu Hsi placed special emphasis on the parts dealing with capping, wedding, funeral, and sacrifice, and he formulated a code of conduct for all occasions from the time of initiation to the end of human life. When people are familiar with what is required on these occasions, they will have no difficulty in other respects of social behavior. What Chu Hsi did is of far reaching significance.

Third, a code of propriety must be practicable, with due reference to tradition and contemporary needs. In the "Preface to the *Family Etiquette*" Chu Hsi commented, "In the times of the three ancient dynasties, the codes of etiquette were complete. However, those extant today, such as specifications of buildings, wares, and clothing as well as the prescriptions of manners and behavior, are not suitable for contemporary society." Because of his conviction that the ancient rules of propriety were obsolete in the Sung dynasty, he came up with his own code of etiquette by "adopting those items that cannot be altered in principle and making minor deletions from and additions to them," with emphasis on "rejecting superfluous decorations and upholding the essential and practical."[47] Chu Hsi was by no means a pedant who stuck to conventions. Certain of the underlying justifications and principles of the ancient codes of propriety remained unalterable, however, because the human feelings of the ancients were not greatly different from those of his contemporaries. For this reason, in preparing the *Family Etiquette* Chu Hsi meticulously studied the codes in the *I-li* in order to fathom their underlying principles and reasons, with the aim of finding out what was unalterable and suitable for adoption in the Sung dynasty. As to those items unsuitable for contemporary society, he had to make deletions and additions as he saw fit. His concept of doing things as necessity demands is far wiser than the pedantic practice of taking the ancient without digesting it. Moreover, in view of what he saw as the prevailing condition of his time—that his contemporaries "either forget the fundamental while attending to superfluous details or neglect the essentials while being devoted to decorative protocol . . . and poor people are particularly worried that there will be no act of propriety on the occasion of their deaths"—he regarded "rejecting superfluous decorations and upholding the essential and practical" as a guideline for his code of propriety, hoping that people at all levels of society, both rich and poor, could adopt it for practice.[48] His intention is quite correct.

Chu Hsi's commentaries on the *Great Learning* and the *Doctrine of the Mean,* which were originally two separate chapters in the *Li-chi,* are his most prominent contribution to the study of *Li-chi.*[49] Since the official publication of his *Collected Commentaries on the Four Books* by the Imperial Institute of Higher Learning (*T'ai-hsüeh*[cz]) in 1211 during the Sung dynasty, these editions have been widely circulated.[50] In 1313 during the Yüan dynasty (1277–1368), Chu Hsi's *Collected Commentaries on the Four Books* was officially designated as the standard reference for official examinations, and the stipulation remained effective in both the Ming and Ch'ing dynasties.[51] It was not until 1905 in the late Ch'ing dynasty that the old examination system was abolished. Therefore, for 582 years all Chinese intellectuals studied the Four Books commented on by Chu Hsi. The commentaries have also been circulated in Japan, Korea, Vietnam, and other countries. In the modern cultural history of China and other Asian countries, no one can match the influence of Chu Hsi. The most mature and refined concepts and theories of Confucianism have been widely propagated through his commentaries on the *Great Learning* and the *Doctrine of the Mean.* This is his greatest contribution to our culture.

However, his incorrect division of paragraphs and sentences and his dubious changes of words and arbitrary annotations has had some adverse influence. This is something we cannot, and should not, defend. For instance, the original text of the *Great Learning* was, and is, complete and systematically organized, as is attested by the T'ang dynasty edition collected in the *K'ai-ch'eng shih-ching*[da] (Classics engraved on stone slabs in the reign of K'ai-ch'eng around 836) and the Sung dynasty block-printed edition of *Annotations of and Commentaries on the Li-chi,* which are practically identical.[52] Because both Ch'eng Hao and Ch'eng I came up with their own versions with the original contents rearranged, Chu Hsi followed with another version based on his own ideas. Because of the broad circulation of Chu Hsi's edition of the *Great Learning,* many students have read only this "standard version" without knowing that there is an original one; on the other hand, those who know that there is an original one have come up with their own rearranged versions, believing, under the influence of the Ch'eng brothers and Chu Hsi, that the original work contains disorganized passages. The result is a multitude of re-edited versions that have rendered the *Great Learning* into something unrecognizable. Such works done by better known scholars include those by Huang Chen[db] (1213–1280), Wang Po[dc] (1197–1274), Ch'eng Min-cheng[dd] (*fl.* 1445), Yang Shou-ch'eng,[de] Kao Kung,[df] Chi Pen,[dg] Liu Tsung-chou,[dh] Ku Hsien-ch'eng[di] (1550–1612), Hu Wei[dj] (1633–1714), Chang Po-hsing[dk] (1651–1725),

Chang Lü-hsiang[dl] (1611–1674), and many others.[53] This kind of scholarship has created confusion for readers while making researchers spend much energy and time on it and sometimes even leading them astray. Although the Ch'eng brothers started the trend, Chu Hsi must also be held responsible for it. The opening sentence of the original text of the *Great Learning* reads: "What the *Great Learning* teaches is manifesting the illustrious virtue, enabling the people to be intimate with each other, and resting in the highest excellence." Following the opinion of Ch'eng I, Chu Hsi commented that the word *ch'in*[dm] (to be intimate) should be changed to *hsin*[dn] (renovate), thus turning an act of humanity, "enabling the people to be intimate with each other," into a rather overbearing action to transform the people. While, according to the former, one may unite oneself with others as a whole without distinction between self and others, the latter builds a barrier between self and others by placing oneself above the group. "Enabling the people to be intimate with each other" is far more broad-minded and gentle-hearted than "renovating the people." One may wonder why Chu Hsi should have made such a change of wording in something which is regarded as the correct expression of the traditional Chinese mind.

As has been explicitly stated in the *Great Learning*, "investigation of things," "achievement of knowledge," "sincerity of the will," "rectification of the heart," "cultivation of oneself," "regulation of the family," "government of the state," and "making the whole world just and peaceful" are steps toward "manifesting the illustrious virtue," "enabling the people to be intimate with each other," and finally "resting in the highest excellence." To be specific, one's "resting in the highest excellence" by way of "manifesting the illustrious virtue" is claimed to make a man "inwardly a sage" while "resting in the highest excellence" through "enabling all the people to be intimate with each other" makes him "outwardly a king" who is able to govern in a kindly way by humaneness. As shown above, "investigation into things" and "achievement of knowledge" are the first steps to these lofty attainments. As has been clearly explained in the opening paragraph of the original version of the *Great Learning*, "achievement of knowledge" means achieving the knowledge of "knowing the root," the knowledge of "knowing what is first and what is last," and the knowledge of "knowing where to rest." The expression "root" refers to "cultivation of oneself" as stated in the passage "from the Son of Heaven down to the mass of the people, all must consider the cultivation of themselves the root (of everything besides)." This is the starting point of all endeavors. The expression "resting" means the ultimate "resting in the highest excellence" through "manifesting the illustrious virtue" and "enabling the people to be intimate with each other," which is the goal of all endeavors. The "root and branches" of things and the "end and beginning" of affairs, which are explicitly stated in the *Great Learning* in terms of "cultivation of oneself," "regulation of the family," "government of the state," and "making the whole world just and peaceful," define the order of "what is first and what is last." With a knowledge of the "root," the order of things, and where to rest, one may achieve "cultivation of oneself" through "sincerity of the will" and "rectification of the heart." The starting point of "achieving knowledge" is "investigation of things"—the "things" that have their roots and branches and the "affairs" that have their end and beginning or, to put it more specifically, the things and affairs of "cultivation of oneself," "regulation of the family," "government of the state," and "making the whole world just and peaceful" for "manifesting the illustrious virtue," "enabling the people to be intimate with each other," and "resting in the highest excellence."

The word "investigation" is a rough translation of the Chinese word *ke*,[do] which can also be defined as "to measure." This definition, originally contained in the *Ts'ang-chieh p'ien*[dp] (Lexicon of Ts'ang-chieh), has been quoted in Li Shan's[dq] notes to *"Yün-ming lun"*[xlr] (On fate and destiny) in the *Chao-ming wen-hsüan*[ds] (A selection of literary works compiled by Prince Chao-ming). This was also considered the original meaning that should be applied to the word *ke* in the *Great Learning* by the prominent Ch'ing scholars Hui Tung[dt] (1697–1758) and Mao Ch'i-ling[du] (1623–1716).[54] The meaning of "measuring" in this context is quite similar to the modern terms "study" or "research." Hence, as explained in the *Great Learning*, the study of, or research into, the "things and affairs" mentioned above will lead to "achievement of knowledge." It appears that Chu Hsi did not seek for the right meaning of "investigation of things" and "achievement of knowledge" in the original text. Instead, he concluded that there was a passage missing in the text, and so he filled in the gap with his "amended" commentary on "investigation of things" and "achievement of knowledge." It is not surprising that many later scholars have criticized his subjective and arbitrary approach.[55] Chu Hsi's explanation of "investigation of things" reads, " 'Investigation' means 'coming to,' and 'things' is similar to 'affairs.' 'Investigation of things' means exhaustively coming to the principles of things and affairs, with the desire that the utmost point may be reached."[56] It is clear that he added "exhaustively" before "coming to" and "principles" to "things and affairs." Thus the passage "achievement of knowledge lies in the investigation of things" is interpreted by Chu Hsi as "achievement of knowledge lies in exhausting the principles." He comes to this interpretation by leaving out the words "coming to" and "things and affairs." This is making commentaries by grafting on words and cannot be considered a serious attempt to seek out the truth. In his explanation of "achievement of knowledge," he comments, " 'Achieving' means 'extending to the utmost'; 'knowledge' is similar to 'recognition.' The term means extending my knowledge and recognition to the utmost, with the desire that there may be nothing which it shall not embrace."[57] Thus, the "explanation" he prepared to supplement the supposedly missing ancient passage reads

The meaning of the expression, "extension of knowledge lies in the investigation of things," is this: if we wish to extend our knowledge to the utmost, we must investigate the principles of all the things we come into contact with, for the intelligent mind of man is certainly formed to know, and there is not a single thing in which its principles do not inhere. But so long as all principles are not investigated, man's knowledge is incomplete. On this account, the *Great Learning*, at the outset of its lessons, instructs the learner, in regard to all things in the world, to proceed from what knowledge he has of their principles, and pursue his investigation of them, till he reaches the extreme point. After exerting himself in this way over a long time, he will suddenly find himself possessed of a wide and far-reaching penetration. Then, the qualities of all things, whether external or internal, subtle or coarse, will all be apprehended, and the mind, in its entire substance and its relations to things, will be perfectly intelligent. This is called the investigation of things. This is called the extension of knowledge.[58]

As can be seen from the above, it is clear that Chu Hsi interprets "investigation of things" and "achievement of knowledge" as something entirely related to the knowledge of man's intelligent mind. This concept, of course, is Chu Hsi's unique and valuable contribution of epistemology—or rather Ch'eng I's contribution, as Chu pointed out in his commentary. Although the concept can provide a philosophical foundation for various kinds of scientific research and study, it appears rather out of context in the *Great Learning*, which is mainly devoted to moral philosophy for the purpose of elucidating the spirit and value of morality.

The *Commentary on the Doctrine of the Mean* is another of Chu Hsi's important works. Explaining its central significance, Chu Hsi has commented after the opening chapter of the book:

First, it shows clearly how the Way is to be traced to its origin in Heaven, and is unchangeable, while the substance of it is provided in ourselves, and may not be departed from. Next, it speaks of the importance of preserving and nourishing this, and of exercising a watchful self-scrutiny with reference to it. Finally, it speaks of the meritorious achievements and transforming influence of sage and spiritual man in their highest extent. The intention of Tzu-ssu[dv] [*fl.* 483 B.C.][59] was that hereby the learner should direct his thoughts inward and by searching in himself, there find these truths, so that he might put aside all outward temptations appealing to his selfishness, and fill up the measure of the goodness which is natural to him.[60]

Again, his comprehension of the subject has the merit of originality. However, it seems that he has left out the important point that the goal of man's efforts to understand and follow the Way is "attainment of equilibrium and harmony." Only through the process of "attainment of equilibrium and harmony" could man come to know the "importance of preserving and nourishing" the path as well as the "transforming influence of sage and spiritual man." A failure to emphasize the key phrase "attainment of equilibrium and harmony" in the opening chapter, which Chu Hsi calls "the sum of the whole work," certainly deprives the following chapters of their central theme while dimming the meaning of the Mean.

Moreover, Chu Hsi's division of the *Doctrine of the Mean* into thirty-three chapters seems fragmented, indicating that he might have failed to grasp the guiding principle and the sequence of ideas of the *Doctrine of the Mean* in its original form. In fact, the chapters designated by him as two through twelve are expositions of the theory of the *Doctrine of the Mean*. To be specific, the discrimination between superior man and petty man is one of the functions that the doctrine emphasizes. Being "without deviation and inclination" as well as "not going beyond or falling short of it" are definitions of the Mean. Legendary sage Emperor Shun's[dw][61] great wisdom, Yen Hui's[dx][62] humanity, and Tzu-lu's[dy][63] bravery are examples given to demonstrate the qualities desirable in the ideal man. The superior man's advance or retreat in the society is used to show that the doctrine of the Mean "in its greatness, nothing in the world would be found able to embrace it" while "in its minuteness, nothing in the world would be found able to split it." This throws light upon the essence and operation of the doctrine of the Mean. According to Chu Hsi's division, the contents from chapter 13 to the sentence "If principles of conduct have been previously determined, the practice of them will be inexhaustible" describe the concrete practice of the doctrine of the Mean. This section, for example, says that honesty and tolerance (*chung-shu*[dz]), agreement of one's words and deeds, doing things proper to one's position, and "being oneself in all situations" are the proper ways for the cultivation of oneself. Harmony between husband and wife, fraternity among brothers, and filial affection towards parents and ancestors are the requirements of "regulation of the family," and examples are given of Emperor Shun's great filial piety and the far-extending influence of the filial dedication of King Wen[ea][64] (r. 1171–1122 B.C.) and Duke Chou[eb] (d. 1094 B.C.).[65] To illustrate the ideal way to govern the states, Confucius' reply to Duke Ai[ec] of the State of Lu[ed] is quoted: "Government of the state lies in getting the right men. Such men are to be got by means of the ruler's character. That character is to be cultivated by his treading in the Way. And the treading the Way is to be cultivated by the cherishing of benevolence." Then there are discussions of righteousness and propriety, which are equally important to the cultivation of oneself. For further detailed elucidation, this section emphasizes that a "knowledge of men" and "knowledge of Heaven" are necessary both for cultivation of oneself and for government of the people. It further defines "knowledge of men" as knowledge of the "five universal obligations" (those between sovereign and minister, between father and son, between husband and wife, between elder and younger brother, and those among friends) and of the "three universal virtues" (wisdom, benevolence, and bravery). No matter whether a man is considered "born with the knowledge," one who "acquired the knowledge by learning," or one who "acquired the knowledge after a painful feeling of his ignorance," he must be "fond of learning," eager to "practice with vigor," and possess the "feeling of shame," so that he can successfully cultivate himself and then govern the people. It is also stressed that there are "nine standard rules" for making the whole world just and peaceful, namely, cultivation of oneself, honoring men of virtue and talents, affection to relatives, respect toward great ministers, considerate treatment of all officers, treating the people like one's own children, attracting all classes of artisans, kind treatment of men from a distance, and cherishing of the princes of various states.

From the words "when those in inferior situations do not obtain the confidence of the sovereign" in chapter 20 to chapter 24 of Chu Hsi's version, the main point is to show that "sincerity" is the "moving force of the doctrine of the Mean." First comes an explanation that "sincerity" is the "moving force of the Mean." It starts by emphasizing that "understanding what is good" and "attainment of sincerity in oneself" are the bases of cultivating oneself and governing others. Then, it divides sincerity into two kinds—one is endowed by nature while the other cultivated by man. On the one hand, to bring into full play the sincerity endowed in man by nature is called "development of nature." From full development of one's own nature, man is enabled to develop the nature of others as well as to develop the natures of creatures and things. On the other hand, "cultivating to the utmost the shoots of goodness in oneself" is the way to exert the sincerity derived from human efforts. Starting from a comparatively narrow sphere and becoming all encompassing, sincerity will become "apparent," "manifest," and "brilliant." It will then "affect," "change," and "transform" all creatures and things. Such a development can only be materialized through "choosing what is good and firmly holding it," "extensive study," "careful reflection," "clear discrimination," and "earnest practice." In the final account, both these kinds of sincerity in their complete state can reach the "equilibrium" and "mean" that ensures full development of oneself and all creatures and things, making man "rank as one with Heaven and Earth."

Chapters 27 to 29, according to Chu Hsi's division, are devoted to "approaches to the Mean." It is necessary for man to "honor his virtuous nature, and maintain constant inquiry and study, seeking to carry it out to its breadth and greatness, so as to omit none of the more exquisite and minute points it embraces, and to raise it to its greatest height and brilliancy, so as to pursue the course of the Mean. He cherishes his old knowledge, and is continually acquiring new. He exerts an honest, generous earnestness in the esteem and practice of all propriety." This the only way to reach the "way of the sage." Moreover, one must have both the necessary "position" and "virtue" for innovating the changes in institutions that can be made by sages. To avoid the possibility that excellently conceived institutions will not be credited by the people, one must make sure that "the institutions are rooted in his own character and conduct, and sufficient attestation of them is given by the masses of the people. He examines them by comparison with those of the three kings,[66] and finds them without mistake. He sets them up before Heaven and Earth, and finds nothing in them contrary to their mood of operation. He presents himself with them before spiritual beings, and no doubts about them arise. He is prepared to wait for the rise of a sage a hundred ages after, and has no misgivings." From chapter 30 on, according to Chu Hsi's division, there are illustrations of the "models of the Mean" with a conclusion praising the greatness of Confucius.

From all the above, it is evident that the general outline of the original version of the *Doctrine of the Mean* is quite clear and easy to grasp. One may wonder why Chu Hsi should have divided it into so many fragments. The most dubious division can be seen in chapters 9 and 12, which are arbitrarily separated at the sentence that reads, "When right principles are opposed and disallowed, the superior man retires into obscurity"[67] (*Chün tzu chih tao fei-erh-yin*[ee]). Chu Hsi claims that the passages before this sentence, including what he calls chapter 11 and those before it, are the words of Confucius being quoted by Tzu-ssu "to complete the meaning of the first chapter." He also maintains that chapter 13, beginning from the above cited sentence to the subordinate clause "it shines brightly through Heaven and Earth," contains the "sayings of Tzu-ssu himself"; this is followed by eight chapters that "complete the meaning of chapter 12 by expositions covering both the 'wide' and the 'secret' as well as the 'great' and the 'minute'."

As can be seen from the different translations cited above, the main question lies in the interpretation of the sentence that the Way of the superior man is "*fei* and *yin*," especially the words "*fei*" and "*yin*." According to Chu Hsi *fei* indicates the wide range of the Way in its application, *yin* indicates the minuteness of the Way in its essence. Such an interpretation indicates that he considers *fei* and *yin* antitheses manifested in the opposites of "essence" and "application" or "function" as well as in "width" and "minuteness." This interpretation seems strained. In the *Ching-tien shih-wen*[ef] (Glossary to Classics) by Lu Te-ming[eg] (556–627) of the T'ang dynasty, it is pointed out that *fei* is printed in another edition as *fu*.[eh] Thus, *fei* is a homonym for *fu* meaning to oppose, to disallow, to frustrate, in their active and passive voices.[68] Thus, the sentence should be interpreted as "When the right principles are opposed and disallowed, the superior man retires into obscurity." Moreover, this interpretation will serve better as a conclusion to the statement immediately preceding it which reads, "The superior man accords with the course of the Mean. Though he may be all unknown, unregarded by the world, he feels no regret." The original meaning of *fei* is expending money and things for similar application as shown in the *Shuo-wen chieh-tzu*[ei] (Explanations and analyses of characters).[69] Chu Hsi strained the original meaning of the word to suit his purpose by regarding "application" as application of the Way. Since ancient times, only heavy spending of money and similar things has been called *fei*, not "wide range of application." It is obvious that Chu Hsi's interpretation is less appropriate than the old one. According to the old interpretation, the passage means: a superior man follows the course of the Mean; he accepts official appointments when employed and retires to obscurity when the right principles are disallowed, always conducting himself in accordance with the Way.

This is the truth of the Mean that can be understood and practiced by common men and women who are ignorant and of low caliber. However, in the utmost reaches of the truth of the Mean, even the sage does not know and is unable to practice it. The entire discourse is a coherent whole that includes the contents of Chu Hsi's chapters 11 and 12. One may wonder why he split it in the middle, claiming that the eight following chapters are expositions covering the meanings of "the wide and the secret" as well as "the great and the minute." For this Chu Hsi can be criticized forgiving strained interpretations and drawing farfetched analogies. There are other similarly questionable points in his version of the *Doctrine of the Mean*. For instance, he has interpreted the word *yung* in *chung-yung*[ei] as commonplace or ordinary. He has designated the sentence that reads "The Master said, 'How is the path of the Mean untrodden!' " as an independent chapter. He has changed the word *su*[ek] (being inclined to) in a sentence to *so*[el] (to examine or to study), which alters the original meaning. And he has combined all the passages about "Duke Ai asking about government" with those discussing "a way to the attainment of sincerity in oneself" into a single chapter.[70]

In conclusion, it can be said with all fairness that Chu Hsi made great contributions to promoting and directing the study of both the *Great Learning* and the *Doctrine of the Mean*. His rearranged versions of these works, although imperfect, have had profound and far-reaching influence over the culture and ideology of China and other Asian countries since the Sung dynasty. As an overall assessment it seems appropriate to regard Chu Hsi's versions of these two significant classics as great accomplishments with small flaws.

Translated by Chou Hsing-chih[em]

Notes

1. *Wen-kuo Wen-cheng Ssu-ma Kung wen-chi*[en] [Collection of literary works of Ssu-ma Kuang], (SPTK ed.), ch. 23, vol. 181, pp. 221–226.

2. *Chu Tzu wen-chi* (SPTK ed.), ch. 14, vol. 227, pp. 212–213.

3. *Ibid.*, ch. 67 and 68, vol. 232, pp. 1237–1238 and 1249–1250.

4. *Ibid.*, ch. 20, vol. 227, pp. 317–319.

5. *Ibid.*, ch. 83, vol. 233, pp. 1502–1503. The three scholars were Ch'eng I, Chang Tsai, and Ssu-ma Kuang. The work is by Chang Shih.

6. Yen Yen was Tzu-yu[eo] (b. 508 B.C.). Pu Shang was Tzu-hsia[ep] (509–420 B.C.?). In *Analects*, 11:2, they are praised as expert in literature. Tseng Shen was Tseng-Tzu[eq] (c. 505–436 B.C.), model of filial piety. Tzu-ssu was grandson of Confucius.

7. *Book of Rites*, ch. 28, sec. 4; and ch. 10, sec. 4, respectively.

8. "Contents" (the portion covering the years from 1217 to 1231), Nan-k'ang Edition of the Sung dynasty which was repaired in early Ming dynasty by the *T'ai-hsüeh*, now in the archives of the National Central Library, Taipei.

9. *Ssu-k'u-ch'üan-shu tsung-mu t'i-yao* (Taipei: I-wen[er] Press, 1933), vol. 2, pp. 466–

467; *Ssu-k'u ch'üan-shu tsung-mu t'i-yao pu-cheng*[es] [The *Ssu-k'u ch'üan-shu tsung-mu t'i-yao* supplemented and corrected], (Taipei: Chung-hua[et] Book Co.), pp. 142–144.

10. *Mein-chai chi*[eu] [Collected works of Huang Kan], (Four Libraries Precious Works ed.), 36:47a.

11. *Chu Tzu wen-chi*, ch. 75, vol. 232, p. 1388.

12. The original edition of *Chu Tzu nien-p'u* in three chapters, compiled by Chu Hsi's disciple Li Fang-tzu[ev] (*fl.* 1214) became extinct. The one re-edited by Li Mo[ew] (in 1552) has been criticized by some for errors and omissions, for Li Mo was a follower of Wang Yang-ming[ex] (1472–1529). Hung Ch'ü-wu[ey] published another edition with further revisions in 1700. The *Chronicle Biography* mentioned here refers to the Li-Hung edition, which records under the 6th year of the *Ch'ien-tao*[ez] reign (1170) that "The *Family Etiquette* was completed when Chu Hsi was forty-one." In the *Family Etiquette* Li Fang-tzu's words are quoted as saying that in the 9th month of the 5th year of the *Ch'ien-tao* reign (1169) Chu Hsi was in mourning for his mother and authored the *Family Etiquette*. However, in the edition by Wang Mao-hung these words of Li Fang-tzu are omitted. Because Li Fang-tzu was a direct student of Chu Hsi, this author considers his words trustworthy. Wang's omission is not entirely justifiable.

13. The same opinion is also stated in Wang Mao-hung's *Chu Tzu nien-p'u k'ao-i*[fa] [An investigation for discrepancies in the *Chronicle Biography of Master Chu*], ch. 1. The statement can be seen in the *Chu Tzu nien-p'u* (Taipei: World Book Co., 3rd ed., 1973), pp. 263–268.

14. *Chu Tzu wen-chi*, ch. 75, vol. 232, p. 1388.

15. The 120 treatises cited in the Chinese version of this paper are omitted in the present English translation.

16. The *Chu Tzu yü-lei* published in Taiwan by the Cheng-chung[fb] Book Co. in 1970 appears to be a very desirable edition. It has an index of personal names, geographical names, and book titles compiled by scholars at Kyushu[fc] University in Japan.

17. The 1725 edition and the handwritten edition of the *Complete Collection of the Four Libraries* are stored in Wen-yüan[fd] Pavillion. Both of them are now in the archives of the National Palace Museum, Taipei.

18. There are the *Jung-ts'un ch'üan-shu*[fe] [Complete works of Li Kuang-ti] edition and the handwritten edition of the *Complete Collection of the Four Libraries*. Both are in the archives of the National Palace Museum, Taipei.

19. *Chu Tzu wen-chi*, ch. 50, vol. 230, p. 871.

20. *Ibid.*, ch. 83, vol. 233, pp. 1503–1504.

21. Both in ch. 67, vol. 232, pp. 1237–1240.

22. *Ibid.*, ch. 42, vol. 229, p. 707.

23. *Ibid.*, ch. 49, vol. 230, p. 847.

24. *Ssu-k'u ch'üan-shu tsung-mu t'i-yao*, vol. 2, p. 527.

25. *Ibid.*, pp. 527–528.

26. *Ibid.*, p. 529.

27. *Ibid.*, p. 532.

28. *Chu Tzu yü-lei*, ch. 57, p. 2135.

29. *Ibid.*, ch. 129, p. 4954.

30. *Chu Tzu wen-chi*, ch. 31, vol. 228, p. 490.

31. *Ibid.*, ch. 63, vol. 231, p. 1170.

32. *Ibid.*, ch. 38, vol. 229, p. 630.

33. Handwritten copy by Ch'en Yi-chen[ff] [Ch'ing dynasty] in the archives of the National Central Library, Taipei; edition in the *Complete Collection of the Four Libraries* in the archives of the National Palace Museum, Taipei.

34. In the *Ch'ing ching-chieh*[fg] [Explanation of classes in the Ch'ing dynasty] compiled by Juan Yüan[fh] (1764–1849).

35. *Complete Collection of the Four Libraries*, National Palace Museum, Taipei.

36. *Ibid.*

37. *Wei-ching-wo*[fi] [Den of enjoying the flavor of the classes] edition published in 1763.

38. Three examples in the Chinese version are omitted here.

39. *Chu Tzu wen-chi*, ch. 59, vol. 231, p. 1081.

40. Three examples in the Chinese version are omitted here.

41. Three examples in the Chinese version are omitted here.

42. *Summary of Contents of the Complete Collection of the Four Libraries*, vol. 22, p. 466.

43. *Book of Rites*, ch. 19, sec. 5.

44. *Ibid.*, ch. 10, sec. 4.

45. *Chu Tzu wen-chi*, ch. 75, vol. 232, p. 1388.

46. *Analects*, 1:9.

47. Preface to the *Family Etiquette*.

48. *Ibid.*

49. The two commentaries are the *Ta-hsüeh chang-chü* and the *Chung-yung chang-chü*, literally the paragraphs and sentences of the two treatises rearranged.

50. See Chang Huang[fj] (1527–1608), *T'u-shu-pien*[fk] [Catalogue of books]; the edition published by T'u Ching-yüan[fl] of the Ming dynasty is in the archives of the National Central Library, Taipei.

51. *"Hsüan-chü lüeh,"*[fm] *Hsü t'ung-chih*[fn] ["Selection and examination, II," a sequel to the *Encyclopedia of Records*], (Taipei: Hsing-hsing[fo] Book Co., 1959), vol. 3, p. 4107.

52. See my *Kao-ming wen-chi*[fp] [Selected works of Kao Ming], (Taipei: Li-ming[fq] Cultural Enterprise Co., 1978), vol. 1, pp. 230–241.

53. *Ibid.*, for accounts of many others.

54. Hui Tung, *Chiu-ching ku-i*[fr] [Original denotations of the nine Classics]; Mao Ch'i-ling, *Ssu-shu sheng-yen*[fs] [Humble opinions of the Four Books].

55. For detailed discussion, see the *Kao Ming wen-chi*, vol. 1, pp. 242–250.

56. For the Chinese original, see the *Ssu-shu chi-chu* (Taipei: I-wen Press), vol. 1, p. 2.

57. *Ibid.*

58. James Legge's translation with minor modifications.

59. The *Doctrine of the Mean* has traditionally been ascribed to Tzu-ssu, grandson of Confucius.

60. James Legge's translation with minor modifications.

61. Legendary sage-emperor, symbol of filial piety.

62. Confucius' most virtuous pupil who died at the young age of thirty-two.

63. His family name was Chung and private name Yu.[ft] A Confucian pupil, he was only nine years younger than the Master.

64. Founder of the Chou dynasty, he was a model sage-king in the Confucian tradition.

65. He was King Wen's son and instituted social and governmental institutions for the Chou dynasty.

66. King Yü,[fu] founder of the Hsia dynasty; King T'ang,[fv] the founder of the Shang dynasty; and Kings Wen and Wu, founders of the Chou dynasty.

67. This is a liberal translation according to my interpretation of James Legge's translation, following Chu Hsi's interpretation, which reads, "The Way which the superior man pursues, reaches far and wide, and yet is secret."

68. *Ching-tien shih-wen* (SPTK ed.), vol. 13, p. 204.

69. *Shuo-wen chieh-tzu* (Taipei: I-wen Press, 1964), p. 284.

70. A detailed discussion of this is found in my *"Chung-yung pien"*[fw] [An investigation into the *Doctrine of the Mean*].

Glossary

a 周禮	ah 論語集註	bo 邱濬
b 周官	ai 孟子集註	bp 家禮考誤
c 鄭玄	aj 四書集註	bq 朱子語類
d 周禮註	ak 仲尼燕居	br 程川
e 賈公彥	al 樂記	bs 朱子五經語類
f 周禮疏	am 學記	bt 李光地
g 杜佑	an 張橫渠載	bu 朱子禮纂
h 通典	ao 儀禮集傳集註	bv 潘恭叔
i 司馬光	ap 南康	bw 書程子禘說後
j 論財利疏	aq 黃榦	bx 樂記動靜說
k 王安石	ar 張宓	by 吳晦叔
l 周官新義	as 楊復	bz 王子合
m 乞修三禮劄子	at 汲古閣珍藏秘本書目	ca 梁萬方
n 周禮三德疏	au 毛宸	cb 重刊朱子儀禮經傳通解
o 周禮太祝九拜辨	av 孝慈堂書目	cc 家禮儀節
p 禮記	aw 王閻遠	cd 楊慎
q 儀禮	ax 鄧鍾岳	ce 王復禮
r 乞頌降禮書狀	ay 四庫全書總目提要	cf 家禮辨定
s 乞增修禮書狀	az 紀昀	cg 蘇軾
t 張栻	ba 胡玉縉	ch 蘇轍
u 三家禮範	bb 鐵琴銅劍樓書目	ci 張敬夫栻
v 書儀	bc 瞿鏞	cj 余正甫
w 家禮	bd 東湖叢記	ck 李季章
x 儀禮經傳通釋	be 蔣光煦	cl 張爾岐
y 言偃	bf 纂圖集註文公家禮	cm 儀禮鄭註句讀
z 卜商	bg 劉垓孫	cn 吳建華
aa 曾參	bh 朱子年譜	co 儀禮章句
ab 子思	bi 王懋竑	cp 禮書綱目
ac 荀子	bj 家禮考	cq 江永
ad 程顥	bk 白田雜著	cr 徐乾學
ae 程頤	bl 家禮後考	cs 讀禮通考
af 大學章句	bm 家禮辨	ct 秦蕙田
ag 中庸章句	bn 應	

cu 五禮通考
cv 陳才卿
cw 開元禮
cx 虞
cy 祔
cz 太學
da 開成石經
db 黃震
dc 王柏
dd 程敏政
de 楊守城
df 高拱
dg 季本
dh 劉宗周
di 顧憲成
dj 胡渭
dk 張伯行
dl 張履祥
dm 親
dn 新
do 格
dp 蒼頡篇
dq 李善
dr 運命論
ds 昭明文選
dt 惠棟
du 毛奇齡
dv 子思

dw 舜
dx 顏回
dy 子路
dz 忠恕
ea 文
eb 周
ec 哀魯
ed 魯
ee 君子之道費而隱
ef 經典釋文
eg 陸德明
eh 拂
ei 說文解字
ej 中庸
ek 素
el 索
em 周行之
en 溫國文正司馬公文集
eo 子游
ep 子夏
eq 曾子
er 藝文
es 四庫全書總目提要補正
et 中華
eu 勉齋集
ev 李方子

ew 李默
ex 王陽明
ey 洪去蕪
ez 乾道
fa 朱子年譜考異
fb 正中
fc 九州
fd 文淵
fe 榕村全書
ff 陳沂震
fg 清經解
fh 阮元
fi 味經窩
fj 章潢
fk 圖書篇
fl 涂鏡源
fm 選舉略
fn 續通志
fo 新興
fp 高明文輯
fq 黎明
fr 九經古義
fs 四書賸言
ft 仲由
fu 禹
fv 湯
fw 中庸辨

20

Chu Hsi as Literary Theorist and Critic

RICHARD JOHN LYNN

Chu Hsi's Theory of Prose

PERHAPS THE ONE most important assertion that Chu Hsi makes about prose is that it should "carry the Way" (*wen i tsai-tao*[a]).

> The way prose *(wen)* carries the Way is just like the way a carriage carries things. Therefore, just as one who makes a carriage is sure to decorate the wheels and shafts, so one who writes prose must be sure to make his mode of discourse (*tz'u-shuo*[b]) attractive, for both wish that people will love and make use of these things. However, if I decorate them and people do not make use of them, then the decoration will be done in vain and will be of no value to the reality of the matter (*shih*[c]). How much the more this is true when it involves a carriage that does not carry anything or prose that does not carry the Tao.[d] No matter how much one might make the decoration beautiful, what good will it be?[1]

This passage is actually a comment on what is perhaps the most famous formulation of the moralistic conception of literature in the Chinese tradition, that by Chou Tun-i[e] (1017–1073).

> Literature is that by which one carries the Way. If the wheels and shafts [of a carriage] are decorated but no one uses it, then the decorations are in vain. How much more so in the case of an empty carriage! Literature and rhetoric are skills; the Way and virtue are realities. When someone devoted to these realities and skilled [in writing] writes down [the Way], if it is beautiful, then [people] will love it, then it will be passed on.[2]

Although Chou and Chu clearly insist that prose should have a straightforward, pragmatic or didactic function, they do not disparage the aesthetic aspects of writing but regard them merely as subsidiary to the pragmatic/didactic function. In this they differ sharply from Ch'eng I[f] (1033–1107) and Ch'eng Hao[g] (1032–1085), who regarded all *wen* (literature as a fine art) as detrimental to the Way.[3] However, Chu was also very careful to insist that good writing is always the result of the author's being thoroughly conversant with and committed to the Way; it is from the Way that fine writing emerges and not, as Su Shih[h] (1036–1101) would have it, the other way around.

> This *wen* is always something that flows out of the Tao, for how might it ever happen that *wen* could actually connect the principles of the Way (*kuan-tao chih li*[i])! *Wen* is *wen* and the Way is the Way. Is not *wen* just like something which helps the rice down when one is eating rice! If one thinks that *wen* connects up the Way, this is but to take the end of it as the beginning and the beginning as the end. How is this possible?[4]

Kuo Shao-yu[j] has analyzed in some detail the formula *wen i kuan-tao*[k] (writing is a means to connect up the Way), which is attributed to Su,[5] so I shall not do more than refer to it in passing. The "rice," of course, is the substance of the meal and the vegetables and meat embellishments that give flavor to the rice as *wen* gives flavor to the Way. This metaphor is consistent with the above carriage-Way metaphor, as well as with the following, which involves the various parts of a tree:

> The Way is the roots and the trunk of *wen*, and *wen* is the branches and leaves of the Way. Let it have its root and trunk in the Way, and whatever is expressed in *wen* will always be the Way.[6]

This last passage is of particular importance because in it Chu immediately goes on to state explicitly how he thinks his view of the relationship of *wen* to the Way differs from that of Su Shih.

> Writings of the worthies and sages of the Three Dynasties all were done from this state of mind, so *wen* was nothing but the Way. In modern times, Tung-p'o[l] [Su Shih] has said: "What I call *wen* must go along together with the Way (*wen pi yü tao chü*[m])."[7] This means that for him *wen* is something that comes from *wen*, and *tao* is something that comes from *tao*, so when one is going to do writing, he immediately has to go out and get a *tao* to put into it! Herein lies his great failing. It is just that his writing is usually so beautiful and marvelous (*hua-miao*[n]) that it keeps this under wraps, but with this he has unwittingly divulged the real nature of his basic fault. According to him, it is always a matter of starting with *wen* and then gradually bringing the principles of the Way into it; it is not a matter of first understanding the principles of the Way and only then starting to write. Thus absolutely everything he writes is deficient.[8]

Kuo Shao-yü has pointed out, in regard to this, that Su Shih insisted that "the Way can be attained to but cannot be sought"[9] and suggests that by this Su meant that experience—action—is the only means to reach the Way; it is the individual and subjective experience of *doing* something—Su's example which Kuo cites here concerns the boys of the South who grow up with water and so are thoroughly adept at swimming by the age of fifteen—that attains to the Way of that something, and, since Su's Way, heavily influenced by Taoism, is a far more naturalistic Way than that of Chu Hsi, it seems to have embraced all things equally, in the sense that all the different *tao* are mutually transmutable, or at least interconnected, so that the practice and realization of one will lead to the realization of others and ultimately to the great Tao which underlies everything. This is why "*wen* and the Way must go along together" and "*wen* can connect up the Way." Chu said that *wen* is a means to carry *(tsai)* the Way, and Su said that *wen* is a means to connect up *(kuan)* the Way. The fundamental difference here is not only due to different conceptions of what constitutes the Way—the object of attainment—but also a difference in the nature of the attaining process itself. Chu insists that the Way has been objectively formulated by the worthies and sages of the Three Dynasties; these formulations were preserved in the Classics (*ching*[o]), illustrated in the histories (*shih*[p]) and explained by learned commentators and thinkers (*tzu*[q]) such as himself. Thus, he believed that the Way could be abstracted from reality and objectively learned, and once learned, it could be taught to others in the same way —by using writing *(wen)* as a means to convey it to them.

Su's approach is entirely different. For him, the Way comes to one indirectly and subjectively through experience and action; any attempt to learn it consciously and deliberately from books, or even by listening to or observing others, is a waste of time and will end in failure. As far as books are concerned, Su also places great importance on them, but he does so for reasons different from those of Chu. Just as one can attain to the Way through the subjective and individual act of writing, so can one attain to it through subjective immersion in books, through a wide-ranging and disinterested exploration which leads to enlightenment. The Way for Su was a diffuse, elusive thing which did not at all lend itself to objective formulation. Chu thought Su's *kuan-tao shuo*[r] (doctrine of connecting up the Way) was harmful nonsense; if Su had lived to see Chu's *tsai-tao shuo*[s] (doctrine of carrying the Way), he would have found it equally harmful and nonsensical; the fundamental differences in their respective basic assumptions make this inevitable. In the words of Archilochus of Paros (eighth or seventh century B.C.), Su Shih was a fox, and Chu Hsi was a hedgehog: "The fox knows many things, but the hedgehog knows one big thing." Isaiah Berlin interprets this enigmatic statement this way:

> [T]here exists a great chasm between those . . . who relate everything to a single central vision, one system less or more coherent or articulate . . . —a single, universal, organizing principle in terms of which alone all that they are and say has significance—and . . . those who pursue many ends, often unrelated and even contradictory, connected, if at all, only in some *de facto* way . . . related by no moral or aesthetic principle; these last lead lives, perform acts, and entertain ideas that are centrifugal rather than centripetal, their thought is scattered or dif-

fuse, moving on many levels, seizing upon the essense of a wide variety of experiences and objects for what they are in themselves without . . . seeking to fit them into, or exclude them from, any one unchanging, all-embracing, sometimes self-contradictory and incomplete, at times fanatical, unitary inner vision. The first kind . . . belongs to the hedgehogs, the second to the foxes.[10]

Chu Hsi also had a great deal to say about another aspect of prose writing closely related to the concept of "carrying the Way"—prose should "communicate ideas" (*ta-i*[t]) and not indulge in "verbal ornament" (*tz'u-hua*[u])—and in this he seems to have been largely in agreement with Su Shih. Su's most famous statement concerning this is probably the following:

> Confucius said, "If words do not have *wen* (patterns/embellishments), they will not go far."[11] He also said, "Words communicate; that is all."[12] Now, if words should only communicate, we may suspect that they are not *wen* (embellished/literary). It is not so at all. To seek the subtleties (or wonders, *miao*[v]) of things is like trying to tie up the wind or capture shadows; we can hardly find one man out of thousands who can make things appear clearly in the mind, let alone making them appear clearly from the mouth and the hand [that is, in speech and writing]. This is what is meant by "words communicate." If words can reach such a state of communicativeness, there will be more than sufficient *wen* (embellishments/literature).[13]

Therefore, for Su the very act of successful communication itself results in verbal beauty; this beauty does not exist apart from its integral role in communication. A number of passages in Chu's writings argue along much the same lines. In the following one he discusses the role of *i*[w] (meaning/intention) in writing and how the great writers of antiquity "wrote as they spoke" and thus avoided all contrivance.

> Someone once asked me about the expressions used in the "*Li-sao*[x]" (On encountering sorrow) and the "*Pu-chü*[y]" (Divination) piece [in the *Ch'u-tz'u*[z] (Songs of the South of Ch'u)], and I said, "From the beginning the sense of these expressions was beyond my comprehension, but once I approached them through the intentions involved I could see what they meant." For example, ". . . be accommodating and slippery, to be as compliant as lard or leather"[14] has the sense of compliantly meeting someone's each and every wish. Expressions such as this are absolutely free of the least impediment. I believe that it is only when someone says such and such on the spur of the moment will it always spontaneously result in good writing. Lin Ai-hsüan [Lin Kuang-ch'ao,[aa] 1114–1178] once said, "Beginning with Pan Ku[ab] [32–92] and Yang Hsiung[ac] [53 B.C.–A.D. 18] writers all contrived their language. Earlier writers such as Ssu-ma Ch'ien[ad] [145?–86? B.C.] and Ssu-ma Hsiang-ju[ae] [179–117 B.C.] only said such and such on the spur of the moment."[15] Now, my own experience has led me to believe that this is so. The ancients were selected for office on the basis of how they could "climb up high and compose on the spot."[16] This surely means both that they had quick-

ness of mind and that they could speak in a freely expressive manner. Some of the ancients regarded public declarations and what one says to be actually the same thing. Writers of later ages just contrived things on paper, and, since it was a matter then of contriving things on paper, Pan and Yang consequently could not manage to be up to the language of earlier times when people such as Su Ch'in[af] [d. 317 B.C.] and Chang I[ag] [d. 309 B.C.] were all extremely versatile rhetoricians and when what was put into the *Shih-chi*[ah] [Ssu-ma Ch'ien's Records of the historian] were always, I believe, things actually uttered in the spoken language of that time.[17]

Here Chu advocates an integrity of verbal articulation in which *i* (intention/ will/meaning) is expressed spontaneously in language that knows no distinction between speaking and writing and thus communicates without the least impediment and contrivance or artifice.

In numerous places in his writings Chu expresses his opposition to what he considers to be artifice in writing—the deliberate cultivation of verbal beauty for its own sake. In a letter to his friend Ts'ai Yüan-ting[ai] (1135–1198) he comes right out and says, "Verbal ornament is certainly without any benefit,"[18] and, whereas he seems to be in accord here with Su Shih in theory, in practice he condemns him along with the other major figures in the *ku-wen*[aj] (ancient prose) movement for paying too much attention to the form of writing at the expense of the substance involved. "In their discursive writings, Han T'ui-chih [Han Yü,[ak] 768–824] and Ou [Ou-yang Hsiu,[al] 1007–1072] and Su do nothing more than concentrate on formal literary style and only occasionally peripherally bring some principles of the Way into it."[19] In another place, Chu suggests that one can even formulate acceptable proportions for the relative amounts of literary embellishment *(wen)* and substance *(shih)* in good writing—with the emphasis, of course, on substance. "In general, in the composition of prose it is necessary to have seven parts substance and two or three parts embellishment. For example, when the venerable Mr. Ou [Ouyang Hsiu] managed to write something good, it was because he kept close to the substance involved and developed it in a clear and orderly manner."[20] Extreme formalism—mannerism—is for Chu a sign of corruption, something which marks a degenerate stage in the tradition of letters. "What people call 'antithetical-parallel' writing deals in smooth-tongued flattery devoid of substance. It is used to toady to popular taste and represents a degenerate stage in writing."[21]

Chu also develops the idea that there is a close connection between artifice and contrivance in writing on the one hand and social-political conditions on the other.

The writing *(wen)* of Chia I[am] [201–169 B.C.] of the early Han era is simple yet substantial *(chih-shih*[an]*)*; the places in Chao Ts'o's[ao] [200–154 B.C.] writings where he discusses the advantages and disadvantages [of policy] are good, but his replies to questions posed by the emperor throw the Way into confusion. The writing of Tung Chung-shu[ap] [176–104 B.C.] is slow-moving and weak. . . . Writing of the Eastern Han era [25–220] is even much worse, since it is marked by a gradual tendency to parallelism (*tui-ou*[aq]) and writers such as Yang Chen[ar] [d. 124] all esteemed trivial detail. . . . With the Three Kingdoms [220–280] and the Eastern and Western Chin eras [265–420] the style of writing became increasingly degenerate.[22]

There is characteristic writing of the well governed age; there is writing characteristic of the age of decline; and there is writing characteristic of the age of chaos. The Six Classics[23] belong to the well-governed age, whereas works such as the *Kuo-yü*[as] (Conversations from the states)[24] are listless and tediously trivial —truly things which belongs to an age of decline! Both the language and the mode of discourse of this time fit with the fact that the Chou was no longer able to assert itself. Coming down later to writing characteristic of the age of chaos, we find this is representative of the Warring States era [403–222 B.C.]. However, this has a robust and heroic spirit which the *Kuo-yü* in its age of decline cannot match. Writing from the Ch'u-Han era [c. 200 B.C.] is really marvelously robust —how indeed could it ever be easy to reach its heights![25]

For Chu, vigor, substance, and the simple and direct expression of values and ideas belong to either the well-governed age or the age in chaos, where the strength and stability of the one provide a necessary nourishing context, and the wide-open but dangerous possibilities of the other supply the stimuli for the hero to perform great deeds and compose great writings. The age of decline provides neither, for then the fabric of society is, in effect, so stretched that its pattern *(wen)* is distorted but not yet broken, and the *wen* of its literary expression reflects this distortion in its use of degenerate mannerisms. This idea, of course, is not new with Chu Hsi but can be traced back to certain statements in the *Book of Rites* and the "Major Preface" to the *Book of Odes*.[26] It is, nevertheless, a basic principle in his theory of prose, one which colors his whole view of literary history and his evaluation of individual figures in the tradition. We shall see later that this holds true as well for his theory and practice of poetry criticism. Now, however, let us see how he applies this to his own age, the Sung era (960–1279).

Writing at the beginning of our own dynasty was always serious and well-seasoned. I once took a look at edicts and other such compositions from the Chia-yu[at] era [1056–1063] and earlier and found that there were some very clumsy usages of language among them. . . . Although this writing is clumsy, yet its expression is forceful and to the point. It has the sense of wanting to be skillful (*kung*[au]) but not being able to achieve that goal; therefore its character is unsophisticated and honest. Coming down to the time of the venerable Mr. Ou [Ou-yung Hsiu], the best of writing then was perfectly fine yet still had this quality of great clumsiness, which did not make it lose its sense of warmth and kindness; but by the time of Tung-p'o [Su Shih], writing already had begun to rush headlong towards excessive cleverness, and, by the time of the Cheng-ho[av]

[1111–1117] and Hsüan-ho[aw] [1119–1125] eras, it had reached an extreme of gorgeous mannerism, which *did* make it lose its sense of warmth and kindness. When the Sage [Confucius] preferred the men of former times in the matters of ceremony and ritual, his reason, of course, was similar to this.[27]

That is, rough-hewn simplicity is preferred to mannered "sophistication." The last reign periods mentioned, of course, signaled the end of the Northern Sung era (960–1126), when the social-political situation was at its lowest ebb and the Sung government was driven out of the North.

In the light of all this, Chu's views of the role of *hsüeh*[ax] (study through emulation and imitation) in the training of the prose writer are rather predictable: (1) he advocates *hsüeh* as the foundation of such training; (2) proper models for emulation are to be found primarily in the ancient period—Western Han and earlier; (3) some great writing defies emulation because it was produced by such genius that, like Ssu-ma Ch'ien's *Shih-chi*, it exhibits no formulaic features and thus has nothing to grasp. Much of what he says about training in prose writing he also says about poetry, with the exceptions that proper models for poetry can be found through the Western Chin era (265–317) and that the true *ku-feng*[ay] (ancient style and spirit) of this poetry was recaptured by Li Po[az] (701–762) and Tu Fu[ba] (712–770), and thus *that* poetry is worthy of emulation as well—whereas Chu had only limited approval for *any* later prose. A good summary of these views is to be found in the following passage:

> For the most part, the writing of the ancients traveled on the correct/orthodox path, whereas those who came later and fabricated things on their own went and traveled on the narrow, tricky paths of heterodoxy. Now, all one has to do is make every effort to keep close to the orthodox path, and in a little while his writing will spontaneously come to surpass that of others.[28]

Chu Hsi's Theory of Poetry

Chu Hsi had a great deal to say about poetry. His collected writings contain many prefaces, colophons and the like that present his views on the history of poetry, its value, nature and function. There is even—as for prose—a separate section of the *Chu Tzu yü-lei*[bb] (Classified conversations of Master Chu) that is devoted to his remarks on poetry (*chüan* 140). He himself wrote poetry in accordance with these views.[29] Of crucial importance for understanding these views are the prefaces to his *Shih chi-chuan*[bc] (Collected annotations to the *Book of Odes*) and his *Ch'u-tz'u chi-chu*[bd] (Collected annotations to the *Songs of Ch'u*) and his equally significant textual study of the collection of poems associated with Ch'ü Yüan[be] (343–c. 277 B.C.) and his tradition.

The arguments presented in the two prefaces reinforce each other and seem to revolve around three essential assertions: (1) Poetry expresses the man, and a careful reading of poetry written by worthy men will help cultivate worthy qualities in the reader. (2) The student of poetry must know the difference between *cheng*[bf] (correct/orthodox) poetry and *pien*[bg] (changed/deviant) poetry —a basic distinction that begins with the poems contained in the *Book of Odes*. "Correct" poetry has both a pragmatic function of providing "models for virtue" and "warnings against vice" and an expressive dimension that reveals proper qualities of restraint and magnanimity. (3) Deviation *(pien)* from the norms of restraint and magnanimity as well as departures from the exemplary functions of poetry inevitably occur when society itself deviates from correct norms, and a poet such as Ch'ü Yüan, living in troubled times, could not help but write *pien* poetry—full of unrestrained and even demonic hatred and resentment. There is still value in this kind of poetry, however, for it teaches by negative example and the reader is admonished that circumstances that provoke such feelings should not be allowed to exist; appreciation of what is being said will lead to the redress of wrongs and the rectification of society. Given the importance of these essays, I shall present here in annotated translation the preface to the *Book of Odes* in its entirety—since these theoretical issues predominate throughout—and that part of the preface to the *Ch'u Tz'u* that is most concerned with theory.

Someone once asked me, "Why have the *Odes* been written?" I replied, " 'Man is born in a quiet state. This is his nature as endowed by Heaven. When he responds to things and is thus moved, this results in the nature's desires.'[30] Having desires, one cannot but have thoughts, and, having thoughts, one cannot but articulate them in speech, and, although one has speech, when it is unable to articulate everything, one has recourse to expressing oneself in overtones carried by sighing and exclaiming, and this inevitably results in natural resonances and rhythms that one cannot keep himself from creating.[31] This is why the *Odes* were written." He then said: "That being so, what is the way by which the *Odes* impart their teachings?" I replied: "Poetry happens when one's *hsin*[bh] (mind/ heart) is moved by things and becomes articulate in terms of the overtones carried by language. Since the heart/mind is moved to both wickedness and virtue, the content of language can be right or wrong. It is only the sage who occupies a superior position from which the nature of his response to things is always correct, and his words, consequently, always have something worthy to teach. Perhaps there might be the case where his response to things is mixed, but there cannot help but be something in his utterances to which people should pay heed. A superior person (a ruler) will necessarily engage in introspection, which inevitably leads to his either encouraging or condemning something. This is also the way that the *Odes* impart their teachings.

"Once when the Chou Kingdom flourished, from above at suburban temples and at court to below in villages and hamlets, the words of all such odes were so pure that none said anything that did not accord with what was right and proper. The sages themselves, to be sure, harmonized their prosodic features and employed them both among country folk and throughout the lesser and greater fiefs, in order to effect moral transformation throughout the world. As far as the odes of the various feudal states are concerned, when the Chou kings made visits to them they were sure to be brought out for perusal so that they could be used in the performance of ceremonies of promotion and demotion. This practice declined after the era of King Chao[bi] and King Mu,[bj][32] for then the odes became permeated with the effects of the gradual loss of kingly power. With the subsequent degeneration that took place after the transfer of the capital to the east,[33] the odes were abolished and no longer discussed. Confucius lived at this time, but, since he failed to obtain an appropriate position, he had no means to put into effect the kind of government in which an emperor or king could properly encourage virtue and chastise evil, promote the worthy and demote the unworthy. This being the case, he took up the texts of the odes, and, after making a critical consideration of them, eliminated duplications, put those in order that were in disarray, and eliminated those that were insufficient models for virtue and insufficient warnings against vice—all this in order to have them accord with standards of simplicity and conciseness and so provide instruction for a very long time, enabling students to have the means to examine right and wrong and allowing the virtuous to find their models in them and the wicked to be reformed by them. Therefore, although his concept of government failed to achieve realization in this one particular age, his teaching actually spread down through countless ages in later times. The *Odes* impart their teachings in this way."

He then asked, "Nevertheless, why do the generic forms of the 'Airs of the States' (*Kuo-feng*[bk]), the 'Elegentiae' (*Ya*[bl]), and the 'Hymns' (*Sung*[bm]) differ as they do?" I replied, "I have heard that of all the odes known as Airs most had their origins as ballads composed in the lanes and alleys of the common folk— what can be called songs sung by men and women to each other, each expressing his or her love. It is only the 'Odes of Chou[bn] and the South' and the 'Odes of Shao[bo] and the South'[34] that were formed into statements of virtue through King Wen's personal moral influence, in such a way that all contain the means to effect the rectification of one's nature and emotions. It is because of this that what they express in words is 'full of delight without passing over into licentiousness or full of sadness without passing over into harmful grief.'[35] Thus, these two sections alone constitute the correct and proper part of the 'Airs of the States.' From the 'Odes of P'ei'[bp] on,[36] the various states differed in whether they were worthy or not, so that what poets expressed after having been moved by things resulted in an uneven variety of depravity and virtue, right and wrong. At this, what we know as the 'Airs' of the former kings underwent a change *(pien)*.[37] As for the sections containing the 'Elegentiae' and the 'Hymns,' these all were composed at the time of the early Chou kings and are the lyrics to the music of the court and suburban temples. Their language is harmonious and solemn, their meaning both broad and dense and their composers very often were of the type that were sages. This is certainly why they have become models for countless ages since—something which no one can ever alter! As for those 'Elegentiae' that had undergone change *(pien)*,[38] these also were written by worthies and true gentlemen who felt sorry about troubled times and felt troubled about society's ills. The Sage [Confucius] included them none the less. The sad and worried yet magnanimous states of mind/heart and the intentions involved to set forth virtue and prevent vice are especially things which the most articulate spokesmen of later ages have never been able to equal. All this is why the *Odes* constitute a

Classic. Through them correct modes of human behavior have seeped down to those below and the Way of Heaven has attained completion among those above —in the course of which not one single principle has failed to be fulfilled."

He then said, "Yes, I agree, but how should one go about studying the *Odes?*" I replied, "One should root himself firmly in the 'Airs of Chou and the South' and of 'Shao and the South' and so seek the essentials inherent in them; he should reach understanding in the 'Airs' of the various states and so become thoroughly aware of the changes that take place with them; he should rectify himself in the 'Elegentiae' and so enlarge his standards; and he should attain harmony within himself in the 'Hymns' and so put his demeanor under complete control. These are the main features involved in studying the *Odes.* After this, he should divide them into stanzas and lines so to get at their main outline; he should do philological explanations of them so to sort out the details and derivations of their meanings; he should chant and intone them so to make them his songs; and he should saturate himself with them until he embodies them completely. He should also examine them in terms of the most subtle and elusive aspects of his nature and emotions and investigate them in terms of what he knows to be the first promptings of one's speech and actions. He need look no further than the *Odes* as far as the Way of cultivating one's person, regulating one's family and bringing order to the world is concerned—for he will obtain all that is necessary here."

The person asking these questions then withdrew in complete agreement with all I had said. At the time I just happened to be engaged in editing these commentaries on the *Odes* and so put all these remarks in order as an introduction to the work as a whole.

Dated the fourth year of the Ch'un-hsi[bq] era, a *ting-yu*[br] year, Winter, the Tenth Month, a *wu-tzu*[bs] day [November 14, 1177], written by Chu Hsi of Hsin-an.[bt39]

If Chu believes the *Odes* to be the best of all directly positive models for moral and literary-aesthetic cultivation, he also believes that the "Songs of the South" in spite of their lack of such exemplary features, can still serve as important stimuli to effect moral transformation and as profound inspirations for the articulation of justifiable anger and resentment.

As far as the character of Ch'ü Yüan is concerned, although his intention and behavior might have exceeded the standards set by the *Chung-yung*[bu] (The Mean) so that he is unsuitable as a model, nevertheless all that he was and did came from a sincere mind/heart that was loyal to its ruler and loved its country. As far as his writings are concerned, although the meaning of his words might tend to be unrestrained and demonic, and hatred and resentment so welled up in them that they are inappropriate as moral teachings, nevertheless all of them are the product of the most honest sentiments of profound concern and sad worry— which he could not stop from feeling in spite of himself. Because he did not know that he should study in the North and so seek out the Way of the Duke of Chou and Confucius, he merely galloped around in the corrupt vestiges of changed *(pien)* airs and changed elegentiae [in the literary tradition of an age in decline]. Therefore, pure-minded Confucian scholars and serious-minded gentlemen might be ashamed to praise him, but if his writings enable the exiled official, the banished child, the estranged or divorced wife, once tears are wiped dry, to sing their laments below so that he who is Heaven to them [whether it be ruler, father or husband] will fortunately listen to them, then, as regards the relations between such ones as these, as well as the virtue inherent in individual human character and in correct human relationships in general, how could these writings fail to promote their mutual development and fail to add weight to the importance of the Three Moral Principles[40] and the Five Human Relationships?[41] These are the reasons why I always find something of interest in what they say and never dare look upon these writings as a mere songwriter's attempts to write literary compositions.[42]

Chu Hsi also used the term *pien* (changed/deviant) in another sense in his critical writings—to mean innovation or variation. For him, the student of poetry has as his goal, first, to acquire the ability to emulate the great masters and, then, to work out of this emulation innovations that will not violate the *cheng* (correctness) these masters maintain for the tradition of poetry as a whole. The tradition, with its rules, is inviolate; it is a sacred trust maintained by each new generation of poets. The student should always strive to effect a tone of magnanimity and restraint and should try to realize those same personal qualities of expression that characterize the works of the great culture heroes of the past. He cultivates himself through the study of them and achieves self-realization himself in the act of composing poetry—a glowing example for his own age and a light for the future tradition. A good summary of these views is found in Chu's "Preface to the *Literary Works of Wang Mei-hsi.*"[bv]

The best qualities of the superior man and the worst qualities of the petty man take external form just as they are determined within in such a way that even in the most subtle aspects of speech and action they always come to light, and how much more this is true in the areas of careers and of writing—especially so for those called "the bright and brilliant." ... I have ... tried this out on the ancients by examining what they had written. In the Han era I came up with Prime Minister Chu-ko [Chu-ko Liang,[bw] 181–234], ... in the T'ang [618–907] Mr. Tu of the Ministry of Works [Tu Fu], ... Ministry President Yen [Yen Chen-ch'ing,[bx] 709–784], ... Ministry Vice-President Han [Han Yü], ... and, in our own dynasty, I came up with the former Associate in the Affairs of Government Mr. Fan [Fan Chung-yen[by], 989–1052]. Although the situations these five gentlemen encountered in life differed, as were the ways in which they established themselves, if one seeks out their hearts/minds, he will find in all of them qualities we call justice and purity of intention, perspicacity and freedom from hindrance, openheartedness and lack of affectation: qualities which could not remain hidden away and can be seen in their careers and in their writings—even in the most subtle features of their calligraphy. One can look upon what they had written and know what their characters were. If one seeks out such things among people of the present day, it would appear that someone such as

... Wang Kuei-ling,[bz] Administrator of the Household of the Heir-Apparent [Wang Mei-hsi, 1112–1171], is an appropriate example. . . . In ordinary life he never pursued any personal pleasures except that he loved to write poetry. This was direct and sincere, straightforward and honest, earnest and compassionate, and grand and sweeping in scope. It was just like his character. He did not indulge in frivolous and ornamental writing, and when he discussed matters, he based himself thoroughly on his own opinions. Thus, since his scope was tremendous, the formal structure of his poetry was wide open and managed to find its way in and out of surprising variations. Superior and magnificent, it moves with supernatural agility. Even those of this day and age who devote all their efforts to writing, surprisingly enough, very often fail to equal him.[43]

Chu was especially hostile to anything in the tradition that smacked of mannerism. He warned the student of poetry away from that of the Six Dynasties era (222–589) after the Western Chin and from Tu Fu's later poetry, that is, that written after his sojourn in K'uei-chou[ca] (766–768)—poetry that he thought was not the honest and straightforward expression of magnanimous states of mind but technical exercises in form as ends in themselves.

For ancient-style verse (*ku-shih*[cb]), one must look at that written during the Western Chin and earlier; such works written then in the ballad (*yüeh-fu*[cc]) and other forms are all beautiful. Tu Fu's verse written before his K'uei-chou period is also beautiful, but in that done at K'uei-chou and later he invents his own rules and standards; this must not be emulated. Su [Su Shih] and Huang [Huang T'ing-chien[cd], 1045–1105] are merely modern poets. Su's talent is of heroic proportions, but he lets everything out all at once so that there is not the least overtone of meaning, and Huang just squanders himself on deliberate calculations.[44]

Chu believes that the poetry of the Han, Wei, and Western Chin eras preserved in the *Wen-hsüan*[ce] (Anthology of literature) compiled by Hsiao T'ung[cf] (501–531), is the best of the post-*Odes* tradition, and anyone who emulates this poetry will achieve, if he has enough talent, great poetry of his own—as does, for example, one of Chu's early teachers, Liu Tzu-hui[cg] (1101–1147).

In both rules and standards and in mood it [poetry by Liu] emulates in every way the ballads found in the *Wen-hsüan* and is not adulterated by popular styles of more recent times. As a result, its spirit and tone are lofty and antique in flavor, and its intonation and rhythm are beautiful and clear. Few people of his own day and age could write anything to equal it. . . . I have always maintained that each and every thing under Heaven has its own distinct method of being done. The student must keep to a proper order and make progress gradually. Something such as the study of poetry also must follow this procedure in its method, and, it is hoped, when one manages not to lose sight of the basic characteristics found in the individual styles of the ancients, after a time he should be able to do innovations on them which no doubt will defy easy estimation of what he can do. However, working innovations as such is a very difficult matter. If one actually effects innovations without violating the *cheng* (correct/orthodox quality) of poetry, then, in an all-encompassing fashion he will gain a marvelous power so that there will be nothing he cannot do. Rather than being unfortunate enough to violate one single aspect of orthodoxy, it would seem, on the contrary, that one should keep to the age-old and proven basic methods that will keep him safe for his entire life. Li [Li Po], Tu [Tu Fu], Han [Han Yü] and Liu [Liu Tsung-yüan^{ch}, 773–819] at the beginnings of their careers in poetry all emulated the poems in the *Wen-hsüan*, and Tu and Han were the most innovative with them, Liu and Li the least. Innovation does not lend itself to emulation, but poetry that is not the product of innovation does. Thus, rather than study from examples of innovation, it would be better to study from examples of poetry that are not innovations. This is the moral behind the story of how the boy of the state of Lu thought he should emulate Liu-hsia Hui.^{ci45} Oh, beware you students and be not beguiled by the notion that you need not keep to the rules—and rashly take such liberties with them that you fall victim to your own self-deception![46]

A number of passages in the *Chu-tzu yü-lei* also praise Li Po for staying close to models in the *Wen-hsüan* and lament the fact that Tu Fu strayed from them in his later work; the following is typical:

> Li T'ai-pai^{cj} [Li Po] absolutely always emulated the poetry in the *Wen-hsüan*— that is why his is always good. The best of Tu Tzu-mei's^{ck} [Tu Fu's] poetry is also modeled after the *Wen-hsüan* poems, but gradually he became lax, and the poems of his K'uei-chou period are altogether of a different order.[47]

In immediately subsequent passages, Chu goes on to castigate Tu's later poetry as "tediously trivial," "lawless and unfit," or simply "incomprehensible"—that is, as mannered in the extreme.

Opposed to this mannerism are the qualities that Chu sees in all great poetry, and these he characterizes in terms of *tzu-te*^{cl} (at ease with oneself/ obtained by oneself), *t'ien-ch'eng*^{cm} (naturalness/sprung from nature), *ch'ao-jan*^{cn} (detachment/transcendency), *tzu-jan*^{co} (naturalness and spontaneity), *tzu-tsai*^{cp} (freedom/carefree spontaneity), and *ts'ung-jung*^{cq} (composure/calm).[48] The meanings of these terms overlap to some extent; they combine to mean genuine personal expression free from artifice of any kind, on the one hand, and tranquility and transcendence of self-centered egotism, on the other. Of course, this means spontaneity within the rules of form and expression of the cultivated individual—the self that stays within the rules of morality (as Chu understands the Way of the Sages). The very highest attainment in poetry, according to Chu, is the expression of a sense of *p'ing-i*^{cr} or *p'ing-tan*.^{cs} After examining a great number of Chu's critical statements containing these terms, Chang Chien^{ct} concludes that Chu's *p'ing-tan/p'ing-i* should be interpreted in eight different ways, regarded from eight different angles: (1) *P'ing-tan* does not mean *k'u-tan*^{cu} (lifenessness and insipidity), and *p'ing-i* does not mean *ch'ing-i*^{cv} (levity and prosaism). (2) *P'ing-tan* and *p'ing-i* signify a higher poetic realm or world than do, to use Chu's own examples, *ching-li*[cw] (exquisite beauty), *hung-wei*[cx] (magnificence), or *kung-cheng*[cy] (precision and orderliness); and the poetry of T'ao Ch'ien[cz] (365–427) best represents this realm. (3) The most precious feature of *p'ing-i* is that it is produced spontaneously and not through conscious effort. (4) There inhere in *p'ing-tan*, under profound restraint, such feelings as *hao-fang*[da] (great vigor and bravery), *kan-shang*[db] (great sorrow), or other sentiments that defy articulation in ordinary modes of discourse. (5) It is very difficult to achieve a sense of *p'ing-tan* in poetry; even such a great master, in Chu's opinion, as Ou-yang Hsiu did not lightly dare to set this as a goal for himself. (6) *P'ing-tan*, like *p'ing-i*, is a wonderful quality that one has to obtain all by oneself without conscious effort. (7) The sense of *p'ing-i* is close to that of *hsien-tan*[dc] (calmness/placidity) but in which one can often see a lofty and far-reaching realm. (8) *P'ing-i* also occurs in prose, but it is of a higher order when it occurs in poetry.[49] The only inconsistency here, when we compare these assertions with what we have already seen of Chu's theory of poetry, especially as it applies to literary history, is the place given to T'ao Ch'ien at the very top of the *p'ing-tan/p'ing-i* scale; he is, after all, a post-Western Chin poet. Chu seems to have regarded T'ao as an exceptional genius who was able to transcend the limitations of his own time and place.

Although the scope of this paper does not allow a detailed examination of Chu's criticism of individual poets—something that Chang Chien does in his book in admirable fashion[50]—we have examined his criticisms of those poets Chu seems to have regarded as the most significant. Even this brief study gives a general sense of what Chu's likes and dislikes were and the reasons for them.

Conclusion

Chu's theories of prose and poetry are thus complementary. Both are predicted upon the assumption that writing is at once a medium of personal expression and a vehicle of moral persuasion. It should be free of superfluous ornamentation and should fulfill these two functions in a clear and direct manner. Both prose and poetry are activities of the cultivated man—with morality and aesthetics combining in a seemingly inextricable way to produce this cultivation. Cultivation in both senses derives from emulation. The Classics provide the ultimate models, with the *Book of Odes* providing the essential first guide to the whole later tradition of poetry. Writings of the early imperial period supply the secondary models—secondary but, because of the more direct linguistic continuity between them and the later tradition, of more practical technical assistance to the student of poetry and prose. The great culture heroes of this time—Western Han for prose and all of the Han, the Wei, and the Western Chin for poetry—are the great writers. They set the standards for the rest of the tradition; emulation of them is of absolute importance in the development of one's own literary art, both in terms of formal style and of expressive qualities. This constitutes, in effect, a literary ortho-doxy, which it is the duty of each new generation to renew and preserve. This duty, however, was not carried out during large parts of literary history when the correct models were ignored and heterodox developments in style and expression took places. These include prose after the Western Han, poetry after the Western Chin (T'ao Ch'ien excepted) and the writing of all later fig-ures who do not incorporate in their own works the correct standards of the past. These the student must guard against and shun as he undertakes his own training. Learning to write, then, is a form of scholarship, just as it is for the student of moral philosophy. Writing, for Chu Hsi, is a thoroughly bookish experience; this viewpoint, not surprisingly, is entirely consistent with the rest of his intellectual and spiritual concerns.

Notes

Chu Hsi's theory of literature and his practical criticism of authors and works have attracted the attention of a number of scholars in modern times. I have found the following works of special value in the preparation of this paper: Kuo Shao-yü, *Chung-kuo wen-hsüeh p'i-p'ing shih*[dd] [A his-tory of Chinese literary criticism], (Taipei: Wen-shih-che ch'u-pan-she,[de] 1979 reprint of the 1934–1947 ed.), pp. 444–450 and 465–469; Lo Ken-tse,[df] *Chung-kuo wen-hsüeh p'i-p'ing shih,*[dg] vol. 3: *Liang-Sung wen-hsüeh p'i-p'ing shih*[dh] [A history of the literary criticism of the Northern and Southern Sung eras], (Shanghai: Ku-tien wen-hsüen ch'u-pan-she,[di] 1961), pp. 189–199; Chang Chien *Chu Hsi de wen-hsüeh p'i-p'ing yen-chiu*[dj] [A study of the literary criticism of Chu Hsi], (Taipei: Commercial Press, 1969). Mr. Chang's book is an excellent guide to the sources of Chu's views; it has saved me an immense amount of time and effort.

1. Chu Hsi, *T'ung-shu chieh*[dk] [Explanations to *Penetrating the Book of Changes*]; see *Chou-tzu ch'üan-shu*[dl] [Complete works of Master Chou], (Basic Sinological Series ed.), 10:180.

2. Chou Tun-i, *T'ung-shu*[dm] in *Chou-tzu ch'üan-shu,* 10:180; trans. James J. Y. Liu[dn] in *Chinese Theories of Literature* (Chicago: University of Chicago Press, 1975), p. 114.

3. See Kuo, *Chung-kuo wen-hsüeh p'i-p'ing shih,* pp. 353–355.

4. Chu Hsi, *Chu Tzu yü-lei* [Classified conversations of Master Chu], (Taipei: Cheng-chung shu-chü[do] ed., 1962 reprint of the 1473 ed.), 139:8a, p. 5309.

5. Kuo, *Chung-kuo wen-hsüeh p'i-p'ing shih,* pp. 341–342.

6. Chu Hsi, *Chu Tzu yü-lei,* 139:19a, p. 5331.

7. This appears to be Chu's paraphrase—to a reductionist formula—of various things Su said about *tao* and *wen;* see Kuo, *Chung-kuo wen-hsüeh p'i-p'ing shih,* pp. 341–342.

8. Chu Hsi, *Chu Tzu yü-lei,* 139:19a, p. 5331.

9. Kuo, *Chung-kuo wen-hsüeh p'i-p'ing shih,* p. 342.

10. Isaiah Berlin, *The Hedgehog and the Fox: An Essay on Tolstoy's View of History* (New York: Simon and Schuster, 1953), pp. 1–2.

11. *Tso-chuan*[dp] [Tso's commentary], Duke Hsiang,[dq] twenty-fifth year.

12. *Analects,* 15:41.

13. Su Shih, *Tung-p'o ch'i-chi*[dr] [Seven collections of Su Shih's works], (SPPY ed.), later collection, 14:10a; trans. James J. Y. Liu in *Chinese Theories of Literature,* p. 130.

14. From the *Pu-chü* (Divination) piece in the *Ch'u-tz'u;* see *Wen-hsüan* [Anthology of literature], (SPPY ed.), 33:4b; trans. David Hawkes, *Ch'u Tz'u: Songs of the South* (Boston: Beacon Press, 1962), p. 89.

15. What has survived as Lin's collected writings, the *Ai-hsüan chi*[ds] (*Ssu-k'u ch'üan-shu chen-pen,*[dt] first series, ed.), does not seem to contain this statement; it is likely that is was part of a letter from Lin to Chu that was not preserved; another such letter does not exist (see 6:8b–9a). However, Lin's view of the gradual "decline" in writing during the course of time—the Han included—is stated in a passage preserved on pages 4:4b–6a.

16. See Han Ying[du] (*fl.* c. 179–157 B.C.), *Han shih wai-chuan*[dv] [Han's external commentaries on the *Odes*], (SPTK ed.), 7:65a.

17. Chu Hsi, *Chu Tzu yü-lei,* 139:1a–1b, pp. 5295–5296.

18. Chu Hsi, *Chu Wen Kung wen-chi*[dw] [Collection of literary works of Master Chu], SPTK ed.), supplementary collection, 2:4a.

19. Chu Hsi, *Chu Tzu yü-lei,* 137:22a, p. 5263.

20. *Ibid.,* 139:20a, p. 5333.

21. Chu Hsi, *Chu Wen Kung wen-chi,* 37:12a.

22. Chu Hsi, *Chu Tzu yü-lei,* 139:2b–3a, pp. 5298–5299.

23. The *Changes, Poetry, History, Spring and Autumn Annals, Rites, Music.*

24. The *Kuo-yü* is attributed to Tso Ch'iu-ming,[dx] a contemporary of Confucius; it records events in the various feudal states from the end of Western Chou up through the Spring and Autumn era (c. 967–c. 453 B.C.).

25. Chu Hsi, *Chu Tzu yü-lei,* 139:1a, p. 5295.

26. See Liu, *Chinese Theories of Literature,* pp. 63–65.

27. Chu Hsi, *Chu Tzu yü-lei,* 139:9a, p. 5311. The reference to Confucius is to *Analects,* 11:1.

28. Chu Hsi, *Chu Tzu yü-lei,* 139:4a–4b, pp. 5301–5302.

29. A study of Chu Hsi's poetry has been undertaken by Li Chi[dy] in "Chu Hsi the Poet," *T'oung Pao*[dz] 58 (1972), pp. 55–119. Several poems by Chu are also translated by Wing-tsit Chan[ea] in "Neo-Confucian Philosophical Poems," *Renditions* 4 (Spring 1975), pp. 12–16.

30. *Li-chi*[eb] [*The Record of Rites*], (*Shih-san-ching chu-shu*[ec] ed.), 37:10a.

31. This paraphrases the *Ta-hsü*[ed] [Major preface] to the *Book of Odes.*

32. King Chao reigned from 1052 to 1002 B.C. and King Mu from 1001 to 947 B.C. —so tradition has it. Chao's reign was marked by luxurious living and extravagant hunting expeditions, Mu's reigned by tours, travel, and costly foreign military expeditions; both signal the decline of central power of the Chou state.

33. This occurred in 770 B.C.

34. The "Chou-nan" [Odes of Chou and the South] are the first eleven of the *Odes* in the Classic and the "Shao-nan" [Odes of Shao and the South] are the next fourteen. They are traditionally attributed to the time of King Wen's reign (1171–1122 B.C.), the very beginning of Chou rule.

35. *Analects,* 3:20.

36. The "Odes of P'ei" are the next nineteen after the "Shao-nan." P'ei was the northern part of the domain of the former Shang kings.

37. The "Major Preface" to the *Book of Odes* states: "By the time the Kingly Way had declined, and propriety and rightness had been abandoned, the principle of government by moral instruction was lost and each state followed a different system of

government, each family a different custom. Thereupon the 'Changed Airs' and 'Changed Odes' arose" (trans. James J. Y. Liu, *Chinese Theories of Literature*, p. 64). Professor Liu comments: "Since the word 'changed' *(pien)* often connotes deviation from the norm and even disaster, the statement implies that abnormal times produce abnormal literature, and that it is impossible to produce normal or proper *(cheng)* literature in a time of crisis" (p. 64).

38. The "Elegentiae" are divided into the "Ta-ya"[ee] [Greater elegentiae] and the "Hsiao-ya"[ef] [Lesser elegentiae]; those that underwent a "change" refer to the latter.

39. Chu Hsi, *Chu Wen-kung wen-chi*, 76:13a–14b. Hsin-an (Wu-yüan[eg] in Anhwei) was Chu's father's native place; Chu usually is associated with Chien-chou[eh] in Fukien, where he lived in his later years.

40. The Three Moral Principles—or Three Bonds or Standards (*san-kang*[ei])—are those that govern the relationships between ruler and subject, father and son, and husband and wife.

41. The Five Human Relationships (*wu-tien*[ej] that is, *wu-lun*[ek] or *wu-ch'ang*[el]) are the constant virtues of a father's righteousness (*i*[em]), a mother's love (*tz'u*,[en] an elder brother's friendship (*yu*[eo]), a younger brother's respect (*kung*[ep]), and a son's filial piety (*hsiao*[eq]).

42. Chu Hsi, *Chu Wen Kung wen-chi*, 76:33b–34b.

43. *Ibid.*, 75:30b–31b.

44. Chu Hsi, *Chu Tzu yü-lei*, 140:1a, p. 5339.

45. Liu-hsia Hui—Hui (The compassionate one) of Liu-hsia [Beneath the willows]. His name was Chan Ch'in[er]; he was a native of the state of Lu during the Warring States era. He once gave shelter to a woman in need and did not take advantage of her. On a later occasion, a woman's house collapsed during a storm, and she sought shelter next door, but the young man who lived alone there would not give her shelter. She complained and asked him why he did not behave as did Liu-hsia Hui, since no one thought anything the worse of him when he gave a woman shelter. The young man replied that if he were a Liu-hsia Hui he could do it, but since he was not, he could not do it—"I could not rely on what I was incapable of doing to emulate something Liu-hsia Hui could do!" Confucius is supposed to have said of him: "Of all those who might want to emulate Liu-hsia Hui, there has never been anyone more fitting than he." See *Shih Mao-shih chuan-shu*[es] [The *Book of Odes* with Mao's commentaries and further sub-commentaris], *(Basic Sinological Series* ed.), 19:113.

46. Chu Hsi, *Chu Wen Kung wen-chi*, 84:20a–20b.

47. Chu Hsi, *Chu Tzu yü-lei*, 140:2b, p. 5342.

48. See Chang Chien, *Chu Hsi de wen-hsüeh p'ing-p'ing yen-chiu*, pp. 29–32.

49. *Ibid.*, pp. 32–34.

50. *Ibid.*, pp. 76–115.

Glossary

a 文以載道	f 程頤	k 文以貫道
b 詞説	g 程顥	l 東坡
c 實	h 蘇軾	m 文必與道俱
d 道	i 貫道之理	n 華妙
e 周敦頤	j 郭紹虞	o 經

p 史
q 子
r 貫道說
s 載道說
t 達意華
u 詞妙
v 妙意
w 意
x 離騷
y 卜居
z 楚辭
aa 艾軒林光朝
ab 班固
ac 揚雄
ad 司馬遷
ae 司馬相如
af 蘇秦
ag 張儀
ah 史記
ai 蔡元定
aj 古文
ak 韓愈
al 歐陽修
am 賈誼
an 質實
ao 晁錯
ap 董仲舒
aq 對偶
ar 楊震
as 國語
at 嘉祐
au 工
av 政和
aw 宣和
ax 學
ay 古風
az 李白
ba 杜甫
bb 朱子語類
bc 詩集傳
bd 楚辭集註
be 屈原
bf 正
bg 變
bh 心

bi 昭
bj 穆
bk 國風
bl 雅頌
bm 頌
bn 周召
bo 召
bp 邶
bq 淳熙
br 丁酉
bs 戊子
bt 新安
bu 中庸
bv 王梅溪
bw 諸葛亮
bx 顏真卿
by 范仲淹
bz 王龜齡
ca 夔州
cb 古詩
cc 樂府
cd 黃庭堅
ce 文選
cf 蕭統
cg 劉子翬
ch 柳宗元
ci 柳下惠
cj 李太白李白
ck 杜子美杜甫
cl 自得
cm 天成
cn 超然
co 自然
cp 自在
cq 從容
cr 平易
cs 平淡
ct 張健
cu 枯淡易
cv 輕易麗
cw 精麗偉
cx 宏整
cy 工整潛
cz 陶潛
da 豪放

db 感傷
dc 閒淡
dd 中國文學批評史
de 文史哲出版社
df 羅根澤
dg 中國文學批評史
dh 兩宋文學批評史
di 古典文學出版社
dj 朱熹的文學批評研究
dk 通書解
dl 周子全書
dm 通書
dn 劉若愚
do 正中書局
dp 左傳
dq 襄
dr 東坡七集
ds 艾軒集
dt 四庫全書珍本
du 韓嬰
dv 韓詩外傳
dw 朱文公文集
dx 左丘明
dy 李祁
dz 通報
ea 陳榮捷
eb 禮記
ec 十三經注疏
ed 大序
ee 大雅
ef 小雅
eg 婺源
eh 建州
ei 三綱
ej 五典倫
ek 五常
el 五
em 義慈
en 慈
eo 友
ep 恭
eq 孝
er 展禽
es 詩毛氏傳疏

21

Chu Hsi and Religion

REN JIYU

A FIGURE OF SIGNAL IMPORTANCE in the historical development of Chinese philosophy, Chu Hsi was, following Confucius (551–479 B.C.) and Tung Chung-shu[a] (176–104 B.C.), the most significant contributor to the completion of the Confucian system. The study of his thought, although an academic matter, is nonetheless relevant to the actual life of the contemporary Chinese people. Whereas the prevailing view in the Chinese academic world has been that Chu Hsi's thought belongs to the realm of philosophy, it is viewed in this paper as belonging to the realm of religion, with his philosophical ideas understood as having been in the service of his religious system.

Sociocultural Conditioning of Chinese Religion

Unlike the natural sciences, religion and philosophy have distinctive national features. A comparison of Chinese culture with the cultures of other nations reveals both similarities[1] and differences. Some distinctive characteristics of Chinese society as compared with the West are the following: the duration of Chinese feudal society was long and stable; its feudal-patriarchal system was more fully developed; the feudal autocracy exerted centralized power; peasant uprisings were more frequent and widespread; and capitalism failed to develop. China has a recorded history of nearly four thousand years, more than half of which were passed under feudalism, and among the elements of ancient Chinese thought that have drawn the attention of the whole world, the most conspicuous is its feudal culture. More penetrating research on Chinese feudal culture would require the common efforts of scholars in such fields as political science, economics, and culture. The present study addresses the problem solely from the perspective of philosophy and religion.

As stated above, one of the characteristics of the history of Chinese feudal society was its patriarchal system, which grew up during the later stages of the clan-dominated communal society. In general, under the conditions of productive backwardness, undeveloped labor skill, and extremely meager output, the social system was to a great extent dominated by blood relationships.

Whereas social and economic development enabled many nations in the world to break the bondage of blood relationships and to establish their state organization on delimited territories, such was not the case in China. Once its state organization had been formed, the old forms of blood relationship left by the clan society were not discarded but, on the contrary, as an effective form of social organization continued to function, regulating and even dominating the activities of the state and society and becoming the mechanism for adjusting social relations. Social clashes created by class contradictions and the disparity between rich and poor were alleviated through clan relationships, and the patriarchal system still firmly bound together the members of a class society through their natural blood ties. Common customs, common psychology, and common norms of behavior retained universal significance in the society. Confucians, in their endeavor to maintain the patriarchal system, constantly made use of its old forms and invested them with new content.

The discussion begins with the Western Chou dynasty (1111–770 B.C.). Having triumphed over the Yin[b] people, the Chou people established their rule over the whole of China and, as a dominating minority, put the conquered majority under their command. Effectively utilizing the patriarchal system of blood relationships, they enfeoffed the aristocrats of their own and related clans and settled them on the principal eastern territories to establish such states as Ch'i,[c] Lu,[d] Yen,[e] and Chin.[f] This system of enfeoffment lasted for seven or eight hundred years, until it was abolished after the unification by the Ch'in (221–206 B.C.), but the patriarchal system of blood relationships survived in new circumstances. After unification under the Ch'in and Han (206 B.C.–A.D. 220) dynasties, the primitive religious rites inherited from the class society were accorded systematic explanations and consistent reasoning, as witness the compilation of the *Li-chi*[g] (Book of rites) at the beginning of the Han dynasty. In the primitive religion, there were no special religious professionals, chieftains having been in charge of the sacrifice. All members of a clan participated in such activities as prayers for a rich harvest, the exorcism of diseases, and avoidance of natural calamities. Productive or social activities were at the same time religious activities, and sacrificial ceremonies within a clan and warfare against external tribes were also carried out under the guide of religious rites. The numerous rituals recorded in antiquity constitute accounts of popular customs of the time. In primitive religion can be found the origins of ceremonies on such occasions as capping, weddings, funerals, sacrifices, military expeditions, the entertainment of guests, festival feasts, and sacrificial banquets.[2]

After prolonged evolution, the culture of the Western Chou gradually developed into the culture of Hua-hsia,[h] which transcended the realm of the Chou people. After the King of Chou moved to the east, the court lost its sovereign status; but the state of Lu, originally the fief of the Duke of Chou[i] (d. 1094 B.C.), preserved the old rites, music, cultural relics, and traditional institutions in their entirety.[3] It was therefore not by chance that Lu and Tsou[j] were the native states of Confucius and Mencius (372–289 B.C.?), the two founders of the Confucian school.

Although there have been different views among scholars as to the relation between Confucius and the Six Classics,[4] all agree that Confucius and his disciples took part in the arrangement of the Six Classics and used them as textbooks to teach their pupils. Among the Six Classics, the records and explanations of the primitive religion were specifically contained in the *Book of Rites* and the *Book of Music*. More broadly, the Six Classics, with their varied contents, also exemplified an outlook on Heaven and man, on society, and on religion, at the very heart of which was the patriarchal system. The teachings of the Confucian Classics such as "venerating Heaven and imitating ancestors," "honoring the honorable and being kind to kindred," and "revering virtue and safeguarding the people" all bore the traces of the primitive religion. Later Confucians, in transmitting these Classics, continually offered new explanations and provided fresh interpretations for them with the result that they became the norms guiding human life. The Confucian Classics have always had a strongly religious character.

The unification of the Ch'in and Han dynasties determined the general pattern of political organization in China for more than two thousand years. The Chinese people have long since thought that unity is normal, division abnormal. Nevertheless, the economy that prevailed in the feudal society was a natural economy in which the produce of the peasants was, save for the portion to be offered in tribute to the state, all to be consumed by individual families and households. Given a closed economic system based on self-sufficiency and on the individual as an isolated unit, it would have been impossible to maintain unity had it not been for the instrumentality of ideological unity. Historically, the attempt to search out ideological unity required seventy years after the unification of Ch'in and Han and culminated when preeminent authority was assigned to Confucianism and a dominant position was assumed by the theological teleology of Tung Chung-shu. During the Eastern Han dynasty the *Pai-hu t'ung*[k] (Comprehensive discussions in the White Tiger Hall) further theologized and systematized the Confucian classical learning. In the past, scholarly accounts of the classical learning of the Western (206 B.C.–A.D. 8) and Eastern Han dynasties have overemphasized its transmission through scholastic or family succession, while its theological significance has been largely neglected. This is an inadequate approach to the subject.

As a result of the prolonged division of a formerly united country during the periods of the Three Kingdoms (220–280) and the Six Dynasties (222–589), the influence of Confucianism diminished, yet there was no corresponding decline in the feudal patriarchal system. Rather, the strength of the nobility and gentry was enlarged and, with it, strict insistence on the teachings of filial piety and fraternal duty and increased emphasis on the study of genealogy. The antagonism between nationalities and the frequent warfare that prevailed at that time prepared the soil for the development of religion, and Buddhism and Taoism flourished. After the unification of the Sui (581–618) and T'ang (618–907) dynasties, Confucianism, Buddhism, and Taoism came to be referred to together as the "Three Teachings," and on occasions of grand state ceremonies, representatives of the three teachings were summoned to engage in discussions at the imperial court. It was at this time that Confucianism began to be generally recognized as a religion.

Chinese Philosophy and Chinese Religion

When the process leading from the confrontation among the three teachings of Confucianism, Buddhism, and Taoism to their mutual interpenetration is examined from a viewpoint of history of human knowledge, the constant progress and deepening of human knowledge can be realized as well.

The history of knowledge of the Chinese people is one with the history of Chinese philosophical development. In the pre-Ch'in period people focused their attention on the Way of Heaven and discussed how the universe had been formed. This period corresponds to the childhood of human knowledge, and Tung Chung-shu's theological teleology did not surpass that stage, a stage still cosmological and not yet ontological. Having experienced several great social upheavals and political changes, people's interest was gradually attracted to an outlook on the Way of Heaven that took into account the more complicated social contradictions. Interest advanced from the problem of how the universe was formed to the problem of man himself in his social context, that is, how the proper nature of man is formed. A theory of human nature had already emerged during the Spring and Autumn (722–481 B.C.) and Warring States (403–222 B.C.) periods, but that was only the beginning. In terms of knowledge, there was steady progress from Confucius' saying that "by nature men are alike; through practice they become divergent,"[5] to Mencius' theory of the goodness of human nature,[6] Hsün Tzu's[l] (c. 313–238 B.C.?) theory of the evil of human nature,[7] Yang Hsiung's[m] (53 B.C.–A.D. 18) theory of the mixing of good and evil in human nature,[8] and Han Yü's[n] theory of the three classes of human nature.[9] Theoretically, however, no great depth had yet been achieved, nor had there begun to be exploration of such problems as What is the origin of the goodness or evil of human nature? What is the relation between human nature and society? Is there any relation between human nature and physiological functions, or between human nature and individual behavior? Does human nature undergo changes, and if so, according to what laws?

After Buddhism came to China, its voluminous scriptures were translated into Chinese, and people found in them a depiction of the world incomparably broader than that found in the Chinese Six Classics. The vivid accounts of human emotion, volition, and psychology found in the Buddhist scriptures were also far more rich and complex than what had been found in the discussions of human nature handed down by the ancient Chinese sages and worthies. People of the Central Kingdom found themselves at a loss when they heard for the first time about karma, the theory of cause and effect whereby past, present, and future lives were understood to be connected.[10] At the same time, human knowledge was steadily making progress. The ever more complicated realities of life obliged people to confront questions of fundamental significance. Why are there calamities in society? Why are there disparities among people in wealth and status? What is the world like, and what attitude should one take towards it? What is the purpose of human life? No concrete science can resolve such questions, though philosophy and religion concern themselves with the attempt to do so. Whether or not their answers have been correct aside, the exponents of philosophy and religion of different times and places have all considered themselves to possess the correct answers. They differed only in their approach, the path of philosophy being speculative, the path of religion being that of faith. Philosophy offers rational explanations, while religion provides emotional satisfaction. Although theoretically speaking philosophy and religion each has its respective domain, medieval philosophy was subordinate to religion, not independent of it. The two domains could not be clearly differentiated by people until they awakened from their long hibernation in the Middle Ages. Only then could they recognize the distinctions between philosophy and religion and apprehend the full significance of philosophy. Further, the level of human knowledge is a reflection of the level of scientific knowledge; the level of scientific knowledge being low compared with that of modern times, philosophy was incapable of rational explanation; resort to religion was inevitable. Even today, the line of demarcation between philosophy and religion is not distinctly drawn by everybody.

After the May Fourth Movement of 1919, Chinese philosophers came into contact with the culture and philosophy of modern Europe and became attuned to the enormous differences between Chinese and Western philosophy. My late professor, Mr. Hsiung Shih-li° (1883–1968), repeatedly emphasized that European philosophy could only provide speculative knowledge and logical methodology but could not teach people the modes of personal practice through which they might attain the spiritual benefits of enjoying peace and establishing one's own destiny. Such a perception is true and valid, and every scholar who really understands traditional Chinese culture will have sensed a difference of this kind, which exists as an objective reality. What needs to be pointed out now is that Westerners too have a need for enjoying peace and establishing destiny; indeed, it is unimaginable that any civilized people should lack the spiritual support for them. Westerners have found such support in religion, while entrusting philosophy with the task of understanding the world.

The Western world experienced its industrial revolution and with it the modernization of its science and its productive forces, which thus prepared the conditions for philosophy and science to be separated from religion. But in China, which experienced not such an industrial revolution but rather the prolongation of feudal society, the conditions for separating philosophy from religion were absent, and philosophy remained undifferentiated from religion and under its domination throughout China's feudal period.

Medieval Western philosophy, too, had been very much concerned both with personal peace and establishing destiny and with the study of cosmology, the object being to unite man with Heaven so that he might attain sainthood and sagehood. Anselm (1033–1109), for example, asserted that faith was the basis for understanding, while understanding might furnish arguments for faith. The time of Anselm corresponds to the reigns from Jen-tsung[p] (r. 1023–1063) to Hui-tsung[q] (r. 1101–1125) of the Sung dynasty, and he was roughly contemporary with Chou Tun-i[r] (1017–1073), the two Ch'engs (Ch'eng Hao,[s] 1032–1085, and Ch'eng I,[t] 1033–1107), Chang Tsai[u] (1020–1077), and Shao Yung[v] (1011–1077). The time of Thomas Aquinas (c. 1225–1274) corresponds to the reigns from Li-tsung[w] (r. 1225–1264) to Tu-tsung[x] (r. 1265–1274) of the Southern Sung dynasty, being somewhat later than the time of Chu Hsi. Western scholastic philosophy had its counterparts to the discrimination between the "Principle of Heaven" and the "human desires," as well as its theories on the person, mind, nature, and destiny. Oriental and Western sages, then, seem to coincide with one another. Some are inclined to compare Kant and Hegel with the two Ch'engs, Chu Hsi, Lu Hsiang-shan (Lu Chiu-yüan,[y] 1139–1193), and Wang Yang-ming (Wang Shou-jen,[z] 1472–1529), and such an inclination has become widespread since the May Fourth Movement. However, it is injudicious to compare different stages of social development, that is, the feudal and capitalist societies, and no trustworthy conclusions can be deduced from such a comparison. There are also some people who think that the School of Principle (Li-hsüeh)[aa] in China and the Buddhist philosophy of India are similar because both are Oriental systems of thought. Actually, the similarity between ancient Chinese and Indian thought derived from the resemblance between their stages of social development. Both China and India were reduced to the status of colony or semicolony before they could formally advance to the stage of modern capitalist society. The similarity between the civilizations of these two great nations lay solely in the fact that both bore the features of antiquity.

What is said here is not intended to deny the distinctive characteristics of the national culture of China, or to suggest that cultural differences are determined entirely by stages of social development. Apart from the features common to all medieval cultures, premodern Chinese culture had its own distinctive feature, namely the feudal-patriarchal system. The Confucian religion of China was created by it in order to render it service, just as ancient Indian philosophy was characterized by its service to the caste system of India. Given the strength, tenacity, and duration of the feudal-patriarchal system, it exerted an enormous influence on traditional Chinese culture, penetrating it to a depth unimaginable to Westerners.

Not only did primitive Chinese thought come under its domination, but even Buddhism, which had been imported from abroad, could not escape being conditioned by it. During the period of more than two hundred years from the Eastern Chin dynasty (317–420) to the beginning of the T'ang dynasty, there arose the controversies over the Buddhist assertions that "a monk should not bow down before a king," or "a monk need not observe secular customs," and all such controversies resulted in the defeat of the monk. The same fate befell the monasteries in their claim of extraterritoriality and the exemption of monks from official punishment. If there were passages in original Buddhist scriptures contradictory to Chinese patriarchal ethics, they would be deleted, modified, or amended in the translation to meet the needs of the feudal-patriarchal system.[11] The highest norm for Buddhists is the *Agama-pramāna* (The norm of Buddha's teachings), an intended violation of which would result in falling into hell or suffering terrible retribution, yet Chinese Buddhists would rather run such a risk than offend against feudal ethics or the *san-kang wu-ch'ang*[ab] (the Three Cardinal Guides and the Five Constant Virtues).[12]

It is everywhere evident that Chinese religions and philosophy were obliged to render service to the feudal patriarchy and the *kang-ch'ang ming-chiao*[ac] (the cardinal guides, constant virtues, institutions, and morals). For example, in the revised edition of *Pai-chang ch'ing-kuei*[ad] (Regulations at the Pai-chang Mountain), a collection of monastic rules of the Ch'an[ae] School of Buddhism, the sovereign is blessed first, followed by the Buddha and the patriarchs, thus illustrating the degree to which Chinese religions were secularized. This secularization is revealed not only in rituals but also in religious theories which were brought into concert with the contemporary feudal-patriarchal system. The essence of religion lies in advocating unworldliness, which requires its followers to be different from members of the secular society both in their living habits and in their world view. But Ch'an, the most influential Buddhist sect in China, held that the Western Paradise was not on that further shore but on this one, that it was not outside the actual world but within it. Deliverance did not involve going to another place to lead a different life, but rather an effort to change one's world view. The practice of Buddhist monasticism did not mean leaving this world in search of a Western Paradise elsewhere. It was necessary only to adopt the Buddhist world view, and the mundane world of daily existence would be one and the same with the Western Paradise.[13]

Even before the School of Principle made its formal appearance, Chinese religions had begun to be secularized. Secularization was a trend common to both Buddhism and Taoism after the mid-T'ang period, with Ch'an becoming the most widespread sect of Buddhism and the *Ch'üan-chen*[af] (Preserving the True State) sect of Taoism also following the path of secularization. Later, in the wake of widespread destitution, clashes between nationalities, and frequent wars and upheavals, and the collapse of the monastic economy during the period from the end of T'ang to the Five Dynasties (907–960), Ch'an was the only Buddhist sect that not only did not decline but spread everywhere. From the confrontation of the three religions during the earlier T'ang dynasty to their confluence in the period from the end of T'ang through the Five Dynasties, the trend toward secularization grew.

The appearance of the School of Principle signified the completion of Confucianism. It might seem that the School of Principle succeeded in displacing Buddhism and Taoism, thus concluding the struggle that had occupied its predecessors for hundreds of years, but this success was only apparent. Unlike a political power, religion cannot be overthrown by any force whatsoever. Especially in the Middle Ages, religion as an ideology had the utmost vitality; it could not be obliterated from history, as evidenced by the fact that several great movements to "destroy Buddhism"[14] in Chinese history all resulted in failure and were all followed by a rekindling among the masses of an even more fervent faith. Advocates of the School of Principle had not deposed Buddhism and Taoism but had incorporated some of their important elements and then erected a sign declaring this to be the Confucian religion.

The School of Principle had its beginnings in the later stages of Chinese feudal society. According to the *Sung-Yüan hsüeh-an*[ag] (Anthology of Sung and Yüan Confucianists), its forebears were Sun Fu[ah] (992–1057), Shih Chieh[ai] (1005–1045), and Hu Yüan[aj] (993–1059); this view, however, was not acknowledged by the orthodox scholars of the school, whose designation of Chou Tun-i and the Two Ch'engs as its founders came to be accepted as the prevailing view. The time of the Five Masters of the Northern Sung (960–1126)[15] coincided with one of the great events in the history of that dynasty— the reforms of Wang An-shih[ak] (1021–1086)—which gave rise to political struggles that persisted until the fall of the Northern Sung. The reason for the failure of the reform lay not merely in bureaucratic mismanagement but also in the inevitable dilemmas attendant upon the later stages of feudal society. Regardless of whether or not reforms were enacted, the situation could not have been remedied. The state of the petty court of the Southern Sung (1127–1279) was even worse, the condition of the economy more parlous, the popular morale still more depressed. The "resurgence" of the Southern Sung was no more than an illusion. Philosophy at that time also confronted a crisis that would not be resolved. This might be described as the idealogical crisis of Confucian philosophy, which was as urgent as the situation calling for political reform. The efforts of the scholars of the School of Principle culminated in the founding of the Confucian religion, a historical mission begun by the masters of the Northern Sung and brought to completion by Chu Hsi during the Southern Sung.

Analysis of Chu Hsi's Theoretical System

Having inherited and developed the idea that "the Ultimateless is also the Great Ultimate" in Chou Tun-i's *T'ai-chi-t'u shuo*[al] (An explanation of the diagram of the Great Ultimate), Chu Hsi established the theory that "principle is one while its manifestations are various," thus demonstrating the relation between the variety and the unity of things and also expounding his idealistic ontology in a comparatively complete way. Having inherited the Ch'engs' proposition that "the nature is principle," he highlighted the objectivity and universality of "principle." Having assimilated Chang Tsai's theory that "the Great Void is material force," he revised Chang's philosophical system by subordinating material force to principle, so that principle became the ruler of material force. Thus he established a theory of cosmology more integrated than that of any previous philosopher.

In respect to the theory of human nature, Chu Hsi accepted the conclusions of his predecessors and developed them further, saying, "that man has his life is only due to the combination of nature and material force. To speak analytically of the combination, the nature is subject to principle and so it is without form, while material force is subject to form and so it has substance."[16] This means that an actual human being is formed when the Heaven-endowed nature pervades the physical nature. The distinction between these two kinds of nature was intended to settle the long-standing dispute in the history of Chinese philosophy over whether human nature is good or evil. According to Chu Hsi, the goodness of human nature which Mencius advocated[17] pertained to the Heaven-endowed nature, for Mencius, focusing only on a human nature that was good and not knowing of the physical nature, could not satisfactorily solve the problem of where evil comes from. As a result, his interpretation of human nature was imperfect. Hsün Tzu's theory that human nature is evil, Yang Hsiung's theory of human nature as a mixture of good and evil, and Han Yü's theory of the three classes of human nature all referred to the physical nature, and they did not understand that the Heaven-endowed nature, which is traceable to the Ultimate, is in itself good. Consequently, their explanations of human nature were also incomplete. Chu Hsi thought that only by strictly differentiating the two kinds of human nature could a satisfactory interpretation be attained. That is why he gave the highest praise to the theory of Chang Tsai and the two Ch'engs on human nature, saying that, "So upon the establishment of the theory of Chang and Ch'eng, the arguments of all previous philosophers collapsed."[18] Thus, by taking the Heaven-endowed nature to be the proper nature of man, it was possible to find ontological grounds for the theory of the goodness of human nature. In Chu Hsi's system, all the myriad things are the embodiment of the Great Ultimate, and when the Great Ultimate is embodied in man, it is called the nature. The Great Ultimate is the most perfect reality, and everything shares its brilliant light. Since it is perfect, its embodiment in human nature should be perfect as well. And since the proper nature of man is good, any defects in the material substance can be diminished through effort.

The crux of Chu Hsi's theory of human nature was that the norms of feudal morality, such as humanity, righteousness, loyalty, and filial piety, are the Heaven-endowed nature. Everybody has these moral endowments; and it is only because of the partiality and obscuretion associated with the material substance that some people are unable fully to develop and actualize this Heaven-endowed nature or morality. Chu Hsi's demonstration served to provide ontological justification for Mencius' theory of the goodness of human nature. Once having been correctly stated, it showed people where to direct their efforts and gave confidence to those who could not yet fully correspond to the norms of feudal morality. Therefore, drawing a distinction between the Heaven-endowed nature and the physical nature was in Chu Hsi's words "a credit to the School of the Sage [Confucianism]." Chu Hsi also thought that the Heaven-endowed nature consists of humanity, righteousness, decorum, and wisdom, which are the original nature not only of man but also of the universe. As he put it, they are "the virtues of Heaven and Earth." "What in respect to Heaven are called origination, flourishing, advantage, and correctness (*yüan, heng, li, chen*[am])[19] are in respect to man called humanity, righteousness, decorum, and wisdom."[20] Chu offered a theoretical justification for the necessity that everyone accept the feudal morality (drawing on Hsün Tzu's view of human nature as evil and the importance of reforming people) combined with a theoretical statement of the possibility that everybody could be reformed into a sage or worthy (developing Mencius' theory of the goodness of human nature).

Chu Hsi also developed a new perspective on the relation between the mind, nature, and feelings. He said, "The nature is the principle of the mind, and feelings are the activities of the nature, and the mind is the master of both the nature and feelings."[21] Using the metaphor of water, he said, "The mind is like water, the nature is like the tranquillity of water, and feelings are like its flowing."[22] Within the nature are humanity, righteousness, decorum, and wisdom; when these are displayed in feelings, they become pity and commiseration, shame and dislike, the sense of right and wrong, and modesty and yielding. From the fact that "humanity, righteousness, decorum, and wisdom are all rooted in the mind," one sees the mind through the nature; and by the fact that the mind of pity and commiseration is the beginning of humanity, one sees the mind through the feelings. Nature is nothing but principle, and so nothing in it is evil, but when it displays itself in feelings, there are both good and evil in it. The mind proper is the "mind of Tao,"[an] and when it is implicated with the feelings, it becomes the "mind of man." Corresponding to the "mind of Tao" and the "mind of man," there are the "Principle of Heaven" and "human desires." So Chu Hsi said, "There is in man only one mind, which represents itself as the Principle of Heaven when it corresponds to the way of Nature, or as human desires when it yields to emotional cravings."[23] Chu Hsi was different from the two Ch'engs in that the latter identified the "mind of Tao" with the "Principle of Heaven," and the "mind of man" with human desires, whereas Chu Hsi associated the "Principle of Heaven" with morality and thought of "the mind of man" not as equivalent to the human desires, which were absolutely evil, but rather as having the potentiality for both good and evil. When human desires are overcome and the Principle of Heaven is revived, there is *jen*[ao] (humanity).

For Chu Hsi, the final aim of man is to seek *jen*. He said, "To conquer oneself and to return to decorum is *jen*.[24] This means that one overcomes personal desires and recovers the Principle of Heaven, and as a result, the substance of the mind exists everywhere and its function reaches everything."[25] "*Jen* is the virtue of the mind and the principle of love."[26] "The way of *jen* is that, being the mind of Heaven and Earth creating things, it is present in things. . . . If it is really preserved as its substance, it will be the source of every goodness as well as the origin of every merit, and that is why the teachings of the Confucian School must persuade its scholars to acquire *jen* devotedly."[27]

These quotations show how Chu Hsi extended the general law of man to the general law of Heaven (Nature). At the same time, he enlarged the general law of nature to apply to man. In his amended commentary on the *Great Learning* in his *Ta-hsüeh chang-chü*[ap] (Commentary on the *Great Learning*), he said,

> What is meant by extending knowledge through investigating things is that the way to extend one's knowledge lies in dealing with things and plumbing their principle. Every intelligent human mind has its knowledge, while everything in the universe has its principle. Only when principle has not been plumbed, knowledge will not be complete. That is why the *Great Learning* at the beginning of its teaching requires that the student deal with everything in the universe and probe deeply to arrive at the limit. When after long striving one suddenly achieves clear realization of the pervading unity, everything is seen clearly within and without, in its coarseness and its fineness, and then the total substance and great function of one's mind are all brought to light.[28]

Thus the investigation of things means "dealing with things and plumbing their principle," and here people are taught to start from recognizing concrete things. The principles to be plumbed include the principles of a blade of grass or a tree as well as the most fundamental principles of philosophy.

Although Chu Hsi stated that we should plumb the principles of the myriad things in the universe, he focused on teaching people to plumb the principles of feudal morality. He said, "Plumbing real principles includes the effort of self-examination. If one merely talks about plumbing the principles of the myriad things in the universe without being concerned with self-examination, he is like a horseman going astray, as it says in the *I-shu*[aq] (Surviving works)."[29] It is evident now that although this theory of investigating things included the element of acquiring knowledge from external objects, his stress was not on knowing the natural world and discovering its laws. His concern was rather with a method for cultivating feudal morality. The object was not to understand the principle of this or that thing, but to reach a state where "everything is seen clearly within and without, in its coarseness and its fineness, and the

total substance and great function of one's mind are all brought to light."
Such a conceptual realm is a realm of sudden enlightenment, a spiritual realm
of omniscience and omnipotence. Chu Hsi said, "When one speaks of knowledge having arrived, one means a knowledge which extends to the principles
of all affairs and things in the world. . . . It must reach everywhere in all
directions, leaving nothing that it does not know, and then it can be said to
have arrived." Pointing to a lamp, he continued, "It is just like the candle
there. Its light shines all over the room; there is nowhere it does not reach."[30]
"To investigate things refers to details, while to extend knowledge refers to
the whole."[31] Again he said, "The mind encompasses the myriad principles,
and all principles are complete within the one mind. If the mind cannot be
preserved, principles cannot be plumbed, and when principles cannot be
plumbed, the mind cannot function to the fullest."[32]

Chu Hsi went from human life to nature, and then from nature back to
man. In his view, Heaven and man share the same principle; they are interconnected and interpenetrating. He had gone beyond the theological teleology
of the Ch'in and Han dynasties based on the idea of a unity of Heaven and
man. Tung Chung-shu had discussed the unity of Heaven and man and said
that Heaven had a will, could be joyous and angry, and capable of reward or
punishment, and that anybody who offended against Heaven would be
punished. Chu Hsi proceeded by following this line, but his reasoning was
more sophisticated. His concepts of Heaven and principle do not reflect such
clear personification but reveal at many points a more reasonable, humanistic,
and rational approach. He said, "T'ai-chi[a] (the Great Ultimate) is nothing but
the highest good and perfect principle. Everybody has in himself a T'ai-chi
and every thing has in itself a T'ai-chi. What Master Chou called T'ai-chi is
an appellation for all virtues and the highest good in heaven and earth, man,
and things."[33] With respect to the existence of things in the natural world, one
can only speak of how they exist and not of their existence being bound up
with the values of good or evil. People do not speak of how good or virtuous
the mountains, rivers, or earth are. For heaven and earth, man and things to
have all virtues and the highest good, they must have been endowed with
moral attributes. Therefore Chu Hsi said again, "The mind of Heaven and
Earth is to create things, and man and things at their birth all possess this
mind of Heaven and Earth to be their own mind. So in talking about the virtue of the mind, although it is comprehensive, analytical, thorough-going, and
complete, it can be characterized in one word: jen."[34] Heaven and Earth and
man all take the creation of things to be their mind, and this mind of creating
things penetrates and displays itself in the myriad affairs and things, in a
blade of grass or a tree, and also in all aspects of social and political life. Chu
Hsi was given to using the metaphor of "the moon being reflected in thousands of rivers" to clarify his reasoning that the same T'ai-chi, or the totality
of all principles, is embodied in everything. If this T'ai-chi must be characterized, the word is jen. As he put it, "The mind of Heaven and Earth has in

itself four virtues, namely, origination, flourishing, advantage, and correctness, and origination dominates all the rest. . . . The mind of man also has in itself four virtues, namely, humanity, righteousness, decorum, and wisdom, and humanity embraces all the rest. . . . When present in Heaven and Earth, the mind is an unbounded one which creates things. When present in man, it is the mind which extends love to man and advantages to things. It embraces the four virtues and permeates the Four Beginnings."[35]

Although the philosophical system of Chu Hsi began with the myriad things in the universe and proceeded from the investigation of things and the extension of knowledge, it ultimately never departed from its primary purpose. Stymied by a return to the ordinary ethical conventions of daily life, it reverted in the end to the cultivation of feudal morality the object of which was to attain *jen*. To investigate things to extend knowledge was solely for the purpose of probing principle and thereby fulfilling the nature. Knowing destiny meant knowing Heaven. In this view, the myriad things in the universe, being originally manifestations of *jen*, were full of vitality and harmony, a fact that was not apparent only because people were deficient in cultivation and delinquent in self-examination. Origination, flourishing, advantage, and correctness were the four virtues of Heaven and Earth, while origination embraced all the rest. Humanity, righteousness, decorum, and wisdom were the four virtues of human nature, while humanity controlled all the rest. The essence of the mind was also the essence of Heaven, or in Chu Hsi's words, "Mind is the virtue of Heaven." Now and then he intentionally drew attention to the interrelation between Heaven and man. This was the common and fundamental world outlook of Sung Confucians. Chou Tun-i would not cut the grass in front of his window,[36] saying, "They have life and vitality as I have." The Ch'eng brothers said, "*Jen* can be seen by looking at chickens,"[37] and Ch'eng Hao said, "*Jen* means forming one body with things."[38]

Chu Hsi criticized the scholars of the Ch'eng School for two sorts of deviation that had appeared in interpretations of their masters' theory of *jen*. The first deviation, represented by Yang Shih[as] (1053–1135), involved understanding the substance of *jen* in terms of things and the self forming one body. The other deviation, represented by Hsieh Liang-tso[at] (1050–c. 1120), involved understanding *jen* as the consciousness of the mind. In Chu Hsi's own view, Heaven and man are interpenetrating, and both realize and embody the *jen* which is the mind to create things. The problem attendant upon understanding *jen* in terms of things and the self forming one body is that in such an idea there are obscurities that "might lead to the identification of things and the self" and to the misunderstanding that *jen*, being a given, requires no effort. Then people would be muddleheaded, lazy, and deficient in vigilant effort. And "if *jen* is understood as consciousness, the obscurities involved in that view may lead to mistaking desires for principle," a deviation which is still more harmful. It is clearly a Ch'an idea. Chu Hsi again and again criticized the Ch'an idea that consciousness is the nature and their notion that "in the eye, it is seeing; in the ear, it is hearing; in the hand, it is grasping; in the foot it is running." According to Chu Hsi, such activities are irrelevant to feudal moral values, and so they are not nature. The difference between man and animals is just that man has the idea of value. Only when seeing, hearing, speaking, and acting are in correspondence with the moral norm are they *jen;* devoid of moral content, they are relevant only to animals instead of man. Chang Tsai said, "All people are my brothers and sisters, and all things are my companions"[39] and "We should establish our minds on behalf of Heaven and Earth and establish our destiny for the people."[40] And Chu Hsi taught people to preserve in their minds a sense of pity and commiseration.

A theory that has exerted widespread influence in a society can never be a fuss about nothing; it must have developed out of experience. Even in the beginning stage of the Northern Sung, conditions were already critical, and there were constant domestic troubles and outside invasions. Wang An-shih's reforms, which had involved the whole political scene, underwent ups and downs until the end of the Northern Sung dynasty, reflecting the political crisis at that time. The failures could not simply be attributed to inappropriate management of the reforms. During the Northern Sung dynasty the economy languished and people were in dire poverty. There was no remedy, regardless of whether or not a reform was carried out. The Five Masters of the Northern Sung were contemporaneous with the political reforms of Wang An-shih, but their theories, unlike the political reforms, proved successful. They and later Chu Hsi of the Southern Sung gradually perfected the ideological system of the Confucian religion. The petty court of the Southern Sung dynasty was in a state even worse than the court of the Northern Sung. With a more difficult economy and a more depressed popular morale, the "resurgence" of Southern Sung was only an illusion and idle talk. In neither the Northern nor the Southern Sung period did social realities give ground for optimism, but the words of the Sung Confucians convey no sense of bitterness or restlessness. They manifested the subtle activating force of nature in all of its vibrancy and the spirit of life in all of its vitality, and the spiritual cultivation to which they devoted themselves was designed to enable them to progress from naturally following the Mean with a bright countenance and upright posture to displaying the dispositions of sages and worthies. In the period of the end of T'ang and the following Five Dynasties, when people had no means of livelihood and even resorted to cannibalism, Ch'an flourished widely and preached everywhere its doctrine of becoming a Buddha or a Buddhist patriarch without reading scriptures or practicing meditation. Such practices illustrate that the religious worldview was a distorted reflection of the actual world.

Some years ago I wrote in an article entitled "On the Formation of the Confucian Religion"[41] that all religions postulate the existence of two worlds, namely, a supramundane spiritual world which is the Kingdom of Heaven, the Pure Land, or the other-world, and, on the other hand, the actual world. In some religions the description of the other-world is very vivid and concrete, an almost unlimited enhancement of all the positive elements in the actual world. Some religions describe the other-world as a subjective and spiritual state, an inclination seen in Chinese Buddhism and Taoism following the Sui and T'ang periods. In such a religious view, leaving the world did not mean abandoning it and searching for peace in some other world or Western Paradise. It was necessary simply to adopt a religious world view in daily life, and the present mundane world would in itself be the most joyous realm of the Western Paradise.[42] In this view every person is a Buddha if he is enlightened by the Buddhist doctrine and adopts a religious world view. The Buddha is within this mundane world, not outside of it.

The School of Principle of the Sung and Ming was just like that. It pointed to the existence of a spiritual state, the "extremely lofty and brilliant way of following the golden mean." One need only remold his world view in order to become a sage; it was unnecessary to remold the world. But the Buddhist theory that one could renounce the world without leaving it of itself destroyed the theoretical integrity of Buddhist doctrine. People could not help questioning monasticism if "carrying water and hauling firewood is the marvelous way." Wasn't the rendering of service to one's father and sovereign also the marvelous way? The greatest social crisis that the Chinese feudal society faced was precisely the problem of how to strengthen and consolidate the order of the Three Cardinal Guides by all means, from political measures to ideological formulations. Both Buddhism and Taoism were willing to do their best to assist in solving this great problem, but their advocacy of leaving the world inevitably represented a barrier. But having gone from the idea that through carrying water or hauling firewood one can perceive one's nature and become a Buddha to the idea that through rendering service to one's father and sovereign one can become a sage or a worthy, the barrier that remains becomes as thin as paper. It is only necessary to break through this paper-thin barrier and the way is opened. Confucianism, Buddhism, and Taoism converge. Viewed historically, it was not only Confucianism that prompted the unity of the three teachings; such unity was also advocated by Buddhism and Taoism. This was a general trend in the development of culture, not something that any individual might have determined. Now the School of Principle became Confucianism, and the old tradition of venerating Heaven and emulating ancestors was invested with fresh content.

Chu Hsi and New China

From the remote past Chu Hsi inherited the orthodoxy of Chu-Szu[au] (two rivers in Confucius' native state of Lu), and from his immediate predecessors he received the tradition of I-Lo[av] (two rivers in Honan, the native place of the two Ch'engs), becoming the most influential philosopher after Confucius. His great influence was of course the result of historical conditions and not solely a matter of his own personal ability. In the period of the May Fourth Movement, people raised the cry "Down with the Confucian Shop," though in reality Confucius bore the blame for others. At that time the struggle to break the hold of old customs involved Chu Hsi rather than Confucius because nearly all the crimes for which people denounced the "Confucian Shop" were those of Chu Hsi and the School of Principle and had nothing whatever to do with Confucius.

Chinese society had hardly passed through a stage of capitalism before passing rapidly into socialism. Lacking the Western tradition of some four hundred years of struggle against medieval ecclesiastical power and authority has resulted in not a few problems for China's socialist construction. The two great slogans of the May Fourth Movement were "Science" and "Democracy." When the sixtieth anniversary of the movement was celebrated some years ago, it was pointed out that these two great aims were still to be achieved. The feudal culture and ideology of China and the Confucian religion, which was so closely bound up with the feudal system, have been far more tenacious than we had anticipated. Observing the course China has followed over the past hundred years and also tracing the course the country followed for nearly eight hundred years after Chu Hsi must be a source of inspiration for every Chinese and for everyone who studies the history of Chinese philosophy. It seems that philosophy and religion are something extremely lofty, and the problems which are discussed and the categories which are raised all remote from the world, but as a matter of fact, they are just a mirror of the actual world.

The Confucian religion was a product of the later stages of Chinese feudal society and, having adapted itself to the circumstances of that time, it became a religion with Chinese features. Yen Yüan[aw] (1635–1704) of the Ch'ing dynasty (1644–1912) also pointed this out saying, "It was not that Buddhism approximated the School of Principle, but that Ch'eng I's School of Principle approximated Buddhism." Of Chu Hsi he said, "He unconsciously committed all the mistakes for which he had reproached Buddhism and Taoism, for instance, practicing quiet-sitting for half a day to observe the disposition before the arousal of pleasure, anger, sorrow, joy."[43] Here Yen Yüan was talking only about one aspect of Ch'eng-Chu Confucianism. Chu Hsi regarded creation as the great virtue of Heaven and Earth, which have in them the mind to create things. There is also in man the mind to love things, a mind endowed by Heaven, and that is *jen*. Without *jen*, a man cannot be human; without *jen*, Heaven and Earth cannot be Heaven and Earth. Chu Hsi's learning was not merely a search for pure knowledge. He himself brought to fulfillment the teachings of ancient sages through practice and application. His understanding of the saying in the *Analects* that "*jen* can be known through examining errors"[44] may be taken as an example.

As to the saying about examining errors . . . it would seem that it does not refer only to one particular person. It is a general theory which explains that the errors made by man are all due to what impels him to partiality, as, for example, liberality or parsimony, restraint or indulgence. So once an error has been made, there is only the selfishness of human desire. If one can perceive through this the defect to which partiality has inclined him . . . one can also perceive the prevailing power of the Principle of Heaven. . . . Hence the saying that by examining errors, one may know *jen*. This means that by examining man's errors and knowing what impels him to partiality, one can know *jen* as well, but it does not imply that *jen* can be known only in this way.

Chu Hsi had not only given such an explanation to the original phrase in the *Analects*, but had also experienced it personally in the teachings of the Sage. He continued,

As for examining one's own errors, I myself had tried but found it unsatisfactory. If I have to examine my errors after having made them, the errors have already become real, and it is too late to examine them. I shall long regret it. This is not the way for me to cultivate my mind, but on the contrary, serves to injure it. If, before making errors, I examine in advance what customarily impels me to partiality then my mind is still clean and stainless, requiring no cultivation or refinement. It seems that the method customarily employed by the Sage for teaching people to cultivate the mind and to attain *jen* would not have been so fragmented as first to have one seek out the defect to which his partiality inclined him and then to examine his mind attentively.[45]

It is clear that the learning of Chu Hsi emerged not out of talk but out of actual personal experience, that it was a learning not of pure speculation but of guidance for behavior, and that it was religion rather than philosophy. Religion teaches not talk but action. From the theory of Tung Chung-shu and the Confucian theology of the *Pai-hu t'ung,* it can be seen that the "Heaven" of the Han dynasty was a personified god, an idea which reflects the level of knowledge of man two thousand years ago. By comparison, the "Heaven" of Chu Hsi is not a lifelike, personified god, but a rational god of the feudal patriarchy. This god is not in human shape but has human nature and "the mind to create things in abundance." The objects of worship in the Confucian religion are Heaven, Earth, the sovereign, parents, and teachers, which might seem to be a manifestation of pluralism, but actually they are only unusual products of the feudal-patriarchal system. Individually speaking, the sovereign represents the feudal state; parents represent the familial authority which is the nucleus of Chinese feudal patriarchy; Heaven is the theological support for sovereignty; Earth is the undergirding for Heaven; and the teacher is one who speaks for the other four and possesses the supreme right to interpret feudalism. It is the same with Buddhism, which venerates the Buddha, the Dharma (law), and the Sangha (clergy) as its Triratna: it would be impossible to propagate the Buddha and the Dharma without the Sangha.

The Confucian religion is different from other religions, and it even upholds the banner of antireligion. It takes the physical nature to be the source of evil, this being Confucians' version of original sin. In advocating asceticism, it teaches people to have little regard for the material life but to be obedient to the Principle of Heaven. It teaches them not to be concerned with reforming the external world but rather to nourish and examine their own minds to detect a single erroneous thought. Chu Hsi's theories were not well understood for a period of time, and so they were put under prohibition. This did not last long, however, and before long the prohibition was lifted, and his teachings were promoted by the state throughout the Yüan, Ming, and Ch'ing dynasties, with his works being used as textbooks for intellectuals in their preparation for civil service examinations. Thus his views were also inculcated into the intelligentsia at large.

The development of productive forces and the economy requires breaking the bondage of feudalism to open the way to capitalism. During the reigns of Wan-li[ax] (1573–1620) of the Ming and Ch'ien-lung[ay] (1736–1795) of the Ch'ing, both industry and commerce developed considerably in certain areas. Had this development not been hindered, China might have kept pace with the world at that time and entered into capitalism. But the forces of feudalism in China were so stubborn and strong that every time a new emerging force grew up, it was repressed. Historians used to say that Chinese science and technology began to lag behind after the Opium War of 1842, but actually they had begun to lose their preeminent position by the middle of the Ming period. Gunpowder had been first invented in China, but the Ming court had to purchase cannons from the West. Chinese navigation, though originally advanced, became backward after the Ming dynasty, and those who circumnavigated the world were not Chinese. In respect to astronomy and the calendar, China had been one of the more advanced countries in the world; but after the Ming period, calendrical calculation also became less precise than it was in the West. Although there were various reasons for the backwardness of Chinese science and technology, the constricting influence of Sung Confucian thought should not be underestimated.

Chu Hsi's theory of investigating things could never give rise to science; it could only serve the feudal-patriarchal system. Likewise, his theory of *jen* could not foster reformers, to say nothing of revolutionaries. His views on investigating things and plumbing principle, or on the person, the mind, nature, and endowment were aimed at defending the feudal order of ethics.

Generally speaking, socialism comes after capitalism. New China, however, did not pass through a developed capitalist society but was established on the foundation of semifeudalism and semicolonialism. Under the regime of the people's democracy, the feudal system of private control of land was abolished without much trouble, but the influence of patriarchal feudalism was not adequately estimated, and there has not been enough time to distinguish carefully between the fine tradition and the dross of feudal culture. The essence of the culture of every nation is the cultural wealth which the masses have accumulated or created through ages; this represents the fine tradition of each respective national culture, while the dross has been left by a few privileged exploiters who used the name of the whole nation to pursue their personal advantage. Many reprehensible activities in the "Great Cultural Revolution," which lasted for ten years and attracted world-wide attention, were done on the basis of feudalistic ideology in the guise of Marxism.

At the core of Chinese feudalism was the feudal-patriarchal system with its theory of the Three Cardinal Guides, a theory which is incompatible with socialism. This same theory is at the heart of Confucianism. If the peasants are under the oppression of the authorities of the state, clan, and deities, they cannot enjoy democracy; if the masses are not liberated from patriarchal oppression but are still subjected to the domination of this or that clan or family, they have no access to democracy. In that the right of young men and women to enjoy freedom of marriage is still interfered with by their parents or the old forces in the society, the new marriage law is designed to safeguard legally the right of matrimonial freedom for young people. Patriarchy and despotic leadership are also vestiges of the feudal-patriarchal system. Such problems no longer afflict Western societies, but in New China they still have their influence and are an impediment to social progress.

The Western world has its own difficulties, such as the weakness of family ties and lack of a place for old people. Some people have found much to admire in the Oriental family system. In the new relationships within a socialist family, the old are respected and the young are cherished, and there are equality and mutual aid among its members, while sons or daughters are responsible for supporting their parents. Such a family relationship is different from the absolute paternalism of feudal patriarchy. The respect paid to parents in a socialist society is not identical with feudal filial piety, because in feudal patriarchy, sons and daughters belong to and live for their parents. It should be noted likewise that a theory may have different functions when it is applied to different social contexts. When the schools of Chu Hsi and Wang Yang-ming were propagated in Japan they exerted a progressive function. In the West, Chinese culture has exerted various influences on different nations in different periods. The reason lies in the fact that a nation must depend upon its traditional culture as the support for its existence and development, whereas a culture imported from outside can only assume an ancillary and supportive role. The thought of Chu Hsi, whether in its positive or negative aspects, could never exert a decisive influence on foreign cultures. However, having been encouraged and inculcated in China by official authorities for nearly eight hundred years, the theory of the Three Cardinal Guides and the worship of "Heaven, Earth, sovereign, parents, and teachers" have conditioned people's minds profoundly and almost irreversibly. In this respect, the personal feelings of a scholar of New China cannot coincide with the impressions of scholars who stand outside the perimeters of this culture.

This symposium is to discuss philosophical problems, and while it seems that what I am dealing with here is not purely philosophical, it is precisely the thought of Chu Hsi. He taught people to proceed from the investigation of

things to the extension of knowledge, attaining sincerity of thought, rectification of the mind, cultivation of the self, regulation of the family, ordering of
the state, and at last bringing peace to the world. The construction of a
socialist country belongs to the category of "ordering the state and bringing
peace to the world," but this cannot be carried out according to Chu Hsi's
scheme. His teachings have been espoused for some eight hundred years, but
they did not solve the problem of how to give the Chinese people enough to
eat and wear, or to make them stand up truly. There are some useful elements
in Chu Hsi's system of thought, but the system of Confucian religion which
he founded is not practicable.

Notes

1. The history of social development shows that, generally speaking, human society
must undergo five stages: primitive society, slave society, feudal society, capitalist society, and socialist-communist society.

2. Recent investigations done among the national minorities of China serve to ver-
ify the records in the ancient ritual texts.

3. *Tso-chuan*[az] [Tso's commentary], Duke Chao,[ba] second year. Han Hsüan Tzu[bb] of
the state of Chin, having seen the rich cultural relics and ancient records preserved in
the state of Lu where he was visiting, exclaimed, "The rites of Chou are all in Lu
now!" See *Ch'un-ch'iu Tso-chuan chi-chieh*[bc] [Collected explanations of Tso's commentary on the *Spring and Autumn Annuals*], (Shanghai: Shanghai People's Press, 1977),
ch. 4, p. 1208.

4. The *Book of Odes*, the *Book of History*, the *Book of Changes*, the *Book of Rites*,
the *Book of Music*, and the *Spring and Autumn Annals*.

5. *Analects*, 17:2.

6. *Book of Mencius*, 6A:6.

7. *Hsün Tzu*, ch. 23.

8. *Fa-yen*[bd] [Model sayings], ch. 3.

9. *Han Ch'ang-li ch'üan-chi*[be] [Complete works of Han Yü], (SPPY ed.), 11:5b–6a.

10. See Yüan Hung[bf] (328–376), *Hou-Han shu*[bg] [History of the Later Han dynasty],
(SPTK ed.), 10:5b.

11. See Chen Yin-ch'ü,[bh] "A Postscript to the Nidāna of Utpala Becoming a Buddhist Nun," in *Han-liu-t'ang chi*[bi] [Collected writings at the Cold Willow Hall],
(Shanghai: Ku-chi[bj] Press, 1980), p. 155. Hajime Nakamura,[bk] "The Influence of Confucian Thought on the Chinese Translation of Buddhist Scriptures," in *Studies on
World Religions*, 1982, no. 2, pp. 26–34.

12. The Three Cardinal Guides pertain to the relationships between the ruler and
minister, father and the son, and husband and the wife. The Five Constant Virtues are
affection between parent and child, righteousness between ruler and minister, order
between seniors and juniors, separate functions for husband and wife, and good faith
among friends, with traditional emphasis on loyalty to the ruler and filial piety to
father.

13. "*Bodhi* (wisdom) is only to be found in one's mind; what use is there of searching elsewhere for the mystic truth? It is said that if one cultivates himself accordingly,

the Western Paradise will be before one's eyes" (the *Platform Scripture, P'in-ch'ien*[bl] *Tripitaka,* "Teng"[bm] 4, p. 7).

14. The sovereigns who took measures to destroy Buddhism were Emperor T'ai-wu[bn] (r. 424–457) of the Northern Wei dynasty (386–535), Emperor Wu[bo] (r. 561–578) of the Northern Chou dynasty (557–581), Emperor Wu-tsung[bp] of the T'ang dynasty and Emperor Shih-tsung[bq] (r. 955–959) of the Later Chou dynasty, (951–960). They are called in history the "three Wus and one Tsung."

15. The Five Masters of the Northern Sung were Chou Tun-i, Ch'eng Hao, Ch'eng I, Chang Tsai, and Shao Yung.

16. *Chu Wen Kung wen-chi*[br] [Collection of literary works of Master Chu], (SPTK ed.), 44:1b, in reply to Ts'ai Chi-t'ung.[bs]

17. *Book of Mencius,* 6A:6.

18. *Chu Tzu yü-lei*[bt] [Classified conversations of Master Chu], (1872 ed.) 4:15a.

19. The Four Qualities of the first hexagram, *ch'ien*[bu] (heaven, male), in the *Book of Changes.*

20. *Chu Wen Kung wen-chi,* 67:21b–22a, "On Humanity."

21. *Chu Tzu yü-lei,* 5:7b.

22. *Ibid.,* 5:12a.

23. *Ibid.,* 78:22a.

24. Quoting the *Analects,* 12:1.

25. *Chu Wen Kung wen-chi,* 67:21b–22b, "On Humanity."

26. *Ibid.,* 67:22a.

27. *Ibid.*

28. *Ta-hsüeh chang-chu,* commentary on the fifth chapter.

29. *Chu Tzu yü-lei,* 18:11a alluding to the *I-shu,* in the *Erh-Ch'eng ch'üan-shu*[bv] [Complete works of the two Ch'engs], (SPPY ed.).

30. *Ibid.,* 15:14b.

31. *Ibid.,* 15:9b.

32. *Ibid.,* 9:7a.

33. *Ibid.,* 94:7a.

34. *Chu Wen Kung wen-chi,* 67:21b, "On Humanity."

35. *Ibid.,* 67:22a. In the *Book of Mencius,* 2A:6, it is taught that pity and compassion are the beginning of humanity, shame and dislike the beginning of righteousness, modesty and yielding the beginning of decorum, and the sense of right and wrong the beginning of wisdom.

36. *I-shu,* 3:2a.

37. *Ibid.,* 3:1a.

38. *Ibid.,* 2A:3a.

39. "Hsi-ming"[bw] [Western inscription], in the *Chang Tzu ch'üan-shu*[bx] [Complete works of Master Chang], ch. 1.

40. *Chang Tzu yü-lu*[by] [Recorded sayings of Master Chang], (SPTK ed.), pt. 2, 6b.

41. *Social Sciences in China* (in Chinese) (Beijing, 1980), no. 1, pp. 61–74.

42. See the *Platform Scripture, P'in-ch'ieh Tripitaka,* "Teng" 4, p. 7.

43. Yen Yüan, *Ts'un-hsüeh p'ien*[bz] [Treatise on the preservation of learning], (Beijing: Ku-chi Press, 1957), pp. 62–74.

44. *Analects,* 4:7.

45. *Chu Wen Kung wen-chi,* 67:15a–b.

Glossary

a	董仲舒	aa	理學	ba	昭
b	殷	ab	三綱五常	bb	韓宣子
c	齊	ac	綱常名教	bc	春秋左傳集解
d	魯	ad	百丈清規	bd	法言
e	燕	ae	禪	be	韓昌黎全集
f	晉	af	全真	bf	袁宏
g	禮記	ag	宋元學案	bg	後漢書
h	華夏	ah	孫復	bh	陳寅恪
i	周	ai	石介	bi	寒柳堂集
j	鄒	aj	胡瑗	bj	古籍
k	白虎通	ak	王安石	bk	中村元
l	荀子	al	太極圖說	bl	頻伽
m	揚雄	am	元亨利貞	bm	騰
n	韓愈	an	道	bn	太武
o	熊十力	ao	仁	bo	武
p	仁宗	ap	大學章句	bp	武宗
q	徽宗	aq	遺書	bq	世宗
r	周敦頤	ar	太極	br	朱文公文集
s	程顥	as	楊時	bs	蔡季通
t	程頤	at	謝良佐	bt	朱子語類
u	張載	au	洙泗	bu	乾
v	邵雍	av	伊洛	bv	二程全書
w	理宗	aw	顏元	bw	西銘
x	度宗	ax	萬曆	bx	張子全書
y	陸象山九淵	ay	乾隆	by	張子語錄
z	王陽明守仁	az	左傳	bz	存學編

22

Chu Hsi on Buddhism

CHARLES WEI-HSUN FU

IN A PREVIOUS PAPER, "Morality or Beyond: The Neo-Confucian Confrontation with Mahāyāna Buddhism," I made an observation that the Neo-Confucian confrontation with Sinitic Mahāyāna is "perhaps the most interesting and significant case of ideological 'love and hate' in the whole history of Chinese philosophy and religion."[1] In continuation with the main line of my philosophical investigation and reasoning there, I wish, in this essay, to examine critically Chu Hsi's critique of Buddhism, Ch'an[a] (Zen) in particular.[2] Very few Neo-Confucian representatives in the Sung (960–1279), Yüan (1277–1368), and Ming (1368–1644) dynasties had studied Buddhism as hard and seriously as Chu Hsi did, nor had any of them attempted a genuine philosophical attack upon Buddhism as thoroughly and devastatingly as he did.[3] He often compared his Neo-Confucian mission of defending the Confucian tradition against Ch'an Buddhism, which he regarded as the most attractive but dangerous heterodox teaching, to Mencius' (372–289 B.C.?) vehement refutation of Mo Tzu[b] (fl. 479–438 B.C.) and Yang Chu[c] (440–360 B.C.?).[4] And he often deplored the fact that a great number of Confucian students and scholars in his times had been one by one drawn into Ch'an Buddhism, which tended to overshadow the Confucian Way in philosophy and practice.[5] Professor Ch'ien Mu[d] remarks, "Chu Hsi had a very clear and true understanding of Ch'an. All the distinctions subsequently made by the Ming Neo-Confucianists originate in Chu Hsi's own distinction. . . . Chu Hsi began to study Ch'an at the stage of puberty, but his realization of the shortcomings of Ch'an was so deep that he naturally felt that he could no longer abide in it. To him belongs the great credit of keeping China from turning into a Ch'an nation."[6]

In his letter to Chiang Yung (Chiang Yüan-shih,[e] 1124–1172), Chu Hsi admitted that he himself had been attracted by Buddhism (and Taoism) for more than ten years but that "I have begun to find the principal direction I should take after my acquaintance in recent years with those who know the Way."[7] He also said elsewhere that he had begun to take a profound interest in Ch'an at the age of fifteen or sixteen, and that he had gradually realized the shortcomings of Ch'an after he met his teacher Li T'ung (Li Yen-p'ing,[f]

1093–1163), who advised him to study the Confucian sayings.[8] According to Chao Shih-hsia,[g] Li made a specific instruction to Chu Hsi concerning the ideological dangers of Buddhism: "What distinguishes our Confucian learning from the heterodox doctrine lies in 'Principle is one but its manifestations are many.' We need not worry about whether 'Principle is one' can be well maintained; what is difficult and crucial is to see the point that 'its manifestations are many.' "[9] Chu Hsi himself recalled: "When I first came to see Master Li, I talked about all sorts of philosophical reasonings (tao-li[h]). Master Li said, 'Why do you engage yourself in so much vain reasoning while failing to understand things near at hand? There is nothing mysterious about the Way. Just try to comprehend the meaning of the task of everyday sociomoral practice, and you will see the Way.' It took me a long time to realize what he said here."[10] Chu Hsi's acquaintance with Li T'ung can be said to constitute the first turning point of his own philosophical destiny; it was indeed through Li's Confucian instruction that Chu Hsi was able gradually to leave behind Buddhism (and Taoism) for an authentic pursuit of the Confucian Way. That Li's influence on Chu Hsi's existential commitment to Confucianism is indelibly strong can be easily detected from those philosophical poems Chu Hsi composed before and after his acquaintance with his teacher. For instance, among a number of poems he composed shortly before his first meeting with Li, the following one smacks of a Buddhist flavor:

> Temporarily I am freed from secular worries and attachments,
> And transcendentally I am one with the Way.
> The door is closed and the bamboo woods are quiet;
> The birds are singing while the mountain rain is subsiding.
> Realizing the absolutely unconditioned (wu-wei-fa[i])
> My body and mind are now at ease.[11]

Just two years after his first meeting with Li, Chu Hsi composed several poems. The last two lines of one of these clearly express his newly discovered Confucian identity: "My secular worries are decreasing day by day;/There is no need to reside in the empty mountain."[12] The "empty mountain" here refers, of course, to the Buddhist (as well as Taoist) way of life detached from everyday human affairs.

After Li T'ung's death, Chu Hsi gradually turned to the Neo-Confucian line of thinking of Ch'eng I[j] (1033–1107) for a fresh philosophical guidance and turned away from Li's teachings of "silent sitting for the purification of the mind" and of "observing the state of nonactivation of human feelings (wei-fa[k])." As we have learned from Professor Mou Tsung-san's[l] careful analysis,[13] Chu Hsi's earnest inquiry into the nature and meaning of both the states of nonactivation and activation of human feelings (i-fa[m]) and of "equilibrium and harmony" (chung-ho[n])—in keeping very closely with Ch'eng I's philosophical line—eventually led him to a new interpretation of "principle is one but its manifestations are many" on the ground of *li-ch'i*[o] (principle/vital force) metaphysics. Chu Hsi's unique resolution of the problem of equilibrium/harmony can be said to make up the second and final turning point of his philosophical development. And it is based on his newly established *li-ch'i* metaphysics that Chu Hsi now thinks that he can make an all-out effort to attack Buddhism in almost all aspects, notably in metaphysical thinking, theory of mind/nature, method of personal cultivation, theory of conduct and action, and theory of enlightenment.

Lacking a complete and solid knowledge of Indian and Chinese Buddhism as a whole in its long and complicated doctrinal development, Chu Hsi is not entirely successful in his criticism of Buddhism.[14] This is particularly true in the case of his often misleading or inaccurate treatment of Sinitic Mahāyāna metaphysics and theory of mind/nature, as we shall see shortly. But he is extremely successful in his critical exposition of the Sinitic Mahāyāna failure to tackle everyday sociomoral problems, which, in his Neo-Confucian judgment, only the Confucian tradition is able to resolve completely and perfectly.

The central thread that runs through Chu Hsi's critique of Buddhism is his Neo-Confucian thesis of "principle is one but its manifestations are many" deeply rooted in *li-ch'i* metaphysics, which he has brought into completion out of Ch'eng I's unfinished philosophical thought. In his Japanese work *Buddhism and Confucianism,* Professor Araki Kengo[p] insightfully observes that "an important motive behind the establishment of Chu Hsi's philosophy is his eagerness to point out the inhumanity of Ch'an experience based on the simplistic view of the identity of primordiality and actuality, as well as to capture the encounter of primordiality and actuality on the level of things near at hand in everyday life."[15] He further states that "the ideological transition from Ta-hui [Tsung-kao,[q] 1089–1163] to Chu Hsi should be regarded as a change of the way to actualize the primordiality rather than as the victory of the Confucian learning over the Buddhist."[16] I tend to agree with Araki's observation here, and I think that what he calls "primordiality" (the original mind/nature) and "actuality" (everyday actualization of the original mind/nature) can be respectively identified with "principle is one" and "manifestations are many," though he never makes this point explicit. Sharing with Professor Araki the view that Chu Hsi's mission lies in a Neo-Confucian transformation of the Ch'an Buddhist way of actualizing the original mind/nature, I would argue that, if Chu Hsi's critique of Buddhism is hard-hitting and constitutes a genuine counter-challenge to Sinitic Mahāyāna, especially Ch'an, which did challenge the Confucian tradition and help to cause the formation of the Neo-Confucian Way, the very success of the critique mostly consists of his ability to expose the Buddhist failure to resolve the problem of everyday (sociomoral) actualization of the original mind/nature, or, in other words, the problem of how to manifest concretely the selfsame principle of the Way *(tao-li)* in everyday sociomoral practice. To extend the various connotations of Chu Hsi's notions of "one principle" and "many manifestations," we can say that the former refers to "sublime transcendence," "reaching the higher spiritual stage," "sudden awakening," "what is above forms" (*hsing-erh-shang*[t]) or the metaphysically primordial, "the heavenly (or moral) nature," Tao[s] (the Way), the Supreme Ultimate, the mind of the Way (*Tao-hsin*[t]), and so on, while the latter refers to "the everyday Mean," "stepwise learning from below," "gradual cultivation," "what is within forms" (*hsing-erh-hsia*[u]) or the phenomenally manifest, "the physical nature" or *ch'i*-endowment, concrete things (*ch'i*[v]), yin-yang[w] (passive and active cosmic forces) and the Five Agents (Water, Fire, Wood, Metal, and Earth), the human mind (*jen-hsin*[x]), and so forth. Despite the fact that Chu Hsi's critique of Buddhism is attempted on the ground of *li-ch'i* metaphysics, the philosophical strength of his critique rather lies in his ability to show the practical sociomoral superiority of the Confucian way of manifesting the principle—however this may be divulged—over the Buddhist way. My principal contention is that neither Chu Hsi nor Sinitic Mahāyāna thinkers (including Ch'an Masters) can win insofar as their dispute over metaphysics and theory of mind/nature is concerned. Chu Hsi can, nonetheless, claim a great ethical victory regarding the question of "actualization of the primordiality" or "making the principle manifest in everyday sociomoral practice." It is in this very sense that Li T'ung's advice to Chu Hsi that "what is difficult and crucial is to see the point that 'its manifestations are many' " can be said to exert a lasting influence on Chu Hsi's criticism of Buddhism, irrespective of whether Chu Hsi himself was fully aware of his teacher's influence. And, if there is any good point at all in Chu Hsi's criticism of Lu Hsiang-shan's (Lu Chiu-yüan,[y] 1139–1193) mind-learning (*hsin-hsüeh*[z]) as Ch'an-oriented or as a vain teaching of sudden awakening, at the expense of gradual cultivation in terms of "holding onto reverential attentiveness or one-mindedness" and "extension of knowledge through investigation of things,"[17] it has to do with the question of how to make the principle manifest, in spite of the traditional understanding that the essential difference between Chu and Lu is that between the thesis of "the nature is principle" and the thesis of "the mind is principle." Let us now examine, in this philosophical light, Chu Hsi's critique of Buddhism in the following order: metaphysics, theory of mind/nature (or metapsychology), method of personal cultivation, theory of conduct and action, and theory of enlightenment (or soteriology). (For the sake of simplification, the two Western terms "metapsychology," which is borrowed from Freudian psychoanalysis, and "soteriology," which is borrowed from Christianity, can be used as terminologically interchangeable with "theory of mind/nature" and "theory of enlightenment" respectively.)

To begin with the metaphysical issue, Chu Hsi, as the greatest Neo-Confucian metaphysician, seems to see more clearly than any other Neo-Confucian thinker that the fundamental difference between Confucianism and Buddhism is metaphysical in nature. Chu Hsi says,

Those who refute Buddhism today rely upon the distinction between righteousness as the essence of the Confucian Way and self-interest as the essence of the Buddhist Way. . . . This distinction is rather secondary. . . . Buddhists take Emptiness as the essence of their metaphysical view. . . . Their metaphysical view is already wrong, consequently all other doctrines they maintain have to be equally wrong. How can it be sufficient to distinguish Confucianism from Buddhism in terms of righteousness/self-interest alone?[18]

Lu Hsiang-shan says that Buddhists and Confucianists share the same view and that the only difference lies in the distinction between righteousness and self-interest. I think this is wrong. If what Lu says were right, we Confucianists and the Buddhists would then maintain one and the same doctrine. If this were the case, can there be any difference at all even in terms of the righteousness/self-interest distinction? The truth is that the fundamental point is different: We Confucianists say all metaphysical principles are real while they say all principles are empty.[19]

Chu Hsi is here highly critical of Lu Hsiang-shan's failure to see the metaphysical, rather than ethical, difference as the most fundamental and essential between the two traditions. He apparently feels that Lu's "the mind is principle" thesis is already very much contaminated by Buddhist Sinitic Mahāyāna metaphysics and metapsychology and that only his own *li-ch'i* metaphysics can serve as the ultimate ground or standard for the Confucian refutation of Buddhism as doctrinally heterodox and ideologically dangerous.

According to Chu Hsi, the metaphysical difference between Confucianism and Buddhism is, first of all, that while Confucianism maintains the moral-metaphysical reality of the Principle of Heaven or Supreme Ultimate, Buddhism reduces everything, whatever that is, to "empty annihilation."[20] From Chu Hsi's vantage point, the Buddhists simply have no understanding of the moral-metaphysical reality of what can be called "the fountainhead" or original source of the ever-creative production and reproduction of all beings, human and nonhuman, in the entire universe—the fountainhead that is divulged in a Neo-Confucian way and expressed as Heavenly Principle or Supreme Ultimate. The Buddhists could never understand the deep and profound moral-metaphysical meaning of the famous line in the *Classic of Poetry*, quoted in the *Doctrine of the Mean*, "The hawk flies up to heaven and the fishes leap in the deep,"[21] which beautifully illustrates the ever-creative operations of the Heavenly Principle in the whole universe. Nor could they comprehend Confucius' words "Like this stream, everything is flowing on ceaselessly, day and night," for they find no real principle beyond or within the transcience or impermanence of the cycle of birth-and-death. Chu Hsi says, "Where there is a thing, there is and must be a specific principle. Those multiple principles . . . all issue from that fountainhead."[22] This fountainhead is none other than what the traditional Confucianists have called the Mandate of

Heaven, which is now metaphysicalized by Chu Hsi as principle or Supreme Ultimate. This fountainhead is the ultimate foundation of the Confucian and Neo-Confucian Way and always allows two complementary—"objective" (the moral-metaphysical approach) and "subjective" (the existential mind/nature approach)—ways of human divulging: "the nature is principle" and "the mind is principle." Chu Hsi's highly celebrated philosophical poem, "Feelings Arising from Reading Books," in Professor Wing-tsit Chan's[aa] following translation, subtly expresses the moral-metaphysical position of the Confucian Way against Mahāyāna Buddhist metaphysics of Emptiness:

> The square pond of half a mou[ab] [one third of an acre] opens up like a mirror.
> Sky light and cloud shadows move together to and fro.
> Let us ask: How can it be clear to such a degree?
> Because there is living water coming from the fountainhead.[23]

Based on his li-ch'i metaphysics, Chu Hsi is further able to say that to Confucianism not only is principle metaphysically real but ch'i[ac]—the primordial vital force penetrating into all parts of the world and man—is phenomenally real as well, and that, in critical contrast, the Buddhists never see into the phenomenal reality of all things but merely try to detect their illusory or unreal nature. Contrasting Taoism with Buddhism, Chu Hsi thinks that the former at least partially preserves the Chinese way of viewing Heaven and Earth, by stressing both being (yu[ad]) and nonbeing, (wu[ae]), while the latter completely reduces the phenomenal reality of everything to pure nothing. To Chu Hsi the Mahāyāna Buddhist notion of Emptiness can only be construed to mean "total nothing," "false illusion," or "unreal vacuity." He says, "Lao Tzu[af] [sixth or fourth century B.C.?] still speaks of being. . . . Buddhists regard Heaven and Earth as illusory and false, and take the Four Elements (Earth, Water, Fire, and Air) as no more than provisionally intermingled with each other. That means: total nothing at all!"[24] He also says, "According to Buddhism, all is just nothing. . . . 'Forms are empty and emptiness is forms.' From ten thousand events and things down to man's one hundred bones and nine apertures, they are all reduced to nothing. The Buddhists eat food all day long and yet they say that they have never bitten a grain of rice; they wear clothing around themselves, and yet they say that they have never put on any piece of cloth."[25]

No Mahāyāna Buddhist would ever accept Chu Hsi's identification of Emptiness with total nothing or unreality. They would rather compare Chu Hsi's lack of understanding of the Mahāyāna notion of Emptiness to the Neo-Taoist Kuo Hsiang's[ag] (d. 312) distortion of Chuang Tzu's[ah] (369–286 B.C.?) Tao or Nothingness as sheer nonexistence. Chu Hsi's distortion of Emptiness as total nothing is definitely influenced by Chang Tsai's[ai] (1020–1077) ch'i-monism or metaphysics of vital force. Chang said that what is really wrong with Buddhist metaphysics is that it "never studies exhaustively the principle, but considers everything to be the result of subjective illusion."[26] He also said, "The Buddhists would never be able to understand heavenly sequence or orderliness, which is the principle of change, manifested in 'the successive movements of yin and yang (cosmic forces of weakness and strength) which cover the entire universe, penetrate day and night, and form the standard of the great Mean in the Three Ultimates of Heaven, Earth, and Man.' "[27] Absorbing Chang Tsai's *ch'i*-monism into his *li-ch'i* metaphysics, Chu Hsi is very sure that he can easily brush off Buddhism, as Chang does, as metaphysically a sheer annihilationism, for it fails to account for the phenomenal reality of the primordial *ch'i* in its perpetual integration/disintegration, in the orderly pattern of yin-yang interaction and the successive movements and transmutation of the Five Agents.

Another important point in Chu Hsi's critique of Buddhist metaphysics is that "while Confucianists regard the principle as neither produced nor perishable, Buddhist take the 'spiritual consciousness' (*shen-shih*[aj]) as neither produced nor imperishable."[28] Sinitic Mahāyāna Buddhists are, Chu Hsi says, impelled to posit an imperishable "spiritual consciousness" despite their assertion that everything is empty (unreal), because they are, in Ou-yang Hsiu's[ak] (1007–1072) words, afraid of death and dying. But from the Confucian metaphysical point of view, "when *ch'i* integrates, there is birth; when *ch'i* disintegrates, there is death,"[29] and there is no reason to presuppose the eternal existence of the so-called spiritual consciousness for the sake of escaping from the cycle of birth-and-death. In short, the respective metaphysical positions of Confucianism and Buddhism can be summed up in Ch'eng I's words "Confucian sages rely upon Heaven, whereas Buddhists rely upon the mind."[30]

From the Sinitic Mahāyāna point of view, Chu Hsi's Neo-Confucian critique of Buddhist metaphysics as sheer annihilationism only exposes his hasty and erroneous identification of Emptiness with total nothing as well as his lack of understanding of the essential distinction between Indian and Sinitic Mahāyāna in metaphysical thinking. First, in regard to the Mahāyāna notion of Emptiness as explicated in the *Prajñāpāramitā-sūtra* (Perfection of wisdom scripture) and Nāgārjuna's *Mulamadhyamakakārika* ("Middle" wisdom treatise), it is entirely free from the man-made duality of being and nonbeing, reality and unreality, (logical) truth and untruth, *nirvāna* and *samsāra* (cycle of birth-and-death), conditioned *(samskṛta)* and unconditioned *(asamskrta)* states of being, and so on; this man-made duality is to be explained as an inevitable result of the nonenlightened being's conceptual fabrications of all things and one-sided fixations of language, thought, and reality on the mundane level *(samvṛti)* of human thinking. The teaching of Emptiness is the Indian Mahāyāna way of reorienting the early Buddhist notions of the nonsubstantiality ("no-self") and relational origination, in order to uncover the true nature of all *dharmas* (experiential factors of existence) as ultimately equal and the same, that is, ontologically nondifferentiable from one another. The teaching of Emptiness is provisionally employed as a pedagogical skill-in-means to remove or transcend all one-sided speculations, which arise as a result of the nonenlightened man's dualistic thinking. The teaching of Emptiness is self-cancellable in the sense that it is to be left behind as "null and void" as soon as all kinds of metaphysical thinking on the so-called "Absolute," whatever that may be, are critically exposed as one-sided. As the Chinese Mādhyamika ("Middle" school) master Chi-tsang[al] (549–623) says, "The refutation of all one-sided views is itself the correct view."[31] Emptiness is not really "empty" if "empty" here is mistaken as "unreal" or "nonexistent"; it is transmetaphysically beyond the duality of reality and unreality, emptiness and nonemptiness, existence and nonexistence, and so on. If Emptiness is one-sidedly hypostatized as "empty," then it becomes what is called "stubborn (one-sided) emptiness," which has nothing to do with "true Emptiness." True Emptiness, Suchness (or Thusness), and the like all transmetaphysically point to the ultimate incomprehensibility of the true nature of all *dharmas* (things, events, phenomena). Paradoxically, the very incomprehensibility here opens up what Lao Tzu calls "the gateway to infinite wonders."[32] Thus, from the Mahāyāna point of view, true Emptiness and wondrous being are one and the same thing. It is in this sense that the teaching of Emptiness always remains open-ended and helps to enlarge our metaphysical vision, allowing us humans to see things as they are in the functional form of holistic multiperspectivism. But the "negativistic" residue is not thoroughly removed in Indian Mahāyāna, as is evidenced by the following quotation from the *Diamond Sūtra*:

> As stars, a fault of vision, as a lamp,
> A mock show, dew drops, or a bubble,
> A dream, a lightening flash, or cloud,
> So should one view what is conditioned.[33]

It is only after the rise of Sinitic Mahāyāna—the philosophy of which covers, among others, the *Awakening of Faith*, the "rounded" teachings of T'ien-t'ai[am] and Hua-yen,[an] and, of course, Ch'an Buddhism—that the unfinished metaphysical task of Indian Mahāyāna is accomplished, by shifting the emphasis from "true Emptiness" to "wondrous being," or more strongly, by transforming the former into the latter. Probably under the profound influence of Taoism and Neo-Taoism, particularly the philosophy of Chuang Tzu, Sinitic Mahāyāna thinkers developed a full-fledged neo-Mahāyāna metaphysical theory—still as a pedagogical skill-in-means—which can be characterized as functionally multiperspectival. I tend to think that, generally speaking, Chinese metaphysics as represented by the Three Teachings of Confucianism, Taoism, and Sinitic Mahāyāna is essentially functional and multiperspectival in nature. Chinese metaphysics is multiperspectival or multidimensional in the sense that it is always open-ended and allows various—higher or lower—ways of seeing things as they are.[34] In Chinese metaphysics, the Principle of the Way takes the place of what is called "Truth" as a matter of objective knowledge in Western metaphysics. Chinese metaphysics is also functional in the sense that the metaphysical terms coined and employed by Chinese philosophers are basically nonsubstantive or nonhypostatic in nature and often contain multidimensional connotations at the same time, examples being *T'ien* (Heaven[ao]), Tao, yin yang, *yu-wu*, and so on. It is especially obvious in the case of Sinitic Mahāyāna that functional terms, such as *t'i-yung*[ap] (substance-function), *i-to*[aq] (one and many), *li-shih*[ar] (principle and events), and *k'ung-chia-chung*[as] (the empty, the provisional, and the middle), are flexibly employed to show the various, multiperspectival ways of seeing the ontological sameness of what Whitehead calls "process" and "reality." The T'ien-t'ai doctrine of the harmonious unity of the Three Truths (the empty, the provisional, and the middle), its all-affirming expression "Every being, be it a color or a fragrance, is none other than a wondrous manifestation of the Middle Way," the Hua-yen doctrine of the Four Dharma-Realms[35] in their nonobstructed interpenetration, or Ch'an expressions like "Every day is a good day" or "Everyday-mindedness is itself the Way," make it abundantly clear to us, if not to Chu Hsi and nearly all Neo-Confucianists, that, in principle at least, Sinitic Mahāyāna leaves no room for any misunderstanding that Emptiness is nothing but total nothing or unreality.

Sinitic Mahāyāna thinkers would even make a forceful philosophical point that their metaphysical teachings as a pedagogical skill-in-means are perfectly open-ended and involve no one-sided human divulging of the transmetaphysically incomprehensible, and therefore that these teachings are far superior to Confucian metaphysics, which attempts to moralize one-sidedly the ultimate suchness or as-is-ness of all things as they are. The Sinitic Mahāyāna claim here may or may not be true. In any case, as far as human metaphysical divulgings of the "Absolute" are concerned, Confucian moral metaphysics, Taoist naturalism, and Sinitic Mahāyāna teaching of "true Emptiness is wondrous being" can be regarded as the three metaphysically complementary ways of seeing things as they are in the functional form of holistic multiperspectivism within the Chinese philosophical tradition. And, from the metaphilosophical point of view, Confucian and Neo-Confucian thinkers must acknowledge the great challenge of Sinitic Mahāyāna metaphysics here.

It is very interesting and significant to note that Chu Hsi on some occasions does make a clear distinction between true Emptiness and stubborn emptiness, which he calls "mysterious (or vain) emptiness." He says,

Mahāyāna Buddhists speak of "mysterious emptiness"; they also speak of true Emptiness. The mysterious emptiness is simply pure vacuum in which there is utterly nothing. True Emptiness is rather that there is something real, and this

true Emptiness is quite similar to what we Confucianists speak of. But they
don't care any bit about heaven, earth, and the four directions; they only care
about one single mind.[36]

Chu Hsi only creates more problems for himself with this statement. For one
thing, he is apparently confusing two different issues—sociomoral and metaphysical. That these two issues can be separated from each other is very difficult for the followers of the Confucian Way to comprehend, for the simple
reason that Confucian metaphysics is always moral-oriented. Whether or not
Sinitic Mahāyānists care about anything at all has nothing to do with whether
or not they are able to see things as they are in the metaphysical sense. Chu
Hsi himself after all acknowledges the metaphysical similarity between Confucianism and Sinitic Mahāyāna, on the condition that the Mahāyāna notion
of Emptiness is not to be misconstrued as "mysterious emptiness." Since,
according to Chu Hsi, this similarity exists, why hasn't he tried to do justice
to Sinitic Mahāyāna metaphysics by clarifying the point? Why, instead, has he
rather stressed "mysterious emptiness" as total nothing, which no Buddhist
thinkers—let alone Sinitic Mahāyānists—would accept as their own view?
Chu Hsi's repeated point that the fundamental difference between the two
traditions is metaphysical and not simply ethical can still stand, for it is certainly true that Confucian metaphysics is moral-oriented while Sinitic
Mahāyāna metaphysics is transmoral, if not amoral, in nature. But if he wants
to change this point and tries to rediscover the metaphysical similarity
between the two traditions, then he must, first of all, remove the confusion
over the two different issues in question. If Chu Hsi were clear about the
metaphysical similarity between Confucianism and Sinitic Mahāyāna in
terms of functional multiperspectivism, wouldn't he have to agree with Lu
Hsiang-shan that the essential difference between the two traditions lies in the
distinction between righteousness and self-interest? Wouldn't he have to
admit that the philosophical superiority of Confucianism over Sinitic Mahāyāna can only be in the field of ethics, and not in that of metaphysics?

As to Chu Hsi's criticism of the Sinitic Mahāyāna theory of imperishable
"spiritual consciousness," it is also based on a total misunderstanding. Mature
Sinitic Mahāyāna thinkers seldom use the term "spiritual consciousness,"
which was probably often used by the early Chinese Buddhists. Those metapsychological terms frequently employed in Sinitic Mahāyāna are: "the
matrix of Tathāgata," "Buddha-nature," "the essential nature of the mind,"
"One-mind," "no-mind," and "the mind of nonabiding"; but these terms are
and must be transmetaphysically emptied of their "own-being." Transmetaphysically, all dharmas, including "Buddha-nature" and the like, are truly
empty, and cannot be said to exist or not exist. In fact, no philosophical-
minded Sinitic Mahāyānist would ever deviate from the teaching of Emptiness and assert the existence of any hypostatic metaphychological entity. The
Mahāyāna theory of Buddha-nature or the like is no more than a pedagogical

skill-in-means created to provide a metapsychological basis for man's existential self-awakening to "true Emptiness is wondrous being." If and when one is ultimately enlightened, the theory itself will have to be left behind as "null and void." In other words, from the perspective of ultimate enlightenment, all *dharmas* are truly empty and the question of existence or nonexistence of Buddha-nature or the like does not arise; from the perspective of nonenlightenment, however, it is of pedagogical necessity provisionally to "posit" the metapsychological reality of the so-called Buddha-nature or "(the mind of) Tathāgata-garbha"[37] for the sake of the average man's existential self-awakening. Chu Hsi's misunderstanding that Sinitic Mahāyānists assert the existence of an imperishable "spiritual consciousness" is not separable from his misunderstanding of the Mahāyāna teaching of Emptiness. Since this point involves the metapsychological issue, let us turn to Chu Hsi's over-all critique of the Sinitic Mahāyāna theory of mind/nature.

In his *Shih-shih lun*[at] (Treatise on Buddhism), Part I, Chu Hsi presents his critique of the Buddhist theory of mind/nature, but the original text is corrupted here and there. Instead of citing this text, I would rather take the following saying of Chu Hsi as his general statement concerning the essential difference between Confucianism and Buddhism in terms of the theory of mind/nature.

As Shang-ts'ai [Hsieh Liang-tso,[au] 1050–c.1120] said, "What Buddhists call nature is what Confucian sages call mind. What Buddhists call mind is what Confucian sages call will (or intention)."[38] The mind is simply that which obtains the principle. Buddhists have never recognized this very principle; they only regard mental awareness and physical movements as the nature. Take seeing, hearing, speech, and behavior, for example. To Confucian sages, seeing has the principle of seeing, hearing has the principle of hearing, speech has the principle of speech, movement has the principle of movement, and thinking has the principle of thinking. . . . Buddhists only take that which can see, hear, speak, think, and move as the nature. It doesn't matter to them whether or not the sight is clear, whether or not the hearing is good, whether or not the speech is proper, and whether or not the thinking is wise. Whatever comes to them horizontally or vertically, they all take it as the nature. They are most afraid of the other people's mentioning the principle; they just want to do away with it. . . . This is exactly the same as Kao Tzu's[av] thesis[39] of "what is inborn is called human nature."[40]

In this passage as well as in many other places, Chu Hsi attacks the Sinitic Mahāyāna theory of mind/nature, again from the standpoint of *li-ch'i* metaphysics. Buddhists are said to totally misunderstand, as Kao Tzu does, human nature, by wrongly identifying it with natural instinct, or with, in Chu Hsi's own words, "mental awareness and physical movements." They cannot realize the truth that the primordial nature of man is imparted by Heaven, which is expressible in Neo-Confucianism as the Principle of

Heaven. What constitutes man's primordial nature is the Fourfold Moral Principle of human-kindness, righteousness, propriety, and (moral) knowledge ever inherent in man's mind,[41] which unites both the nature and the feelings. Without being able to realize the moral-metaphysical meaning of "what is imparted by Heaven is called human nature" in the *Doctrine of the Mean*, chüan 1, Sinitic Mahāyānists have misled us into believing that "natural or amoral functioning of the mind is itself the nature." As Professor Ch'ien Mu remarks, "Chu Tzu's insistence that 'the nature is principle' is specially intended to oppose the Ch'an learning of 'seeing the nature right in the natural functioning of the mind.' "[42] Chu Hsi says, "Buddhists abandon the Tao-mind, but try to seek the precarious human mind and make it function amorally; take away the essential but retain the crude; take human-kindness, righteousness, propriety, and (moral) knowledge as the nonnature, but regard the amoral, psycho-physical functioning before their eyes as the nature. All these have to do with their misconception of the fountainhead."[43] He also says,

> What we Confucianists nourish is human-kindness, righteousness, propriety, and (moral) knowledge; what they Buddhists nourish is merely the seeing, hearing, speech, and movement. To us Confucianists, there are within the whole principle many principles of the Way, each principle having its specific features and specific distinctions between right and wrong. . . . But they only see something chaotic, without involving any specific principles or any specific distinctions between right and wrong. The horizontal is right, and the vertical is equally right; the straight is right, and the curved is equally right. To see things in violation of the principle is this very nature; to see things in accordance with the principle is also this very nature. . . . Therefore, they are muddle-headed and there is nothing right in them. They only recognize that human mind and never care about the Tao-mind. They also say that the mind is all-pervasive and all-penetrating, but, with respect to the moral relationship between ruler and minister, parent and child, elder and younger brother, husband and wife, their mind fails to pervade or penetrate into anything.[44]

The gist of Chu Hsi's criticism here is that Buddhists fail to see the specific distinctions between right and wrong in each and every human situation because they have never tried to realize that "the nature is principle" and that the mind possesses ten thousand principles manifesting the ultimate Principle of Heaven. It is because the mind possesses ten thousand specific principles that one can, on the one hand, "preserve one's mind of Tao and nourish one's nature" to the utmost, and, on the other, fully explore all the specific principles right within things themselves. To Chu Hsi the Heavenly Principle manifests itself in terms of both the specific principles of moral oughtness and specific principles of nonmoral reason inherent in ten thousand things. Chu Hsi says, "We regard the mind and principle as one, whereas they regard the mind and principle as dual. . . . They see the mind as empty and possessing no principle at all, while we see that although the mind is empty it does possess all the ten thousand principles completely within itself."[45] Chu Hsi's saying here is none other than his unique Neo-Confucian reinterpretation or reorientation of Mencius' famous words, "All ten thousand things are already complete within myself."[46]

Another important point in Chu Hsi's critique of Sinitic Mahāyāna theory of mind/nature is that it not only neglects the Tao-mind but fails to realize the limitations of man's physical nature and the selfishness of his material desire. Chu Hsi says, "The learning of the heterodox school . . . does not investigate the limitations of man's physical quality (*ch'i-chih*[aw]), feelings, and desire; capricious will and misconduct is considered perfectly reasonable. This kind of learning is particularly damaging to human affairs. Some Confucianists in our time also tend to follow in the Buddhist wrong steps. We must be careful."[47] Chu Hsi is probably referring to the followers of Lu Hsiang-shan's teaching of "the mind is principle" when he compares "some Confucianists in our time" to Ch'an Buddhists in terms of the total lack of understanding man's physical nature. In another place Chu Hsi says, "Although the mind and principle are one, this truth will not be seen clearly if no attention is paid to the selfishness of *ch'i*-endowment (*ch'i-ping*[ax]) and material desire. . . . That is why the *Great Learning* emphasizes investigation of things."[48] Professor Ch'ien Mu makes a significant remark on Chu Hsi's saying here, stating that Hsiang-shan holds that the mind is principle; this thesis is fundamentally different from the Ch'an thesis. But if one does not recognize that there is still selfishness in man's *ch'i*-endowment and material desire, then one will not know that there are occasions on which the mind does not follow the principle. Further, the principle spreads itself out into ten thousand specific principles amidst heaven, earth, and ten thousand things and phenomena. If one does not make serious efforts in the task of investigation of things but simply says that this mind possesses ten thousand principles, then this mind will become really empty and indistinguishable from the Ch'an mind."[49] Here again, we see a metaphysical and metapsychological reason for Chu Hsi's criticism of Lu's "the mind is principle" thesis as more Ch'annistic than Confucian. Chu Hsi's own theory of mind/nature, which involves the distinction between the Tao-mind and the human mind, is, of course, grounded upon *li-ch'i* metaphysics.

But the most important part of Chu Hsi's critique of Buddhist metapsychology is that, like Kao Tzu, Yang Chu, and some misguided Neo-Confucianists like Hu Hung (Hu Wu-feng,[ay] 1106–1161), Buddhists tend to promote the theory of human nature as neither good nor evil, as against the Mencian theory of human nature as originally good, which must be accepted as the orthodox doctrine by all followers of the Confucian Way. Chu Hsi says,

Primordially, the Principle of Heaven does not have human desire as opposite to it; but since there is selfish human desire, the Principle of Heaven cannot help

competing with human desire for growth or decline. Primordially, good does not
have evil as opposite to it; but since there is evil, good cannot help competing
with evil for either rise or fall. . . . Originally, there is only good and no evil;
there is only the Mandate of Heaven and no human desire. . . . It is all right to
say that the Mandate of Heaven is not confined to things. But to say that it is not
confined to good is to fail to know the reason why Heaven is Heaven. But to say
that good cannot define human nature is to fail to know the original source of
good. In *Knowing Words* (*chih-yen*ᵃᶻ) this kind of argument [Hu Hung's point that
neither good nor evil can define human nature] runs into conflict with the other
points in many places of the same work. Hu's argument is almost no different
from the thesis [of human nature as neither good nor evil] maintained by Kao
Tzu, Yang Chu, Buddhism, and Su Tung-p'o [Su Shihᵇᵃ 1036–1101].⁵⁰

From Chu Hsi's point of view, the Buddhist thesis that human nature is
neither good nor evil falls into "empty silence" and creates an unbridgeable
gap between the primordial nature and the activation of human feelings. (Chu
Hsi sometimes says, "The nonactivation of human feelings is the nature and
the activation of human feelings is good."⁵¹) If Chu Hsi had lived in Wang
Yang-ming's (Wang Shou-jen,ᵇᵇ 1472–1529) time and heard Wang's words
"the original substance of human nature is neither good nor evil,"⁵² he would
certainly have equated Wang's theory of mind/nature with the Ch'an Buddhist one.

Is Chu Hsi's critique of Sinitic Mahāyāna metapsychology fair and sound?
First of all, no Sinitic Mahāyāna thinkers would accept his criticism of the
Buddhist thesis of human nature as "neither good nor evil," for, they would
retort, the criticism here is based on a total misunderstanding or distortion of
the Sinitic Mahāyāna theory of mind/nature, which indeed shares with Confucianism the view that man's original nature or original mind is absolutely
good beyond the duality of good and evil in the relative sense. Transmetaphysically speaking, all *dharmas* are truly empty and the question of the existence/
nonexistence of Buddha-nature or the like does not arise. But humanly (existentially) speaking, it is necessary to develop, within Mahāyāna Buddhism, a
full-fledged theory of mind/nature as a metapsychological basis for man's self-
awakening to his original mind or nature. The Sinitic Mahāyāna deepening
and enrichment of the Indian Mahāyāna theory of Buddha-nature or *Tathāgata-garbha*, by stressing the primordial goodness and absolute purity of
man's mind/nature, must have been under the profound influence of the traditional Chinese—typically Mencian—approach to the problem of human
nature and mind. Despite his nondualistic approach, Hui-nengᵇᶜ (638–713),
the Sixth Patriarch of Ch'an, used, for instance, the terms "the original
mind" and "the original nature"—both of which had been used by the followers of Mencius for a long time—to point to the absolute goodness of Buddha-nature or One-mind. Thus, the difference between Confucian and Sinitic
Mahāyāna theories of mind/nature does not lie in the distinction between
"originally good" and "neither good nor evil" but rather lies in the distinc-

tion between "morally good" and "transmorally (not amorally) good" beyond the duality of good and evil in the relative sense. It is in this sense that Wang Yang-ming's thesis that "the original substance of the mind is neither good nor evil" still remains very much Confucian in distinction to the Ch'an thesis, because of his primary emphasis on the spontaneous extension of man's moral —and not transmoral—mind in dealing with human affairs. In wrongly identifying Sinitic Mahāyāna metapsychology with Kao Tzu's theory, Chu Hsi fails to see the essential distinction between "transmorally good" and "neither good nor evil (in the amoral sense)."

Chu Hsi's criticism that to Ch'an Buddhism "the natural functioning of the mind is itself the nature" is also very superficial, for no Sinitic Mahāyānists have ever held this view. On the contrary, just like the Neo-Confucianists they have consistently applied the typically Chinese thesis of "substance (or reality) and function (or manifestation)" to their theory of mind/nature. For instance, the famous Ch'an expression, "Chopping wood and carrying water: these are none other than a wondrous functioning of the enlightened mind," must be construed to mean that the original mind is the substance while its everyday concrete manifestations in terms of what Chu Hsi calls "mental awareness and physical movements" are the function of the original mind. Again, in the *Platform Scripture* Hui-neng says, "to *nien*[bd] ['instant-thought,' here used as a transitive verb] is to *nien* the original nature of Suchness. Suchness is the substance of *nien; nien* is the function of Suchness."[53] Transmetaphysically, Suchness is the same as Emptiness or Dharmanature; metapsychologically, it is none other than the original mind/nature of man. Chu Hsi's criticism in question, therefore, totally misses the Sinitic Mahāyāna theory of mind/nature as grounded upon the substance/function relationship. And Chu Hsi's following words only create more confusion with regard to his over-simplification of "the natural functioning of the mind is itself the nature."

> Buddhists themselves say that they do understand the mind and see into the nature. But why can their mind or nature not be extended in moral practice? Because they have divided the nature and the function into two separate matters. . . . It is not true that Buddhists do not see into the nature, but when they come to deal with the problem of everyday functioning of the mind, they just say that nothing can be done. Therefore, they abandon the ruler and desert their parents. . . . This is because in their case the nature and the function do not match each other.[54]

In saying here that Ch'an Buddhists "separate the nature and the function as two different matters," Chu Hsi seems to have forgotten what he says in other places about the so-called natural functioning of the mind is itself the nature in Ch'an. And in this saying Chu Hsi again confuses two different issues: sociomoral and metapsychological (as an extension of the metaphysical issue).

Whether or not Ch'an Buddhists "abandon their ruler and desert their parents" is a sociomoral issue, whereas whether or not they see into the nature is a metapsychological issue. Furthermore, how would Chu Hsi explain the apparent inconsistency between his words that "it is not true that Buddhists do not see into the nature" and that "the natural functioning of the mind is itself the nature"—the latter being said by Chu Hsi to be Ch'an's false view of human nature?

As to Chu Hsi's criticism that Ch'an Buddhists pay little attention to the limitations of man's physical nature and the selfishness of his material desire, it is in many ways very hard-hitting, for it is true that because of their primary emphasis on sudden awakening here and now they tend to overlook enormous individual limitations or difficulties involved in their own students' spiritual cultivation for ultimate enlightenment, which is transmoral but can never be amoral. His criticism here can also apply to the Lu-Wang school of "the mind is principle," the cultivational laxity of which eventually led to the Ch'an-like, naturalistic affirmation of "ready-made, innate knowledge of the good" after Wang Yang-ming. Like the "two-way" theory in the *Awakening of Faith*—simultaneous "permeation of Suchness into ignorance" and "permeation of ignorance into Suchness"—Chu Hsi's own theory of human nature that deals with the limitations of man's physical quality (despite the primordial goodness of his heavenly nature) can realistically be said to make up for the high-minded and over-optimistic view held by both Ch'an Buddhism and the Lu Hsiang-shan–Wang Yang-ming School.

As far as the method of personal cultivation is concerned, Chu Hsi's criticism of Buddhism in almost all cases focuses on the Ch'an teaching of sudden awakening, and can be summed up in terms of the following inseparable points: (1) Ch'an Buddhists only aspire to achieve the higher spiritual stage without being engaged in stepwise learning (of the Principle) from below, (2) they totally neglect the task of "investigation of things and extension of knowledge," (3) they only sit quietly without being able to realize the importance of the method of "reverential one-mindedness to straighten the internal and righteousness to square the external,"[55] and (4) the sudden awakening they teach tends to disregard the spiritual and moral significance of the method of gradual cultivation.

First, Chu Hsi is highly critical of Ch'an Buddhists in that they "only speak of 'achieving the higher spiritual stage' while neglecting 'stepwise learning from below.' " But if one neglects stepwise learning from below, how can one achieve the higher spiritual stage?[56] Chu Hsi even raises a great doubt about their ability to achieve the higher spiritual stage, for he reasons that they simply lack a proper method of personal cultivation. He therefore expresses his complete agreement with Ch'eng Hao's[be] (1032–1085) words that "Ch'an Buddhists only aspire to achieve the higher spiritual stage, but is there anything good in their aspiration to achieve the higher spiritual stage?"[57]

Second, from Chu Hsi's point of view of "the nature is Principle," one main reason why Ch'an Buddhists fail to achieve the higher spiritual stage is that they "simply do not engage in the task of investigation of things."[58] In his letter to Hsü Shun-chih,[bf] Chu Hsi stresses this point to indicate one essential difference between Confucianism and Ch'an Buddhism. He says,

> The learning of the sages first consists in the pursuit of *jen*[bg] (humanity) and investigation of things. Therefore, they can, at the moment the feelings are activated, naturally see the distinction between right and wrong or appropriateness and inappropriateness, without missing anything. . . . Now tell me: where does this one instant-thought *(nein)* of Ch'an come from? Can it be called "the original mind"? Can it be called "the Principle of Heaven"? This is just another selfish intention added to the preceding one. . . . This is entirely different from the Confucian sages' pursuit of *jen,* investigation of things, and spiritual nurturing in accordance with the principle.[59]

To Chu Hsi and his followers, the Confucian learning consists of "investigation of things and extension of knowledge" or "thorough exploration of the principle right within things," as the first and necessary step to be taken for one's personal cultivation; this approach is, of course, clearly distinguishable from the learning-as-awakening approach taken by both Ch'an Buddhism and the Lu-Wang school.

Third, following Ch'eng I's method of "spiritual nurturing requires reverential one-mindedness while the advancement of learning consists in extension of knowledge,"[60] Chu Hsi criticizes Ch'an that it not only neglects the task of investigation of things but fails to maintain reverential one-mindedness. Instead, Ch'an Buddhists vainly practice quiet-sitting or sitting meditation. In contrast to Ch'an, Chu Hsi says, the Confucian learning "takes abiding in reverential one-mindedness as the basis and applies exhaustive exploration of the principle in order to enrich the method of personal cultivation."[61] Chu Hsi tried to show the difference between the Confucian method of moral self-vigilance and the Ch'an method of quiet sitting.

> Ch'an Buddhists want to empty this very mind, and the religious Taoists want to preserve this very vital force: all these are a vain artifice. Just try to be morally watchful and careful, then the mind will naturally be preserved forever, with no need of any artificial arrangement . . . *Question:* It seems that Ch'an Buddhists are also able to practice self-vigilance. *Chu Hsi says:* They do it only in the quiet place; their practice is different from ours. They only try to find an expedient short-cut, and escape into the place of quiet seclusion.[62]

Like many other Neo-Confucianists, Chu Hsi occasionally praised highly the Ch'an Buddhist way of spiritual cultivation in terms of sitting meditation and rigorous training of the mind. He says, for instance, that "Ch'an Buddhists indeed make strenuous efforts in this mind-training"[63] and that "once

they attain their Tao, those Ch'an Buddhist monks and their followers simply
enter into deep mountains, live on grass and wood, and nourish their mind for
many years. What a great outlook they exhibit when they come out! So natural, bright, and charming! That is why the worldlings can only look at them
with a sense of awe and admiration."[64] Chu Hsi actually deplored the fact that
so many Confucian students and scholars, including himself when young, had
been attracted by Ch'an because of the practical success of Ch'an discipline
for enlightenment. But Chu Hsi points out the sociomoral meaninglessness of
the Ch'an way of personal cultivation, saying, "Ch'an Buddhists want to
know death first [before knowing life]. They merely learn to maintain the
unmoved mind. Kao Tzu's learning is exactly like this."[65] In contrast, all followers of the Confucian Way must preserve their mind and nourish their
nature for the sake of realizing the Principle of Heaven, which is to be
humanly manifested through everyday sociomoral practice. Thus, in spite of
his occasional appreciation for the success of Ch'an discipline, Chu Hsi makes
it clear that the Ch'an method of quiet-sitting must be replaced with the Confucian method of "reverential one-mindedness to straighten the internal and
righteousness to square the external." As Chu Hsi says, "What Ch'an Buddhists call 'reverential one-mindedness to straighten the internal' is just spa-
ciously empty, and contains nothing at all. In contrast, what the sages call
'reverential one-mindedness to straighten the internal' is deep and profound,
pure and bright, and contains all the ten thousand principles; only then it is
possible to practice 'righteousness to square the external.' "[66] In other words,
Ch'an Buddhists simply fail to realize both "reverential one-mindedness to
straighten the internal and righteousness to square the external," primarily
because their method of personal cultivation lacks a proper sociomoral objective grounded upon the Principle of Heaven.

Finally, Chu Hsi strongly attacks the Ch'an teaching of sudden awakening
in that it completely neglects the sociomoral importance of gradual cultivation, which requires a lifelong task of overcoming the limitations of man's
physical nature as well as his selfish desire. The complete and perfect transformation of the human mind into the Tao-mind necessitates a stepwise Confucian learning—investigation of things and thorough exploration of the principle—and day-to-day moral cultivation. I have translated some of Chu Hsi's
most important sayings on this point as follows:

> "Seeing into man's nature" is a Ch'an Buddhist expression; it means "seeing
> just once and for all." By contrast, the Confucianists speak of "knowing man's
> nature"; after knowing the nature, the nature still requires a full nourishment
> until it is exerted to the utmost. The Confucian task here is gradual and
> stepwise, and cannot be a matter of one or two days' effort. In daily life, once the
> effort slackens it will bring much damage to the mind at that very incipient
> moment. . . . Now the followers of Ch'an Buddhism tend to say to themselves
> that they have, without any doubt, seen into their nature, yet their habitual

nature and desire still remains no different from the average man's. Isn't it the result of an empty talk about "trying to use a broom without seeing any dust?"

I would say that extension of knowledge and investigation of things are the beginning of the learning according to the *Great Learning*. . . . Since the knowledge extended is shallow or deep in degree, how can it be the case that our innate knowledge of the good which is the same as that of legendary sage-emperors Yao[bh] and Shun[bi] is all of a sudden seen? If it were the case, it would be just like Ch'an Buddhist empty talk about "hearing just once amounts to awakening one thousand times" or "direct attainment of enlightenment by one instant leap." This is not the genuine Confucian task of "enlightening one's good nature" and "making oneself sincere."[68]

I would say that not to expect the students to make a jump is what accords with the original nature of the Principle of Heaven; this is not the sages' special arrangement. . . . Take the example of a small tree. It has, of course, the nature of tree, but it is also the tree's nature that its growth requires a gradual nourishment. What is called "expecting the Ch'an novice instantly to attain Buddhahood on the spot" is just like spouting out a mouthful of water on a small tree with a wishful thinking that it will instantly reach the sky. Does this make any sense at all? Even if there were such a magical technique, still it cannot be said to follow the principle. We can again detect selfishness and self-profit in this sort of technique.[69]

Professor Ch'ien Mu makes a very thoughtful remark on the last-cited saying: "It cannot be said that, human nature being originally good, all men can become Yao or Shun with no need to carefully undertake the task of 'knowing the words' and 'nourishing one's vital force.' Some Ming Neo-Confucianists assert that 'the whole street is full of sages' or that 'the tea-boy himself is a sage.'[70] From Chu Hsi's point of view, all these would be close to the Ch'an learning."[71] The dispute between the Ch'eng-Chu School and the Lu-Wang School within Neo-Confucianism involves the methodical question of personal cultivation: gradual cultivation or sudden awakening? This Neo-Confucian dispute is somewhat similar to the dispute between the Southern School of Hui-neng and the Northern School of Shen-hsiu[bi] (605?–706) in the Ch'an tradition. Chu Hsi's warning that the teaching of sudden awakening, often at the expense of gradual cultivation, in both Ch'an and Neo-Confucianism tends to bring damage to Confucian sociomoral practice deserves our special attention, for it seems to me that Chu Hsi's criticism of Ch'an Buddhism and the Lu-Wang School is most forceful and extremely significant when he comes to grips with the question of personal cultivation and conduct as an important and indispensable part of everyday sociomoral practice. Chu Hsi can indeed cite Confucius' example, that even Confucius was able to "follow whatever my mind-heart desires without overstepping the boundary of right"[72] only after he reached the age of seventy, in support of his method of gradual cultivation. The pros and cons of the dispute between the "sudden" and "grad-

ual" teachings cannot be seen clearly without reference to the question of
everyday sociomoral practice in concrete terms of situational appropriateness
of human action.

We have seen that, as far as metaphysical thinking, theory of mind/nature,
and method of personal cultivation are concerned, Chu Hsi's criticism of
Sinitic Mahāyāna Buddhism can be always hard-hitting and forceful only
when the criticism involves his severe attack upon the Buddhist failure to
actualize the primordiality in everyday sociomoral practice as a matter of realization of the Way of *jen-i*ᵇᵏ (human-kindness manifested through gradational
and situational application). Chu Hsi says,

> The learning of Ch'an is most damaging to the Way. Chuang Tzu and Lao Tzu
> did not completely abandon moral principles, but in Buddhism human morality
> is already damaged. As to Ch'an, it has from the outset wiped out all moral prin-
> ciples with nothing left. It is in this sense that the damage Ch'an has brought to
> us is most serious. . . . It is unnecessary to make a detailed investigation in order
> to understand the nature of the learning of Buddhism and Taoism. Their aban-
> donment of the Three Bonds [ruler as the bond of minister, father as the bond of
> son, and husband as the bond of wife] and Five Constant Relationships [parent-
> child, ruler-minister, husband-wife, senior-junior, friend-friend] alone is already
> a grave sin, let alone the other sins they have committed.[73]

Chu Hsi's sociomoral criticism of Buddhism and Taoism here well corresponds with Lu Hsiang-shan's criticism based on the righteousness/self-inter-
est distinction, despite the fact that Chu Hsi himself thinks that the fundamental difference between Confucianism and Buddhism is metaphysical
rather than ethical in nature.

An essential part of Chu Hsi's sociomoral criticism of Buddhism is that it
violates Confucian *jen-i,* which must function as the highest governing principle of human conduct and situational action. *Jen* as humanity or human-kindness constitutes the essential nature of man, and *i* as moral oughtness is, in
Confucian terms, a gradational extension and situational application of *jen* in
accord with the timely Mean. Like Mo Tzu's doctrine of "mutual love," Buddhist teaching of compassion *(karuṇā)* equalizes all kinds of human love—
from love for parents through love for all mankind to love for animals and all
other sentient beings—and entirely ignores the human (sociomoral) necessity
of gradationally and situationally manifesting *jen* or the Principle of Heaven.
Chu Hsi says, "Yang Chu did not even pluck out a single hair to benefit the
world, and yet he said that the world cannot be benefited by a single hair. I
Tzuᵇˡ advocated the doctrine of nongradational love, and yet he said that this
love begins with familial affection.[74] Buddhists want to abandon the relationship of parents, and yet they speak of the *Parents Scripture:* all these are just
quibbles!"[75] He also says, "What Buddhists call compassion has no relation
with the worldly conditions at all; they simply love everything without any
distinction. As to love for parents, they take it as involving the worldly condi-

tions and therefore keeping them from enlightenment; they therefore desert their parents and fail to serve them. But when they see that a tiger is hungry, they give their own body away to the tiger in order to feed it. What kind of moral principle is this?"[76] Again, "Therefore it is said, 'The reality of *jen* lies in serving one's parents.'[77] It is also said, 'Filial piety and brotherly respect are the starting point for the practice of *jen*.'[78] This is why substance [Principle is one] and function [its manifestations are many] are of one and the same source and the manifest and the subtle allow no gap between them.[79] The Buddhist talk about 'true awakening' and 'ability to realize *jen*' is indeed sublime and beautiful. But where is their foundation?"[80] To Chu Hsi, *jen* or the Principle of Heaven is the substance while everyday sociomoral practice is the function, beginning with filial piety and brotherly respect and ending with love for all mankind. But *jen* or the principle must be gradationally manifested as a matter of moral oughtness (i^{bm}); the Buddhist leap beyond the gradational manifestation of *jen* or principle is, therefore, a dangerous violation of the basic moral context of humanity.

To show that Buddhists themselves do understand, however superficially, the meaning of "gradational manifestation of *jen*" *(jen-i)*, Chu Hsi makes an ironical remark: "In the world only this Principle of the Way governs, and no one can escape from it. Take the community of Buddhists and religious Taoists, for example. Although they have tried to abandon human morality, they simply cannot escape from it. They behave like having no parents or children, but they serve their masters and treat their disciples. The senior disciples are called 'elder brothers under the master' and the junior disciples 'younger brothers under the master.' But to protect unauthentic sages or worthies in Ch'an Buddhism is indirectly to preserve the authentic ones."[81] Chu Hsi says further, "Buddhists say that they want to abandon relationships between ruler and minister, parent and son. But they still cannot abandon them. Take Buddhist temples, for instance. There still exist the 'elders' and the like. And the rank distinctions there are very strict. So how can the Buddhists abandon human relations at all? Whatever they say and do is just hypocritical."[82] The Buddhist failure to realize the concrete, gradational manifestations of *jen* or the Principle of Heaven means that there is a total lack of "righteousness to square the external" in Buddhist practice, and this very lack also means that the Buddhist way of "reverential one-mindedness to straighten the internal" is equally wrong. Chu Hsi says thus, "If there is no righteousness to square the external, then even reverential one-mindedness cannot be right. . . . Ch'eng Hao says, 'Buddhists only aspire to reach the higher spiritual stage without engaging themselves in stepwise learning from below. But how can their aspiration to reach the higher stage be right at all?' "[83]

Chu Hsi further criticizes Ch'an Buddhism in that its nondualistic transcendence of all sociomoral distinctions between right and wrong, good and evil, and so on turns everything upside down in daily conduct and situational action. Since this part of Chu Hsi's criticism is most crucial in his defense of the Confucian Way against the Buddhist, I have translated some of the most important and relevant sayings as follows:

> The Ch'an layman P'ang Yün[bn] [740–808] praised "spiritual penetration and wondrous functioning in wood-chopping and water-carrying." . . . But authentic spiritual penetration and wondrous functioning lies in carrying the water and chopping the wood rightly. If the water is not carried rightly and the wood is not chopped rightly, then how can the action be spiritually penetrating and wondrously functioning? What Ch'an Buddhists call "the functioning is itself the nature" is just like this. They never care about the distinction between right and wrong, and only take wearing clothing, eating food, working and resting, seeing and hearing, and other movements as the Way. . . . They don't ask whether these acts or movements accord with the Principle of the Way. By contrast, we Confucianists must seek the Principle of the Way right within these actions or movements. The real Way can be manifested only in this manner.[84]

> What Ch'an Buddhists see is nothing more than "a master" who is always alert. As to the actions taken by this very "master," which do not accord with the principle, they simply don't care. Let us take the example of the heavenly nature of the relationship between father and son. When the father is insulted by someone, his son should come to help him. But this is not what Ch'an Buddhists would do. To them, if the son has the mind of helping his father, he is attached to human affection and his mind becomes deluded. If the "master" is ever alert only in this way, what kind of Principle of the Way can be found here?[85]

> It cannot be said that Ch'an Buddhists do not see into man's nature, but when they come to deal with the functioning of the mind, they say that whatever is done is just right. Therefore, they abandon their ruler and desert their parents and there is nothing they won't do. This is because the nature and the functioning they speak of have nothing to do with each other.[86]

> We Confucianists maintain just one real and true Principle of the Way. Buddhists also say that their own Principle of the Way is true and real. They say, for instance, "Only this is real, the other things are not true."[87] But they speak of the Principle of the Way one-sidedly. They only recognize the human mind. To them, there is no Tao-mind, nor are there human-kindness, righteousness, propriety, and knowledge, let alone commiseration, shame and dislike, deference, and right/wrong. What we debate with them is simply this.[88]

> Buddhists say to themselves that their mind is shining and bright. But without knowing the affection between parents and children or the righteousness between ruler and minister, their assertion that their mind is shining and bright only injures the Way.[89] The human mind is the mind that makes no distinction between right and wrong; the Tao-mind is the mind that makes such a distinction. Buddhists cannot be said to be depraved, but their problem is that they do not have the mind that makes the distinction between right and wrong.[90]

The teaching of our Sage takes "returning to propriety" as the essential. If one only knows how to "restrain oneself" one tends to fall into empty quietude of the Buddhist kind. . . . The learning of Buddhism only involves "restraining oneself" without reference to the task of "returning to propriety." Therefore, their conduct or action does not accord with the Mean. Consequently, they mistake the relationship between ruler and minister as that between parent and child and mistake the relationship between parent and child as that between ruler and minister. So, all distinctions become confused. . . . Therefore, whoever restrains himself must return (restore) his own person to what accords with the sociomoral standard or criterion. This is the meaning of "to restrain oneself and return to the propriety of *jen*."[91]

We have seen previously that, with respect to the method of personal cultivation, Chu Hsi to some extent acknowledges that Ch'an Buddhists are quite capable of maintaining reverential one-mindedness and reaching the higher spiritual stage—though often at the expense of "righteousness to square the external" and "stepwise learning from below." He contends, however, that their failure to accomplish the task of "righteousness to square the external" and "stepwise learning from below" makes their reverential one-mindedness and higher spiritual stage sociomorally meaningless. Here again, with respect to theory of conduct and action, Chu Hsi also acknowledges that Ch'an Buddhists do often restrain themselves and see into the original nature. But, he argues, they have failed to fulfill the sociomoral task of "returning to propriety," and they have not realized the human necessity of transforming the "spiritual penetratingness and wondrous functioning" of their mind into sociomoral manifestation or actualization of the primordial, which is none other than *jen* or the Principle of Heaven. Since they have failed to do so, their self-restraint and insight into the nature also turn out to be sociomorally worthless. Thus, despite his original point that the difference between Confucianism and Buddhism is fundamentally metaphysical, the real strength of Chu Hsi's critique of Buddhism rather lies in his critical exposition of the sociomoral weakness of the Buddhist tradition—even after it underwent a radical sinicization by shifting the emphasis from "true Emptiness" to "wondrous being" in everyday life. In short, the central focus of Chu Hsi's criticism of Buddhism is on the sociomoral issue.

It seems to me, in this connection, that the greatest contribution of Chu Hsi's own philosophy does not, as he claims, lie in metaphysics or theory of mind/nature, but rather lies in his ability to tackle to Confucian problem of "situational weighing" (*ch'üan*[bo]) of the constant moral standard or principle (*ching*[bp]). Chu Hsi may not be able to claim the philosophical superiority of his *li-ch'i* metaphysics and theory of twofold nature over the nondualistic metaphysical/metapsychological views respectively held by Sinitic Mahāyāna and the Lu-Wang School. Nonetheless, the great strength of his method of gradual cultivation and particularly this theory—through in a rather incomplete form —of conduct and action, which I wish provisionally to call "*ching-ch'üan* situationism," can be fully appreciated if ethically contrasted with Ch'an Buddhism, the Lu-Wang School, or any other school that takes a "simple and easy" approach to the sociomoral issues, which only become more and more complicated in accordance with sociohistorical changes. Chu Hsi is certainly entitled to criticize the Ch'an Buddhist nondualistic transcendence of the distinction between right and wrong in human action for the very reason that everyday sociomoral practice, which always requires the fulfillment of the ethical condition of situational appropriateness in any decision making or action taking, must be based on a correct understanding of the situational distinction between right and wrong. To the great majority of nonsagely human individuals, establishment of such a correct understanding cannot be a "simple and easy" matter of sudden self-awakening, whether moral (Lu-Wang) or transmoral (Ch'an); it is rather a life-long task involving constant investigation of things and gradual extension of (moral) knowledge for the sake of properly weighing the situational meaning of the moral principle that is Confucian *jen-i*, as Chu Hsi has strongly recommended. It is primarily because Chu Hsi pays much more attention than any other Neo-Confucian thinker to the ever complicated problem of *ching-ch'üan* in everyday sociomoral practice—the problem that all of us nonsagely humans must deal with from time to time—that he is able to develop his unique theory of gradual learning and cultivation, in order to resolve the problem in the Confucian manner.

We now come to examine the final part of Chu Hsi's criticism of Buddhism, which concerns theory of enlightenment or soteriology. Like many other Neo-Confucianists, Chu Hsi often praises Ch'an Buddhists very highly for their soteriological accomplishment, that they can be even happier than most Neo-Confucianists because of their ability to overcome secular worries and attachments as well as to transcend the duality of life and death, man and the world, and so on. Chu Hsi says, "Look at those Ch'an Buddhists. Although they have no Principle of the Way, they have what they want and rejoice in it throughout their life. This is because they are able to realize what is metaphysically primordial within phenomenal forms."[92] Chu Hsi seems to admit, at least in this place, that insofar as metaphysical thinking is concerned, Sinitic Mahāyānists can reach their own conclusion and live happily on this conclusion. Soteriologically speaking, there is no guarantee that Neo-Confucianists can be as happy as Ch'an Buddhists are simply because they know the Confucian Principle of the Way. Chu Hsi sometimes lamented that many Confucian scholars and students were often lured by material gains or secular titles and failed to recover their original mind or nature, in sharp contrast to those Ch'an fellows who attained Buddhist enlightenment. Chu Hsi says, "Many of our Neo-Confucian old-timers have been benefited by studies of Ch'an Buddhism, and remain unchanged during the most difficult periods of their life. This is because the Ch'an Buddhist way of bravery and vigor, purity and steadfastness, can help man remain stoically content and indifferent, without being tempted and controlled by external things."[93] But Chu Hsi insists that an authentic follower of the Confucian Way should never be envious of the soteriological achievement of Ch'an Buddhism, for the Confucian ultimate concern and commitment is essentially different from the Buddhist.

First of all, while Buddhist happiness lies in transmoral—which is in fact amoral or even immoral from the Confucian point of view—liberation of the mind from what is called the dusty world, Confucian happiness consists in the superior man's gradual realization of the Principle of Heaven by conscientiously fulfilling his sociomoral duties as a matter of heavenly assignment or moral destiny. Man's everyday practice of *jen-i* should naturally lead to supreme happiness in the Confucian sense. Or, to make the point more strongly, man's everyday sociomoral practice (for the eventual realization of the way of inner sagehood and outer kingship) and supreme happiness of life are one and the same thing.

According to Chu Hsi, the essential difference between Confucianism and Buddhism in terms of ultimate concern and commitment can be summed up thus: "Confucianism is ultimately concerned with human affairs while Buddhism is ultimately concerned with the problem of life-and-death."[94] The former is existentially committed to the constant moral perfecting of man and society, whereas the latter is committed to human conquest of transiency and death. Chu Hsi critically contrasts the Confucian and Buddhist views of life and death as follows:

> The creative transformation of Heaven and Earth is likened to a great furnace, in which human and nonhuman beings never cease to grow and regrow. This points to the principle of reality, and we need not worry about the cessation of this creative transformation. Now, Buddhists see it as a vast, vacuous, and quiet thing, and mistake the "awareness or consciousness" posterior to the death of human and nonhuman beings to be the principle of reality. Isn't this wrong? Now, what our Confucian sages and worthies call "to go back in fulfillment and die in peace" is none other than not to miss the Principle of Heaven man has received, so that he can die without any regret or shame. This does not mean that there is one real thing "spiritual consciousness" which can be preserved and held on after man's death so that what Buddhists call "the imperishable" can reside at ease in a dark and empty place. Our Confucian Way that "whether one dies young or old make no difference" and that "one cultivates one's personal life so as to await the Mandate of Heaven"[95] is spontaneously natural, and should not be confused with the heterodox way that focuses only on "the great matter of life-and-death which is transitory and runs fast."[96]

Although he is wrong about the Buddhist approach to the problem of immortality ("spiritual consciousness") in this passage, as I have pointed out previously, Chu Hsi's criticism of Buddhism as unnecessarily over-concerned with man's spiritual conquest of the cycle of life-and-death deserves our attention, for his criticism here is consistent with Confucius' point that man should be concerned with how to deal with human life rather than be worried about what to do about death.[97] Chu Hsi may not be able to demonstrate the soteriological superiority of the Confucian Way over the Buddhist Way, but he has at least succeeded in critically exposing the escapist tendency in and selfish motive behind most, if not all, Buddhists' one-sided (transmoral) conquest of death and attainment of personal happiness and peace. Chu Hsi says, "The shortcoming of Buddhism lies in its selfish aversion. . . . Its shortcoming lies in its indifference and aversion to this-worldly matters and its intention to empty them completely."[98] He also says, "What is called 'nature' is the Principle of Heaven-and-Earth's producing things, as expressed by words like 'the Mandate of Heaven is solemnly unceasing' or 'Great indeed is the ever-creative, primordial source, wherefrom all things are produced.'[99] . . . How can it be selfishly owned by oneself? . . . Buddhists want to empty their deluded mind in order to see into their true nature. I am afraid they will only lose the true nature after death. Isn't their intention egoistic and self-interested?"[100] Although no Ch'an Buddhist would ever say that his attainment of enlightenment means preservation of his own "true nature" after death—for this is rather Chu Hsi's misunderstanding—it is not that easy for him to say that there is not the slightest egoistic motive involved in his personal aversion to everyday human affairs. Buddhism may be able to continue to vie with Confucianism for soteriological supremacy; it may also be able to continue to challenge Confucianism in metaphysical thinking and theory of mind/nature. But its transmoral attainment of enlightenment tends to neglect everyday sociomoral practice, gradationally beginning with familial love and ending with love for all mankind. It is in this sense that Chu Hsi's Neo-Confucian counterchallenge to Sinitic Mahāyāna Buddhism, primarily in terms of sociomoral practice and ultimate concern/commitment, has yet to be met by Buddhist thinkers and scholars.

To conclude, I would like to repeat what I stated at the end of the paper "Morality or Beyond," which appeared eight years ago:

> It seems to me that Mahāyāna Buddhists should learn a good lesson from the challenge of Neo-Confucianism and engage in a necessary and urgent inquiry into the moral dimension of their own tradition, by shifting their traditional emphasis on transcendental truth to a new emphasis on worldly truth in terms of everyday sociomoral practice. This shift of emphasis is not an impossible task, if Mahāyāna Buddhists have a perfect understanding of the principle of the Middle Way as well as of the real meaning of the twofold truth in their tradition. In the past, they tended to regard morality (śila) as primarily a means, discipline, or prerequisite toward the ultimate goal. It is now time for them to develop a new and modern philosophy of the Middle Way by placing equal emphasis on morality as well as on wisdom (prajñā) and meditation (dhyāna). Further, a new moral wine should be put into the ancient bottle full of karunā (universal compassion). But it remains to be seen whether Mahāyāna Buddhists can work out in this

modern age an ethical system to tackle most, if not all, human and secular problems they encounter in everyday life.[101]

Notes

1. See *Philosophy East and West*, vol. 23, no. 3 (July 1973), p. 375.

2. Chu Hsi's writing and recorded sayings on Buddhism can be found in numerous places in the *Chu Tzu yü-lei*[bq] [Classified conversations of Master Chu]. Among the most important primary sources—just to cite a few—are his comments on Buddhism in the *Chu-tzu yü-lei*, chüan 126; his letter to Wu Tou-nan[br] in *Chu Tzu wen-chi*[bs] [Collected literary works of Master Chu], (SPPY ed.), entitled *Chu Tzu ta-ch'üan*[bt] [Complete collection of Master Chu], (Taipei: Chung-hua[bu] Book Co.) 59:22a *ff*; and his letter to Ch'en Wei-tao[bv] in *Chu Tzu wen-chi*, 59:27a *ff*. Among the most notable secondary sources in Chinese and Japanese languages are Tokiwa Daijō,[bw] *Shina ni okeru bukkyō to jukyō dōkyo*[bx] [Buddhism in relation to Confucianism and Taoism in China], (Tokyo: Tōyō Bunko,[by] 1930); Araki Kengo, *Bukkyō to jukyō*[bz] [Buddhism and Confucianism], (Kyoto: Heirakuji Shoten,[ca] 1963); and Ch'ien Mu, *Chu Tzu hsin hsüeh-an*[cb] [A new study in Chu Hsi], (Taipei: San-min[cc] Book Co., 1971), Bk. III.

3. To my present knowledge, none of the Neo-Confucian thinkers had ever studied Buddhism as a whole. Chu Hsi was at least able to study a great number of Ch'an texts, in addition to some of the most important Mahāyāna Buddhist writings. But as Professor Tokiwa critically remarks, Chu Hsi often misunderstood or distorted the meanings of many of those Buddhist texts he had studied. See Tokiwa's book (mentioned in n. 2), pp. 374–378. Chu Hsi was quite familiar with Hua-yen and Ch'an teachings, but his knowledge of Sinitic Mahāyāna—let alone Buddhism as a whole—beyond these two schools was quite poor.

4. See Ch'ien Mu, *Chu Tzu hsin hsüeh-an*, Bk. III, pp. 489–490, 510, 552, and 555. It is important to note that Chu Hsi's *Chin-ssu-lu*[cd] [Reflections on things at hand] has one special chapter (13) on "Sifting the Heterodox Doctrines," in Wing-tsit Chan, trans., *Reflections on Things at Hand* (New York: Columbia University Press, 1967), pp. 279–288.

5. See Ch'ien Mu, *Chu Tzu hsin hsüeh-an*, Bk. III, pp. 509, and 552.

6. *Ibid.*, p. 490. Ch'ien's words that "Chu Hsi has a very clear and true understanding of Ch'an" seem to be an overstatement.

7. *Chu Tzu wen-chi*, 38:34a.

8. Ch'ien Mu, *Chu Tzu hsin hsüeh-an*, Bk. III, p. 1.

9. *Ibid.*, p. 2.

10. *Ibid.*, p. 23.

11. *Chu Tzu wen-chi*, 1:8b. See also Ch'ien Mu, *Chu Tzu hsin hsüeh-an*, Bk. III, p. 7.

12. *Chu Tzu wen-chi*, 2:2a. See also Ch'ien Mu, *Chu Tzu hsin hsüeh-an*, Bk. III, p. 19.

13. Mou Tsung-san, *Hsin-t'i yü hsing-t'i*[ce] [The substance of mind and the substance of nature], (Taipei: Cheng-chung[cf] Book Co., 1969), Bk. III, chs. 2 (sec. 1–6), 3 (sec. 1–4), and 4 (sec. 1–4.)

14. As we shall see, Chu Hsi often fails to distinguish Indian Buddhism from Chinese Buddhism, and, in particular, Indian Mahāyāna from Sinitic Mahāyāna. When he mentions Buddhism, it sometimes refers to Buddhism in general, sometimes to

Sinitic Mahāyāna, and sometimes to Ch'an Buddhism only. But he is probably unaware of the necessity to clarify or specify the meaning of the term "Buddhism."

15. Araki Kengo, *Bukkyō to jukyō*, p. 255.

16. *Ibid.*, p. 256.

17. It is a well-known fact that Chu Hsi often identified, rightly or wrongly, Lu Hsiang-shan's mind-learning with Ch'an Buddhism.

18. *Chu Tzu yü-lei* (Taipei: Cheng-chung Book Co. 1970, 2nd ed.), 126:28b, p. 4872.

19. *Ibid.*, 124:7b p. 4766.

20. *Ibid.*, 113:11b, p. 4380.

21. The famous line appears in the *Classic of Poetry*, ode no. 192, and in the *Doctrine of the Mean*, ch. 33. Confucius' words appear in *Analects*, 9:16.

22. *Ibid.*, 62:16a, p. 2377.

23. Wing-tsit Chan, "Neo-Confucian Philosophical Poems," *Renditions* (Center for Translation Projects, The Chinese University of Hong Kong), no. 4 (Spring, 1975), p. 12.

24. *Chu Tzu yü-lei*, 126:5b, p. 4826.

25. *Ibid.*

26. *Chang Tzu ch'üan-shu*cg [Complete works of Master Chang], (SPPY ed.), 2:2a.

27. *Ibid.*, 2:2b.

28. *Chu Tzu yü-lei*, 126:8a, p. 4831.

29. *Ibid.*, 126:5b, p. 4826.

30. *I-shu*ch [surviving works], 218:1b, in the *Erh-Ch'eng ch'üan-shu*ci [Complete works of the Ch'eng brothers], (SPPY ed.).

31. See Chi-tsang, *San-lun hsüan-i*cj [The profound meaning of the Three-Treatises Philosophy], *Daizōkyō*,ck no. 1852 (col. 45, p. 1).

32. *Lao Tzu*, ch. 1.

33. Edward Conze, trans., *Buddhist Wisdom Books* (London: George Allen & Unwin, 1958), p. 68.

34. I have tried to characterize Chinese metaphysics in general as holistic multiperspectivism in the funtional form in the following papers: "Creative Hermeneutics: Taoist Metaphysics and Heidegger," *Journal of Chinese Philosophy* 3 (1976), pp. 115–143; "The Trans-Onto-Theo-Logical Foundations of Language in Heidegger and Taoism," *Journal of Chinese Philosophy* 5 (1978), pp. 301–333; "The Underlying Structure of Metaphysical Language: A Case Examination of Chinese Philosophy and Whitehead," *Journal of Chinese Philosophy* 6 (1979), pp. 339–366; "Heidegger and Zen*cl* on Being and Nothingness: A Critical Essay in Transmetaphysical Dialectics," in Nathan Katz, ed., *Buddhist and Western Philosophy* (New Delhi: Sterling Publishers, 1981), pp. 172–201; and "Chinese Buddhism as a Existential Phenomenology," in Anna-Teresa Tymieniecka, ed., *Analecta Husserliana* (in press).

35. The four Dharma-realms refer to the four-fold of "the Dharma-realm of phenomena (events, or affairs)," "The Dharma-realm of Principle (which is Emptiness)," "the Dharma-realm of the nonobstructed interpenetration of Principle and phenomena," and "the Dharma-realm of the nonobstructed interpenetration of phenomena and phenomena," these four multiperspectively constituting the true, selfsame Dharma-realm.

36. *Chu Tzu yü-lei*, 126:6a, p. 4827.

37. *Tathāgata-garbha* (the womb or matrix of *Tathāgata*) is a functional term, which

is employed to express the dynamic working of Buddha-nature inherent in each and every sentient being as the seed or potential for ultimate enlightenment. Thus, "the womb of *Tathāgata*"—*Tathāgata* being an honorific title of the Buddha meaning "thus-come or thus-gone enlightened"—gives us a metapsychological explanation of why and how all sentient beings can attain enlightenment or buddhahood at least in principle.

38. See *Shang-ts'ai yü-lu*ᶜᵐ [Recorded sayings of Hsieh Liang-tso], comp. by Chu Hsi (Taipei: Kuang-wenᶜⁿ Book Co., 1972), 2:11b, p. 64.

39. Kao Tzu's naturalistic thesis can be found in the *Book of Mencius*, 6B:1–6. See also Wing-tsit Chan, *A Source Book in Chinese Philosophy* (Princeton, N.J.: Princeton University Press, 1963), pp. 51–53.

40. *Chu Tzu yü-lei*, 126:11b, p. 4838. The *Treatise on Buddhism* [*Shih-shih lun*] is in the *Chu Tzu wen-chi*, extra collection, ch. 8.

41. For Mencius' teaching of human-kindness (humanity), righteousness, propriety, and (moral) knowledge, which Chu Hsi reinterprets as the fourfold moral principle manifesting the Principle of Heaven, see Wing-tsit Chan, *Source Book*, p. 65.

42. Ch'ien Mu, *Chu Tzu hsin hsüeh-an*, Bk. III, p. 498.

43. *Chu Tzu yü-lei*, 126:13a, p. 4841.

44. *Ibid.*, 126:13b, p. 4842 *ff.*

45. *Ibid.*, 126:8a, p. 4831.

46. *The Book of Mencius*, 7A:4. See also Wing-tsit Chan, *Source Book*, p. 79.

47. *Chu Tzu yü-lei*, 12:6a–b, pp. 327–328.

48. *Ibid.*, 126:8a, p. 4831.

49. Ch'ien Mu, *Chu Tzu hsin hsüeh-an*, Bk. III, p. 495.

50. *Chu Tzu wen-chi*, 42:4a–b.

51. *Chu Tzu yü-lei*, 55:1b, p. 2076.

52. *Ch'uan-hsi-lu*ᶜᵒ [Instruction for practical living], pt. 3, sec. 315. See also Wing-tsit Chan, *Instructions for Practical Living* (New York: Columbia University Press, 1963), p. 139.

53. My translation. See also Philip B. Yampolsky, trans., *The Platform Sutra of the Sixth Patriarch* (New York: Columbia University Press, 1967), p. 139.

54. *Chu Tzu yü-lei*, 126:28a, p. 4871.

55. For the origin of the method, see the second hexagram (earth), the *Book of Changes*. See also Wing-tsit Chan, *Source Book*, p. 264.

56. *Chu Tzu yü-lei*, 44:20b, p. 1812.

57. *Ibid.*, 126:18a, p. 4851. See also *I-shu*, 13:1b.

58. *Chu Tzu yü-lei*, 15:17a, p. 483.

59. *Chu Tzu wen-chi*, 39:17b.

60. See *I-shu*, 18:5b.

61. *Chu Tzu yü-lei*, 126:8b, p. 4832.

62. *Ibid.*, 113:4a, p. 4365.

63. *Ibid.*, 125:4b, p. 4792.

64. Ch'ien Mu, *Chu Tzu hsin hsüeh-an*, Bk. III, p. 553.

65. *Chu Tzu yü-lei*, 126:15b, p. 4846.

66. *Ibid.*, 126:7b, p. 4830.

67. *Chu Tzu wen-chi*, 72:31b and 72:32b.

68. *Ibid.*, 72:43a–b.

69. *Ibid.*, 43:12a.

70. The words "The whole street is full of sages" appear in Wang Yang-ming's *Instructions for Practical Living*, pt. 3, sec. 313. See Wing-tsit Chan, trans., the same title, p. 239. "The tea-boy himself is the Way" ["the Way" requoted by Ch'ien Mu here as "a sage"] appears in *Lo Chin-hsi yü-lu*ᶜᵖ [Recorded sayings of Lo Chin-hsi, 1515–1588], (Taipei: Kuang-wen Book Co., 1967), 1:48b.

71. Ch'ien Mu, *Chu Tzu hsin hsüeh-an*, Bk. III, p. 521.

72. *Analects*, 2:4.

73. *Chu Tzu yü-lei*, 126:6b, p. 4828.

74. For the respective teachings of Yang Chu and I Tzu, see the *Book of Mencius*, 3A:5 and 3B:9, in Wing-tsit Chan, *Source Book*, pp. 71–72.

75. *Chu Tzu yü-lei*, 52:34b, p. 2018.

76. *Ibid.*, 126:21b, p. 4858.

77. See the *Book of Mencius*, 4A:27.

78. *Analects*, 1:2.

79. See Ch'eng I's preface to his *I-chuan*ᶜ𐞥 [Commentaries on the *Book of Changes*].

80. *Chu Tzu wen-chi*, 43:9a.

81. *Chu Tzu yü-lei*, 126:7a, p. 4829.

82. *Ibid.*, 126:24a, p. 4863.

83. *Ibid.*, 126:18a, p. 4851. The quotation from Ch'eng Hao appears in the *I-shu*, 13:1b.

84. *Ibid.*, 62:15b–16a, pp. 2376–2377.

85. *Ibid.*, 126:11a, p. 4837.

86. *Ibid.*, 126:28a, p. 4871.

87. This expression appears in the *Fa-hua-ching*ᶜʳ [Lotus scripture]. See *Daizōkyō*, no. 262 (vol. 9, p. 8).

88. *Chu Tzu yü-lei*, 126:14a, p. 4843.

89. *Ibid.*, 12:9a, p. 333.

90. *Ibid.*, 12:18a, p. 351.

91. *Ibid.*, 41:3b–4b, pp. 1666–1668. The words "to restrain oneself and return to propriety is *jen*" appear in the *Analects*, 12:1.

92. *Ibid.*, 62:16a, p. 2377.

93. *Ibid.*, 132:17b.

94. *Chu Tzu wen-chi*, 43:11a.

95. These two quotations are from the *Book of Mencius*, 7A:1.

96. *Chu Tzu wen-chi*, 45:20ab.

97. See *Analects*, 11:11.

98. *Chu Tzu yü-lei*, 126:5b, p. 4826.

99. These two quotations are respectively from the *Classic of Poetry*, ode no. 267, and the *Book of Changes*, first hexagram (heaven).

100. *Chu Tzu wen-chi*, 43:10a.

101. *Philosophy East and West*, vol. 23, no. 3 (July 1973), p. 395. One or two words are slightly changed here. Transcendental (or higher) truth and worldly (or conventional) truth constitute the two inseparable aspects of the Mādhyamika teaching of twofold truth, which philosophically expresses the Middle Way.

Glossary

a 禪
b 墨子
c 楊朱
d 錢穆
e 江泳元適
f 李侗延平
g 趙師夏
h 道理
i 無為法
j 程頤
k 未發
l 牟宗三
m 已發
n 中和
o 理氣
p 荒木見悟
q 大慧宗杲
r 形而上
s 道
t 道心
u 形而下
v 器
w 陰陽
x 人心
y 陸象山九淵
z 心學
aa 陳榮捷
ab 猷
ac 氣有
ad 無
ae 老子
af 郭象

ah 莊子
ai 張載
aj 神識
ak 歐陽修
al 吉藏
am 天台
an 華嚴
ao 天
ap 體用
aq 一多
ar 理事
as 空假中
at 釋氏論
au 上蔡謝良佐
av 告子
aw 氣質
ax 氣稟
ay 胡宏五峯
az 知言
ba 蘇東坡軾
bb 王陽明守仁
bc 慧能
bd 念
be 程顥
bf 徐順之
bg 仁
bh 堯
bi 舜
bj 神秀
bk 仁義
bl 夷子
bm 義

bn 龐蘊
bo 權
bp 經
bq 朱子語類
br 吳斗南
bs 朱子文集
bt 朱子大全
bu 中華
bv 陳衛道
bw 常盤大定
bx 支那に於ける佛教と
　　儒教道教
by 東洋文庫
bz 佛教と儒教
ca 平樂寺書店
cb 朱子新學案
cc 三民
cd 近思錄
ce 心體與性體
cf 正中
cg 張子全書
ch 遺書
ci 二程全書
cj 三論玄義
ck 大藏經
cl 禪
cm 上蔡語錄
cn 廣文
co 傳習錄
cp 羅近溪語錄
cq 易傳
cr 法華經

23

Chu Hsi and His World

BRIAN McKNIGHT

CHU HSI was a man of ideas, a thinker. As such his closest ties were often with men long dead. Even when he dealt with his contemporaries much of his discourse concerned ideas. On this intellectual side of Chu Hsi, and indeed on most other facets of his life, I am ill qualified to comment before such a distinguished gathering of intellectual historians. What I will try to do is more modest, to share some of the results of recent work on other facets of the history of his times—economic, social, and political—so that it may be possible to explore some of the ways in which Chu Hsi exemplified the trends of his times and other ways in which he was atypical.

Perhaps the first thing to be said about his lifetime is that it was a time of peace that was haunted by war. War, and more particularly the occupation of the old Chinese heartland by foreign peoples, lay like a shadow across the Southern Sung (1127–1279). Chu Hsi was born into a time of troubles. Only a few months before his birth in the ninth month of 1130, the fugitive Sung (960–1279) court had been driven to the seacoast in Wen-chou[a] in Liang-che[b],[1] while the enemy ravaged the rich prefectures only a few hundred *li*[c-2] to the northwest.[3] When he died in 1200 the clouds of war were gathering, created by the foolish irridentism of Han T'o-chou[d](1151–1202). And in his middle years, immediately following his decisive break with Buddhism, Chu was deeply involved in the debate surrounding the Chin (1115–1234) invasion of 1161. His passionately argued views of this situation are one clear reminder of his involvement in the issues of the day.

And yet, although Chu Hsi's life was punctuated by conflicts with the Chin, and although he argued his position on war with the north at various times during his adult life, the years of his life were basically an age of peace. By the time he passed from boyhood to adolescence the border with the Chin had stabilized. He did not live to see the Sung invade the north in the early thirteenth century. Only the invasion of 1161–1164 marred a largely tranquil era.

The age was peaceful, but the troubles of the late Northern Sung (960–1126), and the invasion that destroyed it, helped shape the conditions of his lifetime. As work recently done makes clear, there was a widespread change in values and practice among the Chinese elite in the aftermath of the partisan political struggles of the late Northern Sung. Social values, educational practices, attitudes towards politics, and economic relations were all affected by these changes. Chu Hsi's life spans the flowering of the new trends and is illustrative of some of them.

Before dealing specifically with these changes, however, it may be useful to review briefly the economic and political conditions of the years 1130 to 1200.

Economically this period is considered an era of growth, but the rates of growth and other indicators of economic conditions varied from region to region and over time. The overshadowing economic influence of the early years of Chu's life was the conflict with the Chin. One immediate effect of the warfare was a sharp decrease in the supply of coinage. Government issues of coinage fell off sharply. The desperate government responded by issuing bills of exchange designed to assure delivery of rations to the troops and, in some areas, by issuing paper money. In both instances the failure to back the issues adequately led to rapid declines in value. The resultant rise in commodity prices was perhaps especially severe in Szechuan. In other areas of the country this rise in prices continued only until around 1140, after which commodity prices began to decline.

War again disrupted the monetary system in the 1160s, when the Chin invasion of 1161 with its attendant high military costs led for the first time to the widespread use of paper money in the economic heartland of the Sung empire. Paper money had long been in use in certain parts of the empire, but it was the events of 1161 that led directly to the growth of its use in the whole of the Sung state. Insufficiently backed, the paper notes depreciated. The depreciation in turn drove coins out of circulation, either through their being melted down for their ingredients or their being exported to the Chin state or to Japan. The result was a gradual rise in commodity prices for the remainder of the century.[4]

These monetary changes stemmed from fiscal emergency measures forced on the state by military expenditures. The government was well aware of the dangers of resorting to the use of the printing press; and though it was driven to cheapen its money as an emergency measure, the longer-range search for fiscal stability rested on at least three bases—a continuing dependence on the land tax (which brought with it some attempts to reassess landholdings and to reallocate fiscal responsibilities), an increased dependence on the salt monopoly, and the encouragement of foreign trade.

Salt monopoly income played a major role in Southern Sung finances. In 1160 the state derived an income of more than 20,000,000 strings of cash from salt, and although this was slightly smaller than the annual income for salt during the period 1077–1079, it still represented one-third of the state's cash income. This income continued to increase in the following period.[5]

Encouraging foreign trade had been a Sung policy from the beginning of the dynasty, but it took on added importance under the conditions of the 1130s. The government responded by issuing monk certificates to the Maritime Trade Commissions to be used as capital in foreign trade and by establishing new Maritime Trading Commissions, at Wen-chou in 1131, at Chiang-yinᶜ in 1146, and at Sung-chiang in 1163–1164. The state was also active in providing commercial facilities, and, through ship registration, regular anti-piracy patrols, and periodic campaigns against pirate strongholds, in creating conditions conducive to large-scale trade.[6]

Income from foreign trade formed a small if important part of overall revenues during the Southern Sung; the land taxes were the real key to fiscal stability. In trying to assure a steady income from such taxes the Southern Sung authorities at times attempted to have landholdings reassessed. The intent to reassess was expressed in the opening years of the Southern Sung, but no serious action was taken for almost two decades. Then, in the early 1140s Li Ch'un-nien proposed a surveying scheme called "regulating boundaries" (ching-chiehᶠ). The policy was adopted and remained at least nominally in force for eight years, despite local resistance. A somewhat similar scheme was enforced in Fukien during the reign of Hsiao-tsungᵍ (r. 1163–1189).[7]

The state sought in other ways to bolster its income from land taxes and other sources. This was an era when there was an attempt to reduce the fiscal privileges of various groups, including Buddhists and Taoists, the households of officials, and some people who were disadvantaged such as households headed by women.[8] It is apparent, however, that the state was only very partially successful in increasing the efficiency of revenue collection. In an attempt to make collection more effective the state, in the key economic areas of the empire, placed both tax collection and policing powers in the hands of the same village officers, who served concurrently in two different posts.[9] That gross undercollection persisted is suggested by the huge amounts of new income generated in some areas under the "Public Fields" scheme of the closing decades of the Sung, and the great increase at that time in "harmonious purchases," that is, compulsory purchase at prices set by the government.[10] Obviously a great deal of land, at least in some regions, had remained off the tax rolls.

In part this widespread evasion reflected changes in social structure and social attitudes that followed the partisan infighting of the reform and antireform movements of the late Northern Sung, and in part it reflected more immediate changes in patterns of land ownership and land utilization that resulted from the Chin invasions of the 1120s. In the years just prior to and following Chu Hsi's birth in 1130 a wave of refugees fled from the old Northern Sung territories into the south. The major destination was the lower Yangtze valley region, centering on Hangchow and the rich alluvial lands that stretched away to the north and west. One predictable result was a jump in land prices, particularly in Hangchow but also in other favored areas such as the region surrounding Lake T'ai.ʰ Many of the emigrés were powerful officials or members of the imperial clan. Their connections and position put them in an advantageous position to compete for landed property. They could try with varying degrees of success to withhold land from registration or to evade taxes in other ways. Any savings gained in this way were then available for further capitalization in the land, and this in turn by raising their yields added to their wealth.

The economic and social impact of their leveraged capital was further increased by a shift in government emphasis if not in government policy. During the Northern Sung the government was occasionally quite active in water conservancy projects. Although such efforts continued in the Southern Sung they were dwarfed by the effects of privately financed polder (diked field) construction. The increased construction of polders in the Chiang-nan[i] region[11] is one of the striking features of Southern Sung economic development. Such construction increased the value of the enclosed lands but added to the problems of those farming neighboring unenclosed lands, since inadequate drainage channels sharply increased the risks of flooding.[12]

We see emerging a sharper division between the rich and powerful, who were able to build polders and improve the productivity of their properties, and those left outside, who had to suffer the consequences. Oddly enough, the emergence of this group of landlords, often absentee landlords, did not necessarily lead to their domination of local life. In the past some historians, particularly in Japan, have tended to visualize these landlords as exercising a harsh, even a so-called feudal, control over their tenants. Recently, a young historian named Joseph McDermott has gone over the evidence again. He concludes that the social situation on the local level was far more complicated than has previously been supposed, both in terms of variations between regions and in terms of variety within regions. Moreover, the evidence he adduces suggests that in areas like that around Lake T'ai, with many large landlords, actual power to make decisions often rested not with the landlord at all but with his nominal underlings, often his bailiffs and even his tenants. McDermott suggests that the Southern Sung can be seen as consisting of at least six different regions, on the basis of different relationships between landlord and tenant, that landownership was far more widely distributed in south China than some scholars have been willing to admit, and that there was a variety of different kinds of tenants with distinctive patterns of relationships to and obligations toward their landlords.[13]

Perhaps it would be most reasonable if we visualized the majority of the south Chinese peasantry during the period of Chu Hsi's life as being part owners and part tenants, that is to say as people who owned some land, but not enough to support their families. The amount beyond their own property necessary to their support they rented from others, thus becoming tenants, but not tenants on large "manors" as is often supposed.

In only four regions is there evidence of any significant number of landlords who owned more than several hundred *mou*.[14] Even in these regions the evidence for the existence of manors (as these are usually conceived) is ambiguous at best. In the Lake T'ai basin region the large landholdings mostly consisted of many tiny plots scattered over several districts. In Fukien most of the land is reported to have belonged to Buddhist monasteries. These institutions seem to have lost as much as half their land during the course of the Sung; the beneficiaries were probably officials and merchants, but such men rarely owned more than several hundred *mou*. In western Ching-hu[k] West[15] there were landlords who laid claim to large contiguous blocks of land but who could not find tenants to cultivate it. Only for Fu-chou[l] in southern Chiang-nan West[16] do we find clear evidence of a countryside dominated by large contiguous "manorial" landholdings.

Large contiguous landed "manors" were relatively rare; so apparently were tenant-serfs who were bound to the land. Some scholars have asserted that such bondage was common in the southern Sung, indeed that such bondage was the norm. Such assertions ignore the existence at this time of two distinctive types of tenants, the land guest (*ti-k'o*[m]) and the tenant-guest (*tien-k'o*[n]). The land guest was legally classed as his master's servant. The tenant guest was legally classed as his master's tenant, a status inferior to the master but by no means to be equated with the status of servant.

Bondage to the land did occur. It seems to have been most common in the least developed parts of south China such a Kuang-nan[o] West,[17] K'uei-chou,[p] Ching-hu North,[18] and Ching-hu South.[19] In the more developed and economically significant regions of the south, land bondage seems to have been less common.

These patterns of landholding and landlord-tenant relationship are important for what they tell us about local political and social life. Here we see the working out, in the period of Chu Hsi's lifetime, of patterns that derive from changes born ultimately from the impact of the late Northern Sung partisan conflicts. In his recent, as yet unpublished, work Robert Hartwell of the University of Pennsylvania has suggested that the partisan debacle of the late Northern Sung led to a reorientation of the political elite in their attitudes towards the government and government service. His thesis is that prior to the rise of Wang An-shih[q] (1021–1086) Sung politics on the national level was dominated by a group of families claiming descent from families important during the T'ang (618–907). These families tended to seek marriage bonds within this nationwide elite stratum and focused their ambitions on national affairs and national service. The events of the period 1068–1100, however, suggested that national ambitions were chancy. The old nationally oriented elite began to focus its hopes and plans more on their home regions. They sought marriage alliances within their home regions, and indeed tended to pursue careers in government service that were regionally oriented and often occurred largely within the confines of one region. In so doing they were altering their marriage practices to conform to those already dominant among the local elite.[20]

These marriage practices will make more sense if we dismiss from our minds the picture of the Chinese family that has been drawn by such anthropologists as Maurice Freedman. As a result of the work of Freedman and his followers the Chinese kinship system is described in textbooks as an extreme patrilineal system. Robin Fox sums up this view succinctly by describing the system as one in which a woman "on marriage transferred from the lineage village . . . of her birth, and this transfer was for good. As far as her own lineage was concerned, she was lost to it completely and she came under the absolute jurisdiction of her husband's lineage."[21] For the Sung period this just will not do. As Patricia Ebrey has recently shown, Sung families remained interested in their daughters' lives and routinely intervened if they were widowed.[22]

As Ebrey points out, the men of Sung did not divide their kin into agnates (relatives through the male line), cognates (relatives by blood on the mother's aide), and affines (relatives by marriage). Nor did they divide their kin into blood relatives (consanguines) and relatives by marriage (affines) as Americans do. Rather they thought of kin either as agnates (*tsu-jen,*[r] *tsung-tsu*[s]) or as other relatives (*ch'in-ch'i*[t] or at times more specifically *wai-ch'i*[u]).

An examination of legal texts suggests, according to Ebrey, that (1) a person was assumed to be equally tied to relatives through his mother and his wife, (2) he was considered equally related to relatives of his son-in-law and his daughter-in-law, and (3) he was tied to the most nonagnative relatives through his mother and wife, next through his daughters, considerably less through his sisters, and then very minimally through any other connection.

In Chu Hsi's world these ways of defining who was kin were reflected in concern for married daughters and in the establishing of continuing ties of potential support with nonagnatic kin. The interest in married daughters is in turn reflected in the Sung dowry system. The long debate between Professors Niida Noboru[v] and Shiga Shuzo[w] on whether or not Sung women inherited property is in part moot.[23] Professor Shuzo has argued that what unmarried girls received was not an inheritance share but a dowry, but the salient point is that to the men of Chu Hsi's age this dowry was thought of as a type of inheritance share. The dowries are even called *fen,*[x] or portions, just as are the shares of male heirs. Women at times brought land as parts of their dowries and had the right to keep control over what they brought.

Yüan Ts'ai[y] (c.1140–c.1190) suggests one reason why the men of Chu Hsi's world wanted to pass substantial amounts of property on to their daughters. Property carried with it obligations of support. "Nowadays, he says people sometimes have incapable sons and they have to depend on their daughters' families for support, even their burials and sacrifices after their deaths falling to their daughters. So how can one say that having daughters is not comparable to having sons?"[24] Even if it did not come to such a point, in the locally oriented society of twelfth-century China, the other sorts of support that might come from relatives through marriage might be important.

Within the regions that were the focus of their marriage alliances and of their major social and political concern the elite families of Chu Hsi's age sought first for the preservation of their family status and fortunes. In practice this meant a mixed strategy of directing some sons into the path of the civil service examination system but others into commerce or other money-making activities. Work recently done by Robert Hymes at the University of Pennsylvania[25] suggests that families may have directed some sons into the examination life less in the expectation that they might end up with a *chin-shih*[z] (doctorate in letters) degree and an office than that they might earn lesser degrees that did not lead to civil service appointments but did bring with them a certain scholarly cachet, thus making it possible for the families of their bearers to interact on more equal terms with local officials. Hymes's study also indicates that this interlocking group of locally prominent families may well have thoroughly dominated the higher levels of the civil service also, in that most of the *chin-shih* whose kin can be discovered had some sort of relationship, by blood or marriage, with degree holders. Earlier views, which stressed the openness of the civil service system to new blood, defined as men without ties to those in office, needs to be reinterpreted in the light of Hymes's work.[26]

All this has little to do with "virtue" in the philosophical sense. Patricia Ebrey, in an important but as yet unpublished study which centers on a translation of the *Family Precepts of the Yüan Family* of Yüan Ts'ai, argues persuasively that, for members of the local elite (*shih-ta-fu*[aa]) group, the real issue was the preservation of the family fortunes. Yüan Ts'ai, the quintessential representative of this group, argues for his views on the basis of common sense, not the Classics, and reveals the breadth of his humanity by his stress on tolerating the foibles and attitudes of others.[27] Here, as at times elsewhere, it fit with the interests of all concerned to obscure the disparities that existed between the views of different subgroups within the *shih-ta-fu*. The gap between the philosophers and the ordinary members of the group was obscured by the use of a common vocabulary, which meant different things to the different members.

Thus it is not surprising that we see the world Chu Hsi lived in as one dominated on the local level by minor elite families who were able to preserve their economic position for generation after generation by directing some members into money making tasks, and their connections with the official world by directing others (who periodically gained lower degrees if not offices) into civil service competition.

Local elite leadership status in the time of Chu Hsi was attested by the voluntary participation of elite families in projects of value to the community. In the cases of some families that rose to prominence around the time of Chu Hsi's birth, the foundation of their claims to leadership rested on military activities in behalf of the Sung, especially the organizing and leading of local militia groups in the troubled first decade of the Southern Sung. In more peaceful times such acts of leadership were more apt to take the form of the endowing of local institutions, the repair of local facilities, and the provision of welfare and relief in times of natural disasters. Bridges, waterworks, roads, schools, community granaries, all benefited from the financial support of the local elite.

Of particular interest in light of Chu Hsi's attitudes is the involvement of the local elite of his lifetime in the support of Buddhist (and to a lesser extent Taoist) institutions. Robert Hymes's analysis of the community service actions of the elite in Fu-chou, Chiang-hsi, throws light on their attitudes toward religion and toward religious institutions. Buddhism seems to have flourished mightily in the area during the Southern Sung. Hymes noted almost a hundred temples in Fu-chou that were built or rebuilt, received donations of land, or were officially granted titles during the Sung. He estimates that this is no more than half the total number. Where records are sufficient to analyze more thoroughly the work done on these temples, it appears that local lay support was the rule rather than the exception, and many of the families named are known to have been members of the local elite of the area.[28]

At times such participation may have been a mark of social consciousness rather than piety, but at other times it is clear the belief in Buddhism was widely shared. Even stout Confucians participated in such activities, albeit at times with a show of ambivalence. The intertwining of the Buddhist clergy and the local elite is reflected in other ways: in the use of Buddhist monks as managers in the repair of local facilities, or in their being the major sponsors of facilities like bridges, and the building by official authorities of Buddhist shrines to bless the results of such works. Hymes quotes a fascinating passage from the 1220s, a generation after the death of Chu Hsi, which shows the mixture of religious and literati concerns that might be involved in a project.

In the southern part of the district (seat) there is a Buddhist temple. The temple had a pagoda, called T'ai-ho,[ab] which directly faced the district school. By tradition it had come to be called the Writing-Brush. It was built in 1142, but after only sixty-eight years suddenly collapsed. In the four examinations from 1208 on there was not one (from this district) who achieved the *chin-shih*. People's hearts were alarmed . . . they all said: "We must raise up the Writing-Brush!" Therefore they made a joint petition and came to request me (the district administrator) to restore it to its former state. I consequently deputed the prefectural graduate Hsü Te-hsin,[ac] a gentleman of the district (named) Liu Hsieh,[ad] and the monks Tsung-hsin,[ae] Tsung-an,[af] and Miao-tuan[ag] (to organize it) . . . On the top stone were recorded the names of all those to pass the examinations since the beginning of the dynasty, and the thousand names of the Buddha. It was named the Thousand Buddha Pagoda. . . . Work was begun in the fall of 1222, and in the spring (of 1223) it had just been completed, when the Southern Palace announcement [the announcement of *chin-shih*] included the names of Hsü Meng-ling,[ah] T'u Hui,[ai] and Wan K'ai,[aj] all passing together. Then people said: "How quickly the Writing-Brush has responded!"[29]

The elite might also seek the services of monks or temples in caring for the tombs of their ancestors. At times these temples might become the private Merit Cloisters of the elite family involved.

Finally, Hymes notes that the local elite also was a supplier of recruits to the clergy, both Buddhist and Taoist. We have examples of Confucian scholars, and even *chin-shih* graduates, who ended their lives as Buddhist monks, often important and powerful ones. Members of local elite lineages some of whose members were bureaucrats are known to have been high Buddhist and Taoist clergy. In short, religion played an important and pervasive role in the life of Southern Sung China, including that of the supposedly Confucian elite.[30]

One theme that seems to run through many of the descriptions of the Southern (as opposed to the Northern) Sung is what we might call localism or local concern, a deliberate in-drawing of the focus of attention, not, certainly, to the exclusion of national matters, but nonetheless there was a change in the balance of concern. On the microscopic level this change was reflected in the altered marriage patterns described above. On a level above this the decentralization was reflected in the emergence during Chu Hsi's lifetime of what might be called proto-provinces, in the form of four command systems, centered on territorial armies and the hinterlands needed to support them. These command systems gradually assumed many of the functions of the central government. In the case of Szechuan the command system even conducted its own civil service examinations. The systems were integrated with the central administration by giving their officials central government titles, with commissions on detached service for their actual work in the region. Although this use of commands was obviously initially a response to the exigencies of the war against the Chin that was raging as Chu Hsi was born, it remained in use because it made sense in an empire whose economic system was so complex and whose population was so great that with the communication technology of the time close centralized control was no longer feasible. (This complexity is perhaps best reflected in Shiba Yoshinobu's[ak] *Sōdai shōgyō-shi kenkyū.*[al])[31] The Northern Sung central government career pattern, of nationally oriented careers within specific branches of the bureaucracy (such as judicial, fiscal) was replaced during Chu Hsi's lifetime by intraregional careers in a diversity of bureaucratic branches. Policy was adapted to regional problems and reflected the asserted needs of local interest groups.[32]

Below this regional level there was a further decentralizing change, the weakening of the role of the prefecture, which had the effect of increasing the already important role of the district as an administrative unit. This in turn made it possible for local elites to influence administrations in their favor.

The war, which contributed to the emergence of this new local pattern, also helped cause changes in the central administration. The chaos of the late 1120s had resulted, by the time of Chu Hsi's birth, in the loss or destruction of most government records. As a result only the personal copies kept by clerical personnel were extant during the period of recovery, and the clerks used this situation to increase their control over government affairs. In general this has been interpreted as a baneful influence on Southern Sung administration. James Liu[am] has strongly stated the growth of corruption during the Southern Sung, and Miyazaki Ichisada[an] in his earlier writings agreed, though late in his life he came to feel that clerical power was inevitable and not wholly harmful.[33] We can put the situation in perspective if we think of the "corruption" of the clerks as a form of personal favoritism in contrast to objective impersonal administration. Seen in that light the role of the clerks merely mirrors a larger situation, for during Chu Hsi's lifetime a civil service personnel selection system emerged in which favoritism, in the form of the *yin*[ao] (protection) privilege, played a larger role than it did in the Northern Sung.

The works of John Chafee and Robert Hymes suggest that the Sung civil service was by no means an egalitarian and equalizing road to social mobility; the dissertation recently completed by Richard Davis of Princeton makes a strong counterargument. In fact, as Patricia Ebrey has pointed out, the argument is largely a matter of conflicting definitions.[34] The statement that mobility was low is correct, if by mobility one means movement from the non-*shih-ta-fu* levels of society into the civil service. The statement that mobility was high is correct if by mobility one means movement from being a nondegree-holding *shih-ta-fu* family to degree holding. The pattern which fits both arguments suggests that successful candidates, although occasionally drawn from non-*shih-ta-fu* families, tended to come largely from established local elite families, and that these local elite families tended to have affinial if not consanguine relatives who had civil service degrees. Entrance to the examinations also involved securing recommendations, which again tended to the closure of the system. This form of closure was itself largely sufficient during the Northern Sung to make the examination system the route into office favored by the ruling elite for their offspring. Although a great many officials entered service by other routes, and especially through protection, my own analysis suggests that very few men could hope to reach policy making levels in the administration without an examination degree.[35]

However, by Chu Hsi's lifetime the spread of printing and consequently of literacy, combined with the Northern Sung prosperity and population growth, had produced a situation in which competition within the examinations had become forbiddingly fierce. I would suggest that the ruling elite, no longer able to depend on examination success by their descendants, stressed ever more heavily the protection route into office, and more importantly, permitted men who entered in this way to reach at least middle level offices. Richard Davis cites a number of examples from the Shih[ap] clan of men who reached offices of some importance without degrees.[36]

Davis also argues that university reforms, and such innovations as the *pa-hsing*[aq][37] system of recruitment under Hui-tsung[ar] (r.1100–1125), were in part aimed at and had the effect of opening the system to outsiders. He does, how-

ever, admit that "schemes intended to benefit the humble . . . could be manipulated by the elite to their own advantage."[38] Until these reforms have
been further studied it would be premature to decide on the motives of their
sponsors and their effects in practice. What we can safely say is that competition in the examinations had become extreme, that the odds against success
had probably increased, and that families within the elite social stratum, both
the civil service elite and the local *shih-ta-fu* elite, responded in a variety of
ways to the changed situation. Those already in the civil service might seek to
manipulate the system to secure their families continued prominence. Those
excluded from the magic circle of the bureaucracy, by the nepotism of incum-
bents and by the excessive competition of the examinations, reacted at times
by opting out of the struggle. Chu Hsi is in several ways a key figure in providing a legitimizing rationale for and an institutional basis for such renuncia-
tion.

In the end the favoritism reflected in these various changes touched the
imperial clan itself. During Chu Hsi's lifetime the clan used its power to erect
for itself an economic base, particularly in the rich Yangtze delta area (as
noted above). It also at this time began to enter the civil service in increasing
numbers, especially through the examination system but also through specific
acts of imperial grace.[39]

Oddly enough the general pattern of the decentralization of power was
accompanied by an actual increase in the power of the chief ministers, who
came to hold control over both military and civil affairs in their hands.[40] But
this change, which ran counter to the trend toward decentralization, fitted in
perfectly with the trend toward favoritism. There was a continuing problem
with attempts by chief ministers to pack the upper levels of the bureaucracy
with their protegés.

What was the place of Chu Hsi in this changing social, political, and economic landscape? In what ways was he representative of his times, and in
what ways did he stand out as a maverick? The ideal way to answer these
questions would be to present a full-length portrait of Chu Hsi, a true biography. Oddly enough none seems ever to have been written. The closest thing to
such a work may be Ch'ien Mu's[as] *Chu Tzu hsin hsüeh-an*[at] (A new study of
Chu Hsi), but even that impressive work focuses very largely on Chu Hsi's
ideas, to the relative neglect of his life itself. I am not going to attempt here
the audacious task of describing Chu Hsi's whole lifetime in the few pages
available to me. Rather I will focus on one brief period in his life, centering on
the Lung-hsing[au] reign period (1163–1164). By examining Chu Hsi's life during a brief span of years, from the spring of 1162 to the spring of 1164, we can
see in cameo the man and his beliefs.

Li Ch'i[av] has called Chu Hsi "by temperament a Taoist recluse."[41] These
years show both the side of the man of which this is a fitting description, and
the traits and concerns which impelled him at times to violate his desire for

freedom from involvement. In the early spring of 1162 he was living quietly in Wu-fu[aw] village in Ch'ung-an[ax] county in Fukien on the salary he received from a sinecure as the superintendent of the Southern Peak Temple.[42] As his writings of this period show, he was deeply concerned about the war then raging in the north between the Chin and the Sung, but this had little effect on the pace or style of his life. In later spring, about the time when the tenure of his sinecure expired, Chu travelled down the river valley several hundred *li* to Chien-an[ay] county to visit his teacher Li Yen-p'ing (Li Tung,[az] 1093–1163). After meeting in Chien-an, where Li Yen-p'ing's youngest son Li Hsin-fu[ba] was registrar (*chu-pu*[bb]), the two philosophers travelled together back to Li Yen-p'ing's home in Yen-p'ing county. There they apparently spent several months together, discussing Confucianism no doubt, but also the national affairs of the moment. These months show Chu Hsi in a role not unknown from earlier times but made more common by developments of the late Northern Sung, the retired gentleman-philosopher who has refused to participate actively in state affairs. By the style of his life he was already in the process of legitimizing the reclusive alternative to state service, which became more and more popular as entrance to the civil service became increasingly difficult to obtain.

A recluse is not a hermit. We find Chu Hsi in these years enjoying the company of others both in prospect and in retrospect. In one charming preface, which he wrote during the last month of 1162 for the works of his boyhood friend Huang Tzu-heng,[bc] he recalls nostalgically the days of his youth when the two youngsters traveled about together, "played lutes and sang songs, listening to one another, and roaming about without caring if it were morning or evening." He recalls their discussing, as boys of fifteen will do, the profound problems and questions of their lives.[43] More immediately in these years he was involved with the children of his family, as a teacher.

Here, in his role as teacher, we find Chu Hsi again very much a part, cause, and symptom of the developments of his world. His era was one in which the generalized values inherited from the past, and enshrined in the Confucian Classics, were related in increasingly problematic ways to an external world of growing complexity and rapid change. The sociologist Robin Williams has pointed out that one common reaction under these circumstances is fundamentalism—the reassertion of basic values and the identification of these generalized values with the specific goals of the fundamentalists.[44] It was the fortune of Southern Sung China that the fundamentalist par excellence of their age was also one of its most brilliant thinkers. Chu Hsi's fundamentalistic reassertion of Confucian values needs no special comment, but we can see his commitment in a particularly revealing light if we look at the works he finished during the brief span of time on which this paper focuses. It was in these years that he completed his primers on the *Analects*. In his preface to his *Lun-yü yao-i*[bd] (essential meanings of the *Analects*), after a brief resume of the history of commentaries on the *Analects,* he speaks of his difficulties as a boy of thirteen or fourteen in grasping the ideas of the Classics, and his later search for understanding. Then,

> in the Lung-hsing period at the time of the changing of the reign title, I was in seclusion, and had no post. With one or two like-minded men I worked at this task. Zealously I put forth effort. I expunged other writings than those of the Northern Sung Confucian scholars [Ch'eng I,[be] 1033–1107 and Ch'eng Hao,[bf] 1032–1085]. And the writings of (the Ch'eng brothers') disciples and friends I supplemented and fixed, and made of them a book I called the *Lun-yü yao-i.* Since I am of the opinion that if scholars read this book [the *Analects*] they must get a detailed (explanation) of the meaning of characters and special terms from commentaries many (such explanations) offered in commentaries cannot be neglected and expunged. However, insofar as the essential meaning of (the *Analects*) is concerned this book almost (offers us a complete picture).[45]

His concern that students be properly trained in the most basic works is reflected even more clearly in the preface he wrote at this time to his *Lun-yü hsün-meng k'ou-i*[bg] (A catechism on the *Analects* for young students).

> I had already written a preface to the *Lun-yü yao-i* in order to provide it for others to read. On days when I had leisure I read it to my children. Generally speaking, when the various senior scholars wrote, they did not write for children. Therefore their commentaries are brief (in philological) explanation but detailed in expounding the essential meanings. When beginning students read the sentences of the Classics they are not able to understand them. They must again read the commentaries. When asked about the meaning of the works the students are all confused. This can hardly be an appropriate way to teach the young. Therefore I edited and wrote so as to complete this work. Being based on the commentaries my work is a means to master the meanings of the words and terms. By consulting works which explain the language used I have corrected the pronunciations. Thereafter I brought things together from the writings of the various philosophers in order to make clear the essentials (of the *Analects*). Each sentence's meaning was appended to the original sentence. Each section's intent was set at the end of the main section. Also I took things that I had heard from my teachers and friends throughout my whole life and which had been of benefit to me, and occasionally I added one or two items. The beginnings and endings, the subtle and crude, the large and small, the detailed and the cursory, because of my original intention in writing the book I merely aimed at making children's study of the *Analects* easier. Therefore I called it the *hsün-meng k'ou-i.* Since I just used it in our family school I do not dare to make it available to others than children. . . . The commentaries and explanations of this book are clear and detailed. If it is studied every day all will be comprehensible. The expounding of the essential meaning of the book is refined and concise. Intone them and they will all be understandable. On those points we have already understood thoroughly, although we know them, we ought still to study them. . . . Be anxious but do not desire to hurry. Be methodical and do not be lazy. Do not be led by

vulgar teachings, and so desert (Confucian teachings), thinking that Confucian teachings are impractical and dull. Do not be bewildered by heresies. . . . The words of the Sage are the epitome of greatness, centrality, exhaustiveness, and rectitude. They can serve as the standard for ten thousand generations.[46]

As these prefaces make clear, Chu Hsi's faith rested upon two rocks—the unquestioned correctness of basic Confucian values and the fundamental role of education in inculcating these values in the young. To him Confucianism was a good sword and shield. He was the champion of a particular tradition, using tradition in the sense of a universe of symbols that integrated, explained, and justified certain institutional arrangements and the values appropriate to them. The Chinese world of his time was a battlefield between a number of "traditions," using that word in the sense given above. The sharpness of the conflict between these traditions was heightened by the severity of external national problems, and by the increasing competition for certain highly desired social goods, in particular access to office through the examinations. It was part of Chu Hsi's genius to have recognized the central, long-range role of education as a factor in these conflicts between alternate traditions. Chu Hsi's own fundamentalistic stance was both a response to the clash of traditions (and the social groups that were the bearers of these traditions) and an answer to the conflict.

Alienated criticism of those in power is a common response under these circumstances, but Chu Hsi went beyond that in providing a long-term solution embodied in institutional form—a new system of schooling, new in content and to some extent in form. It is not accidental that the man who worked at reviving the schools during his first term of official life, as registrar in T'ung-an,[bh] and who later in his life was to initiate the revival (in a new form) of the *shu-yüan*[bi] (academy) institution, was in the years on which we are focusing, developing curricular materials on very fundamental Confucian texts, both for older students and for the very young. As Linda Walton-Vargo has shown in a study of the rise of *shu-yüan* in Ming[bj] prefecture in the Sung and Yüan (1277–1368), the development of educational institutions inculcating Neo-Confucianism was the key institutional feature in the rise of an orthodoxy during the late Sung. The fundamentalist reassertion of Confucian values, as understood by Chu Hsi, won in the conflict of "traditions" because it struck at the very root of cultural continuity, the training of scholars and teachers who are the key figures in the transmission of cultural values from one generation to the next.[47]

Chu Hsi sought to influence developments in the world he lived in without participating in them. In the long run his approach was enormously successful; in the shorter term he was unable to stay out of the flow of events. He was free to travel about, to visit his teacher, and discuss at leisure the finer points of the Classics, but even in peaceful Fukien, he could not avoid at least intellectual and emotional involvement in larger affairs.

In the ninth month of 1161, a few months before our story opened, the Chin Emperor Hai-ling[bk] (r.1149–1160) invaded Sung territory with a great army divided into two columns.[48] Hai-ling himself led the eastern column, which rapidly overran a number of Sung prefectures. This eastern column eventually drove all the way south to the Yangtze River. Meanwhile, however, the Sung were scoring a series of victories in the far West, aided by timely defections among Chinese officers in Chin service. And in the Chin homeland a coup was brewing.

When he had moved south Hai-ling had sent agents to murder some of his relatives. Among the intended victims was Wan-yen Wu-lu,[bl] a grandson of the Chin founder Akuta and a bitter enemy of Hai-ling. His hand forced by Hai-ling's assassination plot, Wu-lu rebelled little more than a month after the beginning of the southern invasion. Hai-ling's preparations for the invasion had greatly burdened the people in Chin territory, and Wu-lu had little trouble in seizing the Chin capital, where he was proclaimed emperor. Meanwhile, although Hai-ling continued to win victories in the south, he found it impossible to cross the Yangtze successfully. His last serious effort culminated in the destruction of his naval fleet by the Sung forces. Shortly thereafter he was murdered by his subordinates.

The war, however, dragged on, with the Sung armies successful, but not decisively so. The Sung Emperor, Kao-tsung,[bm] (r.1127–1162) then in his mid-fifties, was finding the burden of his role increasingly irksome. In the fifth month of 1162 (about the time Chu Hsi was ending his long visit with his teacher) Kao-tsung named his adopted son Chao Po-ts'ung[bn] heir apparent. A month later Kao-tsung abdicated, and the heir apparent, the Emperor Hsiao-tsung, ascended the throne. Thus, mid-summer of 1162 found the Sung with both a problem and an opportunity. Should the state prosecute the war vigorously in hopes not simply of defeating the enemy invasions but perhaps with the promise of regaining territory lost to the Chin in the 1120s, or should an accommodation be sought? The question sparked bitter debate. It brought Chu Hsi out of his self-imposed seclusion and into the thick of the dispute.

Chu Hsi had by this time left his teacher and returned to his home. But, as was their habit, the two men continued to correspond, writing letters almost monthly. The second letter of the series that began after Chu Hsi's return home was written on the very day when, some hundreds of *li* to the north, the newly enthroned emperor Hsiao-tsung was issuing a call for "frank words" on problems of state. Two months later, in a memorial dated eighth month, seventh day (September 17, 1162), Chu responded. He was newly without a post, the term of his sinecure as superintendent of a Taoist temple having been completed in the fifth month, but he spoke out in no uncertain terms on state troubles and their solutions. His deepest concern was about the Chin enemy. The Chin had occupied "territory which was ours of old, even though through misfortune we lost it." To negotiate for the lost territories from a position of weakness would be both shameful and stupid. Because "the Sung is not able through its own strength to recover the ancestral lands, it thinks of begging for their return from the enemy so as to establish our state. Unworthy though I am I humbly think your majesty would be ashamed to do this." Such an approach would be stupid because, even if by some fluke the Chin agreed and returned the lost lands, a weak Sung state would be incapable of holding on to them. On the contrary, a Sung state strong and virtuous enough to seize the disputed territory by force would find the lands returning to them naturally, and would have no difficulty in holding on to them. The Sung policy of negotiating while hostilities continue is the worst possible solution. It necessarily leaves Chinese councils divided between advocates of peace and advocates of war, confuses those not fully committed to either policy, and enormously strengthens the hand of the enemy both on the battlefield and at the conference table. The proper solution, according to Chu, was neither war at all costs nor peace at any price. Rather it was a cold war. Recall the Sung envoys, he advised. Shut the Sung borders. Concentrate on internal reform and military preparations. Such a policy would hearten the people of Sung, "officers and high officials, soldiers and the common people, the far and the near, those within and those without." With a few years the resurgent Sung state would find the lost territories returning of themselves.[49] Some months later he elaborated on his position.

> I have noted that the people of the present who discuss state policies only have three positions: they say "attack"; they say "defend", or they say "seek peace". But in the affairs of this world what is profitable carries with it injury, and what can be advantageous carries with it losses. Thus, within these three positions there are two points for each. The (policy) of attacking on the one hand involves advancing, but it carries with it the danger of recklessness. The defensive (policy) certainly may be a stratagem which will give you control (over affairs), but it also carries with it the problem of having to be maintained over an extended period. And as for the (policy of) seeking peace, this is the worst alternative. The rights and wrongs (of these positions) are at cross-purposes; their possibilities and impossibilities cancel one another out. In the confusion these talkers adorn their private (intentions) so that the deception cannot be overcome. Even with Your Majesty's discerning intelligence you still will not be able to ward off doubts. . . .

The answer for Chu Hsi was a policy of "no war, no peace." "What needs to be done at present is not to fight, for we lack the means whereby to requite the enemy, and not to adopt a defensive policy, since we lack the means to exercise sufficient control." To sue for peace was even more dangerous. The Emperor ought to forbid discussion of peace as an alternative, and cashier the advocates of peace.[50]

To use the jargon of our day we might say that Chu Hsi was strategically a hawk and tactically a dove. When he discusses the specific aspects of his policy his Confucian convictions become evident. To him the most critical matter is the attitude of the emperor, and that is based on the emperor's having been properly educated. The emperor must make his stand on the basis of fundamental principles. In practical terms this would mean the "rectification of names," that is, the establishing of the proper relationships between ruler and minister, ruler and subject. If this were done one result would be forthrightness. There were those who said, "Pretend peace, talk it, and wait for an opportunity to strike the enemy." Such duplicity was foolish, since it necessarily led to divided councils and opinions, and made concerted activity at a time of opportunity quite impossible. The emperor had to take his stand on principle, to establish the Way among men by enforcing the proper relationships, and to concentrate on internal reforms and strengths. Then, when opportunity did arrive, it could not be missed. Then, because the emperor's intentions were clear to all, the people and the officials would stand united in the face of the enemy. Seen in the light of such solidarity, attack and defense were but parts of an overall policy, and even in defeat there would be a more fundamental victory.[51]

Chu Hsi was certainly a hawk, but a most thoughtful one. His fundamental commitment, which perhaps came to him from his father, was revanchism, and the tone of his writings can only be called proto-nationalist. His analysis of the problem and his operational suggestions are Confucian in the best sense of that word. Perhaps we might credit his teacher in this case, since it seems that Chu did discuss his response to the emperor with Li Yen-p'ing, another believer in the necessity of confrontation if not war with Chin.

Chu Hsi's policies were ignored. The emperor instead accepted the arguments of his minister Shih Hao[bo] (1106–1194). Shih's position, in fact, has a number of points in common with Chu Hsi's, and despite their differences in outlook it would seem that Chu Hsi respected Shih Hao, and it is clear that Shih Hao supported Chu Hsi. But the policy of negotiation won. In the words of Shih Hao:

> Today, the might of [our] armed forces is not yet efficacious, that of [our] people has yet to be rejuvenated [from previous wars], and [our] resources are still inadequate. Were we to suddenly neglect the internal while engaging the external, even if [it led to] restoration of the entire realm, it would still be of no benefit.[52]

Chu Hsi did not take his defeat lightly. Shortly after his famous first interview with the emperor, Chu wrote an angry letter to his friend Wei Yüan-lu.[bp]

> The peace talks have already been decided upon! Wildly improper words have flooded in all directions. This is not a bundle of reeds on which we can cross a stream. The other day I ran into Chou K'uei.[bq] I upbraided him to his face for his lack of righteousness. He said, "This is the big talk of somebody who does not hold power. Now, under the pressure of circumstances, we for the time

being only plan for the moment." I said to him, "The state is a charge for ten thousand years. How can a Civil Councillor make plans for the moment?"[53]

Men like Chu Hsi were especially embittered, as he remarked in a letter to Councilor Lo,[br] when, even in times of quiet and good harvests, the wealth of the people was drained off by the "stingy, grasping" Sung government and handed over to the enemy.[54]

This concern about the war, directly mirrored in his comments on the question of negotiation, is also reflected, though less openly, in the two other critical themes in his addresses to the throne—the problem of favoritism at court and the dangers of Buddhism. In the general discussion of Southern Sung political developments I suggested that some evidence suggests that during Chu Hsi's lifetime there was a subtle shift in the attitude of the Sung elite toward the examination system. Members of the local elites who were not able to place relatives in the elite through the examinations, in part because of the increased intensity of competitions, reacted in part by turning their backs on the examination system, condemning it as a travesty that focused men's attentions on peripheral aspects of the educational process and wholly disregarded the cultivation of the self, which was the only true end of education. Chu Hsi and his educational crusade are centrally involved in this process of alienated rejection. Some of those elite members who had succeeded in entering the ranks of the high civil service often reacted in quite another way. To a limited degree at least they may have downgraded the examinations also, by enhancing the role of the protection privilege so that their kin might have successful political careers without subjecting themselves to the chancy vagaries of the unacceptably competitive examinations. Top positions were still filled by examination graduates, but men who had entered the service in other ways could at least hope to reach middle positions in the bureaucracy. The result of this was a sort of institutionalized favoritism. The increasing number of imperial clan members in the civil service is merely evidence that even emperors were not immune to the mood of the age. Beginning in the 1150s increasing numbers of imperial clan members secured examination degrees, but not by subjecting themselves to the bitter competition of the regular examinations. Imperial clan members were privileged to sit for separate examinations conducted by the Court of Imperial Family Affairs. In 1163 there are said to have been seven hundred clan members sitting for the degree. Small wonder that by the end of the Southern Sung Ming-chou alone could boast one hundred and forty imperial clan members who had gained the *chin shih* degree.[55]

Such favoritism fit in with, and indeed magnified, the tendency toward the packing of offices that had become rampant during the partisan struggles of the late Northern Sung. The Southern Sung symbol of the lengths to which this could go was the figure of Han T'o-chou, the nondegree man who rose to power through favoritism and proceeded to pack offices with his supporters (to the best of his ability) while persecuting his opponents.[56]

To Chu Hsi this trend was anathema. He phrased his objections to the results of such favoritism in terms of the "closing of the channels of communication" and the making of appointments on the basis of long acquaintance rather than on the basis of ability. He focused on the detrimental effects of this development on reform in local areas and the making of national foreign policy, but his objections are at heart general ones. In addresses to the throne he dealt at length with this issue. The fundamental ground of his position is the passage from the opening section of the *Great Learning.*

> Wishing to order well their states, (the ancients) first regulated their families. Wishing to regulate their families they first cultivated their persons. Wishing to cultivate their persons they first rectified their hearts. Wishing to rectify their hearts they first sought to be sincere in their thoughts. Wishing to be sincere in their thoughts they first extended to the utmost their knowledge. Such extension of knowledge lay in the investigation of things.[57]

In the specific conditions of the moment Chu Hsi says that

> whether the people are distressed or have good fortune is, I feel, determined by whether or not the local officials are excellent. This being the case the circuit intendants are the key elements for local governance. The Court is the foundation for the circuit intendants. (Thus, if) one wants the people to be secure in the lands which are their fundament, this then is centered in this Court. Your Majesty may feel that the circuit intendants of the present are corrupt, act cruelly, and injure the people, (but) who among them is not a relative or a hanger-on of the chief ministers and the censors? When these people lose their power Your Majesty should remain aware of their private intercourse, and eliminate it. How could those still in power not be of the same sort of persons? . . . Your Majesty may desire to learn about this, but who will inform you? As to affecting the people, I feel that the matter of first importance is the rectification of the Court. Then these other flaws can be reformed of themselves in a trice, and Your Majesty's intention will have been fulfilled. What in times past was styled "summoning several worthies" is what the world of today calls (summoning) loyal officials and outstanding officers. As to the means whereby to rectify the Court, how could there be any more important than this?[58]

Chu goes on to speak about the importance of using men according to their special abilities, in effect an application of the rectification of names. The emperor is enjoined not to rely on men just because of long and intimate association since that would result in a biased hearing of those officials who were not parts of the long-standing cliques, and also against being moved by private and particular charity, by favoritism under the guise of kindness, since that would prevent reception of the warnings of those outside the magic circle. The emperor having thus rectified himself so that he approached affairs without self-concern and with no partiality would create a pattern of open, unbiased discussion, "and the Court will be rectified. Within and without, distant and near, none will dare not to be uniformly upright." The Court having been rectified, the rectification would spread on down, first to the circuits, and through them to the prefectures and subprefectures. Such local reformation was especially needed at just that moment, when a great plague of locusts afflicted the nation. Elimination of favoritism, and the proper use of personnel which would follow from that, are rooted in the emperor's rectification of himself.[59] The process of this rectification of self is founded upon and in turn interacts with a triumvirate of principles that sum up the proper governance of the world. "Teaching," says Chu Hsi, "is the means by which principles are illuminated, and so provides guidance prior to events. The determination of policy is the means by which appropriate attitudes are nourished and so provides guidance after events. The appointing of the virtuous is the means by which the government is aided, and provides the warp and woof of action during events. The affairs of the world do not go beyond these (principles)." Thus, Chu Hsi's discussion of the third of these principles, proper personnel practices, is accompanied by a long discourse on the first, appropriate education, and in particular, the education of the emperor. In terms of the pressing problems of that moment the lack of proper education for the emperor makes it impossible for him to form correct judgements, since he lacks a solid foundation or starting point. Thus, with regard to relations with the Chin,

> in the midst of darkness these talkers (about peace and war) adorn their own private (intentions) so that their listeners cannot see through their deceptions. Even though the emperor is enlightened he will not be able to make a judgement. Thus, while this is going on he will lack ardent intention. I feel that in this matter the reason that things are thus stems from a failure to discriminate the fundamentals of righteousness and principle, and to a precipitate surrender to the epiphenomena of profit and injury. Therefore I say that in the education of a ruler, coming to understand principle should be placed first. Principle having been understood, then what ought to be done will be done, and what ought not to be done will be stopped.[60]

The key to the understanding of principle is set forth in the *Great Learning*, and consists in the investigation of things. The grasping of principle, distilled out of a study of things, leads to the rectification of self, which makes it possible for the ruler to make correct judgements, and this in turn leads to the rectification of the Court.[61]

In pursuit of this Chu Hsi naturally suggests that the ruler devote himself to the study of the Confucian Classics. His anxiety that the ruler study the Classics is increased by his concern that Hsiao-tsung was being misled by other doctrines. A third theme in these writings is Chu Hsi's concern about the harmful influence of Buddhist and to a lesser extent Taoist studies. We must remember that in 1162 Chu Hsi had only recently succeeded in freeing himself from his previous interest in Buddhism. It is also pertinent to remark that his home region, in which up to this point he had spent almost his entire life, was noted as an area where the Buddhist establishment was extremely flourishing. Most of the arable land in Fukien was reportedly owned by Buddhist temples. It is said that in Chang-chou[bs] they owned six-sevenths of the land and in Fu-chou[bt] one-fifth.[62] The administration was aware of some of the problems this entailed, and indeed had moved to alleviate them. On the day of Hsiao-tsung's inauguration there was an edict concerning the sale of surplus Buddhist temple lands mandated and managed by the local authorities. The economic and social problems stemming from the large number of Buddhists in the region is stressed by Wang Ying-ch'en[bu] (1118–1178) in a letter of 1162. "Generally, if a family among the people has three sons, sometimes one, sometimes two of them will become Buddhist monks." This was done because of the land poverty of the region.[63]

No doubt the flourishing state of the Buddhist establishment in Fukien indicates that here, as in the Hui-chou[bv] area studied by Hymes, the Buddhists received substantial support from the local elite. Given the environment in which he grew up, and the favorable attitude toward Buddhism of many of his peers, it is hardly surprising that the young Chu Hsi was seriously influenced by Buddhist teachings. Nor, on the same grounds, is it surprising that after his conversion from the religion of Buddhism to the quasi religion of Neo-Confucianism, he should be so outspokenly critical of Buddhism.

He had grown up with the religion in Fukien. He was distressed to hear that it was influencing the mind of Hsiao-tsung. In his memorials to the throne he said,

> Your Majesty nourishes the beginning of virtue. Your imperial documents are models, like balance stones, not exceeding what needs to be said, well-sounding and so on. In recent years your sage mind has been seeking the essentials of the great Way. (Yet it is said that) you have to some extend paid heed to Buddhist and Taoist works. (I) shun what I learn by rumor (so) I do not know if this is true or not. But myself, I feel that if this is what has been going on it is not the way to receive the Heavenly Gift. Uplifting the sage spirits treasure was the source of the flourishing of Yao and Shun.[bw] Now, to record and chant elegant (words) is not the means whereby to investigate the source, and to bring forth the Way of good order. (What is) empty and without substance (emptiness and nirvana) is not the means whereby to get at reality and establish the correct.

The proper answer is, of course, to cultivate the Way of the Confucian sages, and Chu Hsi goes on to discourse at length about both the substance and the method by which this should be done.[64]

One suspects that Hsiao-tsung found this Confucian moralizing unutterably boring. He made no great secret of his attitudes. The anecdotist Chou Mi[bx] (1232–1298) recounts an incident that supposedly occurred during a spring tour of West Lake. A young imperial academy student had dashed off a poem that closed with the lines "The next day I put away from me the dregs of the wine, and on the path came seeking the flowered hairpin." Hsiao-tsung laughed and said, "This poem is really good. But that last phrase is a real bit of Confucian sourness," so he altered it to read, "The next day I again rescued the dregs of the wine, and on the path came seeking the flowered hairpin."[65]

Although Hsiao-tsung was certainly not wholly Confucian in his attitudes, he was not insensitive to the strong points in Chu Hsi's arguments. His reputation as one of the best emperors of the Southern Sung is supported by the actions he took or had already taken on some of the problems raised by Chu. On the specific subject of the war he sided with Shih Hao, but he also began some internal changes designed to strengthen the state.

The problems of favoritism, of the packing of the administration with supporters, and of the restricting of the channels of communication were reduced by Hsiao-tsung's policy of never allowing any chief minister to remain in power for any great length of time. The tenures of most such men did not exceed one year.[66]

There was also an awareness in these years of problems of institutionalized favoritism that might arise through systems of recommendation and systems of irregular, i.e. nonexamination, entrance to the civil service. Hsiao-tsung approved policy changes aimed at reducing these problems both before and after Chu Hsi raised the general issue in his addresses to the throne.[67]

This concern did not prevent Hsiao-tsung from favoring members of the imperial clan. The great act of grace accompanying his accession granted favors to some imperial clan members who were examination candidates and to clan members who had lacked official rank.[68] He also extended his grace to other members of the clan,[69] and to the relatives of imperial women.[70]

The need for internal strengthening was also a desideratum that did not need repetition by Chu Hsi. Chu Hsi came from one of the few regions of the empire that was not suffering severe problems. Hsiao-tsung issued a multitude of orders granting relief to local areas during his first two years on the throne. Amidst this collection the Fukien region is mentioned only once.[71] Liang-che and Huai-nan suffered particularly, not just from the invasion but also from locusts and excessive rains. The state responded by issuing a variety of relief orders and by adopting policies designed to provide long-term help to refugees.[72]

Locusts and excessive rains were, of course, not simply disasters, but also signs. In these same years Hsiao-tsung had also to worry about a host of other inauspicious phenomena—astronomical anomalies, palace fires, thunder, and even an earthquake in the capital area.[73] The emperor issued an appropriately contrite edict in response to the plague of locusts.[74] He recognized that such signs might point to specific types of problems, in particular to improperly handled legal cases.[75]

Judicial impropriety was simply one facet of another problem raised by Chu Hsi, corruption in administration. Again, the emperor did not need Chu Hsi to belabor the point. Others, before and after, submitted memorials dealing with specific examples of such corruption, especially on the local level.[76]

Hsiao-tsung responded in part by trying to encourage and reward worthy officials.[77]

All these measures were wholly within the traditional patterns of imperial governance, as were the attempts in these same years to promote better and less expensive government by reducing numbers of personnel, especially clerks.[78] Beyond that, Hsiao-tsung also fitted himself in these opening years of his reign into the Confucian imperial pattern, and showed himself sensitive to the issues raised by Chu Hsi by approving policies that touched on education in the conventional sense and by allowing himself to be subjected to lectures on the Confucian Classics.[79]

Nor was the emperor, despite his personal interest in Buddhism, unaware of the social and economic problems it might pose. Even before Chu Hsi's comments officials had pointed out to him the problems created by extensive Buddhist landholdings in the area around the capital,[80] and although some months after his accession he issued a decree forgiving certain debts of the monasteries in Fukien,[81] he also approved an order in the following year calling for the selling off under government auspices of certain Fukien temple lands.[82]

The new emperor could thus have justifiably responded to the advice of Chu Hsi by pointing to his own record. On a number of points he had already taken actions consonant with the general principles underlying Chu's advice. Only on the issue of the war was Chu Hsi largely ignored. Indeed, in a delightfully ironic response, Chu Hsi's ideas were not used, but Chu himself was nominated for a position in the War College. Chu Hsi, of course, declined, and began a decade of productive writing. His peculiar relationship to the active world, trying to influence it without participating in it, is thus as characteristic of the closing of this brief period with which we have been concerned as it was of its beginning. In 1164 we find him again home in Fukien, again holding a sinecure as the superintendent of a Taoist temple, and again involved in writing on family life. But now, in two symbolic ways his course had changed. His first audience with the emperor signaled his potential importance as a spokesman on national affairs. And he was again a teacher, but, sadly, he had lost his role as student. In the late fall of 1163 Li Yen-p'ing fell gravely ill, and on the fifteenth day of the tenth month (November 12, 1163) he died. The year 1164 was to open with Chu Hsi arriving to mourn his master.

The Chu Hsi who emerges from this reading is a complex man who at the same time embodied and indeed in some cases helped to lead the social trends of his times, but also in other ways was far from representative. Like the elite members hypothesized by Hartwell, he spent the great part of his life in his home region, Fukien, but when he did consent to take an active role in affairs he usually served outside it. Consonant with the picture Hartwell draws, Chu Hsi married a girl from his section of Fukien. Chu Hsi was one of the foremost leaders of the movement to establish an educational system that was fundamentalist, stressed character and behavioral training, and downplayed the importance of the examinations. In this he was the creative spokesman and representative of the social groups that, perhaps out of frustration with the competitiveness of the examinations, were seeking valid styles of life outside the official world. And yet he was an examination graduate himself, who did not scruple to seek support from a government he would not serve. He bitterly condemned the favoritism at the Court, which as we have seen may have been even more serious during his age than in some others because of the growing role of protection in filling civil service posts, but he could also write in the warmest terms to thank those in the government who had intervened to help him get his sinecures. To his benefactor Ch'en he wrote that he was "reverently respectful in receiving the temple scroll." "I have received great kindness from you. Certainly I do not dare to be neglectful, and yet I know not how I can make recompense. . . . Now, because of your strength I have secured a government stipend.[83]

He seems in sum to have been marginal in his place, and ambivalent in his attitudes. He lived a life that was very clearly locally and regionally oriented and that embodied a rejection of much that was characteristic of the central government and its bureaucracy, and yet his concern for China and his feeling of intellectual kinship with his Northern Sung predecessors inevitably led him to suggest national solutions for national problems.

Notes

1. Roughly corresponds to present day Chekiang.

2. A *li* is one-third of a mile.

3. Perhaps the best survey available in English on the Sung-Chin war is found in Edward Kaplan, "Yüeh Fei[by] and the Founding of the Southern Sung" (University of Iowa Ph.D. dissertation, 1970).

4. P'eng Hsin-wei,[bz] *Chung-kuo huo-pi shih*[ca] [A history of Chinese money], (Shanghai: Ch'ün-lein[cb] Press, 1954), esp. pp. 299 ff.

5. Edmund H. Worthy, "Regional Control in the Southern Sung Salt Administration," in John W. Haeger, ed., *Crisis and Prosperity in Sung China* (Tucson: University of Arizona Press, 1975), esp. pp. 111–112. See also Yuki Tetsu,[cc] "Sōdai no tōnan kanmai en-hō"[cd] [The southeastern official sales salt law of the Sung dynasty], *Rekishigaku chirigaku nempo*[ce] [The historical geographical annal] 96/4 (1980).

6. Liu Ming-shu,[cf] "Sung-tai hai-shang t'ung-shang tsa-k'ao"[cg] [A study of the seaborne commerce of the Sung dynasty], in *Chung-kuo wen-hua yen-chiu hui-k'an*[ch] [Researches on Chinese culture], 5 (September 1945), p. 52. On these general developments see Lo Jung-pang,[ci] "China's Emergence as a Sea Power," *Far Eastern Quarterly*, vol. 14, no. 4 (1955).

7. Sudo Yoshiyuki,[cj] "Nam-Sō kyō-to no zei-sei to tochi shoyu"[ck] [The Southern Sung local taxation system and landownership], in Sudo Yoshiyuki, *Sōdai keizai-shi kenkyu*[cl] [Research in Sung economic history], (Tokyo: Tokyo University Press, 1962), pp. 474–500.

8. Brian E. McKnight, "Fiscal Privileges and the Social Order in Sung China," in Haeger, *Crisis and Prosperity,* pp. 79–101.

9. Brian E. McKnight, *Village and Bureaucracy in Southern Sung China* (Chicago: University of Chicago Press, 1971), esp. ch. 5. De facto privileges naturally continued to exist. Some of the best work on such questions is being done by Yanagida Setsuko.[cm] See for example her recent article "Sodai no kan-den to keiseiko"[cn] [The official fields of the Sung dynasty and the powerful households], *Gakushuen daigaku bungakubu kenkyu nempo* [Gakushuen[co] University literature faculty research annal] 26.

10. John Stuermer, "Polder Construction and the Pattern of Land Ownership in the T'ai-hu[cp] Basis during the Southern Sung Dynasty" (University of Pennsylvania Ph.D. dissertation, 1980), esp. p. 177 ff.

11. The Yangtze delta area lying between the river and the hills of southern Chekiang.

12. For Northern Sung water control in this region see Mira Mihelich, "Polders and the Politics of Land Reclamation in Southeast China during the Northern Sung Dynasty" (Cornell University Ph.D. dissertation, 1979). For Southern Sung developments see Stuermer, *Polder Construction.*

13. The original debate in Japan involved Sudo Yoshiyuki of Tokyo University and Miyazaki Ichisada of Kyoto University and their followers. Yanagida Setsuko brought a more balanced perspective to the debate by showing that in part the differences between the two schools arose because their evidence concerned different regions of China. See Yanagida Setsuko, "Kyakko ni tsuite"[cq] [On guest households], *Shigaku zasshi*[cr] [Journal of historical studies], 68/4 (1959), pp. 1–38; Yanagida Setsuko, "Sōdai tochi shoyū sei ni mirareru futatsu no kata; senshin to henkyō"[cs] [Two forms of Sung landholding: advanced and frontier], *Tōyō bunka kenkyujo kiyō*[ct] [Journal of the Asian Culture Research Institute] 29, pp. 95–130. Yanagida also gives a useful survey of the debate. See her "Miyazaki shigaku to kinseiron"[cu] [The historical studies of Miyazaki and recent discussions], in Nohara Shiro,[cv] ed., *Kindai Nihon ni okeru rekishigaku no hattatsu*[cw] [The development of historical studies in present day Japan] (Tokyo: Aoki[cx] Book Co., 1976). For a useful survey in English see Peter Golas, "Rural China in the Sung," *Journal of Asian Studies,* vol. 39, no. 2 (1980), pp. 291–326. Now Yanagida's fine work has been taken one step further. Much of my discussion is based on Joseph McDermott, "Land Tenure and Rural Control in the Liangche Region during the Southern Sung" (Cambridge University Ph.D. dissertation, 1979). McDermott has expanded some of this material in an as yet unpublished article (personal copy).

14. One *mou* equals approximately one-seventh of an acre.

15. Corresponds roughly to present day Hupei.

16. Corresponds roughly to present day Kiangsi.

17. Corresponds roughly to present day Kwangsi.

18. Corresponds roughly to present day Hupei.

19. Corresponds roughly to present day Hunan.

20. The best recent studies of the T'ang and pre-T'ang elite have concluded that most later claims to be descended from the T'ang aristocracy were bogus. See David Johnson, *The Medieval Chinese Oligarchy* (Boulder, Colo.; Westview Press, 1977), pp. 141–148; David Johnson, "The Last Years of a Great Clan," *Harvard Journal of Asiatic Studies,* vol. 37, no. 1 (June 1977), pp. 75–81. For a complementary discussion of the decline of these great families see Patricia Ebrey, *The Aristocratic Families of Early Imperial China* (Cambridge: Cambridge University Press, 1978), esp. 112–115.

Even if such relationships could be traced, the social meaning of membership in the group would have been entirely different under Sung conditions, and in any event such relationship is really peripheral to the major point relevant here, which is marriage and career patterns.

21. Robin Fox, *Kinship and Marriage* (Baltimore: Penguin Books, 1967), pp. 116–117. See also Maurice Freedman, *Lineage Organization in Southeastern China* (London: Athlone Press, 1958).

22. Patricia Ebrey, "Women in the Kinship System of the Southern Sung Upper Class," in Richard Guisso, ed., *Women in China* (Toronto: University of Toronto Press, 1982).

23. Shiga Shuzo, *Chūgoku kazokuhō no genri*[cy] [The principles of Chinese family law], (Tokyo: Sōbunsha,[cz] 1968); Niida Noboru, "Sōdai no kazanhō ni okeru nyoshi no chi-i[da] [Position of women in the Sung dynasty laws on family property], in his *Chūgoku hōseishi kenkyū*[db] [Research on Chinese legal history], vol. 3 (Tokyo: Tokyo University Press, 1962), pp. 365–392.

24. Yüan Ts'ai, *Yüan-shih shih-fan*[dc] [Family precepts of the Yüan family], (Precious Works of the Four Libraries ed.), pt. 1, 25b. Trans. Patricia Ebrey, "Preserving the Family: Yüan Ts'ai and the Culture of the Sung Upper Class" (unpublished manuscript), p. 297.

25. Much of the following discussion of local elite characteristics and activities is based on Hymes's dissertation. See Robert Hymes, "Prominence and Power in Sung China" (University of Pennsylvania Ph.D. dissertation, 1979).

26. I am thinking here particularly of the work of E. A. Kracke, Jr., especially his two articles, "Family versus Merit in the Chinese Civil Service Examinations during the Empire," *Harvard Journal of Asiatic Studies*, vol. 10 (1947), and "Region, Family, and Individual in the Chinese Examination System," in John K. Fairbank, ed., *Chinese Thought and Institutions* (Chicago: University of Chicago Press, 1957).

27. Ebrey, "Preserving the Family."

28. Hymes, "Prominence," esp. p. 50 ff.

29. Chang Hsing-yen,[dd] *I-huang hsien-chih*[de] [Gazeteer of I-huang County], (T'ung-chih[df] ed., 1871), 45b.39a–40a. Cited by Hymes, "Prominence," p. 289.

30. Hymes, "Prominence," pp. 285–295.

31. Hymes, Shiba Yoshinobu, *Sōdai shōgyō-shi kenkyū* (Tokyo: Kazama[dg] Book Co., 1968).

32. For the Southern Sung see Hartwell, "Demographic, Political, and Social Transformation."

33. James T. C. Liu, "The Sung Views on the Control of Government Clerks," *Journal of the Economic and Social History of the Orient*, vol. 10, nos. 2–3 (1967) pp. 317–344.

34. On Sung examinations and opportunity see John W. Chafee, "Education and Examinations in Sung Society (960–1279)," (University of Chicago Ph.D. dissertation, 1979). See also Hymes, "Prominence," esp. pp. 46–105; and Richard L. Davis, "The Shih Lineage at the Southern Sung Court" (Princeton University Ph.D. dissertation, 1980).

35. Brian E. McKnight, "Administrators of Hangchow under the Northern Sung: a Case Study," *Harvard Journal of Asiatic Studies*, vol. 30 (1970). For this study I analyzed biographical information on the approximately one hundred administrators of Hangchow during the Northern Sung. Of the eighty-three men on whom pertinent

information is available, seventy-four (83%) were degree holders. Of the five men who had administered Hangchow before Chen-tsung[dh] (r. 998–1022) came to power (997) only one had a degree. (Of those there serving between the enthronement of Chen-tsung and the end of the Northern Sung ninety-two percent were degree holders. The statistics are similar to those from Fu-chou and Ming-chou.

36. Davis, "Shih Lineage," pp. 120, 201.

37. *Pa-hsing* means the eight virtues of filial piety, brotherliness, kindliness, marital concord, dutifulness, sympathy, and moderation.

38. Davis, "Shih Lineage," p. 24.

39. Yang Shu-fan,[di] *Chung-kuo wen-kuan chih-tu shih*[dj] [History of the Chinese civil service system], (Taipei: 1976), p. 326.

40. Ch'ien Mu, "Lun Sung-tai hsiang-ch'uan"[dk] [A discussion of the power of Sung chief ministers], in *Sung-shih yen-chiu chi*,[dl] [Collected research on Sung history], vol. 1, pp. 455–462.

41. Li Chi, "Chu Hsi the Poet," *T'oung-pao*,[dm] vol. 58 (1972), p. 64.

42. The biographical information used here is drawn largely from Wang Mao-hung[dn] (1608–1741), *Chu Tzu nien-p'u*[do] [A chronological biography of Master Chu], (Shanghai: Commercial Press, 1937), supplemented by materials from Huang Kan[dp] (1152–1221), *Chu Tzu hsing-chuang*[dq] [A biographical account of Master Chu], (Seoul: Uryu munhwa sa,[dr] 1950); Ch'ien Mu, *Chu Tzu hsin hsüeh-an* (Taipei: San-min[ds] Book Co., 1971); Li T'ung, *Li Yen-p'ing chi*[dt] [Collected works of Li T'ung], (Shanghai: Commercial Press, 1935); Huang Tsung-hsi[du] (1610–1695), *Sung-Yüan hsüeh-an*[dv] [Confucians of the Sung and Yüan], (Taipei: Basic Sinological Series ed., 1965).

43. Chu Hsi, *Chu Tzu wen-chi*[dw] [Collection of literary works of Master Chu], (SPPY ed. entitled *Chu Tzu ta-ch'üan*[dx] [Complete literary works of Master Chu]), 75:5a.

44. Robin Williams, "Change and Stability in Values and Value Systems," in Bernard Barber and Alex Inkeles, *Stability and Social Change* (Boston: Little, Brown, and Company, 1971), p. 152.

45. *Chu Tzu wen-chi*, 75:6b.

46. *Ibid.*, 75:7a.

47. Linda Walton-Vargo, "Education, Social Change, and Neo-Confucianism in Sung-Yüan China" (University of Pennsylvania Ph.D. dissertation, 1978).

48. T'ao Chin-sheng,[dy] *Chin Hai-ling ti te fa Sung yü Ts'ai-shih chan-i te k'ao-shih*[dz] [A study of the Chin emperor Hai-ling's attack against the Sung and the battle of Ts'ai-shih], (Taipei: School of Arts, National Taiwan University, 1965), esp. p. 89 ff.

49. *Chu Tzu wen-chi*, 11:6a–7a.

50. *Ibid.*, 13:2a ff.

51. *Ibid.*

52. Shih Hao, *Mou-feng chen-yin man-lu*[ea] [Notes by the Hidden Scholar of Mou Peak] 8:3b. Cited by Davis, "Shih Lineage," p. 97.

53. *Chu Tzu wen-chi*, 24:10a.

54. *Ibid.*, supplementary collection, 5:11a.

55. Hsü Sung,[eb] ed., *Sung hui-yao chi-kao*[ec] [Collected Sung documents], (Taipei: World Book Co., 1965), *hsüan-chü*[ed] [Civil service selection] section 18.22a; Davis, "Shih Lineage," p. 38.

56. Conrad Schirokauer, "Neo-Confucians Under Attack: The Condemnation of the *Wei-hsüeh*,"[ee] in Haeger, *Crisis and Prosperity*.

57. James Legge, *The Great Learning*, in *The Chinese Classics*, vol. 1, p. 358.

58. *Chu Tzu wen-chi*, 11:7a–b.

59. *Ibid.*, 11:8a.

60. *Ibid.*, 13:2a.

61. *Ibid.*, 13:1a.

62. Chizuka Masaaki,[ef] "Sōdai Hoken no shakai to jiin"[eg] [Buddhist temples and the society of Fukien in the Sung dynasty], *Tōyōshi kenkyū*[eh] [Researches on Asian history], vol. 15, no. 2 (1957).

63. Wang Ying-ch'en, *Wen-ting chi*[ei] [Collected works of Wang Ying-ch'en], (Ts'ung-shu chi-ch'eng[ej] [Collection of series] ed.), pp. 145–146.

64. *Chu Tzu wen-chi*, 11:3a.

65. Chou Mi, *Wu-lin chiu-shih*[ek] [Anecdotes of Hangchou], in Meng Yüan-lao, *Tung-ching meng-hua lu (wai ssu-chung*[el]) [A record of dreams of the Eastern Capital, four added works], (Shanghai: Ku-tien wen-hsüeh[em] Press, 1956), p. 376.

66. Wang Te-i,[en] "Sung Hsiao-tsung chi ch'i shih-tai"[eo] [Sung Hsiao-tsung and his times], in *Sung-shih yen-chiu chi*, vol. 10 (Taipei: Chung-hua ts'ung-shu wei-yuan hui,[ep] 1978) pp. 245–302.

67. Hsü Sung, *Sung hui-yao, chih-kuan*[eq] [government offices] section, 10:7a, 11.71b, 26.1b, 26.2a.

68. *Ibid.*, *hsüan-chü* section, 18.21a.

69. *Ibid.*, *hsüan-chü* section, 18.22b; *ti-hsi* [imperial lineage] section, 6:33a, 8.38a–b.

70. *Ibid.*, *hou-fei*[er] [palace women] section, 2:13a–14a.

71. *Ibid.*, *shih-huo*[es] [fiscal affairs] section, 63:20a–22b.

72. *Ibid.*, *shih-huo* section, 1:42b, 3:8a–b, 9b–14b, 6:17a, 18:1b, 61:76b, 63:20a–b, 125a, 127a, 68:62a, 62b, 63a–b, 125a, 125b, 69:61b, 62a; *ti-hsi*[et] section, 9:31a–33a; *jui-i*[eu] [portents] section, 3:6a, 43b, 44a.

73. *Ibid.*, *jui-i* section, 2.6a, 2:18b, 36a, 3:5b, 6a, 38b, 43b, 44a.

74. *Ibid.*, *ti-hsi* section, 9:31a–33a.

75. *Ibid.*, *jui-i* section, 3:6a.

76. *Ibid.*, *shih-huo* section, 9:10a, 11:21a, 65:94b, 69:26b.

77. *Ibid.*, *chih-kuan* section, 30:12a, 48:36b.

78. *Ibid.*, *chih-kuan* section, 6:10a, 9:10b–11a, 10:7b, 28b; *hsüan-chu* section, 23:17b, 24:22b.

79. *Ibid.*, *ch'ung-ju*[ev] [eminent Confucius] section, 1:37a, 38a–b, 7:9a ff.

80. *Ibid.*, *shih-huo* section, 10:16b.

81. *Ibid.*, *shih-huo* section, 63:20b.

82. Wang, *Wen-ting chi*, 13:145–148.

83. *Chu Tzu wen-chi*, 24:10b.

Glossary

a 溫州	f 經界	k 荆湖
b 兩浙	g 孝宗	l 撫州
c 里	h 太	m 地客
d 韓侂胄	i 江南	n 典客
e 江陰	j 畝	o 廣南

p	夔州	bm	高宗	dc	袁氏世範
q	王安石	bn	趙伯琮	dd	張興言
r	族人	bo	史浩	de	宜黃縣志
s	宗族	bp	魏元履	df	同治
t	親戚	bq	周葵	dg	風間
u	外戚	br	羅	dh	眞宗
v	仁井田陞	bs	漳州	di	楊樹藩
w	滋賀秀三	bt	福州	dj	中國文官制度史
x	份	bu	汪應辰	dk	論宋代相權
y	袁采	bv	徽州	dl	宋史研究集
z	進士	bw	堯舜	dm	通報
aa	士大夫	bx	周密	dn	王懋竑
ab	太和	by	岳飛	do	朱子年譜
ac	許德新	bz	彭信威	dp	黃榦
ad	劉炎	ca	中國貨幣史	dq	朱子行狀
ae	宗信	cb	群聯	dr	乙酉文化社
af	宗安	cc	幸徹	ds	三民
ag	妙端	cd	宋代の東南官賣鹽法	dt	李延平集
ah	許夢齡	ce	歷史地理學年報	du	黃宗羲
ai	涂愷	cf	劉銘恕	dv	宋元學案
aj	萬開	cg	宋代海上通商史雜考	dw	朱子文集
ak	斯波義信	ch	中國文化研究彙刊	dx	朱子大全
al	宋代商業史研究	ci	羅榮邦	dy	淘晉生
am	劉子健	cj	周藤吉之	dz	金海陵帝的伐宋與采
an	宮崎市定	ck	南宋鄉都の税利と土		石戰役的考實
ao	蔭		地所有	ea	鄧峯眞隱漫錄
ap	史	cl	宋代經濟史研究	eb	徐松
aq	八行	cm	柳田節子	ec	宋會要輯稿
ar	徽宗	cn	宋代の官田と形勢戶	ed	選舉
as	錢穆	co	學習院大學文學部研	ee	偽學
at	朱子新學案		究年報	ef	笠沙雅章
au	隆興	cp	太湖	eg	宋代福建の社會と寺
av	李祁	cq	客户にてして		院
aw	五夫	cr	史學雜誌	eh	東洋史研究
ax	崇安	cs	宋代土地所有制に見	ei	文定集
ay	建安		られる二つの型—先	ej	叢書集成
az	李延平侗		進と邊境	ek	武林舊事
ba	李信甫	ct	東洋文化研究所紀要	el	東京夢華錄外四種
bb	主簿	cu	宮崎史學と近世論	em	古典文學
bc	黃子衡	cv	野原四郎	en	王德毅
bd	論語要義	cw	近代日本における歷	eo	宋孝宗及其時代
be	程頤		史學の發達	ep	中華叢書委員會
bf	程顥	cx	青木	eq	職官
bg	論語訓蒙口義	cy	中國家族法の原理	er	后妃
bh	同安	cz	創文社	es	食貨
bi	書院	da	宋代の家產法におけ	et	帝系
bj	明		る女子の地位	eu	瑞異
bk	海陵	db	中國法制史研究	ev	崇儒
bl	完顏烏魯				

24

The Problem of Orthodoxy in Chu Hsi's Philosophy

SHU-HSIEN LIU

IT IS A WELL-KNOWN FACT that Chu Hsi was the person mainly responsible for the establishment of the orthodox line of transmission of the Way, the so-called *Tao-t'ung*,[a] in the Confucian tradition. Wing-tsit Chan[b] has reported that "the line, with minor variations, is this: Fu-hsi[c] . . . Shen-nung[d] . . . the Yellow Emperor . . . Yao[e] . . . Shun[f] . . . Yü[g] . . . T'ang[h] . . . Wen[i] . . . Wu[j] . . . Duke of Chou[k] . . . Confucius . . . Tseng Tzu[l] . . . Tzu-ssu[m] . . . Mencius . . . Chou[n] . . . Ch'engs[o] . . . Chu Hsi."[1] In a very influential essay, *Chung-yung chang-chü hsü*[p] (Preface to the *Commentary on the Doctrine of the Mean*) Chu Hsi said,

> The orthodox line of transmission of the Way had a long history. It was reported in the Classics: Yao taught Shun that you must hold fast to the Mean, and Shun taught Yü that the human mind is precarious, and the moral mind is subtle; have absolute refinement and singleness of mind, hold fast to the Mean. . . . From then on, such insights were passed on from one sage to another. . . . Even though our Master Confucius [551–479 B.C.] did not have the position [of a king], yet he had succeeded the sages in the past, and opened up new courses for students in the future; his achievement was greater even than that of Yao or Shun. But in his time there were only Yen Yüan[q] [521–490 B.C.?] and Tseng Shen[r] [505–436 B.C.?] who had learned about the Way and transmitted the line. Then in the second generation of Master Tseng's disciples there was Confucius' grandson Tzu-ssu [492–421 B.C.?]. . . . Still another two generations, there was Mencius. . . . After Mencius (372–289 B.C.?) died, the line of transmission was broken. . . . It was not until the Ch'eng brothers [Ch'eng Hao,[s] 1032–1088, and Ch'eng I,[t] 1033–1107], who studied and regained the insight that the line of transmission which was discontinued for a thousand years was revived.[2]

Professor Chan has noted that although the idea of *Tao-t'ung* may be traced back to Mencius, Han Yü[u] (768–824), Li Ao[v] (*fl.* 798), and then Ch'eng I, Chu Hsi was the first Neo-Confucian philosopher to use the term *Tao-t'ung*,[3] and this idea was taken seriously by his disciples. Chan said:

According to Chu Hsi's pupil Huang Kan[w] [1152–1221], "the transmission of the correct orthodox tradition of the Way required the proper men. From the Chou dynasty [1111–249 B.C.] on, there have been only several people capable of inheriting the correct tradition and transmitting the Way, and only one or two could enable the Way to become prominent. After Confucius, Tseng Tzu and Tzu-ssu perpetuated it in its subtlety, but it was not prominent until Mencius. After Mencius, Chou Tun-i[x] [1037–1073], the two Ch'engs, and Chang Tsai[y] [1020–1077] continued the interrupted tradition, but only with our Master did it become prominent." This view was accepted in the *History of Sung* and by practically all Neo-Confucianists.[4]

Professor Chan further pointed out that Chu Hsi excluded the Han (206 B.C.– A.D. 220) and T'ang (618–907) Confucianists including Han Yü, Li Ao, and also Shao Yung[z] (1011–1077), Ssu-ma Kuang[aa] (1019–1086), and others of the Sung dynasty (910–1279) from the line of transmission for philosophical reasons.[5] His points are very well taken.

The questions I would like to raise are on a different level. We know that Chu Hsi taught something quite different from Confucius, Mencius, and even from Ch'eng I, his own mentor to whom he was greatly indebted. His contemporary and rival Lu Hsiang-shan (Lu Chin-yüan,[ab] 1137–1193) even charged that he had smuggled certain Taoist and Buddhist ideas into his philosophy.[6] My question is, then, are there any real philosophical grounds for him to claim that his thoughts may be traced back to pre-Ch'in (221–206 B.C.) Confucian philosophers such as Confucius and Mencius? Or was he merely borrowing their names to promote ideas that were radically different from what they had taught? Especially in view of the fact that the statement Chu Hsi quoted in his essay—"The human mind is precarious, and the moral mind is subtle; have absolute refinement and singleness of mind, hold fast to the Mean"[7]—is now known to have been taken from a fabricated document, we must have serious doubts. Furthermore, if Chu Hsi is to be regarded as the representative of Sung Neo-Confucian philosophy, an even more serious question would arise: Is the so-called Neo-Confucian philosophy truly a Confucian philosophy or is it rather a radically new philosophy based on Taoist and Buddhist ideas with only a Confucian cloak? Indeed, it is not uncommon for Confucian scholars themselves to attack their own colleagues as being Confucian on the surface but Buddhist in essence. All these issues need to be clarified; otherwise there is no way for us to come up with a clear picture of Sung-Ming (1368–1644) Neo-Confucianism. Finally, when all the smoke is cleared, I would like to reevaluate Chu Hsi's position in that tradition especially with regard to the orthodox line of transmission he himself helped to establish and that dominated Chinese thought for several hundred years. In other words, the problems at issue are: Is there truly any continuity between Neo-Confucianism in the Sung and Ming dynasties and classical Confucianism in the late Chou period represented by Confucius and Mencius, whom the Neo-Confucianists claimed to have followed closely? And are there truly essential differences between Neo-Confucian philosophies on the one hand and Buddhist and Taoist philosophies on the other hand? These are important questions which must be answered by any serious student of intellectual history of Sung and Ming thought. As Chu Hsi had always been in the thick of things, it would be most instructive to study his thought to find clues to answer these questions.

First, let us examine Chu Hsi's attitude toward Buddhism. As is well known, Chu Hsi was fascinated by Buddhism when he was young, but he renounced Buddhism in favor of Confucianism after he studied under Li T'ung[ac] (1093–1163).[8] From then on he made strong criticisms against Buddhism, and yet even in his later years, he still held a high opinion of Buddhism. For example, he said,

> The Buddhists simply do not concern themselves with many things. Their only concern is the self. Although their teachings are incorrect, yet their intention is to take care of the problem of the self. That is why they attracted a number of talents, while we do not have followers. Today's Confucianists who can still hold fast to the Classics merely know how to read and discuss the texts, and when they study history, they know only how to calculate about what is profitable or harmful. But the Buddhists want really to take care of the self and to begin their discipline with the self. If the self is not being taken care of, what is the use to talk about others' strength or shortcomings?[9]

Chu also recognized that "the Buddhists spend a lot of efforts to discipline the mind."[10] What is especially interesting is that Chu Hsi never denied that Confucianists may learn from the Buddhists. He said,

> At first Buddhism had only words; there was not the discipline of preservation and cultivation. It was not until the Sixth Patriarch [of Ch'an[ad] 'Zen'] in the T'ang dynasty that discipline of preservation and cultivation was being taught. At first, Confucian scholars also only had words; they did not practice discipline of the self. It was not until Ch'eng I-ch'uan [Ch'eng I] that discipline of the self was being taught. Therefore it is said that Ch'eng I-ch'uan had stolen from Buddhism for his own use.[11]

It appears that vulgar scholars had as their only goal the seeking of profit. Buddhists, however, turned their attention away from thinking about how to make a profit or to advance their careers in the world. Therefore, Buddhism had a great deal of attraction for Neo-Confucian philosophers, as the primary goal of theirs was none other than to find a way of self-realization. No wonder so many Neo-Confucian philosophers drifted along the paths of Buddhism and Taoism for many years before they returned to the Classics and found that the Confucian way was self-sufficient. It is for this reason that we can easily find a number of similarities between Neo-Confucianism on the one hand and Buddhism and Taoism on the other. But once a Neo-Confucian philosopher declared that he had rediscovered the Confucian way, then more often than not he would have some very strong words against Buddhism. Chu Hsi seems to have followed this pattern. Having been once attracted by Buddhism, he realized even more deeply the dangers of Buddhist teachings, as they appeared to be "very close to the principles and yet they produced a good deal of confusion about learning of truths."[12] When we examine the grounds for Chu Hsi's opposition to Buddhism, we have to conclude that there are indeed essential differences between Neo-Confucianism on the one hand and Buddhism on the other hand. Even though many of Chu Hsi's criticisms of Buddhism were unfair and not supported by good evidence, they were true reflections of Chu Hsi's feelings toward Buddhism.[13] We may say that Chu Hsi had only a rather superficial understanding of Buddhism and that he was merely instinctively reacting to something that posed a serious threat to the very things that he had tried hard to defend. If such is the case, then surely it is impossible to see Chu Hsi as a disguised Buddhist thinker with only a Confucian cloak. As he did not even know much about Buddhism, how could he be able to sell its messages under a different cover? What remains for us to do, then, is to locate the differences between these two different lines of thought.

Let us start with the most obvious. The Confucianists value highly the function of human institutions, while the Buddhists hold a negative or at best a passive attitude toward them. Chu Hsi said,

> It is not necessary to examine the doctrines of Buddhism and Taoism deeply to understand them. The mere fact that they discard the Three Bonds [between ruler and minister, father and son, and husband and wife] and the Five Constant Virtues [righteousness on the part of the father, deep love on the part of the mother, friendliness on the part of the elder brother, respect on the part of the younger brother, and filial piety on the part of the son] is already a crime of the greatest magnitude. Nothing more need be said about the rest.[14]

And these differences are manifestations of profound ontological differences between the two schools. Both schools take problems of the mind and of human nature to be of crucial importance, and yet they have reached completely different conclusions.

> Ts'ao asked how to tell the difference between Confucianism and Buddhism. The teacher said: "Just take the doctrine 'What Heaven imparts to man is called human nature.' The Buddhists simply do not understand this, and dogmatically say that nature is empty consciousness. What we Confucianists talk about are concrete principles, and from our point of view they are wrong. They say, 'We will not be affected by a single speck of dust [such as distinction of right and wrong or subject and object] . . . and will not discard a single element of existence (dharma) [such as the minister's loyalty to the ruler or the son's filial piety to the father].' If one is not affected by any speck of dust, how is it possible for him not to discard a single element of existence? When he arrives at what is

called the realm of Emptiness, he does not find any solution. Take the human mind, for example. There is necessarily in it the Five Relations between the father and son, ruler and minister, old and young, husband and wife, and friends. When the Buddhists are thorough in their action, they will show no affection in these relationships, whereas we Confucianists are thoroughgoing in our action. There is affection between father and son, righteousness between ruler and minister, order between old and young, attention to their separate functions between husband and wife, and faithfulness between friends. We Confucianists recognize only the moral principles of sincerity and genuineness. Sincerity is the essence of all good deeds.[15]

Regardless of whether Chu Hsi's interpretation of Buddhist teachings is correct or his criticism of them sound, the difference between the two positions cannot be overlooked. Chu Hsi sees the contrast between these two positions as follows: "The Buddhists are characterized by vacuity, whereas we Confucianists are characterized by concreteness. The Buddhists are characterized by duality (of Absolute Emptiness and the illusory world), whereas we Confucianists are characterized by unity (one principle governing all). The Buddhists consider facts and principles as unimportant and pay no attention to them."[16] Even though the Buddhists may evaluate the differences between the two positions differently, they must also recognize that there are essential differences between the two approaches. While the ultimate commitment for the Confucianists is *jen*[ae] (humanity),[17] the Buddhists' ultimate commitment is *k'ung*[af] (*shunya* or Emptiness). While the principle the Confucianists realize is *hsing-li*[ag] (principle inherent in human nature), that understood by the Buddhists is *k'ung-li*[ah] (principle as Emptiness). While the function of the mind for the Confucianists is to realize in itself the principles of what is ontologically real, that for the Buddhists is to provide the basis for an illusory phenomenal world through the transformation of the consciousnesses. While the primary goal of the Confucianists is realization to the fullest extent of the intrinsic value in life, that for the Buddhists is to transcend the bitter sea of life and death. In short, the basic orientations of the two approaches are different, and such differences are recognized by both sides. Surely the Confucianists may learn or even borrow something from the Buddhists, and the Buddhists have made adjustment to the Confucian traditions, but the guiding principles of the two schools are different. This fact should never be obscured by apparent similarities that can easily be found in these two schools.

Now, as we have established that Neo-Confucianism is not to be taken as a disguised form of Buddhism, we must go one step further to examine the claim that Neo-Confucianism is the true heir of the classical Confucianism of Confucius and Mencius, the origin of which may even be traced back to ancient sage-emperors. Our investigation shows that the historical grounds for Chu Hsi to make such a claim are extremely weak. Lacking any solid evidence to substantiate the claim of the historical existence of Hsia dynasty (2183–1752 B.C.?), scholars currently maintain that authentic history begins with the

Shang dynasty (1751–1112 B.C.?); beyond this point is the age of legends the authenticity of which are highly questionable. But Chu Hsi's line of transmission of the orthodoxy is based precisely on such improbable stories. Not only did Chu Hsi and other Neo-Confucian philosophers use apocryphal sources; they had a tendency to read their own thoughts into the Classics. For example, in the *Book of Odes*, were the two lines "The Mandate of Heaven, / How beautiful and unceasing!"[18] Chu Hsi remarked that the Mandate of Heaven means the "Way" or the moral order of Heaven; however, in early Chou (1111–249 B.C.) the belief in an anthropomorphic God was still quite strong. Again, in the *Analects* it was reported that "Confucius, standing by a stream, said, 'It passes on like this, never ceasing day or night!' "[19] What was Confucius thinking about? Was he thinking of the unceasing operation of the universe as suggested by Chu Hsi and Ch'eng I? It seems farfetched to think that Confucius' remark was meant to be a characterization of the Way itself (*Tao-t'i*[ai]).[20] Therefore, from a strictly historical perspective we may easily dismiss the story about the line of transmission of the orthodoxy as a big chunk of nonsense. But for scholars of a more sophisticated mind, the investigation of the problem cannot stop here. In fact, the real search has not yet begun, because the problem at issue is not a historical one. The crux of the matter actually lies in one's existential decision over one's ultimate commitment or philosophical faith. And the ultimate concern of Sung learning in contrast to Han learning is beyond any doubt a philosophical one, not a historical one.

Paul Tillich's distinction between Christology and Jesusology is highly instructive for our purposes.[21] Christology concerns the religious faith in Christ, whose message is that the end of this life is the beginning of another life, much richer than this life, while Jesusology studies the historical Jesus by trying to collect more or less probable evidence concerning the man. Tillich says,

> The search for the historical Jesus was an attempt to discover a minimum of reliable facts about the man Jesus of Nazareth, in order to provide a safe foundation for the Christian faith. This attempt was a failure. Historical research provided probabilities about Jesus of a higher or lower degree. On the basis of these probabilities, it sketched "Lives of Jesus." But they were more like novels than biographies; they certainly could not provide a safe foundation for the Christian faith. Christianity is not based on the acceptance of a historical novel; it is based on the witness to the messianic character of Jesus by people who were not interested at all in a biography of the Messiah.[22]

By the same token, Confucianism is not based on the acceptance of a historical legend; it is based on the witness to the clear character of the sagely mind which found its manifestations among the ancient sage-emperors and which is inherent in everybody. Hence, accuracy of historical details is not that important for those who had faith in the manifestation of the sagely mind in the human world. Surely I do not mean that the problems of Confucianists are exactly the same as those of Christians, as the messages they try to convey are different. But without any doubt their problems are parallel to one another. The Confucian message must be traced back to Confucius as the Christian message must be traced back to Jesus as the Christ. It is through a study of the ideals Confucius embodied that we may hope to find the continuity between Neo-Confucianism and classical Confucianism.

When we go back to the time of Confucius, we find that Confucius himself already complained about the lack of evidence to substantiate his claim of knowledge of the spirit and practice of propriety (*li*[ai]) in the Hsia and Shang dynasties, but he never wavered in his faith in the function of propriety as a means to educate people.[23] This shows that even though Confucius showed a genuine love of history, yet what he cared for most were the ideals embodied in the historical legends as he saw them. The same attitude was adopted by Neo-Confucian philosophers. In establishing the line of transmission of the orthodoxy Chu Hsi made it clear that he was following in Confucius' steps, and he explicitly stated that Confucius' achievements were even more important than those of the ancient sage-emperors, as the Confucian ideals were most clearly embodied in the person of Confucius. Now the problem lies in whether these Confucian ideals defended by Neo-Confucian scholars are truly the ideals represented by Confucius himself. The Neo-Confucian philosophers firmly believed that they could understand the sagely mind even though their time was behind the time of the Sage by more than a thousand years. Although there was a variety of opinions among Neo-Confucian philosophers, it is not difficult to find some common characteristics. For the sake of convenience, I shall mention only two. They all believed that man's moral nature is good[24] and that it is an endowment from Heaven; they also believed that Heaven is the ultimate creative principle, which works incessantly in the universe, that can be grasped by the mind. Now, our burden is to show, if we can find them, the foundation of such thoughts in Confucius himself.

On the surface, it seems that we can only give a negative answer. It was reported in the *Analects* that Tzu-kung[ak] said, "We can hear our Master's [views] on culture and its manifestation, but we cannot hear his views on human nature and the Way of Heaven [because these subjects are beyond the comprehension of most people]."[25] But the main interests of the Neo-Confucian philosophers lay exactly in what Confucius talked about least before his students—human nature and the Way of Heaven. If we look into the matter more deeply, however, we shall find that there are indeed seeds in Confucius' thought that may be interpreted in such a way that they are thoroughly consistent with the views of Neo-Confucian philosophers. For example, it was reported in the *Analects:* "Confucius said, 'Shen,[al] there is one thread that runs through my doctrines.' Tseng Tzu said, 'Yes.' After Confucius had left, the disciples asked him, 'What did he mean?' Tseng Tzu replied, 'The Way of our Master is none other than conscientiousness (*chung*[am]) and altruism (*shu*[an]).' "[26] Wing-tsit Chan's comment is as follows: "All scholars agree . . .

on the meanings of *chung* and *shu*, which are best expressed by Chu Hsi, namely, *chung* means the full development of one's [originally good] mind and *shu* means the extension of that mind to others."[27] Although Confucius never specified the one thread that ran through his doctrines, it is not difficult to figure out what it is by looking for cross-references in the *Analects*. For example, he said, "A man of humanity [*jen*], wishing to establish his own character, also establishes the character of others, and wishing to be prominent himself, also helps others to be prominent."[28] Wing-tsit Chan pointed out that "Liu Pao-nan[30] (1791–1855) is correct in equating *chung* with Confucius' saying, 'Establish one's own character,' and *shu* with 'Also establish the character of others.' "[29] If such interpretation is not incorrect, then *chung* and *shu* must be the two sides of the same coin, for they are manifestations of *jen*. And *jen* is without any doubt Confucius' ultimate concern, as he says, "If a man is not humane (*jen*), what has he to do with ceremonies (*li*)? If he is not humane, what has he to do with music?"[30] Ceremonies and music are the two most important means that Confucius relies on to educate people, and *jen* is clearly the spirit under the practice of ceremonies and music. Again, he says,

> Wealth and honor are what every man desires. But if they have been obtained in violation of moral principles, they must not be kept. Poverty and humble position are what every man dislikes. But if they can be avoided only in violation of moral principles, they must not be avoided. If a superior man departs from humanity, how can he fulfil that name? A superior man never abandons humanity even for the lapse of a single meal. In moments of haste, he acts according to it. In times of difficulty or confusion, he acts according to it.[31]

From such evidence we cannot but conclude that *jen* is Confucius' ultimate commitment as well as that one thread that runs through all his doctrines. Therefore, even though Confucius never quite said that human nature is good, he does believe that there is great potentiality in man and that the primary goal of a man is to develop the great potentiality within himself and to help others to develop their potentiality. Confucius was the first Chinese philosopher to give *jen* a new meaning and make it the primary virtue, the foundation of all other virtues. The Neo-Confucian philosophers showed the same commitment to and faith in *jen*. Here it is clear that they were indeed the followers of Confucius, only they attempted to add new dimensions in the understanding of *jen* and tried to describe *jen* in more precise terms.

Now we shall examine Confucius' attitude toward Heaven. It seems naive for Neo-Confucian scholars to believe uncritically that the so-called "ten wings" (commentaries) of the *Book of Changes* were Confucius' own writings and then consider all the views expressed therein to represent Confucius' own position. It is better for us to stick to the most reliable source to study Confucius—the *Analects*. On the surface it seems that Confucius still believed in the traditional concept of Heaven as a personal God, as he said, "Heaven produced the virtue that is in me; what can Huan T'ui[ap] do to me?"[32] And when his beloved student Yen Yüan died, he complained bitterly, "Alas, Heaven is destroying me! Heaven is destroying me!"[33] But we must become skeptical when we find that he also said, "He who commits a sin against Heaven has no god to pray to."[34] It was also reported that "Confucius never discussed strange phenomena, physical exploits, disorder, or spiritual beings."[35] Heaven does not seem to intervene in either human affairs or natural events. We find an extremely interesting conversation recorded in the *Analects.* "Confucius said, 'I do not wish to say anything.' Tzu-kung said, 'If you do not say anything, what can we little disciples ever learn to pass on to others?' Confucius said, 'Does not Heaven (*T'ien,*[aq] 'Nature') say anything? The four seasons run their course and all things are produced. Does Heaven say anything?' "[36] It is clear that Confucius was taking Heaven as his model, while Heaven seems to be the ultimate creative force working incessantly but quietly in the universe. Heaven here shows an impersonal rather than a personal character. But it would go too far to interpret Confucius as taking a totally naturalistic position in regard to understanding Heaven, as he said, "The superior man stands in awe of three things. He stands in awe of the Mandate of Heaven; he stands in awe of great men; and he stands in awe of the words of the sages."[37] Again, he described his own learning process throughout his life as follows: "At fifteen my mind was set on learning. At thirty my character had been formed. At forty I had no more perplexities. At fifty I knew the Mandate of Heaven (*T'ien-ming*[ar]). At sixty I was at ease with whatever I heard. At seventy I could follow my heart's desire without transgressing moral principles."[38] Surely Confucius still regarded Heaven as a transcendent source. Confucius' originality lies in his belief that there is no need to depart from human ways in order to know the Mandate of Heaven. Confucius put the emphasis entirely on man himself. He said, "It is man that can make the Way great, and not the Way that can make man great."[39] And the following exchange was recorded in the *Analects:* "Chi-lu [Tzu-lu[as]] asked about serving spiritual beings. Confucius said, 'If we are not yet able to serve man, how can we serve spiritual beings?' 'I venture to ask about death.' Confucius said, 'If we do not yet know about life, how can we know about death?' "[40] Here we find a model for future generations of Confucian scholars to follow. Confucius taught a humanism without cutting off its ties with a transcendent creative source in Heaven. One reads messages from Heaven in order to find guidance for self-realization in life. Here again Neo-Confucian philosophers followed the lead of the Master. They may be guilty of reading too many things into the texts of the Classics, but in spirit they are surely the heirs of Confucius' teachings.

Contrary to current opinion, which holds that Confucian scholars followed traditions slavishly without showing creative sparks, great Confucian philosophers were never satisfied with what was handed down from the past. Each generation broke new ground and continually added new dimension to the tradition. For example, Mencius surely went beyond Confucius by stating explicitly that human nature is good. By human nature he meant the distinctly human nature that distinguishes man from other animals. He believed that everyone has the Four Beginnings of Humanity, Righteousness, Propriety, and Wisdom in his mind.[41] By fully developing his potentiality, man can then know Heaven. As Mencius says, "He who exerts his mind to the utmost knows his nature. He who knows his nature knows Heaven. To preserve one's mind and to nourish one's nature is the way to serve Heaven."[42] Mind ($hsin^{at}$), nature ($hsing^{au}$), Heaven (*T'ien*) now form an inseparable trio. The *Doctrine of the Mean* went even further by saying that "what Heaven (*T'ien*, Nature) imparts to man is called human nature. To follow our nature is called the Way (Tao^{av}). Cultivating the Way is called education."[43] The Mandate of Heaven now is completely internalized in human nature. "Sincerity is the Way of Heaven. To think how to be sincere is the way of man."[44] Man not only knows Heaven, but acts after the model of Heaven. Thus,

> only those who are absolutely sincere can fully develop their nature. If they can fully develop their nature, they can then fully develop the nature of others. If they can fully develop the nature of others, they can then fully develop the nature of things. If they can fully develop the nature of things, they can then assist in the transforming and nourishing process of Heaven and Earth. If they can assist in the transforming and nourishing process of Heaven and Earth, they can thus form a trinity with Heaven and Earth.[45]

The idea of Heaven as the ultimate creative ontological principle was further developed in the commentaries of the *Book of Changes*. It is said that "the great characteristic of Heaven and Earth is to produce."[46] Again, "The successive movement of yin^{aw} and yang^{ax} (passive and active cosmic forces) constitutes the Way (Tao). What issues from the Way is good, and that which realizes it is the individual nature."[47] From these sources we can trace the development of a creative metaphysics, one which holds that only through the realization of the self can the creative message of Heaven becomes manifest. But in the Han dynasty scholars turned their attention to textual studies and institutional considerations. They were also interested in cosmological speculations that degenerated into astrological speculations or even superstitions. During the Wei (220–265) and Chin (265–420) dynasties Neo-Taoism and then Buddhism became the main streams. The innermost Confucian message was being forgotten. It was under such circumstances that we see the emergence of Neo-Confucianism in the Sung dynasty.

Because the Neo-Confucian movement arose as a Confucian response to Buddhism and Taoism, naturally the Neo-Confucian philosophers received certain stimuli from and in some ways were profoundly influenced by these two schools. But the messages they spread were different. The Neo-Confucianists believed that man is endowed with a good nature and that it is imparted from Heaven, which is none other than the ultimate creative principle that works incessantly in the universe. Such messages were indeed ones that we can find in the Classics, only the expressions of them were quite different. The Neo-Confucian philosophers were totally uninhibited in borrowing from Taoism and Buddhism, and they were vigorous in their drive to open up new vistas for Confucianism. This explains why Chou Tun-i borrowed the Diagram of the Great Ultimate from an unmistakable Taoist source and turned it to Confucian use.[48] The Ch'eng brothers might have borrowed the term *li*[ay] (principle) from the Hua-yen[az] School of Buddhism,[49] but they gave a completely new meaning to it. What is most important for Neo-Confucian scholars is that the essential Confucian message must be fully realized in the self; textual studies or scholarly learning are of only secondary importance. For example, Lu Hsiang-shan said, "If in our study we know the fundamentals, then all the Six Classics are my footnotes."[50] The reason why Lu held such an attitude may be seen from the following quotation:

> The four directions plus upward and downward constitute the spatial continuum (*yü*[ba]). What has gone by in the past and what is to come in the future constitute the temporal continuum (*chou*[bb]). The universe (these continua) is my mind, and my mind is the universe. Sages appeared tens of thousands of generations ago. They shared this mind; they shared this principle. Sages will appear tens of thousands of generations to come. They will share this mind; they will share this principle. Over the four seas sages appear. They share this mind; they share this principle.[51]

Lu firmly believed that because we can find and grasp principles in our own mind, it was not that important for us to study the Classics. Surely Chu Hsi would not go as far as Lu. In fact, one of his criticisms against Lu was that Lu's attitude of completely neglecting Classical studies would have harmful consequences. But Chu Hsi's main concern was also "the study for the self." Even though he spent a lot of time and energy writing commentaries for the Classics, it is by no means true to say that he held a slavish attitude toward the Classics. When he defended Chou Tun-i's essay "An Explanation of the Diagram of the Great Ultimate" against Lu's charges that the diagram was taken from a Taoist source and did not have any foundation in the teachings of the sages, he said,

> When Fu-hsi invented the trigrams and King Wen developed the system, they never talked anything about the Great Ultimate (*T'ai-chi*[bc]) but Confucius talked about it. When Confucius gave interpretations to the *Book of Changes,* he never talked about the Ultimate of Nonbeing (*wu-chi*[bd]), but Master Chou talked about it. Is it not true that the ancient sages and the modern sages were following the same principles? If we can truly see the reality of the Great Ultimate, then we know that those who do not talk about it are not doing too little, while those who talk about it are not doing too much. Why should we have so many troubles concerning this issue?[52]

What is interesting here is that these words could have been said by Lu Hsiang-shan himself. True, Chu Hsi honored the Classics, but only because he believed that there were truths embodied in them. When he wrote the commentaries for the Classics, he was trying to manifest the truths he saw as embodied in them. This was creative work, not just a meaningless paraphrasing of the texts themselves. But what are important are the messages carried by the texts. On this score Chu and Lu did not really differ much from each other. Even Lu never said that we need not study the Classics at all; he simply felt that the emphasis should not be laid on pedantic classical studies per se. But even Chu was merely using the Classics for pedagogical purposes, because he also firmly believed that the mind has the ability to get hold of principles. He was trying to relive the experiences of the sages through studying the Classics with a view to recovering the intended meanings in the texts. Although there are indeed significant differences between Chu and Lu, they agreed on interpreting the Classics in such a way that the Confucian message can be realized in one's life. On this score they were allies.

Now we can clearly define the relationship between classical Confucianism and Sung-Ming Neo-Confucianism. Neo-Confucian philosophers claimed that they were transmitting the Way of Confucius and Mencius, as Confucius claimed that he was transmitting the Way of sage-emperors in the past—Yao and Shun, King Wen and King Wu. The words may be different, but the spirit remains the same. In their studies of the Classics Neo-Confucian scholars sometimes seemed to have done violence to the texts by giving new interpretations, new meanings not intended by the original authors, but they had reasons for so doing. They believed that in essence the sagely mind is not different from our minds and that the principles embodied in the words and deeds of sages in the past are not different from those to be realized in our own lives. And we do find that the Neo-Confucian understanding of men through *jen* and their understanding of *T'ien* (Heaven) have their seeds in the thought of Confucius as recorded in the *Analects*. True, they did break some new ground. For example, classical Confucianism never identified *jen* with *sheng-sheng*[be] (creative creativity) as Neo-Confucian scholars did. But we find nothing in classical Confucianism that contradicts or precludes such development in Neo-Confucian thought. Therefore, we must agree with the Neo-Confucian philosophers when they claim that there is continuity between classical Confucianism and Neo-Confucianism and that they teach something quite different from Buddhist and Taoist thoughts, as these two schools do not believe in the classical and Neo-Confucian views of Heaven as the ultimate creative ontological principle in the universe and man as being endowed with humanity in his mind and nature.

By using these two criteria we can tell easily who are true Confucianists and who are not. A case in point would be Wang Yang-ming[bf] (1472–1529) in the Ming dynasty. Even though he said that "in the original substance of the mind there is no distinction between good and evil,"[53] we cannot say that

Wang was giving expression to a Buddhist view, as Wang clearly submitted to the Confucian views of Heaven and man. What he really meant was only that we cannot give adequate characterization of the supreme good, as it is beyond good and evil.[54] Once he wrote a famous poem as follows:

> The soundless, odorless moment of solitary self-knowledge
> Contains the ground of Heaven, Earth, and all beings.
> Foolish is he who leaves his inexhaustible treasure,
> With a bowl, moving from door to door, imitating the beggar.[55]

We should never take Wang to be a Taoist or Buddhist simply because he used such seemingly Taoist images as "soundless and odorless" and such Buddhist metaphors as "inexhaustible treasure"; the thrust of his thought is totally consistent with Mencius' thought that human nature is good, and he could have easily found his precedent in Confucius' teaching without words and the concluding remarks in the *Doctrine of the Mean:*

> The *Book of Odes* says, "I cherish your brilliant virtue, which makes no great display in sound or appearance." Confucius said, "In influencing people, the use of sound or appearance is of secondary importance." The *Book of Odes* says, "His virtue is as light as hair." Still, a hair is comparable. "The operations of Heaven have neither sound nor smell."[56]

Of course, we can always argue that even the *Doctrine of the Mean* may have already been influenced by Taoist thought. But such arguments, even if they could be proved to be true, could only serve to confuse the issues. The crux of the matter lies in whether the document as a whole as transmitted to posterity is essentially Confucian or Taoist in character. The fact is that no school of thought, unless it is dead, can afford to remain unchanged. In order to revitalize itself or to enlarge its perspective, it cannot but learn from competing movements with a view to adding new dimensions to its own tradition. Only if it has lost the essential character of its own school and adopted the basic outlook of another school we may conclude that a conversion has happened. In fact, two schools of thought intertwining over a long time may share quite a few ideas that from an outside viewpoint may appear to teach the same thing. But if we probe somewhat deeper, we would find that they are actually spreading very different messages. For example, both the Taoists and the Confucianists taught *wu-wei*[bg] (taking no [artificial] action), but they meant something quite different by the term. The Taoists saw nothing positive in human institutions, while the Confucianists believed that the system of rituals and music is so natural for man that it could function so smoothly that no other means would be needed for a sage-king to run state affairs. Let us look at the problem from still another angle. Professor Mou Tsung-san[bh] claims that all the three major traditions in China—Confucianism, Taoism, and Buddhism—

asserted the possibility of what he called "intellectual intuition."[57] It is quite possible that from an outsider's viewpoint these three traditions may be seen to have taught very similar ideas. But these similarities should not mislead us to conclude that the three traditions are really teaching exactly the same thing, or there is no need to find essential differences among these traditions. My personal view is that we must see the development of ideas from a dynamic, historical point of view: schools with vitality constantly enlarge themselves and absorb certain insights from rival schools, but this fact does not make the differences among the schools disappear.

In the above I have shown that there is some justification for the Neo-Confucianists in Sung to claim that they inherited the line of transmission from the classical Confucianism of Confucius and Mencius. Naturally, I do not mean that there is not an alternative way to claim a different line of orthodoxy. In fact, after Confucius died it is said that Confucianism was split into eight different branches, and in Hsün Tzu's[bi] (313–238 B.C.) days he could have claimed the orthodoxy for himself against the rival school of Mencius; then in the early Ch'ing dynasty (1644–1912) people like Yen Yüan[bj] (1635–1704) claimed that the whole movement during the Sung and Ming dynasties went wide off the mark and gave a distorted picture of Confucian teachings. But if you were to go into the circle of faith of Sung-Ming Confucianism, you would see clearly that the program was definitely not just an arbitrary concoction without a rationale among its proponents.

When definite criteria have been established to distinguish Neo-Confucianism from Buddhism and Taoism, many controversies are seen to be unnecessary and avoidable. For example, during the famous debates between Chu Hsi and Lu Hsiang-shan, each side charged the other side with teaching Buddhist ideas.[58] These criticisms are unfounded. The differences are differences within the Neo-Confucian tradition, not those between Confucianism and Buddhism. Their charges against each other only showed their emotional dissatisfaction against a rival school within the same tradition, as they were really worried that their orthodoxy would be usurped by some impure doctrine mixed up with Buddhist and Taoist thoughts.

Our next problem is whether it was Chu Hsi or his rival Lu Hsiang-shan who really represented the orthodox teachings of Confucius and Mencius. On the surface this was never a problem, as we have seen that as a matter of historical fact Chu Hsi almost single-handedly established the line of transmission of the orthodoxy which was unquestionably accepted by posterity. Lu, on the other hand, was completely ignored by scholars until his thoughts were again recognized to some extent by Wang Yang-ming.[59] He never gained such a prominent position that he could be compared with Chu Hsi. But the problem was reopened by Professor Mou Tsung-san's monumental work on Neo-Confucian philosophy, *Hsin-t'i yü hsing-t'i*[bk] (Substance of mind and substance of human nature),[60] and we must reexamine the problem carefully before we can reach a conclusion.

Professor Mou pointed out that although Chu Hsi belonged in the general movement of Neo-Confucianism, yet what he succeeded and developed were Ch'eng I's ideas, which were quite different from what Mencius had taught. Ch'eng I maintained that "love is feeling whereas humanity is the nature."[61] Feeling *(ch'ing*[bl]*)* and nature *(hsing)* pertain to two different levels. Chu Hsi further developed Ch'eng I's ideas by identifying nature with principle *(li)* and feeling with material force *(ch'i*[bm]*)*; the mind *(hsin)* for Chu Hsi is constituted of the most subtle kind of material force, and it has the ability to comprehend the principles in things.[62] But when we go back to Mencius we find that Mencius never used the term *ch'ing* in the sense that Ch'eng I and Chu Hsi used it. *Ch'ing* for Mencius means only *ch'ing-shih*[bn] (what is the case). And Mencius himself never made the distinction between the feeling *(ch'ing)* of commiseration and the mind-heart *(hsin)* of commiseration. What Mencius advocates is that if we can recover our lost mind, then our feelings of commiseration, righteousness, propriety, and wisdom will naturally develop into the virtues of *jen, i, li*[bo] and *chih.*[bp] For Mencius, there is no distinction between the original mind and the essential nature of man. When we fail to follow the naturally good tendencies of our mind and nature because of bad influences from the environment, then evils will ensue. *Ch'i* for Mencius is "the strong, moving power."[63] According to him, "If nourished by uprightness and not injured, it will fill up all between heaven and earth."[64] From these statements we may infer that Mencius did not seem to make a distinction between *ch'i* (material force) and *li* (principle); the material force that filled up heaven and earth is naturally embodied with principles until it is obstructed by adverse influences so that it will deviate from principles. Hence for Mencius, the mind, the nature, principle, and material force all go together when they can perform their proper function according to their essential character without obstructions. This philosophy was labelled by Professor Mou as teaching a straightforward system that implies a creative metaphysics that takes the ultimate ontological principle to be both active and existing.[65]

In contrast to this system, Chu Hsi sees *li* and *ch'i* as pertaining to two different levels. Principles, which belong in a metaphysical realm, are pure, clean, devoid of content, and vast in scope, while material force is that which makes things real and concrete. When this metaphysics is applied to the analysis of man, we get the tripartite structure of the mind, the nature and feelings. Only the nature is principle; feelings are largely constituted of material force, but the mind is made of the most subtle kind of material force and hence it has the ability to comprehend principles and is the key to bringing about the unity between the nature and feelings. The function of the mind is to appropriate principles and make them work in one's life. Therefore, Chu Hsi's philosophy presupposes a dualism that we cannot find in Mencius' thought. However, Chu Hsi did make it clear that even though *li* and *ch'i* must be kept distinct from each other they cannot be separated from each other. It would be quite wrong to read a Platonic dualism into his thought.

Still, there is no denial that his thought was quite different from Mencius' thought in spite of the fact that he wrote his commentary for the *Book of Mencius*. For Chu Hsi, it is futile for the mind to remain in itself; it must direct itself toward principles in order to find any guidance for behavior. Therefore, he condemned those who put their exclusive attention on the mind. And as he saw it, the Buddhists had made great contribution in controlling the mind. Hence, he identified all those who put emphasis on the mind with the Buddhists. This was why he thought Lu was spreading the message of Buddhist teachings. Thus, what Chu accomplished was a subject-object related system in which the vital force of the mind can relate itself to principles that only exist but do not act.[66]

It was obvious that Lu could not be taken as a Buddhist, as he firmly believed that there is intrinsic value in human life and that man is endowed with humanity in his mind-heart. Furthermore, it is simply not the case that Lu did not pay any attention to the concept of *li,* as he declared, "Principle is endowed in me by Heaven, not drilled into me from outside."[67] And he said,

> The mind is one and principle is one. Perfect truth is reduced to a unity; the essential principle is never a duality. The mind and principle can never be separated into two. That is why Confucius said, "There is one thread that runs through my doctrines,"[68] and Mencius said, "The Way is one and only one."[69] [Quoting Confucius], Mencius also said, "There are but two ways to be pursued, that of humanity *(jen)* and that of inhumanity."[70] To do in a certain way is humanity. Not to do in a certain way is the opposite of humanity. Humanity is the same as the mind and principle. "Seek and you find it"[71] means to find this principle. "Those who are the first to know" know this principle, and "those who are the first to understand" understand this principle.[72] It is this principle that constitutes the love for parents, reverence for elders, and the sense of alarm and commiseration when one sees a child about to fall into a well. It is this principle that makes people ashamed of shameful things and hate what should be hated. It is this principle that enables people to know what is right to be right and what is wrong to be wrong. It is this principle that makes people deferential when deference is due and humble when humility is called for. Seriousness *(ching)*[pq] is this principle. Righteousness is also this principle. What is internal is this principle. What is external is also this principle. Therefore it is said, "Straight, square, and great, [the superior man] works his operation, without repeated effort, [and is] in every respect advantageous."[73] Mencius said, "The ability possessed by men without their having acquired it by learning is innate ability, and the knowledge possessed by them without deliberation is innate knowledge."[74] These are endowed in us by Heaven. "We originally have them with us," and "they are not drilled into us from outside."[75] Therefore Mencius said, "All things are already complete in oneself. There is no greater joy than to examine oneself and be sincere (or absolutely real)."[76] [77]

Lu's ideas all came directly from Confucius and Mencius. How can we charge him with teaching Buddhist ideas? His views both of man and of Heaven are totally consistent with the Confucian tradition as set down in the *Doctrine of the Mean* and the "Appended Remarks" to the *Book of Changes*. As he said, "The Way fills the universe. It does not hide or escape from anything. With reference to Heaven, it is called yin and yang. With reference to Earth, it is called strength and weakness. With reference to man, it is called humanity and righteousness. Thus humanity and righteousness are the original mind of man.[78]

Strangely enough, if we follow Chu Hsi and accept Mencius' thought as representing the orthodox line of Confucianism, then Lu stands much closer to Mencius than Chu Hsi. Lu believed that principles naturally flow out of the mind, and so he did not see the need to draw a sharp distinction between the mind and principle as Chu Hsi did. He said, "My learning is different from that of others in the fact that with me every word comes spontaneously. Although I have uttered tens of thousands of words, they all are expressions of what is within me, and nothing more has been added. Recently someone has commented of me that aside from [Mencius'] saying, 'First build up the nobler part of your nature,' I had nothing clever. When I heard this, I said, 'Very true indeed.' "[79]

Not only because many of Lu's quotations came directly from Mencius or because his spirit was very close to that of Mencius, but also for important philosophical reasons we must say that Lu's thought should be regarded as more representative of the orthodox Neo-Confucian position if we should accept the tenets of the school, as Chu Hsi's approach must presuppose what Lu Hsiang-shan taught but not the other way around. Once Lu commented on his difference with Chu Hsi as follows:

Chu Yüan-hui[br] [Chu Hsi] once wrote to one of his students saying, "Lu Tzu-ching[bs] [Lu Hsiang-shan] taught people only the doctrine of honoring the moral nature. Therefore those who have studied under him are mostly scholars who put their beliefs into practice. But he neglected to follow the path of study and inquiry. In my teaching is it not true that I have put somewhat more emphasis on following the path of study and inquiry? As a consequence, my pupils often do not approach his in putting beliefs into practice." From this it is clear that Yüan-hui wanted to avoid two defects [failure to honor the moral nature and failure to practice] and combine the two merits [following the path of study and inquiry and practicing one's beliefs]. I do not believe this to be possible. If one does not know how to honor his moral nature, how can he talk about following the path of study and inquiry?[80]

These criticisms would not be sound if Chu Hsi refused to accept the principle of "honoring the moral nature," but Chu Hsi in fact was pursuing the sagely ideal. For him following the path of study and inquiry was only a means to approach the realization of such an ideal. In Chu Hsi's famous commentary on the fifth chapter of the *Great Learning,* he said,

The above fifth chapter of commentary explains the meaning of the investigation of things and the extension of knowledge, which is now lost. I have ventured to take the view of Master Ch'eng I and supplement it as follows: The meaning of the expression "The perfection of knowledge depends on the investigation of things (ko-wu^bt)" is this: If we wish to extend our knowledge to the utmost, we must investigate the principles of all things we come into contact with, for the intelligent mind of man is certainly formed to know, and there is not a single thing in which its principles do not inhere. It is only because all principles are not investigated that man's knowledge is incomplete. For this reason, the first step in the education of the adult is to instruct the learner, in regard to all things in the world, to proceed from what knowledge he has of their principles, and investigate further until he reaches the limit. After exerting himself in this way for a long time, he will one day achieve a wide and far-reaching penetration. Then the qualities of all things, whether internal or external, the refined or the coarse, will all be apprehended, and the mind, in its total substance and great functioning, will be perfectly intelligent. This is called the investigation of things. This is called the perfection of knowledge.[81]

It is a controversial matter whether anything has been lost from the text of the *Great Learning,* but it is clear that in the supplement Chu Hsi wrote he was expressing his own ideas based on the insight of Ch'eng I as he had understood it. It would be absurd to interpret Chu Hsi to mean that man can be omniscient after he has made a vigorous effort to investigate things and to extend knowledge. What Chu Hsi means is that one may realize the ontological principle that governs the operation of the universe within his own mind after a long search on the path of study and inquiry. But this can be achieved only by the act of a leap of faith. By following an inductive approach we may build up certain empirical knowledge of the world or even formulate a unified theory of the physical universe, but these are not enough to establish a metaphysics of creativity. By the same method we also may learn a great deal about moral practice in the society, but not the realization of the moral principle within the self. Since Chang Tsai, Neo-Confucian philosophers had made a sharp distinction between informative knowledge and moral or ontological knowledge.[82] And the insight can be traced back to Mencius' distinction between the nobler and the smaller parts of man.[83] Only by the realization of the moral and creative nature within man can he truly grasp the profound message of the Way of Heaven. Lu Hsiang-shan's approach followed closely Mencius' approach both in form and in spirit, while Chu Hsi took a roundabout way. But if Chu Hsi did not have an intrinsic faith in the nobler part of man's nature, all the studies and inquiries in the world would not lead him to the kind of "wide and far-reaching penetration" that he praised in his remark. It seems that Chu Hsi believes that one can learn about one's own mind only through its ability to reflect the principles in things, so he dismisses all those approaches that go directly to the mind as Ch'an (Zen) teachings. He does not seem to realize that his own approach would not work if it did not presuppose

Lu's approach, which is essentially no different from Mencius' approach. Can Chu Hsi then dismiss Mencius' teachings as Ch'an teachings? It appears that Chu Hsi enjoys much more the softer light from the moon while refusing to acknowledge that the origin of such light is the sun itself. It is ironic that one who almost singlehandedly established the orthodox line of transmission of the Way should teach only a feeble reflection of the Way, if we may be allowed to use the metaphor to characterize Chu Hsi's position within the Neo-Confucian movement.

To say, however, that Lu's position is closer to the orthodox line of transmission from Mencius does not entail the conclusion that there are not serious limitations and shortcomings in his thought. True, the realization of the moral nature is the primary concern for Neo-Confucian philosophers, but it is not their only concern. One must constantly enlarge his vision and sharpen his skills so that he can help the Way to prevail in the world, and he must also take good care of his physical nature. Mencius' righteousness does not exist only in a transcendent realm; it is realizable in this mundane world amidst the pursuit of profit.[84] Lu's merit lies in his firm grip of the essence, but his door and court are certainly too narrow. His relative neglect of the path of study and inquiry becomes his Achilles' heel. History showed that he was no competition for Chu Hsi, who accumulated so many riches in his formidable scholarly pursuit. From an educational point of view Chu Hsi's gradual approach also has its merit. One needs external help as well as hard work before he can even reach that point of enlightenment that was the only concern for Lu Hsiang-shan. And one must realize his moral nature amidst the entanglement of the physical nature. If one does not pay enough attention to his physical nature, then what he claims to be the manifestation of his moral nature may very well be only a reflection of his physical nature. Although Chu Hsi's position deviated somewhat from the Mencian orthodoxy, yet he added valuable new dimensions to Confucianism. It was through his great scholarship, his indefatigable hard work, and his unquestionable integrity that Neo-Confucianism after his death was honored to be the orthodox line of Confucianism. The result was a most remarkable phenomenon in the development of Chinese intellectual history that Professor Mou Tsung-san characterizes as "the side branch [taking] the position of the orthodoxy."[85] Through a careful examination of the materials available and reflection on the problem of orthodoxy in Chu Hsi's philosophy, I cannot but agree to Professor Mou's observation. After all, Chu Hsi's philosophy has been honored as the unchallenged orthodoxy in Confucianism for the more than six hundred years since the early Yüan dynasty (1277–1368).

Notes

1. Wing-tsit Chan, "Chu Hsi's Completion of Neo-Confucianism" in Francoise Aubin, ed. *Études Song-Sung Studies in Memoriam Étienne Balazs*, Ser. II, No. 1

(1973), p. 75. For a general review of the formation of the orthodox line of transmission, also see Wm. Theodore de Bary, *Neo-Confucian Orthodoxy and the Learning of the Mind-and-Heart* (New York: Columbia University Press, 1981), pp. 2–13.

2. *Chu Tzu wen-chi*[bu] [Collection of literary works of Master Chu], (SPPY ed. entitled *Chu Tzu ta-ch'üan* [Complete literary works of Master Chu]), 76:21–22b. Legendary emperors Yao and Shun were supposed to have reigned in the third millennium B.C. Legendary emperor Yü was supposed to have been the founder of the Hsia dynasty (2183–1752 B.C.?). Both Yen Yüan and Tseng Shen (505–c. 436 B.C.) were Confucius' disciples. Tsu-ssu (492–431 B.C.?), Confucius' grandson, was supposed to have been the author of the *Doctrine of the Mean*.

3. Chan, "Chu Hsi's Completion of Neo-Confucianism," p. 75.

4. *Ibid.*

5. *Ibid.*, pp. 75–76.

6. "Letter to Chu Yüan-hui," *Hsiang-shan ch'üan-chi*[bv] [Complete works of Lu Hsiang-shan], (SPPY ed.), 2:5b–11a.

7. *Book of History*, ch. 3, "Counsels of Great Yü."

8. Cf. Wang Mao-hung[bw] (1668–1741), *Chu Tzu nien-p'u*[bx] [Chronological biography of Master Chu], (World Book Co. ed.) 1A:7–9, 11–13.

9. *Chu Tzu yü-lei*[by] [Classified conversations of Master Chu], (Taipei: Cheng-chung[bz] Book Co., 1970), 8:10a, p. 225.

10. *Ibid.*, 125:4b p. 4792. The Sixth Patriarch of Zen in China was Hui-neng[ca] (638–713). He was originally an illiterate fuel-wood peddler. The story of his achieving sudden enlightenment was told in *Liu-tsu t'an-ching*[cb] [The platform scripture of the Sixth Patriarch).

11. *Ibid.*, 126:29a, p. 4873.

12. "Preface to the *Chung-yung chang-chü.*"

13. For example, Chu Hsi was certainly wrong when he charged that the Buddhists had plagiarized from the *Lieh Tzu*[cc] and the *Chuang Tzu.*[cd] See *Chu Tzu yü-lei*, 126:3b, p. 4822.

14. *Chu Tzu yü-lei*, 126:7a, p. 4829. Wing-tsit Chan trans. and comp., *A Source Book in Chinese Philosophy* (Princeton, N.J.: Princeton University Press, 1963), p. 646. For the sake of convenience I would like to quote from the *Source Book* wherever possible. Hereafter the book will be referred to as Chan, *Source Book.*

15. *Chu Tzu yü-lei*, 126:8b–9a, pp. 4832–4833; Chan, *Source Book*, pp. 647–648. The quotation about human nature is from the *Doctrine of the Mean*, ch. 1.

16. *Ibid.*, 126:7b, p. 4828; Chan, *Source Book*, p. 648.

17. See Shu-hsien Liu, "The Religious Import of Confucian Philosophy: Its Traditional Outlook and Contemporary Significance," *Philosophy East and West* 21 (April 1971), pp. 157–175.

18. *Book of Odes*, ode no. 267, "The Mandate of Heaven"; Chan, *Source Book*, p. 6.

19. *Analects*, 9:16; Chan, *Source Book*, p. 36.

20. *Chu Tzu yü-lei*, 36:21b, p. 1556.

21. Paul Tillich, *Systematic Theology* (Chicago: University of Chicago Press, 3 vols., 1951, 1957, 1963), Vol. I, pp. 135–137; Vol. II, pp. 97–118.

22. *Ibid.*, Vol. II, p. 105.

23. Confucius said, "I can describe the civilization of the Hsia dynasty, but the descendant state of Ch'i[ce] cannot render adequate corroboration. I can describe the civilization of the Yin dynasty [1751–1112 B.C.], but the descendant state of Sung[cf]

cannot render adequate corroboration. And all because of the deficiency of their records and wise men. Were those sufficient then I could corroborate my views" (*Analects*, 3:9). Quoted from Fung Yu-lan,^{cg} *A History of Chinese Philosophy*, trans. Derk Bodde (Princeton, N.J.: Princeton University Press, 2 vols. 1952, 1953), vol. I, p. 55.

24. This point was stressed by *Mencius*, 6A:6. Cf. Chan, *Source Book*, pp. 53–54.

25. *Analects*, 5:11; Chan, *Source Book*, p. 28. Tzu-kung (520–c. 450 B.C.?) was Confucius' pupil. His family name was Tuan-mu,^{ch} private name Tz'u,^{ci} and courtesy name Tzu-kung. He was noted for his eloquence and diplomatic skills.

26. *Ibid.*, 4:15; Chan, *Source Book*, p. 27. Shen was the private name of Tseng Tzu. He was noted for filial piety, and the *Great Learning* and the *Book of Filial Piety* were ascribed to him.

27. Chan, *Source Book*, p. 27.

28. *Analects*, 6:28; Chan, *Source Book*, p. 31.

29. Chan, *Source Book*, p. 27.

30. *Analects*, 3:3; Chan, *Source Book*, p. 24. Even from a statistical point of view *jen* was without any doubt the most central and the most discussed virtue in the *Analects*.

31. *Ibid.*, 4:5; Chan, *Source Book*, p. 26.

32. *Ibid.*, 7:22; Chan, *Source Book*, p. 32. Huan T'ui was a military officer in the state of Sung who attempted to kill Confucius by felling a tree. Confucius was then fifty-nine years old.

33. *Ibid.*, 11:8; Chan, *Source Book*, p. 36. Yen Yüan was Confucius' pupil. He was a quiet scholar, noted for his virtue. Unfortunately, he died early.

34. *Ibid.*, 3:13; Chan, *Source Book*, p. 25.

35. *Ibid.*, 7:20; Chan, *Source Book*, p. 32.

36. *Ibid.*, 17:19; Chan, *Source Book*, p. 47.

37. *Ibid.*, 16:8; Chan, *Source Book*, p. 45.

38. *Ibid.*, 2:4; Chan, *Source Book*, p. 22.

39. *Ibid.*, 15:28; Chan, *Source Book*, p. 44.

40. *Ibid.*, 11:11; Chan, *Source Book*, p. 36.

41. *Book of Mencius*, 2A:6; Chan, *Source Book*, p. 65: "The feeling of commiseration is the beginning of humanity; the feeling of shame and dislike is the beginning of righteousness; the feeling of deference and compliance is the beginning of propriety; and the feeling of right and wrong is the beginning of wisdom. Men have these Four Beginnings just as they have their four limbs."

42. *Book of Mencius*, 7A:1; Chan, *Source Book*, p. 78.

43. *Doctrine of the Mean*, ch. 1; Chan, *Source Book*, p. 98.

44. *Ibid.*, ch. 20; Chan, *Source Book*, p. 107.

45. *Ibid.*, ch. 22; Chan, *Source Book*, pp. 107–108.

46. *Book of Changes*, "Appended Remarks," pt. 2, ch. 1; Chan, *Source Book*, p. 268.

47. *Ibid.*, "Appended Remarks," pt. 1, ch. 5; Chan, *Source Book*, p. 266.

48. Cf. Fung, *A History of Chinese Philosophy*, Vol. II, pp. 435–442. Chou Tun-i wrote the famous essay "T'ai-chi-t'u shou"^{cj} [An explanation of the Diagram of the Great Ultimate. This explanation has provided the essential outline of Neo-Confucian metaphysics and cosmology. Few short Chinese treatises like this have exerted so much influence. This essay is found in the *Chou Tzu ch'üan-shu*^{ck} [Complete works of Master Chou], ch. 1. For a translation of the text, see Chan, *Source Book*, pp. 463–464.

49. Cf. Wing-tsit Chan, "The Evolution of the Neo-Confucian Concept of *Li* as

Principle," *Tsing Hua*[cl] *Journal of Chinese Studies*, New Series IV, no. 2 (February 1964), 123–149.

50. *Hsiang-shan ch'üan-chi* 34:1b; Chan, *Source Book*, p. 580. The Six Classics were the books of *Odes*, *History*, *Rites*, *Changes*, the *Chou-li*[cm] [Rites of Chou], and the *Spring and Autumn Annals*. The ancient Six Classics had the *Book of Music*, now lost, instead of the *Chou-li*.

51. *Ibid.*, 22:5a; Chan, *Source Book*, pp. 579–580.

52. *Chu Tzu wen-chi*, 36:8a.

53. Wang Yang-ming, *Instructions for Practical Living and Other Neo-Confucian Writings*, trans. Wing-tsit Chan (New York: Columbia University Press, 1963), sec. 315, p. 243.

54. *Ibid.*, sec. 101. pp. 63–64: "The Teacher said, 'The state of having neither good nor evil is that of principle in tranquillity. Good and evil appear when the vital force is perturbed. If the vital force is not perturbed, there is neither good nor evil, and this is called the highest good.' "

55. *Wang Wen-ch'eng Kung ch'üan-shu*[cn] [Complete works of Wang Yang-ming), (SPTK ed.), 20:629a–b, trans. Julia Ching,[co] *To Acquire Wisdom: The Way of Wang Yang-ming* (New York: Columbia University Press, 1976), p. 242.

56. *Doctrine of the Mean*, ch. 33; Chan, *Source Book*, p. 113. The two quotations from the *Book of Odes* were taken from ode no. 241 and no. 260, respectively.

57. Mou Tsung-san, *Chih ti chih-chiao yü Chung-kuo che-hsüeh*[cp] [Intellectual intuition and Chinese philosophy], (Taipei: Commercial Press, 1971), p. 346.

58. For a detailed discussion of the debates between Chu Hsi and Lu Hsiang-shan, see Ch'ien Mu,[cq] *Chu Tzu hsin-hsüeh-an*[cr] [A new study of Chu Hsi], (Taipei: San-min[cs] Book Co., 1971), Bk. III, pp. 293–356. See also Mou Tsung-san, *Ts'ung Lu Hsiang-shan tao Liu Ch'i-shan*[ct] [From Lu Hsiang-shan to Liu Tsung-chou], (Taipei: Student Book Co., 1979), pp. 81–212; and Shu-hsien Liu, *Chu Tzu che-hsüeh ssu-hsiang ti fa-chen yü wan-ch'eng*[cu] [The development and completion of Master Chu's philosophical thought], (Taipei: Student Book Co., 1982), pp. 427–479.

59. *Wang Wen-ch'eng Kung ch'üan-shu*, 7:242b–243a, "Preface to the Collected Writings of Lu Chiu-yüan (Lu Hsiang-shan)," trans. Julia Ching, *To Acquire Wisdom: The Way of Wang Yang-ming*, pp. 206–208.

60. Mou Tsung-san, *Hsin-t'i yü hsing-t'i* (Taipei: Cheng-chung Book Co., 1968–69). See also my review of the work in *Philosophy East and West* 20 (October 1970), 419–422.

61. *I-shu*[cv] [Surviving works], 18:1a (Chan, *Source Book*, p. 559), in the *Erh-Ch'eng ch'üan-shu*[cw] [Complete works of the two Ch'engs], (SPPY ed.).

62. See Shu-hsien Liu, "The Function of the Mind in Chu Hsi's Philosophy," *Journal of Chinese Philosophy* 5 (1978), pp. 195–208. Chu Hsi said, "The mind is constituted of the most subtle kind of the material force" (*Chu Tzu yü-lei*, 5:3b, p. 198). He also said, "The whole substance of the mind is clearly vacuous and bright; it comprises tens of thousands of principles" (*Ibid.*, 5:11a, p. 213).

63. *Book of Mencius*, 2A:2; Chan, *Source Book*, p. 63.

64. *Ibid.*

65. Mou Tsung-san, *Hsin-t'i yü hsing-t'i*, Bk. I, pp. 70–74.

66. *Ibid.*

67. *Hsiang-shan ch'üan-chi*, 1:3a; Chan, *Source Book*, p. 574.

68. *Analects*, 4:15.

69. *Book of Mencius,* 3A:1.
70. *Ibid.,* 4A:2.
71. *Ibid.,* 6A:6.
72. Referring to *ibid.,* 5a:7.
73. *Book of Changes,* commentary on second hexagram, *k'un*[cx] (earth).
74. *Book of Mencius,* 7A:15.
75. *Ibid.,* 6A:6.
76. *Ibid.,* 7A:4.
77. *Hsiang-shan ch'üan-chi,* 1:3b–4a; Chan, *Source Book,* p. 574.
78. *Ibid.,* 1:6b; Chan, *Source Book,* p. 575.
79. *Ibid.,* 34:5a; Chan, *Source Book,* p. 582.
80. *Ibid.,* 34:4b–5a; Chan, *Source Book,* p. 582.
81. Chan, *Source Book,* p. 89.
82. "Knowledge gained through enlightenment which is the result of sincerity is the innate knowledge of one's natural character. It is not the small knowledge of what is heard or what is seen" (*Cheng-meng*[cy] [Correcting youthful ignorance], ch. 6; Chan, *Source Book,* p. 507).
83. *Book of Mencius,* 6A:15; Chan, *Source Book,* p. 59.
84. *Ibid.,* 1b:5; Chan, *Source Book,* p. 61.
85. Mou Tsung-san, *Hsin-t'i yü hsing-ti,* Bk. I, pp. 41–60.

Glossary

a	道統	y	張載	aw	陰
b	陳榮捷	z	邵雍	ax	陽
c	伏羲	aa	司馬光	ay	理
d	神農	ab	陸象山九淵	az	華嚴
e	堯	ac	李侗	ba	宇
f	舜	ad	禪	bb	宙
g	禹	ae	仁	bc	太極
h	湯	af	空	bd	無極
i	文	ag	性理	be	生生
j	武	ah	空理	bf	王陽明
k	周	ai	道理	bg	無為
l	曾子	aj	禮	bh	牟宗三
m	子思	ak	子貢	bi	荀子
n	周	al	參	bj	顏元
o	程	am	忠	bk	心體與性體
p	中庸章句	an	恕	bl	情
q	顏淵	ao	劉寶楠	bm	氣
r	曾參	ap	桓魋	bn	情實
s	程顥	aq	天	bo	義
t	程頤	ar	天命	bp	智
u	韓愈	as	季路子路	bq	敬
v	李翱	at	心	br	朱元晦
w	黃榦	au	性	bs	陸子靜
x	周敦頤	av	道	bt	格物

bu 朱子文集
bv 象山全集
bw 王懋竑
bx 朱子年譜
by 朱子語類
bz 正中
ca 慧能
cb 六祖壇經
cc 列子
cd 莊子
ce 齊

cf 宋
cg 馮友蘭
ch 端木
ci 賜
cj 太極圖說
ck 周子全書
cl 清華
cm 周禮
cn 王文成公全書
co 秦家懿
cp 智的直覺與中國哲學

cq 錢穆
cr 朱子新學案
cs 三民
ct 從陸象山到劉蕺山
cu 朱子哲學思想的發展
   與完成
cv 遺書
cw 二程全書
cx 坤
cy 正蒙

25

A Reappraisal of
Chu Hsi's Philosophy

Ts'ai Jen-hou

The Background of Chu Hsi's Philosophy

*The Philosophical Development of the Three Forerunners
of Northern Sung*

IN THE SIX HUNDRED YEARS of development of Neo-Confucianism from the
Sung (960–1279) to the Ming dynasty (1368–1644), Chou Tun-i[a] (1017–
1073), Chang Tsai[b] (1020–1077), Ch'eng Hao[c] (1032–1085), and Ch'eng I[d]
(1033–1107) of the Northern Sung (960–1126); Hu Hung[e] (1106–1161), Chu
Hsi (1130–1200), and Lu Hsiang-shang (Lu Chiu-yüan,[f] 1139–1193) of the
Southern Sung (1127–1179); and Wang Yang-ming (Wang Shou-jen,[g] 1472–
1529) and Liu Tsung-chou[h] (1578–1645) of the Ming dynasty were the central figures. They were mutually related and closely connected, and they were
responsive to one another in respect to the development of philosophical
problems.[1] With the fundamental teachings of the Confucian Classics in
mind, the Confucianists of Northern Sung developed their philosophical
thoughts. They started with the notions of the Way of Heaven (*T'ien-tao*[i]) and
sincerity (*ch'eng*[j]) of the *Doctrine of the Mean* and the *Book of Changes*. Then
they turned back to the notions of *jen*[k] (humanity), *hsin*[l] (mind), and *hsing*[m]
(nature) of the *Analects* and the *Book of Mencius*, and finally ended with the
notion of the examination of things (*ko-wu*[n]) and the investigation of principle
to the utmost (*ch'iung-li*[o]) of the *Great Learning*.[2] In the rise of Sung Neo-Confucianism, cultural and moral consciousness go side by side, and there are
a number of distinguished scholars. Those who could truly understand
and develop the fundamental teachings of Confucius (551–479 B.C.), Mencius (372–289 B.C.?), and pre-Ch'in (221–206 B.C.) Confucianists, and who
could lay down the philosophical pattern of Neo-Confucianism were the three
forerunners of Northern Sung, namely Chou Tun-i, Chang Tsai, and
Ch'eng Hao.

Chou Tun-i, with his "tacit understanding of the mystery of Tao,"[p3]
explained *ch'ien-yüan*[q] (the originator) and *ch'ien-tao*[r] (the Way of Heaven) of

the *Book of Changes* in terms of sincerity of the *Doctrine of the Mean* and thus revived the metaphysical insight of pre-Ch'in Confucianism. Chang Tsai, whose thoughts comprehended the whole process of creation and penetrated the Way of Heaven, nature, and the Mandate of Heaven, talked of the reality of nature (*hsing-t'i*[s]) directly in terms of the reality of Tao, and achieved an appropriate understanding of the *jen* of Confucius and the "original mind" of Mencius. Finally, Ch'eng Hao, with his well-rounded and integrative intelligence, developed the notion of *i-pen*[t] (one source)[4] and completed the model of the teaching of Confucianism that "mind, nature, and Heaven are one."[5]

Tao manifests in oneness whether from the subjective or objective point of view. Tao is nothing other than the moral creativity of "onto-cosmological reality"[6] or penetration of cosmological creation. Consequently, the objective sincerity and the Way of Heaven and the subjective *jen*, mind, and nature are all (1) statically ontological beings, (2) dynamically cosmological principle of creation, and (3) the reality of creation of moral creativity.[7]

The Principle of Heaven (*T'ien-li*[u]), which Ch'eng Hao is said to have realized himself, has precisely these three meanings. Therefore, the Principle of Heaven is a term of far-reaching and pregnant significance. Other terms like the Way of Heaven, the Mandate of Heaven, the Great Ultimate (*T'ai-chi*[v]), the reality of the Great Vacuity (*T'ai-hsü*[w]), sincerity, spirit (*shen*[x]), equilibrium (*chung*[y]), *jen*, nature, and mind all could be covered by this Principle of Heaven, which is the reality possessing creativity and consciousness.[8] The way that Ch'eng Hao realized the original reality of the Principle of Heaven (Tao, nature, mind) existentially echoed the insight of the life of pre-Ch'in Confucianism and thus revitalized and reaffirmed the original patterns of the *Analects*, the *Book of Mencius*, the *Doctrine of the Mean*, and the *Book of Changes*. On the other hand, it continued naturally the philosphical trend opened up by Chou Tun-i, and, having absorbed the contributions of Chang Tsai, completed a system of Neo-Confucian philosophy. This idea of the Principle of Heaven is the ground for calling the Confucianism of Sung through Ming the "School of Principle" or the "School of Nature and Principle." However, the Principle of Heaven is not just a principle. It is also mind and spirit because it is the reality "which is absolutely quiet and inactive and which when acted upon immediately penetrates all things."[9] It is the mysterious reality of "the deep and endless [Mandate of Heaven],"[10] that is, the reality which has creativity and consciousness. It is both being (because it could promote the continuous production of material force 'ch'i'[z] and has creativity) and activity.[11]

Change of Direction

When the Ch'eng brothers were teaching together, their ideas came mainly from Ch'eng Hao. After his death, Ch'eng I taught independently for more than twenty-two years and gradually developed his own line of thought. Following his own simple, straightforward, analytical way of thinking, he under-

stood Tao and nature as merely principle. As merely principle, it is consequently neither mind nor spirit, and Tao and nature can no longer be said to
be that which is absolutely quiet and inactive and which when acted upon
immediately penetrates all things. Without such meaning, Tao as principle
becomes merely being, without any activity.[12] Hence the idea that Tao is onto-
cosmological creativity is lost. The same is true of nature. Furthermore,
Ch'eng I split Mencius' idea of the original mind as nature into three parts:
mind, nature, and feeling. To him, nature is mere principle and belongs to
what exists before physical form, while mind and feeling belong to material
force and to what exists after physical form. (Later Chu Hsi adopted this line
of thought and said, "Mind is the intelligence of material force and feeling is
the change of material force."[13]) As activity could not be attributed to principle (or nature), it must be attributed to material force, that is, mind and feeling. Thus, nature, too, becomes merely being and inactive.

Because of the one-sidedness in his understanding of the reality of Tao and
nature, Ch'eng I's philosophy shows a departure from the mainstream of
Confucianism. However, Ch'eng I himself was not conscious of this change in
direction. Nor were the disciples of the Ch'eng brothers. They simply followed and taught the doctrines of the two Ch'engs, which are basically
Ch'eng Hao's ideas, and did not follow Ch'eng I's new direction. Hu Hung of
the first decades of Souther Sung continued the teachings of the three forerunners of Northern Sung, opening up the framework of concretization of nature
through the mind.[14] Hu Hung's moral practice of upward self-consciousness[15]
in understanding of the reality of *jen*[16] is all the more obviously a direct heritage from Ch'eng Hao, showing no influence from Ch'eng I's new direction at
all. Therefore, up to the time of Hu Hung, and possibly including Chu Hsi's
teacher, Li T'ung[aa] (1093–1163), too, the departure of Ch'eng I from the
mainstream was but an undercurrent which had not attracted the attention of
scholars.

Ch'eng I's approach was made explicit only after Chu Hsi had consolidated
the result of his reflections and investigation on equilibrium and harmony
(*chung-ho*[ab]) in his fortieth year. This was already more than sixty years after
Ch'eng I's death. Although Chu's mind set seems to have been almost the
same as Ch'eng I's, he followed Ch'eng I's direction only after a number of
reflections and digressions. If we take the completed philosophical system of
Chu Hsi as the standard, then his thoughts before forty were but records of
his effort at learning and thinking; they had no "real insight into reality."[17]
After forty, Chu Hsi followed his inclination in agreement with Ch'eng I's
mentality and consciously completed the latter's departure in a natural way,
thus opening up a new philosophical system.

The Relation of Chu Hsi to Northern Sung Confucianists

Traditionally, Neo-Confucianism has been differentiated into the two schools
of Ch'eng-Chu and Lu-Wang. This differentiation, however, is not only in-

capable of making clear the truth of the six hundred years of history of thoughts from the Sung to the Ming dynasty, but is also incapable of revealing completely the whole of the philosophies of Neo-Confucianism. What is generally called "Ch'eng-Chu" refers only to the ideas of Ch'eng I and Chu Hsi, overlooking those of Ch'eng Hao. In contradiction to the facts of the history of thought, the ideas of Ch'eng Hao have no significance in this so-called School of Ch'eng-Chu. According to Ch'eng Hao's teaching, for example, mind, nature, and Heaven (principle) are one, and we therefore not only can say that "nature is principle (*hsing chi li*[ac])" but also that "mind is principle (*hsin chi li*[ad])."[18] But we can not say so in the cases of Ch'eng I and Chu Hsi because for them the mind is the concrete mind that belongs to the realm of material force. It is therefore erroneous in respect to philosophical thought to place Ch'eng Hao in the same system with Ch'eng I and Chu Hsi. The Hu-Hsiang[ae] School of Hu Hung, which carried on the development of the three forerunners of Northern Sung, is in fact the orthodox descendant of Northern Sung Confucianism. Hu's philosophical framework of concretization of nature through the mind and concretization of nature by developing the mind to the utmost[19] has the essential necessity and importance. Though this system declined for four or five hundred years, Liu Tsung-chou echoed this idea of concretization[20] and completed another philosophical system just before the downfall of the Ming dynasty—the end of the six hundred years of development of learning from the Sung to the Ming. Cognizant of these problems, Professor Mou Tsung-san,[af] in his book *Hsin-t'i yü hsing t'i*[ag] (Substance of mind and substance of nature), has differentiated the Neo-Confucian schools according to their philosophical systems. The three forerunners of Northern Sung developed new philosophical ideas but did not divide into different schools. After them, there have been the School of Ch'eng I and Chu Hsi, the School of Lu Hsiang-shan and Wang Yang-ming, and the School of Hu Hung and Liu Tsung-chou. The second and third can ultimately be unified into one school, though they need to be understood independently. As to how this unified school can relate to or articulate with that of Ch'eng I and Chu Hsi, that is another problem. Here we can only assert that the three schools were all guided by a moral consciousness, and with the main themes of mind and nature, completed a grand system of learning that teaches moral cultivation of sageliness within. Professor Mou's division is not based on a subjective viewpoint but relies on objective facts of philosophical systems. He achieved this step by step through a detailed clarification of their philosophy at every level. The crucial point of this clarification, however, lies with the Ch'eng brothers and Chu Hsi.

Ch'eng Hao was a great philosopher among Neo-Confucianists and enjoyed a very prominent status. But we cannot recognize his true face in those chapters (13 and 14) of the *Sung-Yüan hsüeh-an*[ah] (Anthology and critique of Sung and Yüan Neo-Confucianists) concerning him; and more than half of the "two masters' sayings" (chapters 1–10) in the *Erh-Ch'eng i-shu*[ai] (Surviving works of the two Ch'engs) does not identify which were Ch'eng Hao's sayings and which were Ch'eng I's. How, then, can we identify which is which? After careful reconsideration, Professor Mou decided to start with the different mentality of the Ch'eng brothers, to take as standard the four chapters (11–14) of Ch'eng Hao's sayings in the *I-shu* recorded by Liu Hsüan (Liu Chih-fu[aj]), and to include the small number of sayings of the Ch'eng brothers in the first ten chapters of the *I-shu* that had been identified as Ch'eng Hao's.[21] According to these three points, Professor Mou established clues to identifying Ch'eng Hao's insight; then by copying and comparing several times, he finally edited Ch'eng Hao's sayings into eight sections—the Tao of Heaven, the Principle of Heaven, Criticism of Buddhism, the Doctrine of One Source, What Is Inborn Is Nature, the Understanding of *jen*, Calming Human Nature, the Disposition of Sages and Worthies—thus making clear the major ideas and structure of Ch'eng Hao's philosophy. With Ch'eng Hao's philosophy clarified, Ch'eng I's philosophy is also clarified. His sayings have also been edited into eight sections—Principle and Material Force; Nature and Feeling; Physical Nature; Ability and Nature; On Mind, Equilibrium, and Harmony; Abiding in Seriousness and Accumulating Righteousness; Examination of Things; and Investigation of the Principle of Things to the Utmost. Ch'eng I's thoughts and approach have thus been made clear.[22]

Chu Hsi wrote a large amount of philosophical literature. However, his most important formulation and the focus of his hard work is his reflection and investigation on the problem of equilibrium and harmony. This is followed by his discussion in his "Jen shuo"[ak] (Treatise on *jen*).[23] These thoughts emerge only gradually in the process of his own painstaking reflections and through discussions with the disciples of Hu Hung. Only by following this clue of development can we clarify and ascertain the framework and central ideas of Chu Hsi's philosophy.

Chu Hsi seldom distinguished the two Ch'engs, treating them as one person. By "Master Ch'eng," Chu Hsi usually referred to Ch'eng I. Moreover, those ideas of Chu Hsi's that are more definite and well established have mostly come from Ch'eng I. As to Ch'eng Hao's sayings, he usually considered them to be indefinite, too profound, or too difficult for students. In effect, he was not too satisfied with Ch'eng Hao. Of course, Chu Hsi honors Ch'eng Hao, but his praises have nothing to do with Ch'eng Hao's teaching. Therefore, Ch'eng Hao does not have an important position in his mind. As a matter of fact, Chu Hsi transmitted only Ch'eng I's philosophy but not Ch'eng Hao's. As to Chou Tun-i and Chang Tsai, though Chu Hsi honored them very much and drew from their works, he had no real understanding of the key notions of their realization of Tao and nature. Hence, the assertion that Chu Hsi synthesized the School of Principle of Northern Sung into a grand system must be reexamined.[24] With respect to editing, writing of commentaries, and wide and broad academic discussions, Chu Hsi showed definitely the pattern of a grand synthesis. However, to say that Chu Hsi achieved a grand synthesis of the Northern Sung School of Principle involves problems of philosophical systems and approaches to moral practice, which need careful differentiation. These problems should not be skipped over lightly, obscuring the true history of philosophical thought.

Chu Hsi and the Confucianists of Southern Sung

The Relation between Chu Hsi and the Early Fukien School

The two Ch'eng brothers had two bright students, Hsieh Liang-tso[al] (1050–c. 1120) and Yang Shih[am] (1053–1135). The School of the Ch'eng brothers was transmitted by them during the early period of Southern Sung. The teaching of Hsieh Liang-tso developed into the Hu-Hsiang School through Hu An-kuo[an] (1074–1138) and his son Hu Hung, while the teaching of Yang Shih developed into the Fukien School before Chu Hsi.

Yang Shih passed on the teachings to Lo Ts'ung-yen[ao] (1072–1135) and then to Li T'ung. All were natives of the Nan-chien[ap] County of Fukien, hence the Fukien School. Yang Shih talked of *jen* in terms of commiseration and of the reality of *jen* in terms of "the myriad things and I are one." These are obviously ideas from Ch'eng Hao. Even in talking about the extension of knowledge, examination of things, and investigation of principle to the utmost, he did not follow Ch'eng I's approach of a subject-object opposition, and never had the meaning of recognition in terms of knowing and known. Yang Shih proposed to observe equilibrium before feelings are aroused.[25] This is "returning to tranquillity to reveal reality."[26] It is the approach of realizing reality through the moral practice of upward self-consciousness, and is quite different from the way Ch'eng I talked about equilibrium and harmony. Hu An-kuo once remarked that Yang Shih's insight lay in *Doctrine of the Mean*, and "this comes directly from Master[aq] Ming-tao [Ch'eng Hao]."[27] When Yang Shih, a native of the South, left for home and said good-bye to him, Ch'eng Hao saw him off and said, "My teaching goes South from now on."[28] From the line of development of Yang Shih's philosophy, we know that Ch'eng Hao knew his student well.

Lo Ts'ung-yen was a man of earnest devotion who practiced what he taught. He studied under Yang Shih for more than twenty years, working hard to achieve the final goal of sagehood through study and practice. The most essential moral practice he taught is to observe in tranquillity what the disposition is like before the feelings are aroused. This practice of realizing reality through returning to tranquillity to reveal reality is the cornerstone of his philosophy.[29]

Li T'ung studied under Lo Ts'ung-yen at the age of twenty-four; he then led a simple and poverty-stricken village life for more than forty years but felt no qualms about it at all. His teaching also takes the "observation of the original state before the feelings are aroused" as his approach to Tao.[30] Huang

Tsung-hsi[ar] (1610–1695) remarked that this is "a straight approach from Ming-tao down to Yen-p'ing[as] [Li T'ung]."[31] Chu Hsi also said that "this is the formula of moral practice of the followers of Kuei-shan[at] [Yang Shih]."[32] Chu Hsi first went to see Li T'ung at the age of twenty-four, and again at twenty-nine. It was not till he was thirty-one, however, that Chu Hsi formally became a pupil of Li T'ung. Three years later Li T'ung passed away. He never lectured nor wrote any books. It was through Chu Hsi's questioning and recording of his sayings in the *Yen-p'ing ta-wen*[au] (Replies of Li T'ung)[33] that his philosophy has become known to the world. Chu Hsi received from Li T'ung the theme of observing the equilibrium before feelings are aroused and worked very hard on the problem of equilibrium and harmony but could not understand and penetrate Li T'ung's transcendental approach of realization through upward self-consciousness. From the age of forty on, Chu Hsi turned away from Li T'ung's teaching and followed instead Ch'eng I's approach.

Chu Hsi at one point remarked, "I am afraid that Master Lo's teaching, in the final analysis, has a defect."[34] He regarded Li T'ung's teaching as leaning too much toward tranquillity and felt unsatisfied. As to Yang Shih's philosophy, Chu Hsi also criticized it at times. I believe that Yang Shih and his followers have their own importance without Chu Hsi, and Chu Hsi need not be attached to the line of development of Yang Shih, Lo Ts'ung-yen, and Li T'ung to be great. Chu Hsi's own philosophy is profound, substantial, broad, and great, and could simply be called "Chu Hsi's School"; it need not be referred to as "the School of Fukien." Ch'eng I and Chu Hsi form a separate school while Yang Shih's School is but a branch of Ch'eng Hao's. Therefore, the Fukien School of Southern Sung is more properly regarded as belonging to Yang Shih, Lo Ts'ung-yen, and Li T'ung.[35]

It is true that Chu Hsi was a student of Li T'ung, but with respect to philosophical development, Chu Hsi did not transmit the teachings of Yang Shih and Li T'ung. The remarks of Huang Tsung-hsi that "Kuei-shan's philosophy was inherited by Chu Tzu in the third generation and thus became ever more flourishing"[36] is but a vague statement purely from the apparent line of succession. What Chu Hsi made prominent was Ch'eng I's teaching and not Yang Shih's. In fact, the latter's line of transmission ended with Li T'ung.

Chu Hsi and the Hu-Hsiang School and Their Approaches to Moral Practice

After the death of the Ch'eng brothers, their teaching spread to the South. It split into two and centered respectively in Li T'ung and Hu Hung. Both of them were simple, pure, profound, and incisive persons. They were capable of absorbing and maintaining the teachings of Northern Sung and, because of their concentration on and close attention to the essential problems, both established definite approaches toward moral practice.[37] Li T'ung insisted on tranquil meditation to observe the original disposition before the feelings are aroused. This is transcendental realization of reality through upward self-consciousness developed from the realization of equilibrium and harmony to the highest degree discussed in the *Doctrine of the Mean*. This approach is necessarily implied by the idea of returning to tranquillity to reveal reality and also by the moral practice of being watchful when alone. Hu Hung taught immediate realization of conscience wherever it shows itself and positively affirming it to be the reality. This is immanent realization of reality through upward self-consciousness. It was developed from Mencius' idea of collecting one's lost mind and Ch'eng Hao's understanding of the reality of *jen*.

In transcendental realization of reality through upward self-consciousness, one has to be detached temporarily from actual life. This detachment is what is meant by being transcendental. What is immanent is to have no detachment from actual life but to realize reality right here. However, tranquil meditation in detachment for the realization of the reality of equilibrium (the original reality of the Principle of Heaven) is but one step. We need to go further; we must continually purify and cultivate our minds so that the reality of the Principle of Heaven can be actualized in our lives. It can then be concretely manifested in moral actions and create moral values. Li T'ung knew this well, and after pointing out the realization of the reality of the Principle of Heaven through sitting in silence and purifying the mind, he went on to point out that we need "defrosting and warming up"[38] to allow principle to be in harmony with actual affairs and arrive at the universal operation of the Principle of Heaven. These two steps are the philosophical procedures implied by the approach of transcendental realizaiton of reality: Thus, those who are detached must nevertheless return to actual living. Hu Hung, however, taught immediate realization of conscience wherever it shows itself in our daily life and positively affirming it to be the reality. He thus needs no tranquil meditation or detachment. This is what is referred to as "Tao is right here and now." Therefore, though moral practice through upward self-consciousness possesses two aspects, namely, the transcendental and the immanent, the immanent approach is especially essential in the moral practice of recovering one's original mind and is also the essential point of moral practice with respect to sageliness within. Though Hu Hung's philosophy declined after only one generation, the philosophical framework and approach to moral practice that he opened up are of distinctive merit.

Hu Hung once said, "King Hsüan[av] of Ch'i[aw] saw the cow and could not bear to kill it. This is the budding of conscience, revealed in the midst of the pursuing of profit and desires. Once revealed, if one practices and preserves it, preserves and cultivates it, cultivates and extends it so it becomes great, then it will be identical with Heaven. This mind lies within every man. Its beginning of revelation varies. The essential point is to recognize it and that is all."[39] He is following Mencius in pointing out that moral practice starts with the revelation of conscience. He also said, "If one wants to practice *jen*, he must first of all understand the reality of *jen*."[40] This comes directly from Ch'eng Hao's teaching that "the student must first of all understand the reality of *jen*, . . . Understand this principle and preserve it with sincerity and seriousness."[41] Chu Hsi did not understand the meaning of Hu Hung's *Chih-yen*[ax] (Knowing words) and raised eight points in questioning it.[42] Many of the followers of the Hu-Hsiang School responded sharply. Among them, Chang Shih[ay] (1133–1180) accepted most of Chu Hsi's arguments, but he never abandoned the approach of "recognizing first and then cultivating." (This is the only argument of the Hu-Hsiang School that Chang Nan-hsüan[az] [Chang Shih] did not abandon; had he abandoned this, he could no longer be considered a disciple of Hu Hung.) The following explanation shows how Chu Hsi and the Hu-Hsiang School differ in their approaches to moral practice.

What Chang Nan-hsüan referred to as "recognizing first" is recognizing the beginning of the revelation of conscience, that is, beginning to understand the reality of *jen*. This is nothing other than the approach of immanent realization of reality through upward self-consciousness. And what he referred to as "and then cultivating" is cultivating *jen* after its recognition, which is the same as Ch'eng Hao's teaching of "preserve it with sincerity and seriousness." To cultivate here means to cultivate the original mind (conscience, the mind of *jen*). This moral practice is to proceed from the a priori reality of the mind; it is autonomous morality.

Chu Hsi, however, after the age of forty, followed Ch'eng I's teaching of "self-cultivation requires seriousness; the pursuit of learning depends on the extension of knowledge."[43] Ch'eng I kept his eyes on the a posteriori physical mind, teaching that one should cultivate the mind of seriousness which manifests itself by arousing the physical mind into action with solemnity and consolidation so that it can approach the reality of the Principle of Heaven in the sense of "Nature is Principle," and finally turning this physical mind into the mind of Tao (the mind that conforms to Tao.) Chu Hsi followed Ch'eng I's line and developed the pattern of moral practice in terms of "preserving it in tranquillity and observing it in action so that seriousness pervades both action and tranquillity."[44] He also recognized that we have first gradually to cultivate and become clear at the time of tranquillity (that is, when nothing is happening), thus eliminating all selfish desires and impure ideas with a solemn and serious mind, in order to arrive at the state of "being as clear as a mirror and as still as water"[45] and "the mind becoming tranquil and principle completely understood."[46] And then, when action takes place (when we respond to things), we can employ the enlightenment of our knowing mind, which is a manifestation of the cultivated and preserved serious mind, to recognize the change of aroused feelings and make their manifestations conform to principle, thus achieving the harmony in which all feelings attain due measure and degree. Consequently, he could not agree with Chang Nan-hsüan's proposal of "recognizing first and then cultivating," but insisted on "cultivating first and then recognizing."[47]

In fact, both parties understood the terms "to cultivate" and "to recognize" quite differently. Each of them justified what he held on the basis of his own theory and approach and was quite ignorant of the origin of the ideas of the other party. Their argument over which should come first and which later leads, of course, nowhere.

The Contention between Chu Hsi and Lu Hsiang-shan

Both the Fukien School and the Hu-Hsiang School of the early Southern Sung developed the philosophies of Northern Sung. A little later, Lu Hsiang-shan of Kiangsi started the School of Mind based directly on Mencius' teaching. Throughout his life he was Chu Hsi's staunchest opponent.

Starting from the meeting at the Goose Lake Temple in 1175, what is usually referred to as "differences and similarities of Chu-Lu"[48] has been a constant, hotly debated topic. Though it is generally known that the central point of dispute between Chu and Lu centers on the problem of "nature is principle" and "mind is principle," what these two sentences really mean is not clearly understood. In adopting Mencius' teaching that original mind is nature, Lu Hsiang-shan's "mind is principle" implies "nature is principle"; in the works of Wang Yang-ming the sentence "nature is principle" appears more than once.[49] Therefore, it is obvious that Lu and Wang asserted, as Chu Hsi did, that "nature is principle." But Ch'eng-Chu (meaning Ch'eng I and Chu Hsi, without including Ch'eng Hao) could not assert that "mind is principle," because what Chu Hsi understood by "mind," "nature," and "principle" differed not only from Lu Hsiang-shan but also from the mainstream of the Confucian tradition.

To Chu Hsi, the mind is the concrete mind of material force but not the original moral mind of transcendental reality. Nature is what is opposed to mind; it is not the original mind or that which is identical with the mind. Principle is merely principle that has only being but is inactive; it no longer possesses the meaning of mind, of spirit, or of that which is silent and inactive but which when acted upon immediately penetrates all things. It is no longer the principle that is at once being and activity. In a word, Chu Hsi did not understand the meaning of the original mind of Mencius and assigned the mind to the realm of material force. Consequently, he decided that mind is not principle and that only nature is principle (and a mere principle).[50]

Lu Hsiang-shan followed Mencius' teaching that the original mind is nature and hence argued against Chu Hsi. He maintained not only that nature is principle, but that mind, the original moral mind, which possesses its own a priori lawfulness, is principle also. He therefore asserted with no hesitation that "mind is principle." From these, it is obvious that the difference between Chu and Lu centers on the problem whether the mind and nature are one. If the original mind is nature and if mind and nature are one, then the philosophies of Chu and Lu can be unified. If there can be no change in the expressions of Chu Hsi's philosophy that "mind and nature are two" and that "mind and principle are two," then their differences in philosophy are necessarily and definitely beyond reconciliation. The rest of their disputes are unimportant and can be resolved and their entanglements removed. The following paragraphs summarize their disputes.[51]

Extensive Learning and Concentrated Moral Cultivation. Chu Hsi insisted on general survey and broad learning first, followed by concentrated moral cultivation. Lu Hsiang-shan, on the other hand, insisted on discovering and manifesting the original mind first and then turning to extensive learning. Thus in teaching how to learn, the two thinkers differed in their approaches and methodology. But if we consider the matter on the basis of instructions for moral cultivation aiming at sageliness within, this dispute should not be regarded as merely a question of methodology. It should be a question of what is essential and what is nonessential. What comes first or later should be determined by its being essential or not. Seen in this light, the dispute can readily be resolved.

Over-Simplicity versus Isolated Details. Chu Hsi believed that the way Lu Hsiang-shan taught people was too simple, while Lu Hsiang-shan believed that the way Chu Hsi taught people was one of isolated details. To be fair, what Lu Hsiang-shan taught is not *too* simple. Its simplicity and ease is nothing other than the teaching of "simplicity and easiness which lead to the universal principle of all things" in the *Book of Changes*.[52] To be simple and easy is to establish first of all what is important and to discover and manifest the original mind. It is not to teach people not to read. In accusing Chu Hsi of teaching isolated details, Lu Hsiang-shan is pointing out that Chu Hsi's teaching of extensive learning is in fact irrelevant to the moral cultivation for sageliness within and has nothing to do with moral practice. He is not asserting that extensive learning and book reading are isolated details themselves. If this distinction is made, a way can be found to resolve their differences.

Honoring Moral Nature and Following the Path of Inquiry and Study. Chu Hsi thought that Lu Hsiang-shan emphasized "honoring the moral nature" while he himself was more inclined to "following the path of inquiry and study." So he wanted to "do away with the weakness of both and combine what is good in both." But Lu Hsiang-shan asked, "If we do not know how to honor the moral nature, how can we follow the path of inquiry and study?"[53] In fact, there is a first level of following the path of inquiry and study, which is relevant to the honoring of the moral nature, and also a second level of following the path of inquiry and study, which is completely irrelevant or of little relevance to honoring the moral nature. However, since Lu Hsiang-shan referred particularly to the former, and Chu Hsi made no differentiation between the two levels, a deadlock ensued. Today, we see that the second level of following the path of inquiry and study not only does no harm to moral practice, it can also help and enlarge our moral practice. The problem is just that Chu Hsi could not accept the moral creativity of the original mind and Lu Hsiang-shan could not allow the independent significance of the second level of following the path of inquiry and study. Had they calmly tried to understand each other's approach to philosophy, they might have understood each other and found a way of resolution.

In addition to these disagreements there is the dispute on the essay "T'ai-chi-t'u shuo"[ba] (Explanation of the Diagram of the Great Ultimate). In regard to the problem itself, Chu Hsi was more refined than Lu Hsiang-shan, who was merely giving vent to his pent-up feelings on some extraneous pretext. And Chu Hsi's argument is basically correct except in his understanding that the Great Ultimate is merely principle, which is not the original meaning in the context of Chou Tun-i's thought.[54]

Reappraisal of the School of Chu Hsi

Successes and Limitations

In the above, we have undertaken a simple and clear discussion of the background of Chu Hsi's School and his differences and similarities with the Southern Sung Confucianists. We have found that Chu Hsi had no real and appropriate understanding of the reality of Tao and nature as they were understood by the three forerunners of Northern Sung. Chu Hsi totally disagreed with and could not understand Ch'eng Hao's teaching and his discussions on jen and the mind. He was also opposed to Hsieh Liang-tso's explanation of jen in terms of consciousness and to Yang Shih's teaching of the reality of jen in terms of the unity of myriad things and the self. Furthermore, he could not realize or grasp Li T'ung's approach of transcendental realization in moral practice or Hu Hung's doctrine of immanent realization. As to Lu Hsiang-shan's teaching that the mind is principle, which originated from Mencius, Chu Hsi likewise could not understand and, what is more, debated the proposition vigorously. Later on, the School of Wang Yang-ming adopted Lu Hsiang-shan's philosophy and opposed Chu Hsi strongly. Why did these differences arise? We may propose an answer to the question by considering the success and limitations of Chu Hsi in the School of Nature and Principle in relation to the full and limited meanings of the terms "nature" and "principle."

The full meaning of the terms can be expressed by stating that nature is principle—that is, mind, spirit, that which is silent and inactive but which when acted upon immediately penetrates all things and unifies all things. Principle is the principle of creativity that can promote the continual production of the material force; it is therefore both being and activity.

The limited meaning of the terms can be expressed by stating that nature is mere principle—that is, mind, spirit, that which is silent and active but which when acted upon immediately penetrates all things; these things, however, are all detached from the reality of nature and belong to the realm of material force. In cosmology, principle and material force are in opposition to each other; so are principle and spirit. In moral practice, mind and nature are in opposition to each other; so are mind and principle. Principle becomes an ontological static being; it cannot have a creative function to promote continual production and is consequently mere being with no activity.

Studying these distinctions, we can see that the reality of Tao and nature as understood and realized by the Sung and Ming Confucianists does in fact differ in both full and limited meanings. The differentiation of philosophical systems in Neo-Confucianism lies precisely here. Chu Hsi, following Ch'eng I's thoughts and approach, understood the reality of Tao and nature as mere being without activity. Therefore, the meaning of nature and principle that he maintained is the limited one.[55] Objectively speaking, the system that Chu Hsi completed[56] is a system of ontological being. From the view of onto-cosmology, the Great Ultimate or principle is an ontological being, while the myriad aspects of material force result from cosmological creation and evolution. Subjectively speaking, the system that Chu Hsi completed is a system of static cultivation and static apprehension. By static cultivation is meant the cultivation of the physical mind in a static state; by static apprehension is meant the cognitive apprehension of the cognitive mind. Chu Hsi's system, then, is a system of horizontal apprehension. Its approach to moral practice is the approach of outward apprehension.

Because of the limited meaning of mind, nature, and principle in Chu Hsi's system, it naturally differs from the vertical system (with its approach to moral practice through upward self-consciousness) espoused by such philosophers as Lu Hsiang-shan, Wang Yang-ming, and Ch'eng Hao. Chu could not understand those teachings which conceived the reality of Tao, nature, *jen*, and mind as both being and active; it was this misunderstanding that led to the dispute. In other words, Chu Hsi could not understand properly, could not appreciate, and even disliked as a consequence of misunderstanding, all terms that belonged to onto-cosmological vertical penetration (vertical system). And he claimed that everything he was unsatisfied with all belonged to the vertical system. The only person he praised with no qualms at all was Ch'eng I.[57]

The thoughts of Chu Hsi himself are very precise and consistent. As he was also earnest, sincere, and diligent, he could not make many mistakes. His bias or defect lies mainly in his following Ch'eng I's direction and understanding the reality of Tao and nature as mere being without activity. And because of this understanding, Chu's approach to the problem of moral practice also departed from the approach of realization through upward self-consciousness of the orthodox mainstream of Confucianism.[58] Following Ch'eng I's saying that "self-cultivation requires seriousness; the pursuit of learning depends on the extension of knowledge,"[59] he opened up the framework of moral practice by espousing cultivation in tranquillity and observing in action, seriousness penetrating both action and tranquillity, and investigating Principle to the utmost in things at hand.

That Chu Hsi could carry to the utmost the thoughts and approach of Ch'eng I and independently complete a system is indeed a great achievement; through this synthesis he made a significant contribution to the history of culture and thought. However, because his system is not in line with the original archetype of the teaching of moral cultivation for sageliness which had been developed in pre-Ch'in Confucianism, his system is not identical with the tradition of the *Analect,* the *Book of Mencius,* the *Doctrine of the Mean,* and the *Book of Changes.* With respect to Sung Confucianists, Chu Hsi could not be said to be really the great synthesizer of the School of Principle of Northern Sung. He has been the central figure of disputes, and he is certainly the center or focus of philosophical Neo-Confucianism. To take him as the center of discussions of Neo-Confucianism is acceptable, but to take him as the standard is not. The highest standard is Confucius, and Ch'eng Hao can represent the model of Neo-Confucianism. With the mainstream of Confucianism as the standard, the system that Chu Hsi opened up by following Ch'eng I can not be considered a linear descendant. If it is said that Chu Hsi's is also a kind of orthodoxy, his status is due to his being the lateral offspring that becomes orthodox (*chi-pieh wei-tsung*ᵇᵇ).⁶⁰ This distinction has been made by Professor Mou, and I believe that it is appropriate and incontrovertible. It should be understood that to say so is not to downgrade Chu Hsi but rather to reveal his true color. It is to show the real significance of Chu Hsi's philosophy by getting rid of layers of obscurity and obstructions, thus recovering the hidden virtues and profound insights of Chu Hsi. As to his great contribution and influence in culture, philosophy, and thought, they are so well known that we need not emphasize them here.

The Modern Significance of Chu Hsi's Philosophy

Although Chu Hsi's system departed from the Confucian teaching of moral cultivation for sageliness within, his theory on the investigation of the principle of things can achieve new meaning and show its significance for modern times.

According to the maxim "the intelligence of the human mind has cognitive power, and everything has its principle," Chu Hsi put everything into "being so" and "why so." "Being so" refers to concrete things, things as they exist, and "why so" to the universal principle that is in everything. What he referred to as "taking things at hand and investigating the principle to the utmost"⁶¹ means employing the understanding of the cognitive mind to investigate to the utmost the principle of external things. This apprehension of the relation between the understanding of the cognitive mind and the principle in things forms his ultracognitivistic theory of investigation of things.

In Chu Hsi's system, "taking things at hand and investigating the principle to the utmost" is derived from the observations made after the feelings are aroused, but it goes a step further. It still belongs to the problem of the approach to moral practice. Here, the universal principle is the principle that includes the reality of *jen*, nature, Tao, and the Great Ultimate, and hence, in this pattern of "taking things at hand and investigating the principle to the utmost," this principle is posted as the object of the understanding of the cognitive mind. Therefore, the reality of Tao, nature, and *jen* as the principle becomes forever the object, the known, and cannot be the subject, the knowing itself. According to Chu Hsi, the responsive, conscious, cognitive mind is the only subject, the knowing. This being the case, it is no longer possible to ascribe to the substantial reality of mind what has been ascribed to it ever since Mencius: the vertical and morally creative function. As a result, mind and principle become forever two and not one. Even the unity achieved through moral practice is two in one and not originally or truly one. The morality of this kind of intellectualized moral metaphysics[62] is necessarily heteronomous. Only in the principle or Tao that the mind, nature, and principle are one, which is the source of moral creativity, and in moral actions that spring from deep and endless self-consciousness and spontaneity, with self-mastering and autonomy, with self-determination and self-direction, with autonomous command, and with absolute purity, is there autonomous morality. Since the mainstream of traditional Confucianism lies in such autonomous morality, a system of heteronomous morality such as Chu Hsi's obviously cannot be accepted as the orthodox.

Furthermore, though the pattern of investigation is cognitive, Chu Hsi's teaching of "taking things at hand and investigating the principle to the utmost" has no positive significance in the acquisition of knowledge, for the practice of investigation of the principle of existence to the utmost is wholly philosophical—that is, moral—while to be scientific, investigation must probe the definite details (of quality, quantity, relation) of things that exist. Chu Hsi's differentiation of principle and material force does, however, contain the ground that can lead to scientific knowledge: Based on principle, one can establish philosophy and moral theory. Based on material force, one can have positive knowledge.[63]

The former is the main line of Chu Hsi's philosophy, and the latter is brought forth in the process of his "following the path of study and inquiry." Furthermore, Chu Hsi showed much interest in knowledge. For instance, the discussions on heaven and earth and on spiritual beings in the second and third chapters of the *Chu Tzu yü-lei*[bc] (Classified conversations of Master Chu) are all conversations concerning things that exist. Though Chu's explanation of the formation of nature through the production and activity of material force is not up to the scientific level, his view that the production and activity of material force is physical is basically scientific, and it can surely lead to the development of science. Chu Hsi's teaching of "following the path of study and inquiry" and "examination of things and investigation of the Principle to the utmost" possesses implicitly the true spirit of cognitive understanding; it is not simply a kind of empty learning. One of Chu Tzu's outstanding disciples, Ts'ai Yüan-ting[bd] (1135–1198), had especially deep interest in this kind of pure knowledge and showed great talent in this respect. Though this is a kind of old-fashioned, prescientific spirit, it is akin to that of the scientist.[64]

Thus we see how following the steps of "taking things at hand and investigating the principle to the utmost" and going a step further—from investigating the principle of existence to the utmost to investigating definite details of things themselves—can open up the study of scientific knowledge. In any event, the mind that Chu Hsi talks about is the cognitive mind on the level of understanding. Today, if Chinese culture needs more substantial and richer development and needs to give vent to the cognitive subject in order to establish scientific knowledge, then Chu Hsi's (and also Hsün Tzu's,[be] [313–238 B.C.?]) theory on the mind and his intellectual tendency provides a good and ready framework. This is also the hidden virtue and profound insight of Chu Hsi's philosophy that need to be developed.

Translated by Lee Shui-chuen[bf]

Notes

1. This is the conclusion proposed by Professor Mou Tsung-san as a result of his eight years of arduous research in the philosophies of the Sung-Ming period. Cf. his *Hsin-t'i yü hsing-t'i* [The reality of mind and the reality of nature], Bks. I–III (Taipei: Cheng-chung[bg] Book Co., 1968–1969); his *Ts'ung Lu Hsiang-shan tao Liu Chi-shan*[bh] [From Lu Chiu-yüan to Liu Tsung-chou], (Taipei: Student Book Co., 1979); and my *Sung-Ming li-hsüeh: Pei-Sung p'ien*[bi] [The school of principle of the Sung and Ming dynasties, vol. 1: Northern Sung], (Taipei: Student Book Co., 1977); *Sung-Ming li-hsüh: Nan-Sung p'ien*[bj] [The school of principle of the Sung and Ming dynasties, vol. 2: Southern Sung], (Taipei: Student Book Co., 1980); and *Wang Yang-ming che-hsüeh*[bk] [The philosophy of Wang Yang-ming], (Taipei: San-min[bl] Book Co., 1974).

2. The *Analects*, the *Book of Mencius*, the *Doctrine of the Mean*, the *Book of Changes*, and the *Great Learning* may be regarded as the five new Classics of Sung-Ming Neo-Confucianism. Cf. *Hsin-t'i yü hsing-t'i*, Bk. I, pp. 19–20.

3. This is Yüan Neo-Confucianist Wu Ch'engs[bm] (1249–1333) phrase in his praise of Chou Tun-i. See the *Sung-Yüan hsüeh-an* (Shanghai: World Book Co., 1936), ch. 12, on Lien-hsi[bn] (Chou Tun-i), p. 306.

4. *Hsin-t'i yü hsing-t'i*, Bk. II, pp. 18, 103.

5. *Ibid.*, Bk. I, p. 44.

6. "Onto-cosmological" is a term coined by Professor Mou in his *Hsin-t'i yü hsing-t'i*. According to the metaphysics of Confucianism, the principles of ontology and cosmology could be connected and united into a whole. What the Confucianists talk of as the reality of Tao (the metaphysical reality) is not merely an ontological concept of abstract thinking, but the active reality which could all by itself manifest the function of promoting the productive and reproductive changes in the material realm. This reality of Tao is an ontological reality, and is also a cosmological principle of creation and changes (principle of creativity). Hence, Professor Mou coined the term "onto-cosmological reality" to describe it. This term indicates appropriately the characteristics of the Confucian moral metaphysics.

7. *Hsin-t'i yü hsing-t'i,* Bk. II, p. 56.

8. *Ibid.,* p. 19.

9. *Book of Changes,* "Appended Remarks," pt. 1, ch 10.

10. *Book of Odes,* ode no. 267, "The Mandate of Heaven."

11. *Hsin-t'i yü hsing-t'i,* Bk. I, p. 58.

12. *Ibid.,* pp. 58, 59.

13. Following Ch'eng I, Chu Hsi completed the framework of the tripartition of mind, nature, and feeling. His discussion can be found mainly in *Chu Tzu yü-lei,* ch. 5, under such headings as Nature and Principle and Nature, Feeling, Mind, and Will.

14. *Hsin-t'i yü hsing-t'i,* Bk. II, pp. 280, 281.

15. "Upward self-consciousness" (*nih-chiao*[bo]) is a term coined by Professor Mou Tsung-san in his *Hsin-t'i yü hsing-t'i.* The word "nih" is derived from the word "fan"[bp] (return to) as it is used in Mencius' sayings *"Yao Shun hsing-chih, T'ang Wu fan-chih"*[bq] (with Yao and Shun, their nature shows itself directly while King T'ang and King Wu returned to their nature) and "fan-shen erh ch'eng"[br] (return to oneself and being sincere). "Nih-chiao" is put into opposition with "shun-ch'u"[bs] (outward apprehension) to show the difference in the approaches of moral practice between the vertical and the horizontal systems of apprehension.

16. *Sung-Yüan hüeh-an,* ch. 42, on Wu-feng[bt] (Hu Hung), p. 781.

17. *Chu Wen-kung wen-chi*[bu] [Collection of literary works of Master Chu], (Taipei: Commerical Press, 1980), ch. 40, p. 601, second letter in reply to Ho Shu-ching.[bv]

18. "Hsing chi li" is a sentence in the *Erh-Ch'eng chi*[bw] [Collected works of the two Ch'engs], (Taipei: Li-jen[bx] Book Co., 1982), *Erh-Ch'eng i-shu,* ch. 22, p. 293. "Hsin chi li" (Mind is principle) is a sentence in the *Lu Hsiang-shan ch'üan-chi*[by] [Complete works of Lu Chiu-yüan], (Taipei: World Book Co., 1973) ch. 11, p. 95, letter to Prefect Li.[bz]

19. See *Hsin-t'i yü hsing-t'i,* Bk. II, pp. 446–454, 511–513.

20. See Professor Mou Tsung-san's *Ts'ung Lu Hsiang-shan tao Liu Ch'i-shan,* pp. 453–459.

21. *Hsin-t'i yü hsing-t'i,* Bk. II, p. 4.

22. *Ibid.,* Bk. II, pp. 21–249, pp. 251–410.

23. *Chu Wen-kung wen-chi,* ch. 67, pp. 1178–1179.

24. Cf. my *Hsin Ju-chia ti ching-shen fang-hsiang*[ca] [The spiritual direction of Neo-Confucianism], (Taipei: Student Book Co., 1982), pp. 183–185.

25. *Sung-Yüan hsüeh-an,* ch. 25 on Kuei-shan (Yang Shih), p. 552.

26. *Hsin-t'i yü hsing t'i,* Bk. II, p. 477.

27. *Sung-Yüan hsüeh-an,* ch. 25, p. 554.

28. *Erh-Ch'eng chi,* external works, ch. 12, p. 428.

29. *Ibid.,* ch. 39 on Yü-chang[cb] (Lo Ts-ung-yen), pp. 723–728.

30. *Ibid.,* on Yen-p'ing (Li T'ung), p. 728.

31. *Ibid.,* on Yü-chang, p. 727.

32. *Ibid.,* p. 735.

33. *Yen-p'ing ta-wen* was edited by Chu Hsi and included in *Li Yen-p'ing chi*[cc] [Collected works of Li T'ung] as ch. 2.

34. *Chu Tzu yü-lei* (Taipei: Han-ching[cd] Culture Co., 1980), ch. 102, p. 1032.

35. Cf. my *Sung-Ming li-hsüeh: Pei-Sung p'ien,* ch. 18, pp. 462–464.

36. *Sung-Yüan hsüeh-an,* ch. 25 on Kuei-shan, p. 549.

37. Cf. *Hsin-t'i yü hsing-t'i,* Bk. III, p. 9.

38. *Chu Wen-kung wen-chi,* ch. 97, p. 1672, "Yen-p'ing hsing-chuang"ᶜᵉ [Biographical account of Li T'ung].

39. *Sung-Yüan hsüeh-an,* ch. 42 on Wu-feng, p. 781. The reference to King Hsüan is to the *Book of Mencius,* 1A:7.

40. *Chu Wen-kung wen-chi,* ch. 73, p. 1296, "Hu Tzu *Chih-yen* i-i"ᶜᶠ [Doubts on Hu Hung's *Knowing Words*].

41. *Erh-Ch'eng chi, Erh-Ch'eng i-shu,* ch. 2, p. 16.

42. Cf. Chu Hsi's "Hu Tzu *Chih-yen* i-i" in *Chu Wen-kung wen-chi,* ch. 73, pp. 1293–1297.

43. *Erh-Ch'eng chi, Erh-Ch'eng i-shu,* ch. 18, p. 188.

44. This is Professor Mou Tsung-san's summary of Chu Hsi's framework of moral practice; it is based on Chu Hsi's "i-fa wei-fa shuo"ᶜᵍ [On the states of aroused and pre-aroused feelings] in the *Chu Wen-kung wen-chi,* ch. 67, p. 1173, and is also based on Chu Hsi's reflections on the problem of equilibrium and harmony. Cf. *Hsin-t'i yü hsing-t'i,* Bk. III, p. 134, and my *Hsin Ju-chia ti ching-shen fang-hsiang,* p. 189, where a concise account of Chu Hsi's framework of moral practice is presented.

45. *Chu Wen-kung wen-chi,* ch. 64, p. 1126, first letter to the scholars of Hunan on equilibrium and harmony.

46. *Ibid.,* ch. 56, p. 945, letter in reply to Ch'en Shih-tei.ᶜʰ

47. See my *Sung-Ming li hsüeh: Nan-Sung p'ien,* pp. 97–101.

48. Chu and Lu met at the Goose Lake Temple in 1175. From then on their differences and similarities have been discussed. Cf. *ibid.,* pp. 238–268.

49. *Wang Yang-ming ch'üan-shu*ᶜⁱ [Complete works of Wang Shou-jen], (Taipei: Cheng-chung Book Co. 1953), ch. 1, *Ch'uan-hsi lu*ᶜʲ [Instructions for practical living], pp. 12, 28, 35.

50. Cf. *Sung-Ming li-hsüeh: Nan-Sung p'ien,* pp. 187–201.

51. The discussion of the following three topics is based on *Lu Hsiang-shan ch'üan chi,* (Taipei: World Book Co., 1959), ch. 36, the biographical material of his thirty-seventh year in "Hsiang-shan nien-p'u"ᶜᵏ [Chronological biography of Lu Chiu-yüan], pp. 322–323.

52. *Book of Changes,* "Appended Remarks," pt. 1, ch. 1.

53. *Lu Hsiang-shan ch'üan-chi,* ch. 36, p. 325. Chu Hsi's words quoted by Lu are found in the *Chu Wen-kung ch'üan-chi,* ch. 54, p. 897.

54. Cf. *Hsin-t'i yü hsing-t'i,* Bk. I, pp. 404–413. The disputes on the "T'ai-chi-t'u shuo" are found in the *Chu Wen-kung ch'üan-chi,* ch. 2, pp. 14–21.

55. Cf. my *Sung-Ming li-hsüeh: Pei-Sung p'ien,* ch. 7, appendix, pp. 206–213.

56. Cf. *Hsin-t'i yü hsing-t'i,* Bk. I, p. 59; Bk. III, p. 68.

57. Both Ch'eng I and Chu Hsi belong to the system of horizontal apprehension. Their practice of investigation of things and investigating the principle to the utmost is to know (apprehend) the principle of things with the cognitive function of the mind. Such knowing results in the opposition of subject and object, and places subject and object on the same plane (horizontally). Consequently, their system is called "horizontal apprehension." Because the cognitive mind takes this approach to know or to apprehend principle, this way of moral practice is called the "outward apprehension" approach. In the vertical system, what is, in the objective way of speaking, the cosmological production and change is, in the subjective way of speaking, the moral creativity, that is, the vertical penetration of the metaphysical reality which is both being and active. This metaphysical reality is the reality of the Principle of Heaven, in which the

reality of Tao, of nature, and of mind are one. In other words, they are all motivated, created, and substantiated by the reality of the Principle of Heaven, which is the origin of creativity. Here, there is no horizontal opposition between subject and object, but vertical penetrative creativity, and hence it is called the "vertical system." In every vertical system, the approach of moral practice is realization through upward self-consciousness.

58. Cf. *Hsin-t'i yü hsing-t'i*, Bk. II, pp. 476, 477.

59. *Erh-Ch'eng chi, Erh-Ch'eng i-shu*, ch. 18, p. 188.

60. Cf. my *Hsin Ju-chia ti ching-shen fang-hsiang*, p. 176.

61. Chu Hsi's commentary on ch. 5 of the *Great Learning*.

62. See *Hsin-t'i yü hsing-t'i*, Bk. I, p. 97.

63. *Ibid.*, Bk. III, pp. 364–367.

64. Both Chu Hsi and Ts'ai Yüan-ting emphasized not only morality, but also cognitive understanding. Their emphasis on the latter is of special significance to modern Chinese culture in its development of scientific knowledge.

Glossary

a 周敦頤
b 張載
c 程顥
d 程頤
e 胡宏
f 陸象山九淵
g 王陽明守仁
h 劉宗周
i 天道
j 誠
k 仁
l 心
m 性
n 格物
o 窮理
p 道
q 乾元
r 乾道
s 性體
t 一本
u 天理
v 太極
w 太虛
x 神
y 中
z 氣
aa 李侗
ab 中和
ac 性即理
ad 心即理

ae 湖湘
af 牟宗三
ag 心體與性體
ah 宋元學案
ai 二程遺書
aj 劉絢質夫
ak 仁說
al 謝良佐
am 楊時
an 胡安國
ao 羅從彥
ap 南劍
aq 明道
ar 黃宗義
as 延平
at 龜山
au 延平答問
av 宣
aw 齊
ax 知言
ay 張栻
az 南軒
ba 太極圖說
bb 繼別為宗
bc 朱子語類
bd 蔡元定
be 荀子
bf 李瑞全
bg 正中
bh 從陸象山到劉蕺山

bi 宋明理學北宋篇
bj 宋明理學南宋篇
bk 王陽明哲學
bl 三民
bm 吳澄
bn 濂溪
bo 逆覺
bp 反
bq 堯舜性之湯武反之
br 反身而誠
bs 順取
bt 五峯
bu 朱文公文集
bv 何叔京
bw 二程集
bx 里仁
by 陸象山全集
bz 李
ca 新儒家的精神方向
cb 豫章
cc 李延平集
cd 漢京
ce 延平行狀
cf 胡子知言疑義
cg 己發未發說
ch 陳樹德
ci 王陽明全書
cj 傳習錄
ck 象山年譜

26

Chu Hsi and Hu Hung

CONRAD SCHIROKAUER

AN INVESTIGATION into the relationship between Chu Hsi and the "Hunan School" of which Hu Hung[a] (1106–1161) was the leading master can help place Chu Hsi's thought in historical perspective and also cast some light on his intellectual position by considering ideas he rejected as well as those he made his own, for the Hunan thinkers constituted a major tradition of Neo-Confucianism during Chu Hsi's youth in the early years of the Southern Sung (1127–1279).[1] Yet after Hu Hung's death in 1161 and after a change of mind of the part of Hung's chief disciple and Chu Hsi's friend Chang Shih[b] (1133–1180), the Hunan School ceased to function as a separate tradition. Only in recent decades has Hu Hung been examined by Chinese and Japanese scholars.[2] It is the purpose of this essay to consider some of his salient ideas as they affected Chu Hsi and elicited responses from him. But first an overview of the broader Hunan School is in order.

The Hunan School

The origin of the Hunan School is usually traced to Hu An-kuo[c] (1074–1138) who was from Fukien but retired to Hunan.[3] Although An-kuo was not a direct disciple of Ch'eng Hao[d] (1032–1085) or Ch'eng I[e] (1033–1107), he was linked to them through teachers and friends and was regarded by himself and others as belonging to the Ch'eng tradition.[4] By all accounts he was a staunch Confucian, and in a letter to his sons quoted by Chu Hsi in his *Hsiao-hsüeh*[f] (Elementary learning) An-kuo told his sons to aspire to be like Ch'eng Hao and Fan Chung-yen[g] (989–1052).[5] Politically, too, he defended the Northern Sung (960–1126) masters, asserting that they provided the door that gave access to the thought of Confucius (551–479 B.C.) and Mencius (372–289 B.C.?).[6]

Hu An-kuo, however, is best known for rescuing the *Ch'un-ch'iu*[h] (Spring and Autumn Annals) from the opprobrium cast on it by Wang An-shih[i] (1201–1286) and his followers who banned the work from the examination halls, the schools, and the imperial seminar ("classic mat," *ching-yen*[j]). When the Emperor asked An-kuo to edit the *Tso-chuan*[k] (Tso commentary), he decided instead to write his own commentary on the Classic, which he believed Confucius had fashioned into "an essential text for the transmission of the mind" (*ch'uan-hsin yao-tien*[l]).[7] According to An-kuo, the position of the *Annals* among the Five Classics[8] was like that of judgments in a legal tradition. The principles involved remain accessible, for what men's minds have in common remains the same through time. Although worlds apart, later scholars can still have intimate contact with the sages: "the standards of the *Annals* are in us." These were the orthodox standards—such as reverence for the ruler-father—but An-kuo's stress on the difference between Chinese and barbarians, his view that a son is duty-bound to avenge a wronged father, and his suspicion of alliances with barbarians spoke to the times and help to account for the popularity of his work.[9] An-kuo was also the author of a supplement, unfortunately no longer extant, to Ssu-ma Kuang's[m] (1019–1086) *Tzu-chih t'ung-chien*[n] (Comprehensive mirror for aid in government).

Hu An-kuo was helped in his work on the *Annals* by his son Hu Ning,[o][10] who also wrote on the *Annals* but did not attain the prominence of his younger brother, Hu Hung, or of Hu Yin[p] (1095–1156), a nephew whom An-kuo adopted as his oldest son. Hu Yin shared An-kuo's interest in history, as can be seen in his most influential work, *Tu-shih kuan-chien*[q] (Observations on reading history), which had for its purpose the application to history of the principles found in the Classics. It is thus similar in intent to Chu Hsi's *T'ung-chien kang-mu*[r] (Outline and digest of the *Comprehensive Mirror*), which was heavily influenced by Hu Yin's book. Both Hu Yin and Chu Hsi depart from Ssu-ma Kuang in insisting that history be viewed as morality. When the study of Chu Hsi as a historian is undertaken in depth, an assessment of Hu Yin's influence will surely occupy a prominent place.[11]

Hu Hung also contributed to his family's tradition of historiography. His longest, but not most highly regarded, work is the *Huang-wang ta-chi*[s] (Great records of emperors and kings), a history from the beginning of the world to the end of the Chou (1111–249 B.C.) that employs Shao Yung's[t] (1011–1077) system of dating and incorporates, among other texts, An-kuo's commentary on the *Annals*. In his preface, Hung takes up the issue of the relationship between the Classics and history, comparing the former to limbs and trunk, the latter to arteries and veins. In a comment further on in the work he states that the meanings transmitted in the Classics and the facts contained in the histories should be used to correct each other and goes on to say that facts without meaning are totally unacceptable. He does not, however, consider the opposite extreme, presumably because for him the Classics could hardly contain meanings divorced from facts.[12] Hu Hung's moral meanings, not surprisingly, resemble those of his father and brother. Comparing father and son, Chu Hsi remarked that An-kuo was correct in his discussions of the general outline and that while Hung was more subtle in fine points of detail, his general outline had deficiencies. In another short comment Chu Hsi said that although An-kuo's discussions are somewhat careless, they are good, whereas Hung is subtle but makes mistakes.[13]

The Hus' interest in historical studies seems to have been a new development in the Ch'eng brothers' tradition of learning, and Hu Hung may be considered the first Sung philosopher (depending on how that term is defined) to occupy himself with a historical project. Perhaps this concern for history was part of their response to the turbulent and traumatic history of their own era. Another element of this response was an insistence on the need for reconquest of the heartland of Chinese civilization, the Central Plain, occupied by the Chin (1115–1234). The second generation of Hus all refused to serve in the government during the ascendancy of Ch'in Kuei[u] (1090–1155, ascendant 1138–1155). As is well known, Chu Hsi shared not only the Hus' interest in history but also their longing for reconquest of the north and their contempt for Ch'in Kuei. However, he did not by any means agree with all their political or economic views. For one thing, Chu Hsi was much more even handed in his assessment of Wang An-shih. For another, he was critical of Hu Hung's drastic restorationism—advocacy of a return to the institutions of antiquity, including the well-field system.[14]

Another attitude shared by the Hus and adopted by Chu Hsi was their hostility toward Buddhism. At a time when Buddhists themselves showed sensitivity to Confucian concerns and when prominent Buddhists demonstrated their patriotism, many scholars seem to have been quite receptive to Buddhist teachings.[15] The hostility of the Hus thus seems to have been something of an anomaly. Hu Hung as well as Hu Yin challenged Buddhist views, but it was Hu Yin who did so most energetically. He wrote his *Ch'ung-cheng pien*[v] (In defense of revering correctness) with the express purpose of "exposing the depraved heterodoxy" (*hsieh-shuo*[w]) of the Buddhists and rejected any possibility of accommodation with the alien faith. Both the Buddha and Confucius could not be right. They are mutually exclusive. Both cannot stand.[16] Chu Hsi, who approved of this book,[17] came to share this hostility toward Buddhism although it does not appear that the twelfth century added anything to the arsenal of arguments long employed against Buddhists by their enemies.[18]

Early Contacts between Chu Hsi and Hunan Scholars

Chu Hsi's connection with Hunan scholars began very early, primarily through his relationship with Hu An-kuo's nephew Hu Hsien[x] (1082–1162); a friend of Chu Hsi's father, Chu Sung[y] (1097–1143); and one of the three men to whom Chu Sung entrusted the care of his son just prior to his death in 1143. Chu Hsi was thirteen at the time. Hu Hsien was a follower of An-kuo's teachings and during his university years secretly read the writings of the Ch'eng brothers, which were then proscribed. Hsien too refused to serve in government during Ch'in Kuei's time. Instead he returned home and supported himself from the land and by selling medicine. An exemplary Confucian, he was finally prevailed upon to accept a position in the local school.

Chu Hsi records that when Hsien first admonished his career-minded students by citing the *Analects,* "the ancients studied to improve themselves," he was greeted with laughter. However, when they saw that his own self-cultivation and conduct was consistent with his words, they came to respect and believe in him.[19]

After Ch'in Kuei's death Hu Hsien did accept office and in 1159 became a Correcting Editor of the Imperial Library (*Pi-shu-sheng cheng-tzu*). In response Chu Hsi composed two poems generally understood as critical of his teacher's assuming office at his advanced age and after so many years in private life. Chu Hsi and Hu Hung never met, and the only occasion the older scholar commented on the younger was when he saw a poem Chu Hsi wrote in response to a call by friends to serve in government. The men mentioned in the first two lines are Hu Hsien and Liu Kung[aa] (1122–1178), who had become a censor. A rough and tentative translation might run as follows:

> Master Hu ascends the Fragrant Hall;
> Councilor Liu puts on a censor's cap.
> Detaining the recluse in the deserted valley
> A stream's wind and moon want me to look.
>
> In front of the jar window a green screen;
> Evenings the screen and I face one another in quiet decorum.
> A floating cloud leisurely furls and unfurls.
> The everlasting green mountains just green like this.[20]

Hu Hung commented that Chu Hsi showed promise and that his words had substance but lacked function. To admonish Chu Hsi, Hu Hung too turned to poetry:

> The recluse solely loves the mountains' goodness
> Because green mountains remain green and do not age.
> Clouds issue from the mountain and rain on the world.
> Once the dust has been washed off the mountains are better still.[21]

As Professor Tomoeda[ab] has pointed out, Chu Hsi's green mountains remain in motionless tranquillity whereas Hu Hung's encompass movement as well as tranquillity as clouds rise to bring rain. In his collophon to Hu Hung's poem Chu Hsi expresses his regret at never having met Hu Hung. By the time he heard the poem from Chang Shih, Hu Hung was dead.

The Methodology of Self-Cultivation

Hu Hung's criticism came at a time when Chu Hsi, still under the predominant influence of Li T'ung[ac] (1093–1163), followed a theory of self-cultivation that emphasized quiet sitting focused on nourishing the "centrality" (*chung,*[ad] equilibrium) before the feelings are aroused rather than concentrating on scrutiny after the feelings are aroused, a distinction based on the famous passage in the first chapter of the *Chung-yung*[ae] (Doctrine of the Mean): "Before the feelings of pleasure, anger, sorrow, and joy are aroused it is called centrality. When these feelings are aroused and each and all attain due measure and degree, it is called harmony."[22] At issue was the definition of proper Confucian practice, a matter of vital concern.

Chu Hsi quotes Hu An-kuo as saying, "If you just apply yourself to the already aroused condition, there will be no waste of mental energy."[23] The position that self-cultivation should begin in the active phase was generally maintained by Hunan thinkers. The process begins when we perceive the beginnings of the originally good mind/heart (*liang-hsin*[af]) in the course of the activities of everyday life. In Hu Hung this was perhaps most clearly and forcefully expressed in a dialogue with a disciple.

> *Someone asked:* The reason why a person is not humane is that he has lost his originally good mind. Can the lost mind be used to seek for the (true) mind?
>
> *Answer:* When the King of Ch'i[ag] saw the ox and could not bear its being slaughtered, that was the sprout of the originally good mind seen in the midst of desire for profit. Once you see it, hold fast and preserve it, preserve it and nourish it, nourish and fulfill it so that it becomes enlarged. When it is great and cannot be stopped, it will be identical to Heaven. This mind is in (all) people, but the beginnings of its expression differ. What matters is to perceive it, that's all.[24]

When King Hsüan[ah] of Ch'i could not bear to see the suffering of the ox being led off to sacrifice, Mencius told him, "This mind/heart is sufficient to enable you to become a true king."[25] This episode is also cited by Chang Shih in his *T'an-chou ch'ung-hsiu Yüeh-lu shu-yüan chi*[ai] (Record of the repair of the Yüeh-lu Academy in T'an-chou) composed in 1166 where Chang explicitly uses it to provide authority for the argument that it is in daily life that we should look for the beginnings of the virtue of humaneness (*jen*[aj]), the expression of the original mind. "If we examine how during the day we serve our parents, obey our elder brothers, respond to things and deal with affairs, the beginning may appear." A little earlier in the same piece Chang stressed that the Way cannot be divorced from daily life. He then went on to outline a sequence of self-cultivation: "If we are truly able to comprehend it in silence and preserve it, extend, develop, and perfect it and the wonder of life's perpetual renewal flourishes therein, then how can we possibly fail to apprehend the substance of humanness?"[26] Although the influence of Buddhism on Chang Shih is not to be discounted,[27] this position is entirely consistent with that of Hu Hung.

Before considering the theory of mind and human nature on which this concept of self-cultivation is based, it is well to note that it begins with cognition. Hu Hung is quite insistent on this. "Studying the Way is like studying archery. Before you grasp bow and arrow you must first know the target. Only then can you seek to hit the target by accumulated practice." Later in the same discussion he says, "If knowledge is not extended first, you will not know where to end. It is like going somewhere, but the road has many forks. If you do not know where to go, seriousness cannot be enacted and there will be no ruler within."[28] In discussing the perennial question of the relationship between knowledge and action, Chang Shih, too, while strongly insisting that they are inseparable, nevertheless places knowing first: "Knowledge always comes first, and practice never fails to follow."[29]

The conviction that knowledge had priority may also have helped to reconcile an ardent patriot such as Hu Hung to a life of political inactivity during the Ch'in Kuei years, for it assigned a lofty role to the scholar in returning the dynasty to the True Way without which the Northern Plain would remain lost to China forever. The vital role of those who know is suggested by Hu Hung in this observation: "Only after those who wield the axes listen to those who handle the marking line can a mansion be completed. Only when those who handle weapons listen to those who illuminate moral principles can great undertakings be settled."[30] Another passage in *Chih-yen*[ak] (Understanding words) concerning knowledge merits quotation in full.

> People all say that men are born with knowledge. However, they are born ignorant. Knowledge comes after they have been close to teachers and made friends. Thus it is after one knows about dangers that one can plan for peace. It is after one knows destruction that one can plan for preservation. It is after one knows disorder that one can plan for order. With reference to the loyalty of Tzu-wen[al] of the State of Ch'u[am] Confucius said, "He cannot be said to know, how can he be considered humane?" How great is knowledge! Of the ten thousand things in the world none has priority over knowledge. Therefore, the superior man must first extend his knowledge.[31]

Elsewhere Hu states that although people are provided with the Tao,[an] they need study to comprehend it,[32] but he does not specify the content of that study. As may be expected of a scholar who labored long and hard on his large historical opus, Hu Hung was not one to reject book learning or relegate the Classics to a secondary role, tantamount to rejecting the sages.[33]

It is not clear how much emphasis Hu Hung would give to introspection directed toward perceiving the beginnings of the original good mind and how much emphasis he would place on knowledge gained from teachers and books. Since the passages collected in *Understanding Words* are not dated, we cannot delineate the development of his thought. There may have been a change of emphasis during his life, but this is a matter for speculation. What seems most worth noting, however, is that along with the priority given to cognition, his writings advocate both introspection and external investigation even though his position on the former commanded more attention than his quite unexceptional views on the latter.

Once the process of self-cultivation has begun, Hu Hung emphasizes the need for sustained effort and continuing practice and discusses the need for reducing the desires much as had his predecessors. Similarly he emphasizes the extension of knowledge. There is little here that seems new or exceptional. Similarly, others before him, notably the Ch'eng brothers, expounded on the role of seriousness (*ching,*[ao] reverence) a vital quality for Hu Hung as well. "Firmly guarding our mind is called seriousness. By seriousness we nourish our humaneness."[34] Elsewhere, he indicates that the preservation of heavenly principle depends on seriousness.[35] And he remarks that

> the Way of Heaven is most sincere and therefore never ceases. The way of man is to hold seriousness as fundamental in order to seek to accord with Heaven. Confucius progressed from "setting his mind on learning" to "following his heart's desires and not transgressing what is right." That is the perfection of the Way of seriousness. Seriousness is that whereby the superior man completes his life.[36]

Finally, in his record of a study named "Fu"[ap] (returning) after the twenty-fourth hexagram of the *Book of Changes*, Hu Hung incorporated a description of the process of self-cultivation including a statement on seriousness admired by Chu Hsi and later scholars.

> Men are not born to knowledge but depend on events and things for knowledge. Depending on events and things for knowledge, they are deluded by events and things, lose the mean and have no place to stop. From youth to old age they are at a loss like a traveler unable to return home and settle down. Now although we want to dispel external delusions and retain the pure heart of an infant so as to return to the mystery that gave us birth, life cannot be free of events and things and we cannot do away with them and cause them not to be. The way of Confucius is to follow human nature, guard the decree, and share the effort of heaven. Therefore, in handling events and selecting things we do not hate and reject but we must personally investigate them in order to extend our knowledge. Now events undergo all kinds of changes and the stimuli of things are inexhaustible. The way to investigate them must be to make up the mind to affirm the foundation and abide in seriousness in order to hold on to the will. When the mind is set on the exterior of events and things, and seriousness is enacted in their interior, the understanding can be refined.[37]

It is apparent that for Hu Hung as for other Neo-Confucians the mind/heart is at the center of self-cultivation. It is not only the instrument employed in self-improvement but is what makes self-cultivation possible in the first place. It can best be considered in conjunction with the nature (*hsing*[aq]).

The Nature and the Mind/Heart

Hu Hung had a strong sense of the unity of man and the universe, a perception that colors much of his philosophy. For him man is the essence of heaven and earth (*t'ien-ti chih ching*ᵃʳ).[38] Just as heaven and earth are rooted in harmony, as sun, moon, and stars are rooted in heaven, as mountains, rivers, and plants are rooted in earth, so man is rooted between heaven and earth.[39] And he lives in the Way just as fish live in water and plants on land. Removing any of them from their natural habitat leads to disaster.[40] Conversely, the ideal man is perfectly tuned to the universe, for the rhythm of the sage's life corresponds to the waxing and waning of sun and moon and the fluctuations of yinᵃˢ (passive cosmic force) and yangᵃᵗ (active cosmic force). Thus when Confucius attained perfection at the age of seventy, he became heaven.[41]

The basis for this identity is provided by human nature, for man partakes of the nature which is all encompassing. "How great the nature! The ten thousand principles are complete in it. Heaven and earth are established from it. When ordinary scholars speak of the nature, they all alike discuss it with reference to a single principle. None of them have seen the total substance of what heaven imparts."[42] Perhaps we should not be surprised at the failure of ordinary scholars, for the substance of the nature is so great and all-inclusive that even a sage cannot name it. It permeates everything, and although "things have a set nature, the nature does not have a set substance." In its creativity it cannot be checked.[43] It contains everything, and everything is contained in it. "There is no thing outside the nature and no nature outside things."[44]

Although both *li*ᵃᵘ (principle) and *ch'i*ᵃᵛ (vital force, material force) figure in his writings and sayings, Hu Hung has not left a discussion of how they are to be related to each other. But he sees both as grounded in the nature. As just indicated, all principles are complete in it. In addition, as the source of creativity it is also the "root of the vital force": "If it were not for the nature, there would be no things. If it were not for the vital force, there would be no forms. As for the nature, it is the root of the vital force."[45] It is the source: "Water has a spring, and therefore its flow is inexhaustible. Trees have roots, and therefore their lives are limitless. The vital force has the nature, and therefore its circulation is unending."[46]

With a substance so vast that even a sage cannot name it, indeed, without a set substance at all, the nature transcends all distinctions usually made in ordinary language. This includes the distinction between good and evil. "The nature is the innermost mystery of heaven and earth and the spiritual forces; good is inadequate to characterize it, let alone evil."[47] This position seems to imply not only a rejection of numerous earlier theories of human nature but also a departure from the teachings of Mencius whom Hu Hung, like other Neo-Confucians, revered and whom he defended against the critique of Ssu-ma Kuang.[48] Hu Hung explained the apparent discrepancy between his view and that of Mencius by quoting his own father as saying that Mencius' assertion was an exclamation of admiration for the nature and that he was not ascribing to it a goodness that can be contrasted with evil.[49] Chu Hsi traced this thesis through Hu An-kuo back to the Ch'anᵃʷ monk Ch'ang-tsungᵃˣ

(1025–1091), but Hu Hung would, of course, have been deeply dismayed by the suggestion that his teachings were tinged by the Buddhism he so heartily opposed.

Like other Confucians, Hu Hung insistently criticized Buddhists for their withdrawal from active life and their rejection of the ordinary world. For Hu Hung, "all the ten thousand things belong to the nature. The sages completely realized their nature (*chin-hsing*,[ay] developed their nature fully). Therefore, they did not reject things."[50] The Way itself cannot exist of itself apart from things any more than things can exist of themselves without the Way. "The Way has things like the wind has motion or water has a current. Who can separate them? Therefore, to seek for the Way apart from things is simply absurd."[51] The difference between things and the Way is that things have form and number. "What is shaped by shape is called things. What is not shaped by shape is called the Way. Things are restricted by number and have an end. The Way penetrates the transformations and is infinite."[52]

As is well known, the word "*wu*,"[az] here rendered "things," designates living creatures as well as inanimate objects, and there is no reason to suppose that this was not Hu Hung's intent in the passages just quoted. It is intrinsic to his concept of the sage that he does not reject "things" in either sense. It is the function of the sage in the world to see to it that each and every plant and animal gets its due according to the different principles inherent in its individual nature. Hu Hung's concept of things sharing a common nature yet each having its own individual nature is, of course, reminiscent of Ch'eng I's famous thesis that principle is one but its manifestations are many (*li-i fen-shu*[ba]). In any case, no creature is to be neglected; each is to be ranked and valued appropriately. Man, as "the essence of heaven and earth" and the finest *ch'i*, ranks first. "Things" exist for his use, not the other way around.[53]

The sage does not reject "things," nor does he reject feelings and desires. They too stem from the nature. In Hu Hung's version of the water analogy, "Compare human nature to water: The mind is like water running downwards, the feelings like the water's billows, the desires like the waves."[54] The sage has ordinary human emotions, but his operate differently from those of the common person. "Love and hate are human nature. The petty man loves and hates in terms of himself. The superior man loves and hates in terms of the Way. Look into this and you will be able to understand the Principle of Heaven and human desires."[55] The distinction between the Principle of Heaven (*t'ien-li*[bb]) and (selfish) human desires (*jen-yü*[bc]) is as basic to Hu Hung's moral teachings as it is to other Neo-Confucians, but, consistent with his theory of the nature, he sees these two opposites as sharing a common basis. "The Principle of Heaven and human desires are the same in substance but differ in function. They are the same in operation but differ in feeling (*ch'ing*,[bd] situation). The superior man who goes forth to cultivate should deeply distinguish them."[56] The emphasis here is on the need not to confound them.

Neither feelings nor desires are trustworthy, nor can we rely on our sensations. "It is the lot of the multitude to be restricted by what their eyes see and their ears hear."[57] Our feelings may be downright misleading. The fur coat that feels light in winter seems unbearably heavy when summer comes around, even though its actual weight has remained unchanged. Thus the feelings can distort our judgments concerning weight. The same holds for people who rely on their feelings in making moral judgments and mistakenly think that they are acting virtuously.[58] Desires, as well as feelings and emotions, lead people astray. They destroy people's sense of reality and are responsible for the interruption in the transmission of the true teachings.

> Basically life is not to be loved, but people love it because of their desires. Basically death is not to be hated, but, again, people hate it because of their desires. With respect to life, they seek to satisfy these desires, and with respect to death, they fear losing them. Restless on this earth, everyone is occupied with his desires, and the learning of the mind/heart (*hsin-hsüeh*[be]) is not passed on.[59]

However, "love and hate are human nature," and the sage has feelings and desires the same as everyone else. He does not deny these, including the desires for food and sex. "People despise the way of husband and wife because they consider it a matter of lascivious desire, but the sages are at ease with it because the preservation of harmony is its meaning."[60] Sages and ordinary people are endowed with the same human nature, and they do not differ in their essential emotional or psychological constitution. They have the same feelings, desires, and abilities. Even though ordinary people take a dim view of these inborn impulses and propensities, the sage rejects none of them. Sages, like common people, have their anxieties and resentments. But in contrast to ordinary people, they accept these, too. The difference between the sage and the common man is that when the sage's feelings and propensities are aroused, they attain, in the words of the *Doctrine of the Mean*, "due measure and degree."[61]

In a letter to Tseng Chi[bf] (1084–1168), probably seen by Chu Hsi, Hu Hung elaborates on this contrast in terms of the famous passage from the first chapter of the *Doctrine of the Mean*. According to Hu Hung, "the state before the feelings are aroused is empty, tranquil, and without any sign, and all share the great basis (*ta-pen*[bg]) so that even an ordinary person is no different from a sage."[62] This is because this stage refers to the nature. The stage after the feelings are aroused then refers to the mind/heart. Only sages, having fully realized the nature, can remain tranquil when acted on by things.

This does not mean that the mind appears only after it is acted on from without. From the point of view of the outside observer, our humaneness can be seen only after something occurs and knowledge arises, but "in terms of ourselves, the mind 'flows' (*liu*[bh]) in unison with heaven and earth. How can there be an interruption?"[63] Further light is shed on Hu Hung's concept of the mind and its relationship to the nature in a passage in *Understanding Words* in which he employs the distinction between substance and function. After discussing the sages' naming of the Way, he states, "Designating its substance the sage calls it 'the nature.' Designating its function he calls it 'mind.' The nature cannot but be active. Active it is mind. The sage transmitted the mind and taught the world by humaness."[64] Similarly, in another passage, he characterizes centrality (before the feelings are aroused) as the substance of the Way and harmony (after the feelings are aroused) as the Way's function.[65] These descriptions of the relationship between the nature and the mind in terms of the two stages of the *Doctrine of the Mean* and the substance/function dichotomy also fit in with Hu Hung's comparison of the nature to water.

In another passage Hu Hung draws an analogy between the mind (rather than the nature) and water and says that the mind reflects all things as water reflects all images.[66] One of the primary functions of the mind is thus cognition. "There is this mind and then we have knowledge; without this mind, there is no knowledge."[67] Or again, in one of the terse and suggestive sayings included in *Understanding Words,* Hu Hung compares man's functioning in the world with that of the mind in the body: "Man necessarily responds to the world's stimuli just as the mind necessarily knows when the body is sick with pain."[68]

The mind not only knows; it also rules. "The vital force *(ch'i)* is ruled by the nature; the nature is ruled by the mind. When the mind is pure, the nature is settled, and the vital force is correct."[69] This point is reiterated in another passage and extended to "things" *(wu):* "When the nature is settled, the mind rules and things follow."[70] Again, in a passage criticized by Chu Hsi, "The mind is what understands heaven and earth and rules the ten thousand things in order to complete (*ch'eng*[bi]) the nature."[71] Since it is difficult to conceive of a function (mind) ruling over a substance (the nature), the suggestion has been made that different metaphysical planes or dimensions are involved, for example, that objectively the nature is substance, the mind function, but that subjectively the mind rules.[72] This is not to deny the existence of a transcendent mind as revealed in the following dialogue.

A disciple asked: Is the mind subject to life and death?
Master Hu: No, it is not.
Disciple: In that case, when someone dies where is the mind?
Master Hu: You already know of its death and yet you ask where it is?
Disciple: What do you mean?
Master Hu: It is only because it is not dead that you know it. What is the problem?
Disciple: I don't understand.
Master Hu (laughing): Your obtuseness is really too much! If you would consider the mind not in terms of shape but consider the mind in terms of mind, you would understand it.[73]

The point apparently is that mind as such does not die.

The mind is as permanent and extensive as the nature at the same time that it is immanent in everyone and makes sagehood possible. "The mind is everywhere. Based on the transformation of the Way of Heaven, it deals with social interactions, assists heaven and earth, and provides the ten thousand things." The trouble is that people lose this mind because it is obscured by selfish desires. Therefore, we must, as Mencius taught, "seek after the lost mind."[74] This everyone possesses. To deny it for the sake of personal gain is to sink to the level of animals.[75] Conversely, if we perceive it as did the King of Ch'i when he could not bear the suffering of the ox, it can be cultivated and enlarged until it becomes as great as heaven.

Humaneness (*jen*) is the paramount quality of the mind. In nature it is the mind of heaven and earth which inexhaustibly creates, and in man it is what enables him to participate in the operations of the universe. Since everyone has a mind, it is accessible to all. "There are people who lack humaneness, but there is no mind that is without humaneness."[76] As we have seen, "The reason why a person is not humane is that he has lost his originally good mind." When a disciple asked about practicing humaneness, Hu Hung answered, "If you want to practice humaneness, you must understand the substance of humaneness." When further queried about its substance, he went on to say,

> The way of humaneness is vast yet intimate. Those who understand it can understand it all in one word; those who do not understand it will not understand it even after countless words. Those who are capable can demonstrate it with a single undertaking; those who are incapable cannot do so even though they point to countless matters.[77]

This dialogue goes on with Hu Hung denying that the substance of humaneness lies in being one with all things and ends with the disciple leaving in terror. However, in *Understanding Words* it is presented as a single item with the discourse concerning the King of Ch'i which immediately follows it. Understanding the substance of humaneness may thus be described as an intuitive experience of self-identification with the moral and creative force of the universe and as such not attainable by intellectual analysis alone.

Chu Hsi

For a time, as a result of conversations and correspondence with Chang Shih, Chu Hsi was attracted to the Hunan theory of self-cultivation and influenced by it to depart from the teachings of Li T'ung. However, as is well known, he went on to formulate his own theory, developing a synthesis that provides for both preserving/nourishing before the feelings are aroused and for examination after they have been activated, in that order of priority but with serious-ness *(ching)* the predominant quality in both the tranquil and active phases. In the course of working his way through to this position, Chu Hsi became quite critical of Hu Hung and persuaded Chang Shih as well as Lü Tsu-ch'ien[bj] (1134–1181) to join him in a critique of some selected passages which, under the title *Hu-tzu Chih-yen i-i*[bk] (Misgivings concerning Master Hu's *Under-standing Words*) has been preserved in Chu Hsi's collected works as well as in the *Sung-Yüan hsüeh-an*[bl][78] (Anthology and critical accounts of Sung and Yüan Neo-Confucianists) and the *Yüeh-ya-t'ang*[bm] (Elegance of Kuangtung) edition of the *Chih-yen.*

One of the passages from *Understanding Words* singled out by Chu Hsi and bearing directly on the issue of self-cultivation is the one just cited in which Hu Hung states that one must begin by "understanding the substance of humaneness." Chu Hsi points out that when asked about humaneness Confu-cius himself talked to his disciples about methods to seek for it and did not begin by getting them to understand its substance. Chu Hsi further expressed his concern that to have self-cultivation depend on first obtaining knowledge could lead to neglect of everyday nourishing. In his view, the two processes should proceed step-by-step in tandem, although it should be noted that Hu Hung, too, insists on both, even if in opposite sequence.

Chu Hsi's views were elaborated in letters in which he clarifies his rejection of Hu Hung's doctrines.[79] Without the moral effort of preserving and nour-ishing, the mind will become increasingly confused, and if we use this con-fused mind to examine the mind, the confusion will merely be aggravated. Chu Hsi, unwilling to wait for the attainment of intuitive understanding, put his full trust in the mind which is prone to error and confusion. A foundation must be established before meaningful intellectual activity can take place. As he wrote to Lin Yung-chung,[bn] the reason why *Ta-hsüeh*[bo] (Great learning, Advanced learning) begins with the investigation of things *(ko-wu*[bp]) is that the ancients completed their nourishing during their elementary learning *(hsiao-hsüeh)*. However, "People today do not begin with this moral effort, but see-ing that the *Ta-hsüeh* gives priority to the investigation of things, they seek it only by intellectual understanding and do not exert themselves to hold fast and preserve *(ts'ao-tsun*[bq]). Even if they surmise it completely, they lack solid terrain on which they can rely."[80]

Chu Hsi also wants scholars to go through the whole sequence defined in the *Great Learning*—to extend knowledge, make the thoughts sincere, and rec-tify the mind—fearing that not to do so may mislead one into heterodoxy. He is ever sensitive to the possibility of slipping into Buddhism and on occasion suggests minor changes in phraseology to avoid this.[81] Furthermore, he is much concerned to strike a balance. Thus, while nourishing has priority and continues throughout the process of self-cultivation, Chu Hsi describes that process as involving parallel progressions of knowledge from shallow to deep, and action from petty to great. One of his major objections to the Hunan theory was that it lacked balance. As he told Chang Shih, "Now if you insist that it is to be sought in action, this is because you intend to avoid a one-sided reliance on tranquillity, but you fail to realize that, on the contrary, you are relying one-sidedly on action."[82] In this context he warns against falling into the errors of Ch'an.

The differences between Chu Hsi's and Hu Hung's methodologies of self-cultivation are intimately related to profound differences in their philosophies of mind and human nature. For Chu Hsi these are not two aspects of the same reality as they are for Hu Hung. Thus he criticizes Hu Hung for identifying the mind with the state after the feelings have been aroused in contrast to the nature as the state before the feelings are activated. According to Chu Hsi this was an early view of Ch'eng I which he later abandoned.[83] For Chu Hsi the mind is present in both states, and both are found in the ordinary world of experience. In the tranquil state when the feelings are not yet aroused, mind and consciousness are present.[84] It is this which makes this state a proper and necessary object of self-cultivation. And it is itself a state of the mind, not of the nature.

Furthermore, for Chu Hsi mind and nature do not stand in a simple one to one relationship with each other, for he sees the human psyche in tripartite terms. It is the feelings which are the functions of the nature; therefore when the nature is active, Hu to the contrary, it is feelings, not mind.[85] Chu Hsi follows Chang Tsai[br] (1020–1077) in teaching that the mind directs and unites (*t'ung*[bs]) the nature and the feelings. Therefore, he objects to Hu Hung's statement that the mind "completes" the nature and would change his statement to "directs the nature and feelings."[86]

Chu Hsi also objects to the conversation quoted earlier in which a startled disciple is told that the mind does not live or die. He fears that Hu Hung comes close to the Buddhist theory of reincarnation here, although it should be noted that Hu himself subscribed to the Neo-Confucian view of endless creation and rejected the Buddhist concept. Chu Hsi makes a distinction between the mind which "in Heaven and Earth penetrates past and present and does not undergo formation or destruction" and that "within humans where it begins and ends depending of physical form and vital force."[87] This is a distinction also found in Hu Hung,[88] but Chu Hsi goes on to say that if we understand that "principle is one but its manifestations are many" then there is no need to startle students with the theory that the mind does not die. For Chu Hsi, as for Hu Hung, mind has a transcendental dimension since it harbors the Principle of Heaven, but in Hu's less complicated theory, mind itself is transcendent.

Chu Hsi not only rejects Hu Hung's views on mind and its relationship to the nature but pays special attention to the theory that the nature is beyond the distinction between good and evil, a position apparently continued as a

Hu family tradition, for it was defended not only by Hu An-kuo and Hu Hung but also Hu Hung's son, Ta-shih,[bt] as well as Hu Hung's brother, Hu Yin. As already noted, Chu Hsi traced this thesis back to the Ch'an monk Ch'ang-tsung; but according to Chu Hsi, Ch'ang-tsung himself had been very careful to remain within the Mencian tradition and had only maintained that "the goodness of the original nature does not stand in contrast to evil"[89] or, in another version, "[the nature's] perfect excellence does not stand in contrast with evil."[90] But Hu An-kuo and his sons and grandsons went much further and ended in denying the goodness of the nature, much to Chu Hsi's distress.

In a letter to Hu Yin's son, Hu Ta-yüan,[bu] Chu Hsi acknowledged that Hu Hung in *Understanding Words* did not indicate that the nature was not good and indeed intended to exalt the nature. However, according to Chu Hsi, Hu Hung had instead demeaned it, placing it in a remote, arbitrary, confused, and impure position. As depicted by Hu Hung, the nature lacks concrete principles and is turned into "an empty object" (*k'ung-hsü ti wu*[bv]) or, as he says elsewhere, made into something faceless.[91] Thus Hu Hung fell into the mistake made by Kao Tzu[bw] (c. 420–350 B.C.) and long since refuted by Mencius,[92] a mistaken position more recently taken up by the Su[bx] family.[93]

Chu Hsi conceded that the goodness of the original nature which man received from Heaven is of a perfection which does not stand in contrast to evil, and he agrees that the dichotomy of good and evil appears only after there is activity. But he argues that the goodness manifested in activity as a result of man's following his nature (and thus contrasting with the evil which occurs when he fails to do so) is the same as the original goodness of the nature. Otherwise, there would be two goodnesses, an original absolute goodness and a relative goodness. This in turn would entail two natures.[94] Since this is an untenable position, he concludes that there can be only one goodness and that it is therefore proper and necessary to designate the nature as good.

For Chu Hsi the nature as the source of goodness must itself be good. As he wrote to Hu Hung's cousin Hu Shih[by] (1136–1173):

> We can say that the Mandate of Heaven (*T'ien-ming*,[bz] what heaven imparts) is not confined to things, but if we consider it as not confined to goodness, we will not understand what makes heaven heaven. We can say that we cannot speak of the nature as evil, but if we consider goodness as inadequate to characterize the nature, we will not understand where goodness comes from.[95]

He goes on to complain that there are many such discussions in *Understanding Words* that contradict the good passages and come close to Kao Tzu, Yang Hsiung[ca] (53 B.C.–A.D. 18), the Buddhists, and the Su family. Earlier in the same letter Chu Hsi said, "At first there is goodness and there is no evil; there is the Mandate of Heaven and there are no human desires."[96] In a subsequent letter to Hu Shih he voices the same concern: "The nature is called good in order to distinguish the Principle of Heaven from human desires."[97]

The fear that the distinction between the Principle of Heaven and human desires would be obscured also prompted Chu Hsi to take exception to Hu Hung's statement "the Principle of Heaven and human desires are the same in substance but differ in function."[98] His basic objection here is that Hu's formula tends to combine the two opposites into a single entity. He does say that the idea of picking out human desires within heavenly principles and of seeing the Principle of Heaven within human desires is very acute, but he concludes that this should be rejected since the original substance is the Principle of Heaven without the presence of human desires, which appear later. Also, the sages did not teach this kind of effort.[99] In a letter, he further elaborated on his critique of Hu's "same substance, different functions" thesis comparing human growth to that of a tree. What grows straight out from the roots to the trunk, the branches, and leaves and thus conforms to the nature is contrasted to parasitic growths (such as fungi) which grow out sideways. The former are the Principle of Heaven and good; the latter, human desires and evil. The former is proper and has a source, is obedient and correct; therefore it should be fostered. The latter is a misbirth lacking a source, is disobedient and incorrect; therefore it needs to be cut off. He goes on to say that generally good and evil are spoken of in sequence with good placed first. Otherwise, "if we place good and evil east and west, facing each other with neither yielding to the other, the heavenly principles and human desires will issue from a single source and in the state before the feelings are aroused there will already be these two beginnings."[100]

Hu Hung's formulation, however, had considerable appeal. Lü Tsu-ch'ien for one did not share Chu Hsi's misgivings.[101] Yet Chu Hsi remained persistent in his critique. For him a basic distinction was at stake. According to the Hus, "humaneness and nonhumaneness, righteousness and unrighteousness, propriety and impropriety, wisdom and nonwisdom would all become the nature"[102] and, still worse, so would the desires.[103] Substance and function cannot be differentiated. Hu's proposition would lead to the conclusion that the nature is both good and evil. According to Chu Hsi, the Hus were intent on exposing heterodoxy but were unable to avoid placing a foot into it themselves.[104]

According to Chu Hsi, Hu Hung's mistake concerning the moral status of human nature also led him to say, "Love and hate are human nature. The petty man loves and hates in terms of himself. The superior man loves and hates in terms of the Way."[105] In his critique of this passage[106] Chu Hsi charged Hu with treating the nature in terms of love and hate rather than good and evil. Furthermore, to characterize the superior man as "loving and hating in terms of the Way" is to place the Way outside of the nature.[107] Another problem is that according to Hu's statement love and hate appear simultaneously without order of precedence or priority. Yang Shih was correct when he said, "The Mandate of Heaven is what is meant by the nature. The desires are not the nature." Chu Hsi went on to say,

> Love and hate are inherent in the nature but cannot directly be called the nature. Now love and hate are something. To love goodness and hate evil is the rule (tse,[cb] specific principles) of things. "When there is something, there is a rule"[108] is what Mencius meant by "form and body are the nature endowed by heaven."[109] If we now want to talk about the nature and bring up things but neglect the rules, harm will be unavoidable.[110]

Consistent with his stress on the Principle of Heaven and his concern that the goodness of the nature not be compromised, Chu Hsi further said that the superior man follows his nature whereas the petty man violates his nature. He went on to charge that Hu's proposition would lead to "loving what men hate and hating what men love also being the nature."[111] Chu Hsi feared that perverse love and hate would be indistinguishable from principled love and hate.

It is unfortunate that Chu Hsi and Hu Hung never met and that the debate between them necessarily remained one-sided since Chang Shih evidently did not put up a very spirited defense of his teacher's views. It is not the purpose of this paper to attempt to remedy this situation,[112] but we may note that Hu Hung surely would have objected to Chu Hsi's interpretation of a good number of his statements and vigorously rejected the notion that he approximated the Buddhism he wholeheartedly opposed or that by elevating the nature beyond good and evil he had provided equal status for human desires and the Principle of Heaven. He most certainly saw himself as a faithful follower of Mencius.

Hu Hung had a proclivity for short and highly suggestive statements that invite reflection but are open to misinterpretation. A debate might have forced him to greater precision. That there was no such debate was in part due to the times, for it would seem that Hu Hung lived at a time when Chinese intellectuals were fully occupied regaining their bearings following the turbulent years that brought on the shocking loss of North China to "barbarians." Certainly Confucian discourse was far more varied and lively during the second half of the twelfth century, when Chu Hsi was active.

On the other hand, it may also be the case that Hu Hung as a thinker who emphasized the unity of the world had a cast of mind which naturally sought to avoid making too many distinctions; he certainly would have been dismayed by Chu Hsi's criticism that his views implied such things as two natures or a Way outside the nature. Also, as a philosopher who gave such emphasis to and placed so much faith in the mind, he may well have been content to leave it to future minds to intuit the inner meaning of his words. "Understanding words" is, after all, a mental process. Had he so desired, Hu Hung certainly could have spelled out his ideas in some generally accepted format, for instance a commentary on the *Book of Mencius*. As it was, he did not leave a completed work.

In contrast to Hu Hung, Chu Hsi's thought on the nature of man employed such concepts as the physical nature (ch'i-chih chih hsing[cc]) and li and ch'i as well as adopting Chang Tsai's tripartite scheme of the nature, feelings, and mind. Similarly, in Chu Hsi's metaphysics the Supreme Ultimate (*t'ai-chi*[cd]) figures much more importantly than it does in Hu Hung and fulfills the role of linking the transcendent and experiential, a role performed by the nature in Hu Hung. Chu Hsi's system is more complex than that of Hu Hung and his arguments were more persuasive to his own contemporaries as well as to most later Neo-Confucians. His philosophy was better worked out and, as suggested by his resolution of the self-cultivation issue, attained a certain middle ground. Yet Hu Hung left open certain possibilities in Neo-Confucianism and to the degree that his sayings have stimulated present day philosophers, he has helped to fuel Neo-Confucian discourse in the twentieth century as he did in the twelfth.

Notes

1. Yang Shih[ce] (1053–1135) and Lo Ts'ung-yen[cf] (1072–1135) both died in 1135 when Chu Hsi was five years old.

2. Hu Hung is discussed by Mou Tsung-san[cg] in his influential *Hsin-t'i yü hsing-t'i*[ch] [Mind and human nature], (Taipei: Cheng-chung[ci] Book Co. 1968–1969). Cf. the review article by Wei-ming Tu,[cj] *The Journal of Asian Studies* 30 (May 1971), pp. 642–647. Mou Tsung-san's influence is apparent in the useful book by Wang K'ai-fu,[ck] *Hu Wu-feng de hsin-hsüeh*[cl] [Hu Hung's learning of the mind/heart], (Taipei: Student Book Co., 1978). Chu Hsi's critique of Hu Hung is discussed by Ch'ien Mu[cm] in the *Chu Tzu hsin hsüeh-an*[cn] [A new study of Chu Hsi], (Taipei: San-min[co] Book Co., 1980), Bk. III, pp. 198–228. A most valuable sutdy in Japanese is Okada Takahiko,[cp] "Ko Go-hō"[cq] (Hu Wu-feng), *Toyobunka*[cr] [Eastern culture] 10 (1965), pp. 23–33; 11, pp. 30–47. Also see Takahata Tsunenobu,[cs] "Ko Go-hō no shiso"[ct] [The thought of Hu Wu-fe], *Chukyo Daigaku bungaku kiyo*[cu] [Literary bulletin of Chukyo University] 36 (1974), pp. 23–33 and 30–47.

3. For Hu An-kuo's biography see Hu Yin, *Fei-jan chi*[cv] [Collected writings of Hu Yin], (Complete Four Libraries Collection ed.), ch. 25. Hu Hung composed a record of a pavilion his father built in Hunan; see *Wu-feng chi*[cw] [Collected writings of Hu Hung], (Complete Four Libraries Collection ed.), 3:6a–8a.

4. Chu Hsi devoted ch. 13 of his *I-lo yüan-yüan lu*[cx] [Records of the origins of the School of the two Ch'engs] to Hu An-kuo.

5. Chu Hsi, *Hsiao-hsüeh*, external compilation, ch. 1, *Shōgaku*[cy] [Elementary education], ed., annot., and trans. Uno Seiichi[cz] (Tokyo: Meiji shoin,[da] 1965), p. 226.

6. Hu Yin, *Fei-jan chi*, 25:64a–b. Cf. Conrad Schirokauer, "Neo-Confucians Under Attack: The Condemnation of Wei-hsüeh,"[db] in John W. Haeger, ed., *Crisis and Prosperity in Sung China* (Tucson: University of Arizona Press, 1975), p. 165.

7. Hu An-kuo, *Ch'un-ch'iu chuan*[dc] [Commentary on the *Spring and Autumn Annals*], preface.

8. The *Book of Odes, Book of History, Book of Changes, Book of Rites,* and *Spring and Autumn Annals.*

9. Cf. the entry for *Ch'un-ch'iu chuan* in Etienne Balazs and Yves Hervouet, *A Sung Bibliography* (Hong Kong: Chinese University Press, 1978), p. 40; and Mou Jun-

sun,[dd] "Liang Sung Ch'un-ch'iu hsüeh chih chu-liu"[de] [The main stream of Northern and Southern Sung Ch'un-ch'iu studies], *Ta-lu tsa-chih*[df] [The continent magazine] 5 (1952), no. 4, pp. 1–4; no. 5, pp. 18–20.

10. See *Sung-Yüan hsüeh-an* [Anthology and critical accounts of Sung and Yüan Neo-Confucianists], (Shanghai: Commercial Press, 1936), Bk. I, ch. 34, pp. 677.

11. An edition of the *Tu-shih kuan-chien* printed in 1514 has marginal annotations indicating what was incorporated into Chu Hsi's *T'ung-chien kang-mu*. A full study of Chu Hsi as a historian should also take into account his other historical writings as well as his informal remarks.

12. *Huang-wang ta-chi* (Complete Four Libraries Collection ed.), 7:14a; or *Wu-feng chi*, 4:25a.

13. *Chu Tzu yü-lei*,[dg] [Classified conversations of Master Chu], ch. 101 (Taipei: Cheng-chung Book Co., 1970), p. 4100.

14. *Ibid.*, ch. 108, pp. 4262–4263. Also see Hsiao Kung-ch'üan,[dh] *Chung-kuo cheng-chih ssu-hsiang shih*[di] [A history of Chinese political thought], (Taipei: Chung-hua wen-hua ch'u-pen shih-yeh wei-yüan-hui,[dj] 1954), vol. 4, p. 504.

15. Cf. Miriam Levering, "Neo-Confucianism and Buddhism in the Sung as Movements within a Single *shih-ta-fu*[dk] Culture. Buddhist interpretations of Confucian Discourse," paper presented to the University Seminar on Neo-Confucianism, Columbia University, March 2, 1979.

16. Hu Yin, *Ch'ung-cheng pien* (Kyoto: Chūbun[dl] Publishing Co.), 1:12a.

17. *Chu Tzu yü-lei*, ch. 101, p. 4067.

18. Cf. Galen Eugene Sargent, "Tchou Hi[dm] Contre Le Bouddhisme," *Melanges Publies par l'Institute des Hautes Études Chinoises*, 1 (1957), pp. 1–157.

19. Chu Hsi, *Hui-an h'sien-sheng Chu Wen-kung wen-chi*[dn] [Collected writings of Chu Hsi], hereafter cited as *Wen-chi* (Kyoto: Chūbun Publishing Co., 1977), 97:17a, p. 1727. The quotation is from *Analects*, 14:25.

20. *Wen-chi*, 2, 9a, p. 80. These translations incorporate several valuable suggestions made by Professor Mao Huaixin.[do]

21. *Wu-feng chi*, 1:24a–b. Cf. Tomoeda Ryūtarō,[dp] *Shu-shi no shiso keisei*[dq] [The formation of Chu Hsi's thought], (Tokyo: Shunjū sha,[dr] 1969), pp. 63–64.

22. *Doctrine of the Mean*, ch. 1, trans. Wing-tsit Chan,[ds] *A Source Book in Chinese Philosophy* (Princeton, N.J.: Princeton University Press, 1963), p. 98.

23. *Wen-chi*, 70:20a, p. 1285. Also see Okada, "Ko Go-hō," p. 41, where he traces the idea of Hsieh Liang-tso[dt] (1050–c. 1120).

24. Hu Hung, *Chih-yen* (Complete Four Libraries Collection ed.), 4:7b. For a discussion of texts and editions see Takahata Tsunenobu, "*Koshi Shigen-Shigen gigi* no seiritsu jijo"[du] [The circumstances of the composition of *Hu Tzu Chih-yen* and *Hu Tzu Chih-yen i-i*], *Tetsugaku*[dv] 24, pp. 101–111. Many but not all of the translations from Hu Hung have benefited from the comments and corrections of Professor Wing-tsit Chan, and I want to acknowledge my special debt to him.

25. *Book Mencius*, 1A:7.

26. Chang Shih, *Nan-hsien chi*[dw] [Collected writings of Chang Shih], (Taipei: Kuang-hsüeh[dx] Press, 1975), 10:2b.

27. Cf. Tomoeda, *Shu-shi*, pp. 129–130. The influence of Hu Hung on Chang Shih is also discussed by Fukuda Shigeru,[dy] "Chō Nanken shonen no shiso"[dz] [The early thought of Chang Nan-hsien], *Chugoku testugaku ranshu*[ea] [Studies in Chinese philosophy], 2 (1976), pp. 24–41; and in Takahata Tsunenobu, *Chō-Nanken shu jinmei*

sakuin[eb] [Index to names in Chang Nan-hsien's *Collected Works*], (Nagoya: Saika Shorin,[ec] 1976).

28. *Chih-yen*, 4:12b–13b.

29. Chang Shih, "Preface to Discourse on the *Analects*," *Nan-hsien chi*, 14:4b.

30. *Chih-yen*, 3:2b. For the presence of the Way determining whether Chinese or barbarians control the Northern Plain, see the Yüeh-ya-t'ang edition of *Chih-yen*, 6:1a.

31. *Chih-yen*, 5:14a–b. The quotation from Confucius is from the *Analects*, 5:18.

32. *Chih-yen*, 2:1b.

33. See, for example, *ibid.*, 3:12b.

34. *Ibid.*, 3:6b.

35. *Ibid.*, 5:8a–b.

36. *Ibid.*, 4:4b–5a. Reference is to the *Analects*, 2:4.

37. *Wu-feng chi*, 3:5a–b.

38. *Chih-yen*, 3:13a.

39. *Ibid.*, 6:7a.

40. *Ibid.*, 2:12b–13a.

41. *Ibid.*, 1:1b; 2:6b–7a; and 2:1a. Reference is to the *Analects*, 2:4.

42. *Ibid.*, 4:3b.

43. *Wu-feng chi*, 5:53a.

44. *Chih-yen*, 1:4b.

45. *Ibid.*, 3:6b.

46. *Ibid.*, 2:2a.

47. *Ibid.*, 4:2b–3a.

48. See Conrad Schirokauer, "Hu Hung's Rebuttal of Ssu-ma Kuang's Critique of Mencius," *Proceedings of the International Conference on Sinology, Thought and Philosophy Section* (Taipei: Academia Sinica, 1981), vol. 1, pp. 437–458.

49. *Chih-yen*, 4:2b–3a. Cf. A. C. Graham, *Two Chinese Philosophers: Ch'eng Ming-tao*[ed] *and Ch'eng Yi-ch'uan*[ee] (London: Lund Humphries, 1958), p. 45.

50. *Ibid.*, 4:4a.

51. *Ibid.*, 1:8b.

52. *Ibid.*, 3:13b. Cf. Graham, *Two Chinese Philosophers*, p. 34.

53. *Ibid.*, 5:11a and 3:6a–b.

54. *Ibid.*, 2:5a.

55. *Ibid.*, 2:1a.

56. *Ibid.*, 1:5b.

57. *Ibid.*, 1:2b.

58. *Ibid.*, 1:2b–3a.

59. *Ibid.*, 3:1b.

60. *Ibid.*, 1:6b.

61. *Ibid.*, 4:3b–4a. Reference is to the *Doctrine of the Mean*, ch. 1.

62. *Wu-feng chi*, 2:46b.

63. *Chih-yen*, 2:4a.

64. *Ibid.*, 6:1a–b.

65. *Ibid.*, 2:6b–7a.

66. *Ibid.*, 4:13b.

67. *Ibid.*, 2:2a.

68. *Ibid.*, 3:10b.

69. *Ibid.*, 2:9a–b.

70. *Ibid.*, 4:6b.

71. *Ibid.*, 1:1a.

72. Cf. Wang K'ai-fu, *Hu Wu-feng,* pp. 87–88, citing Mou Tsung-san.

73. *Chih-yen,* 4:3a. See also 3b.

74. Cf. *ibid.*, 2:11b. Reference is to the *Book of Mencius,* 6A:11.

75. *Ibid.*, 2:10a–b.

76. *Wu-feng chi,* 5:43b.

77. *Chih-yen,* ch. 4, 7a.

78. *Wen-chi,* ch. 73; *Sung-Yüan hsüeh-an,* ch. 42.

79. Analyzed and summarized by Okada, "Ko Go-hō," pp. 44–46.

80. *Wen-chi,* 43:30b, p. 733, eighteenth letter to Lin.

81. *Ibid.*, 73:47a, p. 1357.

82. *Ibid.*, 30:20a, p. 473.

83. *Ibid.*, 64:31b, p. 1187. Cf. "First Letter to the Gentlemen of Hunan on Equilibrium and Harmony," Chan, *Source Book,* pp. 600–602.

84. *Yü-lei,* 96:8b–9b, pp. 3922–3924, trans. Wing-tsit Chan, *Reflections on Things at Hand: The Neo-Confucian Anthology* (New York: Columbia University Press, 1967), p. 148.

85. For Hu Hung's very different views, cf. nn. 63–65.

86. *Wen-chi,* 73:44a, p. 1335.

87. *Ibid.*, 73:48a, p. 1357.

88. "The mind suffers a hundred ills and one death," *Chih-yen,* 4:7b.

89. *Yü-lei,* 101:25b and 27a, pp. 4110–4113.

90. *Ibid.*, 101:28a, p. 4115.

91. *Wen-chi,* 46:20b; *Yü-lei,* 101:29b, p. 4118.

92. *Book of Mencius,* 6A:1–6.

93. Reference is to the three famous Sus: Su Hsün[ef] (1009–1066) and his sons Su Shih[eg] (1036–1101) and Su Ch'e[eh] (1039–1112). For Su Shih's views see *Su-shih I-chuan*[ei] [Mr. Su's Commentary on the *Book of Changes*], (Ts'ung-shu chi-ch'eng[ej] [Collection of series] ed.), vol. 2, pp. 159–160 which is quoted in Graham, *Two Chinese Philosophers,* pp. 46 and 135.

94. *Yü-lei,* 101:25a–b, pp. 4109–4110, trans. Chan, *Source Book,* p. 617.

95. *Wen-chi,* 42:5a, p. 702, third letter to Hu Shih.

96. *Ibid.*, 42:4b, p. 701.

97. *Ibid.*, 42:8a, p. 703, fifth letter to Hu Shih.

98. Chu Hsi does not object to the second part of the statement.

99. *Ibid.*, 73:45b, p. 1356.

100. *Ibid.*, 59:46a–b, second letter to Chao Shih-hsia.[ek]

101. *Ibid.*, 73:45b, p. 1356.

102. *Yü-lei,* 101:30a, p. 4119.

103. *Ibid.*, 101:30b, p. 4120.

104. *Ibid.*

105. See n. 49.

106. *Wen-chi,* 73:46a–b, p. 1356.

107. Elsewhere Chu Hsi makes the same point but charges that it places principle (rather than the Way) outside of the nature. Cf. *Wen-chi,* 32:6b, p. 522, fourth reply to Chang Shih.

108. *Book of Odes,* ode no. 260, quoted in the *Book of Mencius,* 6A:6.

109. *Book of Mencius,* 7A:39.

110. *Wen-chi,* 73:46a–b, p. 1356.

111. *Yü-lei,* 101:30a, p. 4119.

112. For a defense of Hu Hung against Chu Hsi's critique cf. Mou Tsung-san and Wang K'ai-fu, cited in n. 2.

Glossary

a	胡宏	al	子文	bw	告子
b	張栻	am	楚	bx	蘇
c	胡安國	an	道	by	胡實
d	程顥	ao	敬	bz	天命
e	程頤	ap	復	ca	揚雄
f	小學	aq	性	cb	則
g	范仲淹	ar	天地之精	cc	氣質之性
h	春秋	as	陰	cd	太極
i	王安石	at	陽	ce	楊時
j	經莚	au	理	cf	羅從彥
k	左傳	av	氣	cg	牟宗三
l	傳心要典	aw	禪	ch	心體與性體
m	司馬光	ax	常總	ci	正中
n	資治通鑑	ay	盡性	cj	杜維明
o	胡寧	az	物	ck	王開府
p	胡寅	ba	理一分殊	cl	胡五峯的心學
q	讀史管見	bb	天理	cm	錢穆
r	通鑑綱目	bc	人欲	cn	朱子新學案
s	皇王大紀	bd	情	co	三民
t	邵雍	be	心學	cp	岡田武彥
u	秦檜	bf	曾幾	cq	胡五峯
v	崇正辯	bg	大本	cr	東洋文化
w	邪説	bh	流	cs	高畑常信
x	胡憲	bi	成	ct	胡五峯の思想
y	朱松	bj	呂祖謙	cu	中京大學文學紀要
z	秘書省正字	bk	胡子知言疑義	cv	裴然集
aa	劉珙	bl	宋元學案	cw	五峯集
ab	支枝	bm	粵雅堂	cx	伊洛淵源錄
ac	李侗	bn	林用中	cy	小學
ad	中	bo	大學	cz	宇野精一
ae	中庸	bp	格物	da	明治書
af	良心	bq	操存	db	僞學
ag	齊	br	張載	dc	春秋傳
ah	宣	bs	統	dd	牟潤孫
ai	潭州重修嶽麓書院記	bt	大時	de	兩宋春秋學之主流
aj	仁	bu	胡大原	df	大陸雜誌
ak	知言	bv	空虛的物	dg	朱子語類

dh 蕭公權

di 中國政治思想史

dj 中華文化出版事業委
員會

dk 士大夫

dl 中文

dm 朱熹

dn 晦庵先生朱文公文集

do 冒懷辛

dp 支枝龍太郎

dq 朱子の思想形成

dr 春秋社

ds 陳榮捷

dt 謝良佐

du 胡子知言——知言疑義
の成立事情

dv 哲學

dw 南軒集

dx 廣學

dy 福田殖

dz 張南軒初年の思想

ea 中國哲學論集

eb 張南軒集人名索引

ec 采華書林

ed 程明道

ee 程伊川

ef 蘇洵

eg 蘇軾

eh 蘇轍

ei 蘇氏易傳

ej 叢書集成

ek 趙師夏

27

The Establishment of
the School of Chu Hsi and
Its Propagation in Fukien

MAO HUAIXIN

The Founding of the School of Chu Hsi

THE SCHOOL OF CHU HSI was generally known as the Fukien School, and its propagation and influence in Fukien afforded an embryonic form of its role all over the country in the later generations. The term *chi-ta-ch'eng*[a] (putting together all Neo-Confucian ideas) was first applied to Chu Hsi by his disciples Li Fang-tzu[b] (1214 *cs*) and Ch'en Ch'un[c] (1159–1223). This paper aims at inspecting the validity of the term.[1]

The main current of this school inherited the ideas of the Ch'eng brothers (Ch'eng Hao,[d] 1032–1085 and Ch'eng I,[e] 1033–1107), which were regarded as the most orthodox and pure by the Neo-Confucianists. It did not reject the *hsiang-shu*[f] learning (the study of emblems and numbers) of Shao Yung[g] (1011–1177) although it was considerably marked by the influences of both Taoist and Buddhist ideas. It defined, though not in a written form, the basic classical texts for Neo-Confucianism: among the pre-Ch'in (221–206 B.C.) literatures there were, in addition to the Four Books,[2] the "Appended Remarks" of the *Book of Changes,* the "Record of Music" in the *Book of Rites,* the "Hung-fan"[h] (the Grand Norm) and the "sixteen words from heart to heart" in the "Counsel of the Great Yü"[i] chapter of the *Book of History.* In short, the Fukien School, which brought Neo-Confucianism to its culmination, held an all-embracing attitude toward all branches of the Neo-Confucian ideas. In principle it regarded both Buddhism and Taoism as heterodoxy, whereas in practice it absorbed much from Buddhist ways of thinking as well as from the Taoist view of nature. With regard to the latter it is unfortunate that though Taoism, endowed as it was with the germ of natural sciences, should have exercised its positive effects in bringing Neo-Confucianism closer to science, the historical fact witnessed it otherwise. Taoism only mystified and vulgarized Neo-Confucianism.

According to relevant records, when Yang Shih[j] (1053–1135) a native of Nan-chien[k] in Fukien, left his teachers the Ch'eng brothers to return home in

the south, Ch'eng Hao said, "Henceforth my doctrine is going to the south"
—a saying that became well-known in the history of Neo-Confucianism. Chen
Te-hsiu[l] (1178–1235), a native of P'u-ch'eng[m] in Fukien, an admirer of Chu
Hsi and an intimate friend of Chu Hsi's disciple Ts'ai Ch'en[n] (1167–1230),
remarked in his *Reading Journal,*

> The learning of the two Ch'engs was inherited by Yang Shih, who transmitted it
> to Lo Ts'ung-yen[o] (1072–1135), and Lo in turn transmitted it to Li T'ung[p]
> (1093–1163), who finally transmitted it to Chu Hsi. Thus was the legacy of one
> school.
>   Hsieh Liang-tso[q] (1050–c.1120) transmitted it to Hu An-kuo[r] (1074–1138),
> who transmitted it to his own son Hu Hung[s] (1106–1161), who in turn transmit-
> ted it to Chang Shih[t] (1133–1180). This was the legacy of another school. . . .
> The learning of Chu Hsi and Chang Shih was characterized by what was the
> most essential in it [the learning of the Ch'eng brothers].[3]

This scholastic succession may be illustrated as follows:

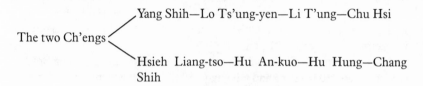

Yang Shih—Lo Ts'ung-yen—Li T'ung—Chu Hsi

The two Ch'engs

Hsieh Liang-tso—Hu An-kuo—Hu Hung—Chang
Shih

Although this relationship of succession may be taken as only roughly correct,
Neo-Confucianists of later generations, including the compiler of the *Writings
of Sung* [960–1279] *and Yüan* [1277–1368] *Philosophers* all shared this view.[4]
    The branch of Chang Shih was called the Hu-Hsiang[u] School. Chang Shih,
son of the famous commander-in-chief Chang Chün,[v] was Chu Hsi's friend in
learning, or, in the words of the *Writings of Sung and Yüan Philosophers,* was
"in the same tune"[5] with Chu Hsi. Because his influence was not very great,
we shall leave him aside. As for the succession from Yang Shih to Chu Hsi, I
am of the opinion that Chu Hsi himself would not acknowledge it; at any rate,
he did not pay attention to it. In the *Classified Conversations of Master Chu*
there are various passages in which Chu Hsi expressed his view that the followers of the Ch'eng brothers failed to succeed their masters. The general
conclusion he reached was that "the disciples of the Ch'eng brothers were far
less in scholarship as well as in insight when compared with Shao Yung and
Chang Tsai[w] [1020–1077]."[6] Moreover, Chu Hsi asserted, "Even at their own
times, gentlemen like Yu Tso[x] (1053–1123), Yang Shih, and Hsieh Liang-tso
did not look like their masters but rather like another school in the making."[7]
    By the end of the Northern Sung dynasty (960–1126), many of the promi-
nent pupils of the Ch'eng brothers such as Hsieh Liang-tso, Lü Ta-lin[y] (1046–
1092), Chang I (b. 1071),[z] and Yu Tso had already died. Only Yin Ch'un[aa]

(1071–1142) and Yang Shih survived down to the early years of the Southern Sung dynasty (1127–1279). Because of their experience and prestige, they were chosen by the royal court as lecturers of Classics to the emperor. Although Yin Ch'un was loyal to his master—he was one of only four people who dared attend the funeral of Ch'eng I, who died in melancholy and oblivion during the political persecution of 1107—he was no more than a pedant; he insisted rigidly on the line of his master's doctrine, but he achieved nothing else. Chu Hsi criticized him, saying, "While lecturing on the Classics to the emperor, there was little in him that was enlightening or encouraging. When he was summoned to the court in the early years of the reign of Shao-hsing[ab] period [1131–1162], all the court placed their hopes in him, looking on him as a semi-god, but what he really achieved was very little."[8]

Yang Shih seemed more energetic, but Chu Hsi repeatedly said of him that he derived his learning from the Buddhist meditation (Ch'an[ac]) sect. Once Chu Hsi said, "Yu Tso, Yang Shih, and Hsieh Liang-tso all began by learning from Ch'an and that practice remained with them long afterwards."[9] He also said, "Yang Shih was promoting the Buddhist tendency."[10] When Yang Shih was introduced by Premier Ts'ai Ching[ad] (1047–1126) to serve in the government during the reign of Hsüan-ho[ae] (1119–1125), he expounded to the emperor only on such topics as the rectification of the mind and the sincerity of the will and other impractical advice. Hence Chu Hsi criticized him: "In times of emergency, the people expected much of him but he behaved incompetently like that. This is the reason why some people ridiculed the Confucians as useless."[11] Elsewhere he remarked, "At a critical time like that, if Yang Shih were able enough to turn the whole situation instantly, it would not be in vain for him to take part in the government. But what he did was no more than to muddle along with others."[12] During the Southern Sung dynasty when the regime in the south began settling down, both Yang Shih and Yin Ch'un enjoyed considerable authority, but as the only prominent pupils of the Ch'eng brothers then still surviving, they failed to bring about anything of significance either in politics or in learning. In the eyes of Chu Hsi, both were undeserved scholars.

Also undeserving of belief, perhaps, was the famous saying, "Henceforth my doctrine is going to the south." It first appeared in the *Kuei-shan yü-lu*[af] (Recorded sayings of Yang Shih), which was written by his pupils. That is one reason why its authenticity is open to doubt. In addition, Hu An-kuo's "Kuei-shan chih-ming"[ag] (Epitaph of Yang Shih),[13] inscribed in Yang Shih's tomb in 3,000 words, did not mention such an expression. As Chu Hsi said, "Many of the historical records are not reliable"[14] and "many of the historical records are incredible."[15] These comments seem also applicable to some messages in the history of Neo-Confucianism.

About Li T'ung, Chu Hsi's own teacher, as well as about Lo Ts'ung-yen, Li's master, passages somewhat critical in tone may be found in the *Classified Conversations of Master Chu*. For instance, about Lo Ts'ung-yen, Chu Hsi said, "Lo Ts'ung-yen's exposition of the *Spring and Autumn Annals* was inferior to Hu An-kuo's, because the latter was much more talented,"[16] and "Master Lo's doctrine [of sitting in quiescence] was after all not so healthy. . . . this is a doctrine that leads to some deviation."[17] About Li T'ung, Chu Hsi said, "Li was not good at discriminating [between] good and evil."[18] "[He] did not give reverence a clear explanation. Therefore people wasted much time trying to grasp the meaning of it."[19] About Li's idea of sitting in quiescence, Chu Hsi said, "If it is only thus, then it looks just like Buddhist meditation and calmness."[20] Thus it seems that the relation of Chu Hsi to his early master Li T'ung was somewhat akin to that of the Ch'eng brothers to Chou Tun-i[ah] (1017–1073). Although he was not without respect, he never took his master as a model. Hence it may be seen that both Huang Pai-chia's[ai] (*fl.* 1695) assertion that "the doctrine of Yang Shih was handed down to Chu Hsi in a course of succession through three generations"[21] and Ch'üan Tsu-wang's[aj] (1705–1755) assertion that "the doctrine of Yang Shih was handed down to Chu Hsi in a course of four generations"[22] were dealing only with superficiality. Had Chu Hsi himself read the above accounts of transmission, he would not have agreed and would have advanced many arguments against such a line of transmission. As a matter of fact, he claimed himself a direct successor of the Ch'eng brothers.

As is well known, the Neo-Confucianism of the Ch'eng brothers took the way of the Mean from the *Doctrine of the Mean* and the Three Principles and the Eight Items[23] from the *Great Learning* as its theoretical foundation. Their method was the cultivation of the self and the regulation of the family, and their aim was to govern the state and to pacify the world. Such a commonplace doctrine was regarded by someone in the Northern Sung dynasty as a proof of *ju-men t'an-po*[ak] (superficiality of the Confucian School).[24] It even compelled the Ch'eng brothers themselves to draw from Buddhist ideas, as can be seen by such slogans as "The principle is one but its manifestations are many" and "Essence and functions are derived from the same origin."

Both Chou Tun-i's "Diagram of the Great Ultimate" and Shao Yung's "Diagram of What Antedates Heaven" were borrowed from Taoist ideas. Indeed, the Taoists carried with them the germination of science and worked out their study of emblems and numbers by making comparison with the *Book of Changes* and its commentaries. The origin of the study of emblems and numbers may be traced back to the study of the *Book of Changes* and the Taoist theory of alchemy in the Han dynasty (206 B.C.–A.D. 220). Inevitably there were mysterious and unscientific elements in it, but Chou and Shao labored diligently in absorbing the intellectual innovations of their predecessors for the sake of formulating a cosmology to the extent the scientific thought at that time permitted. Besides the social phenomena, their system tried also to embrace the natural phenomena in their changes and developments. From the point of view of cultural development, there is nothing reproachable in their efforts.

Although the Ch'eng brothers never mentioned the Great Ultimate or discussed the theory of numbers even though they lived together with Shao Yung for about thirty years, this did not mean that the study of emblems and numbers did not exist by then. The fact that this study had had a long and widespread tradition may fairly be shown by the emergence of the doctrine of Chu Chen[al] (1072–1178), a native of Shao-wu[am] in Fukien and the author of the *Han-shang I-chuan*[an] (Commentaries compiled beside the Han River on the *Book of Changes*), who was generally acknowledged as the past master in the study of emblems and numbers between the Northern and Southern Sung dynasties. The doctrines of Shao Yung continued to prevail in the Southern Sung dynasty. This can be seen in the case of Lin Kuang-ch'ao[ao] (1114–1178), a native of P'u-t'ien[ap] in Fukien whom Ch'üan Tsu-wang described as "having propagated the learning on the Ch'eng brothers into the southeast." Lin once put the question to Chang Shih: "Why did Ch'eng I never speak of emblems and numbers which are found in the *Book of Changes?*"[25] and Chang Shih could not explain this point.

While synthesizing various doctrines of Neo-Confucianism such as that of the Ch'eng brothers, Chou Tun-i, Shao Yung, and Chang Tsai, Chu Hsi was at the same time also in agreement with Lu Hsiang-shan (Lu Chiu-yüan,[aq] 1139–1193) of the School of Mind so far as they both held the fundamental principles of feudalism. As Huang Tsung-hsi said, "Both of them nourished the Three Bonds (*san-kang*[ar]) and Five Constant Virtues (*wu-ch'ang*[as]),[26] both of them upheld the Confucian ethical code, and both of them honored Confucius and Mencius."[27]

Chu annotated most of the Confucian Classics, including the Four Books. In addition, some 100 chapters in his own *Chu Tzu wen-chi*[at] (Collection of literary works of Master Chu) and 140 chapters in his *Classified Conversations* exerted great influence upon later generations and spread his doctrine afar to Japan, Korea, and Vietnam. One of the successors of the Fukien School, Hsiung Ho[au] (1247–1312), a native of Chien-yang[av] in Fukien, had, on the occasion of the founding of the T'ung-wen[aw] Academy, written a poem to the effect that someday the works of their school would be brought to Korea and Japan, and all the world would come for their instruction.[28] This poem witnessed the cultural intercourse between the Fukien School and Korea and Japan during the end of the Sung dynastry and the beginning of the Yüan dynasty.

Chu Hsi was born in Fukien and throughout his whole life he was closely related to Fukien. His teachers in his early years, namely, Hu Hsien[ax] (1082–1162, the nephew of Hu An-kuo), Liu Tzu-hui[ay] (1101–1147), Liu Mienchih[az] (1091–1149), and Li T'ung, were all Fukienese. In his middle age Chu Hsi had been appointed the prefect of Chang-chou[ba] in Fukien for a year. When he was persecuted in his later years he retired to private life in Chienyang of Fukien until his death.

Among the pupils of Chu Hsi there were seven who have been given inde-

pendent chapters in the *Writings of Sung and Yüan Philosophers:* Ts'ai Yüan-
ting[bb] (1135–1198), Huang Kan[bc] (1152–1221), Fu Kuang[bd] (*fl.* 1194), Ch'en
Chih[be] (*fl.* 1230), Tu Yü[bf] (1208 *cs*), Ts'ai Ch'en, and Ch'en Ch'un. Four of
these were Fukienese. In those later years, when he lived in Chien-yang, Chu
Hsi built the Ts'ang-chou[bg] Academy and called himself "the sick man of
Ts'ang-chou." Chapter 69 of the *Writings of Sung and Yüan Philosophers,*
devoted to Chu Hsi's pupils, shows that most of them studied at the Ts'ang-
chou Academy. Of the 156 pupils listed, 81 (51 percent) were Fukienese. In
the beginning of the *Classified Conversations of Master Chu,* the 97 persons
who recorded the conversations are listed. Of these, 31 were Fukienese,
namely, about one-third of the total. For good reason was the School of Chu
Hsi generally known as the Fukien School.

Successors of Chu Hsi and the Propagation of the Fukien School

Ts'ai Yüan-ting and Ts'ai Ch'en

Ts'ai Yüan-ting was one of Chu Hsi's most intimate pupils. He suffered the
Ch'ing-yüan[bh] (1195–1200) persecution together with Chu Hsi under the pre-
miership of Han T'o-chou[bi] (1152–1207) and died in exile in Tao-chou[bj] of
Hunan. On hearing of his death, Chu Hsi lamented and said, "Alas, is it for
you to have such an end? I shall find no more such sophisticated insight, such
excellent talent, such indomitable will, and such indisputable discourse as
yours."[29]

Ts'ai Yüan-ting contributed very much to the formation of the doctrine of
Chu Hsi. He gave much advice concerning the compilation of Chu Hsi's *Ssu-
shu chi-chu*[bk] (Collected commentaries on the Four Books). Chu Hsi's *I-hsüeh
ch'i-meng*[bl] (Primer on the *Book of Changes*) was first written by him. As Chu
Hsi himself observed, "Chi-t'ung[bm] [Ts'ai Yüan-ting's courtesy name] was so
modest that he only put his ideas into my work."[30] Two famous works of his
are the *Huang-chi ching-shih chih-yao*[bn] (A guide to the Supreme Ultimate governing the world) and *Lü-lü hsin-shu*[bo] (A new book on theories of music), both
of which belong to the study of emblems and numbers.

The main works of Ts'ai Ch'en are the *Shu chi-chuan*[bp] (Collected commentaries on the *Book of History*) and the *Hung-fan huang-chi*[bq] (Grand Norm and
the Supreme Ultimate). The former amplifies the ideas of his master Chu Hsi
and the latter that of his father Ts'ai Yüan-ting. The former was written in
line with orthodox Neo-Confucianism. In the year 1313 during the Yüan
dynasty, it was decreed that in the civil service examinations all interpretations on the *Book of History* should follow Ts'ai Ch'en's annotations. Thus
the intellectual influence of the Fukien School was greatly strengthened by
the official status of the book, which ranked together with Chu Hsi's *Collected*

Commentaries on the Four Books and others as the official assignments for scholarly reading.

Huang Kan and Ch'en Ch'un

Huang Kan, a native of Min-hsien[br] in Fukien, was Chu Hsi's son-in-law. Ch'en Ch'un was a young pupil of Chu Hsi's when the latter was the prefect at Chang-chou and again at Chien-yang later. Both of them kept strictly to the teachings of their master and upheld them earnestly.

In the field of compiling the classical documents, Huang Kan continued Chu Hsi's work with his own *I-li ching-chuan t'ung-chieh*[bs] (A general explanation of the *Book of Etiquette* and its commentaries). In the maintenance of the Confucian orthodoxy, he wrote some articles of significance. Like other disciples of Chu Hsi, Huang Kan himself made few innovations and amplifications.

With regard to Ch'en Ch'un, Ch'üan Tsu-wang said of him, "Sometimes he went too far towards opinions different from theirs."[31] In this respect, Ch'en Ch'un was imbued with more sectarianism than Huang Kan. One of the great contributions Ch'en Ch'un made was that he kept strictly to the teachings of the Ch'engs and Chu Hsi in working out his famous *Hsing-li tzu-i*[bt] (Meanings of terms on nature and principle), which endeavors to explain the concepts of Neo-Confucianism.

Ch'en P'u[bu] and Hsiung Ho

Ch'en P'u, a native of Ning-te[bv] in Fukien, and Hsiung Ho, a native of Chien-an[bw] in Fukien, were both disciples of Chu Hsi of the second generation and may be regarded as the junior forces of the Fukien School in the Southern Sung dynasty. Ch'en P'u made a very clear explanation on Chou Tun-i's doctrine of the Great Ultimate while keeping perfectly in line with Chu Hsi's interpretation.[32] Therefore it may well be seen that the followers of Chu Hsi in Fukien did thoroughly understand him and propounded his ideas.

Hsiung Ho was the dean of the Au-feng[bx] Academy in Chien-yang. In his works he cited numerous ancient stories in order to amplify the arguments of the Neo-Confucianists. In his essay *Shang yu san-jen liang-i-shih shuo*[by] (On the three virtuous men and two righteous ones of the Shang dynasty, 1751–1112 B.C.),[33] he argued that the fact that most of the Shang people would not let themselves be subject to the regime of the Western Chou dynasty (1111–770 B.C.) under the reign of King Wu[bz] (r. 1121–1116 B.C.) was a result of the long-time indoctrination of the Shang regime. He therefore concluded that it was of paramount importance to cultivate the minds and customs of society. The proposition that a good political and social order was dependent on good social custom constituted one of the most important arguments of the Fukien School. And it also afforded Hsiung Ho a reason for not serving the Yüan government.

Principles of Neo-Confucianism

Traditionally, the School of Chu Hsi represented the Neo-Confucian ortho-doxy. That this orthodoxy eventually became firmly established and devel-oped was to a considerable degree related to Chu Hsi's synthesis of the doc-trines of his predecessors into an all-embracing system. The two schools of Neo-Confucianism in the Northern Sung dynasty, that is, the School of Moral Principles of the Ch'eng brothers and the School of Emblems and Numbers of Shao Yung, were harmoniously synthesized by Chu Hsi. Thus the camp of Neo-Confucianism was enlarged and strengthened. As to Buddhist and Taoist ideas, though Chu Hsi looked upon them as destructive to morality and both empty and inactive, he still adopted an attitude of acquiescence toward them, especially toward Taoism. He had annotated Chou Tun-i's "Explanation of the Diagram of the Great Ultimate" which was considered to have derived from Taoism, and it was just in this Great Ultimate that the basic idea of his philosophy lay. And it was from the *Hua-yen ching*[ca] (Scripture of flowery splendor) of Buddhism that he borrowed the proposition "Everywhere the moon can be seen when it shines on all the rivers"[34] to illustrate the Ch'eng-Chu proposition "essence is one but its manifestations are many." On his death-bed Chu Hsi told his pupils, "The principle is no more than this. What awaits you is only to practice it hard."[35] No disciple of Chu's ever surpassed him. What the disciples did was only to observe what Chu Hsi had taught. Down to the Yüan and Ming (1368–1644) dynasties, no follower of his over-stepped the scope laid down by him.

During the Ming dynasty, one orthodox thinker of the Chu Hsi School, Hsüeh Hsüan[cb] (1389–1464) said of the *Collected Commentaries on the Four Books,* "It summarized the sayings of all the sages. . . . It is so broad and sub-stantial and yet so penetrating and so sophisticated that not a bit of the ideas of the ancient sages is left undeveloped. Scholars are sure to gain a great deal from him provided they realize and practice single-mindedly his method to achieve progress by thinking and reading."[36] This quotation implies that the comprehensiveness of Chu Hsi's system accounted for its wide propagation and that his disciples and followers in later generations failed to surpass him. The reason for the second point may perhaps be attributed to the fact that within a certain period of history the slumbering medieval society demanded nothing more in ideology from the scholars of that time.

In its contents, the Fukien School comprised all the characteristic features of Neo-Confucianism, such as the regulation of social strata in human rela-tionships, the rejection of utilitarianism in politics, the priority of morality over technique in learning, and the sharp demarcation between the Chinese and the foreigner in international relations. These had formed the fundamen-tal principles of the Confucianists ever since the time of Confucius (551–479

B.C.) and Mencius (372–289 B.C.?); and through the theoretical confirmation by the Ch'engs and Chu Hsi, they assumed the authority of the Neo-Confucian program under the label of a philosophical concept—the Principle of Heaven. About each of these items we shall say a few words.

Social Strata in Human Relationship. The ranks and titles of the feudal nobilities, the regulations of distinctions based on blood lineage, the difference in status between offspring of the wife and offspring of concubines, funeral ceremonies and dresses—all these, though very trivial and formalized, constituted the fundamental laws on which the patriarchal clan system rested. Chu Hsi himself had written *The General Explanation on the Book of Etiquette and Its Commentaries* and left his unfinished works the *"Chi-li"*[cc] (Sacrificial rites) and the *"Sang-li"*[xd] (Funeral rites) to his disciple and son-in-law Huang Kan to carry on. The dogmas expounded in these works have been far from being ineffective in later generations.

In the beginning of the Ming dynasty, Prince Yen,[ce] an offspring of the emperor's concubine, usurped the throne of his nephew Emperor Chienwen,[cf] the legitimate heir-apparent to the throne. This action was in a high degree contrary to Confucian and Neo-Confucian dogmas about the relationship of monarch and subjects. Fang Hsiao-ju[cg] (1357–1402), a famous scholar, opposed Prince Yen and died as a martyr rather than support the usurper. His stand in defiance of the usurpation had a profound influence as a moral example of Neo-Confucianism in later generations.

In the middle of the Ming dynasty Emperor Chia-ching[ch] intended to honor his dead father, who was only a prince in title, as an emperor. Such Neo-Confucian officials as Yang T'ing-ho[ci] (1459–1529) and his son Yang Shen[cj] objected because such behavior does not conform to the manners prescribed in the Confucian Classic the *Book of Rites.*

In the laws of the Ming and Ch'ing (1644–1912) dynasties, there were regulations on the privileges of the venerable, the senior, and the noble which embodied the Neo-Confucian principles of "priority to the prior" and "honor to the honorable." Even such an eminent scholar as Ku Yen-wu[ck] (1613–1682) possessed the privilege of drowning his servant, not to mention numerous other cases of how the lower social strata suffered under such an institution.

It was with a view to maintaining the social order of the privileged that different social statuses were regulated. Feudalism had carried with it innumerable suppressions and persecutions on the people of the lower social strata. In the subsequent development of the patriarchal system, Neo-Confucianism lent a strong hand in supporting and even promoting the same kinds of regulations, consciously as well as unconsciously.

Rejection of Utilitarianism in Politics. This was also a long tradition of the Confucian School. Confucius once said, "A gentleman understands righteous while a little-minded man understands utility (*li*[cl])."[37] Mencius spoke to King Hui of Liang,[cm] "Why must you talk of utility?"[38] In the Han dynasty Tung

Chung-shu[cn] (176–104 B.C.) preached, "So act as to follow the righteous and disregard its utility."[39] Chu Hsi and Chang Shih were on good terms because Chang Shih emphasized the distinction between righteousness and utility.

The distinction between the righteous and the utilitarian did not mean the cessation of all social activities. Chu Hsi himself had engaged in such activities as irrigation and storing up grains for relief. The learning of Huang Kan has been considered a "learning that deals with essence as well as function" because Huang engaged in the cause of defending the city against the invasion of the Chin[co] tribes.

Rejection of utilitarianism seems to mean that one should adhere to Confucian principles rather than trying to attain one's objective regardless of the means. To achieve his goals Shang Yang[cp] (d. 338 B.C.), a Legalist and prime minister of Duke Hsiao[cq] of Ch'in, would only duly mete out rewards and punishments. He vowed and offered an order to win the people's confidence that anyone who would remove a stake from the east gate to the west would be rewarded fifty golden coins. The Neo-Confucianist Hsiung Ho criticized this as "a trick on the part of a little-minded man."[40] Wang An-shih[cr] (1021–1086) was a noted reformer in the eleventh century who carried out his policy of *hsin-fa*[cs] (new law) for the improvement of public finance; this was looked upon by Neo-Confucianists as an exploitation by the government. Ch'eng Hao spoke of him as "squeezing by force."[41]

The method adopted by the Neo-Confucianists was to convince the people by proclaiming some empty slogans such as "urging the people to till the land" and the like and by instructing the intellectuals to observe Confucian doctrines and to study the learning of the rectification of the mind and the sincerity of the will. After obtaining high positions through their successes in civil service examinations, most Neo-Confucianists appeared to be pedantic and impractical and achieved nothing useful in their social activities. Here lay their weak points, which were severely criticized by their contemporary opponents Ch'en Liang[ct] (1143–1194) and Yeh Shih[cu] (1150–1223) and rebuked in later generations by Ku Yen-wu and Yen Yüan[cv] (1635–1704).

The influence that the Neo-Confucian dogma exerted upon later periods should not be underestimated. It is noteworthy that in his tomb inscription for Wei Hsüeh-lien[cw] (1608–1644), son of an upright officer Wei Ta-chung[cx] (1575–1625), Huang Tsung-hsi[cy] (1610–1695) said, "What he emphasized was the governing of the nation which amounts to no more than the learning of utility" and "It is the learning of utility that misled him."[42] Hence it is apparent that Huang Tsung-hsi followed the Confucian tradition and despised utility. As we know, the famous pamphlet *Ming-i tai-fang lu*[cz] (Waiting for dawn: A plan for the prince) usually attributed to him, was full of passages on the topics of utility. Here we find a little contradiction in Huang Tsunghsi's expression.

Priority of morality over technique in learning. In the view of Neo-Confucianists, morality meant the way of Confucius and Mencius. It is what they called the Principle or Way of Heaven. Technique here meant the productive arts or crafts. The view that the former should take precedence over the latter formed a long tradition in the intellectual history of China. In the *Book of Rites* it is written: "The accomplishment of virtue belongs to the nobles and that of technique to the common people,"[43] upon which K'ung Ying-ta[da] (574–648), the famous T'ang dynasty (618–907) specialist on ancient Classics, commented: "By the nobles was meant the kings, princes, and masters. They accomplished their tasks by virtue and hence ranked high. By the common people was meant the musicians and sorcerers. They achieved their tasks by their technique and hence ranked low."[44]

When Neo-Confucianism was prevailing in the Northern Sung dynasty, the emphasis on the priority of morality over technique was very much in vogue. The fact that the Ch'eng brothers never spoke of numbers is a reflection of the prejudice of the nobility that the study of emblems and numbers belonged to the level of technique. Ch'ao Yüeh-chih[db] (1059–1129), an admirer of Chang Tsai, once remarked, "As for the study of terms and numbers, a gentleman learns it but does not take it as essential."[45]

Chu Hsi, whose scope of study extended rather broadly, did not object to the learning of the emblems and numbers. He pointed out that "the study of calendar, jurisprudence, astronomy, geography, and so on all should be paid due attention,"[46] and he knew a great deal about natural sciences himself. Nevertheless, what he emphasized was "the way the *Great Learning* taught people in ancient times," "the Classics of the sages and their commentaries by ancient scholars," and "the way of scrutinizing the principle, rectifying the heart, cultivating the self, and governing the nation."[47]

Through the Chu Hsi School, such an intellectual tradition continued to flourish for centuries. The science and technology introduced from Europe into China by the end of the Ming dynasty, even though far behind the advanced level in the West at that time, was rejected by the Neo-Confucian literati as superfluous artifice, while those intellectuals in favor of it, such as Hsü Kuang-ch'i[dc] (1562–1633) and Li Chih-ts'ao[dd] (1565–1630), did not belong to the mainstream of the literati. As late as the end of the Ch'ing dynasty Chang Chih-tung[de] (1837–1909) when obliged to found the Hanyang[df] arsenal after the European pattern still propounded, "Let Chinese learning be the essence and Western learning be the function."[48] Further, the requirement of the civil service examinations had always been confined within the scope of the Four Books and the Five Classics[49] with very little care for the knowledge of natural sciences. This requirement showed that the Confucian tradition of priority of morality over technique was great enough to determine the cultural policy of the government.

With such a cultural and academic background, it was indeed very difficult for the Chinese to provide a sound basis for the development of natural sciences. It is partly because of this fact that science in modern China and thereby the country's national strength have declined.

Sharp demarcation between the Chinese and the foreigner. This kind of discernment constituted an integral part of the Confucian "significance in the *Spring and Autumn Annals.*" It was recorded in the *Kung-yang*[dg] *Commentary* that "the *Spring and Autumn Annals* endears its own country but not its neighboring nations, and endears its own neighboring nations but not the barbarian nations."[50] Thus a sharp demarcation was set between nations in accordance with their distance from one's own country—a principle which was called "discernment of China and the foreign"—just as that held among relatives, which was called "the gradation of intimacy."

This discernment involved also the love for national independence. In his appeal to Emperor Hsiao-tsung[dh] (r.1163–1189), Chu Hsi repeatedly declared that "the present policy should be no other than the strengthening of national power in defense against the foreigner."[51] This proposal aimed at the resistance by the Sung dynasty against the Chin tribes, but the origin of such an ideology may be traced to the Confucian discernment of the Chinese against the foreigner.

By the fall of the Sung dynasty there appeared such national heroes as Wen T'ien-hsiang[di] (1236–1282), Hsieh Ping-te[dj] (1226–1289), Lu Hsiu-fu[dk] (1238–1279), and Lin Ching-hsi[dl] (*fl.* 1271), whose stories became well known to later generations.[52] Another anti-Mongol hero, Chang Shih-chieh[dm] (d. 1279), came from the rank of low officers and was recorded in history as saying, "Though I know I'd be a wealthy dignitary if I should surrender to the enemy, I would still be willing to die for my sovereign."[53] Here the Confucian obligation of a vassal to his lord found its typical expression.

By the fall of the Ming dynasty Shih K'o-fa[dn] (1601–1645), who defended Yang-chou[do] in the north side of the Yangtze River in Kiangsu; Yen Ying-yüan[dp] (1607–1645), who died to defend Chiang-yin[dq] in the south of the Yangtze; Ch'en Tzu-lung[dr] (1608–1647) and Hsia Wan-ch'un[ds] (1631–1647), who died after being captured by Manchu troops; Liu Tsung-chou[dt] (1578–1645), who died of a hunger strike;[54] and other innumerable examples of loyalty and patriotism, whether recorded or not, can be attributed to the Neo-Confucian teachings on demarcation between the Chinese and the foreigner.

The propagation and influence of the Chu Hsi School was at the same time the propagation and influence of Neo-Confucianism in the Southern Sung dynasty. In the early years of the Yüan dynasty, with its introduction to the north by Chao Fu[du] (*fl.* 1235), Liu Yin[dv] (1249–1293), and others, it gradually gained nation-wide influence. As the most systematic and most profound orthodox ideology, it played a sweeping role for more than seven centuries down to the beginning of the present century. And its merits as well as its demerits should be given a thorough historical analysis and should be neither entirely refuted nor blindly accepted. Historical phenomena are doomed to pass away. It is for us to draw instructions therefrom.

Throughout the last seven centuries the political and cultural history of

China has been closely connected with the development of Neo-Confucianism. Yen Fu[dw] (1853–1921), the famous representative of the enlightenment of the last years of the Ch'ing dynasty, came into contact with Western learning when he was studying in London; during his later years he introduced such scholars as Huxley, Spencer, and Adam Smith into China. It was Yen Fu who remarked, "Today [the nineteenth century] our ideas, manners, and politics may find their causes and results in the history of Sung, Yüan and Ming, either directly or indirectly." This assertion is generally valid. The ideology of Sung, Yüan, and Ming was chiefly the Neo-Confucianism of Chu Hsi, which originated in Fukien. With these words Yen Fu pointed out the significance of the study of Neo-Confucianism and particularly of Chu Hsi.

But the school of Chu Hsi was only one form of Neo-Confucianism. The Neo-Confucianists can be divided into three categories. The first category comprises those who kept strictly to the teachings of the Ch'engs and Chu Hsi. They commented on the Classics and preached the orthodox doctrine to their pupils. It is true that some of them did maintain their principles without regard to their own benefits. But they were pedantic in their actions and incapable of solving impending social problems, thus impressing others with their incompetence. To this category belonged a rather large number of the Neo-Confucianists such as the Ch'engs' disciple Yin Ch'un and Chu Hsi's disciple Ch'en Ch'un. The second category includes those who sought personal benefits under the pretext of preaching Neo-Confucianism, especially after the time when the Four Books and the Five Classics were required for officialdom. They talked about high-sounding moralities, but in reality they did everything they could for their own interests, no matter how ignoble their behavior might be. They were generally called *chia-tao-hsüeh*[dx] (pseudo-Confucianists). Those who paid attention to social problems and endeavored to make the nation well governed by the theories of ancient sages comprise the third category. They were concerned with the practical issues of society and the people and regarded themselves as genuine Confucianists both in essence and in function. This tendency began with Hu An-kuo in Hunan and Lü Tsu-ch'ien[dy] (1137–1181) in Chekiang, both of whom laid emphasis on the *Tso-chuan*[dz] (Tso's Commentary of the *Spring and Autumn Annals*), a classical work expounding more about current politics and less about theories. And the later stream from Ch'en Liang and Yeh Shih down to Yen Yüan who were all very critical of Neo-Confucianism may also be classified in this category.

Ku Yen-wu once observed. "[The Neo-Confucianists] talked about their subtle doctrines all day long while discarding the poverty and misery of the people without any concern."[55] What he criticized here is the weak point of the Neo-Confucianists of the first category. And those whom Li Chih[ea] (1527–1602) blamed and Chi Yün[eb] (1724–1805) and Yüan Mei[ec] (1716–1797) satirized in their works[56] belonged to the second category, the pseudo-Confucianists. As for those of the third category, they had cast off the confines of nonutility. They realized that the discernment of the righteous from utility and acting to follow the righteous while disregarding its utility were mere pompous words. Eventually they were driven to the conclusion that "virtue dwells only where one succeeds in success" (Ch'en Liang).[57] Later, in the last years of the Ming dynasty, Ch'en Ch'üeh[ed] (1604–1677) and Wang Fu-chih[ee] (1619–1692) further developed this idea into a more definite proposition that "the Principle of Heaven consists in human desires"[58] and thus opened the way for further development of the advanced ideology of the age.

What of Chu Hsi? Where does he fit in this scheme? Chu Hsi may be regarded as belonging to both the first and the third categories. In the early Ch'ing dynasty Fang Pao[ef] (1668–1749) in his tomb inscription for Li Kung[eg] (1659–1733) praised Chu thus: "Neither the fames of Chao [Chao Kuang-han[eh]] and Chang [Chang T'ang[ei]] of the Western Han dynasty [206 B.C.–A.D. 8] nor the celebrities of Yang [Yang Lien[ej]] and Tso [Tso Kuang-tou[ek]] of late Ming can surpass [him]."[59] This is, of course, an exaggeration by an orthodox Neo-Confucianist, for after all, Chu Hsi was a theorist rather than a practitioner. A more judicious evaluation was made by Ch'en K'uei[el] (1139–1194), a contemporary of Chu Hsi, who once said, "Lü Tsu-ch'ien read a great many books but to no avail, and Chu Hsi prepared prescriptions but produced no effect."[60] Chu Hsi, on hearing of this criticism, thought Ch'en K'uei very candid in expression and sent his disciples to learn from Ch'en. The famous scholar Wen T'ing-shih[em] (1856–1904), speaking of Chu Hsi's *Classified Conversations,* remarked in his diary, "Chu Hsi's instructions to his disciples were so penetrating that it seemed as though one could look into his heart even after so many generations. . . . But his remarks concerning the military and law were inadequate to gratify the readers."[61] These remarks seems to come nearer than the literary exaggerations of Fang Pao to the truth about Chu Hsi.

Translated by He Chao-wu[en]

Notes

1. The term *chi-ta-ch'eng* comes from the *Book of Mencius,* 5B:1. Li Fang-tzu (Li Kuo-chai[eo]) used the term in his *Chu Tzu nien-p'u*[ep] [Chronological biography of Master Chu] and Ch'en Ch'un in his "Yen-ling[eq] Lectures" in the *Pei-hsi ta-ch'üan-chi*[er] [Complete works of Ch'en Ch'un], ch. 15. Although Li Fang-tzu's work has long been lost, several paragraphs of it were quoted by Wang Mao-hung[es] (1668–1741) in his *Chu Tzu nien-p'u.* Cf. Wang's *Chu Tzu nien-p'u* (Shanghai: World Book Co. 1941), 4B:240, and Ch'en Ch'un's "Yen-ling Lectures," particularly the "Shih-yu yüan-yüan"[et] [Relations with teachers and fellow students], in the *Pei-hsi ta-ch'üan chi,* ch. 15.

2. The Four Books are the *Great Learning,* the *Doctrine of the Mean,* the *Analects,* and the *Book of Mencius.* All these four Neo-Confucian Classics were annotated by Chu Hsi.

3. *Chen Wen-chung kung tu-shu chi*[eu] [Chen Tê-hsiu's reading journal], (1739 ed.), 31:35a–36b.

4. *Sung-Yüan hsüeh-an*[ev] [Writings of Sung and Yüan philosophers], (Shanghai: World Book Co., 1936) ch. 48, p. 846.

5. *Ibid.*, pp. 845–846.

6. *Chu Tzu yü-lei*[ew] [Classified conversations of Master Chu], (1876 ed.), 101:1a.

7. *Ibid.*, 101:2b.

8. *Ibid.*, 101:20b–21a.

9. *Ibid.*, 101:2a.

10. *Ibid.*, 101:19a.

11. *Ibid.*, 101:14b.

12. *Ibid.*, 101:17a.

13. *I-Lo yüan-yüan lu*[ex] [Origin and development of the Ch'eng School], (1886 ed.), 10:1a–6a.

14. *Chu Tzu yü-lei*, 137:11a.

15. *Ibid.*, 93:2b.

16. *Ibid.*, 102:1a.

17. *Ibid.*, 102:1b.

18. *Ibid.*, 103:3b.

19. *Ibid.*, 103:4b.

20. *Ibid.*, 103:4b.

21. *Sung-Yüan hsüeh-an*, ch. 25, p. 549.

22. *Ibid.*, ch. 48, p. 847.

23. The Three Principles are: to illustrate illustrious virtue, to renovate the people, and to rest in the highest excellence. The Eight Items are: investigating things, extending knowledge, being sincere in thoughts, rectifying of the heart, cultivating the person, regulating the family, governing the state, and pacifying the world.

24. Ch'en Shan[ey] (*fl.* 1174–1187), *Men-shih hsin-hua*[ez] [New talks in a proud manner], (Shanghai: Commercial Press, 1910), 10:3a. This saying was also inserted in Ting Ch'uan-ching,[fa] *Sung-jen i-shih hui-pien*[fb] [Collected anecdotes of eminent people in the Sung dynasty], (Shanghai: Commercial Press, 1935), p. 388.

25. *Chu Tzu yü-lei*, 103:8b.

26. The Three Bonds are: "the officer should be subordinated to the emperor," "the wife should obey her husband," and "the son should submit to his father." Those stipulations were proposed by the Han Confucianists and recorded in the *Pai-hu t'ung*[fc] [White Tiger Hall discussions]. The Five Constant Virtues are *jen* (benevolence), *i* (justice), *li* (propriety), *chih* (wisdom), and *hsin*[fd] (trustworthiness). Such kind of composing of virtues was proposed by Tung Chung-shu in his memorial to the Han Emperor Wu.[fe]

27. *Sung-Yüan hsüeh-an*, ch. 58, p. 1068.

28. *Hsiung Wu-hsüan chi*[ff] [Collected works of Hsiung Ho], (Cheng-i t'ang[fg] 1709 ed.), 5:3b.

29. *Chu Tzu wen-chi* [SPPY ed.], ch. 87, p. 1519.

30. Weng I[fh] (*fl.* 1247, a disciple of Ts'ai Yüan-ting), *Ts'ai-shih chiu-ju hsing-shih*[fi] [Lives of the nine Ts'ai scholars], in the head chapter of the *Ts'ai-shih chiu-ju shu*[fj] [Works of the nine Ts'ai scholars], (1868 ed.), p. 2a, "General Narratives."

31. *Sung-Yüan hsüeh-an*, ch. 68, p. 1257.

32. Cf. *Sung-Yüan hsüeh-an*, ch. 64, pp. 1164–1165, a letter by Ch'en Pu commenting on the Ultimate of Nonbeing and the Great Ultimate.

33. *Hsiung wu-hsüan chi*, 4:5a.

34. *Hua-yen ching*, ch. 23, sec. 24; *Chu Tzu yü-lei*, 94:41a.

35. *Ts'ai-shih chiu-ju shu*, 6:59b, Ts'ai Ch'en, *Chu Wen Kung meng-tien chi*[fk] [Memory of Master Chu's death].

36. Hsüeh Hsüan, *Tu-shu lu*[fl] [Reading journal], (Cheng-i t'ang abridged ed., 1866), 2:1b.

37. *Analects*, 4:16.

38. *Book of Mencius*, 1A:1.

39. *Han shu*[fm] [History of the former Han dynasty], (Beijing: Chung-hua[fn] Book Co., 1962), p. 2524.

40. *Hsiung wu-hsüan chi*, 4:9a.

41. *Ming-tao wen-chi*[fo] [Collection of literary works of Ch'eng Hao], (SPPY ed.), 2:4a, "Memorial Protesting the New Laws."

42. *Huang Li-chou wen-chi*[fp] [Collection of literary works of Huang Tsung-hsi], (Beijing: Chung-hua Book Co., 1959), pp. 196–198.

43. *Book of Rites*, ch. 38, "Record of Music," sec. 19.

44. *Li-chi cheng-i*[fq] [Correct meanings of the *Book of Rites*], comment on the above.

45. *Sung-Yüan hsüeh-an*, ch. 23, p. 492.

46. *Chu Tzu yü-lei*, 117:26a.

47. Preface to the *Commentary on the Great Learning*.

48. *Ch'üan-hsüeh p'ien*[fr] [Treatise to promote learning], outer chapters, 3:10a, "Establishing School."

49. The Five Classics are the *Book of Odes*, the *Book of History*, the *Book of Rites*, the *Book of Changes*, and the *Spring and Autumn Annals*. All these Classics were in the past considered compiled by Confucius.

50. *Kung-yang Commentary*, Duke Ch'eng,[fs] fifteenth year.

51. *Chu Tzu wen-chi*, ch. 11, p. 162, "Appeal to Emperor Hsiao-tsung in 1162."

52. Wen Tien-hsiang, a famous writer and patriot, was considered by Ch'üan Tsu-wang as the younger generation of one of Chu Hsi's disciples, Ou-yang Ch'ien-chih.[ft] See the *Sung-Yüan hsüeh-an*, ch. 69, pp. 1301–1302; ch. 88, p. 1664. Hsieh Ping-te died of a hunger strike and was well known by his literary name, Hsieh Tieh-shan.[fu] Lu Hsiu-fu, chief minister in the last days of the Sung dynasty, drowned himself with Emperor Ping[fv] in the South Sea after losing hope of resisting the Mongol invasion. Lin Ching-hsi (Lin Chi-shan[fw]), a native of Wen-chou[fx] in Chekiang, was noted for his safe-guarding and burying the bones of Sung emperors and empresses in the mausoleums at Shao-hsing in Chekiang, which were evacuated and destroyed by Mongol soldiers. All these patriots except Lin were recorded in the *Sung shih*[fy] [History of the Sung dynasty], ch. 418 (Wen T'ien-hsiang), ch. 425 (Hsieh Ping-te), and ch. 451 (Lu Hsiu-fu); and the *Lin Chi-shan chi*[fz] [Collected works of Ling Ching-hsi], in the *Yung-chia shih-jen tz'u-t'ang ts'ung-k'o*[ga] [A series of publications in the Memorial Hall to the Poets of Wen-chow], comp. Mao Kuang-sheng[gb] (1873–1959).

53. *Sung shih* (Beijing: Chung-hua Book Co., 1962), ch. 451, p. 13,274.

54. Ch'en Tzu-lung, an intimate friend of Fang I-chih[gc] (1611–1671), was captured by Ch'ing military in 1647 and drowned himself. Hsia Wan-ch'un, the son of Hsia Yün-i[gd] (1596–1645) who drowned himself in loyalty to the Ming, was arrested and killed by the Manchus after his father's death. Liu Tsung-chou, teacher of Huang Tsung-hsi, had refused to take food and died after the fall of Nanking and Chekiang.

55. *T'ing-lin wen-chi*[ge] [Collection of literary works of Ku Yen-wu], (SPTK ed.), 3:1a.

56. Chi Yün, scholar and editor-in-chief, of the *Ssu-k'u ch'üan-shu*[gf] [Complete library in the four branches of literature], composed a series of fables and anecdotes in his *Yüeh-wei ts'ao-t'ang pi-chi*[gg] [Sketches in the thatched cottage penetrating into the

essence of things] to satirize pseudo-Confucianists. Yüan Mei, significant poet and author of *Sui-yüan shih-hua*[gh] [Sui Garden's critique on poetry], had a creative spirit and stressed the importance of free expression of natural emotions.

57. See the *Sung-Yüan hsüeh-an*, ch. 56, p. 1042.

58. Cf. Wang Fu-chih, *Chou-i wai-chuan*[gi] [Outer commentaries on the *Book of Changes*], ch. 1, the *tun*[gj] hexagram; and Hou Wai-lu's[gk] Introduction to the *Ch'en Ch'üeh che-hsüeh hsüan-chi*[gl] [Selection of Ch'en Chüeh's philosophical works], (Beijing: Scientific Publishing House, 1959), p. 4.

59. *Wang-ch'i wen-chi*[gm] [Collection of literary works of Fang Pao], (SPTK ed.), 10:2a.

60. *Sung-Yüan hsüeh-an,* ch. 61, p. 1112.

61. Wen T'ing-shih's *Lü-chiang jih-chi*[gn] [Diary of travel on the Northern Pearl River] was printed in the Ch'ing-ho[go] [Green crane journal] vol. 2, no. 21 (1934), in Shanghai.

Glossary

a	集大成	ae	宣和	bi	韓侂冑
b	李方子	af	龜山語錄	bj	道州
c	陳淳	ag	龜山誌銘	bk	四書集註
d	程顥	ah	周敦頤	bl	易學啓蒙
e	程頤	ai	黃百家	bm	李通
f	象數	aj	全祖望	bn	皇極經世指要
g	邵雍	ak	儒門淡泊	bo	律呂新書
h	洪範	al	朱震	bp	書集傳
i	禹	am	邵武	bq	洪範皇極
j	楊時	an	漢上易傳	br	閩縣
k	南劍	ao	林光朝	bs	儀禮經傳通解
l	眞德秀	ap	莆田	bt	性理字義
m	浦城	aq	陸象山九淵	bu	陳普
n	蔡沈	ar	三綱	bv	寧德
o	羅從彥	as	五常	bw	建安
p	李侗	at	朱子文集	bx	鰲峯
q	謝良佐	au	熊禾	by	商有三仁兩義士説
r	胡安國	av	建陽	bz	武
s	胡宏	aw	同文	ca	華嚴經
t	張栻	ax	胡憲	cb	薛瑄
u	湖湘	ay	劉子翬	cc	祭禮
v	張浚	az	劉勉之	cd	喪禮
w	張載	ba	漳州	ce	燕
x	游酢	bb	蔡元定	cf	建文
y	呂大臨	bc	黃榦	cg	方孝孺
z	張繹	bd	輔廣	ch	嘉靖
aa	尹焞	be	陳埴	ci	楊廷和
ab	紹興	bf	杜煜	cj	楊愼
ac	禪	bg	滄洲	ck	顧炎武
ad	蔡京	bh	慶元	cl	利

cm 梁惠王
cn 董仲舒
co 金
cp 商鞅
cq 孝
cr 王安石
cs 新法
ct 陳亮
cu 葉適
cv 顏元
cw 魏學濂
cx 魏大中
cy 黃宗羲
cz 明夷待訪錄
da 孔穎達
db 晁說之
dc 徐光啓
dd 李之藻
de 張之洞
df 漢陽
dg 公羊
dh 孝宗
di 文天祥
dj 謝枋得
dk 陸秀夫
dl 林景傑
dm 張世傑
dn 史可法
do 楊州
dp 閻應元
dq 江陰
dr 陳子龍
ds 夏完淳
dt 劉宗周
du 趙復
dv 劉因

dw 嚴復
dx 假道學
dy 呂祖謙
dz 左傳
ea 李贄
eb 紀昀
ec 袁枚
ed 陳確
ee 王夫之
ef 方苞
eg 李琛
eh 趙廣漢
ei 張湯
ej 楊濂
ek 左光斗
el 陳葵
em 文廷式
en 何兆武
eo 李果齋
ep 朱子年譜
eq 嚴陵
er 北溪大全集
es 王懋竑
et 師友淵源
eu 眞文忠公讀書記
ev 宋元學案
ew 朱子語類
ex 伊洛淵源錄
ey 陳善
ez 捫蝨新話
fa 丁傳靖
fb 宋人軼事彙編
fc 白虎通
fd 仁義禮智信
fe 武
ff 熊勿軒集

fg 正誼堂
fh 翁易
fi 蔡氏九儒行實
fj 蔡氏九儒書
fk 朱文公夢奠記
fl 讀書錄
fm 漢書
fn 中華
fo 明道文集
fp 黃梨洲文集
fq 禮記正義
fr 勸學篇
fs 成
ft 歐陽謙之
fu 謝疊山
fv 昺
fw 林景熙霽山
fx 溫州
fy 宋史
fz 林霽山集
ga 永嘉詩人祠堂叢刻
gb 冒廣生
gc 方以智
gd 夏允彝
ge 亭林文集
gf 四庫全書
gg 閱微草堂筆記
gh 隨園詩話
gi 周易外傳
gj 屯
gk 侯外廬
gl 陳確哲學選集
gm 望溪文集
gn 旅江日記
go 青鶴

28

Chu Hsi's Influence in Yüan Times

LIU TS'UN-YAN

CHU HSI DIED in the third month in the sixth year of Ch'ing-yüan[a] (1200) at K'ao-t'ing,[b] Chien-yang,[c] Fukien. This was almost ninety years before the complete annihilation of the resistance of the Sung forces by the invading Mongols, whose empire in China, the Yüan dynasty (1279–1368), was founded in 1277. The Mongols ruled China for approximately a hundred years. During this fairly long period Chu Hsi's influence was felt not only among the Neo-Confucianist intellectuals, but also among the populace at the everyday level, for whom it became a sort of guiding force, both for spiritual and moral enlightenment and for social communication and human relations. Without the tremendous efforts made by the Yüan Confucian scholars who, by and large, followed Chu Hsi's school of teaching, the academic lineage of Sung (960–1279) Neo-Confucianism would have been seriously disrupted under a foreign power whose early nomad rulers would have perceived little difference between the teaching of Confucius (551–479 B.C.) and that of some Tibetan lama or indigenous Taoist patriarch. Had that happened, the chapters on Sung-Ming (1368–1644) Neo-Confucianism in any work of history of Chinese philosophy would read very differently from what they now do.

Despite the fact that the contributions of the Yüan Neo-Confucianists towards the cause of the preservation of Chinese culture were so great, not many analytical studies about them and their contribution to the development of Chinese philosophy have been published. The lack of basic material for study may have been a factor contributing to this neglect. It is only in recent years that scholars have benefited from the publication of a large number of Yüan works produced photolithographically from the *Ssu-k'u ch'üan shu*[d] (A great collection of classical works in the Imperial Library according to four bibliographical divisions)[1] and other rare editions, and so find themselves in a better position than Ch'üan Tsu-wang[e] (1705–1755), the cocompiler of the *Sung-Yüan hsüeh-an*[f] (A compendious study of Sung-Yüan philosophers and their works) who, not being a great bibliophile like Huang Tsung-hsi[g] (1610–1695),[2] the earlier compiler, had to resort to hand-copying a work of Wu Ch'eng[h] (1249–1333) from a private library named Yün-tsai Lou[i] in 1723[3] and to take an occasional risk by borrowing a few volumes of the *Yung-lo*[j] *Encyclopedia* from the Imperial Library while serving as an academician for less than two years (1736–1737) in Peking.[4]

Generally speaking, for the study of the influence of Chu Hsi in Yüan times the existing edition of the *Sung-Yüan hsüeh-an*, initiated and first drafted by Huang Tsung-hsi but revised and completed by Ch'üan Tsu-wang, may still be regarded as the most valuable work of its kind. It is known that Ch'üan began to work on Huang's manuscript in 1746–1747 and had more or less completed the Sung section by 1747, for in that year he planned to send that part of the work to Soochow for engraving.[5] A draft of the Yüan section seems to have been virtually finished in 1754, one year before Ch'üan's death. However, it has been learned that as late as 1776, twenty years after Ch'üan's death, the draft manuscript had not yet been made into a clean copy,[6] and the first printed edition of the *Sung-Yüan hsüeh-an* did not come out until 1838.[7] Although this academic work has such a long history of compilation, its veracity has generally not been questioned, for at least two reasons. First, both Huang and Ch'üan were great historians, and Huang was also a great Neo-Confucianist himself, a disciple of Liu Tsung-chou[k] (1578–1645). Both this work and Huang's *Ming-ju hsüeh-an*[l] (A compendious study of Ming philosophers and their works) were pioneering contributions in their own right; without them, a modern historian of Chinese philosophy of these periods would not have known where to start. Second, as already mentioned, Huang was a bibliophile who could consult his private library of more than 30,000 volumes of printed works, in which were preserved many of the rare works originally in the holdings of the Tan-sheng T'ang[m] of the Ch'i[n] family and the Ch'uan-shih Lou[o] of the Hsü family,[p] both earlier collections.[8] As to Ch'üan Tsu-wang, although he was not a bibliophile he was nevertheless a trained researcher, and in each of the items he inserted or revised in the work he included source material, much of which can be corroborated by articles found in his own collected works, *Chieh-ch'i-t'ing chi*[q] (Collected works from the Pavilion of Clam-gathering).[9] Still, for the convenience of my readers as well as for the sake of an independent scholarship, whenever I cite the *Sung-Yüan hsüeh-an* in the present article, I tried to corroborate it with such available sources as I have also read and sometimes quote separately. With one or two exceptions, it was only in those places where the original texts are no longer extant that I have cited the *hsüeh-an* itself as the source.

The Promulgation of Chu Hsi's Teaching

The teaching of Chu Hsi was said to be unknown at the beginnings of Yüan power until the arrival of Chao Fu[r] (c. 1206–c. 1299), a Confucian scholar who was taken captive in Te-an,[s] Hupeh, in 1235 but was brought back to the North by Yao Shu[t] (1202–1279) and Yang Wei-chung[u] (1205–1259), two prominent Yüan officials. Upon Yao's persuasion, Chao became the first preacher of the Ch'eng-Chu[v] teachings in North China. Scholars such as Hsü Heng[w] (1209–1281), Ho Ching[x] (1223–1275) and Liu Yin[y] (1249–1293) were among his disciples.[10] A very detailed account of this, the "Hsü Chiang-han hsien-sheng shih-shih"[z] (About Chao Fu, the Master of Chiang-han), written by Yao Sui[aa] (1239–1314), Yao Shu's nephew and a student of Hsü Heng, is included in Sui's *Mu-an chi*[ab] (Collected works from the hut of a shepherd) and served as a blueprint of Chao Fu's biography in the *Yüan-shih*,[ac] ch. 189.[11] According to Ou-yang Hsüan[ad] (1283–1357), when Hsü Heng was learning those interpretations from Chao, Chao had to write them down for him from memory, for in the North the Ch'eng-Chu annotations to the Classics were still not available.[12] Yao Shu, Yang Wei-chung, and a few others were the earliest officials who started to print and promulgate the works of Chu Hsi and other Neo-Confucianists in Peking. In the *Mu-an chi* we have:

[Yao Shu] himself sponsored the printing of [Chu Hsi's] *Hsiao-hsüeh*,[ae] (A primer of Classics), *Lun-yü huo-wen*[af] (Questions and answers on Confucian *Analects*), *Meng-tzu huo-wen*[ag] (Questions and answers on the *Book of Mencius*), and *Chia-li*[ah] (Family rituals) and invited Councillor Yang Wei-chung to publish the Four Books,[13] T'ien Ho-ch'ing[ai] to publish the *Shang-shu sheng-shih che-chung*[aj] (An attempt at the proper interpretations of the *Book of History* and the *Book of Odes*),[14] the *Commentary on the Book of Changes* by Ch'eng [Ch'eng I,[ak] 1033–1107], the *Commentary on the Book of History* by Ts'ai [Ts'ai Ch'en,[al] 1167–1230], and the *Commentary on the Spring and Autumn Annals* by Hu [Hu An-kuo,[am] 1074–1138]. They were all engraved in Peking. He still thought that the circulation of the *Hsiao-hsüeh* was not wide enough. Therefore he ordered Yang Ku,[an] one of his disciples, to use the movable type printing invented by Shen Kua[ao] [1029–1093] to publish it, together with the *Chin-ssu lu*[ap] (Reflections on things at hand) and the essays on Classics and history written by Tung-lai [Lü Tsu-ch'ien,[aq] 1137–1181] which were widely spread through the country.[15]

About the teachings being "widely spread" the *Mu-an chi* later remarks, "Today even teachers at village schools for children all over China realize the importance of the *Hsiao-hsüeh* and the Four Books, which they use for elementary courses; and even those in far away lands with tattooed skin, and those who serve as clerks and retainers, even hawkers and people of non-Chinese origin often carry them in their hands and learn to recite the words."[16] This is echoed in the writing of Yü Chi[ar] (1272–1348), who describes the life of Hsiung Peng-lai[as] (1246–1323), a Sung scholar who lived into middle Yüan, leading a simple life as a school teacher in the villages. "Very often he gathered around him more than a hundred pupils. He summarized the gist from Chu Hsi's *Hsiao-hsüeh* for his lecture notes, which were later printed and became a household reader throughout the country."[17]

Even at an early stage of his career, before mounting the throne, Khubilai Khan had instructed Chao Pi[at] to study Mongol and had translated Chen Te-hsiu's[au] (1178–1235) *Ta-hsüeh yen-i*[av] (Exposition of the *Great Learning*) for him.[18] Chen Te-hsiu was a student of Chan T'i-jen[aw] (1143–1206), a direct disciple of Chu Hsi. Yü Chi, in an article on "Posthumous Titles" tells us that Chao tells us that Chao Pi actually taught his Mongolian students the Four Books—presumably including Chu Hsi's commentaries.[19]

The three early Yüan Confucian scholars Hsü Heng, Wu Ch'eng, and Liu Yin have been studied fairly thoroughly in recent years by contemporary scholars in the West.[20] Hsü Heng was known as a staunch supporter of Chu Hsi. Liu Yin showed some appreciation of Shao Yung's[ax] (1011–1077) metaphysical speculations in his study of the *Book of Changes*, but even in those writings he sometimes "wonder[ed] what could have been in Chu Hsi's mind here."[21] An Hsi[ay] (1269–1311) was a follower of Liu Yin because of his deep admiration for Liu's work, though he did not have the chance to know the master personally. In his own writings he revealed his great esteem for Chu Hsi[22] which tallies with the view evident in a number of Liu's own writings[23] and those of Su T'ien-chüeh[az] (1294–1352),[24] a student of An Hsi, and Huang Chin[ba] (1277–1357). The latter maintained that Liu Yin's study of the *Hsiao-hsüeh* grasped the "implied meaning beyond the written words of Chu Hsi."[25]

Of the three, Wu Ch'eng's position seems to differ slightly from those of the other two because of his varied academic background. His native place Lin-ch'uan,[bb] Kiangsi, was a city where Huang Kan[bc] (1152–1221), a disciple and son-in-law of Chu Hsi, was magistrate around 1210. Apparently the teaching of Chu Hsi had been seeded there, although the influence of Lu Chiu-yüan's (Lu Hsiang-shan,[bd] 1139–1193) School was still deeply rooted in the province. One of Wu Ch'eng's teachers was Ch'eng Jo-yung[be] (*fl.* 1260), a disciple of Jao Lu[bf] (*fl.* 1256), who had been taught alternately by Huang Kan, Li Fan[bg] (*fl.* 1198), and Ch'ai Chung-hsing[bh] (1190[cs]) (Li was Chu Hsi's student, Ch'ai his follower). Many of Jao Lu's direct disciples were active in late Southern Sung (1127–1279) around 1228–1259. Only a small portion of Jao's writings are still preserved, partly in Ch'eng Tuan-li's[bi] (1271–1345) *Ch'eng-shih chia-shu tu-shu fen-nien jih-ch'eng*[bj] (A chronologically arranged syllabus for classical studies used in the Ch'engs' family school)[26] and partly in Wu Ch'eng's writings.[27] Wu inherited from Jao some of his skeptical attitude towards Chu Hsi; Wu also came under the influence of Ch'eng Shao-k'ai[bk] (*fl.* 1314), another of his teachers and the founder of the Tao-i[bl] Academy, in Hsin-chou,[bm] Kiangsi, who believed that the different views of Confucian teaching held by Chu Hsi and Lu Hsiang-shan were reconcilable.[28]

Ch'eng Jo-yung was the chancellor of the Lin-ju[bn] Academy in Fu-chou,[bo] Kiangsi (founded in 1248),[29] where Wu Ch'eng, Ch'eng Wen-hai (Ch'eng Chu-fu,[bp] 1249–1318), and Wu Ch'en-tzu[bq] (1267–1339) all studied under him.[30] Ch'eng Jo-yung produced a work *Hsing-li tzu-hsün*[br] (Exposition on words concerning nature and principle), comprising six divisions and 183 items, which was compiled on the model of a similar but shorter work by Ch'eng Tuan-meng[bs] (1143–1191), a pupil of Chu Hsi, which had only 30 items.[31] In Ch'eng Jo-yung's *Hu-feng shu-yüan chiang-i*[bt] (Notes for lectures delivered at the Hu-feng Academy) he says,

> Chu Hsi was a master who came last but benefited from the labors of his predecessors, from Kuei-shan [Yang Shih,[bu] 1053–1135], Yü-chang [Lo Ts'ung-yen,[bv] 1072–1135] to Yen-p'ing [Li T'ung,[bw] 1093–1163]. His teaching is so clear and complete and is suitable for extension for education in the world and for later generations. I have studied the latter part of the collection of his *Literary Works*, and derived some diagrams of the four levels from my understanding of his "Letters in Reply to Liu Chi-chang."[bx] [32] The highest level of study is to aim to become a sage or worthy. The second level is for an understanding of humanity and righteousness and for the encouragement of moral integrity and honor. The third level is for the study of literary works and the last is for candidature at the civil examinations.[33]

He believed that "scholars of the second level have [normally] higher intelligence, are cautious and dutiful, anxious to learn humanity and perform righteous deeds, but, unfortunately, they know very little about the teachings of the sages and their followers which in fact should be the root of their career and the core of their heart. Therefore, it should be our task to rescue them [lest they sink to a lower level] and to extend to them the knowledge and the blood-line of the sages."[34]

Probably encouraged by this kind of preaching, Wu Ch'eng in his *Tao-t'ung*[by] (Body of the transmitted Confucian teachings), citing the words interpreting the first hexagram (*ch'ien*[bz] 'Heaven, male') in the *Book of Changes*, compared Chou Tun-i[ca] (1017–1073) to the primogenitor (*yüan*[cb]); Chang Tsai[cc] (1020–1077), Ch'eng Hao[cd] (1032–1085), and Che'ng I to the developers (*heng*[ce]); and Chu Hsi to the benefactor (*li*[cf]); he reserved the position of prolonger (*chen*[cg] 'chastity') for himself.[35] There is no need for me to mention that Hsü Heng, whose teaching enjoyed more government sponsorship, actually sang a song composed by Chu Hsi at his death-bed.[36]

In an article written in 1341, Yü Chi gave an account of the flourishing of Chu Hsi's teaching since the early days of the dynasty.

> The exposition of the Classics and the Four Books has acquired a settled outlook since Chu Hsi's conciliatory interpretations have been revered and publicized by scholars. They enjoy a very high esteem in the dynasty. His works have been singled out as the standard for learning and now all publications are books of his school. . . . In the prefectures and districts education officers have been appointed for supervision of teaching. The system of the Four Leading Academies[37] set up in the former dynasties has been carried on through the provision of academies for scholars in different parts of the country. Many of them were established because of Chu Hsi. In the prefecture of Chien-yang there are seven, either founded at a place where Chu Hsi once stayed or established to commemorate the memory of Chu's teachers, friends, or even his followers. The K'ao-

t'ing Academy is situated five *li*[ch] [38] west of Chien-yang. At the academy there is a tablet with an article written by Hsiung Ho[ci] [1247–1312] giving a detailed account of its funding.[39]

The Restoration of the Civil Examinations

Ministers and scholars in the reigns of Ögödai (T'ai-tsung,[ci] r. 1229–1241) and Khubilai (Shih-tsu,[ck] r. 1260–1294) had often suggested restoration of the civil examinations, not only because the Chinese Confucian scholars believed that through such a participation in the government it might be possible for them to wrest some power from, or at least to share it with, the Mongol ruling elite, but also because the system embodied a long-standing tradition that had been followed even under the earlier foreign rule, sporadically in Liao (947–1125) but regularly and systematically in Chin (1115–1234). However, the limited examinations for civil servants held in 1237 in Shansi and probably also in Shantung, though with some success, had not been continued; and in the early days of the Chih-yüan[cl] (1260–1294) reign, although Shih T'ien-tse,[cm] a premier, had suggested its restoration to Khubilai in his memorial, his suggestion was never adopted and carried out.[40] In 1267 Wang O[cn] (1190–1273), a Hanlin[co]-Secretary who had also been a *Chuang-yüan*[cp] [41] in the Chin period, expressed concern about the situation in his memorial to the court: "Because the system of civil examinations has been abolished, scholars have lost hope of serving the state. To eke out a living, some have turned to the study of law and articles, to become government clerks. Others have taken up a variety of occupations, such as personal servants to officials, small pedlars, craftmen, traders, and merchants."[42]

After many long-drawn debates and delays, the civil examinations including the examinations for the *chin-shih*[cq] degree were finally reintroduced in 1314–1315, about twenty years after the death of Khubilai. At these examinations the Han Chinese candidates, northerners and southerners as well, were separated from those candidates who were Mongols or scholars of Central Asian ethnic origin, who, although they also studied the Chinese Classics, were to be examined at a slightly lower level. Syllabuses for both levels included the Four Books following Chu Hsi's commentaries, while in the syllabus solely for Han Chinese candidates it was stipulated that for the paper on the *Book of Odes* Chu Hsi's commentary was to be used as principal textbook, for the paper on the *Book of History,* the commentary of Ts'ai Ch'en, and for the paper on the *Book of Changes,* the commentaries of Ch'eng I and Chu Hsi; other earlier commentaries were still permitted for reference purposes. For the paper on *Spring and Autumn Annals* the three traditional commentaries and the commentary of Hu An-kuo were used. Only for the paper on the *Book of Rites* were the ancient commentaries alone to be consulted.[43]

In appearance the Yüan Confucian scholars had scored a great victory in succeeding in introducing so many Neo-Confucian works on the Classics into the official syllabuses, for even in Sung time (about 1196) Chu Hsi himself and his teaching had been once vilified as a hypocrite with bogus learning and the Neo-Confucianist texts had never had such an important place in the examination requirements. However, as early as the latter half of the twelfth century the Sung examinations as a means of selecting talented men to serve the government had degenerated to such an extent that corruption and nepotism had become common pratice, and the material set for scholarly inquiry was really superficial and impractical. In Chu Hsi's *Chu Wen-kung wen-chi*ᶜᵗ (Collection of literary works of Master Chu), chapter 69, there is a long article titled "Hsüeh-hsiao kung-chü ssu-i"ᶜˢ (A private observation on the system of education and civil examinations), written probably in 1180 when he was in east Chekiang, which is also to be found in full in Ch'eng Tuan-li's *Ch'eng-shih chia-shu tu-shu fen-nien jih-ch'eng*, chapter 3. In this article Chu Hsi severely criticizes the examination system of his time for "inequity in quotas for recommending licentiates (*chü-jen*ᶜᵗ) from the districts, and the system of admission to the national university *(t'ai-hsüeh)* which is another monetary allurement." He points out that "the different types of special examinations such as the 'university exams,' the 'exams offered at the bureau in charge of tribute grain,' and the 'attached exams' in practice are but shortcuts to emolument and an open course for one to assume false identity and rush about [seeking] opportunities. Since the substance of virtuous deeds is not valued any more in teaching, the candidates are accustomed to merely write rubbish with bombastic words." As to the ills of this system, he believed that "nothing is more destructive than the production of such nonsensical and absolute preposterous babblings."⁴⁴ As a remedial measure he suggested a plan which may be summarized in terms of six points: (1) "Equalize the quotas for recommended licentiates among the prefectures to boost scholars' morale." (2) "Introduce a new category of candidature for admission to the university according to 'virtuous conduct' so that the moral foundation of the scholars may be strengthened." (3) "Abolish the papers on lyrical poems and literature, and set instead papers on Classics, pre-Ch'in (221–206 B.C.) philosophical texts, history, and current affairs, varying in detail in different years." (4) "For classical study the candidate must follow the teaching of a certain school, and the setting of questions must observe the proper punctuation of the text. In offering answers the candidate must have a thorough grasp of the meaning of the texts, listing systematically the different commentaries and forming his own viewpoint." (5) "Appoint men of integrity to fill posts at the schools so as to attract solid and honest scholars to teach." (6) "Reduce the quotas as well as the number of successful candidates recommended as a result of internal examinations at the university so that exceptional favor will not be abused, and the course of monetary allurement will be blocked off." It may be of interest to know that for classical studies Chu Hsi here recommended, as required textbooks, the commentaries written by Hu Yüanᶜᵘ (993–1059), Shih Chiehᶜᵛ (1005–1045), Ou-yang Hsiuᶜʷ (1007–1072), Wang An-shihᶜˣ (1021–1086), Shao Yung,

Ch'eng I, Chang Tsai, Lü Ta-lin[cy] (993–1059), and Yang Shih on the *Book of Changes,* and the *Chi-chieh*[cz] (Collected explanations) on the Four Books, with supplementary remarks by Su Shih[da] (1036–1101), Wang P'ang[db] (1044–1076), Wu Yü[dc] (d. 1154), Hu Yin[dd] (1098–1156), and so on. He suggested also that a candidate should consult at least two related works in any one particular Classic.[45] Not all of them were necessarily the products of Neo-Confucian scholars.

Although Chu Hsi's "Private Observation" was sharp enough to cut into the crux of the problem, and the changes he put forward were workable and sound, they were never implemented.[46] When in the winter of 1314 the reintroduction of civil examinations was proclaimed and the new syllabuses publicized, Confucian scholars everywhere were pleased, believing that the Mongolian ruler Ayurbarwada (Jen-tsung,[de] r. 1312–1320) had at last accepted the substance of Chu Hsi's words and that the course of classical studies (*ming-ching*[df]) would follow only the teaching of Chu Hsi. Such a program would identify preparation for the civil examinations with the promotion of the cause of Neo-Confucianism, which would indeed be a great conception, surpassing the achievements of the earlier dynasties from Han (206 B.C.–A.D. 220) through T'ang (618–907) to Sung.[47]

As the civil examinations had lapsed for so many years in all parts of China, even officials in the provinces were not too familiar with the arrangements necessary to be made for their reimplementation "and were rather afraid of being unfit for the job."[48] Hsiung P'eng-lai, the classical scholar from Kiangsi mentioned earlier, at the point was contacted by the provincial authorities. For each question they asked Hsiung was able to answer with an appropriate suggestion; after being itemized and written down, these were approved by the central government as a set of universal working rules.[49] Teng Wen-yüan[dg] (1258–1328), another Confucian scholar of the time, was appointed chief examiner for the provincial examination held in Kiangsu-Chekiang in 1314. As he believed that the spirit of the examinations and the legislature reestablishing them entailed the adoption of the ideas found in the "Private Observation" of Chu Hsi, he ordered that a copy of Chu's article be inscribed and posted on notice-boards so that candidates who came to sit for the examination would understand the intentions of the emperor and would not dare to follow the corrupt practices of former times.[50]

In fact, the "corrupt practices" were not so easy to get rid of, even in relation to the peculiar way of setting a question and writing an answer prevalent at the time. In order to rack the brains of the candidates, since Southern Sung tricky questions like puzzles bearing no consequence to real scholarship had often been set. Examples of these were cited in Chu Hsi's "Private Observation." Chu Hsi said,

> [The examiners] aimed at having some novelty so that the candidates were given very unexpected things and were stunned when confronted with them. Two sep-

arate sentences from a text were unexpectedly joined together, and another one was cut into two by arbitrary punctuating of the text. The test was to find out how clever the candidate would be when exposed to such a situation where logical reasoning was impossible and hurried extemporization was needed to cope with the difficulties.[51]

An example cited by Chu Hsi serves as a good illustration of this point. In the *Book of Odes* are these lines

> The doings of High Heaven,
> Have neither sound nor smell.
> Take your pattern from King Wen,[dh]
> And the myriad regions will repose confidence in you.[52]

A tricky question spliced the second line—*Wu-sheng wu-hsiu*[di]—onto the first two characters—*i-hsing*[dj] 'take your pattern from'—of the third line.

Not only did questions such as this type of meritless hotchpotch continue to be set in Yüan times, but many woolly essays continued to be composed according to a stereotyped pattern described by Ch'eng Tuan-li in five words in his *Ch'eng-shih chia-shu tu-shu fen-nien jih-ch'eng: mao*[dk] (to set forth an argument at the beginning of the composition), *yüan*[dl] (to follow up and amplify), *chiang*[dm] (to carry out a proper discourse), *cheng*[dn] (to cite evidence), and *chieh*[do] (to conclude).[53] Ch'eng, who at first had so highly praised the reinstatement of the examinations, identifying it with promoting the cause of Neo-Confucianism, later became disillusioned and declined the honor of serving as examiner.[54] Tai Piao-yüan[dp] (1244–1310) in his "Preface to Yü Ching-lung's *Commentary on Chu Hsi's Hsiao-hsüeh*"[dq] written in 1295, lamented that although the civil examinations helped to popularize the works of Chu Hsi, not many of them were seriously studied. He says,

In my childhood the text of *Hsiao-hsüeh* was taught only by a few aged scholars in the villages and not more than four or five schools. . . . At that time Chu Hsi's works were not yet so well known; people in Chekiang sometimes made copies of the texts from others and in this manner they were circulated for mutual enlightenment. The delight in obtaining a copy of them could be likened to the experience of Yang Hsiung[dr] [53 B.C.–A.D. 18] when collecting vocabulary for his lexicon *Fang-yen*[ds] (Dialects recorded from various states in former Han [206 B.C.–A.D. 8]), or the great enjoyment of Ts'ai Yung[dt] [133–192] when he read for the first time Wang Ch'ung's[du] [27–91] *Lun-heng*[dv] (Discourse weighed in the balance). However, in 1244–1245 [during the reign of Emperor Li-tsung,[dw] r. 1225–1264, in Southern Sung] someone used the ideas of Chu Hsi in writing his examination essays and was highly placed on the scroll of success. Then people from everywhere vied with one another in selling Chu Hsi's books and even in remote place like ours [Feng-hua,[dx] Chekiang] many of his works became available. Those we read which had complete texts were his *Chou-i pen-i*[dy] (Original meaning of the *Book of Changes*), the *Collected Commentaries on the Four Books*, and the *Hsiao-hsüeh*. Other works seemed to be still in draft form, or had been manipulated by others, and were not in perfect condition. Of those three works now only his *Collected Commentaries on the Four Books* is a household collection, the *Original Meaning of the Book of Changes* is studied by only a handful of scholars, while the *Hsiao-hsüeh*, a most useful work for the populace, goes practically unread. Isn't this lamentable?[55]

Yü Chi recorded more than once in his writings a dialogue said to have taken place between Emperor Jen-tsung, the Mongolian ruler who decided to reintroduce the civil examinations at the *chin-shih* degree level, and some of his intimate courtiers. A minister comments that "the trouble about examinations is that each time there are too many successful candidates, and, being a *chin-shih* degree holder, it is again too easy for one to be given a post. Besides, these are inexperienced people and I doubt very much the practical value of such a system." To this the emperor replies, "[I know. But] I would be satisfied if among hundreds or a thousand candidates there emerges one good administrator like Fan Chung-yen[dz] [989–1052] of the Northern Sung [960–1126]."[56] It was customary that *chin-shih* examinations be held every three years; between 1315 when they resumed and 1336 when they were temporarily suspended, there were seven sessions. The system was again resumed in 1343, admitting those who had already passed the provincial examinations in 1336 to the final contest held in Peking.[57]

Ch'üan Tsu-wang seems to have a fairly balanced view of the particular esteem in which Chu Hsi was held in Yüan times. He says, "The teaching of Chu Hsi was particularly revered at the university in Yüan times for the systematization of academic pursuits lest they lapse into a jumbled and inchoate, boundless mass. However, when the *Great Compendium of the Four Books* and similar works were edited for examinations in the Ming dynasty and in which Chu Hsi was again honored, they had little to do with academics. It shows only the narrow-mindedness and uncultivated taste of the rulers."[58] Yet Huang Tsung-hsi believed that "the people of Yüan times knew about Chu Hsi only because his teaching was promulgated in the North by Chao Fu and Hsü Heng. They did not really understand Chu Hsi. However, as Chu Hsi was at the core of the examinations syllabuses, they could not but follow him."[59]

Hsiao-hsüeh and the Four Books

If the ordinary, petty-minded, pedantic scholars of the Yüan failed to appreciate the true value of Chu Hsi, certainly this was not so in the case of other distinguished scholars, whether they served the court or merely led the life of a commoner, taught in the rural regions, or headed a private or locally sponsored academy which was a center for Neo-Confucian scholarship. Nationalistic feelings had been very strong among the early scholars who had been Sung subjects, some even killing themselves to show unyielding loyalty to the vanquished imperial household.[60] However, the process of sinicization was so rapid and so penetrating during the nine decades of alien rule that there were not only quite a few Neo-Confucian scholars such as Tai Liang[ea] (1317–1383), a disciple of Liu Kuan[eb] (1270–1342), and Cheng Yü[ec] (1298–1358) who died for the Yüan cause,[61] but also non-Chinese subjects such as Ting Ho-nien[ed] (1335–1424), a scholar and literary man of Muslim origin, who shared the same commitment and confined himself on a small island off Ting-hai,[ee] Chekiang after the fall of Yüan, refusing to acknowledge Ming sovereignty.[62] When Ch'üan Tsu-wang commented on this he emphasized the moral point by saying that "the duties between sovereign and his subject are duties from which there is no escape between heaven and earth."[63] Probably we could appreciate this sentiment more easily in a Neo-Confucian context.

As a result of the development of Neo-Confucianism after Sung times, the publications of Chu Hsi were highly honored by the Neo-Confucianists in Yüan. I mentioned already the spread over the country of the textbook *Hsiao-hsüeh,* which was unknown in the North before some enthusiastic publicity on its behalf by the minister Yao Shu. Yü Chi, in a composition "sending off" his friend Li K'uo,[ef] wrote,

> The founding of the dynasty began with Master Hsü Wen-cheng[eg] [Hsü Heng]. He was a very sincere scholar. He obtained several works of Chu Hsi at the time when communication between South and North was still subject to blockade. When he had studied them he became even more inspired by the feeling of reverence and alertness which he learned to behave towards people and things. When he was known to Emperor Shih-tsu [Khubilai], his attitude to the ruler was purely according to the course of a Confucianist, and none of the others was his equal in this respect. . . . At that time social customs were simple and honest, and men of talents sincere and plain, so that Master Hsü took the texts of the *Hsiao-hsüeh* as his teaching material. The teaching of sprinkling water and sweeping the floor as well as responding to visitors in conversation was to train pupils to yield to the external circumstances; the strict orders governing leaving and returning home and concerning work and recreation were to nourish their minds; the adoption of the principles of loyalty and filial piety for discourse was to provide them with a moral base; and the more subtle discussion of improvisation in rites and etiquette were for them to have a thorough understanding in practical affairs. Within a few decades nearly all the refined ministers and officials came from his gates. It was all due to his efforts, I think, that people in the country endeavored to learn the teachings of sages and worthies, and the works of Chu Hsi were thus transmitted and perpetuated.[64]

Composition of commentaries on the Four Books which bind together the two chapters (the *Great Learning* and the *Doctrine of the Mean*) singled out from the *Book of Rites* with *Confucian Analects* and the *Book of Mencius* commenced with Chu Hsi, but it was not until 1314–1315, when the first Yüan examination syllabuses were proclaimed, that this practice began to enjoy an even more prominent position. Chen Te-hsiu, the late Southern Sung Neo-Confucianist, "often advised his friends to ponder and digest the contents of the Four Books, before they come to study the Great Ultimate, the 'Explanation on the Western Inscription' and *Reflections on Things at Hand*."[65] This tradition was followed very solemnly by others such as Ho Chi[ch] (1188–1268) and Wang Po[ci] (1197–1274), scholars of Chin-hua[cj] School who were the transmitters of the teaching of Huang Kan.[66] Hsü Ch'ien[ck] (1270–1337),[67] a student of Chin Lü-hsiang[cl] (1232–1303) who was a student of both Ho Chi and Wang Po, published a book titled *Tu ssu-shu ts'ung-shuo*[cm] (A jotter prepared while reading the Four Books) in twenty chapters; an incomplete edition of four chapters is included in the *Ssu-k'u ch'üan-shu*, with yet another edition of eight chapters printed in several other series (*ts'ung-shu*[cn]).[68] It is probably in the lost text of this work that Hsü Ch'ien praised Chu Hsi's *Collected Commentaries on the Four Books* most highly, saying, "A scholar should aim at the understanding of the Sage's mind. Without understanding first the Sage's mind, it will not be possible for one to perform the Sage's deeds. The mind of the Sage is contained in the Four Books, and the explanations of the contents of the Four Books are complete in the works of Chu Hsi."[69]

Wu Ch'eng was an erudite Neo-Confucian scholar who, in his many years of teaching and academic study, commented on nearly every matter raised by Chu Hsi. Many of his carefully considered opinions are found in his "Ssu-ching hsü-lu"[co] (Prolegomena to four classical works), "San-li hsü-lu"[cp] (Prolegomena to the three works on *li*), and so on.[70] He also wrote separate studies on the *Book of Changes*, the *Book of History*, the *Spring and Autumn Annals*, the *Book of Rites*, the *I-li*[cq] (Book of etiquette and ceremonial), and the *Classic of Filial Piety*. In an article entitled "Tseng hsüeh-lu Ch'en Hua-jui hsü"[cr] (Farewell to Mr. Ch'en Hua-jui) included in his *Collection of Literary Works* Wu Ch'eng says,

> Master Chu Hsi had said that there were two "passes" (*kuan*[cs]) in the *Great Learning*. The investigation of things (*ko-wu*[ct]) is the pass from being asleep to being awake, and sincerity of the will (*ch'eng-i*[cu]) is the pass from being a beast to being a human being. To my mind, to investigate is to have a proper understanding, and to be sincere is to put things into practice. When things are investigated, one is awakened from a dream; otherwise one is still dreaming even though one may be described as being awake. When the will is made sincere, a beastly mind may be turned to a human mind; otherwise even one who may be described as a member of human society is still a beast. There are so many people who have read the Four Books and still roam in dreamland and the beast's lair. Should one not be apprehensive of this?[71]

The words of Chu Hsi cited by Wu Ch'eng are included in the *Chu Tzu yü-lei*[cv] (Classified conversations of Master Chu), though in the original *yü-lu*[cw] Chu says that "the sincerity of the will is the pass from evil" to goodness and "from being a ghost to being human."[72] However, Chu's words are correctly cited in Chen Te-hsiu's *Collection of Literary Works* when he is asked by a disciple to elaborate Chu Hsi's views on this point.[73] As we know Chen Te-hsiu's teacher was Chan T'i-jen, an immediate student of Chu Hsi. From writings similar to that quoted above, we can see that the general attitude of Wu Ch'eng towards Chu Hsi was quite respectful. Though sometimes he would reverse his ecstasies of delight over Lu Hsiang-shan's teaching of "honoring the virtuous nature,"[74] nowhere in his writings did Wu deny the enormous contribution of Chu Hsi in relation to the Four Books as a whole, though he would raise arguments against Chu on some individual texts.

Hu Ping-wen (Hu Yün-feng,[ex] 1250–1333) was around 1314–1320 the chancellor of the Tao-i Academy, originally founded by Ch'eng Shao-k'ai to promote the synthesis of the thoughts of Chu and Lu. He was also a friend of Wu Ch'eng. Ping-wen, however, was a staunch supporter of the teaching of Chu Hsi. Commenting on Ping-wen's *Ssu-shu t'ung*[ey] (A thorough study of the Four Books), Huang Po-chia,[ez] a son of Huang Tsung-hsi, said, "Yün-feng [Hu Ping-wen] made a pentrating study of Chu Hsi's *Collected Commentaries on the Four Books*. Jao Shuang-feng[fa] [Jao Lu] was a scholar of Chu's School, yet his views often contradicted those of the Master. Yün-feng wanted to correct his errors, hence in this work he expunged all the passages from the *Tsuan-shu*[fb] and the *Chi-ch'eng*[fc] which were found to contradict Chu Hsi, and added his own views to the relevant text."[75] Huang's comment here, I am afraid, is partly misleading: the *Tsuan-shu* or the *Ssu-shu tsuan-shu*[fd] (Exposition and collected notes on the Four Books compiled by Chao Shun-sun[fe] [1215–1276]) and the *Chi-ch'eng* or *Ssu-shu chi-ch'eng*[ff] (Collected commentaries on the Four Books compiled by Wu Chen-tzu[fg]) are not compilations solely by Jao Lu, although Jao's comments are quoted therein. As a matter of fact, because Hu Ping-wen was not too pleased with these two works, he selected only fourteen earlier works from them to be incorporated into his own and added forty-five others by authors who "strictly followed the sayings of K'ao-t'ing [Chu Hsi]."[76]

"Putting Things into Practice" and "Many Manifestations of Principle"

Chu Hsi's theory of the investigation of things as means of attaining true knowledge had led the Southern Sung scholars to attach very high regard to the practical consequence of things and to applying oneself in action. Wei Liao-weng[fh] (1178–1237), a high official and a friend of Fu Kuang[fi] (*fl.* 1208) and Li Fan, both disciples of Chu Hsi, once wrote to an official of the wine monopoly who had advised him to study Chu Hsi and "hand down his doctrines as if he was his ancestor" (*tsu-shu*[fj]), saying,

I believe that the study of the various explanations of earlier Confucian scholars of the Classics is perhaps not as good as reading the works of the Sage himself.

For without personal investigation on the spot one cannot say that one's understanding of a thing is true. In your letter you advise me to hand down the doctrines of Master Chu as if he was my ancestor. It is true that I have read Master
Chu's works over quite a long period of time. However, in order to seek out the
vigorous spirit of his teaching I would rather find the twigs and the roots of a
tree than appreciate the blossoms of peach and plum carried in the loads of the
peddlers.[77]

In the same spirit Wei declaimed bitterly in his *Chu Wen-kung wu-shu wen-ta
hsü*[k] (Preface to questions and answers on the five works of Master Chu), "So
many books have been printed, and so many theories have been advanced.
The clever ones of our time need only to plagiarize some shallow views and
sell them to the world, without putting any into practice through personal
experience."[78]

Wang Po was known for his acute skepticism in textual study of classical
works; he also held a pragmatic view in analyzing Chu Hsi which was, in fact,
Chu Hsi's own attitude towards human affairs and things. On one occasion
his friend Wu T'ai-ch'ing[l] (*fl.* 1260) planned to use the words "seeking-plea-
sure" (*hsün-le*[m]) to name his study or studio, and Wang was consulted about its
appropriateness. This term had a very clear Neo-Confucian background, for it
was the great master Chou Tun-i who had often taught Ch'eng Hao "to seek
the substance in which Confucius and Yen Hui[n] [79] had found pleasure."[80]
Although the concept had such a deeply-seated tradition and had been
cherished for generations, Wang Po nevertheless viewed the matter negatively
and advised Wu to drop the idea.

To use the word *hsün-le* for a sign-board to be hung in your study is, I am afraid,
contrary to the teaching of plainness and practicality. It seems more to imply an
aspiration for "penetration rising high" (*shang-ta*[o]), and less concern for the
"studies lying low" (*hsia-hsüeh*[p]).[81] To my mind if there has not been any effort
in studies lying low, there cannot be any penetration rising high. Elaborating
this particular case Master Chu Hsi said very firmly citing the words of Yen Hui
himself, that we scholars should set as our goal "enlarging our minds with learning, but restraining them with propriety," from whence we may arrive at a state
of being "unable to give over the study of the doctrines of the Sage even should
we wish to do so," and after we have "exerted all our abilities" we may come to a
position from where it is possible for us to reach our aim.[82] Oh! This teaching is
a perennial one and it may be transmitted far and wide without any ill effect.[83]

Having inherited this spirit of Chu Hsi through the expositions of the doctrines by their predecessors, the Yüan Neo-Confucianists seem to have been
most concerned with the idea that learning must be practical and sincere. As
mentioned already Hsü Heng was praised very highly by Yü Chi for his sincerity and his teaching of "having a thorough understanding in practical
affairs," though elsewhere Yü cited Liu Yin's criticism that Hsü "cheated the

world with Lao-tzu's[q] tricks to save his own skin."[84] Ch'eng Tuan-li, in the General Outlines (*kang-ling*[r]) illustrating the contents of his *Ch'eng-shih chia-shu tu-shu fen-nien jih-ch'eng*, cited these words of Chu Hsi as his keynote: "My lectures and seminars are different from the compositions for civil examination because I want scholars to apply themselves in action."[85] Although his work was mainly for preparing candidates to sit for examinations, and for that purpose it had been proclaimed by the national university as a guide-book for systematic learning of Classics, Ch'eng did include extensive quotations from quite a few earlier Neo-Confucian scholars including Jao Lu and Ch'eng's own master, Shih Meng-ch'ing[s] (1247–1306), who was a third generation follower of Chu Hsi. In the *Ch'eng-shih chia-shu tu-shu fen-nien jih-ch'eng* Ch'eng also cited the previously mentioned quotations from Yen Hui and commented, "To study the texts well and to think very deeply is the requirement for 'enlarging one's mind for learning.' To examine oneself thoroughly is for the sake of the 'restraints of propriety.' "[86] He admitted also that for the compilation of this work he had to some extent relied on the *Chu Tzu tu-shu fa*[t] (Methods of study introduced by Master Chu) compiled by Fu Kuang. Lu Lung-ch'i[u] (1630–1692), an early Ch'ing (1644–1912) Neo-Confucianist, in his colophon to a later edition of Ch'eng's book, says, "The methods for study as found in this work are not Ch'eng's own. They are methods laid down by Chu Hsi."[87]

Cheng Yü, a late Yüan scholar who was described by Ch'üan Tsu-wang as "succeeding Wu Ch'eng in the attempt to reconcile the differences of Chu and Lu," was more pro-Chu than was Wu Ch'eng. He did not actually serve the Yüan court, but when the city of Hui-chou[v] [88] fell to the Ming forces in 1357,[89] he hanged himself while under custody to avoid the humiliation of having to serve two lords. In "A Letter to Wang Chen-ch'ing"[w] he wrote,

> When it came to Master Chu [Hsi] of Hsin-an,[x] [90] he took up the task of analyzing all the works of sages and worthies, compared them and singled out their differences, and found the best possible solutions for each of them. None of the words he said were not acceptable, and he was the one who was able to marshal all the findings in the Classics so that his understanding of them would equal that of the sages Confucius and Mencius themselves. It was he who made our Way as bright as the blue sky and the light of day which shines on the myriad objects and reveals their identities. His teaching may be compared to the highways and the main thoroughfares that lead off in every direction, or to a metropolis where there are numerous shops with tens of thousands of doors and gates open and hundreds of carriages always jamming the roads, and none of the commodities sought by the rich merchants who come to the place are lacking. Surely he discovered the secrets of heaven and earth, and expounded most thoroughly the abstruse theories of the sages and worthies. However, subsequent to this advancement of the sages' teachings, there are now immature youths who babble about "honesty" and "consideration for others," and also illiterates and half-baked scholars who discuss "Nature" and "the Way of Heaven." The teachings

of the sages have now become the learning of hearsay and transmission of mere mouthings. The ancient scholars dealt with facts and real experiences. The more they knew personally the deeper their understanding of the issue. Contemporary scholars apply their minds to what happens a thousand *li* away, but their persons never leave their homes. Therefore, although these people seem to be farsighted, they merely talk empty words. How could we say that this is that most exquisite doctrine with which Chu Hsi educated the world? Who knows the depth of offence against the School of the Sage or the remorse their guilty conscience should make them feel towards Master Chu![91]

Wang Hou-sun[fy] (1300–1376), a contemporary of Cheng Yü and grandson of the great erudite scholar Wang Ying-lin[fz] (1223–1296), castigated in terms similar to those of Cheng Yü the weaknesses of the scholars of his time.

Our contemporary scholars have studied only very superficially the works of Chu Hsi, yet they claim to have obtained the true transmission from Master Chu and look down upon the elder scholars who lived in the Ch'ien-ta[ga] and Ch'un-hsi[gb] periods [1165–1189] and mock them. These elders were actually contemporaries of Master Chu. Nowadays people do not read as widely as they did, but are fond of using jargon about nature and principle (*hsing-li*[gc]) to cover up their ignorance and shallowness. I am afraid that this will lead to being given to exaggeration and fantastic belief.[92]

As a natural corollary of the practice of investigation of things, the theory of "principle is one but its manifestations are many"—another important aspect of Chu Hsi's doctrines—was firmly grasped by the Yüan Neo-Confucian scholars. This may be illustrated again by the teaching of Hsü Ch'ien, the author of the *Tu ssu-shu ts'ung-shuo*. As we know, Hsü was a disciple of Chin Lü-hsiang. The epitaph for Hsü written by Huang Chin says,

[Hsü] was taught by Master Chin [Chin Lü-hsiang] who said, "The study of our Confucianism lies in the understanding of the oneness of principle as well as its manifold manifestations. It is easy to understand the principle is one, but it is more difficult to comprehend the myriad manifestations in which it is revealed." Hence Master Hsü began to learn to differentiate the myriad manifestations, and trace their origin to the one principle.[93]

In the *Po-yün chi*[gd] (Collected works of Hsü Po-yün) Hsü Ch'ien wrote the following in a personal letter to Wu Shih-tao (Wu Cheng-ch'uan,[ge] 1283–1344) to advise him on this point and to quell his doubts.

When Wen-kung [Chu Hsi] first became a student at the gates of Yen-p'ing [Li T'ung], he was still fond of talking in a grandiloquent and general manner. He preferred to refer to the common factors in things, and disliked delving into their individual differences. Yen-p'ing disapproved of this and said, "The doctrine of us Confucianists is different from those of the heterodox teachings in that we understand that although principle is one, its manifestations are many. It is easy to understand that the principle is one, but it is more difficult to comprehend the many manifestations in which it is revealed." Master Chu was moved by these words. Thereafter he worked at careful observation and profound understanding of the truth as may be seen in his writings. In your letter you quoted the words of Master Ch'eng I: 'Learn to be reverent for the nourishment of one's conduct, and to extend the knowledge for the advancement of one's scholarship.'[94] These are of course the guidelines for scholars seeking the Tao.[gf] However, extension of knowledge means one should seek its practical application so that one will be able to gain the full measure of knowledge. It is not intended that the words 'extension of knowledge' should merely be held as a motto. It does not say that because one has understood that principle is one, there is no need for one to further study its many manifestations. The works of Chu Hsi amount to several hundred thousand words. The big as well as the small [issues], the fine as well as the large-scale, the root and the branches, those which are hidden and those which are revealed, are all to be found therein. Even if one studied them sentence by sentence and word by word until exhausted, one would still be afraid of not attaining a complete grasp of his teaching. How much more so if one merely got hold of some of its outlines and forsook its myriad detailed items. It would be too easy to fall into the habit of talking emptiness the way Buddhists do. There have been many contemporary scholars who have not been free of these faults. Would you say that we should follow them?[95]

Many modern scholars have noted that the Ch'eng-Chu theory of "principle is one but its manifestations are many" shows some Buddhist influence.[96] However, according to the *Yen-p'ing ta-wen*[gg] (Replies to queries by Li T'ung) recorded by Chu Hsi, it was Li T'ung's belief that "the crucial point here lies in whether one emphasizes the word *chih*[gh] (knowledge)."[97] Elaborating on this Chu Hsi said, "Because one understands that principle is one, one's feeling of kindness arises. Because one understands its manifestations are many, one's differentiation of righteousness occurs."[98] The Sung-Yüan scholars' interpretation of this saying is more according to its practical side than its metaphysical speculation. This was certainly the view of Hsü Ch'ien and Chin Lü-hsiang. It was also that which led Huang Tsung-hsi, in his *Sung-Yüan hsüeh-an*, to comment:

At the time of Jen-shan[gi] [Chin Lü-hsiang] and [Hsü] Po-yün, most of the scholars in Chekiang were of the School of Tz'u-hu [Yang Chien,[gj] 1141–1226, a disciple of Lu Hsiang-shan]. They sought for understanding of the original substance (*pen-t'i*[gk]). They believed this to be the end of inquiry, and gave no consideration to practical matters and things. They did not understand that substance cannot be separated from the objects themselves. Jen-shan reiterated these words to remedy the illness of the time. This was the blood which pulsed through the vessels and veins of the body for five generations.[99]

In the other fields of study in which Chu Hsi made great contributions—such as the *Book of Changes*, the *Book of History*, and the *T'ung-chien kang-*

mu[gl] (Shorter chronological history of China based upon Ssu-ma Kuang's[gm] [1019–1086] *Tzu-chih t'ung-chien*[gn] 'General mirror for the aid of government'), which was published under Chu Hsi's name although most of it may have been penned by a team of workers led by one of his disciples, Chao Shih-yüan[go] (*cs* 1172)[100]—there are also a number of books written by Yüan Neo-Confucian scholars either with the aim of supplementing Chu Hsi, correcting some of his errors, or simply showing off their erudition and literary brilliance. Among those who worked on Chu Hsi's interpretations on the *Book of Changes* (the *Chou-i pen-i* and the *I-hsüeh ch'i-meng*[gp] 'Introduction to the *Changes* for beginners') was Hu Yi-kuei[gq] (*fl.* 1264), a son of Hu Fang-p'ing.[gr] Both father and son labored on this Classic of divination for decades.[101] Another scholar, Hu Ping-wen, the author of the *Ssu-shu t'ung*, also published his *Chou-i pen-i t'ung-shih*[gs] (A thorough study of the *Original Meaning of the Changes*), probably in 1316.[102] Hsiung Liang-fu,[gt] who was made licentiate in 1317, published his *Chou-i pen-i chi-ch'eng*[gu] (A collected commentary on the *Original Meaning of the Changes*), in which he gathered together many explanations concerning the *Book of Changes* by both Ch'eng I and Chu Hsi, including some of the earlier annotations. His compilation was mainly for the preparation for examinations, for which particular purpose the ancient commentaries on the *Book of Changes* had not been proscribed.[103] Nearly all of these works are included in the *Ssu-k'u ch'üan-shu* as well as the *T'ung-chih t'ang ching-chieh*[gv] (Collected commentaries on Confucian Classics published by the Hall of Ever-reaching Spirit) collected and printed by Hsü Ch'ien-hsüeh[gw] (1631–1694) and Nara Singde[gx] (1655–1685).

In historical research Wang T'ien-yü[gy] devoted fifteen years to the compilation of his *Shang-shu tsuan-chuan*[gz] (Collected commentaries and notes on the *Book of History*), a work of forty-six chapters, to promulgate the teaching of Chu Hsi in relation to this ancient text. He based his study on the earlier commentary on the work by Ts'ai Ch'en, who had received personal instruction from Chu Hsi and whose commentary was on the list of prescribed books for examinations during the Yüan period. Wang also incorporated into his combined commentary some of the notes written by Chen Te-hsiu, for he believed that "the controversies over the text of the *Book of History* were settled by Chu Hsi, and Chu Hsi's conciliatory remarks on these controversies were made even clearer by Chen Hsi-shan[ha] [Chen Te-hsiu]." His work was published between 1308 and 1311.[104]

As has been pointed out, Chu Hsi's *T'ung-chien kang-mu* was probably the work of a disciple or disciples. In Yüan times there were several scholars working very conscientiously to supplement it, following some written notes on its compilation handed down from Chu Hsi. As early as the first years of the reign of Khubilai, Liu Te-yüan[hb] (*fl.* 1260–1263) had compiled a work in several hundred items analyzing Ssu-ma Kuang's chronological annals, and it was found that his rearrangement of the events was very close to Chu Hsi's original plan for the *Kang-mu*. For this achievement he was much admired by

Hsü Heng.[105] Liu Yu-yi[hc] (1248–1332) compiled the *T'ung-chien kang-mu shu-fa*[hd] (On the principles of moral judgement in Chu Hsi's *T'ung-chien kang-mu*) which was favored with a preface (1329) by Chieh Hsi-ssu[he] (1274–1344) as well as a colophon by Ou-yang Hsüan.[106] Wang K'o-k'uan[hf] (1304–1372), a licentiate of 1326 who had a number of publications on classical studies, compiled a *T'ung-chien kang-mu fan-li k'ao-i*[hg] (A study on the differences found in the introductory remarks in Chu Hsi's *T'ung-chien kang-mu*) with the intention of revising some discrepancies between Chu Hsi's original outlines for the work and the published texts prepared by his disciples supposedly in accordance with his plan.[107] There were other works of a similar nature, but the compilations of Liu Yu-i and Wang K'o-k'uan were said to have been consulted most frequently by the Manchu emperor Aisin Gioro Hsüan-yen[hh] (Emperor K'ang-hsi,[hi] r. 1662–1722) in his *Imperial Critical Version of Chu Hsi's T'ung-chien kang-mu.*[108]

Revision and Reconciliation

Although the orthodox school of Chu Hsi had a very strong hold in Sung-Yüan times, it was not completely immune from scholarly criticism from time to time, and some of that criticism from within the school led to revision. Huang Chen[hj] (1213–1280), a late Southern Sung Confucian scholar who read most widely through the classical works in order to promulgate the teachings of the sages, criticized Chu Hsi on a number of issues, though he was still generally recognized as a faithful supporter of Chu. His famous work was his reading notes known as the *Huang-shih jih-ch'ao*[hk] (Day-to-day jottings compiled by Mr. Huang). Praising the objective, unbiased attitude of this work, Huang Po-chia says, "The *Jih-ch'ao* often took into account the good points as well as the limitations of many Confucian scholars and issued a mediating judgment. Even K'ao-t'ing [Chu Hsi] would not go along with it if it was against principle, for he had profound confidence in self-deliberation."[109]

In his notes "Reading the *Book of Changes*" Huang Chen disagrees very strongly with Shao Yung's theory of *hsien-t'ien*[hl] (before heaven and earth or primordiality). He also says,

> There are two major schools of thought in the study of the *Changes*. Those who cherished the Neo-Confucian ideas of principle followed the explanations offered by I-ch'uan[hm] [Ch'eng I]. Those who believed in the idea of the numerical universe *(shu-hsüeh)* accepted the interpretation offered by K'ang-chieh[hn] [Shao Yung]. These two theories were opposites. It was not until the appearance of the *Original Meaning of the Changes* and *Introduction to the Changes for Beginners (Chou-i ch'i-meng)* of Master Hui-an[ho] [Chu Hsi] that the exploration was carried to ancient depths and these two different theories made one. Chu said that the origin of the *Changes* was for divination purposes, and that the primordial diagram introduced by Shao had hit upon this origin, while the explanations offered by Ch'eng, though complete in their understanding of principle, gave

very few demonstrations from a mathematical point of view. Since then, scholars who know very little about the work have followed Chu wholeheartedly. They keep on working on the diagram, thinking very highly of the primordial and relegating post-primordial (*hou-t'ien*[hp]) phenomena to a secondary position. In fact, they have created an antecedent for the *Book of Changes* itself.[110]

Ho Chi, the great master of the Chin-hua School, also wrote a letter to a friend Ch'en Ch'eng-chai (Ch'en Chen[hq]) discussing the diagram. He said, "Although there is the primordial diagram which may be taken as a model for reconstruction, I hold that while the Former Sage and the Latter Sage[111] must each have had a plan of no small magnitude, they would not resort to making drawings of them."[112] Another critical comment appears in a footnote to one of the twenty poems of Chu Hsi entitled "Recollections While Living in Quietude," which Ho annotated. Concerning the *T'ung-chien kang-mu* of Chu Hsi he notes, "There are places where words written down are perfunctory, not being the result of better thought, since Master Chu had to follow the original writings of Wen-kung[hr] [Ssu-ma Kuang]."[113]

Wang Po was in general a devoted follower of Chu Hsi. However, when Huang Po-chia was summarizing Wang's contributions to the advancement of Neo-Confucianism, he said,

> Lu-chai[hs] [Wang Po] was a scholar known to be a very strong admirer of Tzu-yang[ht] [Chu Hsi]. When it came to the *Great Learning*, he nevertheless believed that the commentary on "investigation of things" had not been lost[114] and that there was no need to supplement it.[115] He also thought that since in the "Treatise on Bibliography" in the *Han-shu*[hu] (History of the Han dynasty) the *On the Doctrine of the Mean* is recorded in two sections, it was necessary to establish as a separate piece the latter part of the work commencing with the sentence "When we have intelligence resulting from sincerity."[116] As to the "Interpretation to the Diagram of the Great Ultimate,"[117] he maintained that the sentence "*wu-chi*"[hv] (Ultimate of Nonbeing) . . . referred to the diagram, and would not believe that the Ultimate of Nonbeing was formless, and the *t'ai-chi*[hw] (Great Ultimate) was the embodiment of principle.[118] He also revised some of the sayings concerning the *Book of Odes* and the *Book of History*.[119]

Huang Po-chia also said that Chin Lü-hsiang, a follower of both Ho Chi and Wang Po, and teacher of Hsü Ch'ien, "in his study of the *Analects* and the *Book of Mencius*, had often some original views which had not been discovered by Chu Hsi. Sometimes his views contradict Chu's. He did not contradict the great master so as to gain fame. It was merely because he had the same enthusiasm as Master Chu for clarification of the Tao."[120]

In the atmosphere described above, even in early Yüan the ideal of fresh and dynamic thought did not completely die out. Even Wu Ch'eng, when serving as the Director of Studies at the National University in Peking, instructed the students in the extreme importance of "honoring virtuous nature"[121] which, he said, "should be regarded as the basis of one's learning," for without it "the maintenance of constant inquiry and study would lapse into pettifogging annotations and linguistic trifles."[122] Thus his tipping of the scales was evidently not one hundred percent in favor of Chu Hsi.

Commenting on the *Chung-yung chang-chü*[hx] (A punctuated text of the *Doctrine of the Mean*) and the *Chung-yung huo-wen*[hy] (Questions and answers on the *Doctrine of the Mean*), both by Chu Hsi, Wu Ch'eng says,

> His choice of words is extremely fine and the explanations very detailed. However, being too well chosen, it has become delicate; being over detailed, it has become verbose. If its original was natural and effortless, it is now effete and fragile. If its original was clear and luminous, it is now confused with verbiage. . . . In my early days when I studied the *Doctrine of the Mean* I had different views from those of Chu Hsi. Later I found that mine were very similar to the opinions of Jao Po-yü[hz] [Jao Lu]. I regretted very much that I was born so late that I was unable to be enlightened by him in person.[123]

Another example of Wu Ch'eng's criticism of Chu Hsi may be seen in his *Hsiao-ching hsü-lu*[ia] (Prolegomena to the *Classic of Filial Piety*). Wu Ch'eng says,

> Master Chu said that only the first six or seven chapters of the text are the primary text; the rest are but commentaries written by the Confucian scholars who lived in the states of Ch'i[ib] and Lu,[ic] using the *Tso-chuan*[id] (Tso's commentary) and other works as their sources, and the order of the text had been disrupted as well. My observation is that of the words of the former sages handed down through generations, only the texts of the *Great Learning*, the *Analects*, the *Doctrine of the Mean*, and the *Book of Mencius* are unadulterated; the remainder, which appear in historical and other records, are admixtures and cannot be taken as completely reliable. The *Classic of Filial Piety* is one of them.[124]

The text of this Classic exists in the "old script" and "new script" versions. The "old script" surfaced in Sui (581–618) times, but Wu Ch'eng doubted that it was the text believed in Han times to have been discovered in the walls of Confucius' former residence. Hence he said, "Master Chu followed the 'old script' in compiling his *Corrigenda* for this Classic—and this is something I cannot understand. For if we agree with the commentary of Hsing Ping[ie] [932–1010], it is certain that the 'old script' is a forgery. Besides Master Chu himself pointed out suspicious passages in the 'new script.'[125]

Despite the preponderance of pro-Chu scholars throughout the ninety-odd years of Yüan there were still some Neo-Confucian scholars who followed very closely the teaching of Lu Hsiang-shan. They are represented, in the *Sung-Yüan hsüeh-an*, by Ch'en Yüan (Ch'en Ching-ming,[if] 1256–1330) and Chao Hsieh (Chao Pao-feng,[ig] *fl.* 1348).[126] Hu Ch'ang-ju (Hu Shih-t'ang,[ih] 1240–1314) was originally a follower of Chu's teaching but became an admirer of Lu, while in the case of Cheng Yü it was the other way round, though he still advocated that "we should not say anything deprecatory against Hsiang-shan."[127] Wu Ch'eng, as one of the leading Confucianists in early Yüan and the most prolific scholar among them, had always maintained a conciliatory tone in ideological conflicts. The opposition camp within the fold of Neo-Confucianism, no matter how weak it seemed to be, was only temporarily silenced. As was cleverly pointed out by Ch'üan Tsu-wang in a note of Hsieh Shih-lin (Hsieh Chi-shih,[ii] 1684–1756) discussing the nature of the old version of the *Great Learning*,

> The teaching of Chu Hsi was greatly publicized during the reign of Emperor Li-tsung, led by Chen Hsi-shan [Ch'en Te-hsiu] and Wei Hua-fu[ij] [Wei Liao-weng]. At this time China was still un-unified, and the Neo-Confucian studies were known in the Central Plain only because of their introduction by Chao Chiang-han[ik] [Chao Fu]. This may be likened to the springing forth of buds just by getting rid of their outer scales. After Chen and Wei, there were the Four Masters of Chin-hua in the South who made the teaching flourish, and the North there was Hsü Chung-p'ing[il] [Hsü Heng]. When the country was unified by the Yüan, Chung-p'ing was made the chancellor at the National University and the course of learning also became unified. Scholars such as Ts'ao-lu[im] [Wu Ch'eng] who held a conciliatory attitude towards Lu Hsiang-shan were unable to popularize their views or gain any influence.[128]

But the embers were still there. They would be rekindled when the right wind blew, though that was not to be under the rule of the Mongols.

Notes

1. For instance, *Wu Wen-cheng chi*[in] [Collected works of Wu Ch'eng] in the *Ssu-k'u ch'üan-shu chen-pen*[io] [Rare books published from the Imperial Ssu-k'u Library], (hereafter SKCP), 2nd series; *Shih-shan chi*[ip] [Collected works of Chen Yü] in SKCP, 4th series, etc.

2. Ch'üan Tsu-wang, "Erh-lao-ko ts'ang-shu-chi"[iq] [A note on the holdings in the Erh-lao Pavilion Library], *Chieh-ch'i-t'ing chi* (*Kuo-hsüeh chi-pen ts'ung-shu*[ir] [Collection of basic works for Chinese classical studies], ed.), external collection Bk. VIII, 16:884.

3. *Ibid.*, "Nien-p'u"[is] [Chronological biography], 1:2.

4. *Ibid.*, 1:5–6.

5. *Ibid.*, 1:10.

6. See a note attached to the Table of Contents in the external collection, vol. 6, p. 55; also "T'i-tz'u" [Complimentary remarks], Bk. VI, p. 648.

7. A preface written by Ho Ling-han[it] included in the *Sung-yüan hsüeh-an* (hereafter SYHA) (*Kuo-hsüeh chi-pen ts'ung-shu* ed.), original preface, pp. 1–3.

8. See above, n. 2.

9. For instance, read the "Feng-ta Lin-ch'uan hsien-sheng hsü san-T'ang hsüeh-t'ung yüan-liu cha-tzu"[iu] (A letter to Master Lin-ch'uan, [Li Fu, 1673–1750], discus-

sing the academic backgrounds of the three T'angs in Southern Sung) in *Chieh-ch'i-t'ing chi*, Bk. IV, 34:430–431, etc.

10. *Yüan-shih* (I-wen[iv] Press reprint of the Ch'ing Palace ed.), Bk. IV, 189:2b, p. 2070.

11. *Mu-an chi* (SPTK ed.), 4:1a–2b.

12. Ou-yang Hsüan, "Chao Chung-chien kung tz'u-t'ang chi"[iw] [A note about the temple dedicated to the memory of Master Chao Chung-chien], in *Kuei-chai chi*[ix] [Collected works from the Studio of a Piece of Ceremonial Jade-stone], (SPTK ed.), 5:31.

13. The *Great Learning*, the *Analects*, the *Book of Mencius*, and the *Doctrine of the Mean*.

14. The identity of this work is not yet ascertained. In the *History of Sung*, ch. 202, "Treatise on Bibliography," pt. 1, there is a work entitled *Shih che-chung*[iy] [An eclectic study of the *Book of Odes*] compiled by Liu Yü[iz]; *cf.* Chu I-tsun[ia] (1629–1709), *Ching-i k'ao*[ib] [A bibliographical study on the Confucian Classics], (SPPY ed.), Bk. III, 202:10a, p. 2406.

15. "Chung-shu tso-ch'eng Yao Wen-hsien kung shen-tao-pei"[ic] [Memorial inscription for a tablet laid in the spiritual path leading to the tomb of Lord Yao Wen-hsien], *Mo-an chi*, 15:4b.

16. *Ibid.*, 15:16b–17a.

17. "Hsiung Yü-k'o mu-chih-ming"[id] [Epitaph to Hsiung Yü-k'o], *Tao-yüan hsüeh-ku-lu*[ie] [A record of classical pursuit in the Garden of the Way], (SPTK ed.), 18:170.

18. *Yüan-shih*, Bk. V, 159:13a–b, p. 1792. This is presumably not the same Chao Pi found in Chiang Liang-fu,[if] *Li-tai jen-wu nien-li pei-chuan tsung-piao*[ig] [A combined chart for dates, native places, and biographies of historical figures], (Hong Kong, Chung-hua[ih] Book Co., 1961), p. 388, whose dates are 1297–1353.

19. *Tao-yüan hsüeh-ku-lu*, 12:125.

20. See, for example, the papers contributed to the Symposium on Yüan Thought (Seattle, 1978) by Wing-tsit Chan,[ii] David Gedalecia, and Tu Wei-ming[ij] on Wu Ch'eng, Liu Yin, and Hsü Heng in Hok-lam Chan[ik] and Wm. Theodore de Bary, eds., *Yüan Thought* (New York: Columbia University Press, 1982).

21. "Tu-shih chi"[il] [On divination using milfoil-stalks from a casket], *Ching-hsiu hsien-sheng wen-chi*[im] [Collection of literary works of Master Liu Ching-hsiu], (SPTK ed.), 18:5a.

22. "Chai-chü tui-wen"[in] [Replies to queries while staying at home], *Mo-an chi*[io] [Collected works from a silent hut], (SKCP ed.), 3rd series, 3:1a–5b; "Yü Wu Shu-pei shu"[ip] [Second letter to Wu Shu-pei], *ibid.*, 3:10b–12b.

23. See, for example, "Pa Chu Wen-kung 'chieh-jan' 'chih-fang' erh-t'ieh chen-chi hou"[iq] [A colophon to the two pieces of writings beginning with the characters 'chieh-jan' and 'chih-fang' inscribed by Master Chu Wen-kung], *Ching-hsiu hsien-sheng wen-chi*, 22:5b.

24. "An Ching-chung wen-chi hsü"[ir] [A preface to the collection of literary works of An Ching-chung], *Tao-yüan hsüeh-ku-lu*, 6:72, quoting Su.

25. "Pa Ching-hsiu hsien-sheng i-mo"[is] [A colophon to the surviving inscriptions of Master Liu Ching-hsiu], *Chin-hua Huang hsien-sheng wen-chi*[it] [Collection of literary works of Master Huang of Chin-hua], (SPTK ed.), 21:210.

26. *Ts'ung-shu chi-ch'eng*[iu] (Collection of series ed.), 3:119 *ff.*

27. Jao Lu is also quoted in some passages in Hsü Ch'ien, *Tu ssu-shu ts'ung-shuo* (SPTK ed.), 2nd series.

28. See SYHA, Bk. XXI, ch. 84, p. 120.

29. *Ibid.*, ch. 83, p. 92.

30. "Ku Mei-yin hsien-sheng Wu-chün mu-ming"[iv] [Epitaph to the late Mr. Wu Mei-yin], *Tao-yüan hsüeh-ku-lu*, 18:173.

31. SYHA, Bk. XXI, ch. 83, p. 96.

32. *Chu Wen-kung wen-chi* (SPTK ed.), 53:941–946.

33. SYHA, Bk. XXI, ch. 83, pp. 94–95.

34. *Ibid.*, p. 95.

35. Recorded in his "Hsing-chuang"[jw] (Draft biography), *Tao-yüan hsüeh-ku-lu*, 44:386–387; see also *Wu Wen-cheng chi* (SKCP ed.), 2nd series, appendix, 32b.

36. *Lu-chai i-shu*[ix] [Remnant works of Lu-chai], (SKCP ed.), 4th series, 13:39–40.

37. The Sung-yang[iy] and Sui-yang[iz] academies in Honan, the Yüeh-lu[ka] Academy in Hunan, and the White Deer Grotto Academy in Kiangsi were the Four Leading Academies in Sung times. The Sui-yang Academy is also known as Ying-t'ien.[kb] Sometimes a Shih-ku[kc] Academy is counted as one of the four academies replacing the Sung-yang. Shih-ku was situated in Heng-chou,[kd] also in Hunan.

38. A *li* is one third of a mile.

39. "K'ao-t'ing shu-yüan ch'ung-chien Wen-kung tz'u-t'ang chi"[ke] [At the completion of the rebuilding of a memorial temple dedicated to Chu Wen-kung at the K'ao-t'ing Academy], *Tao-yüan hsüeh-ku-lu*, 36:318.

40. *Yüan-shih*, Bk. II, 81:3a, p. 975.

41. The first among the top three competitors, the highest degree conferred in the state examinations held in the national capital.

42. *Ibid.*

43. *Ibid.*, Bk. II, 81:4b–5a, pp. 975–976.

44. *Ch'eng-shih chia-shu tu-shu fen-nien jih-ch'eng*, (Collection of Series ed.), 3:110; cf. *Chu Wen-kung wen-chi*, 69:1273–1277.

45. *Ibid.*, 3:110–111.

46. *Sung-shih*, Bk. III, 156:10a–11a, pp. 1763–1764.

47. *Ch'eng-shih chia-shu tu-shu fen-nien jih-ch'eng*, author's preface, p. 1.

48. "Hsiung Yü-k'o mu-chih-ming," *Tao-yüan hsüeh-ku-lu*, 18:171.

49. *Ibid.*

50. "Wen-su Teng-kung shen-tao-pei ming"[kf] [Memorial inscription for a tablet laid in the spiritual path leading to the tomb of Lord Teng Wen-su], *Chin-hua Huang hsien-sheng wen-chi*, 26:268.

51. *Ch'eng-shih chia-shu tu-shu fen-nien jih-ch'eng*, 3:115.

52. *Book of Odes*, ode no. 235; Legge, *The Chinese Classics*, vol. 6, p. 431.

53. *Ibid.*, 2:20–21. In recent publications, incidentally, I find John Minford's translation of the famous Ch'ing novel *The Story of the Stone*, vol. IV (Penguin, 1982), ch. 82, may help to offer my readers some insight into the pedantic nature of such compositions.

54. In the epitaph to Ch'eng, *Chin-hua Huang hsien-sheng wen-chi*, 33:343.

55. *Yen-yüan Tai hsien-sheng wen-chi*[kg] [Collection of literary works of Mr. Tai of Yen-yüan], (SPTK ed.), 7:4b–5a.

56. "Yang Hsien-k'o shih-hsü"[kh] [A preface to poems written by Yang Hsien-k'o], *Tao-yüan hsüeh-ku-lu*, 33:290; "Sung Chu Te-chia hsü"[ki] [Farewell to Chu Te-chia], *ibid.*, 34:295.

57. "Sung Wu Shang-chih hsü[kj] [Farewell to Wu Shang-chih], *ibid.*, 34:297.

58. "Yü Hsieh Shih-lin yü-shih lun ku-pen *Ta-hsüeh* t'ieh-tzu"[kk] [A note written to Hsieh Shih-lin, a censor, on the "Old Version of the *Great Learning*"], *Chieh-ch'i-t'ing chi*, external collection, Bk. XII, 41:1270.

59. SYHA, Bk. XXIII, ch. 93, p. 62.

60. "Ta chu-sheng wen Ssu-fu t'ang chi-t'ieh"[kl] [A reply to students' query on the collection of rubbings and inscriptions preserved in the Hall of Restoration], *Chieh-ch'i t'ing chi*, ch. 13, external collection, 47:1389–1390.

61. SYHA, Bk. XXIII, ch. 94, pp. 94–97; also p. 88.

62. "Hai-ch'ao chi"[km] [Sayings recorded from a hideout on the sea], *Chieh-ch'i-t'ing chi*, external collection, Bk. VIII, 18:909.

63. *Ibid.*

64. "Sung Li K'uo hsü"[kn] [Farewell to Li K'uo], *Tao-yüan hsüeh-ku-lu*, 5:65.

65. "Wen T'ai-chi chung-yung chih-i"[ko] [On the meaning of the Great Ultimate and the *Doctrine of the Mean*], *Hsi-shan Chen Wen-chung-kung wen-chi*[kp] [Collection of literary works of Lord Chen Wen-chung of Hsi-shan], (SPTK ed.), 31:494.

66. SYHA, Bk. XXI, ch. 82, pp. 12–13.

67. The dates for Hsü Ch'ien given by Chiang Liang-fu are incorrect. He took the third year of Chih-yüan for 1266.

68. In the *Chin-hua ts'ung-shu*[kq] [Chin-hua series], (SPTK ed.), 2nd series, etc.

69. SYHA, Bk. XXI, ch. 82, p. 39.

70. In *Wu Wen-cheng chi*, ch. 1.

71. "Tseng hsüeh-lu Ch'en Hua-jui hsü," *Wu Wen-cheng chi*, 25:17a.

72. Photolithographic copy (Taipei, 1962) of the 1473 ed., 15:538.

73. *Hsi-shan Chen Wen-chung-kung wen-chi*, 30:469.

74. This is a split of a sentence taken from the *Doctrine of the Mean*, ch. 27. The text in translation reads: "The superior man honors his virtuous nature and maintains constant inquiry and study." See Legge, *The Chinese Classics*, vol. 1, p. 422.

75. SYHA, Bk. XXII, ch. 89, p. 120.

76. *Ssu-k'u ch'üan-shu tsung-mu*[kr] [Bibliographical notes on the *Ssu-k'u ch'üan-shu*], (Taipei: Yi-wen Press, reprint, 1964), Bk. II, 36:4a–5a, pp. 740–741.

77. "Ta Chou Chien-chiu"[ks] [A reply to Mr. Chou, the wine-tax superintendent], *Ch'ung-chiao Ho-shan hsien-sheng ta-ch'üan wen-chi*[kt] [Twice-collated edition of *The Complete Literary Works of Master Ho-shan*], (SPTK ed.), 36:310.

78. *Ibid.*, 55:470.

79. Yen Hui, alias Yen Yüan,[ku] was perhaps the brightest disciple Confucius ever had. He unfortunately died an early death.

80. SYHA, Bk. V, ch. 13, p. 23.

81. *Analects*, 14:37, trans. in Legge, *The Chinese Classics*, vol. 1, pp. 288–289; cf. 14:24, p. 285.

82. For the sayings of Yen Yüan (Yen Hui) in admiration of the Master, see the *Analects*, 9:10, trans. in Legge, *The Chinese Classics*, p. 220.

83. "Fu Wu T'ai-ch'ing shu"[kv] [A reply to Wu T'ai-ch'ing], *Lu-chai chi*[kw] [Collected writings from the Studio of Uncouthness], (*Chin-hua ts'ung-shu* ed.), 7:16b–17a.

84. "An Ching-chung *Mo-an chi* hsü"[kx] [A preface to the *Collected Works from A Silent Hut* by An Ching-chung], *Tao-yüan hsüeh-ku-lu*, 6:72.

85. *Ch'eng-shih chia-shu tu-shu fen-nien jih-ch'eng*, p. 12.

86. "Chi-ch'ing lu Chiang-tung shu-yüan chiang-i"[ky] [Notes for lectures delivered at the Chiang-tung Academy, Chi-ch'ing District], *ibid.*, 3:122.

87. Written in 1689; *ibid.*, colophon, p. 3.

88. Hui-chou comprised six districts in present-day Anhui.

89. See above, n. 61.

90. Former name of Hui-chou, Chu Hsi's ancestral home. His father moved to Fukien Province, where Chu Hsi was born.

91. "Yü Wang Chen-ch'ing"[kz] [To Wang Chen-ch'ing], *Shih-shan i-wen*[la] [Remnant writings of Cheng Shih-shan], (SKCP ed.), 4th series, 3:6a–7a.

92. SYHA, Bk. XXII, ch. 85, p. 14.

93. "Po-yün Hsü hsien-sheng mu-chih-ming"[lb] [Epitaph to Master Hsü Po-yün], *Chin-hua Huang hsien-sheng wen-chi*, 32:328.

94. *I-shu*[lc] [Surviving works], 18:5b, in the *Erh-Ch'eng ch'üan-shu*[ld] [Complete works of the two Ch'engs], (SPPY ed.).

95. "Ta Wu Cheng-ch'uan shu"[le] [A reply to Wu cheng-ch'uan], *Po-yün chi* (Collection of series ed.), 2:28–29.

96. See Fung-Yu-lan,[lf] *A History of Chinese Philosophy*, trans. Derk Bodde (Princeton, N.J.: Princeton University Press, 1953), vol. 2, p. 541; cf. p. 353. Read also Fan Shou-k'ang,[lg] *Chu Tzu chi-ch'i che-hsüeh*[lh] [Chu Hsi and his philosophy], (Taipei: K'ai-ming[li] Book Co., 1964), pp. 45–48.

97. *Yen-p'ing ta-wen* (*Chu Tzu i-shu*[lj] [Surviving works of Master Chu] ed.), 24a.

98. Chu Hsi was quoting from Yang Shih, *Yang Kuei-shan Hsien-sheng chi*[lk] [Collected works of Yang Shih], (1717 ed.), 20:2a, first reply to Hu K'ang-hou.[ll]

99. *Ibid.*, Bk. XXI, ch. 82, p. 41.

100. "Shu Chu Tzu kang-mu hou"[lm] [A colophon to Chu Hsi's *T'ung-chien kang-mu*], *Chieh-ch'i-t'ing chi*, external collection, Bk. XI, 34:1140. See also *Ssu-k'u ch'üan-shu tsung-mu*, Bk. III, 88:23b–24b, p. 1773.

101. For Hu Fang-p'ing and his *Chou-i ch'i-meng t'ung-shih*[ln] [General explanation of the *Introduction to the Changes for Beginners*], see *Ssu-k'u ch'üan-shu tsung-mu*, Bk. I, 3:49a–51a, pp. 105–106. For Hu Yi-kuei and his *I pen-i fu-lu tsuan-shu*[lo] [Notes and commentaries appended to the *Original Meaning of the Changes*], see *ibid.*, Bk. I, 4:2a–b, p. 110; for his *I-hsüeh ch'i-meng i-chuan*[lp] [Subsidiary commentaries to the *Introduction to the Changes for Beginners*], see *ibid.*, Bk. I, 4:2b–3a, pp. 110–111.

102. *Ibid.*, Bk. I, 4:12b–14a, pp. 115–116.

103. *Ibid.*, Bk. I, 4:14a–15a, pp. 116–117.

104. SYHA, Bk. XX, ch. 81, p. 135.

105. SYHA, Bk. XXII, ch. 90, p. 135, quoting the *Chi-fu t'ung-chih*[lq] [Gazetteer of the capital and its surrounding areas].

106. "T'ung-chien kang-mu shu-fa hsü,"[lr] *Chieh Wen-an-kung ch'üan-chi*[ls] [Complete works of Master Chieh Wen-an], (SPTK ed.), 8:73; "Lu-ling Liu-shih *T'ung-chien kang-mu shu-fa hou-hsü*"[lt] [A colophon to *On the Principles of Moral Judgment in Chu Hsi's T'ung-chien kan-mu* written by Mr. Liu of Lu-ling], *Kuei-chai chi*, 7:46.

107. SYHA, Bk. XXI, ch. 83, pp. 98, 107–108.

108. *Ssu-k'u ch'üan-shu tsung-mu*, Bk. III, 88:23b–24b, p. 773.

109. SYHA, Bk. XXII, ch. 86, pp. 29–30.

110. *Huang-shih jih-ch'ao* (SKCP ed.), 2nd series, 6:1b–2a.

111. The Former Sage here indicates the legendary Sage-man Fu-hsi[lu] and the Later Sage, King Wen. For the Primordial Diagram (or Diagram of What Antedates Heaven) and other diagrams see Fung Yu-lan, *op. cit.*, vol. II, pp. 459–464.

112. "Yü Ch'eng-chai Ch'en-kung lun hsien-t'ien hou-t'ien t'u"[lv] [On the primor-

dial and the postprimordial diagrams—to Mr. Ch'en Ch'eng-chai], *Ho Pei-shan i-chi*[lw] [Surviving works of Ho Pei-shan], (*Chin-ts'ung-shu* ed.), 1:7a.

113. *Ibid.*, 3:4b.

114. In Chu Hsi's *Commentary on the Great Learning* he believes that the fifth chapter of the earlier commentary explaining the meaning of investigating things was lost and ventured to supply it, taking the views of Ch'eng I. See Legge, *The Chinese Classics*, I, pp. 365–366.

115. "Ta-hsüeh yen-ko lun"[lx] [On the history of the *Great Learning*], *Lu-chai chi*, 2:2a–4b.

116. "Ku *Chung-yung* pa"[ly] [A colophon to the old version of the *Doctrine of the Mean*], *ibid.*, 5:16b–17b; "*Chung-yung* lun"[lz] [On the *Doctrine of the Mean*], pt. 1, *ibid.*, 2:8b–10b.

117. The Diagram of the Great Ultimate was probably a Taoist creation, but had been used by the Neo-Confucianists in Sung times. See Wm. Theodore de Bary, Wing-tsit Chan, and Burton Watson, *Sources of Chinese Tradition* (New York: Columbia University Press, 1964), vol. II, pp. 457–459.

118. "T'ung Chao Hsing-chu"[ma] [A letter to Chao Hsing-chu], *ibid.*, 7:19a; "Hui Chao Hsing-chu shu"[mb] [A reply to Chao Hsing-chu], *ibid.*, 7:21a–b.

119. SYHA, Bk. XXI, ch. 82, p. 18.

120. *Ibid.*, Bk. XXI, ch. 82, p. 22.

121. *Doctrine of the Mean*, ch. 27.

122. His "hsing-chuang" in *Tao-yüan hsüeh-ku-lu*, 44:386–387; *Wu Wen-cheng chi*, appendix, 26b. For "honoring virtuous nature," etc., see the *Doctrine of the Mean*, ch. 27.

123. "*Chung-yung* chien-ming chuan hsü"[mc] [A brief account on the commentaries to the *Doctrine of the Mean*], *Wu Wen-cheng chi*, 20:5a–b.

124. *Ibid.*, 1:19b.

125. *Ibid.*, 1:20b.

126. See the "Ching-ming Pao-feng hsüeh-an"[md] [Chapter on Ch'en Yüan and Chao Hsieh] in SYHA, Bk. XXIII, ch. 93, pp. 61–63.

127. "Yü Wang Chen-ch'ing," *Shih-shan i-wen*, 3:7b–8a.

128. "Yü Hsieh Shih-lin yü-shih lun ku-pen *Ta-hsüeh* t'ieh-tzu," *Chieh-ch'i-t'ing chi*, external collection, Bk. XII, 41:1269.

Glossary

a	慶元	l	明儒學案	w	許衡
b	考亭	m	澹生堂	x	郝經
c	建陽	n	祁氏	y	劉因
d	四庫全書	o	傳是樓	z	序江漢先生事實
e	全祖望	p	徐氏	aa	姚燧
f	宋元學案	q	鮚埼亭集	ab	牧庵集
g	黃宗羲	r	趙復	ac	元史
h	吳澄	s	德安	ad	歐陽玄
i	雲在樓	t	姚樞	ae	小學
j	永樂大典	u	楊惟中	af	論語或問
k	劉宗周	v	程朱	ag	孟子或問

ah 家禮	cc 張載	dx 奉化
ai 田和卿	cd 程顥	dy 周易本義
aj 尚書纂詩折中	ce 亨	dz 范仲淹
ak 程頤	cf 利	ea 戴良
al 蔡沈	cg 貞	eb 柳貫
am 胡安國	ch 里	ec 鄭玉
an 楊古	ci 熊禾	ed 丁鶴年
ao 沈括	cj 太宗	ee 定海
ap 近思錄	ck 世祖	ef 李擴
aq 呂東萊祖謙	cl 至元	eg 許文正公
ar 虞集	cm 史天澤	eh 何基
as 熊朋來	cn 王鶚	ei 王柏
at 趙璧	co 翰林	ej 金華
au 眞德秀	cp 狀元	ek 許謙
av 大學衍義	cq 進士	el 金履祥
aw 詹體仁	cr 朱文公文集	em 讀四書叢説
ax 邵雍	cs 學校貢舉私議	en 叢書
ay 安熙	ct 舉人	eo 四經叙錄
az 蘇天爵	cu 胡瑗	ep 三禮叙錄
ba 黃溍	cv 石介	eq 儀禮
bb 臨川	cw 歐陽秀	er 贈學錄陳華瑞序
bc 黃榦	cx 王安石	es 關
bd 陸九淵象山	cy 呂大臨	et 格物
be 程若庸	cz 集解	eu 誠意
bf 饒魯	da 蘇軾	ev 朱子語類
bg 李燔	db 王雱	ew 語錄
bh 柴中行	dc 吳械	ex 胡炳文雲峯
bi 程端禮	dd 胡寅	ey 四書通
bj 程氏家塾讀書分年日程	de 仁宗	ez 黃百家
bk 程紹開	df 明經	fa 饒雙峯
bl 道一	dg 鄧文原	fb 纂疏
bm 信州	dh 文	fc 集成
bn 臨汝	di 無聲無臭	fd 四書纂疏
bo 撫州	dj 儀刑	fe 趙順孫
bp 程文海鉅夫	dk 冒	ff 四書集成
bq 吳辰子	dl 原	fg 吳眞子
br 性理字訓	dm 講	fh 魏了翁
bs 程端蒙	dn 證	fi 輔廣
bt 斜峯書院講義	do 結	fj 祖述
bu 龜山楊時	dp 戴表元	fk 朱文公五書問答序
bv 豫章羅從彥	dq 于景龍註朱氏小學書序	fl 吳太清
bw 延平李侗	dr 揚雄	fm 尊樂
bx 劉季章	ds 方言	fn 顏回
by 道統	dt 蔡邕	fo 上達
bz 乾	du 王充	fp 下學
ca 周敦頤	dv 論衡	fq 老子
cb 元	dw 理宗	fr 綱領
		fs 史蒙卿

ft	朱子讀書法	hp	後天	ji	陳榮捷
fu	陸隴其	hq	陳誠齋震	jj	杜維明
fv	徽州	hr	溫公	jk	陳學霖
fw	汪真卿	hs	魯齋	jl	槽著記
fx	新安	ht	紫陽	jm	靜修先生文集
fy	王厚孫	hu	漢書	jn	齋居對問
fz	王應麟	hv	無極	jo	黙庵集
ga	乾道	hw	太極	jp	與烏叔備書
gb	淳熙	hx	中庸章句	jq	跋朱文公傑然直方二
gc	性理	hy	中庸或問		帖真蹟後
gd	白雲集	hz	饒伯與	jr	安敬仲文集序
ge	吳師道正傳	ia	孝經叙錄	js	跋靜修先生遺墨
gf	道	ib	齋	jt	金華黃先生文集
gg	延平答問	ic	魯	ju	叢書集成
gh	知	id	左傳	jv	故梅隱先生吳君墓銘
gi	仁山	ie	邢昺	jw	行狀
gj	慈湖楊簡	if	陳苑靜明	jx	魯齋遺書
gk	本體	ig	趙偕寶峯	jy	嵩陽
gl	通鑑綱目	ih	石塘胡長儒	jz	睢陽
gm	司馬光	ii	謝石林濟世	ka	嶽麓
gn	資治通鑑	ij	魏華甫	kb	應天
go	趙師淵	ik	趙江漢	kc	石鼓
gp	易學啓蒙	il	許仲平	kd	衡州
gq	胡一桂	im	草廬	ke	考亭書院重建文公祠
gr	胡方平	in	吳文正集		堂記
gs	周易本義通釋	io	四庫全書珍本	kf	文肅鄧公神道碑銘
gt	熊良輔	ip	師山集	kg	剡源戴先生文集
gu	周易本義集成	iq	二老閣藏書記	kh	楊賢可詩序
gv	通志堂經解	ir	國學基本叢書	ki	送朱德嘉序
gw	徐乾學	is	年譜	kj	送吳尚志序
gx	納蘭性德	it	何凌漢	kk	與謝石林御史論古本
gy	王天與	iu	奉答臨川先生序三湯		大學帖子
gz	尚書纂傳		學統源流札子	kl	答諸生問思復堂集帖
ha	真西山	iv	藝文	km	海巢記
hb	劉德淵	iw	趙忠簡公祠堂記	kn	送李擴序
hc	劉友益	ix	主齋集	ko	問太極中庸之義
hd	通鑑綱目書法	iy	詩折中	kp	西山真文忠公文集
he	揭傒斯	iz	劉宇	kq	金華叢書
hf	汪克寬	ja	朱彝尊	kr	四庫全書總目
hg	通鑑綱目凡例考異	jb	經義考	ks	答周監酒
hh	玄燁	jc	中書左丞姚文獻公神	kt	重校鶴山先生大全文
hi	康熙		道碑		集
hj	黃震	jd	熊與可墓誌銘	ku	顏淵
hk	黃氏日抄	je	道園學古錄	kv	復吳太清書
hl	先天	jf	姜亮夫	kw	魯齋集
hm	伊川	jg	歷代人物年里碑傳總	kx	安敬仲黙庵集序
hn	康節		表	ky	集慶路江東書院講義
ho	晦庵	jh	中華	kz	與汪真卿

la 師山遺文
lb 白雲許先生墓誌銘
lc 遺書
ld 二程全書
le 答吳正傳書
lf 馮友蘭
lg 范壽康
lh 朱子及其哲學
li 開明
lj 朱子遺書
lk 楊龜山先生集

ll 胡康侯
lm 書朱子綱目後
ln 周易啓蒙通釋
lo 易本義附錄纂疏
lp 易學啓蒙翼傳
lq 畿輔通志
lr 通鑑綱目書法序
ls 揭文安公全集
lt 廬陵鐏氏通鑑綱目書
　　法後序
lu 伏羲

lv 與誠齋陳公論先天後
　　天圖
lw 何北山遺集
lx 大學沿革論
ly 古中庸跋
lz 中庸論
ma 通趙星渚
mb 回趙星渚書
mc 中庸簡明傳序
md 靜明寶峯學案

29

Some Thoughts on Ming-Qing Neo-Confucianism

LI ZEHOU

I

SOME SCHOLARS have compared Zhu Xi with Thomas Aquinas, Spinoza, Alfred North Whitehead, and Hegel. In my opinion the Neo-Confucianism of the Song (960–1279) and Ming (1368–1644) dynasties, with Zhu Xi as its most outstanding exponent, is substantially closer to Kant, for its basic characteristic is to raise ethics to the status of ontology so as to reestablish a philosophy with man as the subject. Its main epistemological ideas such as "extension of knowledge by the investigation of things" (*gewu zhizhi*[a]) as well as cosmological concepts such as the Ultimate of Nonbeing (*wuji*[b]), the Supreme Ultimate (*taiji*[c]), principle (*li*[d]), and breath (*qi*[e] 'ether' or 'material force') actually all serve to establish this ethical subjectivity and raise it to a trans-moral ontological position where it "participates with Heaven and Earth."

"Buddhism looks upon life as illusory and a void and therefore ignores the body to benefit others. Taoism takes one's self as true reality and therefore consumes elixirs to nourish life."[1] Buddhism and Taoism generally evolved their theoretical system and structure by concentrating their study on the life and death, mind and body of the individual. In propagating their doctrines and trying to show that the world is a void and everything is illusory, Buddhists deal with cosmology, world outlook, and epistemology, and this has given rise to well-defined, complete speculative philosophies. The comparatively simpler Taoism is concerned with the making of immortality pills, longevity, and meditation but therefore also has to deal with cosmological theory. These two features of Buddhism and Taoism—individual improvement and the search for cosmology and epistemology—were precisely the basic material that Zhu Xi used to construct his own moral philosophy.

It is well known that the "Explanation of the Diagram of the Supreme Ultimate" (*Taijitu shuo*[f]) by Zhou Dunyi[g] (1017–1073), the first great Neo-Confucian of the Song dynasty, retained a Taoist cosmological model, but what is important here is that Zhou Dunyi concluded from this cosmology that "the sage regulates this by the Mean, correctness, humaneness, and righteousness and regards tranquillity as most important; thus he establishes the ultimate standard for man."[2] In his *Elucidation of the Book of Changes* (*Tongshu*[h]), he stressed sincerity (*cheng*[i]), making this Confucian category his central concept. This shows that he began to integrate the Confucian requirements for practical ethics with the Taoist cosmological diagram in an attempt to build a bridge —the first of its kind—between cosmology and ethics (human rules). He started to follow this sequence: ontology (natural noumenon) → cosmology (the diagram of the world) → epistemology → ethics → ontology.

But it was Zhang Zai[j] (1020–1077) who laid the foundation of Neo-Confucianism. In his essay the "Western Inscription" (*Ximing*[k])[4] and in his other works, he formulated a number of basic Neo-Confucian propositions and principles. Zhang Zai's *Correcting Youthful Ignorance* (*Zhengmeng*[l]),[5] compiled by his disciples, is extraordinarily clear as an example of Neo-Confucianism's systematic structure proceeding from cosmology to ethics.

Zhu Xi consciously assimilated the essence of the philosophies of Zhou and Zhang to establish his system. He as well as Zhou Dunyi, Zhang Zai, and the Cheng brothers (Cheng Hao,[m] 1032–1085, and Cheng Yi,[n] 1033–1107) all loved to discuss the *Book of Changes* because this book is full of the pre-Qin (221–206 B.C.) rational spirit shown in such phrases as "Heaven's greatest value is called life"[6] and "renewing life means change"[7] and served as a weapon for the philosophical criticism of Buddhist and Taoist theories which maintained that existence was illusory, denied the perception of the real changing world, and sought after nothingness or longevity as the unchanging noumenon. As it was necessary to affirm the worldly feudal order in practical life, it was imperative to affirm the real world itself and to go on to discuss and affirm the substantiality of this world and the rationality and necessity of its existence. In contrast to Buddhist philosophers, Zhu Xi never negated but regularly affirmed man's perceptual existence and the existence and value of his perceptual environment and objects (that is, the real world). Zhu Xi's anthology of Northern Sung (960–1126) Neo-Confucians, the *Jinsilu*[o] (Reflections on things at hand),[8] and his *Zhuji yulei*[p] (Classified conversations of Master Zhu) both have devoted their first chapter to cosmology in the form of *li*, *qi*, the Ultimate of Nonbeing, and the Supreme Ultimate; however, these were just preludes to the main theme, which was the reestablishment of Confucianism, with the feudal social system as the ontological axis. Zhu Xi armed himself with cosmological theory to establish a theory of human nature that conformed to the social order in the later stage of feudal society. And so he proceeded from "Heaven" (cosmos) to "man" (ethics) and integrated "Heaven" with "man." However, the *Doctrine of the Mean* and the *Great Learning* were more basic to Zhu Xi than the *Book of Changes,* and the discussions of human nature revived and were as heated as in the pre-Quin period, which shows that human nature played a pivotal role in connecting "Heaven" and "man" and is the key to the transition from cosmology to ethics. It is not cosmology and epistemology but the theory of human nature that constitutes the nucleus of Zhu Xi's system. So, while discussing "the relationship between Heaven and man" (*tianren zhiji*[q]), Zhu Xi was nevertheless different from Dong Zhongshu[r] (176–104 B.C.). "Heaven and man combining into one" (*tianren heyi*[s]) as expounded by Zhu Xi is "the study of the nature of the mind," while Dong Zhongshu's "interaction of Heaven and man" (*tianren ganying*[t]) is an organic system theory with a feedback function.[9] The latter is true cosmology while the former is not. In the latter, ethics is subordinate to cosmology, whereas in the former, cosmology is subordinate to ethics.

Following the Cheng brothers, Zhu Xi criticized the Buddhists for seeking emptiness but still not parting with their bodies of flesh and blood and for holding that everything is illusory but still wearing clothes and eating food to preserve the material existence of the sensual world of themselves (body, life) and their environment (natural and human). Zhu Xi linked this kind of secular commonsensical criticism with cosmology; it was raised above mere common sense to the level of a general knowledge of the "relationship between Heaven and man." That is to say, since man has to eat and wear clothes and "live under this heaven and step on this earth," one must theoretically recognize and affirm "Heaven" and "man" as being substantial and rational in their sensual, material existence. It is also necessary to recognize and affirm that this existence is constantly going through movement, change, birth, and death (cosmology). At the same time, in eating, wearing clothes, and so on, man has a certain purpose in mind and conforms to certain rules and orders; so, theoretically, he has to try to seek, probe, and prove these universally valid rules, orders, and purposes (epistemology). That is to say, within the limited, perceptual, and real (and even worldly, commonsensical) innate laws of human relationships, one must seek and demonstrate the absolute, rational, and noumenal that transcends the limited, perceptual, and phenomenal. For in the eyes of Zhu Xi, it is precisely these rules, orders, and purposes that are the noumena that dominate and control the natural and human sensual real world. The laws, orders, and purposes are thus gradually abstracted from the material world and regarded as the thing that dominates, controls, and rules the latter. Such speculative processes are not rare in the history of either Chinese or Western philosophy; the distinguishing feature of Zhu Xi's philosophy is that the central axis of his theory is a theory of human nature. Thus he brought this question into bold relief; that is, he consciously made the fixed orders, rules, and laws of a specific society (the later stage of feudalism) into the supreme law governing the cosmos.

When compared with Kant's empirical perceptual matter being dominated by a priori categories, this formal structure appears similar, but the internal substance is quite different. The Neo-Confucians regarded the domination of the empirical "human desires" and "humoral nature" by the a priori "Principle of Heaven" and "universal nature" as the completion of ethical behavior. Kant's is an extroverted epistemology, demanding the supply of as much perceptual experience as possible to form universally valid scientific knowedge;

Neo-Confucianism is an introverted ethics, demanding the elimination of as much sensual desire as possible to carry out "universally valid" ethical behavior. Kant's a priori categories (for example, causality) come from contemporary mathematics and natural sciences (Newtonian physics); the Neo-Confucian a priori norms (for example, principle, the Way) are derived from the contemporary social order (feudal legality). Kant, by sharply dividing epistemology from ethics and requiring their mutual noninterference, preserved each one's own independent value; the Neo-Confucians, by mixing the two together, consequently got them too tangled up to unravel, and in fact in Zhu Xi's theory of epistemology completely yielded to ethics.

II

It might be said that Zhang Zai was not entirely aware of what he was doing with his philosophical theory as he proceeded from cosmology to ethics. Zhu Xi, on the other hand, was very conscious of his goal when he likewise started out from cosmology to establish a philosophical system with ethics at the center. If Zhang Zai moved from the external to the internal, with Zhu Xi it was the opposite. It appears that Zhu Xi emphasized "principle" (Supreme Ultimate), which exists in all things and is realized in the self, and that he expounded in various aspects and ever-deepening layers a number of central philosophical categories which focus on the *li-qi* question (such as superior and interior forms, the Way and instruments, movement and tranquillity, Ultimate of Nonbeing and the Supreme Ultimate). And because his studies cover everything, great or small, and his logic is rigorous, he has been compared to Hegel by some scholars. However, I think that we should not allow ourselves to be confused by the outward appearance of a system so complicated and elaborate. Instead I would like to grasp the fundamental point of Zhu Xi's great system, which can be expressed in a conceptual formula such as this: "ought" (human behavior and relationships) = "necessity" (cosmic law).

Zhu Xi's all-embracing world of "principle" is divided to fit this formula: the laws, rules, and order that all things must ("necessity") and people should ("ought") honor, follow, and obey are the "Principle of Heaven." Though it exists together with everything, "principle" is something that logically precedes, surmounts, and transcends the phenomenal world and constitutes the noumenal existence of all things. "After all, before heaven and earth came into being, there was first this principle."[10] "In the cosmos there is only one principle. When heaven has it, it is heaven. When earth has it, it is earth. Among all the things born between heaven and earth, each one also has it, and it is its nature. Its extension is called the Three Bonds[11] and its concentration the Five Constant Virtues.[12] And so this principle prevails; there is nowhere it is not."[13] This "principle" ("necessity") that transcends and dominates heaven, earth, man, things, and events is an "ought" in human behavior and relationships; the two are equal and can be interchanged. "The Principle of Heaven prevails everywhere: summer is gone and winter comes, rivers flowing and mountains static, love between father and son and righteousness between sovereign and ministers, this is all principle."[14] "Everything has an ultimate, the ultimate extreme of the Way's principle. Jiang Yuanjin asked if the humaneness of the sovereign and the seriousness of the minister were all ultimates. The Teacher said, these are the ultimates of individual events and things. The principle of heaven and earth and all things is the Supreme Ultimate. Originally, the Supreme Ultimate lacked this name; it was only the manifestation of virtue."[15] Thus, it can be seen that this cosmic noumenal "principle/Supreme Ultimate" is social and ethical: "It was only the manifestation of virtue." It is a "categorical imperative" which must be followed, obeyed, and implemented by the individual.

> The mandate is just like a command and nature is principle. Heaven uses yin-yang[u] [passive and active cosmic forces] and the Five Elements[16] to create all things while *qi* produces forms, and principle is likewise endowed in them, just like an order or a command. As a result, when people and things are born, each receives its own endowed principle to serve as the Five Constant Virtues; this is called nature.[17]
>
> When man and things are born, they all share the principle of Heaven and Earth as their nature and the *qi* of Heaven and Earth as their shapes. They differ only in that man, receiving within the rightness of form and *qi,* is endowed with the basis to make perfect his nature.[18]

The Mandate of Heaven (principle) is nature. This is what Zhang Zai meant by "universal nature." It is an a priori, necessary demand and norm for the individual. For man's difference from things lies in his having the rightness of form and breath to realize this righteous and principled nature to make perfect his nature. Cosmology turns out to be a theory of human nature; the world of principle turns out to be nature and mandate. This is to say, human relationships, morality, and norms of behavior are derived from the categorical imperative, from the Principle of Heaven, and they have nothing to do with utility, happiness, and sensuous joys. When a man sees a child falling into a well, it is not for material gain or merit that he goes to save it; it is simply something he must ("ought to") do; it is an a priori and categorical imperative, transcending perception and experience, which man cannot resist. It is when contrasted with and opposed to the happiness, joy, and benefits experienced by an individual that the strength of the categorical imperative and the nobility of the morality in human relations became apparent, showing clearly that this is indeed an extremely powerful, rational noumenon transcending all the phenomena of experience. As a matter of fact, this is the problem on which Zhu Xi and the whole of Neo-Confucianism have concentrated. Neo-Confucians emphasized the difference between righteousness and profit and fulfillment of the Principle of Heaven and elimination of human desires, and they stressed that "starving to death is a small matter but loss of chastity is of major importance."[19] Even Huang Zongxi[v] (1610–1695) and Wang Fuzhi[w] (1619–1692), those progressive thinkers of the seventeenth century, were against "sitting in a tub filled with the sticky lacquer of profit and desire"[20] and held that "the distinction between superior and inferior men and the difference between men and animals are but the difference between righteousness and profit,"[21] which shows the continuity of the fundamental spirit of Zhu Xi's philosophy. The latter distinctions were the most prominent expositions of the idea that human relationships and rationality ("righteousness" = "man") have a source and essence different from sensuous desires ("profit" = "animal").

Zhu Xi's statement that "principle is one and its manifestations are many" is essentially aimed at showing that the aforementioned moral behavior possesses a universality similar to law and at proving that moral behavior, connected with human experiences of specific, real, material content, still possesses a nature with a simultaneous a priori rationality and is therefore universally applicable and effective. That is to say, this kind of applicability and effectiveness is not based on and confirmed by experience and fact, but arises from the same a priori rationality (the Principle of Heaven): "All things have this principle and this principle comes from one source. But since the positions they occupy are not the same, the application of the principle is not one. Thus, when applied to the sovereign, it is humaneness; when to the minister, it is seriousness; when to the son, it is filial piety; when to the father, it is affection. All things have this principle but they differ in its use; thus only one principle prevails."[22] "Principle is one and its manifestations are many" as "the moon is reflected in myriad streams," that is, as the moon in Heaven, while only one, still is scattered about the myriad streams and thus adapting to externals can be seen. Here and elsewhere Zhu Xi was not talking so much about the common features of the cosmos and nature but rather demonstrating that morality had the character of universal law and raising this to the level of ontology.

Zhu Xi stressed the realization of this universal law (principle) in practical action and not in speculation. This realization had to be highly conscious, that is, possess self-consciousness. In a certain sense he was seeking ethical autonomy and opposing heteronomy. The self-realization of principle is not an external divine order; even less does it exist for external material benefit or happiness. Zhu Xi wanted knowledge to precede action and opposed blindness and spontaneity in moral conduct. This was so because he wanted to establish this kind of autonomy and attain self-consciousness: "When righteousness and principle are not understood, how can they be practiced? When reason is made clear, then one is by necessity filial in serving one's parents, submissive in serving one's elder brother and faithful in serving one's friends."[23] The necessity here is the categorical imperative (the Principle of Heaven) that must be followed at any cost, and the phrase "when the reason is made clear" refers to the self-consciousness. Investigation of things, extension of knowledge, and fulfilling principle are concepts of an epistemology created to achieve this consciousness. "Investigation of things is to grasp thoroughly the principle of everything; extension of knowledge means that there is nothing my mind does not know. Investigation of things aims at the specific and minute, fragmentary way of learning; extension of knowledge aims at the general and comprehensive."[24] This is similar to Cheng Yi's view that the reason for "investigating one thing today and another tomorrow" was to accumulate knowledge to reach the point where "one day suddenly the whole thing is seen in a clear light";[25] this understanding of the ethical noumenon and its implementation in one's own behavior is self-enlightenment and sincerity. Also because of the stress on autonomy, the Neo-Confucians paid great attention to self-discipline even when alone (*shengdu*[x]) and whether each idea conformed with the nature of Heaven, refusing to be influenced or controlled by the external environment, interests, or desires.

Only after having accomplished the aforementioned can one establish an ethical subjectivity sharing virtue with Heaven and Earth. This subjectivity in fact transcends actual moral requirements and attains the height of an existential noumenon. Thus Zhu Xi's philosophy is a kind of ethically subjective ontology. This ontology demands that one be great among the ordinary, arrive at the highest virtue and practice the doctrine of the Mean, and display the universal necessity and nobility of the moral code in daily life.

Ethical noumenon, nonutilitarian moral imperative, universal laws, and autonomy of the will—in a certain sense Zhu Xi's philosophy is indeed similar to Kant's.

There is, however, a fundamental difference. Apart from the difference in the temporal and class background (the feudal class in traditional China versus the bourgeoisie on the threshold of modern Europe) this results in a difference in the theoretical essence (for example, Zhu Xi lacks Kant's explicit stipulations about "freedom" and "man is the purpose"). Kant made an absolute separation between reason and knowledge, noumenon and phenomenon; practical reason was solely a "categorical imperative" and "duty," which had nothing to do with any feelings and conceptions of the phenomenal world, or with causality, time, and space. This rather thoroughly guarantees its noumenal status transcending experience. Chinese practical reason never separates noumenon and phenomenon and seeks noumenon from phenomenon. Even with the mundane and transmundane, what it stresses is "Heaven and man combine as one." Kant's "categorical imperative" is a pure form of the a priori which is inexplicable and originless (otherwise it would degenerate into the phenomenal realm of causality), while Zhu Xi's "principle" is closely related to man's perceptual existence and psychological feelings. It was not limited to pure form, but had a basis in social psychology. As inheritors of the tradition of Confucius (551–479 B.C.) and Mencius (372–289 B.C.?), the Neo-Confucians clearly constructed the idea of duty and categorical imperative

from a certain sort of humaneness which possessed a content of social sentiment. While Kant did not depart from the traditional Western idea of original
sin and looked upon human nature as evil, Zhu Xi followed Confucius and
Mencius in stressing that human nature is good and implementing basic principles that merged psychology with ethics. The Mandate of Heaven and
human nature, the moral code and human relationships, which had originally
been made so great and lofty, came ultimately down to a psychological and
emotional foundation full of sensuality and flesh and blood. This perception
caused their whole cosmology and world view, devised to confirm the ethical
noumenon, also to carry a humanized, vitalized overtone. The great affirmation of humaneness and compassionate heart and that of the growth and development of the natural realm of perceptions are analogically linked. In Zhu Xi
and Neo-Confucianism, therefore, the natural world of perception and the
noumenal realm of rational ethics not only are not separated but have actually
completely merged with each other. Heaven and man, then, have two aspects:
rational and emotional. This perception led to two popular stories in the Neo-
Confucian tradition: Xie Liangzuo[y] (1050–c.1120), one of the leading students of the Cheng brothers, used peach kernel (taoren[z]) and apricot kernel
(xingren[aa]) to explain humaneness (ren[ab]), reasoning that the fruit pit signifies
life and growth.[26] Zhou Dunyi in like fashion never cut the grass in front of
his window in order to see Heaven's will.[27] "All things are in contentment
when seen in serenity/Sharing with man their wonderful mood through the
four seasons"[28] and "Casually I came to recognize the features of the east
breeze/When all hues and colors made up the spring"[29] are well-known lines
from Cheng Hao's and Zhu Xi's poetry, seeking to feel and reveal human
moral obligations in, and compare them to, life and vitality in nature. This is
one of the characteristics of the Neo-Confucians and that is why they valued
the Book of Changes and the Doctrine of the Mean so highly. They like to talk
about the happiness of Confucius and Yan Hui,[ac] which they regarded as life's
highest realm, and which actually refers to the undaunted, brimming vitality,
belonging to the spiritual realm of teleology, which is ethical and yet trans-
ethical, quasi-aesthetic and yet super-aesthetic. Kant's teleology can be
expressed in the phrase "nature is born of man" and is in a certain sense
objective teleology, with the subjective purposiveness being just the realm of
aesthetics. However, the Neo-Confucians used subjective teleology that
"Heaven and man combine as one and all things have the same substance" to
indicate the trans-ethical and super-aesthetic ontological realm which man can
attain and which is seen as man's highest existence. This noumenal realm is
indeed similar and close to the aesthetic state of mind and nonutilitarian pleasures where the objective and the subjective are both forgotten.

Nevertheless, it is precisely in this respect that there is a tremendous contradiction in Zhu Xi's system. As the noumenal and phenomenal realms are
not distinguished and separated from each other, the noumenal realm can be
pervaded by feelings (as the happiness of Confucius and Yan Hui) and experi-

ences; thus perception itself achieves a significant status. And recognition and affirmation of the perceptual existence of man and the world inevitably leads to recognition of man's sensual desires and needs. Since "Heaven's greatest virtue is life," demands and purposes in accordance with the growth and development of sensual nature, which include *li*, the natural laws of sensual desires are not evil but good. Since principle has to be manifested in *qi*, it is very hard to distinguish between the Principle of Heaven and human desires. Thus, Zhu Xi frequently said, "The distance between the Principle of Heaven and human desires is but a hairbreadth."[30] "When one is hungry one desires to eat; when one is thirsty one desires to drink. How could there be no such desires?"[31] "Though they are human desires, there is also the Principle of Heaven in them."[32] This suffices to show that the rational noumenon (the Principle of Heaven) and the perceptual phenomenon (human desires) should not be opposed to each other. However, the social demands of the feudal ruling class made Zhu Xi take the ruling order and behavioral codes—the laws of the feudal system—of a transient, specific period as the universally necessary, omnipresent "Principle of Heaven" and "Mandate of Nature" to repress and smother man's sensual, natural passions. Asceticism, feudalism, and hierarchy were regarded as the cosmic "Principle of Heaven" and the human "Mandate of Nature." "What is the Principle of Heaven? Are not humaneness, righteousness, propriety, wisdom, and sincerity the principle of Heaven? Are not relations between sovereign and minister, father and son, older and younger brothers, husband and wife, and friends the Principle of Heaven?"[33] Thus, on the one hand, in theory Zhu Xi affirms the existence and development of sensual nature and does not require a separation of the noumenal and phenomenal world; on the other hand, he demands the confinement, repression, and even denial of the needs of man's sensual nature and wants a clear demarcation between the ethical noumenon and the phenomenal world. This major contradiction lay like a time-bomb in the core of Neo-Confucianism.

The theory of mind, first advanced by Zhang Zai and then developed by Zhu Xi, divides mind (*xin*[ad]) into nature (*xing*[ae]) and feelings (*qing*[af]). Nature is the Principle of Heaven and comes from the noumenal world; it is called "unaroused" (*weifa*[ag]) and also the "mind of the Way" (*Daoxin*[ah]). Its content is humaneness, righteousness, propriety, wisdom, sincerity, and other feudal ethics governing human relationships. It is pure reason. On the other side, the human mind (*renxin*[ai]), or feelings, which belongs to the aroused phenomenal world contains such ideas, emotions, and psychological attitudes as compassion, good and evil, modesty, right and wrong. It has perceptual components, or elements related to perceptions. The distinction between nature and feeling actually corresponds to that between Heaven-mandated nature and humoral nature. Just as *li* cannot depart from *qi*, the mind of the Way cannot depart from the human mind but rather controls it. The hypothesis of a dualistic mind made the contradiction mentioned above all the more sharp.

In his early period, Zhu Xi defined nature as unaroused. Mind and nature in this view were still somewhat separate; nature, not being able to penetrate the mind, became external demands and commands. Zhu Xi later came to think that mind should include the unaroused and aroused or both the mind of the Way and the human mind, so that they constitute both noumenon and function, apply to the apparent and hidden, and encompass movement and tranquillity; thus nature as the Principle of Heaven is carried right into the mind inseparable from a flesh-and-blood body. Thus although the mind can be divided into two (the mind of the Way and the human mind), from another point of view the two are combined into one. In short, the rational and the perceptual, social and natural, noumenon and phenomenon, are all concentrated in the same mind.

> Nature is the principle of the mind, feelings are the movements of the mind; the mind is the master of nature and feelings.[34] The mind is like water, nature is like the tranquillity of water, feelings are the flow of nature and desires are the waves of water.[35] The mandate is like imperial ordinances and commands, nature is like functioning bodies, feelings are like measures, the mind is the man.[36]
>
> The mind, when conscious of principle, is the mind of the Way; when conscious of desires, it is the human mind. . . . The human mind emanates from shape and vital power and the mind of the Way originates in nature and mandate. . . . In the human mind, one should also recognize the mind of the Way.[37]

Zhu Xi's view was that the mind of man and the mind of the Way are originally one mind but with division between the Principle of Heaven and human desires. Recognizing only the mind of the Way will lead to a Buddhist doctine. The human mind exists so long as bodies of flesh and blood exist. The human mind contains both good and evil, but the mind of the Way is all good, and therefore one must follow the mind of the Way existing in the human mind. If the desires for eating, drinking, and love are right, the human mind becomes the mind of the Way. The latter controls the former, setting right the desires for eating, drinking, and love. Obviously, the mind of the Way (Nature, unaroused, is purely the Principle of Heaven) exists to control or rule the human mind (Feelings, aroused, can lead to human desires), but the mind of the Way and the human mind must also be only one mind and the former must not depart from the latter.

On the one hand, it is extremely dangerous to have the human mind closely connected with the needs of the natural world of perceptions and the material existence of the human body, because, if not properly handled, it will turn into excessive personal interests and desires and give rise to an outpouring of human desires; this is evil. On the other hand, the mind of the Way has to depend on the human mind connected to material existence; otherwise it cannot exist and fulfill its function. Without this material substance the mind of the Way, nature, and mandate fall into the void. "Nature is only principle; without the *qi* of Heaven and substance of Earth, this principle has no place to reside."[38] Negating this *qi* of Heaven and substance of earth, the human mind and "shape and *qi*" would be the same thing as the Buddhist denial of the material world and sensual nature. Achieving a stable balance between these two aspects, that is, the Mean, became a matter of particular concern to Zhu Xi. It is indeed very hard to call for the unity and merging of principle and desire, nature and feeling, the mind of the Way and the human mind, the rules for human relations and naturalness, since they come from two entirely different and even antagonistic worlds (the worlds of noumenon and phenomenon, reason and perception). The basic Neo-Confucian category of humaneness, for example, is regarded as nature, principle, and the mind of the Way and at the same time as having the perceptual elements or content of spontaneous growth and development. So are categories like Heaven and mind: they are rational but also perceptual, supernatural but also natural, a priori but also empirical, and they encompass morality but also the cosmic order. This contradiction has the potential of exploding all of Neo-Confucianism. But covered up by Zhu Xi's grand cosmological epistemological system, it is not very conspicuous. The theory of mind did not yet occupy a dominant position in Zhu Xi's system and so the contradiction is submerged in the discussions on the investigation of things, extension of knowledge, Ultimate of Nonbeings, Supreme Ultimate, and so on. But once mind became noumenon in the new stage of Ming Neo-Confucianism (the School of Mind), mind became a more central topic in the system and this contradiction inevitably emerged and developed, finally causing the theoretical disintegration of Neo-Confucianism in modern China.

III

In the 1950s I wrote an article on Kang Youwei's[aj] (1858–1927) philosophy, in which I maintained that "in Wang Yangming's[ak] (1472–1529) philosophy, mind is divided into the mind of the Way (the Principle of Heaven) and the human mind (human desires).[39] The mind of the Way opposes the human mind and yet has to rely on the human mind for its existence. Herein lies the inevitable contradiction that is breaking up the entire system. For the mind of the Way must pass through the human mind's perception, feeling, will, and consciousness for its basic concepts, and the innate knowledge of the good conforms to spontaneity. Thus, this kind of consciousness assumes the psychological nature of the human body and is no longer purely a principle of logic. This necessarily leads to the materialism expressed in the sayings 'the Principle of Heaven is in human desires' and '*Li* is in *qi*.' "[40]

This rupture was first manifested in the emphasis on the inseparability of the mind of the Way and the human mind, which often came to be confused and gradually identified with each other. Although Wang Yangming by abstraction elevated the mind of the Way to an a priori height transcending physical matter, it was still not principle but related to body and matter. In this way the rational and the perceptual frequently became one thing or so close as to be indivisible. Advancing one step further, these material things gradually turn into the basis for nature and principle. The logical principle which originally was in a dominating and commanding position actually became an extension and derivative of mind and feelings. Thus from principle and nature to mind was reversed, as was from nature to feelings. Rather than humaneness (Nature and principle in Zhu Xi) determining and governing the compassionate mind (feeling in Zhu Xi), on the contrary, humaneness and fulfilling principle are derived and expanded from the compassionate mind. Since the mind is principle, it cannot be removed from the flesh and body, or better yet has to depend on the body to be able to exist. ("There is no mind without body and no body without mind; when we refer to the function of filling a space, it is body; when we refer to the ruling function, it is mind."[41]) The mind of the Way and the human mind cannot be separated, nor can mind and body. Thus, principle and the Principle of Heaven are increasingly mixed up with sensual flesh and blood and made worldly. This is an inevitable movement in the modern period.

In Wang Yangming's celebrated remarks: "Having neither good nor evil is the substance of the mind; having both good and evil is the movement of the will; distinguishing between good and evil is innate knowledge; doing good and eliminating evil is the investigation of things."[42] Even though he placed mind in a supernatural, trans-moral noumenal realm, it nevertheless has a more psychological nature than Zhu Xi's logical principle. Wang's school focused all questions on the subjective body, the spirit mind, and will, which cannot be separated from the physiological body. His original idea was to turn psychology into ethics in order to instill the social order directly into the minds of the people. However, the result was quite the opposite: his so-called innate knowledge, as good will or moral knowledge, was instead tinged with sensual emotions. His disciples, from Wang Gen[al] (1498–1582) to Wang Ji[am] (1483–1540), either made absence of idea (*wunian*[an]) the principal aim and stressed that the "spontaneity of the unrestrained mind" is capable of attaining innate knowledge or made joy (*le*[ao]) the basis and stressed that "joy is the original substance of the mind": "the human mind is naturally joyful but we restrain it with our own desires . . . Joy is to enjoy this study, study is to study this joy."[43] They thereby developed the School of Mind further in a perceptual direction. Although their referents are not at all sensual enjoyment—perceptual pleasure or natural desire, "spontaneity of the unrestrained mind" and "joy" still mean a certain spiritual satisfaction and belong to the moral realm—they are in some way linked to the perceptual either directly or indirectly and become more and more separated from purely moral commands (Principle of Heaven). Hence there soon appeared formulations such as "restraining desires is not an embodiment of humaneness," and Wang Yangming's School inclined more and more to deny the necessity of the use of external standards to artificially control and repress desires, or in other words to deny the necessity of using abstract, a priori rational concepts to coerce the mind. The doctrine that mind is principle became more and more perceptual;

no longer regarding ethics as psychology, it gradually shifted to accepting psychology as ethics. And logical norms increasingly became psychological needs. The principle in "mind is principle" was increasingly changed from external Heavenly principle, norms, and orders into internal nature, feelings, and even desires. This comes close to the theory of naturalistic human nature of the modern bourgeoisie; human nature is man's natural passions, needs, and desires. This tendency is present in the Taizhou[ap] and the Jishan[aq] schools. After Wang Gen spoke of "love" and Yan Shannong[ar] maintained that to "just follow our own nature and allow for pure spontaneity . . . can be said to be the Way. . . . If scholars first study reason and norms, it will be enough to block the Way,"[44] He Xinyin[as] (1517–1579) said that "nature means taste, sensuality, music, and comfort. This is nature."[45] Liu Zongzhou[at] (1578–1645), wanting to keep the superiority and dominating function and position of the mind of the Way, said, "The mind of the Way is the original mind of the human mind; the nature of righteousness and principle is the original nature of the humoral nature."[46] But his student, Chen Que[au] (1604–1677) said, "Originally the Principle of Heaven was found lacking in the human mind; it is seen precisely in human desires. When human desires are appropriate, that is the Principle of Heaven."[47] "Without human desires, one cannot speak of any Principle of Heaven."[48]

Before them Li Zhi[av] (1527–1602) had already spoken bluntly of selfishness (*si*[aw]) and profit (*li*[ax]). "Selfishness is a man's mind. Man must have selfishness before the mind is seen. Without selfishness there is no mind. . . . If we do not seek profit, it cannot be right. . . . If we do not calculate merit, when would the way be clear?"[49] This is almost totally contrary to Zhu Xi's teaching. Li not only approved of profit, merit, selfishness, and self, but also maintained that they are the basis of righteousness, the way, and the public (*gong*[ay]). From here it was only a short step away to Dai Zhen[az] (1723–1777), who said, "Loving wealth and women is desire; sharing the desired with the people is principle." "What the ancient sages meant by humaneness, righteousness, propriety, and wisdom is not to be sought beyond the so-called desires and is not separated from our flesh and blood."[50] It was again only one further step away theoretically to Kang Youwei. He declared, "Principle is just the principle of man."[51] "We are born possessing desires; it is the nature of Heaven! . . . For our mouths we desire tasty food and for our residence we desire exquisite mansions."[52] It is by no means accidental that such pioneers as Li Zhi and Kang Youwei, who prepared the ground for the modern theory of naturalistic human nature, openly admired Wang Yangming's thought or had direct theoretical connections with his School.

Theoretically speaking, this entire course of development is rather astonishing: from *qi* to *li*, from *li* to mind, and from mind to desires; starting from stressing the distinction between the "Principle of Heaven" and "human desires" and between "righteous and principled nature" and "humoral nature," and ending with "principle is in the desire" and "desire is nature," not to mention the great variety of other details. Beginning as introverted eth-

ics built on extroverted cosmology and finally reverting to psychophysiology
caused the entire Neo-Confucian system to collapse and disintegrate theoretically. Human relations and moral obligations began to be built on real life and
a physical basis of the individual's perceived desires, happiness, and pleasures. The feudal theory of the Principle of Heaven and human nature
changed into the bourgeois theory of naturalistic human nature.

This play of logic had its basis in history. Why did Lu Xiangshan's[ba] (1139–
1193) School of the Mind soon become dormant and nobody pay much attention to it while Wang Yangming, as soon as he raised his voice, win such a
great following and have such great influence all over China? Why were people everywhere so fascinated by Li Zhi though he was imprisoned and his
works were burned? Can we deny that it is obviously related to all the tremendous changes in the economy, politics, culture, social atmosphere, and state of
mind that occurred from the middle of the Ming dynasty?

Apart from moving towards the modern theory of naturalistic human
nature, another characteristic of the School of Wang Yangming is the great
stress on the dynamic role of subjective practice (moral behavior) or the unity
of knowledge and action. It reduces all morality to the self-conscious behavior
of the individual. Knowledge must be action; innate knowledge invariably
acts and self-conscious action is knowledge. That is to say, man's true existence lies in the innate knowledge of behavior and activity and only in this
behavior can he achieve noumenal existence. Man's existence is confirmed
and expanded in the moral behavior of the self-conscious extension of innate
knowledge, just as Huang Zongxi said, "The mind has no original substance;
when perfect efforts are made, it becomes the original substance."[53] Because
of their opposition to knowledge sought purely objectively or divorced from
action, many of Wang's followers became more and more explicit in their
rejection of the Zhu Xi orthodoxy of living respectfully and preserving tranquillity. Instead they adopted an attitude of more active participation and
intervention in daily life. Varied expression of this attitude can be found in
Wang Gen's advocacy of "creating destiny" and "changing destiny" and Liu
Zongzhou's stress on "personal will" and the idea that in the noumenon there
was "the highest good and no evil." All these were to give prominence to ethical subjectivity, wherein the individual's awareness of historic responsibility
and moral self-consciousness played a more significant role and became the
basic spirit and primary theme of the entire theory.

These two aspects of Ming-Qing (1644–1912) philosophy drew the theory
of principle towards mind, demanding that mind should transcend the real
world to become independent and free, and form the noumenon of the cosmos. The former aspect approaches the modern theory of naturalistic human
nature as it denies that man has two minds and eliminates the critical distinction between righteous and principled nature and humoral nature. The latter
aspect, with its emphasis on subjectivity and willpower, exerted a greater or
smaller degree of influence on many people with lofty ideas in later generations such as Kang Youwei, Tan Sitong[bb] (1866–1898), the young Mao

Zedong,[bc] and Guo Moruo[bd] (1892–1978), who used it as a spiritual weapon or support in the struggle against the old society, system, and customs. Theoretically speaking, the former aspect seems more important but did not develop very much. The theory of naturalistic human nature of China's modern bourgeoisie, except for its expression in the new literature after the May Fourth Movement (1919), did not fully develop. Thus, the latter aspect (seeking individual moral perfection, tempering of the will and the martial spirit) became the factor with practical influence. A very interesting phenomenon is that the young Mao Zedong on the eve of the May Fourth Movement commented on Paulsen's *A System of Ethics* and made clear his intention to combine these two aspects by affirming the egotistical basis of sensual desires to enlarge and temper the individual's subjective consciousness and to promote moral cultivation and voluntary autonomy, and by using the spirit expressed in "I am the universe" and "Seize the day! Seize the hour!" to meet and participate is society's real life. However, this grafting was not sustained for long. Sensual pleasure and freedom were far from being fully affirmed and developed theoretically. The subjective ethical consciousness and the voluntary demands instead achieved practical results and excessive emphasis in the long years of hard revolutionary life and military struggle.

IV

What has the philosophy of Zhu Xi left us in China at present? A question of this magnitude goes beyond a single essay. Only a few preliminary points can be suggested here.

First of all, of course, his philosophy seriously poisoned the minds of the people in its several hundreds of years of dominance, leaving in its wake disasters and sorrow. In the words of Dai Zhen:

> The honored use principle to accuse the lowly; the elderly use principle to accuse the young; and the noble use principle to accuse the mean. Though they err in the action, they are said to be right. When the lowly, the young, and the mean argue, though they are right, they are said to be rebellious. . . . Once accused by their superiors with principle, the inferiors become incriminated with countless crimes. When a man is executed by law there are still people who pity him, but if he is killed by principle, who pities him?[54]
>
> What is called principle is the same as what cruel officials call law. Cruel officials used law to kill people and then the later Confucians used principle to kill people. More and more they set aside the law and resorted to principle; and when the accused is doomed to die, there is no remedy.[55]

And in the words of Tan Sitong:

> Vulgar scholars indulged in quoting [Confucian ritual and Neo-Confucianism] which were honored as the Mandate of Heaven that people dared not change and were held in awe as the state constitution that could not be questioned. . . .

Superiors used them to control their inferiors who could not but respect them. And so for the past several thousand years the tragic misfortunes and cruelties of the Three Bonds and the Five Relationships[56] were greatly aggravated.[57]

Where the code holds sway, not only are people's mouths shut so that they dare not speak freely, but their minds are fettered so that they dare not begin to think.[58]

Dai Zhen's and Tan Sitong's angry denunciations show clearly the historical damage Zhu Xi's philosophy has caused to Chinese society and the Chinese people. Since the Reform Movement of 1898, people such as Tan Sitong, Song Shu[be] (1860–1910), Zou Rong[bf] (1885–1905), Chen Duxiu[bg] (1880–1942), Wu Yu[bh] (1871–1949), Lu Xun[bi] (1881–1936), Ba Jin[bj] (1905–), and Cao Yu[bk] (1910–) were full of fighting spirit and won historical fame and the love of the people through their political writings or their fiction and drama, for example, Lu Xun's *A Madman's Diary*, Ba Jin's *Family*, and Cao Yu's *Thunderstorm*. Was this not so because opposition to Neo-Confucianism, especially Zhu Xi, was the basic theme of all of them?

Even today this centuries-old specter still haunts the land of China, although usually disguised, even under the banner of Marxism. For example, Lin Biao[bl] (1905–1972) said, "We must struggle against the slightest thought of private interest"; "let revolution burst forth from the depths of the soul." It is then not entirely understandable that we have adopted an attitude of rejection of Zhu Xi's philosophy since Liberation? Do we not even today still have the historical task of continuing the criticism and rejection of Neo-Confucianism?

Has Zhu Xi's philosophy left mankind something positive? Especially looking to the future, when its particular feudal function will have been thoroughly eliminated, will it have any value left?

Human psychology differs from that of animal insofar as man has human nature, which is a socialized, psychological structure and capacity. For instance, sacrifice of the individual for the sake of the preservation of the community is a form of sensual activity common to both humans and animals. For an animal, this is instinct; but for man, it is conscious, voluntary behavior and is the result of the rational consciousness using, dominating, and controlling sensual activity. What is expresses is the human will's structural power. This rational will as expressed in sensual form is precisely the essence of man and the dignity of human nature as revealed in its confrontation and even conflict with the sensually and physiologically natural desires—survival, joy, and happiness. On this question Zhu Xi undoubtedly made a more profound contribution than the theory of naturalistic human nature.

Zhu Xi raised moral autonomy, the voluntary structure, the sense of social responsibility and human superiority to nature to a high noumenal plane, giving an unprecedented dignity and greatness to man's ethical subjectivity. Perhaps only Kant's ethics compares to it in the history of world philosophy; but as mentioned previously, Kant's moral law possesses a more awesome external orientation whereas Zhu Xi's theory has preserved a more human feeling. To Kant, there is a division between the noumenal world and the natural world, while to Zhu Xi, feelings and principle are in harmony and there is the "unity of Heaven and man." Is Zhu Xi's philosophy, which seeks "harmony of feelings and principle" and "unity of Heaven and man" so to establish a noumenon of human nature distinct from that of the animal, of any significance and value to today's world where some people are spiritually empty, moral values seem bankrupt, and animal-like individualism runs rampant? Its theoretical achievements and world significance are topics that need further study.

Translated by Zhu Zida[bm]

Notes

1. Dao-an[bn] (312–385), *Guang hongming ji*[bo] [The *Essays Spreading Elucidating the Doctrine* enlarged], (SPPY ed.), 8:8b.

2. In the *Zhouzi quanshu*[bp] [Complete works of Master Zhou], ch. 1, trans. Wing-tsit Chan[bq] as "An Explanation of the Diagram of the Great Ultimate" in his *A Source Book in Chinese Philosophy* (Princeton, N.J.: Princeton University Press, 1963), pp. 463–464.

3. In 40 short chapters. Trans. by Wing-tsit Chan as *Penetrating the Book of Changes* in *Source Book*, pp. 465–480.

4. In the *Zhangzi quanshu*[br] [Complete works of Master Zhang], ch. 1.

5. *Ibid.* For translation of selected passages, see Chan, *Source Book*, pp. 500–517.

6. *Book of Changes*, "Appended Remarks," pt. 2, ch. 1.

7. *Ibid.*, pt. 1, ch. 5.

8. English translation by Wing-tsit Chan, *Reflections on Things at Hand* (New York: Columbia University Press, 1967).

9. Dong Zhongshu, *Chunqiu fanlu*[bs] [Luxuriant gems of the *Spring and Autumn Annals*], essay no. 56.

10. Zhu Xi, *Zhuzi yulei* (1473 Jiangxi[bt] ed.), 1:1a.

11. The Three Bonds are those binding the ruler with the minister, the father with the son, and the husband with the wife.

12. Humanity, righteousness, propriety, wisdom, and good faith; or righteousness on the part of the father, affection on the part of the mother, friendliness on the part of the elder brother, respect on the part of the younger brother, and filial piety on the part of the son.

13. Zhu Xi, *Zhuzi wenji*[bu] [Collection of literary works of Master Zhu], (SPPY ed. entitled *Zhuzi daquan*[bv] [Complete collection of Master Zhu ed.]), 70:5a.

14. *Zhuzi yulei*, 40:8a.

15. *Ibid.*, 90:9b.

16. Metal, Wood, Water, Fire, and Earth.

17. Zhu Xi, *Zhongyong zhangju*[bw] [Commentary on the *Doctrine of the Mean*], comment on ch. 1.

18. Zhu Xi, *Mengzi jizhu*[bx] [Commentary on the *Book of Mencius*], comment on 4B:19.

19. Cheng Yi, *Yishu*[by] [Surviving works], 22B:3a, in the *Er-Cheng quanshu*[bz] [Complete works of the two Chengs], (SPPY ed.).

20. Huang Zongxi, *Mingru xuean*[ca] [Anthology and critical accounts of Neo-Confucians of the Ming dynasty], (SPPY ed.), 32:1a.

21. Wang Fuzhi, *Du Tongjian lun*[cb] [On reading the *General Mirror*], (SPPY ed.), 18:14a.

22. *Zhuzi yulei*, 18:8a.

23. *Ibid.*, 9:4a–b.

24. *Ibid.*, 15:8a.

25. *Yishu*, 18:5b.

26. *Shangcai yulu*[cc] [Recorded sayings of Xie Liangzuo], (*Zhuzi yishu*[cd] [Surviving works of Master Zhu] ed.), pt. 1, 2a.

27. Cheng Mingdao, *Yishu*, 3:2a.

28. Cheng Hao, *Mingdao wenji*[ce] [Collection of literary writings of Cheng Hao] 1:6b, in the *Er-Cheng quanshu*.

29. *Zhuzi wenji*, 20:10b.

30. *Zhuzi yulei*, 13:2b.

31. *Ibid.*, 94:38b.

32. *Ibid.*, 31:2a.

33. *Zhuzi wenji*, 59:23b.

34. *Ibid.*, 5:6b.

35. *Ibid.*, 5:10a.

36. *Ibid.*, 5:1a.

37. *Ibid.*, 62:8a–b.

38. *Ibid.*, 4:9b.

39. Zhang Zai brought up the distinction between the mind of the Way and the human mind as the necessary starting point of Neo-Confucianism. Zhang stressed the transcendent character of the mind of the Way. In Wang Yangming, it is the final state of Neo-Confucianism, and he emphasized the dependent character of the mind of the Way. Of course, strictly speaking the "human mind" is not the same as "human desires."

40. *Kang Youwei Tan Sitong sixiang yangjiu*[cf] [Studies of the thoughts of Kang Youwei and Tan Sitong], (Shanghai: Renmin[cg] Press, 1958), p. 89.

41. Wang Yangming, *Yangming quanshu*[ch] [Complete works of Wang Yangming], (SPPY ed.), 3:1b.

42. *Ibid.*, 3:21b.

43. *Mingru xuean*, 32:11a.

44. *Ibid.*, 32:1b.

45. *He Xinyin ji*[ci] [Collected works of He Xinyin], (Beijing: Zhonghua[cj] Book Co., 1960), p. 40.

46. *Mingru xuean*, 62:9b.

47. *Chen Que ji*[ck] [Collected works of Chen Que], (Beijing: Zhonghua Book Co., 1979), p. 461.

48. *Ibid.*, p. 468.

49. *Cangshu*[cl] [A book to be concealed], (Beijing: Zhonghua Book Co., 1959), Bk. III, p. 544.

50. *Daishi sanzhong*[cm] [Three works by Dai Zhen], (Beijing: Pushe,[cn] 1924), Bk. II, p. 12.

51. *Kangzi neiwaipian*[co] [Inner and outer treatises by by Master Kang], *Studies in the History of Chinese Philosophy* (in Chinese), no. 1 (1980), p. 36.

52. *Datongshu*[cp] [Book of great unity], (Beijing: Zhonghua Book Co., 1956), p. 41.

53. *Mingru xuean*, original preface, 1a.

54. *Daishi sanzhong*, Bk. I, p. 14.

55. *Dai Dongyuan ji*[cq] [Collected works of Dai Zhen], (SPPY ed.), 9:7b.

56. Those between ruler and minister, father and son, older and younger brothers, husband and wife, and friends.

57. *Tan Sitong quanji*[cr] [Complete works of Tan Sitong], (Beijing: Sanlian[cs] Book Co., 1955), p. 14.

58. *Ibid.*, p. 65.

Glossary

a	格物致知	ah	道心	bo	廣弘明集		
b	無極	ai	人心	bp	周子全書		
c	太極	aj	康有為	bq	陳榮捷		
d	理	ak	王陽明	br	張子全書		
e	氣	al	王艮	bs	春秋繁露		
f	太極圖説	am	王畿	bt	江西		
g	周敦頤	an	無念	bu	朱子文集		
h	通書	ao	樂	bv	朱子大全		
i	誠	ap	泰州	bw	中庸章句		
j	張載	aq	蕺山	bx	孟子集註		
k	西銘	ar	顏山農	by	遺書		
l	正蒙	as	何心隱	bz	二程全書		
m	程顥	at	劉宗周	ca	明儒學案		
n	程頤	au	陳確	cb	讀通鑑論		
o	近思錄	av	李贄	cc	上蔡語錄		
p	朱子語類	aw	私	cd	朱子遺書		
q	天人之際	ax	利	ce	明道文集		
r	董仲舒	ay	公	cf	康有為譚嗣同思想研		
s	天人合一	az	戴震	cg	究		
t	天人感應	ba	陸象山		人民		
u	陰陽	bb	譚嗣同	ch	陽明全書		
v	黃宗羲	bc	毛澤東	ci	何心隱集		
w	王夫之	bd	郭沫若	cj	中華		
x	慎獨	be	宋恕	ck	陳確集		
y	謝良佐	bf	鄒容	cl	藏書		
z	桃仁	bg	陳獨秀	cm	戴氏三種		
aa	杏仁	bh	吳虞	cn	樸社		
ab	仁	bi	魯迅	co	康子內外篇		
ac	顏回	bj	巴金	cp	大同書		
ad	心	bk	曹禺	cq	戴東原集		
ae	性	bl	林彪	cr	譚嗣同全集		
af	情	bm	朱士達	cs	三聯		
ag	未發	bn	道安				

30

The Korean Controversy over Chu Hsi's View on the Nature of Man and Things

YOUN SA-SOON

I

NEO-CONFUCIANISM of the Sung period (960–1279), which had been systematized by Chu Hsi, was introduced in Korea at a substantial level in the thirteenth century. For about a hundred years thereafter, however, it did not flourish because of the religious, political, and social conditions of the time—especially the dominance of Buddhism, the state religion of the Koryo period (918–1392). Comprehensive studies of Neo-Confucianism began and flourished only with the establishment in the fourteenth century of the Yi dynasty (1392–1910), which adopted it as the official ideology. Since then, both the theory and practice of Neo-Confucianism have been vigorously studied and interpreted in various ways in Korea.

Two remarkable occasions mark the peaks in the process of the theoretical elaboration of Neo-Confucianism in the Yi dynasty. One of them was the debate in the middle of the sixteenth century about the interpretation, on the basis of the theory of li-ch'i[a] (principle-material force), of the Four-Seven Thesis. The other was the debate at the beginning of the eighteenth century about whether or not the nature of man and the nature of things are the same. These two debates were the most controversial issues in the academic circle of Neo-Confucianism, and they remained so until the Yi dynasty ended in 1910. Throughout the whole scholarly history of Korea, one can hardly find any other case in which so many scholars devoted themselves to the interpretation of and the controversy over a single precise subject. The intellectual fervor aroused by these debates eventually resulted in the formation of four schools of Korean Neo-Confucianism: the Toegye (Yongnam[b]) School and the Yulgok (Kiho[c]) School, resulting from the former debate, and the Hoseo[d] School and the Rakha[e] School from the latter. Such being the case, it can safely be said that a study of these two debates would illuminate some important characteristics of Korean Neo-Confucianism.

Issues raised in the former debate, that is, about the interpretation of the

Four-Seven Thesis, are widely known and have been adequately studied.[1] It would not be easy to deal with both of the debates in a single paper. So our concern here will be limited to the latter, that is, the controversy whether or not the nature of man and the nature of things are the same. Since both of the debates originated from Chu Hsi, a study of either of them will help to elucidate not only some theoretical features of Korean Neo-Confucianism but also some fundamental characteristics of Chu Hsi's thought as illuminated by Korean Neo-Confucian scholars.

II

The controversy that centered on whether the nature of man and the nature of things are the same or not began to develop among the scholars belonging to the school of Kwon Sang-ha (*h.* Suahm,[f] 1641–1721), who upheld Chu Hsi's thought by aligning himself with the followers of Yi I (*h.* Yulgok,[g] 1536–1584) and Song Si-yeol (*h.* Wooahm,[h] 1607–1689). Kwon Sang-ha had eight distinguished disciples widely known as the "Eight Scholars of Kang-mun."[i] Among them Han Won-jin (*h.* Namdang,[j] 1682–1751) and Yi Gan (*h.* Woeahm,[k] 1677–1727) were the most distinguished scholars who took the lead in the controversy.

These two scholars took up opposite positions in the controversy. While Yi Gan asserted that the nature of man and the nature of things are the same, Han Won-jin held the contrary view. Their fervent controversy, which continued for years through correspondence, spread eventually even to the people around them—their mentor (Kwon Sang-ha), friends, and relatives. Those who participated in the controversy were divided into two groups; those in support of Yi Gan included such scholars as Yi Jae (*h.* Doahm,[l] 1680–1746), Park Pil-ju (*h.* Yeoho,[m] 1680–1748), and Eo Yoo-bong (*h.* Kiwon,[n] 1674–1744), while those in support of Han Won-jin included such scholars as Yun Bong-gu (*h.* Byonggye,[o] 1681–1767), Choi Jing-hu (*h.* Maebong,[p] ?), and Chae Ji-hong (*h.* Bongahm,[q] 1683–1741). Perhaps coincidentally, the groupings of scholars coincided with their native places. On the whole those from Rakha (Seoul area) supported Yi Gan, while those from Hoseo (Chungcheong Province) aligned themselves with Han Won-jin. Therefore, with its character of provincialism, the controversy whether the nature of man and the nature of things are the same or not is also called "the debate between Hoseo and Rakha." This controversy, as mentioned already, continued for about one hundred years.

The issue of this controversy, before it was inaugurated in detail by Chu Hsi, can be traced back to Mencius. In view of its historical origin, it is not surprising that the full-fledged examination of this issue in Korea was preceded by studies of such scholars as Cheong Shi-han (*h.* Woodam,[r] 1625–1707), Park Sae-dang (*h.* Seogye,[s] 1629–1703), Kim Chang-hyup (*h.* Nongahm,[t] 1651–1709), and Kwon Sang-yoo (*h.* Kugye,[u] 1656–1724). However, unlike Yi Gan's and Han Won-jin's, their studies by and large can be said to be fragmentary and incomplete. One can find in them neither evidence of thorough inquiry nor the trace of arduous debate. They did, however, contribute to the preparation of an intellectual atmosphere in which genuine controversy between Han Won-jin and Yi Gan was made possible. In the following sections we shall examine in detail Han Won-jin's and Yi Gan's opinions, which may be said to form the central ideas of this well-known controversy.

III

Yi Gan, in dealing with the problem about the nature of man and things, called attention to some of the terms used in Neo-Confucianism. He pointed out that *pen-jan*[v] (the original) corresponds to *i-yüan*[w] (the one origin), and *ch'i-chih*[x] (physical quality) to *i-t'i*[y] (different entities).[2] The "one origin" and the "different entities" are the two viewpoints from which the problem about the nature of man and things was discussed. Yi Gan said,

> In terms of "One Origin," both the Mandate of Heaven (*T'ien-ming*[z]) and the Five Constant Virtues [humanity, righteousness, propriety, wisdom, and truthfulness] transcend form and concrete objects (*hsing-ch'i*[aa]). In this case there is no difference of partial (*p'ien*[ab]) and complete (*ch'üan*[ac]) endowment between man and things. This sameness is called *pen-jan chih hsing*[ad] (the original nature).
>
> In terms of "different entities," both the Mandate of Heaven and the Five Constant Virtues are influenced by physical nature. Therefore, in this case, there are many differences not only between man and things but also between worthies and ordinary minds. Thus, where partial endowment prevails, the physical form and destiny (*ming*[ae]) become off balance, and where complete endowment prevails, their physical form and destiny become balanced. This difference is called the physical nature (*ch'i-chih chih hsing*[af]).[3]

According to Yi Gan, the nature of man and the nature of things with respect to "one origin" are the same in that both of them refer to the original nature. On the other hand, in regard to "different entities" they are different in that both of them refer to the physical nature. In view of "different entities," there are many differences among men and among things themselves as well as between man and things.[4] In other words, in view of original nature, that of man and that of things are the same; in view of physical nature, not only the nature of man and the nature of things but also all the natures of individual entities are different from one another.[5]

Of the two viewpoints, which lead to the different conclusions, Yi Gan held the former, which views "the original" as the "one origin." He declared, "Even though nature is differentiated into the original and the physical, what should be given more emphasis is the original."[6] He maintained that in terms of original nature, that of man and that of things are the same.

Han Won-jin thought differently. He also distinguished "one origin" from "different entities" but in terms different from those of Yi Gan. That is, he held that the "one origin" exists "beyond physical nature" or "transcends physical form and concrete objects" and that "different entities" stand "on the basis of physical nature."[7] Therefore, according to his opinion, the nature of man and the nature of things are the same in that they both transcend physical form and concrete objects, while they are different in that they both exist on the basis of physical nature. Here we can see that Han Won-jin, like Yi Gan, also approved that different conclusions could be drawn according to different perspectives. However, Han Won-jin's approach was different from Yi Gan's in that he put more emphasis on the difference between the nature of man and the nature of things. Furthermore, on the premise of his theory of "three levels of nature," Han Won-jin showed that there could be three different ways of looking at the difference between the nature of man and the nature of things.[8] He said,

> In terms of principle but not material force, man and things are in the state of nondifferentiation. In this case we cannot distinguish one from the other by a certain principle or a certain virtue. But all particular principles or particular virtues, that is, the principles of all creatures and the virtues of humanity, righteousness, propriety, and wisdom, are all included in the same universal principle. This principle refers to the nature that man and things have in common.
>
> In terms of the principle of physical nature, the principle of plant is humanity, that of metal, righteousness, and so on. While man, endowed with balanced material force, has balanced nature, things, endowed with unbalanced material force, have unbalanced nature. Thus, in this case, nature for all men is the same, but the nature of man and the nature of things are different.
>
> In terms of principle and material force being mixed together, all creatures differ from one another in their qualities such as hard and soft, good and evil. In this case every man has a different nature.[9]

According to Han Won-jin, both man and things, in view of principle without involving material force, transcend physical form and concrete objects. His position of viewing things on the basis of physical nature can be considered in two respects: one possibility is "to view the human mind with respect to its principle of material force," while the other is "to view principle and material forces as mixed together." Consequently, from the viewpoint that encloses both man and things with respect to principle, the nature of man and the nature of things are the same. From another viewpoint, that is, viewing the human mind in regard to its principle of material force, while the nature of man and the nature of things are different, human nature is the same in every man. According to still another viewpoint, that is, viewing principle and material force mixed together, there are differences in human natures as well as between the nature of man and the nature of things.[10] Of the above three viewpoints Han Won-jin approved of the second and the third, that is, viewing things on the basis of physical nature. Thus, it would be quite natural that he maintained the difference between the nature of man and the nature of things.

IV

It is clear that the difference between Yi Gan's and Han Won-jin's opinions resulted from their contrary viewpoints. If both of them had taken the same viewpoint, whether that of one origin and transcending physical form and concrete object or that of different entities and viewing things on the basis of physical nature, they would probably have had the same opinion. However, a little more thorough examination would lead us to confirm that such difference of viewpoints alone is not sufficient to explain the difference of their opinions. It also resulted from their different use of the term, *hsing*[ag] (nature).

Hsing for Yi Gan meant the original nature and the One Origin. In this case principle refers to the origin of the universe such as the Mandate of Heaven, destiny, or the Great Ultimate (*T'ai-chi*[ah]). In fact, in the course of the controversy he said that the One Origin is the same as the Mandate of Heaven, destiny, the Great Ultimate, the original nature, and even the Five Constant Virtues. According to him, these seemingly different concepts all refer to the principle.[11] He said that the relationship between nature as the Five Constant Virtues and destiny as principle are two different terms for the same thing.[12] To make his point clearer, he said, "Regardless whether it is called the original nature or the physical nature, it refers only to principle . . . If nature can not be substituted for principle, on the one hand, and principle cannot be interpreted as nature, it is beyond my concern."[13] At this point it is obvious that Yi Gan approved of the idea that nature is principle and that principle is one but its manifestations are many as propounded by Ch'eng I[ai] (1033–1107) and Chu Hsi. On the basis of these two ideas he maintained that the nature of man and the nature of things are the same.

On the other hand, Han Won-jin's use of the term *hsing* (nature) was different from Yi Gan's. Of course he seems to have used the term "nature" in the sense implicit in the idea that nature is principle. Such a use of the term was implied when he said, on the subject of transcending physical form and concrete objects, "In terms of principle without involving material force, the nature of man and the nature of things are the same." However, we should also notice that on other occasions he used the term differently. For instance, his emphasis on the difference between the nature of man and the nature of things is based on his use of the term "nature" as "the principle of material force in the human mind." Therefore, even though he referred to nature as principle, nature in this case is different from Yi Gan's use of principle as an abstract universal concept such as destiny or the Great Ultimate. Rather, it refers to the concrete and individual principle inherent in material force.

Han Won-jin's use of the term "nature" is made clearer in his quotation of Chu Hsi's and Yi I's explanations of nature such as "nature is discussed on the basis of physical nature" or "nature is the mixture of principle and material force. Thus principle can be called nature only when it has entered into material force. If principle exists independently out of material force, it should be called not nature but principle."[14] He also used "nature" in this context when he stated that the Five Constant Virtues as nature are different from the Mandate of Heaven or the Great Ultimate. According to him, the Mandate of Heaven and the Great Ultimate refer to things in their completeness and can be applied to everything regardless of physical form or the status of a concrete object, while the Five Constant Virtues refer to the partiality that can be expressed only on the basis of their being physical nature.[15] The Five Constant Virtues for Han Won-jin are no other than "the original nature explainable only in terms of material force."[16] Therefore, the Five Constant Virtues, according to him, are all the more different from the original nature, which can be applied to things in their partiality as well as in their completeness.[17] Thus, Han Won-jin said, "It is true that we can substitute nature for principle, and interpret principle as nature. However, if nature is compared with principle, they are the same as principle, but different as nature."[18]

As we have discussed, Yi Gan put more emphasis on principle, Han Won-jin on material force. With such difference of attitudes or viewpoints, they even differed in their use of the term *hsing*. Their opposite attitudes may also be seen in their mutual criticism during the controversy: whereas Han Won-jin criticized Yi Gan's interpretation of nature to be "vain,"[19] Yi Gan found fault with Han Won-jin's idea of nature, saying, "He misunderstood physical nature as nature."[20]

However, in spite of their different interpretations of nature, each of their opinions may have a rational validity—to the extent that their initial premises and attitudes are granted as acceptable. In other words, if we accept that everything including man originates from the basic principle such as the Mandate of Heaven or the Great Ultimate, we can say that Yi Gan's opinion has a kind of rational validity—for he maintained, on the basis of "nature is principle," that the nature of man and the nature of things are the same. On the other hand, if we accept that nature makes man and things what they are, or that it is a kind of essence that enables one to distinguish species from genus, we can also say that Han Won-jin's opinion has a rational validity—for he insisted, on the basis of "principle within material force," that the nature of man and the nature of things are different. As they believed in their own rational validity, each one was convinced of the correctness of his own opinion while criticizing and opposing the other.

V

As is often the case with enthusiastic and serious debates in general, this debate also extended to issues of a wide scope and came to deal not only with the central subject but also with peripheral problems. Their debate concerning nature, especially, extended to consideration of feelings before they are aroused (wei-fa[ai]), for Han Won-jin viewed nature as principle within the human mind or material force. In their different interpretations on this subject, Yi Gan, with the emphasis on principle and on the nature of the mind, interpreted the state of feelings before they are aroused as goodness inherent in pure principle, while Han Won-jin, with the emphasis on material force and on the function of the mind, regarded the state as the principle of material force which manifests itself either as good or evil.[21] Of course, their interest was centered on the problem about the nature of man and things, not on these related problems. Thus, they focused their discussions on the nature of man and things, especially quoting from the Classics or from the theories of previous scholars. The theory they quoted in common to support their opinion was Chu Hsi's. This fact deserves our special consideration.

Yi Gan, who maintained that the nature of man and the nature of things are the same, once stated, "Since ancient times, principle of One Origin has been said to mean the original nature." He took as examples "the nature mandated by Heaven" stated in the beginning of the Doctrine of the Mean and Chu Hsi's commentary on it, namely, "The nature mandated by Heaven is no other than humanity, righteousness, propriety, and wisdom."[22] Chu Hsi's commentary may be considered in relation to the following remark of his:

> Mandate is equal to a command, and nature is principle. Heaven creates myriad things through yin-yang[ak] [passive and active cosmic forces] and the Five Agents [Metal, Wood, Water, Fire, and Earth]. When material force assumes physical forms, principle is provided for each of them. Thus the procedure of Heaven's creation is like that of giving a command. As the virtues of strength (nature of Heaven) and obedience (nature of Earth) and the Five Constant Virtues result from principle, which is given to every physical form during the process of creation, the principle is equal to nature.[23]

This commentary is tenable on the premise that both man and things retain the principle of the Mandate of Heaven such as the Great Ultimate, and that principle is nature. It therefore supports the opinion that the nature of man and the nature of things are the same. Naturally, this quotation is quite agreeable to Yi Gan, but not so to Han Won-jin.

In this regard Han Won-jin said that in his theory of the nature of man and things the Mandate of Heaven and the Five Constant Virtues were mentioned merely on a general basis, not on the basis of the idea inferrable in the first chapter of the Doctrine of the Mean or in Chu Hsi's commentary on it. And he avoided further comment on Chu Hsi's commentary.[24] However, feeling that such an avoidance alone is insufficient to justify his position, he continued, "[Author of the Doctrine of the Mean] Tzu-ssu's[al] [492–431 B.C.?] intention was different from them. There are two kinds of Mandates of Heaven: that of completeness and that of partiality. The former is applied to man, and the latter to things."[25] With such an interpretation, he tried to transcend the confinement of Chu Hsi's commentary.

With a similar intention, he further quoted Chu Hsi, that is, Chu Hsi's *Meng Tzu chi-chu*[am] (Collected commentary on the *Book of Mencius*) and referred to his idea stated in the *Ta-hsüeh huo-wen*[an] (Questions and answers on the *Great Learning*). He said, "In the *Meng Tzu chi-chu* Chu Hsi said, 'Man and things differ in the genuineness of humanity, righteousness, propriety, and wisdom.' This statement refers to the Five Constant Virtues of different entities."[26] He also said, "In the *Ta-hsüeh huo-wen* Chu Hsi said, 'Only man is created with fair and transparent material force. Thus man's *hsing* is the noblest.' Man differs from animals in this respect."[27]

To have a more thorough knowledge of Chu Hsi's ideas quoted above, we need to examine them in detail. In the *Meng Tzu chi-chu*, Chu Hsi said,

> Man and things cannot come into existence without nature (principle) and material force. From the point of view of material force, man and things do not seem to differ in their sensory function. However, from the point of view of principle, who can say that things are also endowed with genuine humanity, righteousness, propriety, and wisdom? This is the reason why man's nature is good and man is the lord of all creation. Kao Tzu[ao] did not understand that nature is principle, and he confused material force and principle.[28]

And in the *Ta-hsüeh huo-wen* Chu Hsi said,

> Man and things are created in the following order: They are endowed with principle before they complete the nature of strength, obedience, humanity, righteousness, propriety, and wisdom. After they are endowed with material force, they complete the body of spirit, viscera, and skeleton . . . From the point of view of principle, as the origin of everything is one, there cannot be any difference as to nobility and meanness between man and things. However, from the point of view of material force, fair and transparent material force constitutes man, while unfair and opaque makes things. Thus there can be difference as to nobility and meanness between man and things.[29]

Judged by the above quotations from the *Meng Tzu chi-chu* and the *Ta-hsüeh huo-wen*, Chu Hsi seems to have acknowledged somehow the difference between the nature of man and the nature of things. Chu Hsi's ideas, therefore, might prove to be favorable to Han Won-jin. However, we should notice that Chu Hsi's ideas were not only about the difference but also the similarity between the nature of man and the nature of things. Therefore, Yi Gan could also quote Chu Hsi's ideas in his support, and he in fact did.[30] Thus, the controversy between Yi Gan and Han Won-jin on the nature of man and things proceeded along endless parallel lines.

VI

The fact that both of the two scholars, Yi Gan and Han Won-jin, quoted Chu Hsi's idea implies that their scholarly positions remained within the boundary of Chu Hsi's thought. If they could maintain contrary positions on the basis of Chu Hsi's philosophy, it may be said that Chu Hsi's thought itself contained antithetical aspects or contradictions.

To make this point clear let us review Chu Hsi's ideas stated in the *Ta-hsüeh huo-wen* and the *Meng Tzu chi-chu*. First, Chu Hsi's idea in the former work can be summarized by saying that nature (the Five Constant Virtues or nobility and meanness) of man and things is identical from the point of view of principle but different from the point of view of material force. Principle and material force cannot be separated in reality; it involves a contradiction to speak, allegedly for the purpose of theoretical clarification, of the aspect of principle alone or of the aspect of material force alone. Aside from this problem, Yi Gan and Han Won-jin, from the beginning of their controversy, approved of the essential point of the *Ta-hsüeh huo-wen,* that is, Chu Hsi's theory on the nature of man and things formed on the basis of "nature is principle."

Chu Hsi's idea in the *Meng Tzu chi-chu,* however, was different. It can be summarized as suggesting that while from the point of view of material force there is no difference of sensory function between man and things, from the point of view of principle there really is a difference of humanity, righteousness, propriety, and wisdom or the endowment of the Five Constant Virtues between them. In other words, from the point of view of material force there is no difference between the nature of man and the nature of things, whereas from the point of view of principle, there is a difference between them.

In the last analysis, the point of the *Meng Tzu chi-chu* may be said to contradict that of the *Ta-hsüeh huo-wen* (and the *Chung-yung chang-chü*[ap] [Commentary on the *Doctrine of the Mean*]). Thus, it may be concluded that there is a theoretical contradiction in Chu Hsi's idea on the nature of man and things. How are we to interpret this seeming contradiction?

If we probe into the contents of the *Ta-hsüeh huo-wen* and the *Meng Tzu chi-chu,* we can find that each work uses the same terms in different contexts. In other words, we need to call attention to the fact that Chu Hsi used terms such as principle, material force, and nature with different connotations in the context of each work.

Material force, mentioned in the *Ta-hsüeh huo-wen,* constitutes concrete sensory substances, for, with its characteristics of "clearness," "turbidity," "purity," and "impurity", it enables everything to have its own appearance, color, and size. On the other hand, principle is an original, abstract, and universal entity; and since it is usually asserted that principle comes before material force, it is free from material force. Therefore, in this case, nature as principle means the original nature considered in terms of principle being one and its manifestations being many (*li-i fen-shu*ᵃᵠ) in the theory of the Great Ultimate. In this case, therefore, nature, which was called "the One Origin" by Yi Gan, corresponds to the original nature of everything, man and things together. If man and things essentially have such nature in common, the difference between them is reduced to only a phenomenal one.

But the same terms are used differently in the *Meng Tzu chi-chu*. Here, material force is used more as a sensory function or characteristic than as a phenomenal sensory substance. And principle in this work means humanity, righteousness, propriety, and wisdom mentioned in the *Book of Mencius*, 2A:6 and 6A:6, and is believed to be inherent in the human mind. Therefore, it means the principle within material force. Thus, in this case nature means man's essential nature that distinguishes man from other animals. Moreover, nature here can be extended to mean every innate characteristic of things that distinguishes one kind from the other.

Seen in this light, the difference between man and things is made possible essentially on the basis that the original nature is principle. Thus, the difference between them originating on the basis of nonessential and changeable material force is rather negligible. With respect to principle and material force, therefore, the *Ta-hsüeh huo-wen* stands in contrast to the *Meng Tzu chi-chu*. Accordingly, one may insist that the seeming contradiction between the two works is a matter of difference in expression, not in content. Chu Hsi himself might have explained himself in some such a way.

Though such an explanation may be acceptable, this problem may be said to remain unsolved as long as there is a contradiction suggested in the different ways of expression with respect to principle and material force. The difficulty arises because Chu Hsi frequently used the terms "principle" and "nature" interchangeably. Principle, however, has only one usage while nature is sometimes used as the original nature and sometimes as the physical nature. Thus, the obscurity remains because of the difficulty caused by identifying either of two natures with one principle. Viewed in this respect, the difficulty in expression may be thought to be a methodological ambiguity implicit in Chu Hsi's theory of human nature.

The methodological weakness of Chu Hsi's philosophy comes from his wanting to hold to a two-way division of principle and material force. For him, principle and material force are always in contrast, and their characteristics, which are often explained respectively as being above phenomenal forms (*hsing-erh-shang*ᵃʳ) and being within phenomenal forms (*hsing-erh-hsia*ᵃˢ), are also opposed to each other. In addition, the fundamental idea of his theory of principle and material force holds that the phenomenal nature is formed by the inseparable relation of antithetical principle and material force. It may therefore be said that the ambiguity of his methodology resulted from his applying the antithetical and contrary idea regarding principle and material force to an explanation of a phenomenon or a fact.

Can it really be said that Chu Hsi's theory on the nature of man and things has a flaw only in expression and not in content?

VII

We have seen that both the *Ta-hsüeh huo-wen* and the *Meng Tzu chi-chu* mean by principle the original nature, and that each work mentions original nature in different contexts and senses. To use the same term in different senses is the cause of confusion. The contradiction in Chu Hsi's idea discussed above can be said to result from his ambiguous use of a term by employing two contradictory senses of the same term on different occasions.

Nevertheless, it is not likely that Chu Hsi mentioned the original nature without recognizing the two contradictory senses of the word. Rather, the fact seems to be that the twofold meaning of original nature was indispensable in his philosophical system. For, as suggested in his remark "each thing has its own Great Ultimate,"[31] he consolidated the system of "principle being one and its manifestations being many," on the one hand, and followed whole-heartedly Mencius' thought on the other. Thus, it may be that the contradiction implicit in Chu Hsi's view of original nature is unavoidable in his philosophy.

There is a logical contradiction in the assumption itself—that man retains his nature as a thing while at the same time maintaining his unique human nature. Likewise, the two contradictory aspects ascribed to original nature cause difficulties in Chu Hsi's philosophy. In that his "original nature" refers to something original and ultimate, it transcends the category of individuality or of human attribute. On the other hand, original nature without innate human individuality would lose its significance in his philosophy. Therefore, the contradiction implicit in Chu Hsi's philosophy as has been discussed may be ascribed, above all else, to his concept of original nature. We may say, then, that the opposite positions of Yi Gan and Han Won-jin about the nature of man and things are the manifestations of the contradiction implicit in the concept of original nature in Chu Hsi's philosophy.

It must be recalled that the discussion about original nature has axiological implications as well as philosophical significance. It has been already said that according to Mencius original nature refers to humanity, righteousness, propriety, and wisdom, characteristics that in this case indicate the basic goodness of human nature, that is, they are spoken of with respect to good and evil. Similarly, the Great Ultimate as original nature should be considered not only in terms of factual implication as "the sum total of principle of all creation"[32] but also in terms of the value judgment of good and evil as "the standard of supreme good of all creation."[33] Fundamentally, original nature is predicated only on the reality of principle. But considering that principle is inactive in material existence unless it is in conjunction with material force, the reality of original nature as principle is meaningless. The significance of original nature lies in its aspect of value, that is, as supreme good. That Chu Hsi understood the problem is clear. In the *Ta-hsüeh huo-wen* he examines whether the nature of man and the nature of things are the same from the point of view of nobility and meanness.

It is in this ethical context that we can understand the significance of Chu Hsi's idea on the nature of man and things: Chu Hsi's thinking on the difference or sameness of man's nature and things' nature was motivated by his desire to conserve and embody the highest good and noblest value innate in the human mind and to promote a virtuous and meaningful human life commensurate with the status of man as the lord of all creation.

VIII

The significance of Yi Gan's and Han Won-jin's idea on the sameness or difference of the nature of man and the nature of things can also be evaluated in these terms. Like Chu Hsi, they emphasized the value of original nature. Yi Gan, who maintained the sameness of the nature of man and the nature of things on the basis that original nature is the Great Ultimate and Mandate of Heaven, tried to persuade Han Won-jin that "not only the Five Constant Virtues, but also the Mandate of Heaven and the Great Ultimate are all noble and good."[34] On the other hand, Han Won-jin, who upheld the difference of them on the basis of the Five Constant Virtues, told Yi Gan that "the nature of man is nobler than the nature of things."[35]

Judging from the above quotation, we can say that Yi Gan tried to confirm the ignity of human nature by emphasizing the absolute goodness of original nature, while Han Won-jin attempted to establish the dignity of human nature by emphasizing the unique nobility of goodness inherent in original nature. Thus, they have in common the intention of establishing the dignity of human nature as original nature. They differ only in the way of expressing the intention. Therefore, it may be said that the significance of the ideas of these two scholars on the nature of man and things is not different from that of Chu Hsi. They also recognized the sameness or difference of man's nature and things' nature, and then tried to conserve and embody the highest good and noblest value of human nature in order to promote a noble life becoming man as the lord of all creation. Their ideas on the nature of man and things are developments out of Chu Hsi's philosophy, for each stood on one of the two antinomic positions implicit in Chu Hsi's thought.

This controversy on the nature of man and things brought about an important consequence in the intellectual discussion of Korean Neo-Confucianism. With the knowledge and experience accumulated through this controversy and also through the debate about 150 years earlier on the interpretation of the Four-Seven Thesis, Neo-Confucian scholars in Korea began to stop accepting Chu Hsi's thought indiscriminately and to inquire into Chu Hsi's philosophy more carefully and thoroughly. As a result, they came to discriminate in Chu Hsi's thought the points of certainty and uncertainty, inconsistencies due to typographical errors and misinterpretations, and so on. And they tried to sort out problematic points subject by subject. The *Chu-cha eon-ron dong-i go*[at] (The identity of the theory and remarks of Master Chu), which had begun with Song Si-yeol and was completed fifty years later by Han Won-jin, represents one such attempt. This work, motivated by debates centered on Neo-Confucian issues, can be said to be a monumental landmark in the development of Chu Hsi's thought in Korea.

Translated by Sohn Yoo-taek[au]

Notes

1. The Four-Seven debate centers on the issue whether the four moral qualities (humanity, righteousness, propriety, and wisdom) and the seven feelings (pleasure, anger, sorrow, joy, love, hate, and desire) originate from principle or material force. This thesis was introduced in my "A Study on Toegye's View on Human Nature," *A Study on Toegye's Philosophy* (Seoul: Korea University Press, 1980), and in Tu Wei-ming's[av] "Yi Hwang's[aw] Perception of the Mind," *Toegye Hakbo*[ax] [The journal of Toegye study], vol. 19, (Seoul; The Toegyehak Study Institute, 1978).

2. Yi Gan, *Woeahm yu-go*[ay] [Inherited manuscripts of Yi Gan], (Seoul: Cho Yong-sung,[az] 1977), 7:15b.

3. *Ibid.*, 7:16a.

4. *Ibid.*, 7:16ab.

5. *Ibid.*, 7:19ab.

6. *Ibid.*, 7:18b.

7. Han Won-jin, *Namdang jip*[ba] [Collected works of Namdang], (Seoul: Chae In-sik,[bb] 1976), 10:33b.

8. *Ibid.*, 7:2b.

9. *Ibid.*, 7:2b–3a.

10. *Ibid.*, 7:2b.

11. *Woeahm yu-go*, 7:17b.

12. *Ibid.*, 7:18b.

13. *Ibid.*, 7:22a.

14. *Namdang jip*, 11:10a.

15. *Ibid.*, 10:24b, 30b.

16. *Ibid.*, 10:22b.

17. *Ibid.*, 10:30a.

18. *Ibid.*, 10:32b–33a.

19. *Ibid.*, 10:22b.

20. *Ibid.*, 10:25b.

21. *Ibid.*, 11:44ab; and *Woeahm yu-go*, 12:25, 26–34.

22. *Woeahm yu-go*, 12:34b.

23. *Chung-yung chang-chü*, ch. 1.

24. *Namdang jip*, 10:25a.

25. *Ibid.*, 11:16b.

26. *Ibid.*, 10:32a. Chu Hsi's comment is on the *Book of Mencius*, 6A:3.

27. *Ibid.*, 11:1b. Chu Hsi's comment is on the text of the *Great Learning*.

28. *Meng Tzu chi-chu*, 11:88a. Kao Tzu (420–350 B.C.?) was an opponent of Mencius and held that man's nature is neither good nor evil and that righteousness comes from the outside. See the *Book of Mencius*, 6A:1–6.

29. *Ta-hsüeh huo-wen* (Seoul: Kyongmunsa,[bc] 1977), pp. 22–23.

30. *Woeahm yu-go*, 7:18a.

31. *Chu Tzu yü-lei* [Classified conversations of Master Chu], (Seoul: Cho Yong-sung, 1977), 94:365a.

32. *Ibid.*, 94:367b.

33. *Ibid.*

34. *Woeahm yu-go*, 7:19a.

35. *Namdang jip*, 11:24b.

Glossary

a	理氣	t	金昌協農巖	al	子思
b	退溪嶺南	u	權尚游灘溪	am	孟子集註
c	栗谷畿湖	v	本然	an	大學或問
d	湖西	w	一源	ao	告子
e	洛下	x	氣質	ap	中庸章句
f	權尚夏遂庵	y	異體	aq	理一分殊
g	李珥栗谷	z	天命	ar	形而上
h	宋時烈尤庵	aa	形器	as	形而下
i	江門	ab	偏	at	朱子言論同異考
j	韓元震南塘	ac	全	au	孫裕澤
k	李柬巖巖	ad	本然之性	av	杜維明
l	李縡陶庵	ae	命	aw	李滉
m	朴弼周黎湖	af	氣質之性	ax	退溪學報
n	魚有鳳杞園	ag	性	ay	巍巖遺稿
o	尹鳳丸屏溪	ah	太極	az	曹龍承
p	崔微厚梅峯	ai	程頤	ba	南塘集
q	蔡之洪鳳巖	aj	未發	bb	蔡仁植
r	丁時翰愚潭	ak	陰陽	bc	景文社
s	朴世堂西溪				

31

The Tradition of the Way in Japan

Yamazaki Michio

The Tradition of the Way

THE TRADITION of the Learning of the Way originated with Mencius (372–289 B.C.?), who said, "The source of the Learning of the Way is to be found in Yao[a] and Shun,[b][1] and Confucius [551–479 B.C.] inherited it. I live in the time close to that when he lived, and I was born in the neighborhood of his native place. Unless I go forth to transmit the sacred Way, how could it be handed down to posterity? It is myself that can do it, I believe."[2]

Yoshida Shōin[c] (1830–1859) was an ardent Japanese worshiper of Mencius. Though it was forbidden in his country in those days for anyone to go abroad, he intended to board an American battleship anchored in the Harbor of Shimoda,[d] Izu[e] Province, and go to America.[3] To his great regret, he was refused and was captured. He was sent to his native place at Hagi,[f] Chofu[g] Province,[4] and put in prison. Taking notice of the above saying of the *Book of Mencius,* he remarked in his *Kōmōyowa*[h] (The supplemental lectures on the *Book of Mencius*) which he wrote in Noyama[i] Prison, "It is a great surprise that Mencius himself wished to be an inheritor of Confucius. Let us listen to him. We should keep what he said in our minds as long as we live."[5] Yoshida was a man of inspiration and sincerity. He was, in my belief, impressed so deeply by Mencius' saying that he wished to complete the reconstruction that led to the Meiji[j] restoration in 1868.

Mencius concluded his book with the remark "in these circumstances, is there no one to transmit his doctrines? Yea, is there no one to do so?"[6] It means that, if anyone sees and knows the Way of Confucius and does not hand it down, no one will ever know of it. The former "wu-yu"[k] (no one) means to see the Way of Yao and Shun and know it, and the latter "wu-yu" (no one) means to hear the Way and know it, according to the interpretation of Chu Hsi who had followed Lin Chih-ch'i[l] (1131–1162).[7] Mencius, admiring Confucius most heartily, said very firmly, "Who could hand down the Way of the great Sage in later years except myself?"

Han Yü[m] (768–824) in his "Yüan-tao"[n] (On the Way) said, "What I call the

Way is not the Way of the Buddha or Lao Tzu.[o] It is the Way Yao and Shun originated and handed down successively to T'ang,[p8] Wen,[q9] Wu,[r10] the Duke of Chou,[s11] Confucius, and Mencius. It was forgotten after him."[12]

Master Ch'eng,[t13] having taken notice of the saying of Han Yü that Mencius was the purest of the pure and that Hsün Tzu[u] (313–238 B.C.?) and Yang Hsiung[v] (53 B.C.–A.D. 18) did not select the Way in its purity and moreover did not apprehend it thoroughly, praised Han Yü highly for knowing the Way in the true sense a thousand years after the death of Mencius.[14]

Why did the question of the tradition of the Way arise? Mencius regarded Yang Chu's[w] (440–360 B.C.?) doctrine of "for oneself," Mo Ti's[x] (468–376 B.C.?) doctrine of "universal love," and Tzu-mo's[y15] doctrine of "holding the Mean between the two" as obstacles and rejected them. To him, they are heterodoxy.[16] Why is the principle of holding the Mean between the two a heterodoxy? What is the difference between his principle and that of the Mean taught by Yao to Shun? Mencius attacked Tzu-mo for not weighing the circumstances in adhering to the Mean. Weighing means balancing, showing adaptability, shifting to the right or the left according to the weight of a thing. If one does not consider the circumstances in adhering to the Mean, one sticks only to one side and does not see the other side, and in the end he destroys the Way. He takes only the intermediate principle of Yang Chu and Mo Ti in his understanding of the Mean. Chu Hsi affirmed this criticism in his commentary on the passage, saying, "The Mean of the Way of Tzu-mo lacks weighing. Tzu-mo does not weigh even when he takes it. He adheres only to one side of a thing without the consideration of the circumstances." Chu Hsi also said, " 'Being for oneself' inflicts injury upon humanity (*jen*[z] 'benevolence'), 'universal love' does harm to righteousness (*i*[aa]), and holding to the Mean of Tzu-mo hurts the Mean according to the time (*shih-chung*[ab]). *Shih-chung* in the *Doctrine of Mean* denotes the adaptation to moderation, considering the circumstances around."[17]

In the age of Han Yü, the principle of the Buddha and Lao Tzu spread abroad and spoiled the world. Han Yü rose up against them, saying that their principles dispelled humanity and righteousness from the world.[18]

In the Sung dynasty (960–1279), the principle of the Learning of the Way was shown first in the epitaph for the tomb of Ch'eng Hao (Ch'eng Ming-tao,[ac] 1032–1085) written by his younger brother Ch'eng I (Ch'eng I-ch'uan,[ad] 1033–1107),[19] which Chu Hsi quoted in his *Meng Tzu chi-chu*[ae] (Collected commentaries on the *Book of Mencius*).[19] I-ch'uan remarked in it, "My elder brother was the most suitable for succeeding Mencius." In the preface of his *Chung-yung chang-chü*[af] (Commentary on the *Doctrine of the Mean*) Chu Hsi explained why Tzu-ssu[ag20] had written the *Chung-yung.*[ah] He also supplemented it and explained it in detail. He added that in the Sung dynasty the two Ch'eng brothers had succeeded Tzu-ssu.

Now, what is the essence of the spiritual contents of the tradition of the Way? According to Chu Hsi's preface to the *Chung-yung chang-chü,* when

Emperor Yao handed over his empire to Shun, he told him to take the Mean of the Way, and Shun told Yü[ai][22] that it was very easy for one to be misled by one's own avarice and one should endeavor to take the Mean of the Way with great care, adding that it was the very best way to live by in the world.[23]

Huang Kan (Huang Mien-chai,[aj] 1152–1221), the best disciple of Chu Hsi, wrote the *Sheng-hsien tao-t'ung tsung-hsü shuo*[ak] (General treatise on the transmission of the Way of sages and worthies) in which he enlarged the instructions of his teacher, explained the tradition of the Way in detail, and told of the thoughts of ancient sages in thirteen articles with a summary at the end. He said, "It is the principle of Chu Hsi that leads one to knowledge by studies, abolishes one's avarice by dint of self-control, and makes him sincere by abiding in sincerity."[24]

Yamazaki Ansai[al] (1618–1682), foremost in the tradition of the Way in Japan, respected the *Chin-ssu lu*[am] (Reflection on things at hand) and excluded all the explanations written by Yeh Ts'ai[an] (*fl.* 1248), regarding them as unsuitable. He, moreover, published a book written by Wang Ch'i-chih[ao] in the original with his preface. It was by way of this great work in the tradition of the Way in Japan that he exalted the spirit of the *Chin-ssu lu*. He said in his preface in 1670 that the way of learning is for one to achieve full knowledge and to endeavor to practice it, and the only way to accomplish these is to keep one's original mind and cultivate one's nature. The third chapter of the *Chin-ssu lu* is on extension of knowledge, the fourth chapter, on preserving the mind and nourishing nature, and the fifth on conquering oneself; Yamazaki Ansai explained in his preface that abiding in seriousness and plumbing principle depend on self-control.

Inaba Mokusai[ap] (1732–1799) was a student of Sato Naokata[aq] (1650–1719) in Yamazaki Ansai's school. It is said that Mokusai was a great scholar and thoroughly absorbed Yamazaki's studies and learning. His disciple wrote down his lectures and entitled it *Hakurokudo keiji hikki*[ar] (Notes on the announcement at the White Deer Grotto Academy) in 1797. In his lecture he said, "My teacher, Yamazaki Ansai, published the *Chin-ssu lu* in Chu Hsi's original and his own annotations on the 'Pai-lu-tung hsüeh-kuei'[as] (Academic regulations at the White Deer Grotto Academy) with high praise for its author, Chu Hsi." This shows us that Ansai was the originator of the Learning of the Way in Japan. This remark of Mokusai's on Ansai has been highly regarded.

The Principle of Learning

The Learning of the Way means the learning by which one knows the Sage's way of living. It has two meanings: the learning of Confucianism in the broad sense and that of the nature and principle of the Ch'eng brothers and Chu Hsi in the narrow sense. Let us examine more deeply what the true sense of the Learning of the Way is and who has truly transmitted it.

In the preface of Chu Hsi's *Chung-yung chang-chü*, it is said that the commentary was written because Tzu-ssu was worried about the loss of the Learning of the Way. This was the first time that the term "the Learning of the Way" (*Tao-t'ung*[at]) appeared. It had never been used in the time of Yao, Shun, Confucius, or Mencius. It shows that the age of Chu Hsi had become conscious of the existence of heterodoxy.

Satō Naokata wrote the *Dōgaku hyoteki*[au] (The goal of the Learning of the Way), which includes the lectures of Inaba Mokusai. In these Mokusai said, "My father Inaba Usai[av] [1684–1760] said, 'The reason why the term "the Learning of the Way" has come is that the world has declined and heterodox learning has appeared in the world. It has become difficult to recognize whether learning is genuine or not, and the genuine learning came to be known as the Learning of the Way just as gold is called genuine or imitation. Just "learning" would be sufficient, but Chu Hsi called it *tao-hsüeh*[aw] to mean the Learning of the Way.' "[25] Now, Mokusai said in his lectures on the "Pai-lu-tung hsüeh-kuei" as follows: "One should learn as widely as possible, but unless one returns to the two works, the 'Pai-lu-tung hsüeh-kuei' and the *Chin-ssu lu*, his learning is of no use."

Ansai said in the above-mentioned preface, "It is to be admired extremely that the 'Hsüeh-kuei' explains the Way. It is to be read and appreciated together with the *Hsiao-hsüeh*[ax] (Elementary learning) and the *Ta-hsüeh*[ay] (The Great Learning). Few read it because it is collected among Chu Hsi's writings. I hang a copy of it in my study to appreciate it as much as possible. Afterwards I read the *Tzu-sheng lu*[az] (Records of self-examination) written by Li T'ui-hsi [Yi Hwang, Yi Toegye[ba] 1501–1570] to find with great admiration that it dealt with the Way in full details."

Ansai was a man of keen insight enough to find out that Li T'ui-hsi was the greatest scholar on Chu Hsi in Chosen (Korea). Satō Naokata, one of Ansai's greatest students along with Asami Keisai[bb] (1652–1711) and Miyake Shōsai[bc] (1662–1741), wrote the "Tojibun"[bd] (Essay at the time of the winter solstice) for his own students. In it he said that Li T'ui-hsi had been the greatest scholar of the Learning of the Way since Chu Hsi. He had the insight to find this out just as his teacher Ansai had done. Why did Naokata not mention his teacher Ansai as the greatest scholar on the Learning of the Way in his treatise? It was because Ansai advised people to Shintō together with Confucianism in his later years, according to Naokata, while his comrades remained very faithful to the Learning of the Way. Naokata and his circle were against Ansai, because they hated the confusion of the two systems and admired the purity of the Learning of the Way. Li T'ui-hsi's *Chu Tzu shu chieh-yao*[be] (Essentials of Master Chu's letters) and *Tzu-sheng lu* had a great influence on the study of Chu Hsi in Japan. It is to be noted that Satō Naokata and his school regarded the *Chu Tzu shu chieh-yao* and "Instructions to pupils" (chapters 114–121) of the *Chu Tzu yü-lei*[bf] (Classified conversations of Master Chu) as absolutely indispensable for students of the Learning of the Way.

Inaba Mokusai, when he knew that his teacher Yamazaki Ansai had been extremely excited by Li T'ui-hsi's *Tzu-sheng lu*, said, "My teacher Ansai was regarded as a man of obstinate character, but he was so modest as to admire Li T'ui-hsi. Ansai studied so hard on how to cultivate himself that he could appreciate the spirit of the *Tzu-sheng lu* very deeply. It was from his humble personality that he said he owed his notes on 'Pai-lu-tung hsüeh-kuei' to T'ui-hsi. It is very interesting that, at the age of thirty-three [in 1650], he said, at the end of the preface, 'How could I be inferior to him in spite of the difference of our nationalities?' "

Inaba Mokusai's school produced Mikami Zean[bg] (1816–1876), one of the best disciples of Okudaira Seichian[bh] (1769–1822). He wrote the *Fumoto no shirube*[bi] (Guidepost at the foot of a hill) as a guidebook to the Learning of the Way, with a supplemental pedigree entitled "Lineage of the Learning of the Way" separately in Han-t'u[bj] (China) and in Japan. The former part reads: "It came from a high sense of Sato's school, and it is noteworthy that he mentioned Li T'ui-hsi as the last thinker of the Learning of the Way in Han-t'u."[26]

Inaba Mokusai dared remark in his *Dōgaku hyōteki hikki*[bk] (Notes on the *Goal of the Learning of the Way*), "It is the best for our School to regard our teacher Yamazaki as the standard, I think, but I dislike his confusion of Confucianism with Shintō. It was in order not to hurt the Learning of the Way that Satō Naokata wrote the *Dōgaku hyōteki*. The mixture of other thoughts in the Learning of the Way will become an obstacle to it. It is not good for the Learning of the Way. When he listened to his teacher Yamazaki Ansai explaining Shintō, Master Naokata wished that Shintō would disappear like a temporary dream." Then he added, "Some disapprove of me because of my ignorance of Sintō, but it is not true. When anyone speaks of the Learning of the Way, he should mention nobody except Confucius, Tseng Tzu,[bl][27] Tzu-ssu, Mencius, Chou Tun-i[bm] (1017–1073), the brothers Ch'eng Hao and Ch'eng I, Chang Tsai[bn] (1020–1077), and Chu Hsi. I know that I owe what I am to Master Yamazaki enough to be able to preach the Learning of the Way, but when I speak of the goal of the Learning of the Way, I am obliged to mention his faults."[28] I can see from this point of view that certainly it was the keynote of Satō's school to investigate the Learning of the Way thoroughly.

Mikami Zean said in his *Fumoto no shirube*, "According to Chen Te-hsiu[bo] (1178–1235), the origin of the Learning of the Way is to be found in the four words that Yao told Shun and the sixteen words that Shun taught Yü. Out of them came not only the *Ta-hsüeh*, the *Doctrine of the Mean*, the *Analects*, and the *Book of Mencius*, but also all the technical terms in the *Book of Odes* and the *Book of History*. It is a stream of learning."[29] He preached the investigation of principle, self-control, the strict keeping of the Way, and the method of learning which his wise predecessors had shown him.

To return to Satō Naokata, he said in the preface of his *Dōgaku hyōteki*, "The phrase *tao-hsüeh* arose in the Sung dynasty. It was known before Confucius and Mencius that learning meant merely learning the Way, but various names for it came out after Mencius. Inaba Mokusai thought that a goal was needed for the Learning of the Way, and made selections from Confucius, Tseng Tzu, Tzu-ssu, Mencius, Masters Chou, Ch'eng, Chang, and Chu to constitute the *Dōgaku hyōteki.*" Inaba Mokusai wrote in his *Dōgaku hyōteki hikki,* "The book [*Dōgaku-hyōteki*] contains the sayings of the *Doctrine of the Mean* to the effect that the full alertness of the mind to the Learning of the Way is the mastering of the Way by banishing trifling avarices and worldly thoughts so the mind can be purified, and that it is not until one enters into the core of the minds of the sages that one can inherit the Learning of the Way."[30] Another work by Inaba Mokusai, the *Dōgaku nijisetsu*[bp] (A treatise on the term "tao-hsüeh"), is not found in any of his collected works. A copy of it by my teacher, Uchida Shūhei[bq] (1857–1944), is a treasure preserved in the Mukyūkai[br] Library in Tokyo. In it Inaba Mokusai said, "The two words, *tao-hsüeh,* are *tao* (the Way) of *tao-t'i*[bs] (the substance of the Way) combined with *hsüeh* (learning) of *wei-hsüeh*[bt] (to pursue learning) in the *Chin-ssu lu* and mean the Learning of the Way, according to the preface of the *Doctrine of the Mean.*"[31]

Now, Miyake Shōsai, student of Ansai, remarked in his *Kinshiroku hikki*[bu] (Notes on the *Chin-ssu lu*), "The *tao-t'i* in the title of the first chapter means the substance and existence of the Way, which is the object of learning. One would be lost in the Way without the knowledge of it. The title *Wei-hsüeh* in the second chapter means the method of the Learning of the Way. The remaining twelve chapters do not go beyond these two ideas."[32]

Wakabayashi Kyōsai[bv] (1679–1732) was a distinguished disciple of Asami Keisai, and Ono Kakuzan[bw] (1701–1770) was a leading disciple of Kyōsai. The *Kinshiroku kōgi*[bx] (Lectures on the *Chin-ssu lu*) written by Kakuzan is an excellent book. He said, "The Way is the substance of things in their natural state and qualities. Fire dries, water damps, some flowers are red, parents are dear, and children are lovely. They are in the state of nature itself. It is the substance of the Way. It is best for one to act solely according to the substance of the Way. Speaking of *tao-t'i,* it is the foundation of the Way. Where there is *tao-t'i,* there is the Way, and human morality exists."[33] Shōsai and Kakuzan were of the same opinion as Mokusai.

Now, Mokusai said in his *Dōgaku hyōteki hikki,* "The *Chin-ssu lu* by Chu Hsi is the best and ultimate book. One needs no other book than it." He also said in his *Treatise on the Term Tao-hsüeh,*

> It was Yao and Shun who originated the *tao-hsüeh.* When they taught to follow the Mean, it meant the Mean of the Way, and it was to learn it thoroughly and exclusively. When the Learning of the Way has been realized in action, it is to be intimate with the nine tribes as Yao was,[34] and it is the way of Shun to practice the Five Teachings.[35] Therefore, the Way of Yao and Shun is morality itself, while Mencius said, 'The Way of Yao and Shun if filial piety and brotherly respect, that is all.'[36] The principle of Yao and Shun was handed down through

the Three Dynasties of Hsia [2183–1752 B.C.?], Shang [1751–1112 B.C.?], and Chou [1111–249 B.C.] and it was natural that the learning should be the clarification of morality. The Way of the sages is based upon the Five Relations[37] and the Five Constant Virtues[38] which originated from Heaven. They are called the Way, and the learning of it is called Learning. Therefore, in the Learning of the Way, man is united with Heaven.[39]

It was Mokusai who explained uniquely the Learning of the Way by explaining the two words, *tao* and *hsüeh*, for the first time.

He also said,

There are to be seen, in the "Canon of Kao-yao"[by] of the *Book of History*, the Five Standards, which are righteousness, affection, friendliness, respect, and filial piety.[40] This is the learning that keeps people correct and earnest. Heaven, destiny, and nature in the *Doctrine of the Mean* are the substance of the Way, and it is the mastering of learning that makes one cautious and apprehensive enough to catch hold of them. The sentence in chapter 30 of the *Doctrine of the Mean*, "Sincerity is the way of the Heaven," is a statement on the substance of the Way, and it is essential for learning to make sincerity one's own.

Turning to Chu Hsi, affection (between father and son), righteousness (between ruler and minister), separate functions (between husband and wife), order (between brothers) and faithfulness (between friends) in the "Academic Regulations at the White Deer Grotto Academy" are a statement on the substance of the Way; and learning extensively, inquiring accurately, thinking carefully, sifting clearly, and practicing earnestly are the essentials for learning. These are all methods of learning. It is very natural for *tao* and *hsüeh* to go together with each other. Sometimes they go together with each other in heterodoxy although they are wrong. For instance, Lao Tzu taught that the Way is nonbeing. His learning was to nothing. To the Buddha, the Way means death. Their learning was far from the Way. A heretic talks about *tao* and *hsüeh*, but they are different from the Way. What is based upon the Heaven and human morality is called the Learning of the Way, while the other, heterodoxy.

Mokusai continued, "The meaning of the Learning of the Way is explained fully in the 'Pai-lu-tung hsüeh-kuei' by Chu Hsi and the *Dōgaku hyōteki* by Satō Naokata. When one acts in accordance with the two works, one can recognize the meaning and secret of the Learning of the Way."[41] Ansai, originator of his School, wrote, at the age of thirty-three, the *Collected Commentaries on the "Pai-lu-tung hsüeh-kuei,"* admiring and recommending it. Mokusai, following him, brought to a climax the learning of his School.

He also said in his *Dōgaku hyōteki hikki*, "Why did Satō Naokata write the *Dōgaku hyōteki?* The *Chin-ssu lu* by Chu Hsi is the supreme and ultimate book on the Learning of the the Way. Naokata wrote the *Kōgaku bensaku roku*[bz] (Records of encouragement of learning) at the age of thirty-six, selecting Chu Hsi's sayings in order to encourage and promote them; moreover, he wrote, at the age of sixty-three, the *Dōgaku hyōteki* in order to make clearer the end and aim of the Learning of the Way. Naokata advised us to read the *Hyōteki* first, and then the *Bensaku roku*."[42]

How was the principle of the *Dōgaku hyōteki* transmitted to Inaba Usai and his son Mokusai? It is explained in the *Himejima kōgi*[ca] (Lecturer at Himejima).[43] Usai wrote the essence of the *Dōgaku hyōteki*, and sent his son Mokusai to his eight disciples living in Kazusa[cb] Province. The son then presented his father's writings and gave lectures at Himejima on the *Dōgaku hyōteki*, which came to be called *Himejima kōgi*. He moved there at the age of fifty from Edo[cc] (now Tokyo) to devote himself to study and cultivation until he died there at the age of sixty-eight. His writings, which he gave to his disciples, are very valuable for understanding the tradition of the Way from Satō Naokata to Inaba Usai and Mokusai. Mokusai and all his School regarded the *Analects*, 4:8[44] as their doctrine. Mikami Zean, disciple of Mokusai, said in his *Kōshin Zatsuroku*[cd] (Miscellaneous jottings) written in 1860 when he was forty-three, "Naokata adopted the *Analects*, 4:8, as the basis of his learning. My teacher Okudaira Seichian said that the sages of Satō's School would be the same as those of other schools if they did not take much notice of this saying." Zean also said in chapter 14 of his *Ogawa no Masago*[ce] (Real sand in a small river) that one feels joyful when one hears and knows the Way just as a blind man does when his eyes are open and can see things. Satō's School has transmitted lines selected from a famous poem by Chu Hsi: "I salute the mind of a thousand years./The autumn moon shines on the cold water."[45] The passage may be interpreted thus: When I think respectfully of the sages who have been keeping the principle of the tradition of the Learning of the Way for thousands of years since Yao and Shun, it shines and reflects upon my mind, just as the clear moon is shining and reflecting upon the pure water. The autumn moon points to the principle of Yao and Shun and the cold water to the author's pure, unspoiled mind.

Returning to Mokusai once again, he said in his *Dōgaku hyōteki hikki*, "One feels confused until he has heard the Way. When he has heard it, he gets ready for death. The sentence, 'In the morning hear the Way; in the evening, die content!' does not mean one is willing to die actually, but means the importance of the Way."[46] Mokusai also said in his *Dōgaku hyōteki hikki* that the tradition of the Way is not only heard and written, but also to be kept in mind, and that when one has acquired the principle of Chu Hsi, one has gained that of Yao and Shun. He wrote his last book, the *Rokuhachiroku*[cf] (Recorded at the age of sixty-eight) in 1799 and died in the same year. In the book he said that the mind of a sage contains nothing except the mind of the Way, just as the autumn moon reflects on the cold water.

Similarly, Mikami Zean said in chapter 14 of his *Ogawa no masago*, "Mokusai adopts the autumn moon and the cold water which are the purest in the world. The principle of the Way always reflects on the mind, just as the moon shines on the water. It is the tradition of the Way that the principle reflects on the mind." There are two kinds of sages in the tradition of the

Learning of the Way, he said, the perfect and the near-perfect. Perfect sages were Yao, Shun, Yü, T'ang, Wen, Wu, the Duke of Chou, Confucius, certain Confucian pupils, Mencius and the early Sung Neo-Confucianists, and Chu Hsi, while the near-perfect sages were certain other Confucian pupils, followers of early Sung Neo-Confucianists, and followers of Chu Hsi.

Kusumoto Sekisui[cg] (1832–1916) under the influence of Miyake Shōsai gave lectures to Kaizan[ch] (1873–1921), son of his elder brother Kusumoto Tanzan[ci] (1828–1883), which were collected and produced under the title the *Seigaku yōryō*[cj] (Essentials of the Learning of the Sage). It begins with the "Cannon of Yü" in which Shun's doctrines were transmitted to Yü, and ends with the sentence in the preface of the *Chin-ssu lu* written by Yamazaki Ansai. To preserve the mind and nourish nature, penetrate through extension of knowledge and earnest practice, it may be said that he speaks to the point, mentioning the beginning of the tradition of the Learning of the Way and the end of it.

Translated by Etō Hatsumi[ck]

Notes

1. Legendary sage-emperors of the third millennium B.C.
2. *Book of Mencius*, 7B:38.
3. Now Shimoda City, Shizuoka[cl] Prefecture.
4. Now Hagi City, Yamaguchi[cm] Prefecture.
5. *Yoshida Shōin zenshū*[cn] [Complete works of Yoshida Shōin] (Tokyo: Iwanami[co] Book Co., 1939), ch. 3, p. 511.
6. *Book of Mencius*, 7B:35; translation by James Legge.
7. A high official in the government of Southern Sung (1127–1279).
8. Founder of the Shang dynasty.
9. Founder of the Chou dynasty.
10. Son of King Wen and first ruler of Chou.
11. Younger brother of King Wu.
12. Han Yü, *Han Ch'ang-li ch'üan-chi*[cp] [Complete works of Han Yü], (SPPY ed.), 11:5a.
13. The book does not specify if this is Ch'eng Hao's or Ch'eng I's saying.
14. *I-shu*[cq] [Surviving works], 1:3b–4a, in the *Erh-Ch'eng ch'üan-shu*[cr] [Complete works of the two Ch'engs], (SPPY ed.).
15. A sage in the state of Lu.
16. *Book of Mencius*, 7A:26.
17. *Meng Tzu chi-chu*[cs] [Collected commentaries on the *Book of Mencius*].
18. Han Yü, *op. cit.*
19. *I-ch'uan wen-chi*[ct] [Collection of literary works of Ch'eng I], 7:7b, in the *Erh-Ch'eng ch'üan-shu*.
20. Comment on the *Book of Mencius*, 7B:38.
21. Grandson of Confucius to whom the *Doctrine of the Mean* has been traditionally attributed.

22. Founder of the Hsia dynasty, a sage-king in the Confucian tradition.

23. *Book of History,* ch. 3, "Counsel of the Great Yü."

24. *Mien-chai chi*[cu] [Collected works of Huang Kan], (Precious works of the Four Libraries ed.), 36:39b.

25. Manuscript preserved at the Mukyūkai, preface, p. 1b.

26. *Fumoto no shirube* (Tokyo: Dōgaku kyōkai,[cv] 1921), p. 3b.

27. Tseng Tzu's private name was Ts'an.[cw] One of the most outstanding pupils of Confucius, he is in the main line of transmission of the Way.

28. A 1790 manuscript preserved at the Mukyūkai, pp. 6b–7a.

29. *Fumoto no shirube,* p. 5a.

30. Preface to the *Dōgaku hyōteki.*

31. A manuscript preserved at the Mukyūkai.

32. Explanation of the title of the first chapter in his commentary on the *Chin-ssu lu.*

33. Explanation of the title of the first chapter in his *Kinshiroku kōgi.*

34. See the *Book of History,* ch. 1, "Canon of Yao," sec. 2.

35. *Ibid.,* ch. 2, "Canon of Shun," sec. 19. Shun told his minister Hsüeh[cx] to spread the Five Teachings, namely, affection between father and son, righteousness between ruler and minister, separate functions between husband and wife, order between brothers, and faithfulness between friends.

36. *Book of Mencius,* 6B:2.

37. The five relations mentioned in n. 35.

38. Humanity, righteousness, propriety, wisdom, and faithfulness, or the five moral qualities mentioned in n. 35.

39. *Dōgaku nijisatsu.*

40. Ch. 2 in the *Book of History.*

41. *Dōgaku nijisatsu.*

42. Preface to the *Dōgaku hyōteki.*

43. Himejima is in Kazusa, Chiba[cy] Prefecture (formerly Kazusa Province).

44. Here Confucius said, "In the morning, hear the Way; in the evening, die content!"

45. From "Feeling Aroused While Resting in the Study," *Chu Tzu wen-chi*[cz] [Collection of literary works of Master Chu], ch. 4, the tenth of 20 verses.

46. *Dōgaku hyōteki hikki,* p. 12a.

Glossary

a	堯	k	無有	u	荀子	
b	舜	l	林之奇	v	揚雄	
c	吉田松陰	m	韓愈	w	楊朱	
d	下田	n	原道	x	墨翟	
e	伊豆	o	老子	y	子莫	
f	萩	p	湯	z	仁	
g	長府	q	文	aa	義	
h	講孟餘話	r	武	ab	時中	
i	野山	s	周	ac	程顥明道	
j	明治	t	程	ad	程頤伊川	

ae	孟子集註	bd	冬至文	cc	江戸
af	中庸章句	be	朱子書節要	cd	庚辛雜錄
ag	子思	bf	朱子語類	ce	小川乃眞砂
ah	中庸	bg	三上是庵	cf	六八錄
ai	禹	bh	奥平棲遲庵	cg	楠本碩水
aj	黄榦勉齋	bi	麓乃志留邊	ch	海山
ak	聖賢道統總叙説	bj	漢土	ci	楠本端山
al	山崎闇齋	bk	道學標的筆記	cj	聖學要領
am	近思錄	bl	曾子	ck	江東初三
an	葉采	bm	周敦頤	cl	靜岡
ao	汪器之	bn	張載	cm	山口
ap	稻葉黙齋	bo	眞德秀	cn	吉田松陰全集
aq	佐藤直方	bp	道學二字説	co	岩波
ar	白鹿洞揭示筆記	bq	内田遠湖	cp	韓昌黎全集
as	白鹿洞學規	br	無窮會	cq	遺書
at	道統	bs	道體	cr	二程全書
au	道學標的	bt	爲學	cs	孟子集註
av	稻葉迁齋	bu	近思錄筆記	ct	伊川文集
aw	道學	bv	若林強齋	cu	勉齋集
ax	小學	bw	小野鶴山	cv	道學協會
ay	大學	bx	近思錄講義	cw	參
az	自省錄	by	皐陶	cx	契
ba	李退溪滉	bz	講學鞭策錄	cy	千葉
bb	淺見絅齋	ca	姫島講義	cz	朱子文集
bc	三宅尚齋	cb	上總		

Appendix A
Biography of Chu Hsi

Wing-tsit Chan

Chu Hsi's family came originally from Wu-yüan,[a] which was part of Hui-chou[b] Prefecture, earlier called Hsin-an.[c] His father, Chu Sung[d] (1097–1143), moved to Fukien to serve as a district sheriff, and Chu Hsi was born in 1130 when the family was living temporarily in Yu-ch'i (or Yu-hsi[e]), Fukien. He began his schooling at five, and even at that age he was inquisitive enough to ask what lay beyond the sky. At eight, when he was given the *Classic of Filial Piety*, he declared that one is not a man unless one fulfills its ideals.

In 1140 his father, then assistant director in the ministry of personnel (*li-pu yüan-wai-lang*[f]), resigned because he opposed making peace with the Chin invaders and went to live in Chien-yang[g] County, Fukien. Chu Hsi was tutored at home. Three years later his father on his death-bed expressed the wish that he should study with Liu Tzu-hui[h] (1101–1147), Liu Mien-chih[i] (1091–1149) and Hu Hsien[j] (1086–1162). Liu Mien-chih liked him so much that he gave him his daughter in marriage. He obtained the *chin-shih*[k] degree in 1148, at nineteen.

In 1151 he was appointed district keeper of records (magistrate) (*chu-pu*[l]) of T'ung-an[m] County in Fukien and served there from 1153 to 1156. He increased school enrollment to capacity, built a library, regu-lated sacrificial rites, enforced marriage ceremonies, strengthened city defense, and built a memorial temple for a local worthy. Before he went to T'ung-an, he went to see Li T'ung[n] (1093–1163) and on his way back in 1158 he walked several hundred *li*[o] (a *li* is one-third of a mile) to see him again. In 1160 he attended him as a pupil, and in 1162 he visited him again. Through his influence Chu Hsi discarded his interest in Meditation Buddhism (*Ch'an*[p]) and concentrated on Confucianism. The Confucian doctrine as developed by Ch'eng Hao[q] (1032–1085) and Ch'eng I[r] (1033–1107) was transmitted to Li T'ung by Lo Ts'ung-yen[s]

Reproduced, with modifications, from Herbert Franke, ed., *Sung Biographies* (Wiesbaden: Franz Steiner Verlag, 1976), pp. 282–290.

(1072–1135), who had received it from the Ch'eng brothers' pupil Yang Shih[t] (1053–1135). So the Confucian tradition was firmly established in Chu Hsi's early life.

In 1159 Chu Hsi was called to the temporary capital, Lin-an[u] (modern Hangchou), but because someone had tried to block him, he declined. When Emperor Hsiao-tsung[v] ascended the throne in 1162, Chu presented a sealed memorial in which he urged the emperor to practice the Confucian teachings of sincerity of the will and rectification of the mind as taught in the *Great Learning*, not to make peace with the Chin, and to put worthy men in office. In response to an imperial summons, he reached Lin-an late in 1163. At that time the prime minister, T'ang Ssu-t'ui[w] (d. 1164), was intent on making peace with the Chin, but in his three audiences with the emperor Chu Hsi exhorted the emperor to investigate things and to extend his knowledge (also taught in the *Great Learning*), to repulse the Chin, and to listen to the people. At year's end he was made professor of the military academy (*wu-hsüeh po-shih*[x]). He went to take office in 1165, but finding that prime minister Hung Hua[y] (1117–1184) was about to appease the Chin, he returned to Wu-fu[z] Village in Ch'ung-an[aa] County, Fukien, which had been his home since 1143. For the next fourteen years, he repeatedly declined office.

He was extremely productive in this period, writing many books, attracting pupils, and carrying on voluminous correspondence in scholarly discussions. In 1166 he corresponded with Chang Shih[ab] (1133–1180) and others in Hunan on the subject of equilibrium and harmony, believing that these can be attained only after the mind has become active. In further letters exchanged with them in 1169, he came to realize that the attainment can come both before and after, a point which may be regarded as the full maturity of his ideas. He compiled the *Ho-nan Ch'eng-shih i-shu*[ac] (Surviving works of the two Ch'engs of Honan) in 1168, a fact that suggests that by this time he had taken the Confucianism, or rather Neo-Confucianism, developed by the Ch'eng brothers as the orthodox line. In 1172 he wrote the *Hsi-ming chieh-i*[ad] (Explanation of the meaning of the *Western Inscription* [by Chang Tsai,[ae] 1020–1077]) and a year later, the *T'ai-chi-t'u shuo*[af] (Commentary on the Explanation of the *Diagram* [of Chou Tun-i,[ag] 1017–1073]), using them respectively as the ethical and the cosmological patterns for Neo-Confucianism. He regarded these works, however, as of such subtle significance that he did not show them to students until 1188. In 1175 Lü Tsu-ch'ien[ah] (1137–1181) came to visit him, and together they selected from the works of Chou Tun-i, the Ch'eng brothers, and Chang Tsai to form the *Chin-ssu lu*[ai] (Reflections on things at hand). The first anthology of its kind, it formed the broad basis of Neo-Confucian thought, served as the prototype of later anthologies for several hundred years, and was the model for the *Hsing-li ta-ch'üan*[aj] (Great collection of

Neo-Confucianism) of 1415 which came to dominate Chinese thought for centuries. During this visit Lü Tsu-ch'ien arranged a meeting of Chu Hsi and Lu Chiu-yüan (Lu Hsiang-shan,[ak] 1139–1193) at the Goose Lake Temple in Kiangsi to compose their conflicting views. Each, however, continued in his own opinion, Lu Hsiang-shan for "honoring the moral nature" and Chu Hsi for "following the path of inquiry and study." In 1177 Chu Hsi annotated the *Analects* and the *Book of Mencius*, supporting his own interpretations with those of other Neo- Confucianists. He had been working in these Classics for years and he wanted these drafts to represent the highest level of his reconstruction of Neo-Confucianism. But his life was by no means confined to theories. In his village, for example, he established a community granary which provided the surrounding area of some fifty *li* with sufficient food and became the model in many areas for centuries.

In 1179 he became prefect of Nan-k'ang[al] Prefecture (present Hsing-tzu[am] County, Kiangsi). He had refused the appointment twice and accepted only at the strong prodding of Lü Tsu-ch'ien and Chang Shih. While in Nan-k'ang he promoted education, personally lecturing to students every four or five days. He built a temple for Chou Tun-i and reestablished the White Deer Hollow Academy, an important institution which was to play a great role in Neo-Confucianism and which served as the leading academy for hundreds of years. He built dikes and greatly improved measures to prevent famine. In 1180 he infuriated the emperor by sending in a sealed memorial in which he insisted that economic distress, military weakness, and political corruption can be removed only if the ruler rectifies his mind. He invited Lu Hsiang-shan to the White Deer Hollow Academy to lecture, and Lu's lecture on the distinction between righteousness and profit moved his audience to tears. Chu Hsi had the lecture written down for his students, and it was later inscribed on stone.

When his term expired in 1181, he was appointed superintendent-designate in charge of affairs of ever-normal granaries, tea, and salt (*ch'ang-p'ing ch'a-yen kung-shih*[an]) in Chiang-nan[ao] West (eleven prefectures in Anhui and Chekiang). While waiting to take office, he returned home, and when later in the year there was a great famine in Chekiang East (six prefectures in Chekiang), the prime minister, Wang Huai[ap] (1127–1190), recommended that he be given the same position in that area. During the twelve months he held this post, he toured the stricken area extensively and established community granaries; impeached two prefects (including a relative of Wang Huai), two magistrates, and several big families for contributing to the famine; and destroyed Ch'in Kuei's[aq] (1090–1155) temple. He had an audience with the emperor and took him to task for allowing wicked officials to rule. At that time the minister of civil personnel (*hu-pu shang-shu*[ar]), Cheng Ping[as] (*fl.* 1131–1198), memorialized to attack the doctrines of the two Ch'engs. The censor Ch'en Chia[at] attacked the *Tao-hsüeh*,[au] as Neo-Confucianism was then called, as hypocrisy. Both of them were aiming at Chu Hsi, but their attacks did not deter him from promoting Neo-Confucianism. In 1184–1185 he criticized in correspondence the idealistic doctrine of Lu Hsiang-shan and the utilitarianism of Ch'en Liang[av] (1143–1194). Even Lü Tsu-ch'ien was not spared. Two years later in 1187, Chu Hsi was appointed judicial intendant of Chiang-nan West (*Chiang-nan hsi-lu t'i-tien hsing-yüeh*[aw]); but in the sixth month of 1188, before he took office, he had an audience with the emperor during which he emphasized that only when the Principle of Heaven overcomes human selfish desires, when the mind is rectified, and when the will becomes sincere can economic difficulties be removed, the government be reformed, and the enemy be repulsed. By this time, the emperor was tired of his moralizing. He was appointed to be director in the army ministry (*ping-pu lang-kuan*[ax]) but he declined. Thereupon he was told to assume the judicial intendency. In the eleventh month, feeling that he had still not fully expressed himself, he sent a sealed memorial in which he advocated the six measures of rectifying the mind, employing worthy officials, enforcing discipline, reforming social customs, providing for the welfare of the people, and reforming the military. Though the emperor had retired by the time the memorial arrived at midnight, he got up and read it by candlelight. The next morning Chu Hsi was appointed junior expositor-in-waiting (*Ch'ung-cheng-tien shuo-shu*[ay]), but since some officials still considered the *Tao-hsüeh* as evil, he declined the appointment.

From 1190 to 1191 he was prefect of Chang-chou[az] Prefecture in Fukien. He promoted moral education, regulated ceremonies, abolished irregular taxes, prohibited men and women from congregating in Buddhist abodes to recite scriptures, banned nunneries, and impeached a magistrate for profiteering. His recommendations for land and tax reforms, however, went unheeded. In 1194 he was pacification commissioner of Ching-hu[ba] South based at T'an-chou[bb] Prefecture (present Ch'ang-sha, Hunan) for three months, just long enough to persuade rebellious natives to surrender and to carry out some educational reforms. When Emperor Ning-tsung[bc] ascended the throne that year, at the recommendation of the prime minister Chao Ju-yü[bd] (1140–1196) he was made lecturer-in-waiting and propounded the *Great Learning*. He reduced the number of holidays and lectured on every second day. He was awarded an earldom. But then, because he attacked the influential imperial relative Han T'o-chou[be] (d. 1207), he was relieved in spite of the intervention of Chao Ju-yü. The emperor had wanted him only to lecture, not to interfere with his affairs. Chu Hsi returned to Fukien and settled in K'ao-t'ing[bf] in Chien-yang County, about 120 *li* from Wu-fu Village.

By this time Han T'o-chou had centralized power in his own hands. He accused Chao Ju-yü of conspiracy, and Chao fled to Yung-chou[bg] (present Ling-ling[bh] County, Hunan) toward the end of 1195. Chu Hsi drafted a long memorial to attack wicked officials and by inference to defend Chao Ju-yü. His pupils, sensing the grave consequences of such a move, urged him to reach a decision through divination. The result of the divination was the hexagram *tun*[bi] (to withdraw) in its variation of *chia-jen*[bj] (family), whereupon Chu Hsi burned the draft and changed his literary name to Tun-weng[bk] (old man who has withdrawn).

During the almost fifty years after he received his degree, he held office in the government for only nine years and attended at Court for no more than forty-six days. In his three sealed memorials to the emperor in 1162, 1180, and 1188 and in the three audiences with the emperor in 1163, 1181, and 1188 he desperately tried political and moral reforms. In office he proved to be a courageous and effective administrator. But he did not cherish a political career. He declined many positions, notably compiler-designate of the bureau of military affairs (*Shu-mi-yüan pien-hsiu*[bl]) in 1169, librarian of the imperial archives in 1176, another post in the imperial archives in 1181, judicial intendency in Chiang-nan West in 1182, ministry executive in the department of army and junior expositor-in-waiting in 1188, assistant regional finance commissioner of Ching-hu South (in Hunan and part of Kwangsi) (*Ching-hu nan-lu*[bm]) in 1191, and pacification and planning commissioner of Kuang-nan[bn] West (in Kuangsi) in 1192. In 1169 he declined the post of compiler in the bureau of military affairs three times, and between 1170 and 1173 he declined the summons to the capital five times. In 1178 he accepted the post at Nan-k'ang only after four refusals. Often he pleaded a foot ailment but actually he was unwilling to support appeasers and corrupt officials.

A poor man practically all his life, he several times requested and obtained a temple guardianship, a sinecure that enabled him to stay at home with leisure to teach, write, and discuss with the most outstanding scholars of the day. In these ways he dedicated his life to the synthesis and completion of Neo-Confucianism. By organizing the philosophies of Chou Tun-i, the Ch'eng brothers, and Chang Tsai into a harmonious whole, he determined the direction of Neo-Confucianism, completed its theories of the Great Ultimate, principle (*li*[bo]), and material force (*ch'i*[bp]), defined the line of orthodox transmission of the Confucian tradition, brought Ch'eng I's doctrine of investigation of things to the highest point, and inaugurated the movement of overthrowing traditional interpretations of such Confucian Classics as the *Book of History*, the *Book of Odes*, and other works.

But to government officials Neo-Confucianism was a dangerous doctrine. By 1196 their attacks on Neo-Confucianism as "false learning" had become intense. The teachings of Ch'eng I and others were proscribed. The investigating censor (*chien-ch'a yü-shih*[bq]) Shen Chi-tsu[br] impeached Chu Hsi for ten crimes, including "false learning." This action was instigated by Hu Hung[bs] (1163 *cs*), vice-president of imperial sacrifices (*T'ai-ch'ang shao-ch'ing*[bt]), who had been offended because years before when he visited Chu Hsi, he was treated with plain food without wine or a chicken dish. An official candidate, Yü Che,[bu] even petitioned for his execution. As a result of these attacks Chu was dismissed from his compiler appointment and from his temple guardianship as well. Ts'ai Yüan-ting[bv] (1135–1198), whom Chu Hsi regarded as a friend rather than a pupil and with whom he associated longer than anyone else, was banished and was sought for arrest; and in 1197–1198 the attacks on "false learning" became even more severe. In the following year, at his request, his title was removed and he began to receive visitors in the informal attire of a plain citizen. A year later, in 1200, he died. In spite of the political atmosphere, almost a thousand people attended his funeral. When the political climate improved nine years later (1209), he was honored with the posthumous title of Wen[bw] (Culture), and in 1230, he was given the title of State Duke of Hui[bx]; in 1241 his tablet was placed in the Confucian Temple.

During his lifetime Chu Hsi wrote, compiled, and annotated almost a hundred works in the fields of philosophy, history, religion, literature, and biographical writing. Besides those already mentioned, the *Ssu-shu chang-chü chi-chu*[by] (Division into chapters and sentences and collected commentaries on the Four Books) must not be overlooked. In addition to the annotations on the *Analects* and the *Book of Mencius*, this includes the *Ta-hsüeh chang-chü*[bz] (The *Great Learning* divided into chapters and sentences) and the *Chung-yung chang-chü*[ca] (The *Doctrine of the Mean* divided into chapters and sentences). He had been working on these two for years although he did not write the prefaces for them until 1198. The work on the *Great Learning* was never actually finished; three days before he died he was still working on it. In 1313 an imperial decree ordered that his commentaries on the Four Books, which he had published in 1190, be the standard official interpretations and the basis of civil service examinations. They remained the authority until the examinations were abolished in 1905. Thus for almost six hundred years they were virtually the Chinese Bible. His conversations have been collected in the *Chu Tzu yü-lei*[cb] (Classified conversations of Master Chu), 140 chapters, and his literary works in the *Chu Tzu wen-chi*[cc] (Collection of literary works by Master Chu), 121 chapters. His mother, a former Miss Chu,[cd] died in 1169 at the age of seventy. His wife died in 1176. They had three sons, including Tsai[ce] (b. 1169), who rose to be assistant minister of the department of civil personnel (*Hu-pu shih-lang*[cf]), and five daughters, one of whom was married to Huang Kan[cg] (1152–1221), a star pupil.

Glossary

a	婺源	ad	西銘解義	bf	考亭
b	徽州	ae	張載	bg	永州
c	新安	af	太極圖說解	bh	零陵
d	朱松	ag	周敦頤	bi	避
e	尤溪	ah	呂祖謙	bj	家人
f	吏部員外郎	ai	近思錄	bk	避翁
g	建陽	aj	性理大全	bl	樞密院編修
h	劉子翬	ak	陸九淵象山	bm	荊湖
i	劉勉之	al	南康	bn	廣南
j	胡憲	am	星子	bo	理
k	進士	an	常平茶鹽公事	bp	氣
l	主簿	ao	江南	bq	監察御史
m	同安	ap	王淮	br	沈繼祖
n	李侗	aq	秦檜	bs	胡紘
o	里	ar	戶部尚書	bt	太常少卿
p	禪	as	鄭丙	bu	余㗊
q	程顥	at	陳賈	bv	蔡元定
r	程頤	au	道學	bw	文
s	羅從彥	av	陳亮	bx	徽
t	楊時	aw	江南西路提點刑獄	by	四書章句集註
u	臨安	ax	兵部郎官	bz	大學章句
v	孝宗	ay	崇政殿說書	ca	中庸章句
w	湯思退	az	漳州	cb	朱子語類
x	武學博士	ba	荊湖	cc	朱子文集
y	洪适	bb	潭州	cd	祝
z	五夫	bc	寧宗	ce	在
aa	崇安	bd	趙汝愚	cf	戶部侍郎
ab	張栻	be	韓侂冑	cg	黃榦
ac	河南程氏遺書				

Appendix B

Conference Personnel

Administration

Honorary Chairmen: Hung Wo Ching, Fujio Matsuda

Conference Director: Wing-tsit Chan

Conference Committee: Wm. Theodore de Bary, Chairman; Irene Bloom, Wing-tsit Chan, Chung-ying Cheng, Wei-ming Tu

Administrative Director: Stephen Uhalley, Jr.

Assistant Administrative Director: Peggy Blumenthal

Local Committee: Roger Ames, C. Y. Cheng, Priscilla Ching-Chung, Eliot Deutsch, Daniel W. Y. Kwok, Brian McKnight, Stephen Uhalley, Jr., K. N. Upadhyaya

Committee of Conference Historians: Irene Bloom, Peter Bol, Daniel K. Gardner, Michael Kalton, M. Theresa Kelleher, David Gedalecia

Interpreters: Richard Shek, Charles Wei-hsun Fu, Huang Chun-chieh, Shigenori Nagatomo, Wang I-hua

Participants

Panelists

IRENE BLOOM, Lecturer, Department of East Asian Languages and Cultures, Columbia University; Ph.D., Columbia; Mellon Fellow in the Humanities, Columbia; recipient of National Endowment for the Humanities fellowship; co-ed. (with de Bary), *Principle and Practicality: Essays in Neo-Confucianism and Practical Learning*.

WING-TSIT CHAN 陳榮捷, Gillespie Professor of Philosophy, Chatham College; Professor Emeritus of Chinese Philosophy and Culture, Dartmouth College; Visiting Professor of Chinese Thought, Columbia Uni-

---

Data about participants and observers have not been updated since the conference.

versity; Honorary Doctor of Humane Letters, Dartmouth; Honorary Doctor, China Academy, Taiwan; Ph.D., Harvard; former dean, Lingnan University; life member, Academia Sinica; recipient of Guggenheim, Rockefeller Foundation, American Philosophical Society, and National Endowment for the Humanities fellowships; author and trans., *Religious Trends in Modern China, A Source Book in Chinese Philosophy, The Way of Lao Tzu, Instructions for Practical Living, Reflections on Things at Hand,* 朱子門人, 朱學論集, 王陽明與禪, 陳榮捷哲學論文集; ed. for Chinese philosophy, *The Encyclopedia of Philosophy.*

CHANG LIWEN 張立文, Professor, Renmin University, Beijing; contributing ed., 中國哲學史研究; author, 周易思想研究, 朱熹思想研究, 中國哲學史講話.

CHUNG-YING CHENG 成中英, Professor of Philosophy, University of Hawaii; Ph.D., Harvard; founder and ed., *Journal of Chinese Philosophy*; founder and president, International Society of Chinese Philosophy; author, *Peirce's and Lewis's Theories of Induction, Scientific Knowledge and Human Value, The Philosophical Aspects of the Mind-Body Problem* 中國哲學與中國文化; trans., *Tai Chen's Inquiry into Goodness.*

(CH'IEN MU 錢穆, in absentia), dean of Chinese sinology; founder and former president of New Asia College, The Chinese University of Hong Kong; Honorary LL.D., Yale; author of numerous works including the 5-vol. 朱子新學案.

JULIA CHING 秦家懿, Professor of East Asian and Comparative Religions, University of Toronto; Ph.D., Australian National University; author, *To Acquire Wisdom: The Way of Wang Yang-ming, Confucianism and Christianity.*

CHIU HANSHENG 邱漢生, Vice-director, Institute for Research on the History of Chinese Thought, The Chinese Academy of Social Sciences; formerly professor at Fu-tan, Ta-hsia, and Peking Normal universities; author, 四書集註簡論, 宋明理學與宋明學史研究, 理學開山周敦頤, 論伊川易傳, 陳淳的理學思想, 中國思想通史(與侯外廬合著) (4 vols.).

WM. THEODORE DE BARY 狄培瑞, John Mitchell Mason Professor of the University, Columbia University; Ph.D., Columbia; Honorary Doctor, St. Lawrence University and Loyola University of Chicago; former director, East Asian Language and Area Center; chairman, University Committee on Oriental Studies; executive vice-president for Academic Affairs and provost, Columbia; former president, Association for Asian Studies; Guggenheim fellow; author, *Neo-Confucian Orthodoxy and the Learning of the Mind and Heart*; ed., *Principle and Practicality: Neo-Confucianism and Practical Learning, The Unfolding of Neo-Confucianism, Self and Society in Ming Thought, Sources of Chinese Tradition.*

CHARLES WEI-HSUN FU 傅偉勳, Professor of Buddhism and Far Eastern Philosophy and Religion, Temple University; Ph.D., University of Illinois; formerly professor at National Taiwan University, University of Illinois, and Ohio University; author, 西方哲學批判史, *Guide to Chinese Philosophy* (with Wing-tsit Chan).

FUNG YU-LAN 馮友蘭, leading Chinese philosopher; Ph.D., Columbia; Honorary Doctor of Humane Letters, Princeton; formerly professor at Tsing-hua University and visiting professor at the University of Pennsylvania and the University of Hawaii; author of numerous works including 中國哲學史 *A History of Chinese Philosophy*, 中國哲學史新編, *A Short History of Chinese Philosophy*, 新理學 *The Spirit of Chinese Philosophy*.

A. C. GRAHAM 葛瑞漢, Professor of Classical Chinese, School of Oriental and African Studies, University of London; M.A., Oxford; Ph.D., London FBA; author, *Two Chinese Philosophers: Ch'eng Ming-tao and Ch'eng Yi-ch'uan*; *Later Mohist Logic, Ethics and Science*; *Chuang Tzu, the Seven Inner Chapters: And other writings from the book Chuang-tzu*; *Book of Lieh-tzu*.

(HSÜ FU-KUAN 徐復觀, deceased), late professor at Tung-hai University, The Chinese University of Hong Kong, and New Asia Institute; author, 中國思想論集, 中國文學論集, 中國人性論史先秦篇, 公孫龍子講疏, 兩漢思想史 (3 vols.), 周官成立的時代及其基本性格.

HUANG SIU-CHI 黃秀璣, Professor Emeritus of Philosophy and former department chairman, Beaver College (Pennsylvania); Ph.D., Pennsylvania; formerly visiting professor at the University of Hawaii and Ziamen (Amoy) University; author, *Lu Hsiang-shan—A Twelfth Century Chinese Idealist Philosopher*; trans. into Chinese, *George Berkeley's Three Dialogues between Hylas and Philonous and Josiah Royce's Sources of Religious Insight*.

KAO MING 高明, Professor, Chinese Culture University; graduate, National Central University, Nanking; Honorary Litt.D., Konkuk University, Korea; formerly professor, head of department, and dean, National Northwest University; formerly professor at National Taiwan Normal and National Cheng-chih universities; author, 高明文輯, 大戴禮記今註今譯; ed. 中華文化百科全書 (15 vols.); co-ed. 中華大辭典 (40 vols.).

LI ZEHOU 李澤厚, Research Scholar, Institute of Philosophy, The Chinese Academy of Social Sciences; Professor of Philosophy, Hobei University; author, 康有爲譚嗣同思想研究, 中國近代思想史, 批判哲學的批判, 美學論集, 美的歷程.

(LIANG SHUMING 梁漱溟, in absentia), elder of Chinese intellectuals; former Professor of Indian and Chinese Philosophy, Peking University, and dean of Shantung Reconstruction Institute; former member of Na-

tional Defense Council; founder of Democratic League; member of
1946 Political Council; present executive member of Drafting of Constitution; author, 東西文化及其哲學.

SHU-HSIEN LIU 劉述先, Professor of Philosophy, The Chinese University of Hong Kong; Ph.D., Southern Illinois University; formerly
professor at Tung-hai and Southern Illinois universities; author,
朱熹哲學的思想的發展與完成, 中國哲學與現代化, 文化哲學的探討, 生命
情調的抉擇.

LIU TS'UN-YAN 柳存仁, Professor and Head of the Chinese Department,
Australian National University; Ph.D. and Lt.D., Australian Academy
of the Humanities; author, *Buddhist and Taoist Influence in Chinese
Novels, Chinese Popular Fiction in Two London Libraries, Selected Papers
from the Hall of Harmonious Wind*, 和風堂讀書集 (2 vols.).

STANISLAUS LOKUANG 羅光, Archbishop of Taipei and President of Fu
Jen Catholic University; Professor of Philosophy at Fu Jen and Chinese
Culture universities; Doctorate in Sacred Theology, Urban University
of Propaganda and Faith, Rome; formerly secretary general and then
conveyer of the Commission of Asian Bishops; author, *A History of the
Envoys Between China and the Holy See, The Life of Hsü Kuang-ch'i*,
中國哲學思想史 (6 vols.), 中國哲學的展望, 理論哲學, 實踐哲學, 宗教與
哲學, 人生哲學論叢, 新儒學論叢.

RICHARD JOHN LYNN, Lecturer, Department of Asian Studies, University
of British Columbia; Ph.D., Stanford; formerly taught at University of
Auckland, University of Massachusetts, Amherst University, Indiana
University; formerly senior lecturer and head of the Department of
Chinese, Macquarie University, Sydney; author, *Kuan Yun-Shin,
Chinese Literature: A Draft Bibliography in Western European
Languages*.

MAO HUAIXIN 冒懷辛, Associate Professor, Institute of History, The
Chinese Academy of Social Sciences; author, *Study of Shao Yung, Ts'ai
Yüan-ting and Ts'ai Ch'en*.

BRIAN MCKNIGHT, Professor and Chair, Department of History, Uni-
versity of Hawaii; Ph.D., Chicago; Fulbright fellow; formerly professor
at University of Nebraska; author, *Village and Bureaucracy in Southern
Sung China, The Quality of Mercy: Amnesties and Traditional Chinese
Justice, The Washing Away of Wrongs: Forensic Practice in 13th Century
China*; ed., Asian Studies at Hawaii.

DONALD MUNRO 孟旦, Professor of Philosophy, University of Michigan;
recipient of Ford Foundation Foreign Area, Social Sciences Research
Council, and Guggenheim fellowships; former chairman, Committee on
Studies of Chinese Civilization of the American Council of Learned
Societies and member of the Committee on Scholarly Communication

with People's Republic of China; author, *The Concept of Man in Early China*, *The Concept of Man in Contemporary China*.

OKADA TAKEHIKO 岡田武彦, Professor, Kassui Women's College, Kyushu; Emeritus Professor, Kyushu University; Doc. of Lit., Kyushu University; Honorary Doctor, China Academy, Taiwan; formerly dean of the College of General Education of Kyushu University, professor at Seinan-Gakuin University in Fukuoka, and visiting professor at Columbia University; author, 王陽明と明末の儒学, 坐禅と静坐, 宋明哲学序説, 王陽明文集, 劉念台文集, 中国と中国人; ed., 陽明学大系 (12 vols.), 朱子学大系 (15 vols.), 日本の思想家叢書 (50 vols.), 近世漢籍叢刊 (52 vols.).

REN JIYU 任繼愈, Director, Institute for Research on World Religions, The Chinese Academy of Social Sciences; member of the Committee on the Academy's Research Institute on Philosophical Studies; professor at Peking University; lecturer and invited participant at international intellectual conferences in Soviet Russia, Nepal, Pakistan, Japan, United States; visiting professor at the University of Toronto; author, 中國哲學史 (4 vols.), 中國哲學史簡編, 墨子, 韓非, 老子今譯, 老子新譯, 漢唐佛教思想論集, 中國佛教史, 中國哲學史論.

SATO HITOSHI 佐藤仁, Professor, Hiroshima University; specialist on Chu Hsi and the continuator of the Kusumoto School in Japan; comp., 晦庵先生朱文公文集人名索引, 朱子語類語句索引.

CONRAD SCHIROKAUER, Professor of History, The City College of the City University of New York; Ph.D., Stanford; co-chairman, Regional Seminar in Neo-Confucian Studies; author, *A Brief History of Chinese and Japanese Civilization*; trans., *China's Examination Hell—The Civil Service Examinations of Imperial China*.

BENJAMIN SCHWARTZ 史華慈, Leroy B. Williams Professor of History and Government and Director of Academic Policy of the Council on East Asian Studies, Harvard University; former associate director of the East Asian Research Center, Harvard, and president of the Association of Asian Studies; author, *In Search of Wealth and Power: Yen Fu and the West*, *Communism in China and the Rise of Mao*.

SHIMADA KENJI 島田虔次, Professor Emeritus, Faculty of Letters, Kyoto University; author, 朱子学と陽明学, 中国における近代思惟の挫折, 中国革命の先駆者たち, 大学中庸註.

TENG AIMIN 鄧艾民, Professor of Philosophy, Peking University; chairman, Peking Branch of the Society of the History of Chinese Philosophy; co-author, 中國哲學史 (4 vols.), 中國哲學史 (2 vols.).

TOMOEDA RYŪTARŌ 友枝龍太郎, Professor, Seinan University; Professor Emeritus, Hiroshima University; formerly professor at the Army Officers Academy and Tokyo University; lecturer at Fu-tan, Peking,

Taipei Normal, and Korea universities; participant in international conferences; author, 宋子の思想形成, 朱子, 近世の思想 (宋学), 熊澤蕃山集義和書, 新井白石鬼神論, 陸象山文集抄, 朱子の学問論.

Ts'AI JEN-HOU 蔡仁厚, Professor of Philosophy, Tung-hai University and Chinese Culture University; author, 孔門弟子志行考述, 儒家哲學與文化真理, 宋明理學北宋篇, 南宋篇, 王陽明哲學, 新儒家的精神方向.

WEI-MING TU 杜維明, Professor of Chinese History and Philosophy, Harvard University; Ph.D., Harvard; formerly taught at Tunghai University, Princeton University, and University of California at Berkeley; author, *Neo-Confucianism in Action: Wang Yang-ming's Youth, Centrality and Commonality: An Essay on Chung-Yung, Humanity and Self-Cultivation: Essays in Confucian Thought*, and two collections of essays in Chinese.

MONIKA ÜBELHÖR 余蓓荷, Ph.D., Hamburg University; Lehrbeauftragte für Sinologie, Universität Marburg; trans. *Shimada Kenji's Shu shi gaku to Yōmei gaku.*

WEI CHENG-T'UNG 韋政通, Professor of Chinese Philosophy, Taiwan Divinity College; formerly professor at Chinese Culture University and Kuang Wu College of Engineering; author, 中國思想史 (上下), 荀子與古代哲學, 先秦大哲學家, 中國哲學思想批判, 中國的智慧, 中國文化概論, 中國文化與現代生活; comp., 中國哲學辭典; ed., 中國思想方法論文選集, 中國哲學思想論集 (8 vols.).

YU YAMANOI 山井湧, Professor, Daito Bunka University; formerly professor at the University of Tokyo; author, 明清思想史の研究, 黃宗羲; co-trans., 明末清初政治評論集; ed. 朱子文集固有名詞索引.

YAMAZAKI MICHIO 山崎道夫, Professor, Kokushikan University; Emeritus Professor, Tokyo Gakugai University; director and lecturer, Shibunkai; councilor and lecturer, Oriental Culture Research Institute of the Mukyukai; vice–chief director of the Japan Yi Toegye Research Institute; author, 近思錄講本釋義, 近思錄序説, 近思錄, 吉田松陰, 佐藤直方, 西鄉南洲.

YOUN SA-SOON 尹絲淳, Professor and Chair, Department of Philosophy, and Director of the College of Liberal Arts, Korea University; vice-president, Committee on Korean Philosophy; author, *A Study of the Philosophy of Toegye, A Study of Korean Confucianism* (both in Korean).

YING-SHIH YÜ 余英時, Charles Seymour Professor of History, Yale University; Ph.D., Harvard; LL.D., The Chinese University of Hong Kong; life member, Academia Sinica; formerly professor at Harvard, president of New Asia College, and pro–Vice chancellor of The Chinese University of Hong Kong; chairman, U.S. Delegation of Han Studies to People's Republic of China; author, *Trade and Expansion in Han China,*

Early Chinese History in the People's Republic of China, 方以智晚節考, 章學誠, 歷史與思想, 紅樓夢的兩個世界, 中國知識階層史論, 史學與傳統.

Fellows

Joseph A. Adler, Teaching Associate, Department of Religious Studies, University of California, Santa Barbara; Ph.D. thesis, "Divination and Philosophy: Chu Hsi's Interpretation of the *I-ching*."

John H. Berthrong, Research Assistant, Center for Religious Studies, University of Toronto; Ph.D., Chicago, 1979, thesis on Chu Hsi as interpreted by Ch'en Ch'un.

Alison H. Black, Visiting Assistant Professor, School of International Studies, University of Washington; Ph.D., Michigan, 1979, "Nature, Artifice, and Expression in the Philosophical Thought of Wang Fu-chih (1619–1692)."

Peter Bol, Fellow, Society of Fellows in the Humanities; Lecturer, Columbia University; Ph.D., Princeton, 1981.

John W. Chaffee, Assistant Professor, Department of History, State University of New York at Binghamton; Ph.D., Chicago, 1979, "Education and Examinations in Sung Society (960–1279)."

Chao Ling-ling 趙玲玲, Chair, Department of Philosophy, Soochow University, Taipei; Fu Jen Catholic University Ministry of Education National Ph.D., 1974, thesis on Shao Yung.

Ron-Guey Chu 朱榮貴, Graduate Research Assistant, Columbia University; Master's thesis, "A Study of Hsieh Liang-tso (1050–c.1120) as Expounder of the Philosophy of the Erh-Ch'eng."

John W. Ewell, Jr., University of California, Berkeley; Ph.D. thesis, "Tai Chen's Modernist Reconstruction of the Confucian Tradition."

Daniel K. Gardner, Assistant Professor, Department of History, Smith College; Ph.D., Harvard, 1978, "The Classics During the Sung: Chu Hsi's Interpretation of the *Ta-hsüeh*."

David Gedalecia, Associate Professor, Department of History, College of Wooster; Ph.D., Harvard, 1971, "Wu Ch'eng: A Neo-Confucian of the Yüan."

James J. Griffin, Commonwealth Scholar, Edinburgh University; Ph.D. thesis, "Caritas and *Ren*: A Comparative Study of Thomas Aquinas and Zhu Xi."

Russell Hatton, Assistant Professor, Department of Philosophy, University of Delaware; Ph.D., State University of New York at Buffalo, 1979, "A Comparison of *Ch'i* and Prime Matter."

Chin-shing Huang 黃進興, Ph.D., Harvard, 1982, "The Lu-Wang School in the Ch'ing Dynasty."

Huang Chun-chieh 黄俊傑, Associate Professor, Department of History, National Taiwan University; Ph.D., Washington, 1980, "The Rise of the Mencius: Historical Interpretation of Mencian Morality, ca. A.D. 200–1200."

Lionel Millard Jensen, Junior Fellow, Center for Chinese Studies, University of California, Berkeley; Ph.D. thesis, "The Neo-Confucian Mind and Hunger for Wholeness."

Paul Yun-ming Jiang 姜允明, Head, Chinese Section, School of Modern Languages, Macquarie University; Ph.D., University of Auckland, 1976, *The Search for Mind: Ch'en Pai-sha, Philosopher Poet* (Singapore: Singapore University Press, 1980).

Michael C. Kalton, Assistant Professor, Department of Religion, Wichita State University; Ph.D., Harvard, 1977, "The Neo-Confucian World View and Value System of Yi Dynasty Korea"; trans., *Ethics East and West: Western Secular, Christian, and Confucian Traditions in Comparative Perspective* (Seoul: Christian Literature Society, 1977).

M. Theresa Kelleher, Ph.D., Columbia, 1982, "Personal Reflections on the Pursuit of Sagehood: An Interplay of Darkness and Light in the *Journal* of Wu Yü-pi (1392–1469)."

R. Oaksook Chun Kim, Department of Oriental Languages, University of California, Los Angeles; Ph.D., Iowa, 1980, "Chu Hsi and Lu Hsiang-shan: A Study of Philosophical Achievements and Controversy in Neo-Confucianism."

Kim Yung Sik 金永植, Associate Professor, Department of Chemistry, Seoul National University; Ph.D., Harvard, 1973; Ph.D., Princeton, 1980, "The World-View of Chu Hsi: Knowledge about the Natural World in *Chu-tzu Ch'üan-shu.*"

Komiya Atsushi 小宮原, Kyushu University; M.A. thesis, "On the Interpretation of Chou-i by Chu Tzu."

Thomas Hong-chi Lee 李弘祺, Lecturer, Department of History, The Chinese University of Hong Kong; Ph.D., Yale, 1975, "Education in Northern Song China, 960–1126"; author, *Discourses on Sung Education, 1979; The Tradition of Private Lectures,* 1982 (both in Chinese, Taipei).

Okada Susumu 岡田進, Australian National University; M.A., Kyushu University.

Park Yang Ja 朴洋子, Department of Philosophy, Hiroshima University; M.A. thesis, "On Chu Hsi's Lecture at Yushan."

Tim Phelan, Ph.C., Asian Languages and Literature, University of Washington; Ph.D., Washington, 1982, "The Neo-Confucian Cosmology in Chu Hsi's *I-hsüeh ch'i-meng.*"

Sato Akira 佐藤明, Kyushu University; M. A. thesis, "On the thoughts of Lin Hsi-i."

Richard Shek 石漢椿, Assistant Professor of Humanities, California State University, Sacramento; Ph.D., University of California, Berkeley, 1980, "Religion and Society in Late Ming: Popular Morality and Folk Sectarianism in Sixteenth and Seventeenth Century China."

Rodney L. Taylor, Assistant Professor, Department of Religious Studies, University of Colorado, Boulder; Ph.D., Columbia, 1974, *The Cultivation of Sagehood as a Religious Goal in Neo-Confucianism: A Study of Selected Writings of Kao P'an-lung (1562–1626)* (Missoula, Montana: American Academy of Religion and Scholar Press, 1978).

Kirill O. Thompson 唐格理, Instructor, Department of Philosophy, University of Hawaii; Ph.D., thesis on an organistic interpretation of Chu Hsi.

Hoyt C. Tillman 田浩, Assistant Professor, Department of History, Arizona State University; Ph.D., Harvard, 1976, "Values in History and Ethics in Politics: Issues Debated Between Chu Hsi and Ch'en Liang"; author, *Utilitarian Confucianism: Ch'en Liang's Challenge to Chu Hsi* (Cambridge, Mass.: Harvard East Asian Monograph Series, 1982).

Tseng Ch'un-hai 曾春海, Assistant Professor, Department of Philosophy, Fu Jen Catholic University, Taipei; Ph.D., Fu Jen, 1977, "The Meaning of *I Ching* According to Wang Fu-chih's Thought"; author, *The Cosmology of the I-Ching According to Wang Fu-chih* (Taipei: Fu Jen University, 1978, in Chinese).

Ushio Hirotaka 牛尾弘孝, Lecturer, Education Department, Oita University; M. A., Kyushu University, 1975, "On the Thoughts of Yang Ci-hu—the Character of His Mind and Heart Learning."

Ann-ping Chin Woo, Columbia University; Ph.D. thesis on Chan Jo-shui.

Observers

Dr. *Carl B. Becker*, Professor of Philosophy, Southern Illinois University.

Mr. *Matthew A. Levey*, Department of History, University of Michigan.

Dr. *Torbjorn Loden*, Researcher, Department of Oriental Languages, University of Stockholm.

Dr. *Jason H. Parker*, Executive Associate, American Council of Learned Societies, New York City.

Dr. *Robert E. Reuman*, Professor, Department of Philosophy and Religion, Colby College, Maine.

Dr. Gene C. Sager, Professor of Philosophy and Religious Studies, Palomar College, California.

Dr. Harold P. Sjursen 修海樂, Chairman, Department of Philosophy, Augustana College, Illinois.

Dr. Malcolm F. Stewart, Professor Emeritus of Philosophy and Religion, Illinois College.

Mrs. Cheng Sun (Tieh-kang) (Ms. Cheng Kuo 郭貞), Department of Communication, University of Michigan.

Prof. Sun Tieh-kang 孫鐵剛, Department of History, National Chengchih University, Taipei.

Prof. Hiroshi Watanabe, Assistant Professor, Faculty of Law, Tokyo University.

Dr. Sandra A. Wawrytko, Assistant Professor, San Diego State University.

Fr. Benjamin Wren, S.J., Loyola University, New Orleans.

Ms. Loretta O. Q. Pang, Department of History, Kapiolani Community College, Honolulu.

Appendix C

Sponsors: International Conference on Chu Hsi

Individuals

Allen, Leroy Robert; Century Center, Inc.
Ashford and Wriston; Attorneys at Law
Ching, Hung Wo and Elizabeth; Aloha Airlines
Chuck, Walter G.; Attorney at Law
Eu, Edward and Peggy; Universal Motors
Gentry, Tom and Nora; Gentry Homes
Gumpert, Jack; Shirt Stop
Kosasa, Sidney; ABC Drugs
Leong, Harry Y. O.; Oahu Furniture
Luke, Kan Jung; Hawaii National Bank
McCabe, Thomas and Sumie F.; McCabe Hamilton & Renny
Pflueger, James; Pflueger Lincoln Mercury, Inc.
Wong, Harry C. and Nee Chang; H. W. Ching Realty
Wong, Howard and Robert T. W.; Architects
Wong, Estate of Kwai Lun; Hei Wai Wong

Corporations

Alexander & Baldwin, Inc. (R. J. Pfeiffer, Jr.)
Alexander of Hawaii, Inc. (Warren Daspit)
Aloha Airlines (Hung Wo Ching)
American Security Bank (Denis Y. M. Ching)
Bank of Hawaii (Frank Manaut)
E. E. Black, Ltd. (Robert E. Black)
Bishop Insurance of Hawaii, Inc. (Clarence Philpotts)
Chun Kim Chow, Ltd. (Frederic Chun)
B. F. Dillingham Co., Ltd. (Bayard Dillingham)
Foodland Super Market, Ltd. (Maurice Sullivan)
Hauoli Sales, Ltd. (James K. C. Doo)

Hawaiian Dredging & Construction (Paul Banks)
Hawaiian Telephone Company (Don Kuyper)
Hawaii Tokyu Group (Noboru Gotoh)
Hirano Enterprises (Herbert Hirano)
Hong Kong Land Co., Ltd. and Jardine Matheson Co., Ltd. (Robert Sutton)
The Honolulu Advertiser (Thurston Twigg-Smith)
Horita Realty, Inc. (Herbert Horita)
Sheridan Ing Corp. (Sheridan C. F. Ing)
King's Bakery (Robert Taira)
Liberty Bank (Laurence S. L. Ching)
Loyalty Enterprises, Ltd. (Clarence T. C. Ching)
Occidental Underwriters of Hawaii (Siegfried Kagawa)
Okada Trucking Co., Ltd. (Sonny Okada)
Pacific Food Services, Inc. (Andrew Wong)
Pacific Resources, Inc. (James Gary)
Palama Meat Co. (Donald Lau)
Paradise Park, Inc. (James W. Y. Wong)
Richards, Ltd. (Richard W. C. Chow)
Royal Grove Hotel (Leonard K. M. Fong)
Sen Plex Corp. (Francis F. Sen)
Shimaya Shoten (Ichiro Onoye)
Star Super Market, Ltd. (John Fujieki)
Stark Ventures, Ltd. (Bruce Stark)
Richard K. W. Tom, Inc. (Richard K. W. Tom)
WKH Corporation (William Weinberg)
Waikiki Business Plaza (William K. H. Mau)
Wailana Coffee House (Francis J. Tom)
Watumull Brothers, Ltd. (Gulab Watumull)
C. S. Wo & Sons (Robert Wo)

Foundations

Amfac
Atherton Family
C. Brewer Charitable
Governor John A. Burns
Samuel N. and Mary Castle
Finance Factors
Chinn Ho
Louise and Y. T. Lum
McInerny

Index

Ron-Guey Chu has rendered valuable assistance in the preparation of the Index.